The Golden Remembrance

Reawakening One Golden Heart Consciousness

Deborah and Jack Bartello

PUBLISHED BY ONE GOLDEN HEART PRODUCTIONS, LLC

The Golden Remembrance
Reawakening One Golden Heart Consciousness

by Deborah and Jack Bartello
© 2021 Deborah and Jack Bartello
One Golden Heart™
Published by One Golden Heart Productions, LLC

Cover art: Golden Heart Stained Glass designed
by Deborah Bartello, copyright 2012
Editor: Lorien Sekora
Book Design: Chris Molé, booksavvystudio.com

Library of Congress Control Number: 2021914221
ISBN: 978-1-7375405-0-2

First Edition
Printed in the United States of America

Dedicated to All of Golden Life Everywhere

CONTENTS

A NOTE FROM THE AUTHORS

FACT OR FICTION?

To some, Lemuria is a myth, and to others it is as real as the present moment. We are not trying to convince you either way. Our goal is to lovingly offer the story that was shown to us through our inner exploration and guidance.

This book is the result of our 20-year journey of self-exploration and self-discovery on the subject; as well as our experiences with our workshop participants.

We present the material as a work of fiction for two reasons. The first is that the story cannot be corroborated, even though we feel it is true. The second is that the characters in the book are fictional, with the exception of the Golden Masters. Hence, the need to present it as a book of fiction.

The Golden Masters that are presented in the book are real to us and to many. They are not fictional characters.

Regardless of whether this story is true or not, its relevance to our current times is undeniable. Of course, that is for you to discover in the pages ahead.

Part One

Remembering
Golden Lemuria

CHAPTER ONE

PREPARING FOR THE GOLDEN REMEMBRANCE JOURNEY

FRANKLY, THIS IS one of the greatest love stories ever told. It is the story of how our collective Golden Family came to this beautiful and precious planet Earth to create a new and magnificent reality. Back then, our family called this civilization *Lemuria, the World of Golden Love*. Does that include you? Read on to find out.

We each heard the call from far, far away as this glorious planet beckoned, inviting us to join with her in a wondrous birthing of Joy and Creativity.

Coming from many different stars and galaxies throughout the greater Cosmos, each one of us brought the unique talents and gifts that we wished to contribute to this unusual project. We wanted to give of ourselves to its beautiful creation, to open and expand by stretching beyond anything we imagined we were capable of before.

Our goal was not only to do so for our individual soul growth, but to join with that which is bigger and bolder: an entire civilization whose purpose was to devote themselves to Golden co-creation with this planet, the stars, and the many other dimensions of Golden Love that were joining with us from near and far.

It was an experience and expression of a true interdimensional family of many Golden Hearts joining together to deliberately and consciously weave One Golden Heart: a co-creative and interdimensional gift for us all. It was by far the most exquisite experience that could ever be shared; that is how we felt then, and still feel now. It is what we will always be profoundly devoted to.

It was a glorious undertaking that helped each of us become even more magnificent, capable, kind, and strong—more than we had ever thought possible. The experience went far beyond that which can even be imagined by the minds of people today.

❧

The story that unfolds in the pages ahead is the journey of our Lemurian history from the time this planet called us to her, until now. Detailing the establishment of our original Lemurian Creation together, this narrative details how we flourished as a people while deepening ourselves individually and collectively.

We describe the paths that we walked in devotion to our One Golden Heart, our Golden Family, and this beautiful planet with which we will always be deeply in co-creation.

This chronicling of our Golden Lemurian tapestry—in full array of color and texture—is overflowing with beauty, complexity, and substance. Filled with sacred devotion, honor, compassion, and profound love, it is deep and meaningful at every turn. Intricately detailing our enormous challenges as a people, we explore what felt like the shattering of our Sacred Wholeness, our trek through the Gauntlet of Fear, and the final re-discovery of ourselves and our sacred Golden Lemurian Family.

Why are we telling this story?

We are sharing this truth because it was brought to the authors as a mission to be delivered, a story whose time has come. Now is the moment to remember who we are as Golden Ones walking upon this beautiful planet that we call home.

Our Lemurian history contains many splendid gifts that can help us better navigate these modern times; we can draw upon them and be strengthened and empowered as we meet the many challenges that we face in our lives today. Most importantly, these Golden Gifts are essential for the conscious and careful creation of a future for all generations to come. Our Golden Remembrance is both our Lemurian legacy to ourselves, and to the sacred consciousness of all life.

There is nothing small about this book, in size or content, and we realize the sheer volume of pages may be daunting to some readers at the outset. Please be aware that every single page is a step toward the wondrous unfolding and remembrance of your Golden Self. Each page deserves to be read and integrated so that true understanding, clarity, and full remembrance can happen.

As you read on, the benefits of presenting this story as a series of organized steps designed to facilitate this Golden Metamorphosis become apparent. The length of this volume provides a chance to travel through this remembrance process in a most thorough manner, and each completion of the journey's stages prepare you for the next.

The book's many pieces are put together in a precise and deliberate order, and we encourage you to read it in the sequence presented. Doing so will give you the best chance to be truly gifted, and to become clear, thus enabling you to make new choices based on what you discover and remember about yourself as a Golden One.

The actual process of Golden Remembrance takes place through the following steps:

First, we go back to Lemuria of Origin, to the building of our civilization during that period and the experience of our Golden way of being and living.

Second, we describe our understanding of what happened to us Golden Ones from the time of the fall of Lemuria until now.

Third, we explore our subsequent healing and restoration as Golden Ones.

And last but not least is the fourth and final step: the full embrace and conscious re-activation of ourselves as the glorious Golden Ones that we truly are.

You will notice that we have written this book primarily in the present tense, to give you the best chance of experiencing it as fully and directly as possible. At times the storyline will bounce back and forth from past to present, again and again. Through its unique intricacies, you will see clearly how our past affects our present affects our past, etc., and how our perspective can change as a result of our vantage point. The information is also multi-dimensional and inter-dimensional in nature. Often giving voice to energetic subject matter, it affirms that all of life is interactive and communicating. This provides an opportunity for intuitive sensing and relating. The experience can become complete when you are open and accepting to the idea that we operate through our inner senses, as well as our outer. We are all intuitive, perceptive, and energetic Beings that have a more complex design beyond our purely physical senses in the physical world. Our premise is that everything is fundamentally energy in motion: we are ENERGY. We are fluid. It is the way we are. It is the way life truly is.

This book will jog your Golden memory awake. It will move things through you and within you that you have not felt for a long time. You may alternate between feeling elated and celebratory, and even stirred up.

It also presents the entire array of Golden experience. No stone is left unturned and no detail diminished; all has a place and all needs to be valued. It is indeed time to remember ALL of it—not just the beauty and the joy, but also the sadness and the heartbreak, the devastation and the pain that we have walked through to regain ourselves and each other once more.

This pain that we have endured is part of our Lemurian fabric. To heal ourselves from it we need to fully acknowledge and embrace these parts of ourselves. This is the only way it can be witnessed within, and therefore be given the space and understanding it needs for complete healing to occur at last. This is how it will be transformed into love again, and how we will be fully restored to our joyous Golden Wholeness.

Through it all, remember: this is a journey, it is a process that you are moving THROUGH. Keep moving, and things will soon shift and change again.

Indeed, it is time for us to vividly remember ourselves; to remember what we are truly capable of as Golden Gentle Giants who walk on this beautiful Golden planet. We need to remember so that we can shine boldly and brightly once again, and make the differences that we came to offer in this incarnation.

We came here now to reveal to ourselves who and how we truly are. We have struggled and suffered greatly to have this opportunity to remember and to restore ourselves. The time is NOW. The window for this Golden Remembrance is open, and this is the moment we have been talking about, waiting for, and working toward for a long, long time.

As a manual to help all Golden Ones integrate their Golden Remembrance, the information being presented here has been brought forward to help you remember not only that you are Golden, but what that means. Its purpose is to give you the tools to navigate as a Golden One in our present world, and to do so with greater ease, clarity, and alignment—all of which will help you to thrive with passion, purpose, vigor, and joy as the Golden Being that you truly are. This information provides a vehicle through which the remarkable power and gifts of your Golden love can finally be re-embraced and re-activated, thus benefitting all in profoundly beautiful ways now, and into the future.

This book has been written with the help of our Team of Golden Masters, who will guide you throughout this journey. We could say much about each one of them, but would rather you experience them as they reveal themselves to you. Of course, this will require that you remain open to the gifts that they offer, but it is only in being receptive to them that you can discover who they are as they support you on this Golden Remembrance journey—which will be your gift to yourself.

We are ONE People: strong, glorious, deep, and beautiful, and we must remember the entirety of who we are in order to be this again NOW. Our Golden Mastery is needed now. Our unique gifts and talents are needed again now. We are being invited to stand tall and sovereign now. It is time to be Golden Love radiantly outshining now. It is time to be Golden Free now.

For this we have walked through so much. For this, the reward of our One Golden Heart shining magnificently bright and glorious once more is the pure point of it.

We encourage you to stay the course of this book, and to savor it. Do not feel a need to rush through it. Read it at your own pace and in your own time. You will be greatly enriched in many, many ways by doing so. As we have said, it is a love story. The greatest love story ever told and the greatest love story ever remembered.

Let us begin.

CHAPTER TWO

OUR BEAUTIFUL LEMURIAN MISSION BEGINS

ANDAR, MY SOULMATE, walks toward me with a twinkle in his eye and a distinct spring in his step. I know he has something special to tell me, and I cannot wait to hear what it is! As he moves closer, I feel his energy, his excitement, and his joy.

He comes to stand directly in front of me, bowing his head so that his forehead touches mine. This is the special greeting of love and union that we always share. We are of about the same height, and this position fits perfectly for both of us.

We stand here, silent and still, feeling our love for one another flowing like a gentle wave back and forth between us until we are One sacred, sweet joy. There is great comforting sustenance for us in these uniting moments, and we drink each other in completely. Ours is a love that is meant to be as One—a rare and sacred thing that we treasure beyond all else. Such is the depth of our passion and gratitude.

After our few moments of quiet, I can feel Andar eager to burst forth with his news:

"Avalar, my most Beloved one, we have been invited to consider undertaking a new mission of great beauty and magnitude: birthing a brand new Golden Nation in another planetary system. If we choose to do this, we must meet with our Golden Council Leaders now for more information. I don't know all the details, but I do sense that this is going to be sacred and special, beyond anything we have known.

"Providing we both like the plan proposed by the Golden Council, would you, my most Beloved, undertake this mission with me?"

I ponder quietly for a moment, feeling with absolute certainty that this is a Destiny Call for me, and for us. I can feel the joyous song of my Soul. Whatever the details are, I know, without a doubt, that I am IN, full-on IN! My insides are beaming, and I am swept up in the same eager excitement as Andar:

"Yes, my sweet Andar, of course, YES! I am with you on this. I KNOW with every fiber of my Being that this will be an opportunity of greater joy and fulfillment than we have yet known. I feel the calling, and I am

wholeheartedly saying yes to it."

And with that, we join hands and enthusiastically go to meet with our Golden Council Leaders.

∽

Seated at a round, beautifully hand-carved table inlaid with gold, Andar and I are joined by many members of the Golden Council. The air is hushed, but full of excitement and promise. We know these great Leaders well, as we have been in this room and at this very table many times before—but never have we sat holding our breath with such anticipation as right now.

At last, one of the Council Leaders speaks:

"Andar and Avalar, both most respected and Beloved Leaders of Golden Heart, we honor you. You have both had a great deal of experience in birthing and directing new Golden Projects throughout the Cosmos. We are proud of your unique abilities and gifts in this arena, and would like you to consider a similar project—although one of even greater magnitude than has ever been attempted before.

"A new Golden Nation is ready to be born. It is unique in that it will deliberately include the energetic radiance of ALL Golden Forms of Life from other dimensions and planets. It will be as one giant Golden Weave with many Golden Hearts actively joining together to form ONE GOLDEN HEART, thus magnifying the Golden Resonance exponentially throughout the Cosmos. This will provide an opportunity for our Golden Family to expand and strengthen considerably, while also greatly amplifying the infusions of Golden Power that will activate, energize, support, and sustain all the Golden Creations that spring forth from this new Nation.

"Your unique capabilities as Leaders, both individually and coupled, along with the rare gift of your Golden Heart Oneness in your loving partnership, make you the perfect candidates to lead this project. Our hope is that you will agree to do so.

"Golden Beings will be invited from far and wide to actively participate in this new community. Each one will be selected specifically for their unique talents and gifts, and will be asked to contribute these skills toward the birthing and building of this most special Nation.

"There will also be many powerful incoming streams of Golden Radiance from other dimensions, as we mentioned, and these too will be part of the fabric of this great tapestry. This will enable our entire Golden Family, near and far, seen and unseen—from all levels—to boldly shine forth and witness itself in collectively building a far more magnificent contribution

to life than ever before.

"Our goal is to build a stronger, larger, and more vibrantly thriving Golden Family flourishing as One Golden Heart. We do this out of love and profound gratitude to our Maker, to our Source—to that which inspires us all. We do it because it is our nature to love, to grow, to stretch, and to expand. We do it because we are ready to, and because we believe in ourselves and in the joyous Gifts and Power of Golden Love.

"With this having been said, we invite you both, Andar and Avalar, to come on board to get this project underway. If you agree, the first thing for you to do will be to choose the most perfect site, the most perfect home, for this project. We have identified a few Golden Planets that would be suitable for this undertaking, but we will leave it up to you to make the final choice.

"Let us know your decision when you are ready, and we will make plans from there. We are grateful to you both, Beloved Golden Ones.

"One Golden Heart."

With that, Andar and I turn toward one another, and in hushed voices confirm our choice to each other to step up to this beautiful challenge and opportunity. We inform the Council, who respond exuberantly as we all exchange warm hugs of celebration.

We are on our way!

WE MEET OUR BELOVED GOLDEN TERRA

Moving swiftly toward the Gazing Room to view possible sites selected by the Golden Council for our new Golden Nation, Andar and I are so excited that we can hardly contain ourselves. We feel swept up by the beautiful current of Golden Love flowing through this unique project, and its energy feels sweet, kind, and powerful in its grace and purity.

The project seems to be truly alive and birthing itself, as we simply open ourselves to receive it.

Entering the Gazing Room, we step up onto a podium which faces a giant viewing window through which we can see a panorama of planetary systems that are absolutely breathtaking. We are in awe for a moment. The expanse of magnificence which stretches before us moves us both to say a prayer of gratitude to our Creator for such inspiring beauty.

What a sight to behold! As we slowly take it all in, we notice three planets which are more lit up than the others and are calling for our attention. We zoom in on the first one, allowing our senses to gravitate there and to reveal the resonance that this planet holds. It feels simply incredible, but we still have two others to explore.

As we focus in on the second planet, it is as though we are being lifted like dancing lights of joy. We feel good with this one as well—but in a totally different way. Taking a moment, we pull our energies back so that we can see the whole panoramic picture once again.

Now we can see the third planet more clearly. It is a small one that is beaming brilliantly far off in the distance, beckoning to us. We might have inadvertently overlooked it simply because it isn't as large as the others, but the essence of its brightness draws us toward it and piques our curiosity. Instantly, we recognize that its quality is deeper, richer, and more substantial than anything else we have seen. Looking to each other for confirmation, we quickly agree to explore this one further.

Turning our full attention toward this planet, allowing ourselves to be swept in by it, we soon feel as if we are traveling on a pathway filled with recognition. Sensing that we already know this planet well, we wonder, "How is this possible?"

In turn, it's as though she already knows us, and has been waiting for this exact moment!

As her gentle energy holds us strong and secure, tears spring to my eyes. I want to feel more of this. Unable to help myself, I realize I have fallen in love with the beautiful Presence of this planet. Feeling a connection this strong, something stirs deeply in my heart, and my whole system automatically opens in response to the "rightness" of our connection. This is clearly meant to be.

I manage somehow to direct some of my attention toward Andar. I want to check in to see if he is feeling the same way, before going any further.

Turning my gaze toward him, one glimpse into his eyes reveals a separate Universe of pure Gold unfolding within his Heart. Yes, his system has already responded automatically as well. It is as though connecting with this planet has activated depths of powerful knowing and remembrance in him of his greatness and joy—even more than he has ever felt before. The vast treasure of his deep inner beauty is shining boldly, brilliantly, and clearly.

I know and experience him in this moment being truly seen and understood, wholly loved and cared for, deeply supported, and brought to complete peace within. This planet, this beautiful, sacred, glorious planet, is indeed his true and abiding friend. Having brought him more deeply home to himself, it has completely opened him up inside and his Golden brightness is dazzling.

I see wondrous "Universes of Gold" now weaving themselves together in unison and harmony as they bring the entire energetic expanse of Golden Life together in great joy to a meeting point inside of him. Now becoming the "Holder of the Golden Cosmos," he is being deliberately activated as the Golden Bridge between sacred conduits of Golden support and communication from many other dimensions of our Golden Heart family.

I see and feel how deeply moved he is, how his awareness has suddenly opened more than ever in the face of this planet's loving acknowledgement and embrace. I watch as he closes his eyes and begins to cry, tears gently rolling down his cheeks. In this moment I love him more than ever, and my heart swells with passion for him; he is so very beautiful, such a magnificent man to behold.

Continuing to watch Andar, I soon become aware of great Golden Universes opening inside of me, too, although differently. It's as though a great rumbling and rearranging is taking place deep within my Being. My energetic Birthing Canals and Conduits of Creation open more fully, pulling me deeply inside my own Creation Center—deep, deep, and deeper still. I couldn't stop it if I tried, and I certainly don't want to.

I feel my Golden Power and Golden Stability increasing more than ever, feel myself becoming Mother of Golden Creation Birthing. Intense and rich, I feel full of a wisdom and beauty that bursts inside of me; stretching and enlarging me. It is making me incredibly exhilarated and alive while at the same time bringing me to a place within myself that is deep, quiet, and calm. How it all happens in the same moment I do not know, but it does.

This beautiful Golden Planet is moving me, changing me, opening me wide in the most positive of ways, and making my Golden brightness dazzle as well. I feel her energy spiraling through me and expanding me, revealing a sense of her profound wisdom and knowledge, her passion, and her endless caring for life; her intense love of birthing forth and creating magnificence anew—again and again.

What a powerful and gloriously passionate Being she is! And she makes me more completely aware that I am as well.

I feel my intensity of Being beginning to match hers. She is a deep one, and so am I. But what I have known of myself is nothing compared to what will be discovered by being with her in this co-creative endeavor. She is powerful. She is endless, powerful, Golden Goodness.

Suddenly, I also start to weep with tears of gratitude and joy as I recognize how much I have already opened in myself because of her. I know we have found our Golden Home, and Andar knows it too. As we look at each other in the midst of these sensations, we are clearly in agreement that this is THE ONE.

Instantly, we know that it is time to go, to be fully with her in every way. Clearly our new adventure is now in process, our next Creation already being born.

Our energies continue to shift and change even more. Surrendering ourselves fully to her, we begin falling deeper and deeper into her heart. As we are firmly pulled into her resonance our positions adjust, and we move steadily toward her exact location. We are aware that this is happening stage by stage, on energetic levels, and will continue to do so before we become the physicality of it. This destination which we have chosen and wholly committed ourselves to has us eagerly excited as we finally speed toward her—leaving life as we have known it behind forever.

I am aware of Andar gripping my hand. I can feel the electricity moving through his body and into mine, and back again. I feel the Golden Cells of his Being merge and vibrate with mine as his Soul—my Soul, OUR SOUL—beams its dazzling Golden Light. The journey becomes even more focused and intense.

We are being propelled through space and dimensions, the ONENESS of Golden Heart that we have become growing crystallized and strengthened—our One Golden Sound amplified. We feel ourselves "Golden Solidifying"—merging, harmonizing, aligning with and within each other more perfectly than we have yet known. We know this is happening precisely because we are in the process of being aligned as One with the Golden Body, Being, Soul, and Heart of this exquisite Golden Planet. We feel her enveloping us with ALL her love, beyond anything we could have ever dreamed of.

We receive her fully, and in doing so, it is as though she suddenly becomes our everything: Teacher, Mentor, Wise One; our deepest and most trusted friend ever. We want and need to know more, to be moved yet still more powerfully within ourselves. We want to connect with her in a most physical way, to feel her with our bodies as well as our Souls.

At this precise moment of our yearning we feel ourselves landing solidly upon her as everything becomes tactile and physicalized. Our feet gently but solidly touching the ground, we have fully arrived. Yes!

We begin to feel her joy and immense welcome rushing up through the soles of our feet. This is powerful. She is powerful. Andar and I grip each other's hands as we stand shaking like vibrating tops, and it is all we can do to stay upright.

After a few moments, the reverberations begin to subside as we feel ourselves being physically flooded with soft, tender, warm love that makes us tingle and glow inside. She has become so soothing and gentle—what a contrast to the intense vibrating we just went through.

As she touches us with her tenderness, our insides open yet again, creating still new depths of freedom and space. At the same time, our senses become heightened, and we are more alert, activated, and wide awake.

We notice our senses in a profoundly physical way, and smell is first; her moist scent is sweet, rich, and fresh. We breathe in deeply, enjoying it immensely.

Next come the sounds of birds singing, tree limbs creaking gently, and soft winds blowing. Listening intently, we love what we hear.

Next comes the sensation of the air around us, gentle and caressing, it is like silk: soft, smooth, and kind to the skin. Our bodies tingle with its touch, and we are both soothed and invigorated by it. Becoming aware of her soil beneath us, our toes wiggle in delight. The immense pleasure we experience as her physical body touches ours makes us feel warm inside, happy and lighthearted.

Pausing for a moment, aware of her steadiness beneath our feet, of how deeply we already love the pure, joyous physicality of her textures, we feel secure and stable. We breathe in deeply, allowing each breath to penetrate our bellies, connecting ourselves with the ground of this Planetary Being. We feel thoroughly supported, and find ourselves sinking in as we relax fully. It is wonderful to be here.

Slowly turning our bodies so that we can have a 360-degree view, we realize how glorious her beauty truly is. There is so much to take in from her, so many colors, shapes, and textures!

As we look around, she shows us the richness of her landscape, displaying a huge array of her gifts. In one direction, we see fields and meadows, flowers and grasses swaying gently back and forth. Soft, rolling hills provide a backdrop of serenity and peace. Trees and forests open in the distance, with great mountains and their peaks thrusting themselves upward majestically to meet the sky.

In another direction we see gently flowing streams and wide rivers with waterfalls cascading down over one another in joyous abandon. These waters eventually find their way to the coast, where the beaches, oceans, and vistas are magnificent. The richness of color is breathtaking, as are all the undulating, organic shapes and forms. She is simply the most beautiful Body of Life we have ever seen.

Gazing up, our eyes are literally filled with the sky. My goodness! It is the most beautiful blue that one could ever imagine, spreading itself out joyously, high and wide, like a gorgeous cape of endless freedom. As if this weren't enough, stunning rainbows arc above as though for our pleasure alone. We are completely awed and moved by it all.

We breathe it in deeply, continuing to let her endless beauty cascade throughout our bodies and Beings. Our senses remain greatly heightened and energized, and we realize that a pulsating Golden radiance is emanating from her skin and permeating everything—including us.

She sparkles, she shines, she glistens and glows; she positively reverberates with joy. She is complete and utter exhilaration embodied.

Andar and I look at one another in total amazement.

For us, simply being a part of this, being included in this magnificent creation, is far beyond anything that we could have dreamed—and yet, we know this is just the beginning!

Taking a deep breath in unison, we offer up a prayer of thanksgiving. From this moment on, we decide to refer to her as our Golden Terra. Our lovingly beautiful, solid Golden ground.

How happy and grateful we are to be here—to be able to call this our home.

Our Golden Terra Speaks

Still standing quietly with deep gratitude in our hearts we now hear a sound. A gentle hum at first, it gradually increases in depth and intensity as the air begins to vibrate. Andar and I listen intently, wondering what this is. Unexpectedly, the sound moves inside of us, penetrating our cells and filling our bodies until we are shaking with its vibration; we have BECOME the sound ourselves. We look at each other and start laughing—we look so funny wobbling all over the place, all arms and legs flapping around, trying to maintain our balance. After a moment a most beautiful, melodic voice springs forth from inside the sound and all motion stops. Taking a moment to regain our equilibrium, we hear what we intuitively know is the voice of our sweet Golden Terra speaking to us:

"Welcome, my most Beloved Ones.

"I am delighted and honored to have you here. I have been watching you from afar for a long time, hopeful that we would come together like this someday. My longing was what prompted your recognition of me and it is a great privilege to have you here upon me. I know you have chosen me, and I am most pleased.

"I want you to know that I AM HERE FOR YOU. I am here to tend to you, to support you, and to share with you all that I am. I am yours for as long you are here, having waited for an opportunity to grow myself in new and bigger ways for a long time. I know that the plan for us is for you to build a new Golden Nation with me, and that we are doing this together as One.

"I have yearned for this, and yearned for you. I have yearned for greatness of Golden expression beyond what I have known. It is my greatest gift to GIVE to you, and in the giving is my gift back. Giving to you enriches me; giving to you is my heart's fulfillment.

"My Maker is the same as yours. I am as compelled as you are to continually reach and stretch and express more and more of my beauty and endless love. I cannot help but do so, and neither can you. Together, we

have begun to merge and become One. We have started to establish a strong and steady foundation from which to build our future—forming a base that will serve as the greatest platform of Golden Love that has ever been seen, heard, or known throughout the Cosmos. Ours is a great unfoldment, a great revelation of who our Source is through us. A great song of Golden Love to be heard and received throughout all the Planetary Systems of Golden Heart.

"I know that many dimensions of Golden Ones will be joining with us in this great Creation. Together, we will touch with our deepest joys the hearts of all of Life. Together, we will birth anew. Together, we will create Golden beauty beyond measure in the pure exhilaration of being our Source—giving our ALL and BEING OUR ALL.

"Our Golden Power is limitless and knows no bounds. It is up to us to be its joyous freedom and fulfillment. Our guiding force is One Golden Love, One Golden Heart. I love you, dearest ones. As our lives grow together, I will be able to show you this more and more. Thank you for Being. I am happy you are here."

And with this, Andar and I are flooded with her love—intense, deep, and powerful, it sweeps through every part of our One Being. She moves into our One Heart, making it sing a brand-new song of Golden Love and Joy that carries a message of forever, a song of beauty more intense than we have ever felt before. She is loving us so thoroughly and powerfully that we find ourselves overflowing with complete and utter contentment. What an amazing experience this continues to be.

And we love her back. Oh, how we love her back! Over and over again, joyous waves of pure glorious love wash back and forth between us, through us, and around us. For myself, I think I might just burst from the sheer beauty of it. That's how powerful it is.

As I look at Andar, I see that we both know how profoundly changed by her we already are—and in the best of ways. Her giving is our receiving. Our receiving is, in turn, our giving. And so, the circle of endless Golden Loving continues.

Feeling grateful, honored, and filled with peace, we know this is the start of something wondrously powerful, strong, and abiding—and that we and our Golden Terra are part of a truly beautiful Creation:

ONE GOLDEN HEART.

ENTERING THE GOLDEN CORE CRYSTAL

Standing quietly in admiration of our beloved Golden Terra, she speaks softly to us again:

"Come, my sweet, dear friends. I have something special I want to show you. Come with me."

We feel ourselves being gently transported inside of her body. We go deeper and deeper, gliding down in a graceful way. It is effortless and automatic. We can feel the atmosphere changing and becoming, ironically, even more rarified and refined. The air seems to be made of shining bright dancing particles—like tiny diamonds sparkling everywhere. We glide silently through this magical mist.

Gradually our motion stops, and the next thing we know we're standing inside a beautiful cavern-like room. Everything about this place sparkles, as though we are inside a crystal. The sensation is of being not just below the surface of her skin, but deep inside of Terra's Center.

As our eyes adjust to our surroundings, it becomes clear that we are in a holy place of immense sacredness and peace. The atmosphere is glowing softly, bathed in Golden light which now penetrates us right to our Core. Standing on what appears to be a solid bank of crystalline rock, I see how extraordinary this place is; it shines, the light bouncing off wet stone and beautiful gems, and endless crystalline surfaces are all around. Golden radiance highlights the natural designs and patterns on the floor, and everything, every inch of it, feels amazingly rich, alive, and activated.

I look up and see a magnificently faceted crystalline ceiling with vivid rainbow colors emerging from its intricate planes. The organically shaped walls of the room contain varying sized stalactites, shimmering from within with even more vibrant color and light. The atmosphere is whisper quiet, except for a gentle rhythm of water dripping in the background. The sound is of the moist richness and beauty of this Body of Life, ancient and serene.

Aware of the depth and sacredness of the crystal formations, it becomes apparent to us that they are also full of information. It's as though anything we would ever need to know could be answered here, because this place has ALL information from throughout time, dimension, and space. This is incredible! Not only is all of it exquisitely beautiful, but it is also a Golden Library filled with sacred wisdom and knowledge.

We feel profoundly blessed to have been invited here, to know about this, and to be part of this great wealth and wisdom that we will be able to draw upon whenever it is needed.

I look at Andar, and as he reaches for my hand, we both close our eyes and breathe it all in. What a gift we are being given. We are so grateful. We sense that Terra has brought us here not only to feel and get to know her depths, but to also deepen into ourselves. As we experience more of her intricacies in this physical way, her INNER beauties are becoming tangible and accessible to us. In culmination, we feel our own inner worlds of beauty rising more clearly to our conscious awareness, like land masses emerging out of the deep blue sea. We feel as though we are literally being beautified.

We continue to breathe deeply. In fact, breathing seems to be one of the most important things we are doing! It seems to be the way that we are gently adjusting to everything we are experiencing. This is all brand new for us, and it is a lot to integrate. We remind ourselves to simply stay soft and relaxed, and flow.

Noticing a distinct shift in the physical atmosphere, the vibrations around us begin changing again. In one corner of the room we see a small mass of Golden Energy swirling in place. Andar and I watch in amazement as it grows bigger, becoming more and more voluminous and substantial, finally materializing into a beautiful Golden Presence pulsating directly in front of us. Shimmering rays of Golden Love cascade outward and move gently toward us, surrounding our bodies and softly reaching into our hearts. We feel ourselves opening fully and freely to this beauty, and as we do so, the Golden Presence in front of us begins to speak. We instantly recognize it as the melodic voice of our Beloved Terra, only with a more ethereal, even more refined quality to her tone this time. The rhythm of her voice is like a lullaby moving tenderly through us now, its effect blissfully comforting and peaceful. Reaching for Andar's hand, we both bask in the energy gracing us here.

This Golden Presence says:

"My Beloveds, I welcome you again. You stand deep inside my Golden Core Crystal, deep within the Center of my Golden Body.

"I am the Sacred Golden Soul of this Beloved Being, our precious Golden Terra. I am that which moves her and gives her Life. I am the Creation of the magnificent One, our Source of ALL, and I am responsible for this Golden Planet, for her well-being, fruitfulness, and flourishing of all Life as I know it. She is my Body, visible and invisible, and the Sacred Matter that I have become.

"I can express the fullness of Source, of that which birthed me, expressing it freely throughout this magnificent demonstration of physical life. I can exist here, in actual material form, and become ever greater and more brilliant as I so choose and desire.

"It is my dream to fulfill the power of the two greatest abilities that My Source has bestowed upon me—LOVE and BEAUTY—both of which are my most precious gifts to be and to share.

"In light of it all, I have called you to myself as Masterful Heart-Centered Ones who are rich in Golden Love, grateful for the opportunity to serve and amaze our Creator, together, we are here at the delight of our God: we are the receivers and expressors of all that is pure Godliness—what a most sacred gift it is TO BE.

"This Golden Nation that we have chosen to build together will be a radiant jewel in the greater Cosmos. It is only just beginning, of course, but soon you will witness great wondrousness and miracles—great love incarnate, expressing itself freely and vividly for all to witness and enjoy. This is the plan, the intention: an offering back to Life of her own majesty and resplendence.

"Ours is a contribution to ourselves as well, so that we can witness the flowing of pure Golden Life moving through us as an art form, as a dance. It is an exhilaration which inspires Golden Creations for all to see, hear, feel, touch, and be inspired by. Through this, it provides not only for our growth and development as individual Life Forms, but also for ALL Life everywhere—and I mean EVERYWHERE. This is a holy and sacred thing. The gift of this opportunity is rare and powerful, deliberate and consciously co-creative.

"Understanding and utilizing energy in this way is done with great care. As you know, our energies can be directed in whatever way we choose. This means, of course, that we are entirely responsible for all that happens as the result of what we choose to create and energize into, and through: form. The power of our Creations affects the whole—and not just when formalized, but also right from the beginning, as the seed of our intentions, the origin of their purity and power.

"Our Golden Nation is like a grand experiment, although, in truth, it is the gift and prize of which I spoke. Those who come to participate directly in this manifestation of Golden Love have been selected carefully and judiciously. They are well developed, highly talented, and gifted Souls who already know how to direct their energies positively in life-enhancing ways. Extremely skilled in their gifts, they are strong and superior in their abilities to foster that which they bring through into physical—and equally as powerful—non-physical form.

"They have been invited and have chosen to come here to be a part of this grand Golden Creation, and they know what is expected of them. There will be no slackers. This is CREATION raised to new heights, with deliberate intent to beautify and glorify God and the greater Cosmos at large.

"We are doing this to demonstrate that all of us Golden Ones, from all levels and dimensions—seen and unseen—can come together as one great magnificent Golden Heart. This is our purpose, and this we will all do to the best of our abilities, and then some.

"Always striving to do our best, we love to stretch beyond what we thought ourselves capable of. After all, our Source is endless possibility, so who are we to question that? Our greatest love is to surrender to the beauty and magnificence that we are made of, radiating this forth as far and wide as it desires to go. Reaching, touching, and caressing all of life with our dreams and passions fulfilling themselves. There is no end.

"All of this must come from a clear, deliberate, and conscious beginning. The vision must be clear; the seeds we plant most lovingly nurtured, tended to, and adored into Being. The two of you know this well already. Together, united as One, we will continue to expand and foster this masterful Golden Creation.

"As we speak, some of those Golden Ones from faraway places, from other domains and dimensions, are beginning to gather upon my sacred surface. When you return there, you will see that the building of our Golden Nation has already begun and is in full swing. You will be delighted and amazed at the differences you see and feel, even in the short time we have been down here together.

"Know that this Golden Core Crystal is a sacred replenishing ground for you. This chamber, this crystalline sanctuary of mine, is both my Core and my holy Center of Manifest Being. It is also the Golden Center of Great Power for the two of you, providing replenishment and all that you will ever need to sustain yourselves and to thrive as the Great Golden Leaders that you are.

"Come often. Come here together. This is you, AVALANDAR, the configuration of the two of you as ONE being held in my sacred Golden Heart and Being. I treasure you. You are precious jewels to me.

"You are responsible for making sure to receive from me what you need, when you need it. I am here for you absolutely one hundred percent—but *only YOU can choose to RECEIVE that which I have for you. The receiving aspect of this relationship must come from you in opening to what I have for your needs and sustenance. My gifts are here, and your gift to me is to receive them. In this way we all become richer, stronger, and greater.*

"Enter this Golden Holy Place often. Be enriched by me, and by it, in every way.

"Each of you also has your own individual Golden Restoration Sanctuary, where you will receive great balancing and recharging on all levels possible. You will know when to go to these, and know the difference between your need for individual replenishment and your Avalandar replenishment. It will be clear to you always. Know that every aspect of you has been considered by me, and that we are the hub around which, and through which, this great and glorious Golden Nation will be built, shepherded, and nurtured. We are going to give it our absolute joy filled best, that's who and how we are.

"We will call our nation Lemuria—the sweet sound of Mother in a Golden Way. Her name alone will foster great nurturing and care for all of Life, and it will carry great Golden Love and Blessing wherever it is spoken.

"Her power, as Lemuria, is unto itself as an exquisite Life Form. Know this and be clear about it. In this regard she has a resonant Soul that will speak to you when she is ready. As her body grows, she will become clearer to you and to all who are here to express her and everything she stands for, through their Golden Hearts.

"Know that she has begun her Life. She is gathering herself together, collecting all the individual aspects of herself so that she can form something far greater and glorious beyond that which has ever been known.

"Magnificent will be a word used often when referring to her. She will become as a vibrant breath of Beauty, cascading exuberantly throughout the Universes. Her Freedom will cause great stirring for all, enabling them to reach inside of themselves, remembering that they too are magnificent. A Dream that is being dreamed; how beautiful she is already.

"As you know and feel, Beloved Ones, I love you powerfully and with great passion. There is nothing I will not do for you. You are knowing this now. I am you. You are ME. We are One Golden Heart Beating, loving, blossoming, and thriving.

"Great, great joy is ours. Gratitude is our way. Thank you, beautiful Golden Ones.

"I LOVE YOU."

Andar and I stand here marveling at the power of Golden Love that this Great Soul is expressing. It is palpable. It moves us, touching our Center. We feel completely and utterly blessed, included, enveloped, and honored. We are thoroughly loved and adored.

This is the Golden Presence of the Golden Soul of this beautiful planet. She that runs deep and knows much, a Great Soul that is wise and caring; a holder of great treasures for us yet to know and cherish.

Gazing peacefully at this beautiful Golden Soul standing in front of us—feeling the union of all of us together becoming stronger and more tightly woven—we feel as if we have landed in the deepest well of pure grace. Our gratitude is endless.

"Beloveds," the Golden Presence speaks one last time. *"There is one more stop to make before you return to my surface. Come with me and we will prepare ourselves."*

CHAPTER THREE

ESTABLISHING OUR SACRED GOLDEN FOUNDATION OF LEMURIA

ANDAR AND I FOLLOW the graceful Soul of Golden Terra as she leads us along a narrow corridor, its atmosphere glowing with soft light reflected off still more crystalline-faceted walls. We are silent as we move toward an arched opening.

Suddenly, vibrant golden sparks burst forth from the opening itself, arcing like shooting stars into the night sky. Our hearts beat faster with growing excitement and anticipation. The energy feels almost electric, reverberating in our direction and beckoning us forth.

Arriving at the edge of the opening, Terra suddenly stops. Holding us with her earnest gaze, she turns and says quietly:

"Breathe. Let us breathe together for a moment. You have now come to another deliberate choice-point of this journey, a moment to consciously CHOOSE, yet again, if you still wish to move forward in this way. This pathway heralds uncharted territory, a brand new direction for you and all those that you love.

"Give yourselves permission to let go of all that you have known, all that you have thought, all that you have ever dreamed of. Look deep into your hearts and ask yourselves: is it truly my choice to move forward into a reality that is far greater than I have even imagined? Am I ready for this? Is this what I truly want to do?"

At Terra's urging, Andar and I close our eyes to look deep inside our hearts. It is obvious from the way she is speaking to us that this decisive moment is particularly significant, a point at which we must choose whether to "take the leap and jump off the cliff together." It's big—and our hearts are loving it! They are bursting open, eager to go forth.

When we finally open our eyes and look at each other, the answer to these questions from our Golden Hearts as One is a resounding "Yes!"

The compelling urgency of our Destiny, combined with the effervescence of joy rising in us, now opens us even more—when suddenly, our bodies begin to vibrate with the pulse of Terra's Golden Soul again. In this moment we feel ourselves aligning with her still more deeply, as our choice has been made and our shift set into motion.

With a powerful sense of purpose in her voice, Terra says, *"Let us go now. You are ready."*

We step forward through the opening and find ourselves standing inside an enormous great Golden Hall. It feels like a Golden Temple. Golden Light is emanating from every part of it, causing it to shimmer and shine. A sensation of Golden vitality permeates everything, including us as well. We hear the sweet song of joy in the air, as if all are on the verge of celebration. It is all so wonderfully alive and exuberant.

Andar and I look around, intrigued by all that we see. There are huge sweeping archways rising gracefully to a peak in the ceiling, as if the energy is thrusting itself upward joyously to meet the Heavens. Around the perimeter of the room, we see what appear to be smaller private sanctuaries, tucked away behind smaller archways. Each one feels like it holds the promise of something special inside, gifts waiting to be opened. We find our curiosity piqued, and it becomes obvious to us that this Great Hall has many wondrous layers to it—that it is intended for great things. Its atmosphere of sacredness and God centeredness fills us as we breathe in its beauty, savoring the sensations of it all.

Patiently waiting to see what happens next, we notice a group of Golden Beings emerging from one of the smaller sanctuaries. Andar and I look at each other with surprise. We know them; they are old and dear friends of ours. We return our gaze to them, watching them move across the floor toward us like Golden Gentle Giants gliding on air. They are tall and graceful, and it is obvious by their bearing that these Beings are Golden Masters of a very High Order, each of them exuding a sense of serenity, a peace that is sublime. Andar and I walk forward to greet them, overjoyed that they are here.

We all exchange fond greetings, after which we are invited to follow three of them back into one of the smaller sanctuaries at the farthest corner of the room.

Our Sacred Golden Foundation Begins

Stepping down into the small, private sanctuary, we are met with the soothing fragrance of musk and roses. Andar and I inhale it deeply—right down to our toes. The lighting inside is subdued in comparison to the brightness out in the Great Hall, creating an aura of wondrousness and serenity—the center of the room is bathed in a soft, Golden glow. We can feel the sacred here.

We are aware that the Golden Soul Energy of Terra is here with us as well, as she continues enveloping us in her tender loving care. We know she is here to add her support and her grounding to this occasion.

One of our dear friends beckons Andar and I to the center of the room to stand facing him. Our eyes gaze at him—it is our most Beloved Sananda, shining like the Heart of the Golden Sun. The purity and power of his glowing Golden Radiance touches us deep inside as we rejoice in his unique and splendid beauty. The three of us have journeyed together many times during our evolution, creating and fostering many projects of Golden Love. We have also established Golden Stations throughout the Greater Cosmos and, through it all, have become a very specialized and spectacular Golden Team. Andar and I sense that this moment in time is bringing us to new heights of co-creatorship, so blessed are we to be embarking on this new Golden Project together.

I look deeply into Sananda's eyes, and he into mine. I love him so much. More clearly than ever, I acknowledge how deeply I KNOW this Being. This beloved Friend of my Soul has been with me for what feels like forever, and I love him dearly and trust him completely. He gazes back at me with such tender kindness that tears well up in my eyes and roll slowly down my cheeks. I feel deeply touched, cared for, loved, and recognized.

Andar, still by my side, is experiencing the same communion as I am, being moved deeply in the same way. Something special and deliberate is happening here. Although neither of us yet understands exactly what, or why, we both know we are poised just on the edge of it.

Compelled now to shift our gaze toward our other two dear friends, each on either side of Sananda, we look first at our Beloved Saint Germain, and then at our Beloved Mother Mary. Their pure Golden Goodness and Power move through us like deep waves rolling steadily across the ocean floor, and we feel their great love for us as well. Acknowledging the powerful bonds here shared as long time Golden Soul Friends, we know that we are indeed one Great Golden Family that has already traveled far, and achieved much, in our loving Golden Creatorship.

And here we are together again, facing the beginning of something grand and glorious: a new adventure which is a rare and wondrous opportunity to birth, establish, and spread great Golden Love far and wide.

Golden Sananda begins to speak:

"Dearest Avalar and Andar, we welcome you on this sacred occasion in this holy place. It is indeed a great honor to be together once again.

"You are both outstanding Leaders of Great Golden Heart. We know this. We honor you with all the love in our hearts and our Souls. We are most grateful to you, and for you. Thank you for choosing to be the Golden Leaders Incarnate of this new and sacred Golden Nation that we are here to build. Know that we are all in this WITH you. This, we pledge.

"Today, as we acknowledge the strength of bonds already shared, our love deepens even more. Together, we will be building our Golden Foundation of Lemuria here. This will be a great Golden Configuration, a strong and intricate grid which serves as the base for all the Golden Lemurian Creation yet to come. This is our fundamental energetic Golden Configuration which will hold the Golden Consciousness for all that is then energetically and physically manifested forward. Building this foundation is a prerequisite for our Golden success to come. We ask that you be patient as we take this building process one step, one layer at a time. You will see that it involves the planting and setting down of several different layers, each one as a focused concentration of the Golden Love in our hearts.

"Each layer adds to the next, creating substance and texture to form the solid, steady, and sustaining base our Golden Creations require to be born, to be strong and well-supported. Our movement is focused and clear, steady and deliberate. It is the beginning of the creation of our beloved Lemuria through Divine, deliberate energetic patterning. Each step, each level and layer are critically important and significant—and they are all essential for the strength and success of the Whole.

"We are together now to join with each other more deeply and fully than ever before—heart and soul, mind and body, breath and life, water and blood—to form a Sacred Union, a Sacred Trust, and a Sacred Marriage between us all. Our pledge to one another with Golden Love and Devotion is a promise to nurture and foster this sacred Golden Project throughout our lives from this moment on."

Sananda's voice is rich with emotion and intensity, sweeping us into a current of pure Golden Reverence that compels Andar and I to drop to our knees, bowing our heads. We feel deeply humbled and profoundly blessed. The energy of this holiness washes through us, inspiring and uplifting us in every way. Our Beings hum with delight. We are glowing.

Sananda reaches his hands forward, touching us both on the shoulder, then placing one hand on each of the top of our heads as he continues to speak:

"We have been working our way toward this Golden Creation for a long time—it is precisely what we have been striving for. We now come together to establish ourselves in an even stronger union, a stronger weave, and a stronger Oneness to meet the great opportunity ahead.

"Stand now in this knowing that I speak of."

Sananda signals to us, but as we try to rise, Andar and I hesitate. Weak and wobbly on our knees, we are unable to get back up on our feet! Sensing that our inner terrains have suddenly shifted enormously, we pause, giving ourselves a moment to take a few steadying breaths. At last we stand, carefully facing one another. Reaching out to hold hands, we gaze tenderly into each other's eyes, surrendering completely to the pure power of our Golden love. In a single heartbeat all separation between us is completely and utterly dissolved.

Suddenly, there is no me; there is no him. There is only we—us, and then, finally—One.

ONE GOLDEN ONE.

From somewhere deep inside our Golden Core our energies have merged in soft, undulating waves of Golden Love and Light. Spiraling up like glowing rainbows weaving in and out, they pull us gently toward one another and we physically touch—body to body, heart to heart, skin to skin. Physical forms yielding, our Beings open wide. Our Spirits begin dancing, swaying back and forth like happy palm trees in the wind, infusing themselves into and through each other in a beautifully fluid but deliberately defined and intricate pattern.

Swirling, soaring, singing with pure joy, our Golden energy radiates brightly, expanding ever outward—well beyond the confines of this small room. What a glorious sensation! Becoming lost in our senses, breathing deeply and singing praises to one another and to our Maker, we feel blessed and adored by all of Life. We rejoice again and again.

After a few moments the intensity gradually subsides. Aware of a natural pulse of our Golden Oneness beating in our hearts and flowing through our breath, our energies feel soft and pliable—yet solid and grounded at the same time. We shake our heads to clear our minds as it dawns on us what has happened: our new Golden patterning has been born. It is exquisite and holding steady and strong.

Yes, our Golden Oneness has become ONE GOLDEN CONFIGURATION that has now been laid down and anchored. Through the mists of our realization we hear the crystal-clear voice of Sananda speaking to us again, beckoning our awareness back to him, and to the others that are present with us:

"Our Beloveds, from this moment on you shall be known, even more powerfully than ever before, as Golden Avalandar. It is the Sound and Song of the Union of the two of you as Golden One—forming the creative and sustaining base from which this Golden Nation will be led and will flourish.

"You, as Avalandar, are the 'Human Golden Power Battery.' You are the fostering love which has chosen to devote itself, and its life, to this Creation. We honor and bless you for this, and are deeply grateful.

"Your Ground of Being as Golden Avalandar is solid and secure. It is steady, strong, Pure, and Sacrosanct. You are GOLDEN CLEAR, and your vibrant, Golden, nourishing waters run deep.

"Rejoice in this fully and freely, then rejoice even more, as it is the achievement of Great Golden Love manifesting itself forth anew."

We pause, taking deep Golden Breaths, slowly integrating all that is happening in us, as us. Allowing it to be, we feel complete joy—and deep gratitude.

After a few moments of silence, Sananda speaks again:

"Beloved Avalandar, just as your loving GOLDEN ONENESS has birthed itself into a new and rich Golden Configuration, so is the loving Oneness of all of us here together now ready and yearning to birth forth anew. This is our Sacred Golden Union expanding our Sacred Golden Configuration."

Gathering ourselves into our small circle with hearts joined, Andar and I, Sananda, Master Saint Germain, Mother Mary, and the Golden Soul of Terra weave our Golden Love together until we are no longer individuals, but one glorious Golden Harmonized unit. We are vibrating now as ONE more deeply integrated and splendid Golden Team. United in this way, we have added yet another layer to our Sacred Golden Configuration. This is Golden Creation being born.

The only sound in the room is our breath as One, the beat of our One Golden Heart: steady, strong, and peaceful.

Aware of a powerful strength anchored in my body and Being, this new, even deeper sense of being grounded and secure in my base permeates me. It is unlike anything I've known before. In an instant, I KNOW that I am and will continue to hold steady no matter what—always.

Feeling so happy, I yield even more as I dissolve completely into something far greater than myself.

When ready, our awareness gently returns to our physical surroundings, our hearts joy-filled and grateful for all that has taken place here. We stand quietly until Sananda speaks again:

"From this point on, we are harmonized as One Golden Foundation, woven together by our powerful Golden Love for one another and our endless love for our Creator, that which gave birth to us and sustains us always. Our weave, our formation, will never break; it will never be torn or compromised. It is indelible and impermeable. Holy and Pure, it is Sacrosanct. We are bound by the love for all that we create from this sacred Union—Golden and Free. We pledge ourselves to all of this from this moment forth."

Sananda's impassioned words reverberate inside the small sanctuary, charging the atmosphere with Golden Power and Purpose as our Union resonates with this truth. Our palpable love and gratitude, illuminating all as One, is strengthening us like never before:

"We bless this Golden Union today and our Golden Configuration that has expanded because of it. We are forever grateful.

"This is the beginning of our Sacred Golden Foundation.

"WE ARE ONE.

"WE ARE ONE GOLDEN CONFIGURATION.

"WE ARE ONE GOLDEN HEART."

As our ceremony comes to a close and we prepare to return to the Great Hall, the unmistakable sound of giant wings beating joyously together reminds us that the Divine Golden Angels and Archangels have joined with us to pledge themselves to our blessed Union today.

Step by step, this now forms the sustaining platform for an even greater Golden Foundation to be born.

OUR SACRED GOLDEN FOUNDATION EXPANDS

Slowly moving back out into the Great Golden Hall, we are greeted with a wondrous sight. While we were tucked away in our private ceremony, many Golden Ones from all walks of life have congregated here and are greeting and celebrating each other. The air is charged with excitement and anticipation as everyone knows they are here for a very special reason. Delighting in this beautiful gathering, we move slowly toward the other end of the room, signaling to everyone that it is time to start settling down. At last, all is quiet.

Sananda steps forward to speak:

"On behalf of everyone, I welcome you all, beautiful Beloved Golden Ones.

"You have been invited here today for the important purpose of marking the beginning of an entirely new movement for all of us, and for the Golden Cosmos at large. Because of its significance, this is still, again, another conscious choice point for each of you. And, even though we know you are here because you want to be, we ask that you once again declare your CONSCIOUS CHOICE to be an active and integral part of what will take place here today, and henceforth. Once you have said 'yes,' please know there is no turning back. You will already be an essential, entrusted, and activated cog in this sacred wheel.

"Before we go any further, please take a moment of quiet introspection to check in with yourselves, with your hearts. Then choose, if you wish, to fully participate in this next mission together. When you are absolutely clear that your choice is to move forward with us, please signal this by joining all of us in a circle around the room. Thank you, we honor you all."

The circle takes shape quickly as Sananda steps into its center, accompanied by Master Saint Germain and Mother Mary.

Sananda speaks again:

"Blessings, Beloved Golden Ones. We honor and thank you for being here with us in full conscious consent, as well as in full conscious Presence.

"We are gathered here now to expand our Sacred Golden Configuration, which will serve as the Sacred Golden Foundation of our blessed Lemuria. Initial stages have already been established and anchored in, and now it is time to set down its remaining layers. Together, our Golden Love will continue to be the architect and builder of our expanding, co-creative tapestry.

"While this Union, this Marriage of all of us together as One Golden Holy Sacrament, involves all of the two-legged ones, along with our Golden Terra, it also includes the Animal Kingdom, Nature, and ALL of the Creations of this beautiful Planet: the Natural World, the Elementals, the Seen and Unseen vibratory Golden Life Forms. In addition, it also includes the many radiant voices of Golden Hearted Ones from the Stars, and from farther off in the Cosmos, and beyond."

As Sananda pauses for a moment, a great whooshing sound suddenly erupts throughout the Great Hall. Pouring forth into the room with great excitement are hordes of Golden Energies of varying shapes and sizes. Every single level of Golden Life is represented here.

Not only do we see many other Golden Two-Legged Ones, but we also see and sense incoming Radiant Streams of Golden Life Forms arriving from many dimensions, near and far. Fairy, Devic, Water, Air, Wind, and Fire Beings. Elementals. Representatives of the Tree, Rock, Soil, Flower, Insect, Bird, and Animal Kingdoms. Representatives from the vast Sea World. More Golden Masters, Golden Angels, and Golden Archangels and others from the Golden Celestial Realms. Indeed, the entire array of Golden Family is represented here with great joy and enthusiasm.

Their unique energies, sounds, and frequencies vibrate as they fill up the entire room to the very top of the ceiling, until the air is thick with rich and pulsating Golden Life celebrating.

It is an enormous and breathtaking Golden Convergence. A joining together of powerful Golden Light and Love FAR beyond anything that Andar and I have ever considered even remotely conceivable. Such is the vastness of this gathering, this supremely joyous event and amazingly momentous occasion.

Noisy exuberance continues to reign, as this vast panorama of radiant Golden Energies swirl all around the Great Hall looking for a way to align and settle down. Finally, it somehow happens, amazingly so, and together, we form circles within circles with hands and hearts joined.

Our attention is now drawn toward the center of the innermost circle, where we begin to hear what sounds like a deep and beautiful heartbeat. It soon becomes obvious that this is the Golden Heartbeat of our splendid, beloved Golden Terra. This becomes our point of focus as we all simultaneously register that this Great Hall is located within her Golden Core Crystal. We smile, as the sound of her comforting, steady, Golden Heartbeat fills the space in and around us.

Within seconds, our heartbeats coalesce with hers, and we become ONE Golden Heartbeat. We each send our devotion to her, honoring her deeply as the exquisite and generous Being that she is. Loving her more than words can say in this holy moment, we feel strong and sustained in the energy of her Golden Body and Light; and as we love her, she loves us with equal intensity.

Soon, we see the manifested energy of her Golden Soul standing quiet and clear in the middle of our circle. She is splendidly beautiful as her voice emanates from her presence:

"Blessed Ones, I love you. I love that you have all chosen to be here with me. I love and feel you honoring me right now. I know that we all know and feel the tremendous inspiration of our Source, our beautiful Creator that has birthed us forth and given us the opportunity of this life. It is made even more special because we are traveling on this journey together and will create great love because of it. This is a unique and remarkable adventure that we are embarking upon. I am so grateful that you have come. Thank you. With all my Heart and Soul, thank you. I love you."

Bathed in her powerful love and gratitude, everyone sinks more deeply still into the sound of our one Golden heartbeat. As Terra said, we all feel the depth of our love for our Maker, and we cherish this opportunity to forge new pathways of love, to spread forward the wonders that rise from our most intimate and precious devotion with our Source.

Enriched by the reverence that permeates this room, Andar and I feel compelled to join with Terra in the center of the circle. As we patiently await her next move, we are acutely aware of the increasing excitement in the room as everyone prepares to expand our Golden Foundation, ready to add more layers of patterning and purpose.

At this precise moment, Terra's Golden Soul energy reaches forward and spreads out, wrapping us all securely as she breathes her breath into our bodies with a whooshing sound like a giant bellows expelling air. We feel ourselves becoming huge inside, as if our inner space is expanding well beyond any physical boundaries. Our energies continue to move outward, eagerly stretching into the ethers far beyond the planet. We reach still further until we know we have touched what was destined to be met. Hearts beating faster now, our breath quickens for a moment—until suddenly, everything becomes quiet. A new pulse is felt, steady and rhythmical.

We have just merged with the essence of something else sacred and special, something glorious that previously felt very far away. We realize we have become one with all the Golden Stars and entire Golden Cosmos beyond. We feel the electrical sensation of our patterning expanding, adding new levels to form a bigger and more intricate, splendid design. Our beautiful tapestry of Golden Love becomes even more magnificent.

We hear Terra's voice reverberating in us:

"Beloveds, we are now inexorably joined with all the Golden Stars, all the Golden Energies in the Golden Cosmos, and beyond, that have ever been. Expanding and strengthening our foundation still more, this greater gathering of Golden Love into your cells is establishing powerful interstellar conduits in your bodies, hearts, minds, and all your senses.

"I urge you to soften inside, and to breathe slowly and deeply. Allow all of this to integrate now and settle into position comfortably inside of you. Welcome it, rejoicing quietly as you feel our growing configuration taking place."

We continue to feel this glorious energy filling us, combining with the pure strength and grounding of Terra coming up through the soles of our feet. It is a strong and powerful sensation. We hear again the deep resonance of our one Golden Heartbeat, which now sounds even richer, signaling that we are growing bigger and more inclusive—and because of this, even more Golden radiant. The foundation of our One Golden Family is increasing in size, strength, and complexity as our new balance and patterning is anchored in. Taking slow deep breaths, we integrate this until we are saturated with great peacefulness, a sign that this process is now complete.

Terra confirms this as she says, *"Golden Ones, yes, this Golden Integration is now indeed complete. Our Sacred Golden Configuration and thus our foundation is even deeper, stronger, and more radiant than before. Job well done! What a masterpiece we are creating."*

Smiling with pride and affection, we beam at one another. Stretching our love out like this feels so good—and what a beautiful result.

In the midst of our glowing, Andar and I suddenly become aware of Terra's focus shifting directly toward us. She holds us purposefully in her energy as she speaks what is in her heart:

"My most Beloved Avalandar, I thank you yet again for being the Great Golden Leaders Incarnate of what is becoming our Beloved Lemuria. You are the Golden Hub around which she will continue to be created, through which the vast Golden Energy Streams will flow, and the incoming Golden Conduits of the Sacred Stars and Cosmos will have their presence here with us. YOU are the Holders of Great Golden Love and Light. You are the Shepherds that will see this through. You are the Masters through which this tapestry, this magnificent Golden Creation, will continue to be steady, move forward, and flourish.

"We come together as One Golden Configuration, but you are the pioneers that make this even possible. You are the Golden Leaders who have agreed to incarnate and guide this project and its purpose from here, you are therefore the ones through which all this manifestation can start to physically take place and grow. I will be grateful to you forever. We will all be grateful to you forever."

And with that, a roar of thunderous applause rings out as cheers fill the air:

"We love you, Avalar and Andar! We love you, Avalandar. WE ARE WITH YOU. We are with you. ALWAYS, ALWAYS, ALWAYS!"

Momentarily taken aback by this unexpected outburst, Andar and I turn to each other in complete surprise. Powerful waves of Golden Love and joy from everyone present are suddenly pouring into us, filling us with such sweet sensations of warmth and caring. Our hearts burst wide open with total love and gratitude in return. Back and forth we go for a few moments, all of us infusing each other with our tender love and caring. We are extremely grateful for one another.

It is a most special communion, one which Andar and I realize is not just about the immense Golden Love that we all share, but also the respect, support, and loyalty we have for each other. It is about the power and passion of our One Golden Family and the message that although each has our own role to fulfill and our own position to hold, we are all in this TOGETHER, cheering each other on heartily. We are a splendid Golden Team resonating together, aligned in love and working as One toward our goals. We are One Golden Team, One Golden Family united, sustained, and strong. The strength of this powerful solidarity is brought home to us, and we embrace it wholeheartedly.

Tears of gratitude glisten in Andar's eyes, and my own as well. We are profoundly moved by what is happening. Suddenly, the energy shifts and Andar and I both burst out laughing! We are overflowing with so much love, joy, and well-being going back and forth that we just can't help ourselves. Soon, everyone else is joining in our laughter as our celebration grows. What a truly exhilarating experience.

COMPLETION OF OUR SACRED GOLDEN FOUNDATION

We savor how much we love our Golden Family, and how diverse it is. There are so many of us here, of all shapes and sizes, and from many walks and dimensions of life—but the common thread that weaves us together is the fiber of our Golden Hearts and our devotion to all that this means to us. Collectively, we praise our beloved Source for our joyous freedom to BE—and to be One Golden Family. How delicious it is.

In the midst of our joy, Sananda's voice rings clear:

"Golden Ones, yes, this family is beautiful, unique, wondrous—and enormous. There are so many of us from all over that grace our lives. We sing our praises to them whenever we are close in body or in thought. This loving acknowledgment reaches everyone because we are interwoven, and our adoration uplifts us all.

"While it is important and beautiful to focus your loving on the Whole, it is also essential to focus it on YOU. This is what we are going to talk about now. Naturally, this leads you home to our beloved Creator.

"Now it is time to focus yourselves in your praise of our Source, in praise of you, the magnificent creation of our Source that you are.

"Golden Ones, you are divine. Stand in this now. Receive yourselves. Open your Inner Senses still more. Feel your passion for that which created you, our Divine Source and Inspiration. This is the bedrock of you, the Being that you are, the life force that breathes you and moves through you. Beautiful are you, this radiance. Splendid are you, this grace. Happy are you, this delight. Inspiring are you, this joy. Serene are you, this peace. This, your treasure, Ground, and Sacred Center. This, your eternal Heart beating.

"How passionate you are!

"How full of life you are!

"Rejoice now!

"You are beautiful!

"We give thanks for you.

"As you already well know, this is where you always begin, with any creation that you make. You always devote yourself to giving praise to this Divine Energy that you are made of, first and foremost. In your solid Oneness with your Source, all is clear and easeful, your Heart full with the endless gift of loving. You praise the splendid beauty of you that is the wondrous manifestation of our supreme Creator. You are God's precious gift of love BEING, a blessing for us all.

"Standing inside your devotion, you shine: full, radiant, strong, graceful, and steady. You feel the magnificent gift of Golden Love that your Source has blessed you with that empowers you and inspires you to new heights of glorious creativity. It fills your heart, moving you as you give thanks and praise now. Doing so anchors this deeply.

"You are standing strong in this Golden Love—purposeful, bold, and brilliant. You are Golden Purpose inspired, empowered to reach forward in the divine act of creating more beauty from its greatness, expressing joyously, sharing freely its wondrous treasures. You give praise to this now. In this you stand strong, Golden Love gloriously outshining. We give thanks for the Unique Golden Blessing that is you.

"So it is with our Golden Configuration. Our Golden love, passion, and purpose are being set down in a deliberate pattern with a deliberate purpose and Divine goal. This energy is collecting, stabilizing, and organizing itself into this solid energetic base that holds the intention and frequency of our intended outcome: Golden Lemuria, flourishing and free.

"We are continuing to add layer upon layer to this patterning as we deepen into our love of our Source, ourselves, one another, and our entire Golden Family, vibrating as One Golden Heart. This is the Golden energy that our configuration holds strong and steady for us, anchored in as our secure foundation from now on. This is Golden Intelligence. It is Golden Love designing and building. It is One Golden Heart being set in motion. We acknowledge and praise this.

"Even though we will be adding still more layers to it, I ask you now to BE the Golden Configuration that we have established. Own it. You are in it. Stand firm in its support and radiance. Breathe it in gratefully and praise it as you breathe out. As it supports you, you support it. Feel here how your gratitude and your praise anchors it throughout your conscious awareness. Feel how strong, how steady this makes you feel. Feel how strong and steady this makes our Golden Family feel. From this foundation, we can do anything.

"We give praise to this now."

We all stand firmly focusing ourselves, connecting deeply with the stability and richness of our Golden Configuration, giving thanks for it, and praising it with all our hearts. As we do so, we feel supported and secured and the energy feels solid, just as Sananda said. Powerful strength rises in us all, giving way to new and abundant confidence and clarity. Yes. This is the sensation of deliberately grounded Golden Anchoring and Power. It makes us feel huge and steady, releasing great joy within that which is now compelled to outshine, express, create, and share. Being us is a rich experience with bold intentions. It feels amazing to feel so Golden strong and steady.

Sananda speaks:

"Yes, you are consciously aware now of the power and strength of what we are setting down here, of our Sacred Golden Configuration. From this anchored position, I invite you to share your Golden Love, experiencing what that is like. Be conscious of how this action of sharing enriches you—it is not only a gift for the receiver, it is a gift to you.

"We will begin with our beloved Terra."

Gently, our focus is drawn back to Terra again: she is such a mainstay of ours. We feel her energy of strength and support moving up through our feet, and our legs, up into our hearts and psyches. It gently spreads throughout our bodies. She is comforting and stabilizing, grounding and peaceful in us and around us. She provides substance to our energetic experiences and enables us to feel and be anchored in physically; steady in a way that we need as long as we are incarnate. We are grateful to her for all of this and so much more.

"Consciously direct your Golden Love, now," Sananda continues. *"Breathing it deeply and fully into Terra, into her Golden Cells."*

We begin pouring our love for Terra directly into the cells of her body. We breathe, exhaling our joy into her, knowing that she is receiving us fully. It feels marvelous to love her, to feel her drinking it in as she is touched and enriched by us. Feeling filled with her tender love in return, our sharing continues. It is a powerful sensation, shining brightly in our mutual Golden Loving.

Slowly, our collective energies begin to coalesce into one solid pillar of Golden Being. Again, it feels profoundly solid. It is strong and radiant and outshining; our Golden Breath moves deeply in and out, our Golden Configuration becoming still stronger, more intricate, and more anchored.

My heartbeat changes, pulsing differently than ever before.

I am aware of my eyes, Golden and focused inward toward myself. I am acutely aware of my Golden body, my Golden Blood coursing through me.

I become aware of the Golden cells, atoms, and molecules that make up my physical body.

I am aware of the Golden Waters, spreading through the pathways of my body and flowing on their Golden course.

I feel the radiant brilliance of the Golden Crystals that are inherent in all the fluids of my body, forming their brilliant patterns of intelligence and order.

My Golden Heart beats with the pure joy of being alive and free.

I am the Golden ecstasy of loving—and being loved.

I am Golden Love personified, alive and flourishing.

We all are.

Solidly together, our Golden Love softening us all still more, we yield ourselves to one another at this deeper level, surrendering our borders as individuals, allowing the integrity of our Souls to continue weaving us together as ONE Golden Body.

We breathe, and it is the sound of One breath.

We pulsate, and it is the sound of One pulse.

Our hearts beat, and it is the Sound of One heartbeat.

We are ONE UNIFIED GOLDEN ENERGY FIELD.

One Golden Heart.

This is our Golden Configuration expanding again—adding still more layers of texture and substance—becoming a giant, exquisitely textured, beautiful Golden Tapestry. Our Sacred Golden Foundation is becoming stronger, larger, and more potent, anchoring it all in. I feel it holding the resonance, the sustaining grace from which all of Lemuria will continue to be conceived, birthed, and built, from which we can now grow and expand still more.

Through all of us, Golden Lemuria is birthing herself, her dream being made manifest. THIS IS GOLDEN LEMURIA. A Golden Gift being born, and a Golden Gift being given.

What exquisite joy this is! How powerful and beautiful.

I feel my chest opening, and my voice ushers forth a most beautiful note. My Golden Heart needs to sing; it needs to express this glorious joy that I am filled with. My Golden Song rings out loud and clear.

I realize I'm not the only one singing—we are ALL singing as one joyous Golden body, One Golden voice, One Golden Heart!

"Golden Love, clear as day.

"Golden Love in every way.

"Golden Love is here to stay.

"We are Golden Love!"

The Sound and the Song reverberates throughout the Hall, extending well beyond it now until it reaches the outer cosmos, where it is heard and RECEIVED. And, in that moment, our Song is responded to in kind as sensations of glorious Golden Love and Harmony stream in from afar: a Golden Love Song sung back to us in matching pitch and volume. We rejoice yet again in the ecstasy of our Oneness with ALL Golden Ones everywhere—on every level and in every dimension. Our celebration rings out and crescendos joyously.

Through it all, Sananda's Golden Voice takes the lead to masterfully guide our chorus along its way, finally bringing it to its conclusion. We sing our last notes and settle back in with hearts and souls vibrant and ecstatic. One huge happy Golden Family—there is nothing like it.

Through our joy and celebration, the final Golden threads of our beautiful tapestry have happily woven themselves together and anchored everything in perfectly.

With a great big smile on his face, Sananda speaks proudly:

"Beloved Golden Masters of breathtaking Brightness, yes, indeed, we have been born anew today, bigger and better than ever before. Our full Golden Configuration is now complete and sacrosanct. Our Golden Foundation fully set.

"We are now woven together as one Golden tapestry, one Golden Configuration, sustaining and inspiring new life, new creations from which ever more Golden Radiance will be born.

"Feel us in all our Golden Glory. Witness us. We are one strong, clear, Golden Unified Field. Our Golden Configuration is impenetrable. Our Golden Fabric woven together forever.

"We are One Golden Heart—eternally pure, strong, steady, and sustaining.

"We are One Golden Heart, in joy resounding.

"We are One Golden Heart, beautiful and free.

"We are One Golden Heart, outshining forever."

SACRED GOLDEN VOW

The richness of Sananda's voice moves through the group as we absorb his words and their meaning. A great hush descends over all of us—we are aware of how Golden illuminated we truly are.

Our brilliant light, intense as one giant GOLDEN GEM, is now fully energized and activated. All our love shines out, radiating like glorious waves from this expanded magnificence that we have become: our Passion, Devotion, Tenderness, Kindness, and Caring. It is all here, along with so much more.

Deeply humbled by the enormity of this beauty that we feel, we all drop down to our knees, coming into prayer position.

Sananda's splendid voice rings out clearly as he speaks on behalf of all of us:

"Beloved Golden Ones, it is from this solid foundation of our Golden Oneness that we can now make our Sacred Golden Vows.

"From this moment forth we vow to serve, support, protect, and nurture our One Golden Heart. We vow to love, honor, and cherish her with all our Heart, Soul, Body, and Being.

"We vow to love one another and all that we stand for, now, and in the future. We vow to love, honor, and protect our Golden Sacredness at all costs.

"We vow to nurture and support our One Golden Heart in all her Beauty and Magnificence. We vow to tend to her and her Greatness, and all the gifts which she births forth. We vow to honor her as she leads us on her Golden Path of Goodness and Glory.

"We vow to keep her steady and sovereign, safe and protected, free and flourishing, forever.

"She is ever Pure, Divine, and Sacrosanct. She is ever Alive—and she is EVER FREE.

"From this moment on, we pledge ourselves and our lives to our One Golden Heart, forever.

"This is our Sacred Golden Vow. Our Golden Word is Sacrosanct."

As Sananda speaks we feel the power of his words. We feel the power of our immense devotion. To say we love our One Golden Heart is an understatement. To say we adore her, worship her, live for her, and strive for her would be much more accurate. SHE is now the reason we will get up in the morning and create gloriously throughout our day. She is now our Sunrise and our Sunset, and all our moments in between. She is now the totality of our Golden Love unified and shining, the reality of who we have become and now stand for. There is no turning back. There is no being anything less than this pure Beauty. This pure Goodness. This pure Magnificent Golden Love in all its fullness.

We inhale, we are grateful for this.

We exhale, we praise this.

WE ARE ONE GOLDEN HEART, FOREVERMORE.

THE SOUL OF GOLDEN LEMURIA SPEAKS

What more is there to do or say? We feel complete now, and ready to go forward.

We are many Golden Ones beaming with eagerness and anticipation, we are ready to take flight and soar. "When?" We wonder.

Ah, but here comes Sananda, who would have us be still for just a few more minutes, as he says:

"Golden Ones, dearest friends of my heart. Now that we have successfully created our Golden Configuration that serves as the steady and sustaining Sacred Golden Foundation for our future, it is time to rise to Terra's surface and get on with building our wondrous Lemuria on all levels. There are many Golden Ones there who are already active in this process of building; they have been participating in and receiving all that we have been doing here and celebrating along with us.

"As you know, we have established and set the energetic patterning in place that will now be the base for our physicalizing all that Golden Lemuria wishes to be. Our success is ensured precisely because we have applied our energy and focus toward building and anchoring such a strong and reliable energetic foundation. This is the Golden Way of Creation. It all begins in the ethers, in the energy fields, in the consciousness—in the Golden Heart. And from there it spreads forth like a beautiful dream finally waking up— unfolding, stretching out and coming to life, bold and beautiful.

"With this in mind, there is one last gift for you to receive before we leave here and create our new life on Terra's surface. It is the gift of Golden Lemuria herself, as if she has already been born and is alive and well. This is the outcome of our Golden Oneness, our love, our devotion, our unified commitment—that she can now come to life, can be real and fully expressed.

"Listen now as she speaks and gifts herself to you, so that you can treasure this in your Golden Heart forever."

Starting quietly at first, and then gaining in intensity and volume, we hear a sound that moves from a whisper, to a hum, to a song. It is the most beautiful thing I have ever heard, and it brings tears to my eyes to be in its presence. It is Golden Grace incarnate. The feeling of it glides and soars and moves joyously through us all. From within the song, her voice speaks:

"Beloved Gentle Golden Ones, I am the Golden Soul of Golden Lemuria. I love you with all my Heart, all my Being. I am truly grateful to you—to each of you, to all of you—and all of you as ONE.

"You are giving me Life. You are birthing me through your Golden Hearts, and through your devotion to this Golden Greatness of Soul and Heart. I am overjoyed to be born, and to become the Guiding Light that will direct and serve you forevermore. You have created me from your own deep and ever-abiding yearning and love.

"I AM your pure Golden Love Incarnate. Everywhere that I am, everywhere that I go, everything that I breathe, is pure Golden Love. My name, Lemuria, is, in and of itself, a divine and exquisite Golden Blessing.

"I have a purpose—a great purpose. I shall extend and express myself to the fullest of my joys and capabilities, all in the name of one goal only: our ONE GOLDEN HEART.

"Far and wide I will reach, deeper and higher I will touch, more and more I will love. This is precisely my plan, my vision, my intent, my exquisite and profound endless joy. There is no end to who I am in this way. There is no end to my loving; and my love creates beauty everywhere.

"You and I are One. I am born from you. All that I am is you.

"Mine is the Soul of Golden Harmony—the sweet, sweet sound of our Source, our loving, our joy, our GOLDEN FREEDOM.

"Let this Golden Birthing begin now. We are One Golden Heart, expressing our Golden Love here on Golden Terra in all its beauty and power, and when ready, setting it free to spread far and wide.

"We are One Golden Family. We are One Golden Love. We are One Golden Harmony. We are One Golden Heart.

"Peace, Joy, Love, Beauty, and Blessing Forever.

"I love you."

And with that, the Golden Voice of Lemuria sings out one final Golden Note of exuberance and power, of strength and love, which uplifts us all. Even when this Golden Note is done, the reverberation remains in the room for several minutes—and the sound and feel of it has never left our bodies.

Standing together in these final moments our hearts overflow with joy, gratitude, and sheer delight. We smile, we hug, we laugh. What a wondrous and miraculous gift we are a part of.

We feel empowered: we are crystal-clear. Our Life as One Golden Heart stretches out in front of us, a beautiful Golden Path of Possibility. Now we are FULLY ready, let's get on with it!

BACK ON THE SURFACE OF TERRA

The next thing we know, Andar and I are suddenly standing on top of Terra's surface! With our feet planted firmly on her solid ground, our stance is secure and steady.

Layer upon layer of gridding has been achieved, so that now our Golden Foundation is fully formed, strong and stable. Everything has been done to ensure exactly that. From this well-grounded and established platform, we can create anything and it will have "legs." It will be sustained and fortified, capable of magnifying and birthing forth anew and anew. It is ready.

Looking at each other purposefully we take in a deep breath, then share a wink and a smile.

We are ready, too. YES, GOLDEN ONWARD!

CHAPTER FOUR

LIFE IN LEMURIA

*Life in Lemuria is like opening the oyster shell
to admire the most exquisite pearl ever seen.*

NOW THAT WE HAVE RETURNED to the surface of Terra, we marvel; what a Blessing this all is. How utterly SPLENDID, everything is so rich and abundant.

Andar and I take stock. Looking around we see that great progress has already been made in the creation of our beautiful Lemuria.

Golden Ones everywhere are hard at work building homes, schools, and Temples—all that will be needed for our great civilization to live with ease and efficiency. There are also many Golden Ones out wandering to get the lay of the land and to begin the great Golden Bonding process with Terra and her whole array of wondrous beauties.

There are many of us Golden Ones who will choose to live outdoors and let our camps reflect our inner natures in this way. We ALL get to be our authentic selves. It is up to each one of us to ensure that our needs are met, and that we have the right atmosphere to support us in our daily living and Sacred Creativity.

Delighted to see that everything is progressing so well, Andar and I each head off in separate directions to explore for ourselves. At the end of the day, we'll reconnect and make final plans for our domestic and work-centered Creations together.

As I step along, I notice that the air smells wonderfully fresh and clean. I breathe it in deeply and love how it makes me feel—juicy and alive! How glad I am to be a part of all of this, how grateful to Golden Terra for bringing us all here. She is a Beauty who offers us such abundance with her endless gifts. I sense the strength, excitement, creativity, and resourcefulness that all of us Golden Ones co-creating with her can bring to fruition—all that we dream is possible, and then some.

❧

It is now late afternoon following a productive and busy day, and we have gathered together in a beautiful open meadow, especially designated as our Holy Meeting Ground. A happy place, with spring flowers bursting up everywhere as butterflies and dragonflies buzz about delightedly, it feels magical and divine.

Our group is large and somewhat unwieldy, as we do our best to gather and organize ourselves. Once settled, we all sit quietly, taking a few moments to enjoy the sweet beauty.

Finally, Andar arrives to take his position on the little rise in front of us so that everyone will have a clear view of him. A handsome and robust man, he exudes passion and vitality. He is a supremely capable Leader who invigorates others with his own strength and enthusiasm.

Focusing our attention on him, we can feel his appreciation for us all. Even though some people here are just getting acquainted, it seems like we are all old friends already.

We fold our hands and close our eyes as Andar speaks a Blessing:

"Dearest God, our most Beloved Source and Provider, we honor and love you in every way. We thank you for this beautiful place, for our beautiful Golden Family here as One to express our Hearts and Souls to you, to one another, and to our Beloved Lemuria. Thank you for this opportunity to flourish in your Grace, and to create this wondrous Nation. Thank you, our Beloved Source: eternally, we thank you."

Opening our eyes, we feel the joy of this special moment as Andar continues to speak:

"Beloved, dearest Golden Ones, welcome.

"This marks our official Greeting Ceremony, the first of many such gatherings in this beautiful spot. On behalf of Avalar and myself, welcome. How grateful we are that you're all here with us. Ours is a magnificent Project, this building of our great Golden Nation, Lemuria. What a grand and glorious opportunity it is for all of us.

"We know you have each come from afar, and have brought your unique talents and gifts of Being and Creativity. You have been chosen, and you have chosen, to participate with us in this remarkable endeavor.

"It is up to each of you to find yourselves at Home here as you create an environment that suits and supports you. After this, we will gradually move toward a greater development of the Whole, but for now please focus on your individual and small group needs.

"Plans for further expression will come soon enough. Life is abundant on our Golden Terra, and I know how excited you all are to begin getting GOLDEN CREATION underway—which is of course our point and purpose in being here. Bless you all.

"We love you, and are honored to be in your presence. We are with you all the way. Glory be to Lemuria! One Golden Heart."

Standing up to take my rightful place beside Andar, I look out at the many happy Golden faces in front of me, and I am moved by how beautiful they all are. Their love shines out, touching everything all around us, as I begin to speak:

"I welcome you as well, dearest Golden Ones, and I am so glad that you are here. It is an honor for me to be with you, and I look forward to all our days ahead as we get to know one another better, as we share the gifts of who and how we are.

"To commemorate this moment, I wish to sing a song in praise of the pure joy of our Being. I dedicate this to our beloved Source of all Beauty everywhere, as I give thanks for all of you and our wondrous Lemuria.

"Blessings, blessings, blessings Be.

"We are here, and we are Golden Free.

"Ours is a Planet that shines so bright,

"Morning, noon, and through the night.

"Ours are days that are filled with love,

"Beauty and Sacredness, beneath us and above.

"We rejoice in our Union, with gratitude to thee,

"We are Free, we are Free, we are Golden Free!

"Long Live Lemuria.

"One Golden Heart.

"Hallelujah!"

After a joyous round of applause and some happy chatter, everyone sets off to take care of business at hand. There is a lot to do, and everyone is eager to do it.

Still having much to do with my own preparations, I decide to spend some time communing with Terra in one of the places that has special meaning for me. Making my way in that direction, a prayer moves happily through my heart.

"My Beloved Terra,

"Land of my Golden Heart and Soul.

"I love you so.

"Yours is the Rock upon which I stand, the ground upon which I sleep, the air through which I breathe, and the wondrousness through which I am inspired and revitalized.

"Yours are ALL things Beautiful, Sacred, and Holy.

"Your Light shines so bright.

"You are love.

"I love you.

"Thank you. Thank you. Thank you."

As I offer my love to Terra in this way, I am aware of her joy bouncing inside of my heart and I chuckle in response. She makes me feel so happy.

Soon, I arrive at the outskirts of one of my restorative places, my very own Golden Sanctuary beneath the Stars. There is a small crystalline field leading up to it, and as I cross it, I enjoy the sound of "crunch, crunch, crunch" as the Golden Crystals—one of my greatest Allies through life's journey—greet me through my feet. Walking across their beds, I am grateful for their friendship and our mutual love fills my heart.

I come to a small cave hidden amongst a group of trees on the outer edge of the field. This cave, inside a beautiful Golden illuminated rock, was offered to me by Terra as a sacred place in which I can be rejuvenated and lovingly recharged.

Each Golden One has been offered a personal Sacred Golden Sanctuary from Terra, tailored for their unique needs, designed to nourish and revitalize them perfectly. Spending time in these special natural places "clears us, polishes us, and makes us shine." We need these Sanctuaries; they are imperative for our balance and well being.

Sitting peacefully in my own beautiful cave, I feel my love for Lemuria being stirred. It is so strong that it sometimes makes my heart ache. It runs deeply—along with the intense caring I have for all the Golden Ones that are an integral part of Her, and of me.

Her Soul comes to me now, and as I feel her Presence, I open my heart to hers. She hums to me at first, and I am soothed by her calming tone as she gently sings the words *"I love you"* as a sweet, sweet song before she speaks:

"I love you. I love you. I love you.

"YOU are my Beloved Sacred One, my Avalar, who guides and leads all these Beautiful Golden Ones who are also my Beloveds. Our love together is the essence of Golden Heart, and all that we achieve here we do because we love doing it. It is that simple.

"Our Love is Beauty. We are Beauty. All that we create is Beautiful. We are Divine.

"I am enriched, and I rejoice in your tender love for me.

"I love you."

I feel her love wrapping me in a rich, warm cocoon. Steadying and soothing, it makes my cells sing with complete happiness. Oh, how I love Beauty! And I know that this is Her moving me, touching me, empowering me with her joy.

"Yes," I think to myself. "There is so much Beauty. It constantly and continuously weaves in and out of itself, bursting forth and creating these most exquisite creations of ours. We are Blessed."

Pondering this, a big smile spreads across my face as I realize the cells of this blessed cavern are smiling back, along with the Soul of Lemuria herself. I am being bathed in this joy, and vitalized by it. What a wonderful start to another day.

Standing up and stretching for a moment, I bow in honor to my Sacred Sanctuary, then prepare to re-enter the world outside with another good chuckle, as I think to myself "Onward girl, there are things to attend to."

Golden Gratitude Ceremony at Dawn

Arising every morning at Dawn to greet our beloved and most Glorious Golden Sun of Lemuria, we know how blessed we are to be a part of this beautiful Sacred Golden Nation. It is our Love that makes us come alive, breathe deeply, and give thanks for all the richness surrounding us, for all the incredible beauty that fills us up day in and day out. How precious this is.

When we look at each other, no matter where we are or what we are doing, we see each other's Golden Glow shining radiant and strong. We care deeply for one another; we care deeply for this beautiful Ground. We care deeply for our Beautiful Sacred Sun; we care deeply for our radiant Stars above.

We all know we are a part of one another, and because of this knowing, we understand that whatever we do affects everything and everyone. We live by this.

Well aware that it is our loving that enables Lemuria to exist, we are also aware that it generates deep kindness that we express every day in many ways, large and small.

Kindness comes from caring. Caring comes from our open hearts. Our open hearts come from our Source; we were born open hearted, we live open hearted, and we are open hearted.

In this, we know we are strong, Golden Strong. And we are grateful.

Looking around in delight, I make my way toward our Morning Ceremony on this beautifully serene start to another day. With the night sky having begun her change, the coming of the sunrise and her exquisite morning colors will begin to show at any moment.

By the time I arrive at our Ceremony site there are many Golden Ones already gathered closely together. Holding hands, their heads tilt upward as they prepare to receive the Sun. Those who are further away from this site, and unable to attend, stand in this same position as if they were here with us. This is our Point of Golden Uniting each day. During this sacred worship, when we give and receive thanks for one another, our focus is on our Source; on our Being, our union, and our Golden Lemuria. Blessing the Golden Sun as it comes to shine down upon us, we drink in its love that so nourishes us.

Our morning Ceremony is essential to us. We know we are One Golden Heart, and our morning gathering reaffirms and confirms this, day in and day out. It is a way of tending to our own garden, of making sure all is well and watered and in its proper place. In this way, our loving as One family is acknowledged, adored, and strengthened every day, thus enabling the greatest love possible to spring forth from this nurtured base. This is our time to spread our gratitude for all of this forward, into the day.

Oftentimes, our ceremony is a singing one, while at others we may simply stand quietly together in silence.

On this particular morning, the song in our hearts echoes throughout this beautiful land.

"Blessing, Blessing, Blessing this day;

"Thank you, dear God, in every way.

"We are Golden Ones through and through,

"One Golden Heart, kind and true.

"One Golden Heart, forever free,

"Thank you, dear God, we bow to thee.

"What a beautiful Golden Day is here,

"One Golden Heart, joyous and clear.

"In love, in life, we hold you true,

"Thank you, God, for this is you,

"Glorious One Golden Heart we are.

"Hallelujah!"

And with that, our love and praise for all that is dear pours from our hearts. Like a gushing fountain, it bathes us all in its freshness and Golden Glow. It lifts our spirits, enhances our Beauty, and fuels us in every way. We know we are One, and it feels fantastic. We feel loved, strong, and ready for our shared endeavors. Golden Love is everywhere, Golden Love in every way! What a way to start the day.

Fully refreshed and invigorated, we head off in our various directions with a bounce in our step and enthusiasm in our hearts. Yes, Golden Day, here we are!

GOLDEN TEAMWORK

All feel the joy of our loving kinship and our One Golden Heart. All are deeply aware that without each other, we wouldn't be here doing this. Although we would no doubt be expressing our God-given talents more independently somewhere, somehow—which would be great in and of itself—it would be nothing like this. And while never minimizing the profound contributions made by each of us as individuals, all know how special it is to be together as one glorious, deliberate Golden Team.

We understand the sheer magnitude of this shared project, and know that it requires many individuals who can count on each other to bring forth this particular Golden Expansion. As the physically embodied members of this huge Golden Team, we also recognize the need to be greater than ourselves, to surrender completely into our wholeness as a community to ensure success. All that we create and build is dependent upon our yielding to all of this.

Through our Golden Teamwork each can discover a greater and more Golden Empowered US. We love the surrender, love completely giving way to that which is purely God's plan. We love the expanded, strengthened, and more textured us that is created.

As time goes on, we adore each other more and more. Strongly and supremely One Golden Family, it is a sacred thing to have a beautiful union such as ours, to share a far greater purpose than we could ever achieve on our own—or even conceive of, for that matter.

The very gift of this expression, of this Golden Union, enables us to know a different form of loving. A unique and splendid creation springs forth from this conscious joining, merging into One in our sacred Golden Hearts. This love power of the Golden Energy that we have become is the Golden fuel that aligns and strengthens us. And it is this which empowers us to meet our new challenge as One Golden Lemuria.

The Golden Energy also powers our connectedness and our wealth of Being. Our Source gave us this gift because we have earned it, because we are capable and trustworthy, and because we are wise enough to use this power only in life-enhancing ways.

As a transformational property, the Golden Energy is highly refined energy that can be received only by those who are Masters. An upgrade in frequency, it enhances everything that we create, as well as all of our experience: consciously creating Golden Lemuria means our Golden Energy increases exponentially.

All profoundly grateful for the opportunity of this experience, we consider it a Gift, a Blessing more exhilarating and empowering than any we could have imagined. Loving our dearest Golden Lemuria impassions and illuminates us, and our hearts glow with gratitude for all that we are discovering and sharing. Our united movement as One Golden Heart is becoming richer and deeper by the minute. How divine it is.

THE GOLDEN TEMPLE

Walking the grounds, Andar and I decide to check on the building progress. The air is humming with activity and it is obvious that everyone, while busy laboring, is having fun doing so. Their Dreams are becoming manifest. It is exhilarating to watch.

There are many different styles of buildings unlike anything we have ever seen before, some of them being enhanced with all kinds of unique elements that make each one stand out as a truly masterful work of art. The array of unusual architecture somehow all fits seamlessly together. Uplifting to the eyes and senses, it transports us to other lands, to other waves of energetic radiance. How extraordinary it all is.

We find ourselves drawn to one structure that stands separately from the rest. A very large building that feels significant in some way, it has a dome shaped roof with a twelve-pointed diamond star rising right out of its top.

Moving closer, we see that the roof glistens and is composed of Gold. It is etched with diamond shaped patterns inlaid with colorful gems, which create a stunning mosaic that sparkles vibrantly in the morning sun. When the eye finally meets it, the Diamond Star at the pinnacle takes one's breath away. The whole visual is uplifting and magnificent, exuding a sense of richness, power, and purpose.

As we enter through its front portals, we instantly feel a sense of calm grounding, coupled with euphoria. What a wonderful combination. Walking further inside, an atmosphere of welcome envelopes us and ushers us forward. Somehow, it feels as though this place recognizes us and is grateful that we are here. It is comforting and comfortable to us, and we each find ourselves relaxing into its embrace in a noticeable way.

We pause for a moment and gaze around in wonder at the Golden Light which glows throughout. Several Golden archways stand gracefully around the large central space, their tips arcing up to a peak high in the ceiling as if they are reaching triumphantly toward the Heavens. Thinking to ourselves how familiar it all feels, we soon recognize why: although smaller in size, this is an exact duplicate of the Great Golden Hall inside of Terra's Core Crystal, where the Golden Configuration was birthed earlier.

Delighted, we also notice that it contains all of the energetic essence of the Golden Configuration. Aware of the tangible quality of Harmony and Golden Oneness, along with vibrations of our Golden Song from that earlier birthing moment, our minds are flooded with sacred memories of when the Golden Foundation was born.

Both of us feel the glorious Presence of the Soul of Lemuria here as well. We realize this building was erected in this specific location, not only as a representation of the symbol of our Sacred Golden Vow and Golden Configuration, but also as a physicalized Touchstone for all of this powerful and glorious energy. It is truly a tangible reminder from which we can draw great strength.

This is THE place where we will meet again as that Sacred Golden Foundation to restore and realign ourselves, as our purpose grows greater and greater every day. Here, everyone can meet with all dimensions of Golden Life, just as we did inside Terra earlier.

Standing quietly and drinking everything in, Andar and I are touched by it all. Knowing how important this place is, and will continue to be, we offer up a prayer of gratitude and blessing for its generous gifts and beauty. In doing so, we intuitively hear that this building will henceforth be referred to as "THE GOLDEN TEMPLE," whose anchor has now been set. We both take a deep breath and register the power and stability of this truth.

Leaving this sacred place, more peaceful and strengthened than before we entered, the solid support we feel shows us how powerful and helpful its medicine is. It will continue to be for all of us: a gift of pure, substantial sustenance straight from our essential Golden Foundation.

We make our way outside again with great gratitude in our hearts, veering off toward a clearing where progress is being made on additional gardens and natural, preserved areas. We see many Golden Ones focused on communing with Unseen Elemental Energies manifesting an array of fascinating formations that are being calibrated and stabilized into the soil and atmosphere. Here, too, each specific aspect of design will radiate the energy of its purpose directly into the etheric field of Golden Consciousness.

It is beautiful and truly empowering, with much to learn and fully take in. But this will happen over time as we all teach one another about the energies of these different gifts—why they are here, and how they benefit us, individually and together. Indeed, not only are we here to Create, we are also here to learn from and educate each other.

All aspects of Life in Lemuria are busy now. We will check in again as this wondrous Golden progress continues.

∾

Dear Reader, at this point, perhaps you are wondering how elemental Gold relates to the Golden Energy that we have been discussing. The elemental Gold in Lemuria, a precious metal which is a manifestation of the Golden Lemurian Energy, is used ornamentally in some of our buildings—like The Golden Temple described above, for example.

And while we also have gems, many of which are encased in elemental Gold, our focus is always on the Golden ENERGY, so please understand that our focus is not about the elemental Gold.

In present-day there is much focus on the elemental Gold, and understandably so, since it represents material wealth and abundance. But what's missing is the understanding and recognition of the *energy* behind the elemental Gold, which is vitally important to our well-being.

In Lemuria, we knew that we were fed by the Golden Energy. Our appreciation of the beauty of the element included not only what it represented to us, but also the energy behind it. We simply were not fixated on the element, as is often the case in current times.

You may also be wondering about other sources of nourishment that we might have. Frankly, physical food is quite secondary, as we are fed by the life force of all the elements: Sun, Moon, Stars, Terra, water, and air. We are also nourished by the life force emanating from plants, trees, flowers, the animal kingdom—indeed from the entirety of Golden life everywhere. You see, we commune with *all* of it.

While the term "breatharians" refers to those who do not eat, who live simply by breathing, we are "Golden Life Force-arians," completely sustained by the Golden Life Force which emanates from everything, everywhere. It comes in through the crown at the top of our head, from our feet firmly planted on Terra— and enters our Golden Hearts in the form of love, Golden Love.

We are Golden Ones—Golden Illuminated, Golden-filled, and Golden-nourished. And, yes, we also eat and drink when we so desire, grazing from time to time on wild fruits, nuts, seeds, and vegetables. We also drink extremely potent water, which is filled with life force, nutrients, and minerals—and is much like eating more solid substances.

However, eating truly is secondary, filled as we are with Golden Life Force. While some of our fellow Golden Ones do cultivate plants simply because this resonates with them, it isn't necessary. Thanks to Terra, we have everything we need, and are extremely grateful to her for providing us with bounty on all levels.

Overall, our Golden Love and our full expression of this enables us to feel wonderful all the time. We all love, and are loved by, our Golden Life Force. The many expressions through which this flows truly provide all the nourishment we need abundantly.

❧

Andar and I spend many nights under the stars, falling asleep to the sound of Terra's lullaby. Although our Golden Home has already been built, we so enjoy sleeping outdoors that we rarely use it for that. Awakening now with his warm body next to mine, I am filled with a rush of gratitude—for him, and for all the love and beauty that we share. Ours is a love that knows no bounds, our Oneness a gift that brings so many more gifts of us to me. Tenderly, I gaze at him and marvel at the pure splendidness of him. He is such a wise and gentle man, strong both in body and heart.

Suddenly thinking about how much he makes me laugh, I chuckle. I don't know quite how he does it, but he manages to bring so much lightness, laughter, and a sense of easefulness to all of us. Everyone loves him, and he is greatly valued.

Smiling, I reach gently to wake him, lightly stroking his head until he slowly opens his eyes. He gazes back at me with a twinkle in his eye, his love reaching right into my heart to blend with my own deep love for him. I melt, and chuckle again. What a great blessing this man is to me. I treasure him with all my Being, and look forward to yet another beautiful day spent with him.

Finally managing to get up from our cozy nest, we hurry to join with the others at our Dawn Ceremony. Everyone else is already there, standing quietly in silence as the Golden Sun shines directly upon them like a blessing from Heaven. It is a perfectly glorious morning, pastel colors spread across the sky, a breeze just high enough to tickle our noses, the birds providing all the music we need right now as we offer our prayers and praises. With our Golden Day acknowledged and now brilliant before us, everyone leaves to get started on their morning activities. Andar and I decide to walk around a bit to see what progress is being made out and about.

Almost everyone continues to be busy at their task of organizing, creating, and building—some adding final touches, others focused on new designs to expand what they have already completed. We stop and chat with various Golden Ones here and there, occasionally pausing to admire the energetic handiwork of the Golden Elemental Worlds as well.

There is much to look at, feel, and admire, and Andar and I are filled with gratitude for all the Golden Ones here. As we watch them at work, their exquisite energy and physical beauty is inspiring indeed. Tall in stature, they radiate Golden Energy streaming from their hearts—just like the rays of the Golden Sun that shine down upon us from afar.

And, being like the Sun, we all thrive in her Presence. We need and value her, adore and worship her. Without her, there would be no us, here and now. There would be no life forms thriving and flourishing as they are. Beauty would not be visible without light to reflect it, or reflect upon it. This would be an entirely different world, made up of something else. We love Our Golden Sun. It is most precious and Sacred to us.

All Golden Ones understand there is nothing here to be taken for granted, that it is a gift. But while it is a privilege and a sacred Honor to witness, learn, and Love, it is not always an easy undertaking and is quite demanding of who we are. And, although we absolutely love and thrive on this, it is challenging at times, stretching each of us in many ways and on many levels. Living our natural excellence all the time, we are highly charged, highly fueled, and highly inspired. Being here is an opportunity to achieve great things, to live and express pure greatness itself. We are strong, we are bold, we are capable, and we are bright. We are steadfast, dedicated, and devoted. Our Golden Path is open: we are in complete Golden Freedom.

What do we do with this? We pay close attention and tread consciously with great care and tenderness for all of Life. Honoring and respecting ALL Golden Life Forms means we listen to them, consciously considering each of our actions every time we birth a new Creation. And, in turn, we feel enormously respected, honored, and cared for. We trust in this because it is the truth of our experience.

Lemuria is no place for slackers, it is for Heightened Ones only. We are Golden, glad, and grateful, and always aware of the need to use our unique gifts wisely and well. Every day provides an opportunity for each of us to understand ourselves better, and to appreciate the talents granted to us by our Maker. Yes, we earned these gifts long ago, but we've been developing them ever since, and coming here has amped everything up considerably.

This challenging experimental ground is ONLY for the strong, and everything that we produce needs to be strong. Toward that end, each of us learns daily what it takes to strengthen our Creations, to "gift them out." Because of this training, these Creations maintain their substance, can flourish and then expand forth from themselves in ongoing positive and productive ways.

Andar and I are well aware of all that was learned by the Golden Ones from the shared Golden Configuration and Foundation building process. Multi-layered, textured, and strongly woven, it required great love and patience, clear focus and strong intention. It provided each of us with a chance to witness, firsthand, what all of this truly means within the context of that kind of energetic patterning. Because of their participation in the design, texturizing, and stability of that Foundation—which we are all an integral part of, all Golden Ones now know how to do this for all the Creations they bring forth as our beautiful Lemuria grows.

One of the greatest challenges the Golden Ones find here is the shared gift of Harmonization, which is instinctive and integral to our design. Clear, and constantly at work, Harmonization can be a tall order on a scale such as this. Because we are actively and intentionally inter-dimensional, inter-stellar, and inter-cosmic, our Harmonizing Aperture is open in a particularly expanded way.

With outgoing conduits always open, back and forth, it is effortless for us to instantly share and communicate our needs. We can also choose to commune with, and love, all Golden Ones everywhere. Our incoming conduits, also always in service, result in us receiving vast amounts of information—for ourselves, others, individual projects, and this Golden Project as a Whole.

Some would probably consider having such expansive and open conduits daunting. We do not. While it expands and challenges us, we relish it. It enables us to BE our Bigness. We are Gentle Giants, after all.

All of us are also well-developed Masters, and used to the "tall order" idea of Life. We thrive on it. We love feeling the strength of our spiritual muscles; love using them as we witness their ever-increasing capability. We love our continual self-discovery, and are richly rewarded for our efforts by what we can achieve.

Loving and being loved is the greatest privilege there is. It is the most sacred act that our Maker has infused us with, and we do not take this lightly. We are poignantly aware that loving and being loved is a deep current inside of us, it is a never-ending well—as long as we maintain clear sight from whence it comes and let it flow freely.

We speak about love a great deal in this book. Of course we do. It is who we are and what we are made of. This is not said lightly. We, as Golden Ones, know with every fiber of our Beings that love is our life force itself, that which we are made of, that which moves us, nourishes, and sustains us. It is multi-layered, multi-faceted, deep, abiding, endless, miraculous, magnificent, moving, touching, gentling, nurturing, soothing, inspiring, uplifting, harmonizing, and healing. So many wondrous words, and more, to describe it. Adding to the equation is the gift of Golden Energy that we have been given. It heightens the love that we already know as us, making us even more grateful for the awareness and feeling of this magnificence, every second of every day.

Our waters run deep. Our compassion and sensitivity, our understanding of life at its very essence and purity, defines us. We are constantly being touched and inspired at our core, as well as touching and inspiring just as deeply. Our communion with all Golden Life, seen and unseen, is stirring. It moves us and can make us weep with joy and thanksgiving for our family, our caring, and our sharing. Our joy, our gratitude for life is truly endless.

Our Devotion to our Source, and to all that is related to it is ESSENTIAL.

Paying attention to our gratitude and devotion to our Creator is the pivotal point of all that we are, of all that we will ever be. We are only as inspired as our ability to receive that which is our Source. We are only as impassioned as we are fueled by that immense driving and compelling Source, Our Creator of all Beauty. The strength and power of our Hearts, of our Golden Loving, depends upon this.

Yes, this has been spoken about at length already, but it all bears repeating. It is that important.

Our Sacred Centers are the Core of everything that we do and are. Every day, in every way, must be a gift back to our Creator, a celebration and recognition of this Divine Source of all that we are. This is how we live and thrive. We pay attention, and we make it central. We never lose sight of this, period. We love and treasure this. It makes us be the very best that we were born to be.

WE ARE ALL Golden Gentle Giants. Strong, and completely capable, we are not only beautiful, but also wise, loving, caring, kind, gentle, compassionate, and clear.

The word Giants not only describes how we look as shining, radiant, Golden Illuminated Beings, but also perfectly describes how we are in our natures. We are thoroughly generous in who we are.

Golden Terra is a Golden Gentle Giant too. As Andar and I continue to explore everyone's creations, we can feel how deeply all the Golden Ones care for her, how everything they create is perfectly attuned to her. Clearly, they are devoted to her. They need her. She is Lemuria's Treasure.

There is no question as to how much joy and peace our beloved Terra brings us. She is why we can be here as Lemuria. Speaking and singing our gratitude and praises to her often, we celebrate her in many ways.

We also hold sacred the power of Sound, and we know how well the energy of our words and songs transmit our messages of love to her. These are our Love notes to her. She thrills us, and we want her to know this every single day.

In light of this we dance for her, dance upon her, and dance with her. The energy and intention of our dancing moves her, as she receives our love fully. She feels it all, and we know this because we can feel her feeling us. It is obvious in the way our energies align and resonate. It is wondrous how such a simple and beautiful pleasure that we share in this way creates great joy that benefits everyone.

We also paint pictures and make sculptures for her, using her own natural elements. We create these visuals to show her how we feel about her. To reflect how we see, sense, and experience our profound joy for her and her majesty. It is another way that we share with her; a way that we love and acknowledge her Beauty, and show her that we do.

Dancing, singing, and creating artistic masterpieces are three of the most potent ways to express our adoration to her. We do these with complete abandon and in total celebration for her, and with her. She is our Muse as well as the recipient of what she inspires in us.

We sing, we dance, draw, sculpt, and paint—prolifically.

We also touch her beautiful body with great tenderness often. Yes, we love the sensuality of her—the textures, sensations, colors, and smells. We hold pieces of her elements in our hands, admiring and loving them deeply. In so doing, we know we are also admiring and appreciating all of that which makes up our own bodies. It is soothing for us to do this, joyous for us and for her. It is a true acknowledgement and appreciation of our true elemental natures, of our true Oneness with Terra. We are made of the same stuff, and it is all beautiful.

We also speak our hearts with her, confiding in her as friend, confidante, and companion. Yes, she is our Provider, but she is also our Friend, Teacher, Guide, and Inspiration. She KNOWS us and understands our needs probably even before we do. She soothes and gentles, strengthens and fortifies, balances and inspires, fuels and empowers us. She speaks to and enriches us and all our senses, on every level. She adores and loves us—and we adore and love her.

To be loved and adored by Terra is immense and exhilarating. Her passion is vast, and her beauty profoundly moving. Her nourishment is complete, and there is absolutely nothing mediocre about any of it. It is like being continually flooded with Golden Brightness. Powerfully rejuvenating and exquisite, we soak it up with our entire Beings. She loves us so well, and continually teaches us more and more about love through her own generosity of spirit, her own wisdom. She makes all the difference in our lives: it is truly a privilege and honor to be her Family.

We are each the hub through which our wondrous creations are made manifest. Therefore, we must realize and understand the magnificence that we each are. Each of us is aware of the responsibility to recharge and replenish ourselves daily in this. The act of Creation is as much receptive as it is proactive. We know this. We understand the balance. Without going within and receiving our Creator, we are not fed or inspired. And if we are not, then we do not possess the juice necessary to create.

Our individual Golden Sacred Sanctuaries, received from our Beloved Golden Terra, are where we can be restored and refreshed. These are our personal and private domains, not to be shared with anyone but our Creator. About this we are clear. Being within these sanctuaries is a sublime and extraordinary experience, a time to surrender. TRUST is known and enhanced between Self and Source.

In all ways, on all levels, we are replenished during these moments of deep, penetrating solitude and Golden Grace. Without this amidst our day, we would gradually become diminished and flat, and would flame out. Our Golden Glow would be no more. Our Golden Power to thrive and create would be gone.

Extinguished.

We KNOW this, and so time spent in our Sacred Sanctuaries is our gift to ourselves, to our Source, and to our Beloved Golden Terra, whose strong and steady support we are also aware of during these most intimate of communions. This sacred time is also a gift from our Self, our Source, and our Beloved Golden Terra. We know we need this to be here—to be a part of our One Golden Family, our One Golden Heart. And of course, we want this. It IS our passion.

We bask deeply in the joy of being in the Heart of our Source, when we are fully Golden Bathed and Golden Replenished. It is indeed Golden Medicine for every level of our precious Beings, and we are extremely grateful. After receiving this replenishment, we can then bring forth whatever we are inspired to create with abundant enthusiasm and passion.

At the end of each day, when all is said and done, we gather at dusk for our Evening Devotion Ceremony to honor all that has taken place since Dawn. An equally powerful time, this is when the light changes again, and the atmosphere moves into Golden Night.

Gathering together in groups, or standing alone wherever we are in full energetic participation with the Whole, we honor and acknowledge the beautiful Golden Day that has been received and shared. With all the love in our hearts, we give thanks for our Blessings as we bow to our Creator once again.

"Thank you, dear God, for this beautiful day,

"This Golden Day in every way.

"Thank you for Life and for each other.

"Thank you for our Golden Terra Mother.

"Blessings, blessings, blessings we sing,

"For you, for us, and for everything.

"It is with great joy that we greet our sleep,

"Knowing that, in your heart, our Golden Bodies you keep.

"We love you, adore you, we thank you again,

"For this beautiful day as Golden Family and Friends.

"One Golden Heart.

"Hallelujah."

Once again, our Devotion is our Golden Love expressing—strong, deep, and palpable. We know this and we love this. Every action in our lives demonstrates our awareness of this. We are pleased, blessed, and grateful. How many times will we talk about being grateful in this book? MANY!

Our daily lives in Lemuria continue to be rich and varied, with our Golden Solidarity growing and expanding. We flourish as a People, bringing through many new souls: birthing new children and new energetic forms of Golden Radiance. It is a sacred bowl of truly joyous Golden Activity.

Every day is pure joy for Andar and I as we behold everyone going about their lives, creating the vast array of wondrousness from which we all benefit. We are extremely proud of each and every Golden One. As we've already said, we are witnessing great things. These miracles, small, medium, and large, all have potency and purpose, and they are all working toward the betterment of Golden Life. Each Creation builds on the one before it. It is like a great Golden Stepping-Stone Process of Development.

What are we doing with all these wondrous Golden Creations of ours? Certainly, they enhance us greatly. They also make our Nation strong and outrageously beautiful, inside and out. Daily, Lemuria becomes an even more extraordinary sight to behold, an even more incredible feast for all the senses. There is immense power in this Beauty, and the impact it has on all of us is profound. It deeply affects ALL our senses, and shapes our internal and external direction. It uplifts and illuminates us powerfully.

This is because Beauty is the pure song and loving of our Soul. It is the language of our Soul expressing and radiating. This not only uplifts our hearts and minds, but it also raises our frequencies to a very high level of refinement and radiance that is expanding and life-giving. Beauty also has the power inherent within itself to birth great healing and restoration. Never ending, it is the continuous song of our Soul: exquisite, pure, simple, divine, and free. It has a huge impact everywhere, on every level. We speak about Beauty often, and that is because its gifts are so potent and life enhancing. It is essential to understand this.

It is because of the healing and restorative capabilities of Beauty that some of our Creations are deliberately being made with the future in mind. They are being placed in sanctuaries for safe keeping and will be brought out and utilized in times to come. Nothing is wasted here, and none of our Creations are for naught. They all have a purpose which will indeed be fulfilled—if not now, then later.

Who knows what the Great Future holds? We only know that our precious Lemuria is our Divine and Sacred Womb of Golden Creation. Here, we are utilizing all our Creation and Birthing abilities and becoming powerfully adept at what we do. We are super strong and super Golden. Each Creation makes us stronger and more Golden Substantial as individuals, and as One Golden Family, One Golden Heart.

Our love for creating is endless. There is nothing like it, really. Birthing forth our Golden Creations in such a conscious and deliberate way, and knowing they are being received as those aspects of us are being born, is a magnificent feeling for each of us. Birthing and giving are tremendously fulfilling. But being RECEIVED is also one of the greatest gifts of all. Powerful and empowering, it makes us all want to continually create more while we encourage each other to do so as well.

As time passes, Andar and I see that the Golden Light shines more brilliantly here every day. Its radiance and color are deeper and even more richly vibrant, shining with glorious intensity everywhere.

The energy of this Golden Light is the rich radiance of our Pure Golden Love embodied, individually and collectively. It is the outshining of our great Golden Love expressing. Lemuria, the encapsulation of all this, is the container and conduit for its growth, magnifying its expression and expansion as time goes on.

Our lives continue to be full and fruitful, overflowing with joy, passion, and abundance. We are passionate about Being, passionate about creating, passionate about loving and sharing.

Passionate about our Source, as well as our Golden Family everywhere, this devotion further unites us—enabling us to be stronger than we ever dreamed possible.

Our Golden Nation is becoming vast, our Golden Love more potent and powerful. All are well aware of this, and all respond to and respect it enormously, directing it wisely and well. We have become one strong and steady Golden Station, solid and sustaining in our own right.

We are Golden Empowered and Golden Powerful. We are One Golden Heart.

Now, dear reader, we ask that you take some time and close your eyes:

Imagine yourself walking on Golden Terra as the Golden One that you are. How does it feel? What does the air feel like? What is your connection with Terra like? How do you feel about your fellow Golden Ones? Feel in your heart what it is like to be free. Feel what it is like to express the highest and greatest of who you are. What do *you* do to create?

As you look around, what is it like to see beauty everywhere, to feel deeply connected and in tune with all of life? Your heart is Golden, you are Golden. What does that feel like?

To drop into your Golden Remembrance, you will need to let go of much of what you associate with present day Earth life. For this you must let go of all fear. There is only harmony, love, connection, and creative expression in your Golden Remembrance. Allow yourself to let everything else go, and have your experience. Allow yourself to open to this.

Take all the time you need. Go back into your experience more than once to reconnect with your Golden Self. Breathe in the Gold. Let it re-emerge in your memory, your heart, and your Being. Allow the Golden Love to carry you along, further and further, as you deepen into a knowing of your True Golden Self.

CHAPTER FIVE

CHANGE IS COMING

THE COUNCIL MEETING PRIOR TO THE SHIFT ON TERRA

A S ANDAR AND I WAKE UP, we sense an energetic shift going on in and around Terra. Although it seems like any other morning, something is different and it is unsettling to our systems. Even though we don't feel it in the physical realm yet, we can tell it's coming. Knowing that we need to find out exactly what is going on, it comes as no surprise that we receive a telepathic call from the Sacred Golden Council Leaders to meet.

In an instant, we are energetically transported back into the Golden Meeting Room inside the body of Terra, where we had originally met with the Council back at the start of Lemuria. We are joined by many Golden Masters, including Sananda, Mother Mary, and Master Saint Germain. Seating ourselves around the same round table as before, we take a moment to greet one another and collect ourselves until Master Saint Germain stands to speak:

"Dearest Golden Leaders, Avalar and Andar, we bring you here today to discuss news of great import and impact. I will get straight to the point, as time is of the essence. There are great cataclysmic waves coming to the surface of Terra. All that you have created is about to be destroyed, to be swept away. Lemuria as you have known it will be no more. That is a fact. And while the reasons why this is happening are not important, what is important is understanding that there is no circumventing these planetary changes: they are inevitable and unstoppable at this point.

"Our purpose right now is to decide what to do for Golden Lemuria and her Life Forms, given these circumstances.

"This Council has known for some time that these changes might occur. There was no certainty that this would be the course of things, but we knew preparation was essential in case these events came to pass. As a result, we have explored and discovered possible options for Lemuria's survival and continued well being during this time.

"It has become clear to us that there are two viable choices: one is for Lemuria to simply move herself to another location within the Great Golden Universe and to continue on a different planet. After great adjustments, of

course, this would be a natural and relatively easy transition that would enable you to carry on as you have. It wouldn't be Terra, but it would be another location that suits everyone. I repeat, it wouldn't be Terra. She is a special One.

"The other option that was explored at length was presented to us by the Soul of Terra herself. She suggested depositing yourselves, and all the Golden Energy you have established on her surface, deep down inside her body. She has offered to safeguard all of you and ALL the Golden Energy until it is no longer necessary, and her surface is cleared enough for you to return there and rebuild.

"This offers an extraordinary opportunity, unlike anything ever endeavored for such an extended period. It will admittedly be an enormous challenge for every one of you, but will contain enormous gifts which can strengthen and deepen your relationship with Terra, and with yourselves as a Nation.

"You would live deep inside her body, to be cared for and nurtured, taught and guided by her. It would be a rare opportunity to be engaged with her Life Force and Soul at this most intimate level. Your involvement with one another, with all the Golden Life Forms, would take place in a concentrated way, far beyond any kind of closeness you have yet experienced. As I said, there has been nothing like this before—yours would be the first inner terrain trek of its kind.

"It would ask that you be willing to commit one hundred percent to staying INSIDE of Terra during the entire duration of this experience, and to following through on the growth and changes that this would bring. Living in this highly concentrated way for such an extended period has the potential to fortify and unite you enormously as a Golden Family—in ways you cannot even imagine. This could be something you will never have a chance to experience again.

"How will it be exactly? That is for all of you to find out. No one knows—you are the first.

"We cannot recommend which choice to make. We can only deliver this information, and leave the decision up to you. Because we know you to be wise and loving Leaders, we will support you in whichever choice you make. Both are viable, just vastly different.

"Take time now to discuss this with each other, but keep in mind that we have to act quickly."

Andar and I both feel somewhat breathless, and sit for a moment, stunned by this sudden occurrence. However, familiar with meeting challenges of great magnitude, we are aware we need to focus and gather our strength—both in ourselves, and each other. Knowing there is important work to do now, we get up and leave the room to collect our thoughts and make our choice.

We spend a short time weighing both options, but the answer soon becomes clear: our mutual decision is to unconditionally support our Lemurian Family in whatever choice they make. As the Council stated, either choice is viable, just vastly different—and we will lead our Golden Ones in the direction they choose to go.

Returning to the Meeting Room, we announce our decision to the Council, who confirm their support and commitment to provide whatever is needed accordingly. We then return to Terra's surface to gather our Lemurian Ones together to share the news. It is time to give them an opportunity to make their choice as One Body.

MEETING WITH OUR GOLDEN FAMILY MEMBERS

Andar has contacted everyone telepathically, and we are gathered together at our outdoor Meeting Sanctuary. Those who cannot physically attend have been alerted to participate energetically. Aware now that our Golden Family members have also felt the changes coming, we see that many of them are alarmed; clearly unsettled, they want to know exactly what is going on.

Andar is the first to speak, his reassuring voice ringing out loud and clear:

"Blessings, all Golden Ones here from far and wide. Great, great, great Blessings to all. Thank you for coming. Even though you do not know the details, I know you already sense the significance of what I am about to say.

"An immense life-altering event is about to take place in, and on, our Beloved Terra. Changes are already apparent within her energy fields, within her body itself, and will soon be manifesting on the surface of her skin. They will powerfully and directly affect all of us.

"There are great waters coming: the oceans will rise and sweep uncontrollably across these beautiful lands. Everything in the path of these waters will be demolished, completely flooding over all of us, and all we have created here.

"This marks a sudden, dramatic, and radical change for us. We have no choice in this matter: these cataclysmic events are naturally occurring and cannot be staved off by anyone or anything. The great waters will take over,

and that is that. That is a FACT.

"We meet here today to decide how we wish to proceed, given these inevitable circumstances. I realize that you are in shock at this news. I also know you have sensed it coming to varying degrees in your own systems. This is what you have felt. This explains the sensations you have been experiencing.

"We understand that you feel alarmed. We also know you are strong, steady, and centered. Able to respond to whatever comes next, you are well accustomed to meeting challenges of all kinds—with this situation presenting the biggest one yet, by far. Please take a moment to breathe into your ability to stay focused and clear in the face of what is happening.

"I am standing here not only to tell you of these impending changes, but also to inform you of the two choices we have for how to proceed. We know, given the Sacred Vows that we have all made, that abandoning our Project Lemuria is not even up for discussion. With that said, let us discuss how to move forward to continue our Creation.

"The first option available to us in this circumstance is that we can leave Terra now. We can take all that we have established here energetically and move ourselves, move our Lemuria, to another planet within the great Golden Universe. We could do this fairly easily, and it would enable us to carry on as we have, although in a different place far from here.

"The second option is to do something entirely new and unknown, to surrender to an experience we cannot even fathom right now. This choice, which comes from our beloved Terra herself, has the potential to enrich us all greatly and make us much, much stronger as a People, as One Golden Nation. Because this is her invitation, I will let her speak to you about it."

We sit quietly, watching as the presence of the great Golden Soul of Terra manifests herself into energetic form. As she does, we can feel her energy sweeping through us, enveloping us in her loving, steadying cocoon of strength and reassurance.

The Voice of her Soul touches us all:

"Beloveds of mine, Golden Beauties everywhere, I invite you to come and live inside of my Golden Body whilst all these great changes take place on my surface. I invite you to bring into me all your Golden Selves, your Golden Energies, and all the Golden Radiance you have established throughout our time together thus far. I rejoice at the possibility of your depositing all this inside my belly, inside my Golden Core. I am honored to safeguard and protect this, and all of you, for as long as you need.

"*I will understand if you decide to go elsewhere, and will certainly honor and support that, if it is what you choose to do. I know what I am suggesting will bring about challenges you will not have to face elsewhere. I hear your thoughts, and already understand your two major concerns: one is the state of what you call confinement, the other is your expectation of an absence of Golden Sunlight. In both cases, these concerns are unfounded. You do not know what my insides truly hold for you at these levels, these depths that I am offering you.*

"*What if you discovered that being taken care of by me would bring you greater freedom and liberation than ever before? What if I showed you the extent to which I am nourished by the Golden Sun, just as you are? I have absorbed it, just as you have, and there is much Sunlight stored inside of me. These are just two of the things you will find if you choose to inhabit my inner terrain.*

"*However, the most important thing I wish to speak about is our sacred Golden Love, our sacred Golden Union. We are already so intimately close, and this can continue to grow even deeper and more powerful.*

"*I know how to greatly take care of you. I will honor you, adore you, nurture you, and tend to your every need. I will guide you along, teaching you many new things about myself, and about each one of you. We can continue to grow and flourish together. You will be safe in me, and with me. As you already well know, you can depend on me fully.*

"*We are Love. We are Family. You are my greatest joy. It would deepen me, and my joy, if you would let me do all of this for you. This is both my gift, and fulfillment of my Golden Sacred Vow to you. We are One Golden Family, and we can remain One Golden Family, if you so choose.*

"*You are my Golden Heart's desire. I love you...forever.*"

With that, her Golden Caring fills us yet again. It gently penetrates our hearts in the most touching of ways, and we melt in her love. A few moments later, as her energies gradually disperse, we are all left with a profound sense of clarity and complete peace. Suddenly, what had seemed alarming has been replaced with an unshakeable faith that all is well, and will remain so.

We close our eyes and say a prayer of thanks. Terra has made our choice clear to us, and we know now what we must do.

Andar and I energetically scan all the Golden Family as one Body. Has the choice been made? Yes! All Golden Ones, seen and unseen, have unanimously chosen Terra. There is joy ringing out everywhere as we feel our own jubilation coupled with Terra's euphoria. We remain One Golden Family, and we are all enormously pleased.

Now everyone is eager to prepare for our new life, and while we wait for further instruction from Andar, I take the podium:

"Congratulations our most Beloved Ones. You have made the choice that Andar and I were hoping you would. It is what is in our hearts as well. Our purpose now is to lead you in this chosen direction to the best of our abilities. We are most happy and proud to do so.

"Yes, this will be a vastly different experience for all of us. Making this choice opens us up to new growth, to a multitude of brand-new frontiers within Terra, within ourselves, and within our Golden Family. There are many, many things to be discovered—much beauty, and many gifts that are yet to be revealed.

"This is a rare opportunity that Terra is offering us. This concentrated experience of Golden Family Living and continued Golden Creation, in this way, has the potential of deepening our union like nothing else could possibly ever do. This can only benefit us greatly, both as individuals, and as One Golden Heart.

"Thank you for making Terra your choice. We know how committed you are and that you make this decision consciously, with an understanding that you will follow through with whatever this choice brings—in its entirety.

"Know that we will be within Terra for a considerably long time. We will be living inside her Body as long as we need to while these natural changes take place on her surface, and until conditions resolve themselves. It may be quite a long time—but we can do this and do it well. When the time is right, and her surface is ready for us again, we will re-emerge and build anew.

"We recognize and honor you. We honor the depth of your love for Terra. Honor you for all that we have created with her thus far. Honor your devotion to this beautiful sacred marriage we have with her, and your desire to allow it to continue and grow. Most importantly, we honor your trust. Your trust in Terra, your trust in yourselves, your trust in us, your trust in our One Golden Family, and your trust in our Source to see us through.

"Yes, this is indeed a great leap of Golden Faith. Let's do it with totality, reverence, thanksgiving, and joy. Let's give it all we've got—and then some!"

I look around and see faces beaming with Golden joy. They are wide open and available, completely committed and surrendered to whatever this adventure will bring. Rejoicing in them, I love them fully. They are Golden Love Incarnate, and their Golden Light is shining brightly.

Both Andar and I know, without a single doubt, that all their Spirits are Golden Strong. That they have all it takes to meet this new challenge of ours with grace and equanimity.

Andar steps up to the podium, ready now to give detailed instructions about moving forward:

"Let's rally now and do the work necessary to move down inside Terra's Body.

"Each of you will gather your Golden Energies, and all the Essence of the Golden Creations you have manifested here on Terra's surface. Assist your families, friends, and fellow Golden Ones in collecting the entirety of this, then energetically bring it all back here with you when you are done. This meeting place will become our Golden Departure Station: we will congregate here before entering Terra's body.

"Time is short, so let's get on with it! We are with you. Blessings.

"One Golden Heart."

With that, the Golden Ones disperse and enthusiastically get on with the tasks at hand. Time is indeed short. There is a great deal to do, and we must do it with absolute thoroughness.

Andar and I look at each other and smile. We have no idea what to expect, but we are happy. It feels right, it feels good, and it feels natural. Golden Lemuria continues—with our Beloved Terra. What an adventure this is!

CHAPTER SIX

LIFE INSIDE GOLDEN TERRA

INSIDE GOLDEN TERRA WE GO-A NEW LIFE BEGINS

GATHERED NOW at our Golden Departure Station, we are finally all set and ready to go. The air is filled with anticipation and urgency—there isn't much time before the waters come.

We all know we are poised on a precipice of immeasurable change. There is no compass, no manual, no way of knowing how to place this pending reality into any context of understanding to date. This is simply a great leap of Golden Faith, and all we have to lean into is our Trust—and Terra.

I am the only one who knows, even though it is as yet a piece of the whole picture. I, Golden Avalar, have spent many extended periods of time inside of Terra, learning from her, being infused in special ways with her powerful depths of Golden Energy. She has been mentoring me, helping me to become a Golden Battery for her so that I could also hold her energy for the benefit of other Golden Ones and our Golden Project at large. This has been one of my primary responsibilities as Golden Leader alongside Andar, and a big part of my skills as Mother of Golden Creation Birthing. Because of my experience inside Terra, I know I must take the reins now and lead the way.

With the presence of the Soul of Terra now permeating my Being, I hear the gentle voice of her Spirit:

"Everything has been prepared inside of me. I am ready whenever you are."

Turning to my Golden People, I ask that they close their eyes. Lifting my voice, I begin:

"Golden Beloved Ones, Golden Family of my Golden Heart, we are about to take a brave leap of faith as we pour ourselves into this beautiful sacred vessel of Golden Terra. She is our Mother, our Teacher, our Leader, and Sustainer—just as she has always been, but now even more so. We do this with the knowledge that all will be well with us, and with our Golden Treasures that we bring.

"We shall soon begin the deposit of ourselves and our Golden Essences deep down inside of this most blessed Being. I will lead you on our journey

until the point that Terra takes over fully. But before that happens, let us pause; this very moment, right now, is most sacred.

"Let us give thanks for all that we have known, loved, created, and built here upon Terra's most exquisite and divine surface. Let us give thanks and hold dear ALL the Beauty we have known here; all the beauty Terra has gifted us with through our senses and our everyday living, breathing reality.

"We now honor all that we have been and known here. Let us bow to this and give great thanks."

Getting down on our knees, we all tenderly kiss Terra's beautiful ground. Our kiss is our love letter of forever gratitude to her for all we have known and shared to date. Our kiss is our promise to never forget her in this way. Our kiss marks a touchstone of memory of all that we have become.

Placing our hands now on her precious ground, we gently blow Golden Love into her, as her surface receives us. And as our hearts fill with her loving, grateful response, we become complete. This chapter of our lives, of our Golden Lemuria in this way, has now come to an end.

Avalar continues:

"Golden Ones, we pledge ourselves now to the grace and glory of Lemuria inside of Golden Terra. This is our Golden Heart's desire. This is our Sacred Golden Vow fulfilling itself as our new life begins. The moment of departure is here. We are ready, and Terra is ready.

"Golden Ones, I ask that you turn your attention toward me so we can begin blending the totality of our Essence into one Golden Body."

With that, they turn and breathe their love into me. Together, we take several deep breaths of Golden Essence of Golden Power, as our bodies begin to vibrate and shake. I hear the rush of wind in my ears, feel the caress of a breeze on my face. My focus turns inward, my Inner Vision pulsing, I know what my job is—and I am ready to do it.

This is the beginning of new Greatness for us, and as Our Golden Energies fully merge and become fluid and formless, we coalesce into a single Golden Energy Body. Becoming a spiral, weaving and undulating in a pattern of beauty and grace, we fall into brand new depths of total surrender and dissolve completely into One Golden Harmony. As One Body, our journey inside Terra commences.

My energy is in the center leading the way, and I hear Terra's voice as I feel her pull, deliberate and strong. Suddenly, I know it's time to let go, and as I release my Lead position, she gathers us all carefully into herself. She is our Leader now, our Matriarch. Everything that happens from here on will be under her care.

❧

Dear Reader, are you still with me? Let your mind go, let your eyes close. Let yourself remember this journey and how deliciously free and fluid you felt. Ours was not to be in control here; ours was to let go and be absorbed into the most exquisite sensations of Golden Tingling we had ever felt, or ever known. More so even than we could ever have imagined. Be with us dear Reader, be with us now.

We are glowing, vibrating, pulsating. Our cells begin to sing, soft sounds at first, then growing louder and stronger as we travel down, winding through great energetic spaces—high, low, narrow, open, large, and small. As the journey continues our colors change as if we have all become a rainbow shifting from one vibrant hue to another.

Suddenly entering a huge body of warm water, our motion slows and we soften and separate from one another ever so slightly. Finding ourselves being gently settled into a great soothing Golden Pool, we grow still.

Terra's voice is clear and present:

"Welcome Home my most beautiful Beloved Golden Family. I rejoice in you being here. Welcome, welcome all.

"You have entered my Inner Home, my Sanctuary of Greatest Strength and Well-Being. It is here that I come to meet my Creator, here that I come to pray for all that is dear to me. I have brought you here because this is my Home—and my Home is now your Home. You all live in me now, and I will take good care of you and all the Golden Blessedness of your Being.

"Because it will take a little while for your energies to adjust to this transition, it is important that you stay gathered like this to acclimate to the pulse and resonance of Golden Life as it is in here. Huddling together energetically and physically will also allow the enormity of you to settle into my Body. Any feelings of disorientation will not last long. You are adapting naturally as we speak.

"Allow my soothing waters to bathe you, to wash you anew. Now that you have entered my Golden Core, you are being Golden Birthed into levels and frequencies of deeper, ever-greater expansiveness, wellness, and under-standing.

"Your Consciousness is changing. Your Systems are changing. Your Bodies are changing. YOU are changing, forevermore.

"You have chosen this. You have chosen this because it is your Golden Heart's desire. You know this is true. You know you are Safe, Home, and Free—inside of Me."

As we continue to literally loll around in these divine Birthing Waters, listening to Terra's soothing voice, our calm returns as we are brought to a sweet sense of peace and serenity. Having made it to our intended destination completely intact, we know all is well—supremely well. We are safe in loving, gentle, strong, and capable hands; and it feels wonderful.

Terra begins to sing a beautiful lullaby that cradles us in her heart and soothes us like a mother would a newborn child. Enveloped and cocooned as we are in this total love and commitment, we feel her Presence like none other: deep, fathomless, and sustaining. Strong and serene, she is absolutely PRESENT.

We melt again, unable to do anything else. We languish here happily, and let be what is.

"I love you, I love you, I love you," she sings.

"I am here, I am here, I am here.

"You are safe, you are whole, and you are beautiful.

"In my Body, you are crystal clear.

"Know that Life is good now,

"That in all ways you are FREE.

"Blessed and beautiful are you, my loves,

"Blessed and beautiful in me.

"Peace you are. I love you. You are Home, Golden Home."

Her singing permeates our cells, unwinding us as we organically continue to separate. Returning now to our individual forms—limbs stretching, toes uncurling, hair streaming out in the warm waters—it feels great to be alive, and so delicious to be in here.

I recognize that in the time we have been luxuriating in Terra's Golden Birthing Waters, the fluid that surrounds us has enabled all the initial system adjustments to happen. Without feeling wobbly or shaky, we are now acclimated to being here, having been naturally re-patterned by our own inner wisdom to accommodate our new life.

Opening our eyes and looking around curiously, we can see luminescent crystalline walls sparkling more than any beautiful jewels we have ever seen. Sounds of water flowing in the background indicate there are streams and water-falls of some kind nearby, while an abundance of moisture in the air is causing our bodies to feel supple and alive, refreshed and renewed.

Feeling compelled to move out of the Pool, we all emerge and stretch our legs, curious to know what it's like here. We start exploring, walking through wide, then narrow passageways, climbing across great shelves of glowing rock along our way. It is fascinating in here; organic, moist, and vital.

With the air now changing, the fragrance of flowers delights our senses. We wonder how this could be possible, then remember the Soul of Terra explaining how there is plenty of Sun inside of her. Of course, there could be flowers! As we continue on, the sweet aroma grows stronger, filling our senses with lush sensuality. Greatly intrigued and curious, we wonder what we will discover next.

As we round a corner we squeeze, still huddled together, through a series of narrow corridors. Suddenly, the sense of restriction disappears completely as we enter a giant opening that stretches high and wide. Feeling like we have been pulled through a chute into a new world, a new atmosphere, and a new consciousness, nothing could have prepared us for what we see next: a vast expanse of wide-open sky beneath which flowers, flowers, everywhere stand tall as they sing and wave to us. With their song permeating our hearts and Souls we feel loved, welcomed, and honored.

Suddenly and quite unexpectedly receiving this richly colorful and fragrant gift, like the most beautiful present ever, we find ourselves with mouths open in a state of glorious wonder. We have no idea what to do with all of this, no frame of reference. Life inside Terra is beyond anything we could have possibly imagined it would be.

What an awakening!

A shift in the movement ahead reveals the beautiful energy of Terra's Soul rising in the midst of this glorious field of flowers, as she speaks to us in a voice overflowing with love:

"Beautiful Golden Ones, I know you have hardly even arrived, and already you are experiencing gifts beyond your imaginings. Welcome to my first lesson for you, Beloved Sweet Ones. My first gift is to teach you how to 'Receive Your Life' at levels you have been completely unaware of.

"Now that you are here, you are being flooded with a particular sense of breathlessness which tells you something far greater than you have dreamed is indeed happening for you. This sensation will happen again and again, but will never grow old for you. You will never become immune to the truly heightened frontiers of Beauty here; expanding you, amazing you, and taking your breath away.

"You will, at some point, begin to fully accept that you are, in truth, seeing and witnessing yourself. You are Beauty greater than you have ever dreamed or imagined. You are all of this.

"RECEIVE YOURSELVES. RECEIVE YOUR LIFE NOW.

"Choose to make this simple movement within your psyche, this subtle shift over to a different vantage point, a different window of understanding. This choice will allow you to absorb your own depth and expression at these new levels.

"BE PRESENT AS YOU ARE NOW. LET THIS NEW YOU, BE.

"Again, welcome Sweet Golden Ones. I love you."

And with that, Terra's Soul begins to giggle and laugh delightedly, so pleased with herself for being able to surprise us in this most beautifying way. This is clearly one of her favorite things to do, and with that, we watch as she disappears completely into the flowers.

Suddenly, all is quiet, and here we stand, thinking to ourselves, "This IS a trip!"

More Details About Life Inside Golden Terra

How do we spend our days and nights, you ask?

That is a very good question.

Let me first explain that we do not have any differentiation between day and night anymore. Our every moment simply blends from one to the next. We sleep and restore whenever we feel the need, allowing ourselves to receive the bounty of nourishment that is here for us.

There is, indeed, sunlight down here. Although not exactly as the Sun is on the surface, it is the radiant glow and warmth of the Sun that Terra has collected inside her crystalline forms. And as she exudes this Radiance, we are warmed and bathed by its Presence.

We live mainly in her cavern-like spaces, all of which are remarkably beautiful. Within their many different shapes, sizes, and configurations, these caverns have walls, ceilings, and floors that are speckled with jewel-like crystals. Our living spaces glisten and glow, continuously bathing us in the dancing prisms of light and ever-changing colors that the crystalline forms emanate.

There are also many other natural forms of Life that we enjoy down here: pools and ponds of Golden water, small streams, waterfalls, natural springs, and sauna-like grottos that are therapeutic and cleansing. We enjoy bathing in these often and always emerge thoroughly rejuvenated.

Despite living in close quarters, we each have ways of finding solitude and personal space by going into our own Sacred Sanctuaries. These are now energetic spaces which mimic the atmospheres of our Sacred Sanctuaries we had above surface, and we can access these "energy cocoons" through our intention whenever we want to.

Our systems have instinctively adapted to this environment, and have been naturally geared to a much slower mode since we've been down here. We spend much more time focusing inward, and are getting to know ourselves in much deeper ways, which is turning out to be greatly empowering. Whenever we feel like it, we can also travel, shifting our energies to expansive frequencies and states, stretching out and feeling that exuberance which we so love. Many of us do this more often than others, depending upon personal needs.

The spaces of open meadows and fields with the sky overhead, which I described earlier, are unique and wondrous. They are unexpected and always liberating to be in. Although they have clear boundaries around their edges, they nonetheless have the quality of openness and spaciousness which is potent and satisfying. In them we are physically free, and feel nourished in this way as well.

We come often to these open meadows for our dances, as we often have gatherings of this kind that are significant and celebratory. Rejoicing in our lives is essential to our personal well being, and to the overall balance and health of our community. We have an actual NEED to do this; to remain strong, clear, and connected to our lives, to Terra, and to our family and Creator. It also keeps us well connected to our intrinsic and abundant joy.

Celebrating our achievements is important as well, marking those memories of our success. But it is simply the act of rejoicing in our BEING ALIVE—of expressing our gratitude for this and all the gifts we hold near and dear—that make these gatherings most essential. They are a chance for all of us to share and rejoice, to have fun and celebrate our One Golden Heart with all the exuberance that we are. These celebrations are essential to our flourishing.

Being so deeply inside of Terra has not changed our intimate connection with all the Golden Ones far beyond here. We are perhaps even more interwoven now because of having more time and energy to spend in conscious communion with our Golden Family at large—and we use this time wisely. Our quiet, grateful, loving moments are "love notes" to all of them, to our Source, to whomever and whatever has moved us and stirred our hearts in meaningful ways. Our loving *is* a Creation, the most beautiful Creation of all.

While there are times when some of us may feel a growing frustration and sense of confinement due to our circumstances, for the most part, we have learned to channel the intensity of this energy into our inner learning and expansion. Knowing why we are here, and that we have consciously CHOSEN this, helps us to maintain a beneficial focus for ourselves and our purpose. Giving ourselves permission to receive ourselves in ways that further our understanding of who and how we are helps us to support each other as well.

Facing ourselves this deeply shows us how much more beautiful we are than we had previously realized. As appreciation of our subtle nuances grow, we admire each other's character and unique essences more than ever. We fit together perfectly. And although it may be like a puzzle at times, it is one we welcome and explore with curiosity.

Our understanding and experience of ourselves as One Golden Family continues to intensify. We were close before, but now we are extremely close. We love this; we love ourselves, and we love each other enormously. It is wondrous to be intimately connected in this way, and to harmonize even more substantially while feeling the effects of this deepening bond throughout our time here.

Our Golden Weave, our Golden Tapestry, now grows exponentially stronger by the minute as we become more One than we could have possibly fathomed before. We lean into each other and depend upon each other. We need one another, and accept this. Grateful for this special union, our love for each other is palpable. We know this—and it feels completely right.

The love that blossoms is astounding. Ah, what love can do when touched, expressed, and allowed to flow abundantly. It seems there is never any end to it, and we surrender to this truth, basking in it with pure joy and gratitude. We welcome our harmonization, because this is what nourishes and inspires us all, individually and collectively. In this we are strong—super strong.

We each get on with our own creative projects, embracing the opportunity to more closely examine aspects of our personal process. Having inner time to unwind, observing exactly how we do things in our creative freedom, fosters our abilities and creative natures, enabling us to be even more skilled and successful in our endeavors.

We find ourselves infinitely more focused and deliberate. It is as if we are living suspended in yet another, still deeper, Golden Womb—a concentrated Golden Laboratory out of time, space, and expectation. We are here to continue our Lemuria, yes, but it is also a priceless opportunity to explore ourselves, our Golden Family, our Creativity, and the nature of Creation itself.

Who better to teach us than one of the greatest Creators there is: our beloved Terra. As we live and study with her our Vision becomes clearer, more refined, more powerful. We understand with greater depth and feeling many things that are important to us. Learning by leaps and bounds, we are all growing immeasurably. Terra teaches us constantly, and throughout it all we simply become better people, better Golden Creators, and a better One Golden Family.

～

We are growing exponentially, learning and deepening as we go. With Terra's focused training and wisdom, we are becoming more consciously aware of our self-trust, of the pathway to our own vast inner strength and resources.

"You are Sacred Golden Temples embodied," she says. *"And you need to deepen your CONSCIOUS knowing of your Sacrosanctedness, so that you will engage fully with your inner reservoirs—that which is most sacred, private, and holy within you.*

"There is always room for more self-knowing. This enables you to recognize and know your profound TRUST IN YOURSELVES, letting you RECEIVE this more and more fully into every single nook and cranny of your awareness. Acknowledge it, feeling how it keeps you centered, strong, and steady; understanding how it opens doorways to your holiness.

"Come, let us practice this together as One, right now."

We are sitting in her Core Crystal, breathing slowly and deeply as we await her instruction. Soft, vibrant light emanates from the walls around us, and a glow rises from the cavern floor. You would think it might feel cool in here, but not so: it feels warm. Once again, we are being bathed by Terra, only this time not by her Golden Pool but by her radiant, luminescent Beauty. We are having a Beauty Bath, a sensual experience that makes us soften, yielding in delight.

She tells us, *"Life is always birthing itself. It never stops—and never, ever will.*

"The more conscious you can become of this Truth, the greater will be your abilities to consciously and carefully direct this force in and through yourselves when you choose to.

"Breathe, my beloved Golden Ones. Simply breathe with me. Inhale my scents, my textures, my sensations of serenity, peace, and love. This is here for you. Sink in and feel your systems opening to this more as you are warmed and welcomed by me.

"We are going to deepen now. Crawl inside of yourselves and enter your Sacred Core Within. Feel your pulse, and the pulse of our Creator. Give in to our Creator now, simply because you want to, and because it makes you feel good inside. It is your Purity, your Golden Purity, that reaches up and touches your psyche at this moment. You recognize, yet again, that you can birth because you have been birthed. You are at the Heart of Creation because you are born from this. You ARE this.

"Your trust in yourself is your Trust in your Source. It is one and the same. Drop your Trust deeper now, let go of you and become your Source.

"You are Golden Sacrosanct. You know this. Embrace this, and feel your gratitude. Revel, rejoice, and relax into it thoroughly."

We feel ourselves dropping much, much deeper, traveling to levels within never consciously reached before. Terra's energy pressing down does not permit us to give up, or to be distracted. Our Guide, she is also our Mother Task Master in these moments as she applies an unrelenting pressure. Knowing this is needed to open our psyches to that which we are made of, her sustaining faith in us is welcome. Her great strength is what enables us to go deep and discover new realms of ourselves.

"There is a time when simply allowing is the key," Terra says. *"And then there is a time when desire, intent, and laser focus is the key. I press you, yes, but I am not forcing you. It is my pressure that enables you to remain focused and centered on your quest. Never underestimate the power of forces that would distract you from your course, if they want to. Learn well how to remain absolutely clear and deliberate—no matter what. Become greater Adepts at this now, and continue to focus on strengthening this as we live here together. Vitally important, this is an essential key to our effective Creatorship."*

We feel greatly stirred and shifted inside as Terra continues to move us. Knowing her pure strength, we feel her immense power steadily permeate us as we let go, drop down in, then yield to that which is our own vast Greater Intelligence. Being fortified by her as she expertly guides us into enormous reservoirs within is an extremely empowering sensation. We continue to breathe, continue to deepen and receive ourselves.

Terra says:

"I know you are already Master Creators, great Golden Ones, Leaders in your fields. I commend and honor you absolutely. And yet, you and I know that there is more. There is always more strength to know, clarity to have, Self-trust to fully embrace, and love to pour forth.

"I ask you, what internal muscles need to be developed to make yourselves even stronger, more brilliant, and more you?

"Reflect on this. Ask yourselves, 'What more is there for me to learn about myself—my abilities, my joys, my power, and my heart? What deliberately breathes me, inspires me, focuses me, propels and compels me?'

"This condition of living inside of me makes everything close, concentrated, and crystal clear. It is ripe with information about you as well as for you.

Seize this more, welcome this more, and utilize this rare opportunity still more. I am here with you, supporting you every step of the way. I KNOW who you are, and you are finding out."

We ponder all of this for a moment, knowing Terra's deliberate streamlining of our awareness causes us to further seize the opportunity of our circumstance. She is enabling us to be greatly illumined and empowered, deepening us intensely into our true freedom of Being. She is stimulating us to profoundly KNOW and FEEL ourselves, our Being, our Center—and to stand steady in this no matter the outer circumstances. She is training us to become more focused, deliberate, and strong, inside and out.

Terra speaks again:

"I am a Being of much abundance, many avenues of Creativity, and many exhilarating expressions of my own Creator. You are getting to experience my richness, my strength, and my power more and more, the longer you are here.

"But what you are truly experiencing as well is the deep richness of YOU. What you are truly experiencing is the immense Power of you. What you are growing into is the true strength of you.

"Being inside of me you are able to face yourself fully, without distraction. How exquisitely beautiful is that? How exquisitely beautiful are you? How enormously strong and powerful are you?

"I wish you to delve deep, to bring these answers and these energies up from within the great and powerful internal storehouse of you. There is still much more to you than meets your eye. Be sustained and strengthened from within.

"Go deep, and deeper still. Go right into the Center of your most private, personal, and Sacred Holiness inside. Abide there and BE this.

"Set yourselves free."

❧

Dearest Reader, in the previous pages of this chapter, as well as the remaining ones, Terra is mainly in charge. This is HER time to Mother, guide, and teach us whatever she feels we need to know during our inner stay with her. A rare and sacred opportunity for this kind of extended intimacy with her, we are seizing the day.

Because of this, Andar and I assume more of a backseat position. It is a deepening, quiet time and space for all of us, with Andar and I frequently going into our own retreat state so that we, too, can benefit from Terra's many sacred gifts and teachings.

We are certainly still actively engaged with, and part of, everyone's daily life. Watching over and guiding in our own ways, we gather wholeheartedly with them during times of celebration or counsel. But as you already know, and will continue to learn, it is a deeply internal time of growth for everyone, and Terra is The Great Mother throughout: all receive exactly what we need from this wondrous experience, indeed far more than we ever knew we needed. It is truly remarkable.

∾

At this point in our story we are happy to introduce you to "The Golden Witness," one of the voices you will read going forward. An integral member of our Golden Family, this particular Golden One has volunteered to be the story-teller, when needed, and speaks on behalf of the Golden Family group.

You will love her, and love getting to know her, as she is a great spokesperson, a generous and kind Soul, and indeed, fiercely devoted to our One Golden Heart consciousness. Since she will reveal herself in the pages ahead, we will simply let you discover more about her for yourself.

We invite you to join us and The Golden Witness as she helps to carry us forward in our story.

THE GOLDEN WITNESS SPEAKS

We are all gathered now in Terra's favorite Sacred Sanctuary. She has called us here for another one of her sessions that we have fondly dubbed "Lessons from Terra."

We LOVE being taught by her. She is a magnificent catalyst for our personal expansion, and we are all benefitting so much from the changes happening inside of us.

As we sit waiting patiently for our session to begin, I find myself pondering our experience here thus far. We have been living inside of Terra for what feels like a long time, even though our experience within her is timeless. Our longevity has been up to each Golden One, just as it was on Terra's surface. Some of us have decided to remain ageless, while others have not, depending on our chosen roles and purposes. Regardless of age, however, we have all grown enormously thanks to Terra's tutelage.

I feel wiser, and much more mature, than I have ever known myself to be. Looking around at my Golden Family, I can see that they all feel precisely the same way. We have become more content in ourselves, literally. We have more "content," more substance—and we are more peaceful.

Already strong Creators, to be sure, we now feel more serene inside this ability of ours. There is a quieter rhythm to us, like still waters which run deep. We have drunk in and absorbed much of Terra's beauty while here, learning that there is always much more than meets the eye. Having also learned to break through any previous "ceiling" in our imagination, we simply know now that there are no limits—ever.

This makes what we create inside of her that much more precious. Before this experience, we might have thought that we need wide open spaces, a boundless sky which stretches out forever, to feel the freedom to be our unique selves, to spread out our Creative wings. Down here, we recognize that this is simply not true.

We are each *our own* wide open space, so it is up to us to be the expansiveness of our own natures. This we have learned we can be and do anywhere, no matter the conditions; no matter the amount of space.

We are vast, free Beings. We all have large, beautifully outstretched wings whenever we wish to spread them. We do this no matter where—because we can. And we can—simply because we are.

The Creations which we birth forth now happen in a more concentrated way. We can still have the full breadth, depth, and intensity of them, but on a much smaller scale. We do not feel deprived of the space we need to create, or for our Creations to be realized and to flourish. We simply do it in a different manner, which renders it vastly more potent. Becoming adept in these skills not only benefits us now, but will also serve us greatly in our future.

Learning how to make our Creations more potent, more alive and fruitful—and therefore, much more powerful—has been a groundbreaking training for us. And this "laboratory" has enabled us to experiment with our creative energies in ways that would never have occurred to us before. Necessity is the Mother of Invention, and in terms of Creatorship our circumstances have forced us to grow in ways far beyond any previous parameters and abilities.

Who knew?

What a Gift! And one that will last forever. We are so grateful. I am so grateful.

My thoughts are gently but firmly being brought back to the present moment, as Terra's energies move in more closely, focusing us all to receive her.

Her energies now collecting in and around us, she touches each one of us deeply with her loving kindness. Knowing that we are each special to her feels wonderful indeed.

Terra says:

"Golden Ones, there are a few more things I wish for you to know before your lives change again; before you leave here and return to my surface. We do not know yet exactly when this will be, but no matter when, you will be well prepared and ready.

"I wish to speak to you today about how deeply you love one another. We have spoken much of this, I know, but there is still a reverberation which wishes to be felt and experienced. It is the One Golden Heart that I speak of now, referring not only to all the love that you know and feel right here inside of me—for yourselves, for one another, and for me—but also your love for the larger Family. All the Golden Seen and Unseen Ones, all the Star, Cosmic, Angelic, and Sacred Golden Ones far and wide. Our Golden Family is multi-dimensional, vast, and beautiful.

"Reflect now on our One Golden Heart, so strongly exquisite, so pure and deeply devoted to all of our love that it holds, generates, and radiates. Its sound is pure and crystal clear, its Presence sublime. Collectively, we have birthed this.

"Throughout our time together as Lemuria, we have made this palpable, real, and alive in the Golden Cells of the Golden Universe. It guides us and leads us now, standing strong and steady as our Golden Beacon, our Golden Lighthouse. It is ours to continue to take good care of, to foster and nurture to the best of our abilities. It is our responsibility and our Sacred Vow to do this. In turn, it is up to us to allow it to enrich and nurture us along all the avenues of our lives, wherever they may take us.

"Your abilities to draw from our One Golden Heart whenever you need to—cherishing and embracing it, feeling its Presence inside and around you—have grown infinitely stronger. You are no longer the same as you were when you first came in here to me. You know this.

"You have grown immensely, becoming more powerful, more conscious, and more awake. Your Golden Hearts are much stronger, your Vision clearer, and your Self confidence more compelling. Your Golden Light is vastly more radiant and magnetic. The question is, what will you choose to do with all of this newly discovered and developed Golden Love and Golden Power?

"What will you focus on? What will you create? What will you do, being YOU?

"These are questions you cannot answer right now. I know this. So perhaps you wonder, 'Well then, why is she even asking us these questions?' My

reason for doing so is because I want to sow seeds.

"I want you to ponder these questions, and allow them to percolate. Each time you do, you validate and confirm the growth that you have made here. This is enormously strengthening for you. It brings those gifts still more clearly into Vision—into your awareness, front and center.

"What is most important about all of this is the intrinsic wisdom of your loving, and the healing balm inherent within it. What is important is to share and extend this, and to realize, even more, the great and glorious freedom it contains.

"Your Loving Muscles are strong, and always have been. Having carried you throughout your evolution, they will continue to sustain you through whatever your pathways hold.

"You are love, and you know this. BE this now, even more consciously and deliberately, and even still more. Welcome your adoring Source gently filling you up, still more."

We each sit still and open our hearts, receiving ourselves and our Source in this glorious way. We all feel Terra's largeness as well, her full-bodied breath, moving inside of us. We sink into this, knowing it is opening us up wider and wider. We rejoice in feeling the sensations of our Goldenness, in how much pure love we are. Terra urges us to stretch out in this still more, guiding us now to connect with the Golden Energies of our Golden Loved Ones everywhere. As we finish, finally and fully, she speaks with delight in her voice:

"We welcome to our hearth all the energies of the sacred Golden Ones everywhere. We invite you now to be with us, to merge and mingle inside of our Golden Hearts. We acknowledge you and welcome you joyously.

"Why exactly are we coming together like this? What is so special about this gathering? I will tell you.

"We have come together for one profound and simple reason—to witness each other.

"I ask you to WITNESS EACH OTHER NOW."

Suddenly it feels as if my whole chest has burst wide open, and I feel a pressure inside my heart. It is a good pressure, the pressure of Presence that is so much bigger than myself that it overwhelms me.

Greatly stirred, I hold my face in my hands, and my breath catches, this experience moving me like a giant wave spreading across the ocean floor. With a sudden and intense clarity, I realize that WITNESSING is a sacred and most powerful act of Love. Seeking to change nothing, it does not evaluate, assess, or judge. It only stands, front and center, in the "Presence Of."

As I witness, standing still with eyes open, senses aware, heart fully acknowledging what is right in front of me, it is breathtaking and beautiful. I understand that it is necessary to our well-being—and as I am witnessed in return, I shine.

I understand clearly in this moment what witnessing is. It is being fully seen, heard, felt, and included. It is being honored. It is being acknowledged and recognized as a VALUABLE AND VALUED LIFE.

I start to cry. This simple act of love is so profound and reverberating. These are not tears of sadness, or even of joy. They are tears of being deeply and most tenderly touched and moved.

I am witnessing, and I am being witnessed. How beautiful this is. How beautiful we all are.

One Golden Family.

One Golden Heart.

I could cry these tears of loving resonance forever. That is how profound this is for me.

PART TWO

WHAT HAPPENED?

CHAPTER SEVEN

The Ascent

Preparing to Resurface: Andar and Avalar Meet with the Sacred Council

AVALAR SPEAKS:

It's time. Andar and I both KNOW it. Feeling strongly compelled now to return to the surface of our Beloved Terra, it is apparent that our extended time of being with her in this most special way has come to an end.

A collective restlessness has become evident in the Golden Ones inside our beautiful world of Terra, and she feels it as well. The time to leave has arrived, with all of us ripe and ready for whatever comes next. Such is the process of Creation: ceaselessly moving and changing, adapting and rearranging.

With a telepathic call from the Golden Sacred Council having just been received, Andar and I prepare to meet with them to get our instructions. Taking a moment to hold hands and breathe deeply together, our love flows through us, bringing perfect balance and clarity. Our combined focus now firmly engaged, it is with readiness that we return once again to the Sacred Council Meeting Area and the room with the circular table.

Quietly taking our seats, we greet the rest of the Golden Masters who are present. There is a moment of silence to honor each other through our hearts, then Sananda stands to address us. As he looks at Andar and I with immense love and gentleness, we both melt into his Golden Clarity. My own Inner Eye expands as it reaches into his, and in this moment, we become one and the same. Seeing through his awareness just how much activity is anticipated—the sheer volume of change, the need to deliberately focus in unfamiliar ways—I understand how great the challenges ahead of us truly are.

Although details have not yet been revealed, my sense is that it will require the entirety of all that Terra has nurtured in me, in all of us, during our time here together. With Andar obviously having a similar experience of clarity, I see his conduits being lit up with an activation of new levels of ability. A completely new set of channels, developed in his system while we've been down here, are now being energized as they are brought to full power. And the same is true for me: all our circuitry and development as Avalandar is now being strongly activated, and rising to our conscious awareness. We are being prepared and charged up, there is no question about it.

After a few minutes, we feel the energies begin to even out and become softer. Taking deep breaths, our systems regain their balance, and we are grounded in our seats once more as Sananda begins to speak:

"Beloveds, Andar and Avalar, you are both strong and mighty leaders. Your Hearts are pure and deep. You carry within you the blueprint of Lemuria, sacrosanct and strong. Your job ahead is to continue to hold this foundation of wholeness, purity, and love that has become all that Lemuria is—One Golden Heart.

"Your job as Avalandar is to treasure this, to keep it secure, well, and strong; breathe into it, worship it, adore it. Nurture it and love it deeply. Drink from it, and be constantly nourished and restored by it. It will never be compromised. You know this. It cannot be compromised because it is sacrosanct.

"At any time of new change such as this, the Ground of Golden Being needs to be fortified and reaffirmed. This is what these moments with us now are all about. In our presence, you know the strength of our complete and utter love for you; of our support for you and all that you stand for, forevermore. WE are with you. Always, Always, Always.

"You are the carriers of this Golden Love, this One Golden Heart, and our One Golden World. You are the Golden Treasures that embody and hold this all together, safe and sound. This is what is being asked of you from here on in. This is what you have been prepared for. This is your Sacred Vow in action.

"Know that you are filled with this, and always will be. No matter what the future brings, your WHOLENESS IS INTACT. Your Wholeness will never be compromised. You are sacrosanct, and you always will be.

"You are the Holders of the Golden Light, the Golden Love, the Golden Configuration, the Golden World, and the One Golden Heart. THIS is AVALANDAR.

"Terra, her Soul, Body and Being, is with you always—inside of you, around you, and through you. She is the glue that holds you together and restores you to Peace, Golden Peace, every time you think of her; she will provide you with all that you need, just as she always has.

"She lives fully inside of you now. We are with you in this deep and powerful way as well, and together, we make One Golden Family. You know this to be so.

"Take a moment now to feel this truth and inhale it deeply inside of your hearts, your minds, your bodies, and your Souls. Avalandar: Golden Love Sacrosanct—Pure, Whole, Joyful, Clear, and Free.

"Let this guide you, be you, and sustain you throughout all that is ahead. We can give you no further information, no details, or anything that would alter your perception about the future.

"But what you do know is that you now enter the Great Unknown. You two have taken such leaps many times before, and you know exactly how to be present and fluid with whatever Life brings. Your Conscious Choice has been made, and you have been well prepared to receive the Life that awaits you.

"Your joy and your power are strong. You are members of One Golden Unified Family, and always will be. We always will be. Go forth with joy and passion. Be all that you can Be. We love you and honor you.

"We are ONE with you forevermore. One Golden Heart reigns supreme. You are this: Golden Avalandar."

With that, Andar and I feel ourselves taking one last deep, loving breath with the Council. Although unable to know what our future holds, we feel strong and supported beyond any level we have consciously known before. And that is all we need.

As Andar and I leave the Golden Council for one last meeting with our Beloved Terra, a depth of clarity and focus warming our hearts, we feel positive indeed about returning to her surface.

ANDAR AND AVALAR SAY FINAL GOODBYES INSIDE TERRA

Andar and Avalar Speak:

"Thank you, our most beloved Terra. Thank you for everything that you have given us and our Golden Family.

"Our time inside of you in this deep and holy way has been a gift greater than we could have ever dreamed or imagined. You are in our Heart, Soul, Body, and Breath. You are in every cell of us. We love you so very much, and we deeply honor you.

"We know you are always with us, always around us, always here for us. Your heart is ours, and ours is yours, forevermore.

"Your Great Golden Body has kept all of us safe and well, allowing us to grow profoundly during our time with you. We know that even after returning

to your surface our intimate connections with you will only develop and deepen still more. Our life up top is unknown right now, but we know it will be filled with you and our deepest connection always.

"You are a Beauty, a Golden Beauty. Thank you from the bottom of our hearts, our dear-hearted one.

"Forever thank you.

"We Are One Golden Heart."

Andar and I, down on our knees, both feel unable to express enough gratitude and love for this divine and beautiful Being. What an honor it has been to be here inside of her: to grow so intimately with her. What a gift to be guided, tended, cared for, loved, and mothered by her. What a privilege it has been to have been taught and illuminated so powerfully by her.

It has changed both of us forever.

Feeling her energy rocking me ever so gently, my eyes fill with tears—but my heart is oh, so full. This enduring steadiness will remain inside of me always. This faith and security that only she could have provided is mine forever more. I am solid as a rock, clear as a bell, fluid as an ocean. All that she is, I have become.

Looking deeply into each other's eyes now, Andar and I can see how profoundly she has affected our union, not just with her, but with one another. Our base of Avalandar is stronger, more loving, and more powerful than ever before. We feel fully charged, filled up like great batteries with Golden Illumination, ready to take on our new lives and all that they ask of us. Ready and eager to return to the surface to build anew, we look forward to seeing how Lemuria will grow during this next phase.

In our absolute joy we feel the energy of Terra's magnificent Golden Soul caressing our hearts, as she speaks to us now:

"My Beloveds, as you know, you are not leaving me. You are simply 'changing your station,' going from down here to up top again. All that you have grown into, and all that you know of me, is an intrinsic part of your fabric. It will always remain thus. You know this, strong and clear.

"You also know how profoundly I love you, and that I hold you near and dear, always. I am your refuge and your home, always. I am here for you in whatever ways you need, always. You know you can count on me, as I have so lovingly shown you. I am so happy to have had the chance to take care of and provide for you in the ways that I have.

"Things, as you know, will change now. But they will only change on the outside, not the inside. You will always be Golden Avalandar, no matter what.

And our Golden Family will always be One Golden Heart, no matter what.

"As you move back up to my surface, you know it will be radically different than it was before you came down inside of me. Do not be daunted by this difference. Do not be disturbed or disappointed if it does not meet your expectations. It is hard not to have preconceived ideas based on experiences of the past. But know that your true vision is clear and open. As great Golden Leaders, well equipped and highly developed as you are, you can meet Life as it meets you. And you will continue to successfully guide your People, just as you always have.

"This is a brand-new chapter. I rejoice in all that we have been, and look forward to all that we have yet to become. I love you, dearest Ones. I love you with all my Heart and Soul and Body and Being. We are One. We are One Golden Heart. Forever.

"Let us go now and speak to all the Golden Ones. I know of their restlessness and aching need to take the next steps of growth and change. Such is the way of Life, always growing and always changing.

"Bless you, Beloveds. My heart is yours, we are GOLDEN ONE.

"I love you."

And with that, we are transported by Terra into the midst of our final meeting with all the Golden Ones inside her to discuss strategies for our return to her surface. As always, she continues to guide our way with tender loving care and supreme purposefulness.

THE FINAL ASCENT MEETING

Andar and I, along with the Golden Soul energy of Terra, now face many eager eyes in this crowd of beautiful, shining Golden Ones. We can see how brightly lit up they all are—like exquisite diamonds sparkling in the morning sun. Their Golden Radiance is strong and vibrant, their hunger to again experience the expansiveness of great open sky evident. As they look at us with complete unabashed faith, we are pleased to see the confidence they have in us. Their trust in the next steps of their lives, and in us to lead them, is clearly unwavering and absolute. Their collective Choice to accept whatever might occur and remain on Terra—made so long ago, before the great cataclysms, has carried them well. It continues now, bringing them steadily forth into the great mystery of what lies above.

There is also a restlessness, an agitation, which Andar and I know is nothing more than an indication of how truly ready they are to joyfully and faithfully create anew on Terra's surface. Having become empowered and matured by being with Terra, there will be no holding them back, with forward being the ONLY motion they want now. THEY ARE READY, and are just about bursting at the seams.

There is a need to calm them down, so that they can receive our instructions. We are thankful that Terra's Golden Soul energy is moving forward to command the stage. As her soothing energy of love sweeps throughout the group, the Golden Ones are simply melting and sitting back, powerless in the face of her tender loving care. Being ever so gently bathed in Terra's peace, they are all managing to collect themselves as her energy begins to speak:

"Beloved Golden Dear Ones: yes, I know well how eager you are to get on with things. How well I understand the driving need to create in a bigger and more expansive space. This is what you have worked toward—this reentry onto my surface. Knowing it will be very different from what it was when you left, I admire the fact that you bring fresh eyes, hearts, and minds. This is what it asks of you. This is how it will be able to respond fully to you.

"Together, we will rebuild. Together, we will embrace whatever our future brings, our Golden Hearts devoted, resilient, and strong.

"You have prepared yourselves for this, and I have done my part to assist you. Together we have done well, exceptionally well. You deserve to be proud—proud of yourselves as individuals, proud of yourselves as a beautifully strong and deeply loving People.

"Yes, you are ready for whatever comes next. Yes indeed, you are good and ready now.

"Know that I am with you—always, always, always. My Heart, my Soul, and my Spirit ring out loud and true inside of you. I am the Ground you can always count on, no matter what you are creating, no matter what you are building, no matter what you are sustaining. I live within the very cells of your Being, as you live in mine. I am always here for you, inside and out.

"Let yourselves have your future. Walk the pathway that is set in front of you, knowing that every step will make you still stronger, bigger, and brighter. There is no end to what your Golden Creativity can realize, and it is in the action of your creations that your dreams truly do come true.

"Great Golden Ones, I encourage you to focus yourselves now, to express your Golden Centeredness that we have spent so much time maturing together. You are all Golden Masters in your own right—strong, clear, clever, and adept. Stretch those hard-earned Golden Muscles, rely upon them,

and witness them growing even stronger still. OWN the Golden World that you make, now and in all your futures, for there is no end to your Beauty, Creativity, Passion, and Love. There is no end to you. Ever.

"Bless you, Great Ones. Thank you, from the bottom of my Heart and Soul, for the love that we have shared during these times together. Thank you for touching me deeply, and allowing me to touch you in kind. I love how much you love me, and am eternally grateful for this. And I love how much you let me fill you and nourish you with my love always.

"We are ONE and continue to be so, forevermore. So much love we are, Golden Love. Golden Glory is ours.

"I love you.

"One Golden Heart Forever."

Andar and I gaze out at our Family, seeing many eyes now filling with tears, hearing quiet sobs throughout the crowd. Terra has touched us all deeply, yet again. Taking a few more moments to feel her grace, each one of us privately speaks our heartfelt gratitude to her for the gifts and the splendidness of living inside her. Our closeness with her is palpable, as we conclude this wondrous and powerful chapter of our Golden Lives, knowing that all we have shared with her will remain with each of us forever.

Gradually, Terra's energy dissipates as she leaves us with her gentle Golden Godspeed, and we all bring our focus back to the task at hand. There is much ground to cover, with very specific steps that must be followed. Andar steps forward to address the group:

"Beloved Golden Ones, my beautiful Golden Family, I love you. We love you.

"Avalar and I are extremely proud of all that you have grown into and become during our time inside of Terra. You are strong and steady Golden Leaders now, Masters at what you do and Masters of Golden Being.

"What awaits us up top is a mystery, and we cannot have any pre-conceived notions about what we might find. Terra's surface has been completely altered, reborn in ways that we cannot yet fathom.

"We must each hold steady, giving ourselves complete permission to meet this unknown future with open minds and hearts, but also with much care and discernment. Since we do NOT know what awaits us, we must simply observe and see what we find.

"Once we emerge onto what will hopefully be dry land, we will regroup, then make decisions as to how best to proceed. Right now, because this is

*as far ahead as we can plan, we must take it one step at a time. First step
is to get ourselves back up there!"*

Suddenly, the enormity of what is happening begins to sink in. We are really
and truly going to DO this! We are going to make this change! Once again, everyone takes a deep collective breath to remain steady and calm as Andar continues
with his instructions:

*"Initially, we will send out our highly trained and Masterful First Scouts.
Depending upon what they report back to us, we will then send out another
Team of Scouts, and then another, until we are sure all is ready for the
rest of us to emerge.*

*"Know that we are at first only emerging as a People. We will not be ushering
up the fullness of our Golden Energies until we know what we are dealing
with. These will be sent up to the surface on an as-needed and as-ready
basis. In the meantime, Terra will continue to take good care of them for
us inside of her body, as she has done for so long now.*

*"In terms of our actual ascent itself, once the Activation Charge for this has
been turned on, there will be no turning back. The energy will be powerful,
so please know this: the only direction to go will be UP. Focus yourselves
on this highly charged, vibrating current. Allow its strength and power to
propel you upward to where we need to go. The ride promises to be bumpy,
but it will happen quickly, with no effort on your part. Simply let go, and
allow these energetic forces to carry you.*

*"As we near the top, you will feel the energies gradually slowing down.
We will stop our motion at a point just prior to the surface, where we will
gather to make an evaluation and receive reports from our Scouts. Then,
when ready, we will emerge through Terra's crust back out onto land. The
men will go first, followed by the elders, and then the women and children.*

*"It is essential to understand that this entire process will be quite rapid.
The more you relax and soften, the easier and more comfortable it will be.*

*"Before we complete our final preparations, there is one last detail that
must be addressed. Avalar, please come forward to say a prayer for our
safe travel, blessing us and this new journey we now embark upon."*

I step up to take my place in front of our beloved Golden Ones. As I gaze
out at them, love and pride well up in my heart. These are truly beautiful Souls,
all of whom I love very deeply. Feeling the strength of our power and weave as
ONE in this moment, I send my own prayer of thanksgiving to our Source for

the exquisite tapestry of Golden Harmony that we embody.

Avalar speaks:

"My dearest Golden Ones, I bring to you my heart and soul. I am exceedingly proud of you, and honored to be able to call you Family. I love you enormously. You are all courageous and resilient, strong and capable. You are filled to overflowing with joy and the pure radiance of your Golden Hearts. During our time together inside of Terra we have grown to know one another so well. We have all been inspired by the beauty and grace that we have discovered in each other.

"As you know, we are One and will always be thus. Our fabric is powerfully enmeshed, and our One Golden Heart beats joyously throughout.

"As we enter this next venture of ours, I acknowledge and honor our sustaining Golden Oneness yet again. It is the nature of who and how we are. It is the pledge, the sacred vow we have made from the beginning of our Lemuria. We are ONE Golden Family, and in this we stand forever. We keep this always in the forefront of our vision as the motivating and inspiring element in everything we do and are. This Truth is at the heart of all our Lemurian Creation. We bless this and are eternally grateful.

"As we prepare to leave the bosom of Terra to re-enter her surface domain, we do so with gratitude and blessing for her, for ourselves, and for our Golden Family near and far. Having been brave in our trust of Life, and in making necessary changes in the past, our courage has rewarded us greatly—beyond measure. And so it is again: another change, another point of courage, another passageway of Trust.

"Before we embark on this new adventure, let us bow our heads and pray that all will go well, and that we will again rise triumphant and strong; radiant in our Beauty, Love, and Creativity as One Golden Family.

"Our most Beloved Source, that which created us and all that we hold dear, we thank you from the bottom of our hearts and Souls. We ask not only for safe travel to our intended destination, but to emerge intact and whole upon the surface of our beloved Terra as well. We ask for your guidance and empowering support to help us in fostering and nurturing this new birthing of ourselves well, with clarity and wisdom.

"We receive you, now and always, our Beloved Source, honoring you with all that we are, grateful for the wonder and beauty of Life that we have been gifted with and now revel in. Thank you, our most Beloved Source.

"We are One Golden Heart—forever grateful.

"Golden Blessings abounding.

"We thank you."

As I end the prayer, a soft breeze touches my face, no more than a whisper. It is Terra reminding me that the light of day, the freshness of that sweet Golden Air above, will be mine again soon. I murmur a soft thank you to her, then open my eyes to joyously face our future.

"We are ready now," I say. *"The Golden Wind will carry us up, and forward."*

We all feel like we are poised on the edge, a quickening vibration in the air indicating that we are about to launch. Andar steps back up to the front of the crowd to speak his final words:

"Golden Ones, we ask that you stand steady now, and await our final signal.

"Remember, we have made the Choice to do this one hundred percent. We are ripe and ready, and fully committed. There will be no altering of our direction; there is only one way now, and that is UP!

"Get ready for a bumpy but exhilarating ride, we will see you at the top, Golden Godspeed."

THE ASCENT

Avalar continues:

All standing still, holding our breath, the Activation Charge is finally turned on. We are off!

There is a great rumbling sound. Pressure in my ears is building. I know I need to stop bracing myself, and simply let my breath go, but it is difficult to do. I focus more intently on easing up inside and trying to maintain as soft a stance as possible, managing now to lessen at least some of the jostling that is taking over my body. What we were told certainly seems to be true, as the thrusting of upward power has an incredible force, and any tightening up only makes the sensation of turbulence more uncomfortable.

The reverberation in my ears is getting louder now as my whole body begins to shake. The intensity of it increases and I feel like my teeth are going to start rattling inside my head any second. Somehow, I manage to open my eyes to check on everyone else. A quick glance reassures me that they are okay so far in the face of this powerfully intense upsurge that has taken over, and which is propelling us upward. We are moving very fast, the momentum charging us through what feels like many different layers and levels of energy and matter.

Finally the intensity lessens and I know that we are arriving closer to the top. As we slow down, there is enough space for me to be aware of my whole system rapidly recalibrating itself to accommodate the vibrational frequency required for life back on Terra's surface. I welcome this instinctive intelligence and try to stay as soft as possible. I am grateful to have this ascent almost over with.

Focusing back on my deeper breathing, I suddenly become aware of a very odd sensation at the periphery of my energy field. What is that? I turn toward it, streamlining my inner vision in that direction to investigate. I immediately sense that whatever it is, it is deeply out of balance with us. Unsettled, I check again to confirm. Yes, it is still there, vibrating close to our energy fields and feeling increasingly disturbing. Something here is definitely not right. I know it. Suddenly, my senses go into high gear, registering alarm.

Looking around, I don't see that anyone else is aware of this, but as soon as I reach for Andar's hand, I know he is, and already on high alert.

"Beloved," he says gravely. *"This is not as we expected it to be. I know there are Foreigners here—and I suspect they are not friendly. I am clear about this already. We must proceed with great caution. It may be that you and I will have to go into crisis mode and change our positions. With the rest of the Golden Ones rising rapidly, we already know there is no stopping our emergence."*

Without any hesitation, he opens his conduits to engage with the First Scouts in an attempt to halt their surfacing, but it appears they have already moved forward, and are emerging as planned. All we can do now is await their incoming signals, and hope that all is well.

As we finally come to a stop just below Terra's surface and regroup, it is obvious that the rest of the Golden Ones also realize all is not well. They don't know exactly what is going on, but there is alarm and confusion in the air.

I telepathically ask them to please remain focused and calm. They are doing so, but with hesitation. They are all braced and cannot help their vibratory response, which I understand.

Andar, now steady and focused, instructs me:

"You and I need to move our positions, Beloved. NOW! I need to expand my sensory energy body and find out what is going on out there. You need to go into safekeeping as YOU are the one holding the energy of the Golden Configuration securely right now. We know you cannot sacrifice this at any cost, so please move yourself now in order to do so. From there, you will be able to stretch your sensors to witness clearly what is taking place.

"Do your best, Beloved, as will I. We are the Leaders, and this is what is required

of us. I will fill you in as I gain information and counsel.

"*All the others should be well taken care of by the Guides and Scouts that are here to show them the way out. There is only one way to go, and that is forward. You are my Beloved Avalar, I am your Beloved Andar. We are Avalandar.*

"*We are One, forever.*

"*I must go now.*"

With Andar's attention and focus bursting outward, the energies of Terra and our One Golden Heart draw me in, placing me in safekeeping so that I can fulfill my vow of holding the Golden Configuration Energy. From here I am secure and steady, able to expand my conduits to be the Sacred Witness and Record Keeper for everything that will come next. I am removed from the huddled closeness of my Beloved Family, and although I must stand alone, I will remain one with them energetically.

At this point, dear Reader, I turn the story over to the Golden One who has volunteered to be the storyteller for this next sequence of events, our Golden Witness.

THE GOLDEN WITNESS SPEAKS

What has this ascent been like for me so far? Well, we've been traveling at a very high speed, with an awful lot of bumping and jostling around. However, since Andar prepared us well for this commotion, I have been able to stay open to it, and am truly thankful for its ability to propel us into our new life. Gratitude, always my greatest ally and comfort, is something I use often when facing unknown situations—and this is certainly one of those!

I am excited. We are returning to Terra's surface to create our New World. Onward, I say!

As I begin to slow at last, I know we must be arriving close to Terra's surface. Suddenly, my blazing enthusiasm is dimmed by a sense of something else, a nagging disturbance that I do not recognize. Part of me says it's just part of this new unknown, so relax and let go. Remember to stay soft and pliable. But it isn't just me. All of us, as a group, have now entered a state of tension. Reminding myself over and over to remain soft, I keep thinking it's the powerful upsurge that has caused us to feel this way, and will soon pass as we are arriving at our destination.

My inner talk which usually calms me is doing nothing right now, it's not working at all. My system seems to be getting more tense, tightening by the second, all of which tells me that something else truly is going on. I feel increasingly uneasy as we slow further, gradually coming to a complete stop. Now what?

Wow, we are so tightly pressed together, I wasn't aware of how almost on top of one another we had become. There is still excitement, yes, but we are all sharing this sense of alarm as well. What could possibly be the reason for this?

But this is not the time for seeking answers, everything is happening so quickly. We can't even pause for a breath because our group leaders are ushering us forward with such haste, our energies now being somehow propelled through the top layers of Terra's crust and out onto her surface.

My goodness, I have literally just burst right out of Terra's body and am actually standing with both feet squarely planted on her ground! Is that the Sun I feel, and the morning dew on my skin? Am I smelling the sweetness of her fresh, delightful air? Am I seeing the beauty of her clear blue skies? No! I am not! What is happening here? All I can see around me is gray, the air smells bad, the ethers are not clear and sparkling the way they used to be and are dull and heavy. I do not know this aura. I am not familiar with this, and I don't know what it means.

Suddenly, I hear high pitched screams piercing the air! I am taken aback, unable to breathe. What is happening here? My head is reeling; I'm trembling uncontrollably and cannot understand any of this.

All my Beloved Ones around me are in a panic too. Their energy systems are buzzing frantically in an unfamiliar way. What is this we are feeling? What is this we are in?

Oh, no! My arm is seized by something I do not recognize—its shape is human, and it is covered in big pieces of black armor. It is cold steel, huge and powerful—and it is hurling me through the air!

Now I'm on my back, with the wind knocked out of me. There is a haze of loud shouts and terrified screaming all around, but none of it can actually register because I am being attacked again!

This is complete agony: powerlessness. I am shattered, Body and Being. Screaming from this unbearable pain in my body, I cry out even more loudly from the agony of this assault on my blessedness, my holiness, my sacredness.

Please, God, let me die! I know the same thing is happening to the rest of my loved ones. Screams of agony continue to rent the air and there is blood everywhere. Swords of steel are clanging, killing and destroying. I can take no more. All these sounds of my Golden Family Members dying are torturous.

I am dying, finally, thank God. A sword has passed through some part of me, and I am leaving this body now. I hover outside of it, watching for a few seconds as I see the panorama of horror playing out in front of me. Thankfully, I can no longer feel anything. All I see is devastation and its brutal, bloody mess.

As I turn to go, I notice others close to me are doing the same. Joining hands, we move upward together in a new direction of awareness—back up into the state of our Golden Souls. Our time on Terra is now over.

"That sure was a short stint on the surface!" I don't know how it is possible to have any sense of humor at all at this moment, but I still seem to be able to look at the lighter side of things—and I am glad to be out of there! I am here now with many other beloved Golden Ones in our Soul State. What a relief, and what a contrast!

I can see our Beloved Leader Andar talking with a group of the Family, deep in concentration over what he is hearing. Something in me relaxes at the sight of him, and I feel a sense of relief, of peace for a brief moment, knowing we are in good hands.

I'm being swept up in the throng of those Golden Ones who are here, and I feel content to simply be with them—but now several Golden Angels have gathered around us, and we are being whisked off somewhere.

In no time at all we have arrived in a beautiful place of sanctuary and softness, along with many other loved ones who are also here. I am now being told that this is where we will heal from our recent trauma—and my response is a grateful yes!

I am surprised, however, that I still don't really feel anything; what we went through seems like a fading mirage right now. Am I numb, or is it just that it is so far away in frequency and vibration? My mind already seeks to know the lessons from what just happened. With no resistance to it or about it, I am able to be with it all.

I am being led to an invitingly soft, cushiony kind of bed where I immediately lie down with relief and gratitude. "My, oh my, that was a trip," I think to myself. And not at all what I had expected, though I thought I had erased all expectation prior to our ascent. In any case, the strongest residue of the experience is a distinct memory of what felt like a complete SHATTERING. In fact, I can still hear the sound—like a huge mirror breaking into a million, trillion splintered pieces as shards of glass hurl outward into the great universe beyond.

I do feel broken, and am aware of a potent, highly charged package of energy encased within my being that is holding a state of complete fracture. But it is not only my fracture that I feel, it is the fracture of our ENTIRE GOLDEN FAMILY. It feels like the fracture and shattering of our woven tapestry, our Golden Oneness.

It is a bizarre and strange feeling. If I didn't know better, I would say I was bleeding—profusely. I would say that my entire sense of wholeness has been shattered forevermore. I feel greatly and deeply wounded, and don't how I will ever be able to recover from an injury such as this. It feels deeply penetrating, so central in my core.

But I also sense new conduits already spreading inside of me, creating new pathways and patterns that are now wound-related and wound-oriented as result of this shattering experience. "Wow, that's fast!" I remark to myself. It's like a new me is already busy building itself. But the trouble is, it's a new form of me that I do not want. I can see why healing is vitally necessary at this moment. There is no question, I am ready and willing.

I hear Golden Angels singing to me, to the many of us who are here, all lying down cozy and snug. As we hear their soft lullabies we are soothed and gentled.

Finally, I feel ready for sleep. Relaxing further into my soft downy bed, I am aware of a profound sense of exhaustion. With a prayer for healing on my lips, I fall into a deep Soul Slumber and soon disappear...

I am Soul within Source.

I am Soul of Source.

I am Source.

I am One.

Everything is melting. Blending. Swaying on a soft, pastel-colored breeze.

I am brushed gently with love.

ALL IS ETERNALLY WELL...

Aliyah's Story

My name is Aliyah, and I am the daughter of Avalar and Andar. In Lemuria, my gift is to work with the children, who I love.

Known as the Golden Baby Caller, I summon these precious Golden Beings forth, prepare their way, and attend to them after they arrive. Teaching, guiding and inspiring them, I also work closely with pregnant women and new mothers after their babies are born.

I am a Golden Midwife, with Teams of Midwives that I train, work alongside, and shepherd. All in all, it is a large scope of responsibility and I love every single minute of it. In addition to loving my job, I love my purpose, my talents, and my gifts. Most of all, I love being in service to my Golden Family.

Although I am not literally the only one responsible for birthing our Golden People, occasionally thinking of myself as such helps me to remain clear and focused. Having a constant awareness of being accountable to our expanding families and our civilization, both on Terra and beyond, is essential.

I honor my work, and honor myself for doing it. I am strong, and have enormous power which I use wisely and well. I KNOW I am a true Golden Master, and I love this about myself. I love all the challenges and responsibilities that go with it.

I see this same Self-Awareness in both of my parents, who are our Golden Leaders. They have to be this Self-Aware, as do I. They are such an inspiration to me, and to all of us here. Loved, honored, admired, and respected—as individuals, a couple, and our Leaders—they are both great Gift Givers. We all absolutely adore them.

And they absolutely adore each other. Sweet and touching to watch, they are an inspiration for all of us as we witness the power and amazing grace of their Oneness. In addition to the deep devotion they have for each other and for their love, they love life and cannot get enough of it.

My parents have an enormous capacity to embrace the Unknown, to step fully into New Frontiers. I don't always know how they do it, but they are extremely adept at this. They NEVER shrink. Never flinch, never show up less than one hundred percent—and then some.

Always FULL ON and FACING PRESENT, they hold vast expanses of Golden energy from all domains, near and far. Suffice is to say, they are our Golden Leaders because they are so masterful.

As true Golden Masters of the Highest Order, I am enormously grateful to them. Grateful to be their daughter, I would follow them to the ends of all the moons and back. We are One. I am very close, and completely interwoven with them, as they are with me.

My father is my rock. The absolute ground in the picture of my Being, which enables me to hold many dimensions of Golden energy, pre-manifest and manifest. This is all an enormous plateful for me. Certainly, I am well-skilled, and it is well within my Mastery, but my father has always been my steady one. He lit up my life early on with his tender, loving care and joyfulness, and absolutely adored me, which I knew—always. He was the reason I came, the one who called me in—but I called him in, too.

My mother, well, there's a talent if I ever saw one. She and I are absolutely alike, absolutely in sync. Although our terrains of Golden Mastery are quite different, we are both intimately attuned to, and responsible for, Energetic Golden Creation. I have learned an extraordinary amount from her throughout my lifetime. As my Teacher in many ways, she is also my reason for coming here; she called me in too, and I her. She lives in my bones, as does my father.

My mother and I work together, preparing the energetic grids which receive the new Souls coming in. Working extensively with the Natural World and the Unseen Golden Ones, we build necessary stabilizing platforms for incoming Golden Souls. It is often like planting and grounding vibrant, sometimes unwieldy Rainbows; it is a fine art, and can be quite a challenge.

When my mother and I combine our gifts for this energetic work it is the most exquisite dance of loving creation imaginable—completely full of love and joy. Thanks to the sheer exuberance of birthing, and the potent power of facilitating these miraculous happenings, it feels like riding inside the exhilarating cocoon of Source.

My mother has also taught me much about devotion. One who is powerfully devoted, she makes no bones about it. When she loves, she loves passionately; when she cares, she cares deeply; when she is committed, she is in one hundred percent—and then some.

We are all keenly aware of her Oneness with Source; of how profound that is for her, inside and out. Although we are all this way, of course, her strength, clarity, and receptivity go well beyond what the rest of us know. That is one of the many Gifts she thoroughly expresses—and thorough she is.

My mother frequently goes off on her own to spend much needed time inside the Core Crystal of our beloved Golden Terra, where she is replenished.

My father, on the other hand, spends a great deal of time within the Golden Star Systems, which is natural and effortless for him because of how he is designed.

Adored and respected by many, he has a great ability for organizing important details, with an eye for clear insight throughout. But it is his tender heart, coupled with his jubilation, that what we all love and do our best to absorb whenever we are around him. His humor is infectious, and his laughter is the greatest sound in the whole universe. He is such a powerful and touching influence in my life, and always has been. Both of my parents are. I am deeply grateful for them— eternally so.

My own husband, a dear man and an outstandingly talented Scout and Leader in his own right, has a huge all-encompassing energy. Boisterous and funny, he loves me very much, and I him. We do not have the same profound coupling as my parents, but then they have theirs for specific reasons that are essential to Lemurian Leadership.

I am happy with my own family life, and love my two beautiful children with all my heart and Soul. Although I tend to many other children, these two sweet ones are my absolute treasures, and mean more to me than anything or anyone. That's the Truth. I often feel that they are truly my reason for being. They nourish and feed me immensely, and I love them powerfully.

When the time comes for us to move down inside of Terra, I am thrilled. Not because I want to leave the surface, but because this is a rare opportunity for me to experience a deeper intimacy with her—to personally discover the fine power and brilliance of Creation at her Core. The prospect of this excites me enormously, as I want to KNOW it and OWN it in myself. I know that Terra, as my Mother in this way, can impart and infuse me with a new breadth and depth of Being that I would never otherwise know. She can light up so many new fires of ability inside of me, and I can hardly wait to experience those yet untapped talents. This is extremely exciting for me.

Everything that I was hoping for is indeed taking place while we've been inside of her. Being mentored by her in this most powerful and wondrous of ways, my perception of myself, and of life, is changing radically. I am being Goldenly Altered, far beyond who and how I was before. Every moment spent inside of her has been my sacred gift and Golden Homecoming. I never knew what I was missing.

The babies who are coming in during this time are super-powered in special ways, thanks to Terra's potent and concentrated inner environment. I know they are coming in precisely for this reason, and that we will all, as a People, benefit greatly from the gifts of these special Souls. Although I do not yet understand all the fine details of this, I know it is so; it will certainly be revealed in time.

This experience inside of Terra, for all of us, is raising us to new heights and abilities as a People, clearly upgrading us in our Golden Wholeness by setting the bar still higher. We are substantially stronger, more effective, and more powerful in every way—including some new ones. Being the lucky ones in the Cosmos to be having such an amazing experience, we are indeed blessed.

Our time inside Terra is full, with much growth and strengthening happening for all of us. I have no idea how long we have been down here, and it doesn't seem to matter. Everything just keeps humming along—until, in a moment, it all changes. A shift happens. A moment of readiness to make a big change and turn toward a new direction: upward! Yes, we are going back to Terra's surface.

I am READY. My system overflows with Terra's potency and power and it is time to spring forth. Quite suddenly, we are all feeling this way.

Fully charged and fired up, thanks to her, we are ripe and ready to discover what her surface will offer us, no matter what it looks like—or how it might have changed. Now well equipped to create anew, we are all buzzing with excitement as Terra's love shines proudly over us. Everything starts to quickly align with this new course, and before we know it, the time for departure has come.

With our impending ascent upon us, my dear husband, who is heading up the Team of First Scouts, has already gone up to the surface to prepare the way for the rest of us. Praying for him and his successful journey, my knowledge of how skilled he is at his job fills me with confidence. Although I wish he were here with me now, I know I will be seeing him soon.

Standing ready with my two children, my parents, and many new mothers and babies surrounding me, I know the plan is for us to be the last to surface. We have been told our emergence will happen rapidly once it begins, so vigilance is necessary for us to all stay connected. I know I am responsible for my group, and even though I'm excited about our new venture, I put this on hold so that I can be fully present and focused on the job in front of me.

I take a deep breath as I squeeze my children in closer to me…and suddenly, we are on our way!

The turbulence and jostling begin right away—quite vigorously, in fact. I am momentarily startled. But then I remember my father telling us that this commotion should be expected, and I am able to settle in with it somewhat. Our speed increases rapidly, and my children and I cling to one another desperately as this wild ride carries us upward. We are shaking and vibrating all over the place.

Somehow, we manage to hold on, although just barely, until finally, thank goodness, we begin to slow down, and then stop. What a relief! I'm so glad it wasn't a longer journey. At last, my body stops shaking and my balance returns as I press my children even closer. I quickly check around to make sure my group is in order and see that, yes, it is and everyone is doing fine.

It dawns on me abruptly that my parents aren't here with me. They were when we started off, where are they now?

I start to feel uneasy about this, but then remind myself that they are no doubt attending to others elsewhere, as I am here. Still, I wonder.

I am given no more time to think about this however, because after this short pause, the energy starts propelling us again, pushing us this time through what feels like a very narrow space. I hope it will finally lead us out to the surface. I feel myself becoming disoriented again, and grab my children to make sure they are close. This last part of the transition doesn't take long, and suddenly we burst out into wide open space. My goodness, we've just popped out of Terra like popcorn flying right out of the pot.

Amazingly, we have all landed on our feet, with a great big poof of dust rising and swirling around us, as evidence that we have indeed hit the ground. After a second, we catch our breath and as the air clears, we start to inhale deeply. Oh, how I have longed for this moment. Give me the first sweet scent of Terra's divine fresh air.

What meets my nose, however, is not at all what I expected. With no time to question it, I am suddenly thrown off balance by all the jostling of the young mothers and children who are now pressing in on me. Why aren't they spreading out, for goodness sake? Give us all some space, please!

And then I see why.

Large hulking beings wearing black steel armor are coming right at us!

Human in shape, I see they have sharp spikes pointing out from their body armor, and are brandishing clubs and other weapons in their hands. I stand frozen, all senses in high alert to the danger that we are in.

They are huge, and there are so many of them. Suddenly they are upon us, pushing, prodding, and yelling out strange and vicious sounds. They goad us repeatedly, as if they are wanting to toy with us just because they are so much bigger and stronger than we are.

Many of the women are rolling themselves into balls, their arms wrapped tightly around their young ones, trying to protect them. I too am holding onto my two little ones for dear life, but what can I actually do to protect them? We are powerless against these monsters. We all strengthen our grip on each other, pressing ourselves even closer together to create a protective exterior around our children. The monsters come at us still, yelling, leering, jabbing at the air with their weapons.

Their goading becomes more aggressive and they start ramming us with their clubs, lifting them higher and hitting some of the women as hard as they can. We try to fend them off, to fight back, but it's useless, and it just makes them more determined, more violent.

Suddenly, one of them grabs one of the women, throwing her to the ground and killing her. Other monsters are taking her child, only to kill her as well. I have never in my life imagined anything could possibly be like this. I am stunned, shocked, utterly horrified.

The rampage escalates. There is screaming all around us, and bloody bodies are being thrown everywhere.

Suddenly, for some reason, it all goes silent, and I cannot hear anything. I only see mouths wide open, faces distorted, eyes popping with terror. I look down and see that my two young ones are terrified, but still here with me. What can we do?

We must run! I grab my children up into my arms, and with lightning speed am somehow managing to get through all the confusion and brutality. As I run, I see the violence but continue to HEAR NOTHING.

There is no sound. In a way, this makes the sight even more horrific, more acute. More unrelentingly unforgettable. Gasping for breath, I am somehow still running. How am I managing to do this? I don't know, and don't care; I only want to get to safety.

Out of nowhere, one of the monsters is hurling himself toward me. I fall face down on the ground, winded and stunned. My ears are knocked open and I hear my children screaming. Now I can hear all the sounds—the shouts, the pleas for help, the screams of agonizing pain.

My older child is now bleeding profusely. Oh, my God, NO! My youngest has been fatally wounded. Oh, my God, NO! I am being attacked as well, but I don't even care at this point. It is painful. Brutal and vicious. But it is nothing compared to witnessing my two little ones dying.

I lunge for them. My youngest, I can see, is now dead. My oldest is watching himself bleed to death. As I look into his eyes, I see an image of his father, and instantly know that something terrible is happening to him as well. My son sees me for an instant through the haze of his own agony—a look of pure love mixed with spasms of pure pain. "Help me, Mama," his eyes plead. "Help me, please. I need you."

I reach out to touch his face with my hands, but an angry metallic arm is pulling me away, flinging me violently through the air. Now I have landed a few feet away from my children, completely dazed and breathless, and see they are both dead. I have failed to protect them. This is my fault.

Now, more monsters are on top of me. They are hurting me, but I really don't care. I just want to die—now, please! One of them stabs me viciously—and I am gone, finally.

I stand over my body, watching this desperate, brutal scene for a moment, and I am anxious to find my children. I ache to be with them. I need to see them and hold them right now.

As I leave the physical domain and rise upward toward my Soul State, my children are the only thing on my mind. The scene below me, the entire gruesome and heartbreaking theater of it all, is fading. It is still happening, but I am grateful to be disconnecting from it. Looking up, I feel my own spiritual energy pulling me upward in a tender and effortless way. My mind, or what was my mind, begins to let go and drop away. My memory of what just happened and where I have been, now fades as well.

I see the Souls of my two children up ahead of me being greeted by Golden Angels and the Golden Guardians of the Spiritual Realms. Skipping and dancing along, they do not see me, do not yet know that I too am here. A smile spreads across my face as I see them whole, and yes, even happy. Nothing could make me feel better than this right now. I can breathe deeply again.

I call to them. Their faces instantly light up like giant sunbeams at the sound of my voice. Their joy at seeing me well and intact is just like mine for them. Kneeling down, I pull them into my arms as I press them close to my bosom, enormously relieved and so very happy. Their sweet scent fills my Being, their love so strong, I melt.

The Golden Angels and Guardians stand close by as we huddle together in this moment of tender reunion. Gesturing, they beckon for us to follow them into a small sanctuary infused with soft soothing light of varying colors. There are many children in here, as well as many of my dearest young mothers. What a celebration this is. For a moment, we all share warm hugs and breathe together with no thought—just closeness again. We are all greatly relieved.

My children are invited to go with a group of small Golden Angels to an area where many of the other young children are being soothed and tended to. I sense this is important restoration for them, let them go for now, knowing they are in good hands. One of the Sacred Guardians comes over to me, beckoning me to follow him. His presence is kind and gentle, and I am aware that his request of me is important. I look over to my children, and notice that there is a serenity about them that tells me that all is well. I follow the Sacred Guardian.

I am led to a small chamber nearby where I find my parents waiting to welcome and reassure me. We are so happy and relieved to see each other. There are warm hugs all around, all of us deeply grateful that we are together again. After a moment, we sit quietly, waiting for my father to share what is in his heart.

I sense in this moment that nothing about the surreal travesty that just happened on Terra is over yet, although we are in the Spirit world. Lemuria is still alive, and in great need of our help. It's an odd mix of emotional sensations: faded memory and present reality, coupled with urgency about the future. I am still somewhat stunned, but also feel alert and focused, aware of the sensation of many compelling challenges calling at the edge of my awareness.

With great gentleness my father finally speaks:

"Aliyah, our dearest One, here we are. There is much to tell, many questions to answer, but there are more pressing concerns to talk about first." He reaches out to hold my hand firmly in his. *"It is your husband, Artemus. You have undoubtedly already sensed that he has fallen on troubled circumstances. I must speak to you about this so that you can hold him whole in the Light of your loving heart.*

"As you know, being First Scout Leader he went out ahead of the rest of us with four others of his Team to assess how Terra's surface may have changed during our time below. We expected a post-emergence report from Artemus that would help the rest of us to be informed, and better prepared. But his communication was never received.

"We waited, and after considerable time, one, and only one, of the Scouts was able to notify us. Although he was able to return, from the sound of what took place, it was a miracle that he made it back.

"According to him, when the Team surfaced, they hardly had a chance to look around before they caught sight and smell of many, many Alien strangers. They certainly hoped they might be friendly. We knew before surfacing that we might meet others from other places who had come here during our absence—and, should this happen, hoped we could develop a friendship and have an agreeable alliance with them. Coexisting in any form of mutual positivity would certainly be an acceptable outcome after

our having been away from Terra's outer environs for as long as we were.

"*The plan was for the Team to begin to make headway in that direction, if this was indeed the case. It was obvious right at the outset, however, that an alliance was not possible with these strangers. Friendliness from them, in any way, was not their plan. They had no intention of sharing this territory with us, or with anyone else for that matter.*

"*Your husband was the first to be seen. There were many of these Aliens milling about, and the Team happened to surface close to where they were, leaving the Scouts no chance of being able to observe from a hidden position. After spotting Artemus, the Aliens immediately alerted one another, surrounded the Team, and swarmed in. The Scout that returned said he was only able to get back because he had been the last one out, and managed to lay lower than the rest. Somehow, he had remained unseen.*

"*This is his account of what happened:*

"'*The Aliens surrounded all of the Scouts, except for me, and shouted in an unfamiliar language. They were clearly unfriendly, and not interested in forging any kind of connection—or of having any exchange whatsoever. As I watched, it became obvious that they just wanted to taunt the Scouts and get rid of them, make them go away.*

"'*At first, there was a lot of noise and yelling, but no actual violence. But the longer the Scouts were there, the more agitated these Aliens became. Finally, it was as though their threshold was reached, as if they simply couldn't stand the idea of anyone else being there. After pulling out clubs, knives, and other kinds of weapons, they began threatening the Scouts by lunging at them, but stopped just short of wounding them.*

"'*Artemus simply stood there, passively watching, unflinching in gaze and posture. You would have been proud of him. His courageousness was palpable, his strength of Spirit quiet and focused as he took it all in rather than reacting. I knew he was gathering information, even in the thick of this strange and obviously very dangerous situation.*

"'*The other Scouts were also holding their ground, but were more actively involved in defending themselves and protecting each other. They were even trying to distract the Aliens from Artemus so that he could, in fact, take everything in. This was his purpose, and he was doing his utmost to gain as much information on all levels that he possibly could. He was the one responsible for recording everything, so it could be brought back home.*

"'Finally, the Aliens decided on a more aggressive action. They grabbed Artemus and the other Scouts, then abruptly hoisted them up and took them away. At this point, I was alone, only able to know what ensued because of my sensory conduits. Fully connected to my Teammates, but powerless to help them now, I knew it was essential for me to find out the rest of what happened as best I could, so as to bring this information home.

"'I discovered that after the Scouts were taken, they were brutally and relentlessly tortured. The Aliens were demanding information on the rest of us. I have no idea how they knew there were more Golden Ones about to emerge, but their sensors, however they worked, informed them of this. It was obvious that these Aliens have highly sophisticated information systems, being as aware as they were of things they should not have known.

"'I could tell, by using my own energy sensors, that Artemus was the one who fared the worst, by far. Although the others were tortured as well, they used most of their tactics on Artemus, recognizing him as our leader. They used everything they could to get him to break.

"'Finally, after a long, long time of immense and unrelenting pain and agony, he did. His Spirit broke. He broke. I only know this because I know him well, because our conduits of communication and friendship are so strong, I simply KNEW.

"'I could feel him breaking, as if he was shattering and being ripped apart at the same time. I felt his Spirit being crushed and collapsing from this agonizing intense pain that was beyond bearing, and I knew in that moment that he would never be the same again. Knowing him as I do, I also knew he would always blame himself. That he would never, ever forgive himself.

"'Whatever techniques of torture they used convinced him that he was responsible for the slaughter of his people, and that he had betrayed us. I know he didn't. I know he didn't utter a single word, not one. But he doesn't know this, and believes that he revealed information about our whereabouts. In truth, he spoke absolutely no word at all. Not a single one.

"'What I know is that these Aliens somehow already knew that we were coming, and already knew our exact location of re-entry. I do not know how, but that is my observation. And, Artemus our Leader is still there. They have not killed him. He has not died.

"'They plan to use him, to program him through brainwashing to make him one of their own. This is my account of what happened. I am deeply sorry that I do not have different news to report.'"

My father finishes speaking, weeping with the deepest sorrow. And so are we. Reaching out to console one another, our hearts ache with despair for how Artemus has suffered in this way. Knowing this is not the end of his suffering, but only the beginning, makes this heartbreak even worse.

There are depths of reverberation about this that, were I still in my physical body, would certainly be shattering me into a million different pieces; would now be crushing the life and breath out of my body and Soul. But I am here in Spirit, where thankfully it is possible to understand things in a vastly different way. I know Artemus' pain, but am not inside of it, the way I would be otherwise. Somehow, I have a stillness about it and know that even in the midst of this tragedy, everything is going to be all right. This may sound strange to you, dear Reader, but it is true.

What stands out most strikingly to me is the clarity that I have for the need to act; to take some serious action in regard to all of this. That is what my system is compelling me to do.

The question for me now is simply how to save Artemus from this excruciating experience. And knowing he is not the only one suffering in this way, I will remain steadfast in my determination to do whatever is needed to help all of the others as well.

My father speaks again:

"Artemus is a broken Golden One now. His Spirit is empty, his psyche primed and ready for whatever the Aliens want to do with him. He is defenseless, powerless, and knows us no more. Indeed, he knows no one, not even himself.

"We know this will be a long, hard journey for him. His devastation and self-blame will be ruinous to whatever remains of his Golden Heart. All we can ask for is hope and perseverance. All we can do is pour our love into the wounds of his Soul, witnessing and waiting for the return of something that will shake him out of his pain and self-torture.

"He is now a Lost One, and we must pray for him. We must hold him steady in our Golden Flame of Love while doing what we can to soothe his broken Soul. He was a Great One—so great that his fall is far more devastating. It is completely shattering. What we also know is that it could have been any one of us.

"Everyone has their breaking point. His was tested, and found. It could have happened to any of us—and the truth is that this has not only happened to him, not by any means. He is one of what will be many, many Golden

Ones who will end up utterly lost and broken.

"We have much work ahead of us. Avalar and I must move swiftly now to a meeting place with the Golden Council where we can view everything and make clear plans. We love you dearly, our Beloved Aliyah. We are deeply sorry for your husband's plight. He is precious to us, as you well know. We will all do right by him. You know this."

Looking at both of my parents, and feeling so much love flowing between us, I know we are One in our hearts, minds and Souls. I know that Golden Grace will indeed guide our way, as it will for everyone. We are One Golden Family—no matter what, no matter where, and no matter when.

Leaving them now to return to my children, I realize it will be essential to spend some time in recovery so my system can be soothed, rebalanced, and realigned after all that has happened.

The Golden Angels are just ahead of me, once again beckoning me to follow, and I can see my children standing there with them. I know that great Golden Healing awaits us all, and that we will receive everything that we need to be restored.

CHAPTER EIGHT

LIFE IN SPIRIT:
COLLECTING OURSELVES

AVALAR SPEAKS:

Andar and I are aware that the Golden Ones everywhere are shaking, shocked, and stunned. We can feel the enormity of this in our systems as if it is our own. The delicate nature of our family's pure and refined balance has been disturbed and disabled. To the Golden Family everywhere, the recent events on Terra have felt like a complete shattering. And not just within individual members, but for the entire Sacred Golden Tapestry. What does this mean, then, for each of them, for all of them? These are the questions that are desperately being asked. There is massive internal confusion; our entire Family, now heartbroken and disjointed, feels deeply isolated—as if they have been hurled out into some cold, heartless void.

This is the most contrary state for Lemurians. Our bond up until this point has been so strongly interwoven, with everyone feeling solid and secure as ONE. Alas, no more.

And while these horrific events seem to have ruined all of that on many, many levels, in other ways it really is not the case. But for now, it feels like a FRACTURE to Golden Ones everywhere.

Andar and I, well aware of this multitude of reverberations, recognize the deep wounding of our beloved Golden Family. Except for the two of us, and our select Golden Team who also hold the Sacred Configuration steady and secure, everyone else remains in a deeply traumatized state.

Still, we know that no matter how it looks and feels, ALL IS ACTUALLY WELL. Our Golden Tapestry may have a delicate, refined nature, but it is powerfully strong, unshakably grounded, and secure in itself. We built it that way from the beginning, and have been adding massive layers and textures of further fortification throughout our time of Golden Creation together. The truth is, it is simply IMPOSSIBLE to break, much less shatter into a million pieces. We, as One Golden Family, have ensured that this is so—no matter what.

However, along with our select Golden Team, we are the only ones who understand this right now—as we will for a long time to come.

Right now, the Golden Family feels broken. The Fracture is loud, and the sound deafening. The memories of what just took place on Terra are vivid and raw, with their details—sights, sounds, and smells—ghastly, appalling, abhorrent. Every accompanying sensation is still jarring to our Sacred Golden Souls. The Golden Ones are wounded, and now it is time to take care of them. Deep Healing must begin.

Andar and I lock hands and hearts and move forward. We find ourselves entering a Golden space of Peace and Tranquility, a gift we are being given of a respite amidst the storm. It is imperative that we let go of all the highly charged reverberations we have been feeling, and re-engage our energies with one another fully to be clear and focused on the job at hand. Releasing it all, we blend our Sacred Golden Heart energies and restore. We are ONE, no matter where we are. Golden Avalandar lives on, no matter what dimension we are in. Our hearts meld together until they are humming a sweet song. Soon, we are refreshed—and ready for whatever comes next.

THE GOLDEN COUNCIL MEETS IN SPIRIT

After being called to meet with the Golden Council, Andar and I have arrived to find them already hard at work in the Golden Meeting Room, looking over the drawing boards of what has taken place—not just on Terra, but throughout the entire Golden Universe as well. With so many pieces to our Golden Pie, so many areas where this devastation has been felt, we understand that they are intent on rewiring the Golden Fields before conclusions are drawn and misunderstandings become patterned into the whole. We must act swiftly but gently here. Tenderness is needed, and delicate work is required by everyone, with much to do and many to attend to.

The Sacred Golden Configuration is lit up in the center of the drawing panel. Andar and I step into position and feel ourselves being fully aligned with its current. It charges us up, radiating wave upon wave of Golden Essence, ensuring that we are crystal-clear and sovereign in this way. WE ARE the Golden Configuration. It has always been our job to hold this intact, no matter what—and it will continue to be so.

WE are the Central Point from now on. We will be the physical Golden Leaders for the reclamation and restoration of Lemuria.

Recharged as we are now by this powerful, rich Golden Essence, we feel strong, confidant, and clear, ready to meet all that awaits us. Avalandar is steady, solid, and radiant.

Turning toward the Golden Council, we meet the eyes of our Beloved Golden Sananda looking upon us with pure love and tenderness.

Sananda speaks:

"Beloved Leaders, Avalar and Andar, we honor you with all the love in our hearts. We know what you have been through, what you are experiencing, and all the trauma that now resides in Golden Ones everywhere. Knowing that this has, indeed, been an unspeakable shock, we fill you with our strength and support as we gather here together to face these circumstances.

"What has taken place on Terra has felt like an enormous shattering, for Lemuria and for all Lemurians everywhere. This we know, and this we feel. But this has also been a tremendous opening to our strength, to our Golden Empowerment, and to the building of new Golden Muscles for our future. Indeed, this has THRUST us into new frontiers of ourselves, individually and as a Family. I will not speak any more about this right now, but mention it so you will understand that in truth there is purpose and service to it all. The building and powerful strengthening of these muscles, which will take place over the next many generations, will stand us in good stead when we have future need of them.

"We pledged our Sacred Golden Vow long ago, and we will uphold it. Sit, while we view the present and all that is needed for now. We will focus on this, and only this, so that we can face it with clarity, understanding, and wisdom. We will persevere. This is what we do, and this is how we are. Lemuria lives on, no matter what, and we are all ensuring this.

"Bless you both, for the strength and capability that you continue to demonstrate through your faith and conviction. You are both unwavering in this, as you always have been, and always will be. Our One Golden Heart is your greatest treasure and meaning. As you serve it, it serves you.

"We all thank you for your skills. We thank you for your vision, perseverance, and unwavering love. We all honor and love you both so very much."

Andar and I are both deeply touched by Sananda's words, welcoming his strength and conviction as it buoys us. We continue to be our splendid Golden Team, forging ahead now to meet these new challenges.

Returning our attention to the drawing board, we confer and deliberate back and forth until a feasible plan has been designed. Knowing first and foremost that there are many Golden Ones who are still on Terra (some lost and hiding, some who have escaped and are in hiding, and many others who were taken prisoner by the Aliens), it is clear we must go back to rescue all of our Golden Family. This is our absolute number one priority, above all else.

Sananda's wise counsel continues:

"The time has come to gather the Golden Ones who are here, to explain what transpired, and to inform them as to what is ahead.

"Reverberations of these recent events have been felt everywhere, on all levels: seen, unseen, near, and far. What has happened to those Golden Ones on Terra has shaken the weave of the Golden Tapestry throughout the Cosmos and beyond, because we are completely interconnected. Being woven together as ONE, what happens to one happens to all. While we need to address these circumstances individually, we must also do so in regard to the Golden Family as a whole. This is the plan, as agreed upon, thus far.

"Andar, for the immediate future, you will be the one who addresses the concerns that the Golden Ones far from Terra are experiencing. You will head up a Team to see what is needed in those locations and dimensions, with many more of us here working with you on this. Once that is well underway, you will also be responsible for overseeing many of the Rescue Missions on Terra, actively leading those who will be returning to find our lost Loved Ones.

"Avalar, your task will be to energetically shepherd these Golden Teams of Rescuers who return to Terra, staying connected while witnessing them and their experiences. Andar will be doing this with you as well. The Golden Ones will continually need to be reassured that they are not lost, even though they feel that they are. By witnessing them and staying attuned to what they are going through, you will ease their Golden Hearts—which will keep these Dear Ones alive, activated, and connected to the Family, no matter how lost they feel. It will also be your job to BE with Terra herself, doing whatever is needed to nurture our Sacred Connection with her as you keep it strong, clear, and actively engaged.

"And last, but certainly not least: Andar, you will be responsible for ensuring that Avalar holds steady in the face of all the energetic information she receives and records; while you, Avalar, will ensure that Andar holds steady in his Golden Balance while taking care of his responsibilities.

"For the two of you, this will all be done successfully because you ARE, and will constantly drink and draw from, AVALANDAR.

"Avalandar IS the reason you have been successful in all that you have done regarding Lemuria, and this will continue to be the case. This is absolute.

"We now enter a long and rich period of rescuing. Having vowed to always

take care of one another—as we have done since our inception—this is what we will continue to do. NO GOLDEN ONE WILL BE LEFT BEHIND. NOT A SINGLE ONE. On any level, anywhere. We will devote our lives now to ensuring that this is the case, such is the profound depth and powerful truth of our love, our loving.

"And we will succeed! This, I can assure you. We will succeed one hundred percent. The Restoration, the Remembrance, and the Reactivation of the Golden Family upon Terra and throughout the Golden Universe will indeed take place. We will all see to it that this is so.

"Right now, let us bring our focus and energy to the moment at hand. It is time to attend to the needs of all our Beloved Ones who are here with us in our Golden Spiritual Domain, many of whom are already receiving treatment in the Spiritual Healing Sanctuaries. Their vibrational patterns are being calmed and healed, their equilibrium restored following their devastating experience on Terra.

"We will proceed gently, and with great tenderness for all of them, assessing who is ready to move forward with the Rescues, and letting those who need more healing to remain in repose for as long as necessary.

"We have a lot of challenging work ahead of us as these turbulent times continue. Let's proceed while doing the best we possibly can, with our attention always on our goal. Golden Lemuria lives! We are One Golden Heart, forever."

And with that, we disband, our responsibilities clear and leading the way.

Meeting with All in the Spiritual Domain

The Golden Witness speaks:

Dear Reader, as I described in my earlier account, I entered a state of deep healing and repose with Source, dissolving completely into my Creator's Divine Oneness.

Now...I awaken.

I am purring gently in my cocoon of love, feeling renewed and refreshed. A clear sense of purposefulness has returned.

My Soul Energy now looking to rejoin the rest of my Golden Family here, I feel myself floating toward a gathering place to meet them. Yes! I see them now, and I am delighted to notice that they appear refreshed and renewed as well.

The Golden Council soon arrives as well, along with our Beloved Leaders

Avalar and Andar, Sananda, Master Saint Germain, Mother Mary, and several others whom I also know. They gather together in front of our group, gazing intently at each one of us. My Soul starts to tingle all over as they witness me with their loving kindness.

Amidst the joy of being understood, vaguely painful sensations begin rising from somewhere inside of me, reminding me of my recent trauma and devastation. These memories which I had pocketed away are now surfacing in the face of being so lovingly witnessed, heard, seen, and understood.

It is a moment that we all share here together, an individual and collective memory being honored and acknowledged for all its depth, breadth, and pain. If we did not love so much, we would not feel so much. There is a richness in this, beauty that speaks of our love and tremendous devotion that is holding all this pain, that remembers this pain. It now keeps this pain encapsulated in a tight little bundle within our physical history. It is faded and forgotten here, yes, but never forgotten on Terra. It will always be there—until such time as it is revisited and healed.

Feeling my memory being witnessed and connected with, like a delicate finger gently touching a sore spot, I am reminded that the pain is still there. It will call to me over and over again until I go back there to be with it again. It needs me, needs me to respond to it, to witness it, own it, and release it. This is the healing that is needed.

Everything I have been through is being honored and understood at this meeting, sending a current of healing gently through my energies, uplifting me and fortifying me. I rejoice at my sense of belonging: forever one with The One Golden Heart Consciousness and my Golden Family.

Sananda steps forward now, the warmth of his splendid crystal clear eyes loving us, loving me, and I glow. We all glow. We are one powerful, radiant Golden Light, growing stronger and brighter by the second.

Sananda speaks with great tenderness:

"Glorious Golden Ones, I stand before you to honor you, and to share with you in our One Golden Heart.

"I know what you have been through, and feel the pain of this immense Fracture inside of you. At certain levels of your awareness, I know you believe our One Golden Heart has been greatly wounded, that the mosaic of our Golden Tapestry has been shattered beyond your comprehension. I know you feel as though your Golden Wholeness will never be restored again. I also know that here and now you feel refreshed and renewed, but that all these other feelings that I speak of remain present in your awareness.

"This is good. This is how it needs to be. I say this because you need to NOT

FORGET. Please bear with me as I explain.

"You must carry the memory of this pain—not the details themselves, but that sensation of shattering. Of being violently hurled into some unknown place in the galaxy. Of being forgotten, abandoned, left stranded. You need this memory to be clear, so as to stay connected to those Golden Loved Ones who are still back there, who are calling to you through pain of their own.

"We are talking now about going back to rescue them. These are precisely the conduits that will enable you to locate them so you can do this. This is why we are all here right now: to prepare for the Rescues of all those Golden Ones that we so greatly love, our Golden Family, wherever they are.

"We all took a sacred pledge long ago to one another, to our One Golden Family, and to our One Golden Heart. And we have all lived by this vow of pure love and devotion, which asks now that we step up and do whatever it takes to find all the Golden Ones. We must restore ourselves as our One Golden Family, whole and sacred. I know how strongly you feel about doing this. Your Golden Hearts speak for themselves.

"I ask each one of you to focus, to breathe into your own memories of that pain, and become aware of the distant sounds of those still left behind on Terra. Take this moment to feel them, to hear them, and to witness them as I stand here witnessing you. Go back there right now and let them know, if even for a fragile second, that they are, in fact, not alone. That we hear them and feel them from here. That we are going to rescue them and bring them back home to the Golden Fold of our loving.

"Take a moment to do this now. Each one of you, and all of you as One."

As I close my outer eyes and feel my senses traveling back through time and space, I am suddenly there again, back on Terra. I can hear much moaning, wailing, and crying, deep heaving sobs that speak of the unbearable pain of deepest loss. I didn't know there were so many still here. Their hearts are breaking, this I can feel. And they are bleeding. They don't know what to do. They have been disconnected from the rest of us, wrenched away from the fold, and are now desperately broken in themselves. They feel as though their insides have been blasted out, and they've been left with gaping holes where their Golden Wholeness used to be. They are empty and agonized—clutching their bellies in a vain attempt to hold together what's left of their shattered pieces. It is beyond bearing.

I had no idea of the pain that was here—the intense and unbearable agony of it. I had been given release from it when I left my body, but now, back here once again, I know it thoroughly. During the horror that caused this, I was too involved to feel and know the pain of others, or of myself, in this way. I did not comprehend what I now know, that our One Golden Heart seems like it is bleeding. Each of its wounds are the shattered pieces of the missing broken ones.

Now, I understand. My own heart bleeds, as does theirs; my own Soul feels shattered, as does theirs.

In this moment, I understand that there is a sickness that has descended upon us all. It is the searing pain of our wreckage, the agony of our disconnection, the shattering of our Golden Shining, the deep pain of our Golden Souls, and the violent ripping apart of our One Golden Family. It is all of this and much, much more. We feel broken—in ourselves, and as One.

From this time forward, this will be spoken of as our Lemurian Soul Sickness, and I sense it is going to last for a long, long time. As Sananda said, keeping the shattering experience clear in my memory bank will be the only way to pick up the threads of our Lost Ones. It is only because I can hear their cries and feel their pain that relocating them will be possible, with these threads forming a network of communication lines that can reconnect us.

Sending a prayer out to them now, I let them all know that I feel them, I hear them, and that I will be returning to bring them Home. We all will. That's a Golden Promise.

Upon finishing my prayer, my awareness leaves Terra and I find myself instantly back in the Spiritual Domain. I am amazed to find that I am intact here—and still refreshed. But I know where I have just been, and exactly what needs to be done now. Feeling ready, and with a desire to reenter the physical domain, there is an urgency in my Soul to do the deed of rescuing, to get it done soon, so we can be One Golden Family again.

All of this takes place in a fraction of a second, as I look up and see Sananda's loving eyes still witnessing me. Only now I see that he knows that I KNOW. The energy of his gaze confirms that I have been lit into action through my heart's understanding; that this exercise was successful and is now complete. I am ready. I have the clarity, the understanding, the motivation, and the determination I need to get on with my mission.

And I see this is certainly true for everyone. There is a sense of shared urgency in the air, with the entire group wanting only to find out when, where, and how.

Andar has now stepped up, and is getting ready to speak. I send my love to Sananda, and thank him for making all of this crystal-clear to me. His Golden Blessing comes back swiftly, with a promise to steadfastly accompany us through-out our upcoming missions.

I know the surface of Terra is not like it used to be, but she is still our Terra. We are One with her and all that we had with her as our Golden Lemuria is securely tucked away, safe and sound inside of her, along with our hope for a brighter future. No one knows how far off that will be, but it will probably be a very long time, judging by the scope of what lies ahead.

The reality is that the surface of Terra is now inhabited by some other kind of consciousness. It is into that maze we must go to find those we love, and to bring them Home. So be it.

Andar Speaks and Plans are Made

What a blessed Leader Andar is. I am extremely grateful to him, and to Avalar, for being who and how they are. I have always been able to count on them; I know that this dramatic change in the course of our history only fuels their powerful faith in all of us, and our One Golden Heart. No one doubts their ability to guide us through this daunting new task, our most challenging yet. Together as One we will surely succeed.

Andar's gentle but powerful voice fills the entire space, as he so lovingly recognizes each one of us:

"Beloved Golden Ones, I stand here in complete honor of all that you are, and all that you have been throughout. Our unexpectedly catastrophic re-emergence on the surface of our Beloved Terra, which contained unforeseen circumstances beyond anything we could have imagined, has altered the course of our history in many ways, and on many levels.

"We will discuss this further when the details of what could lay ahead for us are presented. But because each one of you must make your own choice as to whether or not to return to Terra to participate in the Rescue Missions, we will first cover some matters that may affect your decision. This is all far more complex than meets the eye, and some of you will be asked to remain out of the physical body, so as to assist with the missions from here. All decisions will be based on whatever best supports the WHOLE, and we'll talk about this too when the time is right.

"For this moment, let us pause and breathe into our Oneness. Know that as you receive this information, your clarity about your path will become obvious.

"I love you. I am here with you. And I am here for you. We are One Golden Heart."

The intensity of Andar's heart, and the unmistakable strength of his Being, accompany his words. Breathing into our Golden Oneness, and into the continuing dedication of our Golden Hearts, despite the unknown paths that lie ahead,

I realize it is essential that I open myself to receive everything that is about to occur in this sacred space. Thankfully, the intense vibration of the importance of the work to be done here helps focus my ability to do so.

Andar, rock steady as always, continues:

"While the situation on our Beloved Terra has certainly changed due to the altered level of consciousness that now resides there, rest assured that our sacred Golden Energies are still intact. Terra sequestered these Energies back inside of her body for us, where they will remain safe and sacrosanct, until such time as we have completed all of our Rescue Missions—and when everything is ready for us to reestablish ourselves again as our Golden World. We know we will succeed, as it is destined to be. Knowing this will help you to focus on your purpose, because until that time, what faces us WILL NOT BE EASY.

"In order to make these Rescues we must return to Terra, and to the consciousness of what we now refer to as The World of Mondor, which is what the Aliens call their domain. It is not that Terra herself has become any of this, certainly not. It is only that Mondor is the collective consciousness field of the Aliens that now dominate her surface.

"Based on our observations, we are referring to these Aliens as the Heartless Ones, or the H-O for short. They do have some version of a working heart as a muscle, but they do not have any Sacred Heart Consciousness activated. Because of this, they are, for all intents and purposes, heartless. They do not live, breathe, think, or act from their Heart Center. Love is not their language. And they are not governed by Love, but by an endless hunger to Dominate.

"These are the facts, which you need to accept and understand thoroughly. This is what is there now. If you do not accept this information, you will be unable to navigate this terrain, and therefore, your rescue efforts will be in vain.

"Open your eyes to these Aliens, the H-O, on Terra. See them clearly and understand how they work. The more you know, the better off you, and everyone else, will be.

"Take this moment to perceive them through your inner lens of clarity and observation."

Opening myself to travel, but with a different intention than previously, my awareness immediately takes me back to Terra again. I am here, this time, to see and feel what the H-O are like.

I land. I feel cold. It has nothing to do with the weather. It is a cold steel-like feeling around my heart and my psyche. I am suddenly aware of sensations of energy that are completely foreign to me—empty, sharp edged, vacant. I sense many H-O just living their lives. Having given myself permission to observe their thinking processes for a moment, I realize that what I am aware of is exactly how they are.

I feel their cold calculation, with no warmth and no thought beyond self. Controlled by a mechanical force, and simply doing whatever is put into their heads, they are nothing more than robots with human looking bodies. And while they still seem human, their heart space is dead. They are devoid of feeling or concern for anything beyond themselves and their scope of doing.

They identify only with a cold hardness and they MUST DOMINATE. That is the voice of their programming, and to do so they must CONTROL. Anything in the way of this has to be annihilated, without question—period, end of story. They are not capable of anything else. It seems there are other governing H-O somewhere controlling them, directing their every move. It's obvious that this is all far more complex than meets the eye.

Enough of this! I instantly move my attention away from it all and back into my Self. Whew, thank goodness the warmth and sensations of my own energies are rapidly returning.

I am now acutely cognizant of the contrast between these Aliens and us. They have no recognition of Source: they do not identify themselves with anything aligned with greater wisdom, love, harmony, or peace. What I sense is something different, and completely foreign to me.

What I sense is that they have a well delineated form of energetic weaponry, which is something called FEAR. Apparently, it is their greatest and most effective weapon to date.

This word Fear is hard for me to even roll around on my tongue. It is a language I do not speak, one I have never encountered before. In fact, there is no such energy that exists in my design as a Lemurian. As I said, it is completely foreign to me.

What I do recognize in this moment is that the word Fear contains the quality of feelings I experienced with the trapped Golden Ones earlier. Their pain was rife with this element, and I am only now recognizing this clearly. This tells me that Fear has taken over and that it is through this that they, and their circumstances, are now being controlled. The Golden Ones are being manipulated like puppets on a string. In fact, they are being directly controlled through their highly sensitized systems and Emotional Bodies.

Our Golden Emotional Body, an essential and highly refined aspect of how we Lemurians commune, is a large part of our telepathic connection system. The H-O are somehow able to capitalize on this highly developed refinement, having found a way to work right through our own natural conduits to control us. They are using the conduits of our psyches as well, which are also very sophisticated. In this regard, as they assert their power, they disable us by affecting our emotional energies, our psyches, our systems.

The Fear frequency, intensely jarring and agitating to our sensitive systems, also creates weakness and pain. With no protective buffer, our Golden Ones are constantly bruised while being stuck in what can only be called a "Mantle of Fear." Like a heavy cloak they cannot discard, it is always there, no matter what. It veils them as to who they truly are, controlling them and affecting their every move, thought, inclination, and reaction. Since it feels like it has power over them, it controls their lives as it relentlessly seeks to dominate their every breath, their every moment.

I'm suddenly feeling my own energy being pulled inside the whirling vortex of this Mantle of Fear, with no buffer between myself and its roughness. I feel extremely unprotected, unsafe—words that I have never used before. This state of vulnerability and powerlessness is new for me, and indeed I have no reference for it.

I understand now why Andar insisted we come and get this education prior to actually entering this domain. I would have been completely lost without it. I would only have lasted a nanosecond, and been unable to accomplish anything helpful for my loved ones at all. Clearly, the more I comprehend about this state of Mondor and the strange inner workings of the H-O, the more successful I will be in my Rescue Missions.

I'm doing my best to breathe deeply, but it's extremely difficult. I feel confined and restricted, and my Spiritual System is telling me it is time to pull out of here.

As I quickly leave the Mantle of Fear behind, I find myself forcefully expelling the energy of it, like a giant bellows releasing its compressed air. I do this several times, and when my system informs me it is clear, I depart fully from The World of Mondor.

In an instant, I am back in our Spiritual Domain, completely refreshed and bright once again. The contrast is amazing. Inhaling deeply, I appreciate my lightness and warmth, inside and out. What a relief! That was quite an education.

Andar speaks:

"Well done, Beloveds! Very well done, indeed. Now you understand better the maze of what you are asking yourselves to enter."

We feel Andar's admiration for our efforts as we pause to quietly absorb what just happened, what we just experienced. The reality of it begins to dawn on us more fully and we register how daunting this could turn out to be. It is indeed far more complex than we had thought.

"Now what?"

CHAPTER NINE

Re-entry Training

A NDAR CONTINUES TO SPEAK:
"*Every time, before you enter Terra for a Rescue Mission, you will be consciously and deliberately putting the Mantle of Fear over yourself. You will do this because if you don't, you will stand out when you land there, bright as day. And you won't survive for a millisecond.*

"*Donning this Mantle will accomplish a number of things. First and foremost, and with no small degree of irony, it will protect you in the very place where its absence would literally jeopardize your survival. Wearing it will hide you by shrouding your Light, and therefore provide much needed camouflage: it is ONLY by appearing to fit in that you will be able to traverse Mondor without being disturbed.*

"*Secondly, wearing the Mantle will enable you to access the fear conduits and subsequent information which will direct you to the many Golden Ones who are being held prisoner. Sadly, most of those who avoided capture during the initial emergence have since been discovered; their Golden Light was so bright that it made them instantly visible to the H-O. Others, who amazingly have not yet been caught, remain stuck where they are and unable to move, as doing so would expose them. Their only concern now is how they can best help those who have been taken prisoner—but they are at a loss, because they are so easy to spot. This is an unfamiliar situation, and they have no way of discovering the Mantle of Fear and its camouflage effects. If and when you find these particular Golden Ones, it will be up to you to educate them, so they can veil themselves.*

"*Without wearing the Mantle you will also have no bridge of communication through which to locate the imprisoned ones, as they are already trapped in the Mantle themselves. You need to be willing to enter the world of Mondor on its terms, and in this specific manner, or there is no point in your going—no point at all. Without the Mantle, you will be exposed much too quickly to get anything done, and you will be unable to pinpoint the location and circumstance of the Golden Ones you are trying to Rescue.*

"*However, even though the Mantle will serve you in these ways, it is also* absolutely TOXIC to ALL Golden Ones. I will provide more information momentarily, as it is essential that you become aware of the risks of going to Mondor, so you can make an informed choice about participating in any Rescue Missions. Avalar and I, who have already been there, witnessed firsthand what is going on, and understand the potential problems for any who return.

"This Mantle of Fear that you will need to be encased in is overloaded with frequencies and vibrations that are in direct opposition to your own: you are Golden. Fear does not exist within you or your design, anywhere. Therefore, wearing the Mantle is going to be extremely agitating and disorienting.

"Even with the management techniques we will be teaching you that will enable you to navigate some of the deleterious effects, the Mantle will still be enormously challenging for you to live within, even for a short while: fear is noxious, debilitating, and all too often destructive. Be clear on this, KNOW this. And weigh it well as you deliberate.

"I know you have had a taste of what being in Mondor is like, following your personal explorations of the H-O just now, but there is also this: once you have donned the Mantle of Fear, there is a definite risk that YOU WILL FORGET YOUR GOLDEN SELF.

"In addition, returning repeatedly will be necessary, and the more Missions you undertake, the more this Mantle will erode your memory. It is quite possible that you will become greatly disconnected from yourself, the Whole, and your entire memory of the Golden World.

"Added to all of this will be the enormous challenge of what must be endured in order to make these Rescues. Should you ever be found out, you will either be persecuted or instantly killed. Depending on the outcome, this could mean great suffering in many ways. This part of your trek, which is unavoidably painful in its own right, will most likely include experiencing the fear and terror of it all. Why? Because you will be wearing the Mantle of Fear, and you will be inside it—you will be inside ALL of it.

"Again, ironically, this is where the positive service of the Mantle of Fear will come back into play: as an effective veiling agent it will, to some degree, numb the most acute pain around any persecution you may experience. Although the entirety of your suffering cannot be removed, it will reduce some of the extremes.

"And, while none of these painful experiences will be as shockingly intense *as they were in your first emergence experience, they will assuredly be very difficult.*

"Once released from the physical body, however, you will be free of it all, as you well know. Whatever vibrational residue remains from your experiences will be repaired at the right time, and in the right ways for you. This is guaranteed.

"These are the known risks you face in order to bring Home our beloved lost and broken Golden Ones. While there are perhaps many more which are as yet unknown, please know that the greatest price you may pay is the forgetting of your Golden Self, just as they have. And we understand that is a very high price indeed."

The Golden Witness speaks:

I can't imagine this at the moment. I simply cannot even conceive of this kind of deep forgetfulness that Andar is speaking about. I have concerns, yes, about the persecution and pain, but somehow, I know I will emerge with a sense of elation once a Rescue is made and more of my Golden Family are brought back into the fold. But...the forgetting, that one just blows my spiritual mind! I am SO THOROUGHLY GOLDEN. How would I ever lose touch with that, forget that? Even from this new vantage point it seems absolutely baffling to me.

Andar speaks again:

"I know how complex some of this sounds, how daunting and potentially pain-filled. It is not for the faint of heart—but then, Lemurians are definitely not faint of heart! We are exactly the opposite, so strong in Heart that it defies explanation.

"If I didn't know the strength of your Sacred Vows, if I wasn't sure beyond a shadow of a doubt of your determination and your devotion, I wouldn't come to you with this. But I know you, and I know that you will stop at nothing to help one another, so powerful is your loving.

"And, although I speak of all these risks, there is also a light at the end of this tunnel of disconnection and forgetting.

"Avalar and I, along with other Golden Masters throughout the Star Systems—including Terra and many of the Golden Energies in the Unseen Worlds—are keeping the Golden Configuration of our One Golden Heart whole, safe, and sacrosanct. We always have, and always will, no matter what. It is our responsibility to do so.

"What this means is that once ALL of the Rescues have been successfully

completed, we will step back in and remind you of who you TRULY are. We will be the ones who bring you back Home, once you have brought the others back home. This is a Sacred Promise, and our Sacred Vow to you. This we guarantee.

"We will do what is effective in restoring your Golden Memory Banks so you can be your clear, healthy and happy, beautiful Golden Heart Beings once again. We will all be restored as One Golden Family and One Golden Heart; on this you can depend.

"What is also true, is that even when veiled by the Mantle of Fear, you will experience a flickering of that which is sacred and alive deep down inside of you. It may only be a faint knowing at times, while at others it may shine crystal-clear—if only for an instant: it is Your Golden Connection.

"You will feel it speaking to you unexpectedly, although you will be unable to sustain any memory of it while in the Mantle. The veil you must wear will make this connection feel elusive, as if your grip on it is slippery. But you will, nonetheless, have a sense of something special within you. Something bigger and brighter that IS YOU deep inside the Core of your physical memory: and you may or may not remember that it is your Golden Self.

"In this way, your Golden Being will ensure that it stays alive and well, safely held within your deepest self, during your journey through the Gauntlet of Fear. While this may all feel daunting, it is an apt description of the literal and figurative path you will travel while in Mondor.

"Indeed, you will come to know the Gauntlet of Fear very well. Circumstances will be such that you must return to it again and again. These Rescues are going to take many incarnations to complete, as each time you may only accomplish a portion of your task. The obstacles will often be so strong that you may, in fact, not make much progress at all in regard to actual full Rescue success. But then, at other times, you will make huge progress. It will vary. You have to be willing to allow for both—please know it's all forward movement, no matter how small."

At this point Andar stops talking, and there is a sudden pause in the energetic fields. It is time out for stillness and Presence. There is much to take in here, and it ALL sounds challenging—not just some of it.

As Andar's voice fades away, his love moves through me. I become his strength, his clarity, and his passion. He fortifies me with all of this now, so my senses and my Soul remain strongly focused, confident, and clear. Amazingly, I feel my own

Golden Power increasing, not diminishing, with all the information being received. I am aware that I am taking it all in as facts, without emotion, and that doing so will help me face these experiences that lie ahead without flinching when the time comes. It is all preparation; I am the strength of my Spirit, the determination of my Soul, and the enduring love of our One Golden Heart. And it is the same for all the Golden Souls who are here with me.

Andar's voice returns:

"The goal of most of your incarnations from this time on will be to gather as many Golden Ones as you can—to find them and physically Rescue them, if possible, and to 'Tag them' if not.

"I will explain Tagging now. There will be many Golden Ones who are so buried inside the H-O domain that they cannot be physically Rescued, having become lost to such an extent that they will have become more and more enmeshed in the H-O energy patterning. Although you will still be able to find them, hear them, and see them energetically, there will be absolutely no chance for actual physical Rescue. In these cases, you will utilize the energetic lines of communication to Rescue them in a purely sensory way. This is what we mean by Tagging.

"You will energetically Tag the pinpoint of Golden Light that still lives in their hearts, however faded or diminished. You will touch their Golden Heart with your own, making an indelible imprint of your witnessing and discovery of them. This is the actual Golden Tag and will be stored as a future lifeline.

"The Tagging will then be in place from this point forward. It will be as an activation that is dormant until such time as they regain their awareness enough to consciously feel a sense of Golden possibility again. When this happens, no matter how far in the future it might be, they will be able to pick up the Golden Lifeline and find their way Golden Home, back to their Golden Heart.

"Sadly, some captured Golden Ones will resist all rescue efforts, even the Tagging. These Golden family members have experienced enormous pain in ways that have gone beyond their ability to bear. They have lost all sight and sense of their true Beings in any way, on any level, and know nothing but the H-O's control of them. They have been taken deeper and deeper inside the web of fear and have become as one with it.

"These Golden Ones have become completely lost and broken; lost to

themselves, but also lost to the Heartless Ones. They cannot help themselves. Deep down there is an unconscious part of them that is condemning themselves for what they have done, and for what they are continuing to do—precisely because they are so completely lost. They consider themselves absolutely beyond redemption, and therefore they truly believe they are unworthy of being Rescued. These are the ones that we ache for the most."

When I hear this, I am stunned. This could have happened to any one of us.

My heart opens and reaches out. In this moment I recognize that, in fact, I am witnessing those Lost Ones who are still back on Terra who are in exactly this situation. They cannot and must not be forgotten as Golden Ones. They must not be left behind because we do not recognize them anymore. My heart aches to look deeper. Isn't their Golden Light still alive, somewhere inside?

Andar's voice answers me:

"Yes, we need to see beyond their lostness, as their Golden Light still burns deep inside of them, however faintly. It may feel to all of us that it has been snuffed out, but it IS there. It will never be lost, as it cannot be—ever. We will be patient until we find it, and then that is what we will Tag.

"Sadly, these Lost Ones are going to reject any attempts to save them and will thwart all who get close to them. A few of you will be trained to deal specifically with these situations by using a highly specialized approach. It is fraught with risk, and only those with appropriate skill sets can even attempt such difficult Rescues.

"We know how enormously challenging it will be for those of you who choose to go back to Mondor. We do not mean to minimize the risks, or take for granted that any of you will even decide to go. But the fact remains that our Family is not whole. It's as though our One Golden Heart is bleeding and is wounded and shattered. These missing members of our Golden Family are proof of this.

"Unless we go back for them, it will not only be that they will remain lost in perpetuity: we will be lost as well—because what happens to One happens to All. WE are the only ones who can restore our original Golden Family. We are the only ones who can make ourselves whole again—but we cannot do it from here. We must go back to where the shattering happened, and to where the Lost and Broken Ones still remain.

"For those of you who choose to participate in these Rescues, this marks the beginning of a very long and arduous journey. It will constitute lifetimes of feeling the weakness and woundedness of our seemingly shattered Soul

and retrieving and regaining our strength and Oneness as a result. We WILL become stronger because of this. That is a fact. We will, because we will have to, in order to endure. And we will endure, because that is what will heal us, and restore our One Golden Family, our One Golden Heart.

"Ours is a Golden Creation of Love. It always has been. And this pathway forward is a testimony of the depth and power of our loving. Remember this. These Rescue Missions and the determination and courage to go through whatever is asked of us in order to restore our One Golden Heart is, in itself, our profound love in action.

"Absolutely no Golden One will be left behind—not one. Our Golden Love Story continues. We will persevere, just as we always have, and to the very best of our abilities. We will see this through, precisely because that is how much we love one another, and ourselves.

"We are Lemurians. We are Golden Gentle Giants. We are powerful and capable people who love deeply and are magnificent in our abilities to create from this loving. And this will be no different; we will rise to meet this challenge, and we will succeed.

"Everyone who goes through this will come out the other side and be healed of any and all residue when the job is complete. Avalar and I promise you this. This is our sacred Vow.

"So...my Beloved Ones, it is time for you to make your informed and conscious choice. Do you wish to participate in these Rescue Missions? Do you choose to do whatever it takes to do this?"

Andar steps back, giving us all the space we need to be able to see the whole picture for ourselves and make our own choice. I already know full well what my answer is, but to underscore this, my inner vision shows me exactly what it would be like if we all just walked away and left all those Golden Ones behind. I can hear their cries and feel their pain. I know that the agony of this brokenness would hurt my heart and haunt me for the rest of my evolutionary path. Refusing to take action on behalf of my entire Golden Family would utterly destroy me, and I could not live with that, not on any level.

What has happened to them has also happened to me, and I feel a great urgency to get on with this now. I MUST go. I NEED them. I need to restore my Family. I love them so dearly that I don't care what the price is. My love is far greater than any pain anywhere; and I absolutely trust that we will all be saved in the end.

With my choice crystal-clear, my Soul expands enormously, fortifying and strengthening me. My determination to restore my Golden Family is solid and unwavering, and I know that this will carry me through these journeys and into the maze of Mondor to rescue my loved ones.

I can do this. I will do this. YES, I CHOOSE TO DO THIS!

And this is true for all of us here. I am ready. We are ready. Let's bring our Golden Family Home again—One Golden Heart!

It is clear to all of us that Andar is proud of the choice we have made and is dedicated to helping us in whatever way he can.

He continues to speak with gratitude in his voice:

"Beloveds, bless you for all the love in your hearts, and for your willingness to physically enter this unchartered territory to bring our Golden Family home.

"There are many more details to discuss about the Rescue Missions ahead, and much preparation awaits. Because further education and training is required to meet the enormous challenges that await you in Mondor, we have designed what one could call a 'spiritual boot camp'—an intensive training ground to provide you with all you need to know.

"You will disperse into small groups now, according to your skill sets, and be taken to designated Golden Training Pods where you will learn how to traverse Mondor. Be prepared for some more energetic gymnastics.

"Thank you again, Beloved Ones, for all the love that you are. Thank you for your beautiful Souls and all your wisdom of Infinite Being. We will speak together again soon. Bless you all—One Golden Heart."

Master Saint Germain Leads the Way

Waiting patiently in our Golden Training Pod, I am surrounded by ten other members of my Golden Family. It feels small and cozy, like a cocoon, and the atmosphere is calm and purposeful.

My thoughts turn to the missions ahead, toward what it will be like in Mondor. I am curious. It was one thing to go there energetically in spirit for information gathering, but quite another to be there in the physical, and actually wearing "Mondor camouflage." My ponderings are distracted by the scent of an exquisite, familiar fragrance that can only mean our dear friend and Teacher Master Saint Germain is near. It is such a pleasure to see him.

He smiles enormously in greeting and takes his place within our circle. His fragrance fills me gently, and the beautiful violet energy that radiates from him touches my Soul, inspiring me instantly. Everything feels intensified, more awake and purposeful. I know we are being prepared to receive the training that is here for us.

"Beloveds," Master Saint Germain says, as his beautiful Golden Heart bathes

us in his love. *"I know this is an important time for you, and for all of us in the course of our Lemurian History. While these events have marked a new path, unplanned and unexpected though it may be, the truth is that once we chose to remain with Terra in the face of those earlier natural disasters, we were also consciously choosing to stay no matter what circumstances that choice might present. And so, here we are. In our hopes, plans, and dreams for our re-emergence onto her beloved surface, we did not know what we would find. Certainly, we never thought it would be thus.*

"With the course of our plans and our history having changed once more, here we sit, preparing to understand exactly what all of this means and what it asks, of all of us.

"The state of things is as it is. The only question is: how do we choose to meet it?

"First of all, remember that we are a strong, beautiful, wise, and loving People. Our way is to love. Our way is to create Beauty. Our way is Harmony. And our way is One Golden Heart. As you have personally found—both through your own emergence travails and your energetic return for information gathering purposes since—none of this is true for the Heartless Ones. This is why we must begin right there, with our DIFFERENCES. Acknowledging and accepting these, and allowing for them, will be the only way forward.

"In our plans to return to Terra and walk inconspicuously amongst the H-O, we must adapt ourselves to ensure the success of our missions. Andar has already spoken to you at length about this and given you all the reasons why, as well as the risks involved.

"Now, I would like to talk to you about the subject of Imprints. Understanding the nature of Imprints is essential, because you will be relying on this as you 'bob and weave' your way through Mondor. I use these particular terms because you will indeed be bobbing and weaving in and out of Imprints—of all kinds, on several different levels—and it will be your flexibility throughout that will determine how much you forget, or don't forget, of your Golden Self while you are there.

"Some circumstances will be far more extreme, and therefore more challenging than others. However, by the time we are done here in our Training Pods, you will have developed enough skill to traverse the different domains of consciousness with the least amount of disturbance and disconnection possible to your greater Golden Selves—all things being relative, of course.

"Keep in mind, initially, that your systems automatically shut down your most Sacred Golden Conduits at the first hint of threat during the Emergence Experience. The wisdom of protecting these pathways of access to our Golden Treasure will always be top priority. Shutting them down was ABSOLUTE, and will remain so until sometime in the future when we deem it safe to open them up again. Avalar will be addressing this more with you later on.

"At this time, however, what you must understand about this shutting down is the position it has placed you in, in regard to your relationship with yourself: access to your deeply-rooted Sacred Golden Circuits, which have always been your solid internal Ground and Anchor, is no longer available to you. The question is, where does that leave you?

"Please understand that not ALL of your Golden Power has been secured away—only the deeper levels of it. Under normal circumstances, your Sacred Golden Conduits would always be in engagement with the vast reservoirs of our Golden Treasure that Terra is safeguarding for us within the depths of her Golden Heart. However, now that those paths of access are no longer open, it changes the balance of things.

"You are a radiant Golden Being, of course, no matter what. You still have your own sustaining Golden Truth to keep you centered. But relative to who you TRULY are, the absence of your deeper conduits will leave you feeling wobbly and untethered at times. And, while this does not help the situation, we all understand its necessity.

"As you all well know, when in your full Goldenness, you are immense. But the current circumstances, and the Mantle of Fear, will cause you to shrink down and become small, relative to who you truly are. This is unavoidable at this time.

"You will have sufficient Golden Ground and Anchor within yourselves to function, but you will not have the vastness of your full Golden reservoir to draw from, the way you always have. Please know that you will get used to this sensation, and be able to adapt to your new, temporary design. The more you incorporate this into your understanding now, the better off you will be.

"That completes the first part, and the second may make you chuckle for a moment.

"The truth is, if you did have the full use of your Golden Conduits, you would not, in any way whatsoever, be able to put on the Mantle of Fear without it instantly being zapped into Gold. It is simply the power and ability of you; you would only be able to wear it for a millisecond before it was transmuted. So, the fact that you will not be in your fullest power means that you will be of even greater service to the rescue of our Loved Ones. As Andar has explained: without the Mantle, you would be unable to accomplish the Rescues at all.

"Let us move on now, to the subject of Imprints.

"As you have already experienced from your recent energetic trip to Mondor, a new circuitry is now governing the consciousness on Terra that is not ours. And, while this new Imprint is the MASS CONSCIOUSNESS of the H-O, it does NOT mean that our Lemurian Imprint is not still fully there—it is. There are simply different levels of Imprints occurring simultaneously. Ours was fully established at first, only to be followed by theirs. It is not stifling or burying ours, but simply coexisting. One is not, in any way, canceling out the other. They are both fully alive.

"Even though, as we have already made clear, the Golden Configuration has been tucked away, the Golden Imprint that remains is still intact—no matter what you might experience to the contrary. Our Golden Imprint is still there. It is quite possible that you will become greatly disconnected from yourself, the Whole, and your entire memory of the Golden World available to you, especially without access to the deeper Sacred Conduits. You are certainly substantial enough to sustain your footing as the Golden Ones that you are—you just won't have the full embodiment of it, because as stated, the Golden Configuration has been safely stored inside Terra.

"By wearing the Mantle of Fear, you will automatically adapt to the H-O Imprints. You will be traveling their energetic conduits, their pathways, as Andar has already told you. While these will lead you directly to the imprisoned Golden Ones, know that being immersed in the H-O energy will interfere with you and your Golden Self—of this you can be sure. This is a fact, not a maybe.

"Your systems run completely counter to the Fear Imprints that The Mantle cannot help but implement. You are designed in the opposite manner of the H-O, so their agitating Interference will be constantly disruptive. The term 'Interference' refers to any and all Fear energy that comes in to disrupt us in any way. While attempting to disempower you completely, it will strive to distort your design, and interfere with you at every turn. It does not want you there, and it will make your lives miserable—but only if you let it.

"We will be addressing Interference in much greater detail later on so that you will be able to prevent this as much as possible. For now, please *understand that the extent to which you lose your Golden Memory will be the extent to which Interference can get in and disrupt you. This weakens you further, leaving yet more room for it to gain a foothold. There may even be a point where some of you become so disconnected from your Golden Memory that you will not be able to stop this Interference from taking over. You may feel as though you are being energetically pummeled, in varying degrees, all the time.*

"Interference could affect you physically, showing up as aches and pains in various parts of your bodies, sometimes moving through quickly, while at others lingering. For each of you, this will be a different picture, according to your own unique design and where you have already been weakened through the Emergence Experience. What you can be certain of is that Interference will target those weakened areas, at whatever level they exist, often endeavoring to weaken them even more. Again, whatever it takes to disempower you, is what the H-O will seek to do.

"I know that what I am telling you probably sounds overwhelming right now. I understand. But let yourselves get used to the idea of what I am saying, and you will see the picture of it begin to make sense. Gradually, you will find that it becomes as information in a guidebook, helping you navigate your path. You won't resist; you will simply observe.

"Take heart, my Beloved Friends, remember you have all of us to help you. You have the Golden Angels and Nature, and you will have enormous support going in. You will be able to turn to a variety of resources for help. However, you must always remember that throughout the duration of these Rescues, while this support will sometimes be quite obvious, there will be times when you will literally have to reach out for it, and let it in.

"The Mantle's veiling will make all of this blurry and quite difficult at times. The weight of it might even make you feel like it's too much effort to ask for help. But let us be clear: ASKING FOR HELP, AND OPENING TO IT, IS THE KEY. Although you may need to open the door, help will always be right there for you—always. Just remember to reach. Deposit that information into your systems now, please."

I feel myself understanding exactly what Master Saint Germain is telling us about all of this so far. I find myself opening up, deliberately reaching further and further, ASKING for help and support to come in and be here for me. I don't need it right now, I know that. But I will, and I want it to be second nature when I need to open up and seek sustenance in times ahead.

I stretch still more—and allow. It feels really good. I say a prayer to plant this motion deliberately in my system, knowing full well it will be there when I need it. With this information now firmly deposited within, I am ready for what is next, just as Master Saint Germain speaks again:

"Let us begin our gymnastics training!"

With energies shifting, I become Self-centered all of a sudden. My own energies turn away from the other Golden Souls here, as I enter my own private inner universe. Aware of Master Saint Germain in here with me, as close as my own breath, I feel the timbre of his voice flowing through me as he guides me along:

"Focus and draw your Golden Energies into yourself, my Dear One. Feel them intensifying as you embrace and appreciate them. BE now all that our Divine Source has made you. Love that which you are, and love all that you express and birth from this."

I feel myself tingling all over, my energy strong, clear and radiant. Suddenly, my memory banks take me back to our Original Lemuria, and I feel myself inside the conduits of that experience, traveling along those Golden Pathways of complete Oneness. My heart is filled with immense joy and gratitude as Divine Love pours through me. Exhilarated and vibrant, I am fully free, awake, and alive.

I am singing out my song of love for all to hear. I cannot help myself. My joy has to bubble out of me, to share itself. Complete in this moment, body glowing and heart singing, my spirit soars. I am Golden Wholeness—one with my Divine. There is no richer, happier, brighter me than this. I am Love, and I am loving. I am loved. Love is all there is, and all the brilliant expressions of it are what I am right now.

Traveling along these precious Golden Pathways once again, and paying attention to them as never before, I see them clearly as actual textured, substantial conduits that encase and hold my experiences. It's like a beautiful, intricately designed flower layered with many glorious memories. I understand it, for the first time, as an Imprint—just like Master Saint Germain said.

It is as a living, breathing life form of our Lemurian resonance and radiance. These textured layers of our experiences, and the energies that we have imbued them with, are the laying down of our Golden Energetic History in the physical world. As a description of all that we have been, where we have been, and how we have been, it's the Living Legacy we leave wherever we go. This design of our Great Golden Weave made real in the physical ethers as the Imprint of our Golden Consciousness is alive and well, and thrives no matter what.

Drinking in this information, I see it now through new eyes. It was there all along, but I just hadn't understood it in this way before now—I never really thought about it. I was simply living, breathing, and Being. I didn't realize that along with the rest of my Golden Family members, I was in the process of actually laying down these energies in a specific design; that they were forming an Imprint, and creating something glorious that would live in the ethers forever. Now I see that this is something we will be able to return to some day. With a smile warming my heart, I tuck this information away, carrying it with me like a backpack filled with treasure.

My attention returns to our "classroom," as I hear Master Saint Germain's voice again:

"Keep this in the forefront of your awareness as you completely shift gears, moving now, back to Mondor to retrieve the sensations you experienced when you recently arrived there and encountered the H-O."

Suddenly in Mondor once again, feeling the hardness and the Heartlessness, I realize it has already laid down its Imprint as well, and continues to do so. Moving inside this imprint now, I can feel no heart, only the stony emptiness with its intent to dominate, no matter how and no matter what. It is chilling.

Traveling now, inside the conduits of this Imprint, bothers me tremendously. However, it is what I have agreed to do, so I remain, in spite of the sour taste in my mouth. I squirm, and as my system continues to react in discomfort, agitation, and even outrage, I hear Master Saint Germain shushing me tenderly, pacifying my spirit, and soothing my Soul:

"This is simply an exercise, Dearest One. Let it be for now, as it is quite temporary. The more you let go, into it, the more fully you will comprehend it: this is your education. It's all right. I am right here."

I surrender, aware that if I am to succeed in making a Rescue, I need to know what this is going to be like. I urge myself to feel the energy here; hard and angular, closed and unrelenting:

"Notice exactly what this is like," Master Saint Germain continues. *"Notice the Imprint design of this fear-based Consciousness."*

By paying attention to the design aspect, as Master Saint Germain has instructed us to do, I see how hard and jagged its edges are.

Master Saint Germain speaks again:

"Now, pause with this. Remembering your experience of our original Lemurian Imprint from a few moments ago, see the two Imprints side by side. Briefly observe them, and when you are ready, start moving back

and forth between the two, noticing the distinct differences, the specific boundaries, the disparate energies. Practice bobbing in and out, pausing for a count of ten in each."

I have difficulty at first, because each time I go into our beautiful Lemurian Imprint I don't want to come out. However, knowing what I need to do and why, I take a deep breath and get on with it. Pretty soon, regardless of the discomfort, I am indeed bobbing and weaving back and forth between the two Imprints, realizing that it is precisely the clear contrast between them that is making this easier to do—I am also grateful that they each have such distinctive boundaries, and are contained unto themselves.

"You may stop now," I hear Master Saint Germain saying. *"Please leave the imprints and return yourselves fully here, and to Pure Spirit, so we can discuss your experiences. Tell me what you learned."*

Many of us respond without hesitation:

"I learned what I am not."

"I learned how flexible and resilient I am."

"I learned that I CAN actually do this."

"I learned that I'm still GOLDEN ME, no matter what Imprint I am moving in or out of."

"I understand more fully how the Lost Golden Ones are feeling in Mondor, which makes me want to help them even more than I did before. I want them to know they are not stuck in the H-O Imprint forever. I want to give them a glimpse of hope that they will, indeed, be set free."

"I learned that I need to improve my skill in this to be able to get the job of rescuing done successfully. I didn't like the exercise, but since I need to get better at it, let's do more."

And for myself, gratitude is what I am moved to share with the group. "It is giving me a first glimpse into how hard this might actually be, and I am deeply grateful for this training and preparation—no matter how uncomfortable."

Master Saint Germain gazes at us with tender loving care. His energies are wise and brilliant, and he fully understands all of this, and us, as he continues:

"In addition to this practice, which makes you flexible and resilient in the art of moving in and out of these Imprints, the greatest gift which you can, and must, take from all of this is: LEARNING TO REMAIN CRYSTAL-CLEAR ABOUT WHO YOU ARE AND WHO YOU ARE NOT. WHAT IS

YOUR TRUE ENERGY AND WHAT IS NOT, no matter what energies you are in, however foreign, and no matter how interfering they may be.

"With your clarity solidly in place, there is nothing they can do that will disturb your Golden Centeredness. You will remain Sovereign throughout, period."

I get the point. He made it with a zing—reverberating right through me, making me sit up even straighter, and with a more determined focus.

Master Saint Germain continues:

"Achieving this clarity is what you are here to do. We will be continuing to practice all of this, and more, until you are fully skilled in all the areas that are needed. And, when we are done, you will make a conscious deposit of this knowing and ability deep down in your systems, so that it will all be instinctively available to you when you need it.

"Some of you may wonder how much of this you will actually remember once you are veiled inside the Mantle of Fear in Mondor, especially since Andar mentioned that it may cause you to forget who you truly are.

"We have no way of knowing right now how much of this you will, in fact, remember—and thereby be able to utilize. However, anchoring this into your systems deliberately assures the best chance that these skills will rise up instinctively when needed. We will all continue to prepare you as best we can by providing an energetic manual for navigating the terrain of Mondor, and the many challenges that will present themselves.

"For now, I ask that you stay in full Presence, with no projecting into the future beyond what is required for this strength training."

At Master Saint Germain's request, I center myself with no other thoughts besides the present. I feel strong and secure in my Soul that all is well, and my faith is limitless. I am whole, willing, and wanting to do exactly what is in front of me. I know I will have exactly what I need, when I need it.

My position clear and sovereign, I hear Master Saint Germain chuckling in my ear, *"Blessed One, job well done. When nothing fazes you like this, you are Home Free."* I laugh back, "I learned from a True Master."

"All right everyone, let's take a break," says Master Saint Germain. *"You have all worked hard, and it's time to recharge. I ask you now to detach from our gymnastics and let yourselves go into repose. Detach completely, Beloveds, let go to receive your restoration.*

"I love you."

Drifting off while falling gently into the arms of my Source, I soften and become ONE. It's time to rest.

RE-ENTRY TRAINING CONTINUES

Hearing Master Saint Germain firmly but gently calling, I feel myself returning to my Soul Awareness. As my individuality begins to take shape again, I am warmed by the sight of my friends here in training with me, and my love for them bubbles up happily. I know these are difficult circumstances that we are addressing, but we are all in this together, still learning and growing as One. I am grateful to be here.

Everyone finally reoriented, Master Saint Germain directs us back into our training/practice mode:

"Welcome back, my Beloved Ones. I see you had a good rest and repose and are now ready for more. Next on the list will be energetically going back to Mondor to travel the Imprints, only this time with a slight variation on the theme.

"You will begin by becoming your original Lemurian Imprint. Feel those strong upsurges of Goldenness coursing through every ounce of your Being, and overflowing, as you inhale and exhale thoroughly. Please proceed."

Instantly back in the Lemurian Imprint once again, it's as if I have returned to my Golden Physical Body, my cells tingling and alive with joy and creativity. I breathe deeply, awash with Golden Joy fortifying me in every way. I feel the strength and steadiness of my true nature, my Golden Roots anchoring down deeply, my Golden Feet deliciously happy once again. Standing tall and still, my body feels as steady as a rock, glorious Golden Love outshining. I love being truly Home back in Lemuria. With a smile on my lips, I say a prayer of thanksgiving for the richness of all that I am knowing now.

In this state, I hear Master Saint Germain's voice again from afar, directing me to wrap myself up in this package of sensation, and secure this strongly inside my internal "Golden Library."

"You have record of all that you have experienced and all that you wish to draw from at any time, Beloveds. All that you need is inside of you. Take this moment to make this clear imprint in your own Golden Psyche of this solid, substantial KNOWING that you have all that you will ever need.

"Feel the illuminated streams of energy ushering forth from your inner wisdom and clarity. Recognize these as pathways of remembrance that can be drawn up into your conscious awareness and experience at any time,

in any future. These belong to you. These are facets of your own Personal Golden Imprint and design.

"Even with the deepest of your Golden Cords in Sanctuary, remember, as we have already said, you have enough of your Golden Knowing and Experience still available to you that you can draw up these Golden memories—and their wisdom and insight—at any time. These are Golden Power Points for you to utilize in any given moment, anywhere at all.

"Make note of this, inside. Impress this into your existing Imprint of YOU. Make this 'deposit' into your physical system and psyche, consciously anchoring it in, please."

I do as Master Saint Germain requests, feeling myself growing sturdier and more empowered as a result. I am in complete ownership of myself more consciously than I have ever been, and I love it. I am truly peaceful, anchored as a strong Golden Pillar, and steady no matter what.

He continues:

"Good job, everyone, great job! Once again, feel your Sovereignty, your Stillness, and your Strength as we now shift gears.

"Re-enter the Imprint of Mondor, but instead of focusing on the energy of the H-O themselves, feel yourselves standing inside the ATMOSPHERE of this consciousness. It will overwhelm you, if you let it, so the practice here is to hold firm in the face of whatever comes your way—no matter what you feel or become aware of.

"Remain centered in and true to YOU and only you, in these moments. Do not shut down your senses. Instead, open them up further, so that you KNOW exactly what you are standing in.

"You can never afford to lose your grip on your awareness of where you are, or what is there. Shutting down your senses and just 'holding your nose to get through it,' will only WEAKEN YOU and make you vulnerable to being overwhelmed and derailed by the energies coming your way.

"The training here is meant to provide the opposite by staying open in order to know and see, because ALL that you sense will be vital information. And, at the same time as you are registering this information, stand Sovereign in you. Be you in the midst of what is not you.

"Breathe. Stand steady. Keep your focus on your Center and on what is going on around you, all at the same time. You can do this. You are supremely capable of doing it and doing it well."

All of a sudden, my body begins to shake uncontrollably, as if I am rattling around in a storm of chaos and commotion. That's right, I remind myself, this is the atmosphere of the H-O. I feel blitzed and shocked at being instantly upended. Weakened and caving in, I am nothing more than a leaf being blown around by a gusty wind. "How can this possibly be?" I say to myself. "I was strong and steady a moment ago. How can I suddenly be so weak and thrown off like this? What happened to me?"

I hear Master Saint Germain's voice directing me:

"Take a deep breath, this is entirely the H-O atmosphere. It is all Interference at work, doing exactly what we knew it would. It is doing its best to overwhelm and disempower you. So, why then is this a surprise?

"When you find this to be no surprise, you will have mastered this practice.

"Focus on your breathing, and the steadiness of your feet which are, in fact, still holding. Bring your attention to what is INSIDE of you, and let the rest go.

"Gather yourself. You're doing great. This is the CONTRAST of the H-O energy to yours. This is the contrast of the H-O atmosphere to yours. Yes, it is strong and it is powerful, but it is NOT more powerful than you. It is just different.

"You FEEL like you are being hurled around in it and overtaken by it, but in truth, you are not.

"You feel like you are losing your grip, but you are not.

"You feel like you are weakening and slipping, but you are not.

"It's all just waves of different chaotic energies slowly penetrating over and around you, sometimes rumbling quietly, and sometimes crashing loudly through. They want to pull you into their Web, their patterning, and their Imprint. They are deliberately and systematically endeavoring to upset and dislodge your own Golden Balance and Steadiness. These energies want you to lose yourself and become them. This is how they operate.

"The Truth, however, is that you are still standing strong—Sovereign, and completely steady in you, and fully Golden Centered, no matter how it may appear. Come back to this knowing with me."

I resolutely focus on my breath, naturally quieting myself in the process. To my utter amazement, I actually become still again. Here I am, standing in the midst of this crazy chaos, and I am utterly still and peaceful! I am standing my own ground, steady as a rock.

I realize I am slowly but surely ADAPTING, that's what this process is. Maintaining my own Centeredness, I open again to what is around me, and stand clear, steady and peaceful, while also being acutely aware of the chaos and clanging commotion that I am swimming in. I manage to hold my balance steady for much longer this time, but I know I need to practice until I am unwavering, no matter what. The more I practice, the more this instinct will anchor in.

With dogged determination, I persevere, repeating the exercise until I achieve my goal. Finally, Yes!

I feel Saint Germain's presence with me. He is smiling broadly, as he says:

"I am proud of you, Beloved Golden One. You are holding strong in the face of this potentially jarring and turbulent energy. Be cognizant of the streams of energy ushering up from your inner wisdom that we spoke of earlier. Consciously draw them into your psyche, and remain aware of how they stabilize and bolster you further. Embrace the clear Golden Power that you are, with joy and thanksgiving, knowing that your recognition of it anchors you even more. Be deliberate. Be conscious. Yield to this inside.

"Soften within and be strong throughout. You will feel the steadiness of your 'rock' increase; your energies of Golden Sovereignty becoming strong, bright, and bold. So solid, in fact, that nothing can interfere with you—absolutely nothing at all.

"From here, you will make the wisest of choices, no matter where you are and no matter what is around you. Inside, you will be clear, confident, and decisive; your KNOWINGS will shine the way. This is what will ensure the safest and most efficient Rescue. Job well done!"

Feeling myself leave the atmosphere of Mondor, I blow out the energy to clear my system before alighting back into my pure Soul State. Whew, what a trip that was! My senses are still vibrating with the stimulation of the experience, as Master Saint Germain's voice rings joyfully:

"Beloveds, what a great success that was, I applaud you."

His exuberance and enthusiasm for our accomplishments is uplifting, and I feel bathed in his delight.

Master Saint Germain continues:

"You now understand how your ability to hold strong in the face of such contrasting energies will enable you to traverse the inner conduits of Mondor. Take a break now, please. Go into repose, and I will let you know when it is time for more practice."

As another pause for recharging begins, I feel myself gliding inward, becoming Source, and losing all identity of my individuated self. Relieved and at home, I have disappeared, yet again…

AVALAR'S MESSAGE TO THE READERS

Fear is the turbulence that is born in the vacuum
Of separation between Source and Self.
The energy of Fear arises as a signal that
Something has gone awry.
Sacred Wholeness seems to have disappeared.

In the following pages of this chapter, the subject of fear will be discussed at length. I am aware that fear is not something people typically want to hear about, talk about, or even think about—much less read about. It can be upsetting. So many people would rather avoid it, or run away from it. In fact, just knowing that we will now be discussing fear at length may cause you to consider skipping this section—but please don't. Please hear me out first.

I understand completely why one would react this way to fear. The subject is so emotionally charged that it can be extremely uncomfortable in the body, the emotions, and the entire system. But this is Fear doing exactly what it does best: engendering more fear. In fact, just thinking about fear can make one nervous. There's already enough fear in the world, so why read about it? Again, I totally understand.

One fact, however, can help you in overcoming this apprehension: there IS a way to stand strong, centered, and steady in the face of fear. But it is impossible to achieve if the subject, and the feelings it brings up, are continually avoided.

Later in this chapter, different levels of fear will be discussed as they pertain specifically to the Golden Ones and the Rescues. This important information can bring you to a greater, and more objective, understanding of what fear is all about—its different levels and intensities, and how to meet it in a more peaceful way, both in terms of the Rescues, and in regard to current everyday living. You will learn ways to stand still and Centered in the midst of it, thus gaining greater ability to face it and not be adversely affected by it.

Know too, that as Golden Ones in your present-day reality, you incarnated this time to BE GOLDEN. And the only way to ensure that you succeed at this is to divest yourselves of fear. Be aware of your own fears, and acknowledge them so they can be transformed by your love. Be aware of the fear around you, and acknowledge that it is not your own.

Many of you Golden Ones who participated in Rescuing often buried the fear you felt deep within your system, so that you could simply move forward with the job in front of you. In reading these pages, those old pockets of fear may be stirred up as they are heard and acknowledged at last. Know this, and please be gentle with yourselves. It will pass. You will feel relieved by caring for yourself in this way.

In the current times, it seems like fear is everywhere. It is in the "airwaves," as one might say. Through technology, you are being bombarded 24/7 by news and information, most of it fear-based. It is intense and overwhelming, overloading your systems with too much of it, too much pain.

Many people have ongoing fears about survival, in terms of themselves, and their loved ones. "Am I safe? Are my children safe? Do we have enough food, water, and adequate shelter? Are any of us going to get sick? Do I have enough money? Will I be able to hang onto our money, and take care of myself and my family? What's going on with the environment? Is the air safe to breathe? Is my food safe to eat and my water to drink? Is there enough of it?

"And what about the ongoing wars, violence, poverty, and sickness, the danger of unchecked pandemic? The devastation of nature and our natural resources? What about the animals, and our balance of life? Will the planet survive? WILL WE SURVIVE?"

I could go on, but I won't. You understand what I am talking about.

Consider what it would be like if all the news and information you received was about the inspirational and caring things that people do, the differences they make in many ways, the miracles that are occurring every day that enhance and improve the lives of all on this beautiful planet? How would that make you feel? Afraid? I don't think so. I think it would inspire and motivate you to help in all of the ways that you can. It would help bring you to honor the goodness in your life, and to share it, instead of being afraid.

Given the amounts of fear the world currently experiences, the more you understand it, the better. I urge you not to be afraid to learn about it. This knowledge and insight will serve you in positive ways, making you stronger and more empowered. As pervasive as Fear is, recognize, too, that it is but the symptom, not the cause. Personal disconnection from Source is the cause.

Fear has been in human consciousness on this planet for a long, long time. There is no denying this. So much of the suffering around us is because of fear in one way or another. While many are convinced that our times herald Consciousness upgrade and renewal, this can only happen once the cause of suffering is acknowledged, and the energy of it set free. Only then will there be a renewal, and a transformation that embraces the compassion, caring, and wisdom that can stand where fear has been.

Everything begins and ends with Consciousness. Become that responsible human that is awake, and willing to look at what is going on beneath everything else—willing to not only face the fear, but also committed to repairing the disconnection that causes it. This begins with oneself and moves out from there. Embrace your Heart and return to Source—only love will be outshining.

Please understand that the information presented here is an education pertinent to the Rescues, first and foremost, but can also be applied to your daily life in the world of today. Indeed, there are many parallels, as you will soon discover.

You will find that the education provided here is multilayered, with the levels of fear becoming more intense as you read on, giving you ever greater insight into the deepening degrees of "lostness" experienced by many Golden Ones captured in Mondor.

Even if you do not relate to these levels of fear yourself, you will at least understand the plight of many of our Golden Family who have been, and still are, struggling and suffering in these ways. Your energy of understanding and compassion for them will support them greatly through the ethers, bolstering them to find their Golden Way Home. The more you stay steadfast while reading this material, the deeper your compassion will go and the more they will all be graced by your gift.

I thank you for this and urge you to read this chapter in its entirety with all of this in mind.

Thank you for your caring and kindness.

Golden Blessings.

Re-entry Training Continues

Master Saint Germain resumes:

"In this next phase, our focus will be on emotional grounding and psychic equanimity, both of which address the issue of personal balance. So far, you have been building these muscles. Now, we are going to strengthen them.

"Before any practice work can take place, I will be educating you about the intricacies of Fear at three different levels:

"PART ONE: The Overall Nature of Fear.

"PART TWO: Interference.

"PART THREE: Perpetration.

"Let us begin."

PART ONE: The Overall Nature of Fear

"You already know that the energy of fear is a foreign element, as it does not exist within your Lemurian Design. Because you are Whole, fear cannot exist in your design. You have no Fear. That's a fact. Period.

"That said, in order to succeed at Rescuing, you already know you will need to don the Mantle of Fear when you enter Mondor. In that way you will take on Fear, but as a garment only.

"Our training continues to focus on strengthening your ability to remain as connected with your Goldenness as possible, while at the same time remaining securely camouflaged in the domains of Fear. To successfully navigate through the Fear-based conduits of Mondor, it is imperative that you fully understand the complexities of this energy of Fear, and the potent and powerful impact that it has.

"Keep one thing in the forefront of your mind, however: you are NOT there to CHANGE Fear, or to alter it in any way. You are not there to fight it, resist it, or judge it. You are not there to actually become it, or have it become you. As I said, it will remain as a garment only.

"Remember, YOU ARE ONLY A VISITOR IN MONDOR.

"Remember, YOU ARE ONLY THERE FOR THE PURPOSE OF RESCUING OUR GOLDEN LOVED ONES, AND RESTORING OUR GOLDEN FAMILY.

"This energy of Fear will be your greatest challenge in a variety of ways. Just when you think you have a handle on it, it will take you by complete surprise. It will consider you a threat because it will intrinsically sense that you are different from it, and not in a way that supports it. It will perceive itself as your opponent and seek to control and dominate you. This is how it works, how it is programmed. It cannot help but do this. This is its design. I guarantee that it will do everything it can to suck you in, to completely derail and disempower you. This is what it has already done, to one degree or another, to the Golden Ones in Mondor.

"Understanding Fear thoroughly, and knowing its nature, behaviors, and complexities will strengthen your ability to remain balanced and Centered in the face of it, thus rendering you absolutely immune to its manipulations.

"As you can tell, Fear is no lightweight. It can be an extraordinarily powerful energy. We know this and accept this. And yet, is it stronger than the power of our Love? No, absolutely not. However, wherever it dominates, it can only do so because of its ability to obscure the design of Love. It can drive

the energy of Love down so that it FEELS as though Fear is more powerful. It's an odd sensation, as you will soon find out.

"In terms of its nature, the energy of Fear is simply an agitated, embroiled upset in the system of Life. Understand that it is born out of, and lives, directly in a place of disconnection from one's Source—that empty, gaping hole where the comfort, caring, and security of Source should be. Our Source is our Creator, the Provider and Sustainer of all of our Life. When one is lost from Source, for whatever reason, the turbulence and agitation of fear is generated.

"In such a state we are disconnected from our Whole, and our systems recognize that it is not right. This space is a knowing, a sign and a signal that something has gone woefully wrong. The sensation of upset, if not repaired soon enough, can escalate into the spiraling energy called Fear. It can become like a virtual tornado, beginning in a slow, deep, disturbing motion, and then gathering tremendous momentum with alarming speed. It can devastate everything in its path, if it wants to.

"Once it reaches this level of intensity, it can feed on itself and multiply in a variety of ways, all of which become expressions of Fear made manifest. At this point, it can project itself everywhere like a contagious disease.

"I am well aware that these are strong words I am using. Am I giving it more power than is due? No.

"Fear is an energy that has the ability to overwhelm, distort, and disarrange harmony. It can seemingly obliterate Wholeness in a heartbeat. Its very presence can generate and elicit more Fear in an instant. In this way, it is toxic, and can subjugate all that is its opposite—in this case, LOVE.

"How? How exactly does this come about? It's all in the nature of one's REACTION to it. Let's look at this now.

"The typical reflex, when dealing with the energy of Fear, is to literally freeze on it. Why? Because to the system, this invasive, overpowering energy feels like it may obliterate it. It takes one's breath away, while eliciting a preservation response to contract, protect, and hide.

"This state of contraction is like caving in on one's Self. And right there is Fear's power. That millisecond of freezing is when it grabs hold to take charge, and from that instant, unless stopped in its tracks, it will dominate. Once Fear is in charge, the reaction to Fear becomes more Fear itself. This is how it feeds on itself. At this point, with its stronghold on the system, it *instantly obliterates one's strength, clarity, and balance: it has successfully become a disabling agent. And once it owns the space, it can do whatever it wants. From there, it can instantly spread like wildfire in the ethers—to anyone and everything.*

"And this infectiousness is its greatest power; which is how it can multiply itself."

The Golden Witness speaks:

In response to Saint Germain's words, my system suddenly goes into some kind of agonizing contraction. I feel a clenching in my middle as if an iron fist is gripping me there and will not let go. It's a horrible, sickening sensation, and one which is incredibly painful. It feels so foreign and so unlike me.

If I was in a body, it would be akin to my breath being cut short, to the wind being knocked out of me. My gut feels like it's in a vise, and I am gasping for air. What just hit me?

I hear Saint Germain on the periphery of my senses, saying:

"Yes, this is precisely the reaction that I am talking about, like a collapsing inward. It is the exact opposite of how a Lemurian is designed, which is why it is so painful. You have gone from a supremely expanded state to one that is severely contracted, in less than the blink of an eye—and it is a shock to you. All too often, before it can even register, it's suddenly GOTTEN YOU; this is what makes the situation even more challenging.

"It is this REACTION to it that I am endeavoring to neutralize. It is imperative to be clear about its potency, and its behavior, in order to maintain your emotional balance in the face of it—equanimity throughout is what we are striving for.

"Take a deep breath, it is over. I can see you understand my point now."

As I breathe deeply, and stretch out again, the internal clenching dissipates, and my own fluidity and well-being return. Thank goodness! Those were some truly excruciating moments.

Master Saint Germain continues:

"As I said earlier, Fear is the driving weapon of the H-O. They are sophisticated and adept in their use of it, and so it is wise not to underestimate how effective and skilled they are in this arena.

"We know this about them. We accept this and work accordingly.

"They can be them. We can be us. Again, we are not trying to change or

alter them in any way. We simply need to be crystal-clear about what we are dealing with here.

"We'll take a short break now, as your systems need to rest. This is a lot of information to absorb, so we must take it step by step, layer by layer. Thank you for your willingness to be here for this today."

And with that, returning to my Source, I am once again bathed in my own Light of Golden Replenishment.

RE-ENTRY TRAINING CONTINUES
PART TWO: Interference

It was a short break, but I am emerging refreshed and crystal clear, thanks to you, dear Source. Master Saint Germain is wasting no time, however, as he now addresses us again.

"Now let's talk about the next level of Fear: Interference, another systematic method that the H-O employ with absolute precision. As previously defined, Interference is literally the insertion of Fear in precise and strategic ways. Having already discussed this subject to some degree, we are now going to take a much closer look at it.

"As I told you earlier, the H-O are highly skilled in their use of Fear as a weapon. They have found it to be something that works very effectively on Lemurians, and so they have devised all kinds of ways for Interference to be implemented.

"Because of its amorphous and insidious nature, recognizing Interference is often difficult. It can be tricky. You need to develop eyes, ears, and nose for it—literally training your senses to detect it before it catches you.

"It is crucial that you be well enough prepared for this level of Fear, so we will return to it again and again throughout this journey. For now, because we have discovered that the H-O are extremely sophisticated in how they go about their interfering ways, please remember the following fact at all times:

"THE PRIMARY PURPOSE OF INTERFERENCE IS TO DELIBERATELY SABOTAGE THE GOLDEN ONES' CONNECTIONS TO THEMSELVES, TO THEIR SOURCE, AND TO EACH OTHER.

"Interference is used to deliberately confuse and disable you. It disconnects you from your Golden Centeredness, and prevents our Golden Family from connecting to one another, gaining solidarity, and thereby gathering momentum.

"*The H-O's purpose is to block and prevent Golden Power from rising up and prevailing, both personally and collectively. They have no idea what Golden Power means, but they do know that it is a force to be reckoned with, and thus must be kept down at all costs. Also, it is simply their way and their patterning to overpower—period.*

"*They will do everything they can to dominate, control, and thwart us. And so far, it's working, mainly because the Golden Ones are greatly outnumbered.*

"*Let's now discuss exactly HOW they use this Fear.*

"*Interference is often generated by finding an individual's weaknesses, then inserting Fear energy directly into those areas. The Golden Ones, still traumatized by the shattering experience following the re-surfacing, are vulnerable, and their wounds painfully raw and sore. The H-O capitalizes on the weakness created by that shock, deliberately injecting Interference. They are thus able to magnify this weakness and the Interference itself.*

"*Interference CREATES complete energetic distortion. It is disruptive and divisive, and its constant 'static' can obliterate one's personal signals, distorting Lemurian wiring with a distressing effect on our natural design and connection to Self.*

"*Since we Lemurians are such highly refined, sensitized Beings, acutely attuned to the energy of our own inner workings, this is especially traumatizing and disabling. THIS is why the Golden Ones in Mondor have lost sight of themselves and who they truly are. Furthermore, the disruptive static of the H-O Interference is UNRELENTING: it never lets up.*

"*It is the Golden Emotional Body that takes the biggest hit. Because we Lemurians are so fine tuned and complex in our Golden Emotional Bodies, we FEEL things extremely deeply. We are easily affected and impacted by emotional states of energy. The H-O have learned this about us, and now use this to the hilt.*

"*It is primarily through the Emotional Body that the H-O interferes with us. By thoroughly engaging these emotional conduits, they create an open doorway through which Interference can rapidly spread—deeply distorting the psyche, etheric patterning, mental constructs, and the physical body.*

"*The most insidious thing about this is that the sensations of it all seem so real, you think it is all coming from inside of you. You believe that these emotions and thoughts are YOURS, that they are your own beliefs—when, in reality, none of them are. Absolutely NONE. It is Interference at work creating great self-doubt and crippling confusion inside your systems, thus enabling it to succeed in its goal to upset and unbalance you.*

"However, while these effects appear to be total, there is actually one exception: the Golden Heart. This the H-O have NOT been able to touch, and NEVER will. But they have been able to blur, distort, and sometimes even bury its signals, creating further pain of disconnect and isolation. We will address this more later on."

As I hear Master Saint Germain talk, I find this all hard to fathom. I cannot even remotely imagine being distorted in this way. It all seems vastly removed from my own reality, and impossible, given the design of our Golden Fiber. Every part of me rebels against this information.

And yet, I know he wouldn't be talking about it at all, much less to this extent, if it wasn't something for me to watch out for. I realize I must let go of all my reservations about it and give what he is saying full consideration. I have to be willing to learn about it, so that when it comes my way, I'll recognize it.

I deeply love and trust this beautiful Golden Being, Master Saint Germain, who has always been a kind, loving, clear, and Guiding Light for me and for all of us. I know he KNOWS. I open my mind, willing to listen now as he continues educating us.

"All of this explains one way the H-O have found that they can control us effectively. You will discover, upon reaching the Lost Ones, how extremely successful they have been with this approach.

"As you are well aware, your highly developed and refined sensitivity has enabled you to become the beautiful and vastly creative Lemurians that you are. This state of rarified Beauty exists precisely because you have cultivated and developed your sensitivities exquisitely. Your natural design has earned its right to shine brilliantly—it didn't just happen. You worked hard for this refinement, and it is a testimony to your superb abilities as the embodiment of true love, compassion, and Golden Creative Brilliance. You honor your instrument in this way.

"During your journeys in Mondor, your well-developed sensitivity is the very thing that can enable you to infiltrate its corridors and not be discovered. You will be highly attuned to the ins and outs of where you are, of who and what you are dealing with.

"Your sensitivity will ultimately provide the gift of insight that leads you to the Lost Golden Ones, in spite of the deeply veiled fog of those Mondorian pathways.

"We must ensure, however, that these sensitivities which enable success in your task do not become vulnerabilities, which can cause you to likewise be ensnared by the Web of Fear.

"Yes, in volunteering to make these Rescues, you must wear the Mantle of Fear itself, so you will, by consent, already be caught in the Web. But this does not mean that you have to be ROBBED by it.

"You can WEAR it, knowing you are wearing it by CHOICE. You can remain clear in the knowledge that it is NOT WHO YOU ARE; that it is just a temporary camouflaging garment, enabling you to accomplish your task—period. You know this already, but it bears repeating.

"The degree to which you can maintain clarity is the degree to which you will not forget who you are, and the degree to which you will not be drowned in the Fear-based Imprint.

"Are these strong words? Yes, and deliberately so. But this is the truth of the situation for those Golden Ones lost in Mondor, as it stands so far.

"Let us take another short break before discussing still deeper levels of Fear that you must also understand. For now, please soften inside yourselves, and go into repose."

I recognize that I am finally absorbing the information that Master Saint Germain is giving us, and tucking it away for later use. Before I drift off, I take a moment to honor my sensitivity and the many gifts it provides, reflecting that it is impossible to imagine who I would be without it. Eternally grateful for all the beauty in my life that it also supplies, I ask this sensitivity to continue to stand STRONG and CLEAR in ME during the times ahead: that it keep me well-centered, and capable of fulfilling my purpose in the best way possible for all.

Off into repose I go, knowing I will return fully refreshed and ready to hear what is next.

Re-Entry Training Continues

PART THREE: Perpetration

Master Saint Germain speaks:

"Welcome back, Beloveds. Let me begin by saying that one must never be complacent about Fear. It is insidious and manipulative. You will hear me say this quite often, because it truly bears repeating. By its very nature, the energy of fear can often be slippery and elusive.

"As I said earlier, just when you think you have a handle on Fear, it will come at you from another direction, from another person or circumstance that you may not have even remotely considered. Appearing unnoticed right out of the ethers, you won't even realize what is happening, as it suddenly grows and spreads. Not only is it contagious, but it is almost as if it is always listening, always aware of you. Don't pretend otherwise, or you will indeed be duped and become another powerless puppet on a string.

"In Mondor, Fear intends to run the show, a fact that we accept and handle accordingly. My point is this: when you are there, don't be surprised by the surprises. Always be cognizant, aware, present, and as prepared for the unexpected as possible. This is the kind of terrain you will be in.

"No amount of thinking otherwise will make you exempt. This is the Terrain of Mondor. I am giving you these characteristics based on its current design and Imprint, which is its reality so far.

"You have chosen to go there for an honorable purpose for which we are all truly and deeply grateful. BE PREPARED. STAY AWAKE. STAY AWARE. That is what our training time here together is focused on.

"As Lemurians, you have enormous, inherent talents for natural shape-shifting and adaptation on energetic levels that will enable you to camouflage yourselves quite easily. The H-O doesn't know this about you. In these ways, they can be duped by you. Keeping yourselves under their radar prevents detection of who you truly are, which, as you know, gives you a free path to traverse the Mondorian Imprint. Because of this you will be able to locate the sounds, sights, smells, and Golden Patterning of our Lost Ones. The Golden Flame in your heart will guide you directly to the Golden Flame within theirs—no matter how lost they have become. Know this. Count on this. It is the Truth.

"Once in Mondor, you will find yourselves traveling deeply inside of the Web of Fear, whose pathways you must penetrate. At some point, you may be right inside the Perpetration aspect of Fear, so the more you know about this, the better off you will be.

"Get ready to move into some really deep territory now.

"As you know, when our Lemurian Family experienced the shattering of disconnection during our re-surfacing, a weakness was created that made the Golden Ones in Mondor vulnerable to the manipulations of Fear by the H-O. It is directly into this weakness that the H-O applies their skill at planting Fear and multiplying it. Once this is well underway it establishes an actual energetic force field, a Web, into which anyone can be ensnared. Many of the Golden Ones are now caught and trapped inside this Web. This is where they live.

"Further explanation about this energy of Perpetration will help you understand the challenges it presents, as it can seemingly alter one's psyche, emotion, and consciousness. It seeks to re-configure the natural patterning in one's circuitry in order to take control of it. If this occurs, it is like being re-wired, and Perpetration can now direct the show, as it has gained the power to do so.

"To summarize, Perpetration, as we have defined here, is the state of being sucked in and taken over by an outside force of Fear that, after catching you in its Web, will do all it can to keep you there.

"It does this so that once you are in ITS control, you will do whatever it wants you to. Having robbed you of your individual power, you will have become just another one of its pawns. Its intent is to collect as many pawns as possible, since its ability to dominate gains even more power with greater numbers. This Web is hungry, it devours. This is what Fear can do.

"Sound gruesome? I know it does, but I'm being graphic here for a reason. It can be this powerful, and you absolutely must know this. Many of the lost Golden Ones are now re-configured into the Imprint of Fear, and are controlled and distorted by it ALL THE TIME. It is happening in varying degrees, to be sure, but it is happening, nonetheless. Now totally disabled, with their Lemurian Design completely obscured from their psyche as if it never existed at all, their circuitry is being interfered with all the time.

"They are indeed lost—to themselves, to each other, and to us—although some are more lost than others. In order to bring them Home, you must face the reality of this Perpetration by acknowledging and accepting what has happened. Pretending otherwise negates the obvious and discounts this sickness that has taken them over—and then they will never be recovered, and our One Golden Radiant Heart will never be restored.

"What happens to one, happens to ALL of us. What is perpetuated for one, is perpetuated for ALL. Take stock now, and feel the Lost Ones for yourselves."

Before Master Saint Germain has even finished his sentence, I feel myself suddenly overwhelmed by heavy waves of despondency and despair, as if a thick, black cloud has just descended upon me, leaving me utterly sad, utterly lonely.

I yearn for my heart and my Wholeness. I ACHE for it. Feeling profoundly confused and lost, I don't know where to turn. Now adrift in a murky fog; spinning, woozy, and broken, I want only to curl up and die.

My body aches; my mind is a blur. My Soul hurts; my heart bleeds.

I yield, and let all these sensations pour through me as I experience the intense pain and anguish of my beloved Golden Ones in Mondor. Loving them more than life itself, I feel their pain as if it was my very own. My heart reaches out to them, and I ache to go and save them.

Master Saint Germain's voice continues:

"Yes, inherent within this state of 'lostness,' you will feel the anguish of our Golden Ones who are trapped in pain and isolation. You will hear their profound plea for help, their call of desperation to be returned Home, to be returned to all of us. They beg to be saved. Their pain will reach you and move through you deeply. It will penetrate your entire Being. You will want to respond to it instantly, automatically, even without thinking. You will literally ache to join with them and save them—NOW.

"Your love for them, your longing to instantly let them know that you are there to Rescue them, will be hugely intense and powerful. I know that your desire to go directly to them will be instinctive and automatic. This is how much we love one another, and how bonded we are.

"And yet, this is exactly when I encourage you to STAND BACK instead. Stand back, assess, and pay attention. BE ALERT. Bring your awareness of the H-O back into focus. It is only by doing this that you will be clear, and able to make the best possible choices to succeed in this rescue.

"If you do not stop before you act, there is a good chance that you, too, will simply be sucked right into the same pain that they are in. Remember at all times that the energy of the Perpetration is incredibly sticky. It is like quicksand—suddenly, you are in it and sinking.

"And then, to put it bluntly, you are of no use to our lost Golden Ones. Suddenly as lost as they are, you will not be able to help any of them get out. How sad that would be."

I am brought up short by Master Saint Germain's words, as I comprehend his message. Of course. In order to be able to help my Loved Ones, I must maintain the necessary degree of objectivity to avoid becoming lost myself. I remind myself here that my personal balance is critical, that I must keep my wits about me at all times, while at the same time retaining the information about my Loved Ones who need me. I pray for strength to be able to hold this balance and to do it well.

Helping those I love depends upon it.

Grateful for Master Saint Germain's guidance, my attention returns to his voice:

"Let me give you still more details about this Perpetration.

"For those Golden Ones caught in the Web of Fear at this depth, it is both blinding and paralyzing when in the throes of this unexpected reality. It veils them from all that was previously meaningful. Their confused state then allows Fear to further weaken them by relentlessly disconnecting them from their personal power—hindering, disrupting, and interfering with them at every turn. Most of this happens to varying degrees at any level inside the Web, but even far more intensely for those who are lost to this extent.

"I think you now understand how unrelenting Perpetration is. It has a singular goal of eroding and ultimately destroying Self-Trust, which is your Wholeness and your Power. After systematically having their Sacred Wholeness broken down, a Golden One in the throes of the weakened state that follows will be at the mercy of the H-O.

"For a Golden One, the dissolution of Sacred Self-Trust is like a slow death.

"Once perpetrated like this, it is as if they are living in darkness—and if they are able to see themselves at all, they will observe themselves doing the bidding of the H-O and feel powerless to do anything else. Thus, while feeling like a stranger to themselves, rather than being cognizant and Present, everything about their usual thought patterns continues to be disrupted and confused; they remain unable to alter their course, because the energy of the Web prevents them from doing so.

"Those who have been completely sucked into this Web no longer know themselves and are numb all of the time. Now true Sleepwalkers who are lost to themselves, they will remain so until something or someone somehow wakes them up to what is happening.

"In this state of disempowerment, they are easily brainwashed and manipulated, controlled by the H-O through a snap of the fingers or a wave of the hand. At any moment, they could break entirely and become as one of them, with no consciousness of it at all. That is the ultimate in being lost. This is H-O Perpetration at work.

"For a truly Lost Golden One, this level of Perpetration appears to rob them of their very Soul."

Reeling from this information, I suddenly find myself gasping for air, doubled over and clutching my belly as if I am trying to hold my insides intact. I can still hear Saint Germain's voice somewhere in the background, but it barely reaches me:

"The degree to which any of this happens depends entirely upon the level, upon the depth, of self-forgetting that has occurred because of it all."

My hands go to my head, and I am cradling my brain in an attempt to save myself. Horribly dizzy, all of my energies spinning and tilting off axis, I feel thoroughly sick inside, as though I might slip away from myself at any moment.

Feeling like I may never be the same again, the sensations continue to overwhelm me before they finally, thankfully, begin to ease up. As my full focus returns to my true Self, I register that this is but a HINT of what it is like for some of the Lost Golden Ones in Mondor. This is the energy Master Saint Germain is talking about. How will I ever be able to withstand these conditions? All of a sudden, I'm unsure of surviving this kind of situation.

Surely, he will have something positive to say now. Something, anything, to help get all of us through this.

Master Saint Germain continues:

"Please understand, there are many different levels to this Web of Fear. This complete picture was presented for you to understand the depth of lostness that is currently being experienced by some of our beloved Golden Ones. Now you know.

"Having thoroughly covered it all, we can now talk about how to get out of this Web of Fear.

"No matter what level one has gotten sucked into, getting out of this sticky haze, this controlling Web, would seem extremely difficult. First, you must be able to see that you are in it, admit it to yourself, and be clear about what is going on. This is, by far, the most important thing—calling its bluff, so to speak.

"Second, it requires a full commitment to freedom.

"And third, it calls for letting go.

"You'd think great strength of pure will, a determined force, would be needed to extricate yourself from this Web, but it is quite the opposite. A gentle softening into Golden Surrender, with a focus on your Golden Breath, just as we have been practicing in this training, is the only action required.

"The truth is, THE H-O CAN NEVER ROB A GOLDEN ONE OF HIS OR HER TRUE GOLDEN BEING. THAT IS IMPOSSIBLE!

"But if Fear can cause a state of complete erosion of Sacred Self-Trust, and

what feels like a complete internal disconnection, then it will SEEM to a Golden One as if this has actually happened.

"Do you understand what I am saying here? Am I being clear?"

Something is shifting in my field of vision. Gazing at Master Saint Germain, the image of a river filled with murky water suddenly appears between us and is expanding alarmingly fast. The water is getting darker and darker, the surface is churning wildly, and it's growing even wider and more turbulent as each second passes.

Our shores are growing further apart, and Master Saint Germain is becoming smaller and smaller. I might lose sight of him altogether! As I reach out, I feel nothing. He is gone. The picture has stopped, the river has vanished. Feeling desperately isolated, I weep uncontrollably, unable to make sense of all of this.

But now, here he is once again, standing in front of me, clear as day and larger than life. As his eyes look right into the heart of my Soul, his love washes through me, re-igniting my own.

Master Saint Germain says softly:

"I was making a point, Beloved. This is the start of a greater understanding into how losing one's Self might feel."

In the next instant, suddenly bathed in the love of my own Source, I take a deep breath and let joy and relief rush through me as Master Saint Germain continues:

"I have explained many things about Perpetration today, but as the true power of it can only be known through actual experience, you are all going to get more of a taste of it now—at least on the energetic levels.

"As has been the case in our previous practice sessions, know that this is simply an energetic practice and that you ARE NOT THIS. When returning energetically to Mondor now, feel your way through the Web of Fear with the intention of discovering more about these levels of Perpetration we have discussed. Thanks to your most recent trip there, you will have confidence in your Centeredness, no matter what you are experiencing.

"Let's get on with it!"

Energetically returned to Terra once again, I am being swirled gently back into my original Lemurian Imprint as a way to steady and strengthen myself. My mind clear, my senses bright, all thoughts are of love and compassion. With heart wide open, I am grateful to be alive, and ever so grateful to be FREE. My passion for freedom is strong.

I hear Master Saint Germain's voice clearly in my right ear, directing me, as

I feel my own joy rising up to greet him.

"Take a deep breath, Beloveds, inhale your Goldenness deeply. Feel how much you are shining. Radiate your joy and love out into the universe with abandon. Feel how good it is to be you.

"Savor it now. Rejoice in it now. It is you being truly YOU."

Taking in many deep breaths as my Goldenness pours through me, I feel like a glorious fountain overflowing with endless beauty and grace. I LOVE being ME. It feels so good.

Master Saint Germain continues:

"Take one last deep breath, Beloveds. When you are ready, exhale, yielding to what is next. Now we are going to shift gears. Onward!"

Oh no, suddenly, I'm stuck inside some sort of sticky Web that won't come off. Somehow, it's gotten me in its grip and won't let go. No matter how hard I try to extricate myself, its hold on me increases, and I can hardly breathe as it tightens around me.

At first, I notice it's strongest around my middle, only to move to my head, and then my inner eyes. It overwhelms me, and the rest of my senses are now being shut down. My brain becomes foggy, and I can no longer think clearly. It is vaporous and suffocating. My Being has become small, my breathing labored, and my sense of self completely clouded. I feel weak, completely weak, throughout my entire system—and disabled. I wish I could "straighten up and fly right," but I can't. I am immobilized, not just in my body but my psyche as well.

This must be what it feels like to be robbed of oneself, as Master Saint Germain described earlier. I have never experienced anything like it. It is completely overwhelming. As it penetrates deeper, I am literally experiencing myself LOSING me. My emotions are shifting in a way that is unfamiliar to me, being "torqued out" right in front of my eyes, and I can do nothing about it. I am being deliberately upset, emotionally yanked around like a helpless puppet on a string.

My system is being distorted as my head fills with static. All my senses and signals are being tampered with, my patterning and my circuitry feel like they are being rewired.

Is this true? Is this really happening to me? Am I being shaped and formed into an entirely different composition than I have known myself to be? Am I being redesigned by some kind of outside force?

A loud buzzing in my ears pesters me, blocking any connection to the sound of my own inner song. I wish it would go away. I swat at it in frustration, but that doesn't change anything. It simply persists, agitating me more and more. It's amazingly disruptive. It gets louder and then quieter, then louder again—it just won't stop! I am helpless to do anything about it.

There's a terrible smell now. This noxious odor has got to be toxic. It's filling up my cells, weakening me further. I dare not breathe, but of course I need to. Everything in me is contracting. My inner senses are disappearing, I am going numb. Who or what am I becoming? What is happening to me, what should I do?

Shocked by it all, Saint Germain's whisper is barely audible:

"Breathe into me. Breathe into me. I am holding you steady. You are not losing yourself. It just FEELS like you are. Don't resist. You need to KNOW what this is like. I've got you. You are secure."

Yielding to his support, my confidence in my own centeredness restored, I realize it's just that I don't FEEL like ME. It's like I have become a different person who is in the process of being controlled, reshaped, and reprogrammed into something else.

Knowing that Master Saint Germain has me securely in his hold, I allow myself to go further into this uncomfortable experience. Part of me wonders why I am doing this to myself, but another part compels me forward for further understanding and insight. My own wisdom reminds me that I am in the Rescue Training, and that I need this information in order to help those I love. I take a deep breath and pray for strength.

I have no fear, and yet, I find I am terribly afraid. How peculiar that feels. Now what?

I hear faint cries in the distance. I know those voices—they have the resonance of my Golden Family Members. My heart lurches toward those sounds, and my system instantly starts to clear. I am still inside the sticky Web, but my heart understands something: yes, I had to come INSIDE this Web in order to find my lost Loved Ones. This confirms to me that I have made the right choice to go through this, and I feel bolstered as I move forward.

Listening more intently, I know my Loved Ones are trapped here inside; lost, and unable to remember who they are. Their pleas for help penetrate my heart, lighting the fire of my purpose. My clarity prevails as the final traces of fog in which I was stuck completely dissolve from my psyche. My purposefulness has fully cleared my own way. The Fear is gone. I become unveiled, and even with the lingering threads of stickiness pulling at me and the static continuing in the background, I reach out toward the sound of the suffering cries. I can't help but do so.

Suddenly, Master Saint Germain's voice steps in to stop me, as he reminds me to stop myself. Yes, that's right, now I remember. I must step back for a moment to assess the situation properly before rushing in. I must open my awareness to EVERYTHING that is around me, and then proceed gently. We're only here to get a sense of the experience while exploring the feel of it all.

I'm sensing some kind of opening in front of me now. With Master Saint Germain's continued support and presence, I feel strong enough to investigate further. Okay.

I move in the direction of the opening, and suddenly find I've landed inside some kind of conduit, a tunnel that is filled with sounds of sorrow echoing off its walls. This tunnel has somehow formed itself out of the sound waves of the pain experienced by my Lost Loved Ones, and I am certain this is my direct link to them.

Leaning my energy into the sounds, opening wide to them, they come alive and I feel like I can almost TOUCH them. Their energy is palpable, and my Presence lights up at this closeness. I flash for a moment on Andar teaching us about Tagging earlier and now understand the possibility of doing that successfully through this kind of communication line that is highly energetically charged. I tuck this insight away for future use, grateful to at least have a more direct vibrational sense of what he was referring to. Since I am not actually physically embodied right now, I remind myself that I am not here to do any Rescues at this time. That being said, all the information that I am gaining during this trip will definitely stand me in good stead when they begin.

Now, returning to my present exploration, and convinced that this tunnel will lead me straight to my Golden Loved Ones, I immerse myself fully into its energetic current, riding it like a surfer rides a wave—Strong, Clear, Focused, and Balanced. I am literally "surfing the Web!"

Moving quickly at first, the pace of the current has now slowed considerably, giving me more of a chance to scan what is going on around me. Reminding myself that I need to stay aware of my surroundings at all times, I pause in my motion to take stock.

Yes, the sticky threads of the Web are still here, flailing around me as if they desperately want to trap me more deeply inside the Interference again. I can almost feel the Web's frustration that I am here in its midst but not behaving the way it wants me to. I am not reacting to it nor going weak, so it has no control over me. I can feel the energy of it attempting various ways to try and disable me—all to no avail. I know it will keep on trying, because that is simply what it does. That is its PROGRAM.

Solidly and consciously Centered in my own design, my own true Configuration, I recognize that right now, Fear and I are simply in the same location. Different and separate from each other, we are co-existing, as two different Configurations, as two different Consciousnesses—but in the same place. I accept this.

It's simply the way that it is.

We are each doing what we are here to do. I have no "reactivity" to Fear now. By only WITNESSING it, and merely observing, I have become immune and impervious to it. I do nothing to try to alter it. It can be itself, and I can be myself.

This perfect point of balance is exactly what will enable me to Rescue successfully.

Now that I have achieved the ability to hold myself steady and Centered inside the Web of Fear, I am ready to get on with it. Thanks to this trip, I have learned more about the terrain here, gained greater insight into what my Loved Ones are experiencing in captivity, and discovered that it is indeed possible to hear them, feel them, and connect with them in this maze of static and interference. All of this, and everything else that our Training has given us, has instilled confidence and unshakeable faith in my ability to meet and succeed at what lies ahead. I have been prepared, and I am ready.

Standing strong and resolute in my final moments here, I expand my heart and send out a powerful wave of love toward the cries that still call to me. My message is clear:

"I HEAR YOU.

"I HAVE FOUND YOU.

"I WILL BE BACK TO RESCUE YOU.

"I PROMISE."

Suddenly everything shifts, and I am out of there—out of the Web, out of Mondor, and out of Terra.

Again, blowing out the energy of that experience like a giant bellows expelling air, I return fully to my Spiritual Domain with a lightness in my heart. The possibility that our lost Loved Ones will truly be saved has become a tangible reality to me now. I smile and turn to see Master Saint Germain positively beaming at me, as he says:

"Job well done, my Beloved One. You have mastered the terrain, and you are ready for the missions ahead. I congratulate you.

"Know that I will always be there with you, holding a steadying presence in whatever ways you need. We are in this together—all of us. We are all helping one another and persevering until the job is complete.

"I salute you now, for your devotion and strength, knowing full well the depths of love that will sustain you in the days ahead, enabling you to reach those Lost Ones who are so precious to us all.

"Blessings to you, Great Golden One. Golden Blessings and great gratitude to you. Thank you."

I bask in the warmth of Master Saint Germain's blessing, as I feel my Source calling to me, beckoning me to come Home for restoration. I send a wave of gratitude to my beloved Teacher before I go, thanking him for all that he has given me that will enable me to move forward with skill and confidence. His wisdom, along with the others who have stepped up so adeptly, has made all the difference. I am profoundly grateful.

Gently, I turn to go. My Source awaits me…

∽

"Hallelujah, everyone!"

A beautiful, melodious voice has awakened me back to my small group. Mmm, do I smell roses? Oh, how wonderful: this particular beautiful aroma can only mean one thing—our divine Mother Mary must be here. Our Golden Comforter and Guide, she who walks with gentleness and love is also fierce and commanding, as only a Mother can be.

Mother Mary speaks:

"My Beloved Sweet Ones, I too am here with you, to offer my blessing and wish you all great Golden Godspeed. Please know that my heart and Soul will accompany you. We do this together.

"The steps ahead will be rich with new experiences, many of which will be transforming and illuminating for you. Your muscles, having been well trained, will be tested, but also strengthened enormously. And the power of your Golden Love will prevail.

"There are many lifetimes of Rescues ahead for you all. You will stay the course, and see it through to the end, because this is the Vow and Pledge you have made. Go with my love, and with all the love of our One Golden Heart.

"It is with our deepest thanks that I honor you now, rejoicing in your courage, and celebrating the journeys you will make to restore our Golden Family. Please call on me whenever you need to. You know I am here for you.

"We are One Golden Heart. Blessings and Golden Godspeed forever."

Deeply moved by Mother Mary's love and steadfastness, I know she will be there for me, and for all of us, every step of the way. Tucking this certainty deeply inside, like I would a precious jewel safely pocketed away for the future, I love her more at this moment than ever before. Knowing already that she will be one of my "rocks" throughout the challenging times ahead, I whisper to her with endless appreciation in my heart, "Thank you, my Beloved Mother, forever thank you."

CHAPTER TEN

THE RESCUE MISSIONS

RESCUE MISSIONS SEND-OFF

THE GOLDEN WITNESS SPEAKS:
We are gathered together in the Golden Spiritual Domain's Hall of Wisdom, waiting for our Beloved leaders Andar and Avalar to come and give us their final words before we depart for Mondor.

All of us are nervous and jittery with excitement and apprehension. Although we are eager to be reunited with those we love who have been lost for so long, we are nervous about entering the "Great Unknown." It looms large, and we feel as though we are all "parachuted up" and about to take the leap.

What exactly is about to happen? What will it all look, feel, and be like? The buzz of our nervous chatter and stimulation charges the air, and the tension of New Creation can be felt throughout. We are embarking on a new adventure— one with such a poignant goal, and much earnest preparation.

The aura of expectation fills the air. We can hardly contain ourselves…waiting.

At last, I see Avalar and Andar walking gracefully across the stage in front of us. They are holding hands and moving in what can only be described as the "rainbow of their sacred union." Their profound love for one another radiates so beautifully that it is palpable; it has always been thus.

With hands still entwined, they take their positions behind the golden podium that stands at the front of the stage. Their presence is both purposeful and peaceful. I am grateful for their stillness, as I am feeling restless with readiness to go.

There they stand, our beloved and beautiful Golden Leaders; strong, proud and clear, full of love and respect for us all. We can feel it pouring forth from their eyes, their hearts, and their Beings. It can be felt throughout, moving through each one of us like silken water.

I feel my heart flutter and open wide toward them, moving instinctively into their hearts. I have known them for a long time, and we have all been through so much. We are close, and I love them completely.

Right now, it's as though they are me and I am them. I breathe in their gentleness and their strength, and sink further into the comfort of their soothing presence. I feel their graceful energies bringing me steady confidence and reassurance about what lies ahead.

After a few minutes, Avalar steps forward and begins to speak:

"Beloved Beauteous Ones, the time has come. Your training—as much as we could possibly give you—has been completed, and you are ready to embark on the missions for which you have courageously volunteered. We thank you for this. We are grateful for the power of your loving and for your unwavering devotion to our Golden Family.

"At this time, we have no way of knowing how much of your training will be consciously remembered as you arrive in Mondor and begin traversing the Web of Fear. What we do know is that you have planted it all deep inside of you, and it will emerge automatically as much as possible, whenever needed.

"We also know that no matter the degree to which you are able to hold the memory of your True Being, you will, minimally, have the distinct sense that there is, and always has been, something special, strong, and sacred inside of you. This will be your Golden Flame letting you know it is still there and that it burns forever bright, no matter what. It is this Flame that will drive you and compel you on your way. It remembers its task, goal, and purpose, and it always will. This instinct to proceed in whatever way you find yourself moving will be the power which guides your course and clears the way for the successful Rescues of those you love.

"All the while that you are in Mondor accomplishing your missions, Andar and I will be with you. We will be Witnesses to everything that you experience. We will be gathering all the information needed so that, at the end of it all, we will be able to help you, as you will have helped so many others. Our vow is to then Rescue you—to Rescue the rescuers.

"When all is said and done, and all the Rescues have been completed, everyone will be brought home to heal and restore. This is when we will step in and remind you all of who you are and who you truly have been all along—no matter how lost or veiled you may, at that time, find yourselves to be. This will be when we help you to divest yourselves of all the pain of the Rescues and the attendant forgetfulness that may have taken over your daily lives.

"By virtue of being in Mondor and of sacrificing yourselves for the greater good of the whole—and becoming contracted in that Imprint—you will probably suffer to one degree or another. You already know this to be so. This 'woundedness' will be what we will help you attend to, to nurture and heal back to Golden Wellness.

"It will be at that point that we will help you to remember the great Golden Gentle Giants that you truly are and have always been, and the true and immense power of your great Golden Light.

"Andar will come forth momentarily and voice this for himself, but at this moment, I want you to know fully that this is my pledge to you, my beloved Golden Ones: I vow to you, with all my heart and Soul, that I will do everything in my power to enable you to remember and regain yourselves, to know your victory and to stand strong, bright, and shining like Golden Stars again throughout our great Universe.

"I vow to do whatever I can to enable you, once again, to remember and sing your own unique song of Golden Joy—and to let everything else that has happened become as a distant dream which will gradually fade and dissolve.

"Know, without a doubt, that your strength and wisdom—hard won following these upcoming experiences—will remain. You will be grateful for this, and for the tremendous love and compassion that will have grown ever greater and deeper as a result.

"This strengthening and growth will then enable us all to meet the challenges of Grace and Beauty offered up in that new time, far ahead, when our day to flourish again as One Golden Heart will have arrived.

"I tell you these things now, not to distract you or give you false hope; these things I KNOW—and these things you must know as well. It will all be remembered in your Golden Cells and will offer up still more reassurance and determination to persevere during the journeys ahead when you will surely need it.

"So, take heart my Beloveds. You are ready. I love you and I go with you. We are One Golden Heart. I will see you in Mondor.

"You will feel me from time to time, and you will know that I am watching and supporting you, hearing and feeling you. I will be your WITNESS. And as I said, when it is all done, I pledge to bring you Home. Know this.

"I love you, Golden Ones—forever. Golden Godspeed."

And with that, Avalar presses her hand to her heart in gratitude and steps back.

I find myself crying quietly at her words. I have known her love deep inside of me before, but never as touchingly as this. She has penetrated straight through to my Core and I know, without any hesitation, that she will help me surface and feel the light of day at our journey's end. I know she is with me and I KNOW she will truly help me come home. I tuck this safely and securely into my heart. I am so grateful for her.

After a moment, my attention returns to the podium, and I see Andar stepping forward to speak:

"My beloved Golden Ones, I honor you. You have all volunteered to make this Rescue Mission and to do whatever it takes to bring home the rest of our Beloved Golden Ones. You have stepped up of your own volition, and have consciously and clearly chosen to make this Rescue of our Golden Family—no matter the cost.

"As you already know, there will be a measure of pain involved in this sacrifice, as well as many difficult challenges. I am not going to sugarcoat this in any way. I assure you, it will be daunting—often. But your Golden Hearts lead the way, and you have been trained and well prepared to meet any and every challenge.

"You are all strong and mighty Golden Ones: bold, brave, and resilient. I know you. I know you will do this to the very best of your abilities, no matter what. I salute you and I honor you. I have complete faith and trust in you.

"I also have your back, as does Avalar, and you know this. I know that each one of you will remember the most important thing: you must do your best to STAY THE COURSE.

"As I have previously explained, as soon as you don the Mantle of Fear you may forget who you are and why you went—you might stumble or even fall. And yet, as Avalar has already said in her own way, your internal heart's compass will always propel you forward, driving you to persevere with a life's course which you may not fully comprehend.

"Your heart will know, and your heart will guide you. Your Golden Heart will give you glimpses of your True Being, which will flash through you and continue to carry you forward on your Destiny Path. These will be moments of great clarity, moments when you remember that there is something else, something greater and deeply powerful within you, something sacred and precious and purposeful. This 'something' will sustain you. You will grab this knowing and hold it in an iron grip throughout your progress. It will come and it will go, but like the Sun in the sky, it will always be there.

"It will also be your deep connection with those that you love, the sounds and sensations of those you are there to Rescue, that will bring you continued

strength and faith to endure whatever is necessary to accomplish your task.

"And in this, there will be moments of great joy—greater joy than you can remember ever experiencing. It will radiate deeply inside of you, inside of your senses and inside of your knowing. It will activate your faith that somehow all is well, and that this is a good thing that you are doing; that it has a point and a purpose and that it is love-based and love-fulfilling for all involved. It will move your heart profoundly. It will bring you great comfort and renewed purposefulness.

"I urge you to take heart in these experiences, as I know you will. Savor them, and let them replenish you throughout. Rejoice in your joy. Embrace it and surrender to it: it is truly who you are.

"It will be the joy of knowing you have Tagged those who have been lost to us that will continue to bolster your confidence and resolve. You will know that you are achieving a purpose which may well be outside of your clear, conscious remembrance. It matters not what you remember. The levels of veiling that you experience will have no bearing upon your compelling drive to keep moving in your chosen direction of Rescue. You will not be able to hinder that, and you will not want to.

"But know that you will not always understand yourself and the reasons for the movements that you make. You may not always feel clear, not at all. You may be confused and flailing much of the time, but this will not deter you. You will get up and keep moving. You will bounce back and be restored, even when you think you won't.

"You will gather your courage and continue to put one foot in front of the other. YOU WILL SUCCEED.

"Why? Because that is how deep your devotion goes; that is how powerful your love for our Golden Lemurian Family truly is.

"As Avalar has already told you, she and I will be there with you, witnessing all of you. Together, we will hold the torch of remembrance for you. Together, in our own ways and in our own areas of expertise, we will be witnessing all that happens while you are in Mondor, so that we can then build the bridges necessary to your own remembrance when this is finished. On this you can depend. This is my vow to you as well. This is my sacred pledge. Avalar and I make this Golden Vow to you together, as One."

At this moment, as I had with Avalar, I feel Andar's love penetrating within. His power is so stabilizing and strengthening that it practically takes my breath away. I drink in his confidence, and I am grateful to him for his presence and steadiness—like a rock throughout my life.

I am also grateful for the strength of their union. I know it isn't just one or the other—but the combination of both of them, woven and multiplied into something even greater and more powerful—that will endure and help sustain us all throughout what is ahead. Thus, it is with our Golden Family.

I relax more into myself as Andar continues:

"And lastly, know that, as always, Nature will be your greatest Ally. She will guide and direct you. She will feed, soothe, inspire, and help restore you to your true balance and internal grace. She will nourish your senses and remind you of Goodness and Beauty. She will verify and remind you that you are of value—an essential cog in this wheel. She will protect, cleanse, and steer you clearly on your path.

"Nature will be your Ground. She will be your Godsend and your Angel. As ever, she is a Central Member of our Golden Team. In Her we dwell safely and in peace."

At the completion of Andar's speech a great hush comes over the Golden Hall. Everyone is deep in recognition of the Truth of his words, and of this final opportunity to feel the love that binds us together as One. We inhale it, drinking it in as fully as we possibly can. It will hold us and carry us through; we know this to be so.

I look around and see that everyone is once again preparing to go. Just as I begin to wonder when we will begin our journey, I see a shining Golden Aura entering from the side of the stage. As this gorgeous Golden Energy increases, our beloved Golden Master Sananda appears within the center of it. He stands before us in his full brilliance, glowing and pulsating. The mere sight of him causes us to take a sudden breath; he is exquisite, beautiful beyond measure.

I am swept into a giant wave of his pure Golden Love. I hear the sounds of Golden Angels with their wings beating joyously around all of us. We are touched and moved, overcome with joy.

His love fills us, and we forget for a moment why we are here, except to receive him.

Sananda speaks:

"Most Beloved and Blessed Golden Ones, I am here. I am here now to bless you and give my Golden Blessings to this upcoming mission. Along with me are all the Angels and Archangels and Blessed Golden Ones that will be shining Light for you, and clearing your paths to clarity as you make

your way through the labyrinths of Mondor.

"I am here to let you know that I belong to you—truly. I am with you in every breath and every beat of your heart; in every word, thought, and reflection of your dreams. I am with you at every move, at every moment. Know this. Turn to me, and I will help you with all that I can and in every way that you may ask of me.

"This mission, and those that follow, are of a divine nature. Every Rescue of a loved one that you make, every Tagging that you accomplish, restores that piece inside all of us that had gone missing. As each of our Golden Ones is brought back to the fold, we as Golden Ones become more and more whole. Every step you make is a great leap for all of us. Know this. Know how grateful I am for you—for your Light, for your Love, and for your never-ending devotion.

"Who would I be without you? Who would we all be without you? You are essential to all of us, because there is only one YOU. We all praise, love, and support you. We are all with you. We all make this movement as One.

"Please know this now, more than you ever have. YOU ARE NOT IN THIS ALONE. You are loved, sustained, supported, watched out for, and watched over. Thus is the way of the splendor and devotion of our vast Golden Family. Our powerful love for one another is palpable. It moves as one singular breath—deep, sustaining, focused, and strong.

"We each move inside of that breath, flowing wherever our Golden Love directs us to go."

As Sananda speaks, my tears flow freely again. I feel his abiding presence and powerful love shifting me into still greater alignment and purposefulness. It's as if my courage is growing into a gigantic tree: solid, stable, steady, and clear. I breathe in, and allow myself to deepen and expand in this way.

His Golden Grace pulsates evermore throughout my being as he continues his message:

"We stand now on the precipice of a new edge of our experience. We prepare to take this leap and trust our hearts, as we have throughout all the stages and steps of our lives together so far.

"This trust is well placed, as you know. Solid and strong are we in Golden Heart. Everlasting and resilient are we in Golden Soul. Ever divinely guided and inspired are we in every step we take.

"Hear me throughout your upcoming journeys as I whisper to you. Feel

me as I inspire and uplift you. Receive me as I love and strengthen you, bringing you all the courage and clarity you call for.

"Yours is a blessed path, one of great beauty and illumination. Let us join hands now and go forth. This marks a new day, a new way, and a new opportunity to be restored again.

"Your steps will be those of Golden Grace and your hearts will be fueled with the passion to bring restoration home to us all. Golden Godspeed, I say to you now.

"We go as One: One Great Golden Heart. Breathe into me as I breathe into you, and know that all is well and that this is our divine destiny unfolding. I belong to you—One Golden Heart, Forever."

As Sananda leaves us a deep stillness washes over all. We are powerfully moved by his loving message and brought to a knowing that, yes, indeed, all will be well. Without a shadow of a doubt, we know this to be true. And yes, we each know we are not alone.

We are given barely a moment to collect ourselves again, before Andar returns to center stage. His stride is purposeful and his face intent. We all know that it is finally time to go. We know exactly what we need to do.

We gather ourselves up and follow Andar, who leads us silently out of the Golden Hall. We make our way down to the Transition Corridor, which will ultimately transport us to the Doorway to Terra. We arrive at the Locker Room, where our garments for Terra Embodiment await us.

We know that once we put these Mantles on we will rapidly begin to forget. We also know that all too quickly we will begin to feel the quaking of Fear: the Mass Consciousness vibration of Mondor. This is not a state that will be a "maybe." This is a definite.

Reentering the Mass Consciousness of Fear is the only way we can retrieve our Golden Lost Ones, because that is where they are. We have to go there—we have to become that. It is the only way; I know this well. We all know this, and yet now that the moment is here the reality sets in with a thud.

I reach for my "overcoat," my Mondor Mantle. Before I put it on, I say a prayer of thanks to it for enabling me to navigate my destination's terrain. I bless it with love and gratitude, and ask that it carry me through to my Heart's Desire: the reuniting of my precious Golden Lemurian Family.

I put it on. Now there is no turning back—and everything changes in a heartbeat.

Avalar's Song of Hope

As I leave the Spirit World and move steadily through many dimensions toward Mondor, I hear a crystal-clear sound wafting through the ethers. I recognize that sound and I recognize that voice: it is Avalar singing.

She is singing to all of the Golden Ones everywhere with a song of hope and a call of salvation.

"We are coming, Blessed Ones.

"We are on our way to you now.

"Soon you will feel us once again.

"Soon you will know you are no longer alone.

"We are coming to Rescue you.

"Take heart.

"We are coming now.

"We will find you.

"WE PROMISE."

THE GOLDEN WITNESS ARRIVES IN MONDOR TO BEGIN HER RESCUE MISSIONS

As I travel from my Soul State to Mondor, I am aware of moving through changing dimensions. The sensations of increasing density are newly apparent to me—different from the training practices that I completed earlier with Master Saint Germain. The energies that I am traveling through now are becoming thicker, in relation to what I expected. I recognize that this is because I am FULLY here this time.

I am getting closer and closer to Mondor. I can feel tension growing in my body, and I am becoming aware of a growing pinpoint focus, which is gradually narrowing my field of vision. It is helping me to feel clear, and I am grateful. I need this clarity, as it is directing my way.

I know I am going to Mondor to make a series of highly specific Rescues. Each of us who has volunteered for these Rescue Missions has been assigned different Golden Ones to attempt to track down, as well as specific locations to work our way through within the various circles of the H-O.

Since this is our first Rescue Mission, there will be a lot of new types of information gathered, which will hopefully make future Rescue Missions even easier. I hope so—and will soon find out.

The ride is growing bumpy now, and I can feel myself losing some of my clarity. I was told this would happen, and relax into it. I know from our training that remaining soft in the face of the Mantle's effects will prevent it from further clouding my head.

Finally, I land. My feet are on Terra, and the ground feels hard beneath them. The soil is dry, and the air arid. There is dust invading my nostrils, and a steady wind blows around me—I am in desert country somewhere.

I find my mind going somewhat blank, and I shake my head in an effort to clear my thoughts and keep my senses open. It's challenging, as I feel so foggy here. I am aware that I am a woman in my early twenties.

I look down at my feet and notice that I am wearing leather sandals. My clothing seems to be some kind of a sleeveless tunic that covers my legs, all the way to my ankles. Made of a rough kind of material, I know that this garment is not about beauty, but is made simply of what is available and practical. It allows me to move easily, and I appreciate that. I know it sounds silly, but in this foreign land I am grateful for this small thing.

Although I have a family, biologically speaking, even more importantly there is a sense of having a spiritual family of other like-minded women. I find this both comforting and amazing, because at this moment, I realize that I am here in a very dark time of consciousness. I can feel it deeply. Of course I am in a dark time: this is Mondor.

I follow this line of thinking, and immediately have a knowing that I am not only here for Rescues, but to lighten the load of this heavy consciousness and do my part to break through, back to the clarity of Golden Heart. Everything in this incarnation will be about that and in relation to that, including the Rescues. Many of my beloved spiritual sisters have been trapped inside the Web of Fear, and it is my job to bring them out. They are all lost, specific to their experience, but thankfully none of them have been fully broken and completely taken over, yet. At least, that's what I have been told—although we all know that what the future holds remains to be seen.

I hear the sound of sweet, gentle singing. I look over to where it's coming from, and see a young girl. She is my younger sister, and she is bent over a water source. Filling a large earthen jug and singing softly, I can tell she does so much of the time. She is dear to me, and we are very close. Although quite a bit younger than I am, the age difference doesn't get in the way of our joy and sharing. Our hearts are exactly the same: Golden.

Hmm. I hear that word in my thoughts, "Golden." I can hear myself having thought it, and I wonder where it could have come from. How do I know that? What exactly does it mean? I shrug my shoulders and let the question go. How I know isn't clear, but that isn't important—I simply know.

I go over to my sister, and we begin to chat with one another about the tasks of the day, the ordinary comings and goings of our lives in this time and place. We decide to head back to our house, now that the water jug is full. There are many chores yet to finish.

As I walk through the doorway of our home, I see my mother. I hear her mumbling something quietly to herself as she goes about her household activities. She is absorbed in what she is doing and doesn't seem to notice me at first. I spend a moment just watching and welcoming her in my heart. I know and love her deeply, and yet she is different from me.

I am a "God lover." I define God as all things beautiful, sacred, miraculous, and far, far greater and wiser than I am. That's simply how I know myself to be. I have always been this way, it seems. Even as a young child, I was aware of the sensation of a reverence inside of me. I don't know where it came from, as my mother, sweet as she is, has never been this way. She is often lonely and somewhat dulled in her affect, like there is a slightly grayish cloud around her.

My sister and I, on the other hand, have always carried some kind of special light inside of us. I guess we were just born that way. I talk about this feeling of reverence whenever and wherever I can, and to whoever will listen. I know there is risk in doing this, because people may think I am not right in the head, but I often cannot help myself. My heart opens up like a fountain bursting forth, and my mouth starts talking like it will never stop. I listen to myself sometimes, and am amazed.

"Where does all of this come from?" I wonder. And then I forget about myself and look into the eyes of the people to whom I am speaking. I see how hungry they are. I feel how alone they feel. It's obvious to me that they have been looking for so long for something that would comfort them and give them a greater reason for living. Our time and life are not easy. We all need something that propels us forward, that moves us and inspires us—especially the women.

I am lucky. I hold something deep within me that I know is very special. It is a secret that I want to share. I know that many of these women around me don't feel this way inside, and yet I also know there IS something special within each one of us—within all of us. How come I know it and they don't? I don't know, but I just know the difference between us. I can feel how lonely, lost, and often empty they feel—like their Souls are dry somehow, just like the soil and air around us.

I recognize all of this in those around me, and I know that my words of joy and beauty are like a soothing balm that feeds them and gives them hope—more than hope. Somehow, it is changing how they are feeling about themselves. I see and feel that. It gives rise to their own Light within, somehow. I know the impact that I am having upon them when I share so deeply, because I see they are growing stronger in themselves. In this way, I know that I am a Leader, and I feel deeply responsible for that.

And yet again, as I stated earlier, this is a very dark time. I am literally at risk because I am different, and that danger is compounded when I speak with others. I also know of the risk that these women take in coming to listen and share with me; the danger of spending anything longer than mere moments with me.

The governing authorities of our time and place don't like this. They watch all of us, all the time. Those who stand out are perceived as a threat. They want to keep us all subdued; they want to control everything and everyone.

I often ask myself, "Why do I continue to speak as boldly as I do?" And then the answer comes to me, again as clear as day. For me not do so would feel like dying. I, too, am hungry. I am hungry to feel this resonance and reverence pouring through me. This is my Soul speaking. This is my Soul, loving and sharing what is right, what is good, and what is beautiful. I cannot hold back. I find I am unable and unwilling to do so—I am incapable of abandoning my own truth in such a way.

My younger sister is one of my most avid fans. We are careful when we speak of such things, pretending often to simply be going about our daily chatter. But when there is a gathering of our Soul Sisters, she is always there. She watches out for me, just as I watch out for her. It's intriguing to see in one so young, but then I've always known she was more of an old soul.

For a moment, I find myself wondering where my father and brothers are. I'm sure they must be off somewhere doing man's work, although my younger brothers could be busy with their friends. I am not close with them. We are quite different, just by virtue of our genders. There is definitely a distinct difference between the male and female roles in our culture and society—the males dominate, that's the way it is.

In any case, I know I have a job, a purpose, and a specific gift to give: to touch as many of us through my heart as I can. My heart is that of my Soul, it is my Heart of God: that's what I call it. And now, I also call it Golden, because that description was given to me and fits me perfectly.

Time speeds forward, and I am in another time and place.

I find myself hurting now. My body aches, and I'm exhausted and spent. It's been another hard night of searching for my lost loved ones. Several of my Soul kin were trapped by the authorities a long, long time ago. These are the main Rescues that I came here to specifically fulfill, and the time has come for me to take action. All things are ready, and I can feel that clearly now.

What troubles me the most is that I have already spent so much time traveling around, searching for these lost ones that I came here to find, but their exact location continues to elude me. This is not a good sign. I am aware that I am going to have to go deeper inside the labyrinth to find and Rescue them—and it is becoming more and more complicated the longer I wait.

My senses tell me that the time is getting closer to when the inner doorways may be impenetrable, and I would like to get my Loved Ones out of the Web before they are completely lost to themselves. If there is any degree of heart awareness that is still alive and well within them, I will be able to get them out physically—otherwise, it will simply be a Tagging process which, while adequate on the one hand, could cause more suffering than necessary. It seems like it has taken forever for me to find them, even to this point.

The Veil of the Web is dense and consuming, obliterating my clear focus and ability to locate while staying centered. The signal-receiving capacity needs to remain clear, but the Web can cause distortion, rendering those centers useless and immobilized—until they are no longer available. Then it's like being lost in a hazy maze, with all the senses becoming blocked.

I stop and stand still for a moment, allowing myself to find a silent space deep within. I center my focus and ask my inner wisdom, "What do I do now? Where do I go from here?"

I take several deep breaths, and feel my sacred centers responding. Something shifts, flexing to open and receive. I open still more and listen. I wait patiently.

A vague sense and sensation of my Loved Ones rises up in me. Where are they, exactly? I know in this moment that they won't hear or feel me at all, but God willing, I will hear and feel them.

I pray once again, "Dear God, my dear Reverence in Me, show me now where they are. Enable me to locate them, so I can bring them home. If this is their calling and their destiny at this time, then may it be so. I am here for them. May this Rescue be successful."

I feel a strong urgency to shut down all of my outer senses and literally curl up close to Terra. I move away to a quiet spot behind some trees, where I know I will not be seen. I sink to the ground and ask my Mother, Terra, for help as well, "Where are they?" I ask. "I am here. I am listening."

Suddenly, my heart center opens and begins to vibrate. It's not so much my whole inner sensory system, as it is focused solely in my heart. It's like a natural water spring that opens out of a rock bed. It begins to stream forth from me, and I know that it's as though this loving heart "water" is actually doing the locating. I feel it searching. I feel it listening and responding to signals on the other end. I have never experienced my system working quite this way. I marvel at its integrity, wisdom, and intelligence in this moment. I know that I am being gifted, right here and right now.

My inner ears are activated as well. I can hear something. I can hear sounds, human sounds. I soften inside and open still more. The sounds become more obvious to me. I recognize them as sounds of pain. They are soft wailings that are gradually getting louder and clearer to me. I know that it is my kin, because I know the flavors of those voices. I am momentarily overjoyed that I have connected with them, but at the same time, my heart is breaking; I can feel their pain as if it is my own.

They are lost—I had no real idea of the depth and breadth of it. I am able to feel and sense clearly how overtaken by the Web they have become. They are overpowered by FEAR, and I know that this is not a good sign. It means that they are even more deeply lost in the Web than I thought. I know that it has lured them in somehow. It has sucked them in, and they are unable to control any of it. Their minds are fogged, confused, and jumbled. Foreign to themselves and to me, and more and more "brain dead," they follow robotically: utterly controlled by those in domination.

I find myself praying now with greater yearning. I KNOW that if it is their destiny to be brought out of the intensity of this Web, then it will happen. If not, they will be Tagged and will recover further down the line of their history. I say to myself, "Is it possible this freeing up could happen now, dear God? Is there any way this can be? Show me. Help me, I am listening."

I feel God responding to me. Instantly, I am being pulled into the Web myself—this wasn't quite what I had in mind!

I cannot afford to lose sight of myself in all of this; without a clear sense of self, I am useless to them. I hear my inner wisdom speaking to me, "Move through it. That is the only way out. Go into it, and become as one with those you seek. TRUST. Trust in your own God center."

I know there is no turning back for me. My heart clearly feels strong, courageous, and undaunted. This is what I came here to do, and this is what I will now do to the best of my ability. I have a knowing that God is on my side, that some kind of freedom awaits us all.

So, I let go, I do not resist; I surrender to that which is pulling me in. I surrender deliberately and consciously.

I am tossed, turned, and tumbled in a fog of amnesia. Perhaps it is the loss of many memories that are floating around in this vaporous miasma. Maybe all of this amnesia is the lost mind and memory of our loved ones. Whatever it is, I am not comfortable. I dislike being so disconnected. It's a very strange sensation. For an instant, I flash on a voice from somewhere that once said to me, "Breathe. Recognize the DIFFERENCE between what is you and what is not. Acknowledge this. Witness this. Do not fight it. Witness it and BREATHE."

And so, I breathe. I breathe like there is no tomorrow—great, big breaths, slow and steady. In so doing, things start to clear. I am better able to see the contrast between my inner Center, and that which has enveloped me and is pressing in on me; pinning me down, turning me upside down and inside out.

"Hello," I say to this energy, and find myself almost overwhelmed by even that. It is all I can muster, but amazingly, it seems to be enough.

I see it, and it sees me. We are different, co-existing in this very moment. I stay true to this course of positioning. How did I learn to do this? I haven't a clue. I just know that right now it's like old hat to me. Thank God.

I continue to travel further and deeper into this vaporous, hazy fog, this sticky Web. I notice that whenever I even begin to form any mental judgment about it, it tightens and becomes heavier and more devouring. I stop that, as it clearly does nothing for me.

Instead, I hold the position of "Hello," and that seems to make the intense power of it slide off, relieving me to a large degree.

And then, all of a sudden, out of the blue, I physically feel the BREATH of those loved ones I am seeking. Oh my gosh, I am that close to them! They must be right here. But why, then, can I not see them?

I hear and feel them just fine—but why can I not SEE them?

My eyes are all clouded up, and I didn't even know it. I was trying so hard to see clearly, and I realize now that my struggling and straining only blocked my vision. I take my attention off my eyes for a moment and turn to my nose.

I can smell them. I can SMELL my loved ones. I can also smell the toxic, noxious odor of what I now know is fear. This FEAR is like an entity that is alive in its own right; writhing, leering, and undulating in front of me. On the one hand, it is the ugliest thing I have ever seen. On the other, I know that if I make that judgment about it, it will grow stronger and more massive, more devouring of this space, place, and everyone in it—including me.

Instead, I stop my thought process and simply say "Hello" again. Fear doesn't know what to do with that. It hangs there, undulating still. It doesn't get bigger or smaller. It just is.

I take my attention off of it, as I recognize that I am not here for it. I am not here to change it or do anything about it. All I need is my clear-sightedness back, and all the rest will take care of itself.

With this understanding my attention comes back to my eyes. "Dear God," I say. "Please help me to see clearly." Suddenly, I see a beautiful Being emerging through the fog. She feels so familiar to me—I don't know why or from where, exactly, but she is so familiar that it is like a flame bursting open inside my own body, my own heart. I feel suddenly GOLDEN.

She whispers to me like a soft song, her voice is that melodious. *"I am Avalar,"* she says. *"We are Golden Family. I am here to honor you."*

I become aware of a great Presence right next to her, yet another exquisite Being—masculine, and steady like a rock. *"I am Andar,"* he says to me. *"We are here together to witness you in this great moment. Everything is ready. Do what you are here now to do, with all of your heart."*

And with that, ALL of my senses—including my eyes—become crystal-clear, as if no fog or veil had ever even existed. A space of complete clarity opens up, and I can see at least five of my dearest ones right here in front of me. They are bent over in their pain and emotional gripping of their souls and psyches, but I have found them. Yes, I HAVE FOUND THEM!

My Heart Center opens fully and gushes toward them in jubilation. I know I need to love them more gently now, in order for them to receive me, but for a moment, I simply cannot help myself. I am so glad and so happy. I know they are suffering right now, but I also know that soon they will be free from this. They are momentarily startled by me. It is enough to jar them awake, and I see the fog and blankness in their eyes gradually lifting. They RECOGNIZE ME. Brightness begins to move into their eyes again.

It dawns on them what is happening as they realize what this means for them. Suddenly, with a great burst of joy, their own hearts stretch wide open to me, their energy reaching out, aching and yearning to connect.

"I love you, beautiful Golden Ones," I say to them all. "I honor you. I honor your beautiful Golden Hearts."

Instinctively, the pure radiance of my Golden Love pours through me and into them. It penetrates their hearts and Souls, scooping them up and vigorously fanning the Golden Flame within their hearts—strong and clear, bright and bold. Their Golden Hearts quicken; they start to vibrate and glow. They become luminous and radiant with Golden Love, shining powerfully as Golden Light. They look like splendid Golden Jewels, shining forth for all to see and receive. They have COME HOME to themselves. They have been Rescued. I know this, and so do they.

I know that no one else but our little group can see us right now. No other energy can disturb this in any way. We are in a completely protected vortex, out of time and space. Avalar and Andar are sheltering us all. They are standing strong and clear, letting me do my job, letting me fulfill my vow and my purpose. Their honoring and witnessing of me right now makes me strong. It makes me know that I am viable, valid, and REAL. It confirms that what I am doing is actually happening.

We all move together physically now, huddling in a group, merged and breathing as One. We inhale the scent of our loving—savoring it, finally quenching our thirst for one another and for the union of our little Golden Family right here, right now. We stay huddled in this way for a few minutes, quietly and deeply engaged, oblivious to all else.

I become aware of Avalar and Andar's steady presence again, and they are signaling to us to move out of our little huddle and gather ourselves for what is next. I feel the strength of their love for me and for us all.

I refocus and turn my attention back to my five beloved ones standing close with me. I know that we are not out of the woods yet.

"Walk away now," Andar says in a loving but clearly commanding voice. *"WALK AWAY, AND DON'T LOOK BACK. JUST KEEP WALKING."*

I take the lead, and together as one body the six of us turn. Drawn forward, we are propelled, compelled by a sensation of energy that is palpable. We are in complete Golden Protection and complete Golden Direction.

I know that Avalar and Andar are standing back, waiting to see us fully leave. They are holding the ground for our safe and expedient exit from the Web. They are holding the space of possibility for the absolute completion of this Rescue Mission.

I focus only on walking purposefully now, on holding strong to these beautiful bodies that, for these moments at least, are in my charge. Once we are freed from here I will let them go—but not until then. I strengthen my grip on them, knowing that this is necessary. It may be too tight, but it is way better than where they were.

We keep walking, and walking.

Gradually, the air begins to clear somewhat. I recognize that we are emerging from the fog, the haze, and the Veil of Fear. It is a changing of the state of consciousness. The location may be the same, but the consciousness is different.

Finally, we come to a clearing and my legs start to slow down. All must be well, otherwise this wouldn't be happening. We all stop together, just breathing for a moment.

I hear two beautiful voices whispering alongside each other in my inner ear, *"All is well. You are all free. Go forward, and do what your destinies call you to do. Blessings, Golden Love, and great Golden Thank You."*

I know it is Avalar and Andar talking. I reach back to them for a second, touching them with my everlasting gratitude. I know that this has been a Golden Team effort in every way. I am moved by it all, and deeply relieved.

The six of us stand here, holding hands and remaining close for a while longer.

Finally, we are all able to stand back and really look at each other. What beauty! What love and joy we behold in each other's faces. We all have tears in our eyes, rolling down our cheeks with abandon. We thought this moment would never come.

FREEDOM!

We inhale it. We totally absorb its sensations within us right now. Freedom is ours again.

FREEDOM IS OURS AGAIN.

There is simply no sensation or feeling like it. We are all GOLDEN CRYSTAL-CLEAR again. We breathe this, and we breathe this some more. We are shining, and we are bright. We are fresh and renewed and clean. We inhale the scent of this freshness and savor it with all of our might.

We stand here quietly, in complete and total Golden Love. Our hearts are completely flooded with gratitude.

After a few moments, all of these sensations gently soften down, just like we knew they would. They are not gone; they have simply been pocketed deep inside of us for safe keeping and further growth. We know instinctively that we cannot shine our brightness outwardly in Mondor in the way that we would love so much to do—not right now, anyway.

Yes, our Golden Consciousness is alive and well and free again. But in this location of Mondor, we need to remain judicious and wise about revealing that openly.

As these five beautiful women look at me now, I know how precious I am to them—as they are, and always will be, to me. We give each other a giant hug of gratitude and love forever. We will never forget this.

It comes time now for us to disband and go our separate ways. We each have further tasks ahead of us, and further Rescues to make.

Now that these five beloved ones have been freed, they know even better how to free others. This will be their natural gift back to the Golden Heart. Each one Rescue one; once Rescued, Rescue some more.

We each go off in our separate directions with joy in our hearts.

As I walk away, I have a pure and deep elation pulsating through me such as I have never known—or perhaps I have at some other long-ago time. It is a sense that my wholeness is restoring and strengthening, and that I have done right and done well. I have done all of it to the absolute best of my God-given ability.

Yes, I have succeeded. Yes, I have triumphed. Yes, I have fulfilled a piece of my sacred vow fully.

I have learned a lot along the way, and will use it all wisely in the future. I pause and give thanks to God, to Avalar and Andar, to the Golden Grace, and to our One Golden Heart. Thank God I am aware of this. Thank God I can so fully love and feel love in return.

GREAT BLESSINGS FOR THIS DAY!

I move forward with a spring in my step and a song of Golden Hallelujah in my heart.

⌘

Dear Reader, you may be celebrating with me right about now. But you may also be saying, "That's great, but it was only five Golden Ones that were Rescued."

And I say to you, "Yes, but that five will beget how many more Rescues? It all adds up, you know. We do our best and let it fly forward from there."

As I said earlier, "Each one Rescues one. Each one Rescued, Rescues some more."

Again, it all adds up. It is truly a steady journey of perseverance and faith. Keep going for it fully, and our "One Golden Heart Whole Again" is inevitable.

Native American Rescue

I am a young Native American boy, about eleven years old. I am standing with my feet planted firmly on the ground. I am keenly attuned to my beloved Terra. She is my true Mother and I love to feel my feet walking upon her. I can sense her voice and energy coming up and throughout my body with every step I take. She fills me with her loving nourishment, and I feel vitalized and strengthened by her. I feel that her blood is my blood; we are one and the same, she and I.

I know that, as a tribe, we are all intimately connected with Mother Terra. I also know that my relationship with her is obviously different from the others; my entire life and Being are one with her. She is precious and personal to me, and I feel like I can never get enough of her. I love her deeply, and she loves me back in the same way and more. Whatever I need, she is right there for me. She is my joy, my peace, and my companion; my playmate, my heart, and my soul. She guides me and watches out for me always. I know this.

I spend a lot of time outdoors, of course. We all do. But for me, I need to go off by myself a lot of the time. I am definitely a loner. I realized early on that I am not like the other children. I am somehow quite different from them, and I know it's my unique connection with my beloved Terra that makes me so.

Every morning when I wake up, I wonder what she and I are going to do today. How is it going to be? I am eager to be with her—communing, playing, and being delighted by her ever-amazing miraculous creations. She makes my heart strong and joyous.

I belong to a tribe that is exquisitely beautiful and harmonious. We live a quiet, gentle life, and things are simple for us. It is one harmonious flow, joy-filled and flourishing. I have a mother, a father and several brothers and sisters. I am definitely the quiet one amongst this happy, raucous group. I love them all completely, and I know that I am well loved in return.

My family and friends seem to respect and love that I am different. They consider me special. They know that my depth of connection with Terra is a gift not just for me, but for all. They call me "The Gifted One," and they both honor this and do their best to foster it. All in all, my life is good. It's sweet and simple.

Time moves forward now. I am older, about twenty or so. As a grown man I am strong, well-muscled, and tall. Agile, nimble, and athletic, I carry a bow and arrow on my back. While I know how to use it skillfully, I find I don't relate to it all that much. My focus remains on the deep communion I have with Terra. It is from her that I draw my strength and well-being.

As I am walking through the woods at this moment, I can hear the sound of the trees, leaves, and creatures, all in communion with me. My life continues to be full and filled with these communications and sensations. However, right now, I seem to be worrying too. My awareness tells me that something is about to change for all of us, but I don't know what it is. I just know that it is alarming me from deep within, and making me feel agitated and uncomfortable. I know that there are many people in my tribe that are worried, and I worry about their worry, because that is not a good sign.

I continue on with my walk in the woods, disturbed, as I think about all of this. Suddenly, I stop dead in my tracks. I am acutely aware that there is something very wrong. I look around and see nothing out of place here, but I have an intuitive knowing that back at our camp, something dreadful has happened. I have to get back there right away.

I start to run as fast as I can. Alarm bells are going off inside of me, and I can't get there fast enough. I am panting heavily. As I come out of the woods toward the open pasture where we've been living for some time, I stop suddenly...frozen.

A horrible sight plays out in front of me. I see my people being viciously brutalized. Gut-wrenching screams are rending the air, and there is bloodshed everywhere. I see many white-skinned soldiers who are viciously striking at and killing everyone. It is a massacre—cold and cruel.

I try to run, to help, to save, but my feet are frozen to the ground. Terra has me in an iron grip, and I cannot move. She is commanding me:

"Stand still, right here. Watch this. You need to see it all. You need to know; you are the Witness."

I freeze, stuck like a stone, helpless and powerless. I cannot move; therefore, I cannot help. Not only that, but I cannot even close my eyes or my ears to the sounds and sights. My system is making me watch it all. It is all being indelibly printed in my psyche. I am stunned, and I am shocked. I am completely horrified.

Somehow, in the midst of all this pain, my sight draws me to two Braves standing on the outskirts of the scene. They are from another tribe. It becomes clear to me that they were the ones who led the white man here, and I am confused for a moment. I don't understand why they would have done this. They are of our kin, albeit another tribe, but kin, nonetheless. Why would they do this?

My senses return to the scene playing out in front of me, and my shock hits me again, full force. This is agonizing in every way. I am shattering inside.

Finally, the white soldiers are done, and suddenly, they are gone. Where there were piercing screams and agonizing cries for help, now there is only heartbreaking, deathly silence. And blood. There is blood everywhere.

I remain immobilized and stunned. I don't know what to do. I don't know what to do with what I am looking at.

Terra speaks to me again, and she says, *"I am going to release your feet. Go over there now. Go over there. You need to know."*

She lets go of me, and I walk toward this bloody place. I stumble desperately amongst the bodies of my dear ones, in hopes that some of them, even one of them, will still be alive. They are not; no one is. They are all dead—dead, dead, dead.

What do I do now? My heart is numb. My senses are numb. I feel so sick inside. I fall to the ground gripping my guts, my mouth opening in a silent, anguished cry. I can hardly breathe, and my heart has broken into a million pieces. I am in agony, I just want to die myself. I ache beyond bearing.

I don't know how long I am here, but slowly I become aware that some members of my tribe are emerging from the woods and coming toward me. I realize that there are a few of the young braves and older men and women who must have fled, attempting to take the younger women and children with them—as many as they could, anyway.

As they get closer, I can tell that they are stunned and shattered, just like me. We are all in this nightmare together. Maybe we will wake up now and find out it was a bad dream. But of course, that doesn't happen.

They reach my side and we huddle together, arms around each other, numb, our souls broken. No one says anything for some time. But mixed into the depths of our despairing is our gratitude for one another. It is warm and alive.

After quite some time, we move away from the scene in the pasture and back into the woods close by. Safe for the moment, we are finally able to speak. We talk about what just happened, and share why we weren't amongst the dead as well. They tell me that they had been recently instructed by the Elders to do what they just did should our camp ever be in danger. I tell them about my experience with being frozen to Terra—gripped and positioned so I could only witness. We look at each other, not knowing why we have been the ones left here.

It becomes obvious to each of us what we need to do next. We need to attend to those who have died. We need to honor them, as is our custom, and do what we can to enable them to have safe journeys to the Spirit world. It is our responsibility to do so, even in the midst of such pain.

As numb as we are, we manage to bury our dead, to pray over them and for them. We do our best to clean up this sacred place and remove the damage of violent memories. We do what we can to bestow a kindness here, so that this cruelty can be repaired, instead of leaving it to fester here forever.

Finally, when we are all done, we pack up the belongings of our shelters and whatever else we need. We know we are leaving this pasture forever, never to return. We sweep the ground and ask Terra to help us and guide us as we set out for a new place to live. We go silently, as we each put one foot in front of the other, moving blindly toward anywhere but here.

We travel for a long time. We ford streams and hear waterfalls. There are many nights and many dawns. With each one, I feel Terra trying to restore us as best she can, soothing us and bringing us strength and comfort. But our hearts still remain heavy, buried with our loved ones back at our village.

We keep walking. We walk because our grief makes us too numb to stand still. One day, out of the blue, there is a sudden change for me. There is a moment when we come across a beautiful, bubbling stream, and it grabs my attention and holds me there. I look at it, and my awareness somehow begins to open up again. It dawns on me that this water is bubbling along as if it has not a care in the world. I see tadpoles in it, and butterflies hovering here and there. They are laughing softly together and telling me gently and sincerely to lighten up. They tell me our loved ones are not dead, they are just gone from here.

They say to me:

"Your loved ones remain ever alive and well, and they remain in your heart. Don't let your grief take away your own life. You are too gifted to not be open to love, too gifted to be closed up anymore. The light of life wants to touch you. Please let your gift back in."

In my next heartbeat I can feel my mother, Terra, opening up a door inside of me. I realize with sudden clarity that I am here for a purpose and a reason greater than myself, and greater than I know right now. The sun is shining, and I feel it warming my skin. My senses are waking up, somehow. I hear Terra say to me, *"It's a new day now. You must move forward. You are the Leader now. You are here for greater things. Let's go. This is a good home for all of you."*

I gaze around at my people that are here with me, and I see that they want someone to tell them that it is time to put their burden of despair down. It's too heavy, and it makes their steps falter. They want me to tell them it's okay to stop. So, I do.

I tell them we need to build our new life in this sweet place. I tell them that doing so will begin to ease the burdens of our grief and give us a reason to find and feel our hearts alive again. I tell them it's a new day and that we can grow strong again. We all know that our loved ones who died would want us to carry on and flourish; and we know that our beloved Terra will help us. Our tribe is still alive, and we are still able—we still have each other.

We do this. We begin to live again, as though life is our gift and living it more fully is what we give back to those we love in Spirit, and to our Creator. We actually begin to flourish again in our own quiet way. Babies are born, everyone matures, and our Terra guides us steadily throughout it all.

There is one large caveat, however, of which there is no denying. And that is, of course, that the massacre that happened has changed us indelibly. We are never the same again. We are always hyper-vigilant and aware of what can lurk around the corner. But we also can't help ourselves in another way; in our hearts we are also so in love with life that we allow ourselves to start dreaming again, to dream of the future and its many possibilities—and we make our dreams come true, as many as we can.

In the midst of all of this restoration and new birth I continue to lead the way and, as always, to live and breathe with inspiration and guidance from my beloved Terra. I am also deeply aware of many of my loved ones watching over me, and all of us, and I am grateful.

Gradually, I find that my sadness fades and my true joy begins to take a stronger hold again. There is still one thing, however, that stays in the background of my thoughts, bothering and agitating me: I think of the two Braves who led the White Man soldiers to our dwelling place before the massacre happened. I continue to be confused about why they would do this. It disturbs me as to why they would betray their own in this heartless way. What would make them do this?

I think about it often, but with no clear answer. The white man, I know, is blatantly ruthless, greedy, heartless, and hungry to dominate; I know this about him. But my cousins of native blood? This I do not understand.

I try talking to Terra about it, but this is the one time that she is silent. This surprises me greatly. She offers up nothing about this. So, here I am with this unresolved irritation that never leaves me. It's like an itch that I cannot scratch. It remains, at times in the background and at others in the fore, bothering me.

There is something about those two Braves that continues to haunt me.

And yet, time moves forward. It is another beautiful day, and I am taking a much needed walk in the woods. I have a few moments where I can slip off by myself and commune with Terra and with Nature. I sink into myself with the pleasure of it all, and take a deep breath. I love my solitude, but I don't get much of it these days with the many responsibilities as Leader, and my attention always seems to be in demand.

As I move leisurely along on the path through the trees, I become absorbed in my thoughts, pondering my role and the ins and outs of it all. I love being a Leader, and I know I am doing it to the best of my ability. I reflect on the fact that so far, all is going well, and I am pleased about this. It makes me wonder what else I can bring to my people to help us grow even stronger. I continue to amble along the path through the woods, enjoying it all enormously as I become further lost in my thoughts.

Suddenly, my senses shift abruptly. I become aware of something strange around me. I don't like the feeling; it isn't a good one. The hair on the back of my neck stands up, and my senses go on alert.

I hear some branches snapping in the trees over to my right, and I know there is someone there. I am being watched. I know it; I hear what sounds like a bird call, but l know that it is not a bird—it's a message signal.

Crystal-clear images start to flash in my mind's eye, as I know there are two people watching me. Right now, they don't know that I know they are there. They are hidden and well camouflaged. I see with my inner eye that they are not of my tribe, but they are of my native kind.

As I move forward, my senses wide open, I become aware of a familiar flavor. I can almost smell them. I realize I know these ones. These are the two Braves that I saw before at the scene of the massacre. It's them, I know it's them; they led the white soldiers to our camp.

I have a split second of indecision. What to do next? If I do anything differently, anything other than walking along the way I have been, they will know I am on to them. I know I can't run, and I know I can't stop; either way, I am dead.

My senses are on high alert, and I feel sick. Suddenly, the memory of the massacre fills my brain. The sounds of screaming—so much blood. The agony and the pain being inflicted on my loved ones fill my vision and seize my senses as if it was all happening again right now. Only this time I am not powerless. This time I am not frozen to Terra. This time I can move and do something about it.

Aggressively, I reach for the arrows in the quiver behind my back. It's a powerful, automatic response. I load up my bow, and I am ready to pull it. The game is up now.

Suddenly, I see the Braves moving out of the trees. They are drawing their own weapons, reaching for their tomahawks that they are about to use against me. We are in this moment, in this second, hovering on the edge of violence. Someone is about to die. Count on it.

And then the world shifts again—as aggressive as I am feeling, as ready to kill as I am right now, I am frozen, yet again. Oh, no. Only this time, I see I am not the only one that has been stopped dead, frozen in their tracks. The Braves have been as well.

I see them, and I feel them. They see me, and they feel me. And yet we are all frozen in position, immobilized in this time and place. Terra has her grip on my ankles again. I cannot move; I can hardly breathe. Time and space stand still. We are suspended in this moment. What is this that is happening?

My thoughts disappear. My mind is blank, and I become aware only of a sensation moving closer to me through the mists of this timelessness. It is an energy form, a Presence, a Being. As it moves gracefully to my right side, I become aware that it is a strong and vibrant masculine Presence, that his color is blue and gold, and that his energy is thoroughly peaceful and kind. I hear Terra telling me to pay attention—to watch, listen, and trust.

She says to me, *"There is something very special here. Let it happen. This is a moment for which you were born."*

This beautiful figure, this man, reaches out his hand to me, and I hear him saying, *"My name is Andar. I know you. I am here to help you, my Golden brother."*

Beside him, I see another figure emerging—this time, a woman. I see her beautiful rays of purple and gold mixing softly with the blues and golds of Andar. My instinctive knowing is that she belongs to this man and this man to her, and there's something so gentle about them both together that it stirs my heart deeply.

She tells me that her name is Avalar, and that she and Andar are Golden Ones. She shares with me that they are here to help me fulfill a promise that I had made at another time. Suddenly and softly, she starts to sing. Mixed in with her song are soft whooshing sounds, like a quiet wind blowing. It penetrates me and moves me deeply.

I become aware that all of the heightened aggression that had been controlling and fueling me so powerfully a few moments ago, is now completely gone. In its place my heart, and all its love and gentleness, is opening wide. "What is happening here?" I think to myself. "I don't understand."

In my confusion, I experience an instant of complete panic, as I realize I no longer have the shield of my defenses in place. I become afraid, as I feel too vulnerable. And yet, I cannot stop my heart opening. I cannot stop falling into the love of it.

Avalar keeps singing, my heart keeps opening—and I keep falling into it.

Soon, I feel a wave of Golden Energy filling up my chest. It's bright, alive, intelligent, and magnificent.

Avalar stops singing and says:

"Golden One, Andar and I honor you. You are so beautiful. Your heart knows what to do next. We are here to witness you. You will all be set free from your pain."

She points to my heart, and then she points to the hearts of the Braves still standing frozen, close by. Avalar continues:

"Look inside their hearts, and what do you see?"

I look at the Braves, at their faces still frozen in a grimace of aggression. I look into their hearts and in each one I see a faint, but clear, flickering of a Golden Flame. I see that these small Golden Flames are like pilot lights that have been inside them always—potent and alive. The Braves have been completely unaware of them, but they have been there, nonetheless.

As I continue to look at these Golden Flames dancing and pulsating, I find myself becoming mesmerized as images of their histories open to me. I find my gaze shifting first to one Brave, and then to the other. They both show me now that they were once Golden Hearted Ones, alive and radiant, strong and clear in their strength and passion. Then, they begin showing me the opposite, as their stories of devastating pain spill out, presenting themselves to me in vivid detail.

"I don't want to know all of this," I think to myself. I hear Terra telling me in a gentle but commanding voice, *"Simply listen, watch, and witness."*

I surrender. The heartbreaking stories of the Braves unfold, and I see both of them being taken prisoner by what feels like supremely heartless soldiers. They are violated, beaten, and tortured. They are crying, begging for mercy. They cannot stop the pain. I see and feel in their bodies and in their psyches that they have become delirious with this unrelenting torture.

It's like they are being burned inside, their hearts and their loving gentleness extinguished because of the ruthless pain that will not stop. I can hear the crackling of each of their spirits, the breakdown of their minds, their hearts being fractured, and their true natures being obliterated.

My heart opens to them in response to their agony. I reach toward them in compassion and an instinctive yearning to help. I feel their pain as if it is happening in my own body. I feel the pain of being broken like this—of being crushed.

I become clearly aware that they know not who they are anymore. They are not the Golden Ones with Golden Hearts open and trusting anymore—and they have not been, not for a long time. My question has been answered. I understand fully now how they could have betrayed us all without even being conscious of what they were actually doing. Truly, they were no longer themselves.

I ache for them. These two Braves, once so bright and brilliant, have been cruelly broken. As clarity and understanding dawns on me, I see Avalar blowing in their direction again, making that soft whooshing sound like the wind. The vibration of what she is doing is actually fanning the Golden Flames within their heart spaces.

I hear Andar telling me, *"Now you may Rescue or Tag them. You see clearly: this is yours to do. Only you can do this. We are here now to witness you Rescuing them in this way."*

My Golden Instincts take over, as if they have been waiting for exactly this moment. I realize that this was my promise, to Rescue these two lost Golden Ones so they could find their way home again. This was a vow that I made a long time ago.

I feel the floodgates of my heart bursting open with Golden Light. In its own intelligence, it reaches over to theirs with pinpoint focus, and carefully but deliberately touches the fragments of their brokenness, the splinters of their pain. As this happens, their Golden Flames inside their hearts grow brighter and brighter, as if they are being restored to their original life. Their bodies start to glow, inside and out.

I am amazed at this, truly and utterly amazed. Everything is changing.

I become aware now that my own body and Being is Golden Glowing too. In this moment, I understand with certainty that the imprints of pain, and those accompanying of violence, aggression, and defense, are all being altered and reconfigured in the three of us. It's as though it is all being moved to a new framework, based on the vibration and restoration of Golden Heart. History is changing; it's all being moved into a position of Harmony. I don't quite understand, but I know it is so.

Andar and Avalar continue to stand strongly here with me and the Braves, supporting us and all the movement that is taking place. I can feel Terra sending her fortitude up through my feet, holding me powerfully in her own Golden Love.

I look at the two Braves now, and then at myself. I see that we are the same—Golden Beings, lit up and bright-eyed, with hearts open and spirits engaged. We are vibrant with all of life and with what lies ahead, buoyed by freedom. We are all glowing together as if this is the way we were designed to be: Golden Glowing as One.

I marvel at all of this. The feeling and the sensation are far beyond anything I could have ever imagined. It is crystal-clear to me that this is precisely why I was "saved" from being killed at the massacre. I see clearly now why I had been so agitated by these Braves since then. In truth, they had been calling me. They were lost Golden Ones, and they had been calling me to save them and help them remember themselves in this way.

This was the promise I made long ago. This was the vow that I came to fulfill. THIS is what I was born for. This was my purpose in coming and staying. My destiny was to be a part of this exact Golden Moment and of these Rescues—and the shifting tides toward a new possibility of restored Golden Peacefulness and Harmony in the future.

I hear Andar speaking to me now in a clear voice, filled with exuberance and victory, "*The Rescues are successful and complete. Job well done, our Golden Brother.*"

The strength of his Golden Love pours into my heart, and I feel waves of pure joy coming into me from both he and Avalar. Their gratitude is so strong that it almost takes my breath away. It makes me feel so beautiful inside.

Andar gestures to the two Braves shining brightly, and tells me:

"*Know that they will be just fine. They will both come to the end of their incarnations in a natural way. Then they will move up and into their Soul selves with new clarity and choices. They will have their own plans for their Golden Return Home in future incarnations. The Golden Rescue Tagging that has been successfully accomplished today will ensure that this is the case. Throughout time, and their varying life experiences, their Golden Flames will lead them Home. This is now guaranteed.*

"*This is what you have brought to them, on this day. You have fulfilled your Golden Vow and Golden Purpose beautifully, our dear Brother. To you, we are all eternally grateful. All Golden Life everywhere blesses you and thanks you.*"

As I feel this reverberating throughout my being, my heart soars. I know that my eyes are bright and my voice in the future will ring crystal-clear. I feel my Soul at peace with a sacred purpose now fulfilled. I am filled with the rightness of it all. It is as if there is a well of joy that comes from deep down inside of me.

Andar steps forward again, and with a wave of his hand indicates it is time to go. I know I need to leave now, and that the suspended time and space is over.

Andar says to me, "*Golden Brother, you will leave first. You must walk away now, and don't look back. Just walk on. We will take care of the rest. Golden Godspeed.*"

Instantly, I feel the grip of Terra loosen on my ankles, and I know she is about to propel me out of this vortex of suspended time and space. I know that in some ways it will be as if none of this ever happened—and in others, it will remain a constant and continuous soothing Golden Balm in my heart and in my Soul.

I know I have done something profoundly right today, and I know it has changed me. I know it has changed the two Braves. I sense that even the reality of history past has changed, now altering future possibility—all of it for the good, all of it for the Golden Good.

Abruptly now, Terra turns my body in another direction and pushes me off. *"Time to go now,"* she says clearly. *"Just walk, and you will know when the time is right to stop."*

I'm walking. I keep walking with purposeful strides, knowing that soon I will arrive at whatever location she deems right. I know I am being moved out of that suspended space and that I am crossing a dimensional bridge that will take me back to the direction of my tribe.

And then, suddenly, it's as if my normal everyday senses return to my awareness. I hear birds again; I see the leaves fluttering. I hear the sound of a stream bubbling; I see clouds floating through a beautiful blue sky above. There's a spring in my step, as Terra continues to propel me forward.

Finally, she brings me to a standstill a short distance from home. I see that no one else is around, and I am grateful for that, because I suddenly feel an aching need to drop to the ground and press my belly to hers. I need to feel her heartbeat through mine. I need to hear her speak to me about what just happened. I need to know, from her, that this experience was real. I need her to confirm this for me.

I move to the ground and stretch my body out on top of hers. I feel good, strong, and alive. She begins to speak to me, moving through me with her voice and her energy in a way that only she can. I listen to her and receive her with all of my Being.

She begins to tell me of the space that is possible wherein beauty lies and loving reigns. She speaks of new ways of being, responding, and understanding:

"Violence only ever begets violence only ever begets violence—no matter which end of it you are on. You must trust that there is another way, and that it is only through this other way that freedom, for you and for all, can happen.

"Now that you have witnessed and experienced this movement back into Golden Harmony, you know that this is possible. In the past, it would have seemed like an impossibility to you, but now you know differently.

"Golden Heart is capable of great things. Harmony is its nature. Honor this, and you will witness how this automatically changes your life each and every day. Give it its due. Hold strong to all that you have just been gifted, and witness the motion from this that can indeed alter all the lines of history, carrying forth a new way into the future lines of life to come.

"This is the way of true freedom—for you and for all Golden Ones, every-where—Golden Peace, Kindness, Gentleness, Understanding, Love, Compassion, and Forgiveness. This is what the human heart has longed to remember.

"As this progresses and takes hold again, all of history will rise to meet it. The Golden Imprint will live and thrive here again."

I know that what she is telling me is beyond my capacity to understand fully right now. As she so often does, she is steering me into a future yet to be revealed. But I know it will come. This dream of Golden Harmony will become an ever-increasing reality—someday, somehow.

Terra concludes:

"My Dearest One, know that what has taken place today is not only real, but quite important as well. Let it wash through you in the days ahead, and gradually you will see an even clearer picture of it all. For now, just let it percolate. For now, celebrate. You did a great job today. You fulfilled your Golden Vow with great love and courage.

"I thank you, my most beloved. All the Golden Family everywhere thanks you, forever."

And with that, I bless her for her words and kindness and get up, finally ready to go. I know it is time to return home.

As I head back toward my tribe, my heart is so full of Golden Love and Gratitude that I feel like a giant fountain ready to spill over. I am sure everyone will feel it, and that brings me joy. I love being a Leader—and especially one who has been graced with this much love to share. It is bigger than me, so much bigger than me.

My Golden Heart sings, and I know that all is better than it has ever been. I feel healed, Golden Healed.

BIRTHING RESCUE

I am a woman, standing and waiting in a dark, damp, dirty underground cell. There are torches hanging on the walls, and the light is playing off the beads of moisture that are dripping down from the ceiling. It is quiet and eerie, and the air is filled with tension. I understand why.

This cell has been set up by the Heartless Ones as a "delivery room" where the pregnant women prisoners are brought to deliver their babies. On the table right now is a young woman who has been in labor for a long time. We have all been waiting patiently for her delivery moment to arrive.

I am watching the midwife help her. Standing next to the midwife is a soldier who is here to monitor the situation. We all know why he is here. If the baby is a girl child, this soldier will be the one responsible for taking this child and literally doing away with it.

The Heartless Ones have put a ban on female children. No more are to be allowed to live. This is the way of it, period.

I am here to save this child, no matter the sex, and her mother as well. In fact, we all are.

All of us in this room are playing a part, appearing outwardly to be various members of the H-O when, in actuality, we are well-camouflaged Golden Ones. We have found our way here by stealth and secrecy, and we have succeeded in duping the H-O with our scheme. It has not been easy, but so far so good. We excel at what we do, and having already made many Rescues, we have learned well how to hide and mask ourselves in order to accomplish our missions.

And here we are again.

Our plan is to Rescue both this mother and her child and take them back to safety. We live here in this dark time of consciousness, with the Mondorian heartlessness governing everything and all of us in one way or another.

As Golden Ones, we are constantly in varying levels of danger, and we know it. This particular Rescue team that I am a part of is well aware that we continually need to hold ourselves as close together as we possibly can. If, for some reason we separate and become isolated from one another, that is when the veil of fear and forgetfulness will fog us over entirely. The Web of Fear will suck us in and disable us even more than it already has. After that, we will start to completely lose the memory of who we are and why we are here. We have done several Rescues as a team in this incarnation already, and we know it is imperative to stick together, no matter what. Our lives depend upon it.

We don't come out much during the day. We meet at night in the woods, in safe shelters that are removed from the crowds of people. Ours is a band mostly of women—birthing sisters we like to call ourselves—who are here primarily to Rescue and care for the pregnant and new mothers and all of their children, born and yet to be born. We live in our natural habitat in the woods, and have set it up to be a safe haven of sorts. In this way, we are able to take care of the women and their babies to the best of our abilities, given all the circumstances that we have found ourselves in. So far, we have managed to stay off the radar of the H-O.

We know it's only a matter of time before they discover us. It always is, but we don't dwell on that at all. Instead, we focus on being here fully and doing what we are here to do. We have several men who are part of our group that watch out for us and keep us protected as much as possible. The babies are so important to us Golden Ones, and we place them as a top priority when it comes to our Rescue Missions.

For our particular Rescues, it is our teamwork that enables us to be successful at all. Other types of Rescues by the Golden Ones are done more independently, depending upon the circumstance, but that isn't the case with any of ours. This means that we need to stay united as one body all the time, and we have. We all need each other greatly. We depend upon one another and are linked by an indelible bond of trust and Golden Solidarity. It's the Sisterhood, plus the few men who watch out for us, that fuels us, feeds us, strengthens us, reinforces us, and enables us to be strong and remain clear—as clear as we can in this foggy, dense H-O terrain.

We know what the H-O are up to. We have been here before, and will be again. So far, we have been able to Rescue a number of the expectant mothers. Locating them before they were close to delivery, we brought them into our nesting place so that they could deliver their children with us. But there have been some mothers that we have not been able to Rescue. They have simply been too closely guarded in captivity. The H-O are keeping them that way because they are hopeful that they will deliver male children, who will then be taken and raised as H-O warriors over time.

Right now, the girl babies are apparently expendable. This particular Rescue that we are making is of a young mother who is masterfully skilled in the art of birthing and healing herself. She is a great wise one, and knows only too well what might be in store for her child. We are eager to bring her back into our fold—as we are with all of the lost Golden Ones. She has been a prisoner for quite some time, having been captured during an earlier Rescue attempt herself, and we have been following her whereabouts ever since, hoping for the chance to get her out of the hands of the H-O. We were hoping to Rescue her before her baby was born, as it would be much easier to get her out. But that has not been the case.

Back in the cell, I am intent on finding out how our young mother is doing inside her psyche. As I watch her, I can see that she has significantly lost her memory of herself and become disconnected and blank looking. I know that she has been cruelly treated and become yet another Lost One, wounded and almost broken by the H-O. I can only imagine the details. It is the enormity of the soul pain that emanates forth from her that makes my heart weep. My soul reaches out to touch hers. I know that she doesn't know I'm here to help her right now, but soon she will. I am grateful that this may mean the end of her misery.

I know that part of our Rescue here will not only be to ensure that her baby remains safe, but that this beautiful woman be restored to her Golden Heart once again as well. The latter part is my job. I know I won't have much time to accomplish my mission after her delivery, but I'm going to do my absolute best. We want and need her to come back to us—as we do with all the Golden Ones. That is our only purpose in having come to Mondor at all.

I say a prayer for Golden Safekeeping for everyone involved in this mission. A short while later, our young mother delivers her baby, and indeed, it is a girl child, just as I had suspected it would be. The midwife finishes the delivery with expert hands, and the baby is passed to the soldier, who immediately leaves the cell. Somehow, he will make his way to our forest hideout, and I will see him there soon. It is my job now to bring the mother out.

I walk over to her and gaze into her eyes. She is tired, spent, and sore. She looks at me, and at first, her gaze is still blank and empty, but then slowly it dawns upon her who I am, and she smiles weakly in recognition. She knows me, and we have a strong bond together that goes way back. I look into her heart, and see that she has been weakened greatly and that her sense of herself has begun to be compromised by the H-O.

I am acutely aware of the presence of possible danger for both of us, and I know that time is of the essence. I take her hands in mine and look deep inside her heart, reaching into her as far as I can with my love, gentleness, and compassion. I speak to her softly, "I know you have suffered greatly, my beloved sister, that you are worried about your baby and her life as well. I know that you yearn to be free of this place, and that is exactly why I am here. We have taken your baby to safety, and I am here to get you out as well. I am asking you to trust me. Trust me with all of your heart, please."

She looks back at me, and I know that some part of her registers exactly what I'm saying. I am relieved, because I was concerned that perhaps she might have lost herself too much already to be able to be even this clear. But then I remember that she has made Rescues herself, and that she brings that instinct to the situation.

She nods her head and begs me with her eyes to free her from her lost self within. Without her determination and will to survive, we will not make it out of this Web in one piece. We both know this.

I place one of my hands on my heart and the other gently upon hers. I close my eyes and begin to breathe, deep Golden breaths which come from deep inside my Golden Core. I feel my Golden Energies rising up, soaring through my heart, right over into hers. I feel them touching her Golden Flame and making it quiver and pulsate, reigniting it again with power and deliberation. I hear her catch her breath and then steady herself, as she feels her own life force kicking into gear again. I open my eyes, and she is smiling at me—this time with renewed life and vigor that is no longer asleep. I see the beginnings of fierce determination, coupled with an opening back into remembrance and reconnection. I am thrilled. She is recovering herself more quickly than I had dared to hope.

I know we have to go—now. We are out of time, and I know it. I pray that she is truly ready for the trek ahead of us. I reach for her, and she leans into me. As she does so, I become aware of another presence that has come into this room. I quickly glance over to see who it is, and smile in total relief as I recognize our beloved Andar and Avalar. They are such a welcome sight. Hallelujah!

They stand next to me, holding the hands of our sweet new mother firmly in theirs, and breathing deeply into her body and her entire system. They breathe their own Golden Life Force and fortitude directly into her, and she slowly finds herself able to stand upright on her own. She is wobbly, but at least she is up. Seconds pass as she somehow grows strong enough to become steady. As quickly as possible she readies herself, telling me that she is able to make our exit. She knows that time is of the essence.

Andar and Avalar move with us for a short way and then stand back to ensure that we will make it safely out of here. They have wrapped us inside a Golden Cocoon of Love and Protection, and I know that all we need to do is to keep walking and moving with forward momentum and focus. They will take care of the rest.

My sweet friend, this new mother, is sore and still very tired, but also extremely determined. As she leans on me, I find physical strength that I didn't even know I had. It comes from the certainty that somehow all is well and will continue to be. I trust my faith and my instincts, and am grateful for the path of Golden Safety that has opened up in front of us. We are directed and propelled further and further outward, until finally we are free of the maze.

Gradually, the air begins to clear and my senses become lightened. We are still in forward motion, and my sister's weight is making me falter a little. She is losing strength quickly, and I pray that we will make it the rest of the way. Somehow—I don't know how—we manage to do it.

Finally, the momentum that has been propelling us so fiercely begins to slow down, and I see that we are near what looks like our beloved forest home. Oh, I am so glad! My spirits rise, enabling me to take the last weary steps toward home.

We are both tired, but buoyed, as we finally enter back into our little camp. We are greeted warmly by the love and tenderness of our sister clan. They take charge of our new mother, bringing her straight to her new baby. At last, I know that it is alright for me to let down my guard and take care of myself. It has been an arduous and nerve-wracking undertaking, and I am relieved and grateful to be home with everyone, safe and sound. I go off alone to rest and recuperate.

Out of the blue, I hear the energetic voices of Andar and Avalar soothing me, telling me all is well. They softly congratulate me on a thoroughly successful Rescue and expedient journey home. I feel their love and gratitude permeating my heart as they let me know in a soft whisper that soon they will come join us for a ceremony of thanksgiving and blessing for the newest member of our Golden Family and her sweet Golden Mother. They encourage me to relax, and allow the Golden Healing to restore me, as it knows so well how to do.

Later on, we celebrate. We are all overjoyed at the return of our fellow sister and her baby, and it feels great to be together again. Our numbers are growing stronger, and this is important and gratifying.

We dance together tonight as we rejoice in the bonds of our Golden Sisterhood. I feel loving hands joined with mine, and as I look up at the night sky, I am eternally grateful for all of us. I know that we must never let the female spirit die. I know that the feminine nature in all of us, in men and women alike, is the birther of all Golden Creations. This must be kept alive, activated, and strong, so that it can deliver its gifts forward in all of its miraculous ways and forms. Without it, our Golden Way will not survive, much less ever flourish again.

Here together, we attend to the feminine power, constantly receiving and honoring its vast wisdom and intelligence. We do our best to keep it strong and vital, to support and nurture it through our Beings and actions on a daily basis. We each know our responsibility in this, and we give thanks that we can foster the birthing of life, both physically and energetically. We love what we do. We love our Golden Feminine Natures and our abilities to birth in all ways. We love our Golden Family.

This is our Life. At its Center is our One Golden Radiant Heart, alive and well, right here.

As our celebration winds down the night deepens, and the moon rises. I hear the gurgles and squeaks of new babies in the background, and I smile quietly to myself. I give thanks to my Source and to my Golden Heart. I know that at least for now, all is well, and I can sleep.

Golden Goodnight.

RESCUED BABY BECOMES A RESCUER

I am the girl baby that was Rescued in the Birthing Rescue. Even as an infant, I knew I would grow into a woman who makes many Rescues in her own right, precisely because of that.

My mother has told me the story—many, many times—of when she and I were Rescued that night in the delivery cell. She told me how a special group of Golden Ones disguised themselves and made their way into that bleak, heartless place to save me as I was being born.

Each time she tells me the story, it fuels me somehow and makes my blood tingle. I know I will become a really strong Rescuer myself when it is my time to do so. I can feel this knowing, and my future success, in my veins. It is a destiny call that empowers me—right from the start.

I recognize that I am here in this place called Mondor, but I also know that it is not where I belong. I am simply here as a visitor, knowing full well who I am as my true self. I know I am the heart and soul, spirit and being of Lemuria. I just know it. I am a Golden One. I have managed to keep a very strong and open connection with my Golden Fuel, even though I am here in the midst of this discordant consciousness. It is turbulent on this Mondorian terrain, and quite difficult for any Golden One to traverse. I have come in the hope of not only making Rescues, but also to be a clear voice of Golden Remembrance for all the other Golden Ones around me.

I intend to remind them that they ARE, in fact, Golden Ones; that no matter how much they may have lost sight of that, or how disconnected they may have become, this is their truth. I want to help them to keep an even stronger hold on this Golden Knowing, because I know they need it now more than ever. Many of them are growing weary of being here.

I am a strong one. I am Golden Crystal-Clear inside of my Being. It's simply the way I am built. And, because I am a Lemurian, I am naturally a Sensitive: aware of everything. I am acutely affected by the constant bombardment and jangling experience of being here—it is so noisy and turbulent, chaotic and disharmonious. In fact, it is completely out of harmony with life.

In that way, everyone and everything is wounded in varying degrees, relative to who they are. The constant noise and discord of this upset creates great pain. It is jarring and bruising for the Golden Ones—and for all Golden Life, period. We all feel it, and it has an effect. In truth, there is no way to be inured to this. All around me are Golden Ones who have become more and more lost because of it: they are numb and unable to feel their sensory systems.

I am aware that they've become overwhelmed by the deafening clang and pain that they feel here, as well as what they've had to watch and hear about. It is a constant assault for the Golden Ones. Acts of brutality and heartlessness are soul crushing for us, and, here on Mondor it is a continuous, unrelenting thing.

What I observe is that many Golden Ones just can't stand it anymore. It has bruised, bombarded, and beaten them until they cave in and shut down. Others have tried their best to "wall up," if possible. Most of them can't, but they try. How do you build a defense against this kind of interfering onslaught, this kind of "weather?" It's like being in a storm of garbage all of the time; it is a corrosive and ultimately eroding environment that eats away at the purity of the soul, at the psyche and the light. Sometimes it's a vicious blow, and at others an unrelenting yammering, hammering, chipping away that goes on and on.

This is what it is like here. If I was to write a newspaper article about the experience of the Golden Ones here, this is what I would say: this is the name of the game in this kind of terrain, and we knew it before we came. We were as prepared as we could be, but there still remains the actual doing and experiencing of the reality. How do we cope, other than flailing around, caving in, and being wounded both inside and out? Our systems take a beating with this kind of jarring heartlessness. Our systems suffer.

I see the Golden Ones doing their best to stand strong, and they certainly can to a degree. They can weather this—and we can get our job of Rescuing done—providing we are reminded of the pure strength of our organisms; to be reminded of the truth of who we are, and to realize that what feels like suffering inside is actually only on the outer periphery of us. We need to remain clear. We need to avoid over-identifying with it and becoming it, and see that it is only an effect, and not a reality. Not for us.

We are Golden Beings: bright, strong, and clear. If we can hold on to that as much as we possibly can, we can weather anything. We can get on with going further and deeper into this maze of fear, and succeed in locating and saving those that are crippled and broken. We can do our job of getting in and out to complete this process of Rescues. And we need to be reminded that we are not broken—as many times as it takes. That's the truth.

We are strong and powerful, and we have what it takes to do this, even though the Mantle of Fear has darkened our memory of who we are. As much as I understand this veil, I know that nonetheless we came here with enough self-connection to do this, otherwise we would not have chosen to do so.

The truth is that our hearts are completely devoted. It is our vow to bring our Golden Family home, and our vow is invincible. It is our fueling force. It is medicine, and it is food. It is the grace and sanctity of who we are. It is our love.

It is precisely our heart, power, and purpose that drove us to come back to Mondor—and it is that which sustains us each time we return. Someone else might say, "You've got to be crazy to go there." And yet we say, "Crazy or not, we're going, because this is where we've got to go to get the job done and bring everyone home to restore our Golden Sacred Configuration. This is where it all happened, and this is where we've got to be. We've got to make it work."

So, we keep coming back. We continue to ask ourselves to travel through this terrain of contracted consciousness, which is based on heartlessness and fear. We know that we simply have to walk through it to get to where we need and want to go, no matter the circumstances we meet, no matter what happens to any of us who are doing the Rescues.

Although it sounds crazy, we don't really care what happens to us. The priority is to return everyone to the fold again. Yes, we all know that we're probably going to face a difficult demise. We knew that before we came—what else can you expect from heartless consciousness? Nobody is looking forward to that. I'm not saying that. But we carry within us the ability to meet even that challenge, believe it or not, and to bring forward all that we are, to carry us through those difficult—and what could be perceived as totally unconscionable—assaults.

We are fearless; we do not know fear. It has been said many times that fear is not in our design, and that is the truth. We are strong, and we know exactly what we are doing—and exactly what to expect. We know who we are dealing with, we knew all of that before we came. But our Golden Ones are lost and stuck, trapped inside the Web of Fear of the Heartless Ones—and we are here to get them out and bring them safely home to the Golden Consciousness, period.

I'm just a young child, and I know all of this; or rather, I may look young, but I am not.

I grow, maturing into a young woman. As I said earlier, I am a real sensitive—of course, and thank God I am. If I wasn't a sensitive, I wouldn't know anything. I wouldn't be able to feel how my loved ones are feeling. I wouldn't be able to help; I would be as blind as a bat. What good would I be then? Why bother coming? Of course, I'm sensitive. I am, in fact, highly sensitive. I am masterfully sensitive, and I love this about myself.

It is something that gave me tremendous joy in Lemuria, and enabled me to realize the full range of my gifts and abilities. This was true for all of us. Our sensitivity was highly developed, and we were there and involved in the Lemurian Project largely because of this refinement and ability. My role was that of Birther. I was one of the leaders of the Golden Birthing Clans, and they called me the "Baby Caller." It was the sensitivity of my Golden Instrument that I relied upon the most, and which allowed me to commune with those incoming souls prior to conception. I was the one who was able to provide the proper and necessary Golden Runway for them to come in on.

But I digress, and can tell you more about that at another time.

For now, I simply wanted to say a few words about how the power of my sensitivity serves me. I would like to offer that, yes, in a place like Mondor, it is this same sensitivity that can make such a journey even more challenging, because much of the input is so toxic. Quite literally toxic, it can clog up my works and make me sludgy and crapped up. I have to constantly keep an eye on this. My state of being and wellness is entirely dependent upon detoxing my sensory systems. I do my best to hold the image of a bellows pushing out that debris, so that I am not becoming inundated in the crap storm.

Moving forward…

I have been a busy woman. I have successfully completed many Rescues so far, and there are still more to go. It's getting tiring and exhausting for me to be here. I am aware that soon my Rescues, for this lifetime, will be fulfilled. I take a deep breath, and dig deep within myself for sustenance.

As I do this, I can feel my Golden Heart alerting me that it is time to get on with the Rescues that are now ready for me. My task is to focus on a handful of pregnant women who have been trapped deeply inside the Web, and who have forgotten, to a large degree, who they are. And yet, growing life inside of them in the way that they are is actually something that keeps their Golden Creative Juice alive and connected to their psyche.

But it's a stormy ride, and they suffer and worry greatly. It is all so confusing, and they don't know what to do about their babies. I realize the question could be asked, "Well, whose babies are they? Are these babies from the Heartless Ones?" My answer to that is no, they are not from the Heartless Ones. These women were taken when they were already pregnant, and that's why they were taken. That's exactly why they were taken. The Heartless Ones wanted to study them and keep the babies for themselves to turn into little heartless citizens. It breaks my heart to even talk about it.

As I enter this maze now, I know what to do, and I know that I am not alone in this Rescue. Avalar and Andar are with me right from the start, and there are many other Golden Ones present as well, because this is about the babies. All of us Golden Ones are precious, but the babies and the unborn babies and the carrying mothers are our most sacred responsibility. It is one which we all take seriously, and always have. It is such a privilege to receive new life, new Golden Life.

My plan is to go in and bring these mothers out. I will then return them to our camp in the forest, and ensure that the babies are born in a Golden Way—it is imperative that baby and mother alike not be compromised further.

I follow my nose as I get closer and closer to the women, and pretty soon my sensors pick up exactly where they are. I am well camouflaged, as I've done this several times now. I know exactly what to do, and how to do it. I am a strong Rescuer, and will stop at nothing to fulfill my purpose.

I continue to get closer to them, and have soon found their huddled silhouettes, which fill a small dark space that is dirty and uninviting. In the midst of the filth, fear, and horror are five beautiful bellies: round and vibrant. They are just the way they should be, and I feel good about that. The mother's faces are in stark contrast, however. Pale, sad, and despairing, they speak volumes about the deep pain of dire circumstances. Having worried themselves sick about their babies and what the future holds for their unborn children, it has become too much for them to even think about, and they are gravely distressed.

The women feel deeply alone. Yes, they have each other, and that is a comfort, but they feel utterly alone, because none of them has a single answer for what is to come. They seem to have lost their ability to soothe one another, and are isolated unto themselves—trying to survive.

I seem to have come just in the nick of time, but am suddenly overwhelmed by their sadness and worry. I can feel how lost and confused they feel, how alone they are in this cold, dirty place. As I approach them, I do so in silence. I need to be quietly present here for a few moments. I energetically reach inside of the mother's bellies, acknowledging and checking in on the unborn babies. I say hello to these growing little people. I let them know that things are going to get better now.

I bless them and blow them a Golden Kiss. They are little Golden Lights in there, some bigger than others. They begin to wake up, and to feel me. They respond to what I am saying, and forget for a moment that they, too, have felt lost and abandoned in a way. Because their mothers are deeply fearful, there has been a profound disconnect between mother and child. As a result, the babies feel abandoned by that safe, secure bond that would otherwise be present. I understand that it is all so upsetting.

After a few moments of soothing the babies, I make my presence more obvious to their mothers. I am still silent, but my inner voice reaches out to them gently, letting them take their time to recognize that I am even here. It takes them some time, because of how shut down they've become. But slowly and surely they sense my presence, and when one wakes up and looks in my direction, I look right at her, and her eyes start to clear. This recognition becomes transferred to the others, and they all start to perk up.

I see Mother Mary now, who is with me always. She stands behind each one of the young mothers for a moment and showers them with her love and support and strength. I see a protective cocoon beginning to build around us all. Avalar and Andar are standing beside me, and together, the four of us are making this Golden Cocoon more and more substantial. Suddenly this dank, dark cell becomes a beautiful and blessed space—Golden and light-filled.

Avalar turns to me and says, *"It is time for the Rescues, our Beloved One. Do what you do so well. We are here to witness you in this glorious happening."*

My heart opens, as it knows full well how to do, and my Golden Love reaches over toward these five pregnant mothers. It streams right into their hearts, lighting up their inner Golden Flames and pouring down into the hearts of their babies inside their bellies. Everything suddenly begins to burst open with this light, expanding rapidly. The babies' response is so strong that, in turn, it fuels the mother. This is how it should be. Things begin to look the way they are supposed to—pulsating Golden Cords of Love between mother and child: vibrating, feeding, reassuring, soothing, and nurturing. Everything is turning to Gold.

It is a glorious and magical experience.

I watch, misty-eyed, as I see the women remembering themselves again. Their hearts are lit up and their bodies are filling from within. Their cells are finally getting the true sustenance they need as their Golden Light moves up into their heads, then down through their arms and legs—filling their bellies to overflowing. Suddenly, they each remember that they have not been here alone and they turn toward one another, joining hands in gratitude and sharing. It is a beautiful moment of Golden Mother Love gathering all around.

After a few more minutes of watching them become restored, Andar steps forward. *"It is time,"* he says. *"It is time to go. Take all of this Golden Energy with you. You will be safe and protected as you exit this Web."*

We are all eager to get out now, but we know that we cannot leave too fast. We need to be thorough in taking all of this Golden Energy with us, so that the Heartless Ones don't sense we have been here. I ask the Golden Angels to be with us, and to see to whatever needs to be taken care of properly, so we can leave this place. They tell me to breathe in my own Golden Lightness now, and that this will make everything much easier. As I do this, I know that everything is shifting, preparing for our exit.

Finally, Andar gives the signal that all is ready. *"You must all leave now,"* he says in a commanding but gentle way. *"Turn and walk away. Walk, and do not stop until you know it is time."*

As Mother Mary leads the way, I position myself in the center of these women. Around all of us is our Golden Cocoon, shielding and protecting us, propelling us forward.

We walk on...and on.

Gradually, as always happens, the air begins to change and lighten, and we feel ourselves emerging out into a much clearer space.

Finally, we come to a stop near our camp where we will soon join many other young mothers and their children. All is beginning to feel well with us, and we know that we have been delivered out of the Web and back into our own Golden Forest Sanctuary.

I turn to face these sweet, kind, gentle young mothers and we join hands. Standing in a circle, we are filled with grace and thanksgiving for each other; for our liberation, our love, and our Golden Awareness. They look into my eyes and I am flooded with their gratitude. My heart overflows back to them, and we share these precious moments of love before we all go our separate ways.

I am moved by how beautiful these women are, and by how their bodies are filled with such illumination from their little ones inside. It feels good to know that the deliveries ahead will happen in a safe and sacred place, and as close to the true Golden Way as we can all manage.

Finally, I know that I need to go. I feel Mother Mary around me, telling me that she and the Angels will take good care of these women and their babies. She tells me that it is time for me to tend to myself, and sends me off on a wave of love and congratulations for a job well done. I hear the same being whispered by Andar and Avalar, wherever they are right now.

As I walk away, I feel elation mixed with triumph and exhaustion. I am aware that Golden Joy is everywhere—right here, right now—and I am grateful to it and for it. But the truth is that I am tired; I am deeply weary. I realize that this is often the case for me these days. I have done a lot of Rescues and I'm exhausted, but it is a good tired. It is energy well spent.

All I know right now is that I need to go. I need to leave this place and go home and rest. My Rescues are over.

THE SCOUT'S RESCUE

I am a male in my early twenties, a Golden One. I am standing on top of a hill and breathing in the toxic air that surrounds me. I am aware of feeling a strong sense of responsibility.

In this particular incarnation I am a Scout for my Golden Ones, and have led many Rescue Missions already. I have gone into many different levels of "lostness" inside the Web of Fear, and have been working my way in deeper and deeper, each one more than the last.

I work with a team of five other scouts, trading off and on as to who is actually leading Rescue parties into the Web, and who is doing the actual Rescue act itself.

None of us take our responsibilities lightly, and we are well aware that we depend upon each other heavily. Our teamwork is outstanding, and we are exceedingly proficient at what we do.

Prior to leading a Rescue party in, I have already spent a great deal of time and energy deciphering the exact location of the lost Golden Ones, and determining the safest way to get to them. The labyrinth inside the Web of Fear is intricate, and it weaves its web on all levels—not just the physical, but also the emotional, energetic, and etheric. It is a highly sophisticated and interwoven configuration.

It is all too easy for a Golden Rescuer to enter the Web of Fear so deeply that they forget who they are and get lost. They can not only lose their ability to find those they are looking for, but also to retrace their steps out once they are inside. That is one of the biggest challenges and risks of going into the deeper inner weaves of the configuration.

One has to be fully focused and clear, and know exactly what they're dealing with. The more one's senses are open, the better off they are. It is my job to essentially "canvas the Web," and decipher what these different levels of perpetration are, how they are moving and working, and ultimately, exactly how and where they are hiding our Golden Ones.

It is a fine art, and I take none of it lightly. I carry what many would consider to be a heavy sense of responsibility, but truly, it is that I completely own and understand my purpose, and am fulfilling it to the absolute best of my ability.

It demands that of me. There is no mediocrity allowed here, not that I would do any less than my best anyway, but this is a tall order job. It is one which requires excellent skills. I know this, and I am this. Every time I am preparing to do a Rescue Mission, I feel the intensity building inside of me, as a sense of heightened urgency and weighted responsibility. Even though this is a task of Light, it is very serious—one wrong move, and it's all over.

I don't feel the impact of the Golden Light until I'm involved in the actual Rescue act itself—whether as the one doing it, or standing by and bearing witness. Even then, of course, the opportunities for jubilation are short-lived, because we need to get ourselves and everyone out of there as quickly and carefully as possible—but those moments of full-on Golden Grace, although brief, are deeply sacred.

Uplifting, empowering, and exhilarating, I am gifted by them and further motivated to sustain my purpose, even though there are many risks involved.

I know I am a great gift to the whole Golden Family. It is a blessing for me to be able to do my utmost in making freedom a reality for us all. It is a privilege to be who I am, able to accomplish as much as I can.

The Rescue that I am about to make is of at least one Golden One, although I hope it can be more. It is of the original scouts from our Lemurian Emergence that have become so lost that they have actually been thoroughly broken. They are now identified as Heartless Ones themselves. They have been manipulated, brainwashed, and rewired in a certain way so that they now believe, think, and behave as H-O themselves. This is tragic but true.

They have absolutely no memory of any of their Golden History or who they truly are, or even any connection to any active heart-consciousness. This puts them in an entirely separate realm, and asks something completely different of me. This is the tallest order that I've had to fulfill, and the probability of making an actual physical Rescue is extremely unlikely. We will see how it is when I get in there, but I am hoping to accomplish a Tagging, and maybe even more than one.

It is time to go. Nothing more needs to be said about who I am and what my life has been so far.

I am strong and clear. I am on purpose, and am going in alone this time. This is my choice. I feel that I wouldn't want to bring anyone else with me into this depth of the configuration of darkness. Several of my Golden Family on the outside know that I am going in, and if I don't come out, they'll know what happened to me. It won't be pretty, but they'll know—and it will just be one of us who has been compromised, instead of several.

I go in, knowing this risk. I am completely aware of the possible danger in regard to my own well-being, but I need to do it. It's who I am. I feel compelled; it is a deeply personal need for me to step up with the skill set that I have developed, accomplish this task, and fulfill this purpose—because I know that I am capable of doing it. I am one of the few who can.

As I travel deeper into the Web, I am passing through all of the stages and levels I have been in to lead and make Rescues so far. It feels like I'm on a train, and the scenery is passing me by quickly. Because it's such familiar ground, I know what it asks of me.

At last, I arrive at the very last place that I was able to reach previously. I stop and pause for a moment to regroup, and to check everything in myself and ensure that I am ready to move forward. I become aware of the energetic presence of Master Saint Germain. He is on the edge of my peripheral field, and I instantly take a deep breath, glad to know that he is so close with me on this job.

I see him giving me the thumbs up, and I feel his message impressing itself upon me. *"All is well,"* he says. *"We're all together in this. You can do this. You are well prepared."*

I love this Being. I am so grateful for his encouraging words and strengthening presence, right here and right now. I drink it in like a tall glass of water. It focuses me even more and steadies me for the trip ahead.

I am ready to move forward. I activate my energetic sight similarly to how it would be if I actually donned a pair of night vision goggles. Now I can scan the area to see who is here, and where, and to learn what the H-O energetic frequencies are doing.

The H-O have their own scanning frequencies that are all geared for two things: the first pulls Golden Ones in, and the other keeps them out. Contradictory, I know, but true. Either way, I cannot risk being seen or sensed.

I make my way in and out of the H-O's range, skillfully maneuvering my body and my own frequencies so that I am not detectable. Soon, I begin to hear the footsteps of H-O soldiers—loud, thumping, and noisy. There are a number of them here.

I am aware that I am close to some kind of a training camp for the Heartless One's soldiers—but it's not only a training camp, it's also a command center. I am deep inside the Web of Fear now. This is where the apparatus of the Heartless Ones operates: it's their operations center. I have never been in here before. As I scan and observe, I am shocked. I feel my blood running cold. They are so thorough—far beyond what I had perceived. In its own way, it is remarkable.

I am aware that the H-O seem to have every aspect of daily living of the Golden Ones covered. They can see all the people. They are in command, in charge, and can see everyone going about their business. Wherever they want to target to see something more closely, they can. They have their eyes on everyone.

Seeing it right in front of me like this, up close and personal, renders me speechless. It shows me that it's real, and shockingly so. I take a deep breath, and steady myself fully into this understanding. I can handle this. I'm not here to argue with it. I accept it, and can subsequently proceed accordingly. My shock gradually lessens, and I become clear again.

I take a closer look. One of the main things that I become acutely aware of now is that the H-O will stop at nothing. They simply will NOT STOP. This is who they are. This is what they do. They have no compunction about doing this, absolutely none. They don't feel it. They don't have conscience; they don't have caring or heart. And furthermore, they don't seem to get tired, or need any of what we would consider rest periods to restore themselves or balance any of this out.

They are like machines. They go on and on, and will continue to do so. Realizing this so clearly almost takes my breath away; the reality of it is profoundly extreme.

If I wasn't who I am, recognizing and admitting the ceaselessness of it all would make me spin—spin completely off my center. That would be it. It feels like it could take over my mind and my mental structure. It's so thick, hard, and completely unrelenting. It is full of motion, determined and automatic motion. It could completely catapult me right off my center. In this moment, I understand all too easily how this could happen.

But I am who I am; I draw deeply on my skills and manage to remain clear and unaffected. I continue to observe and, again, I become aware of Master Saint Germain on the periphery, holding a steady space for me, a balance point. And there are other ones like him doing the same. I thought I was here alone, but now I see and feel that I am not. Apparently, this is turning out to be a group Rescue. There aren't other Golden Ones here with me physically, but there are other Golden Supports and Assists, energetically. This is an extremely important piece of work. It has taken us a long time to get to these lost Golden Ones, and finally we are here. In a way, this is the end of the line.

I keep watching and sensing, and the H-O continue not to have any idea that I am here. I have been able to completely camouflage myself and my radar and, thankfully, they don't see me or even sense that I am right here in their midst.

Over to my right, I begin to pick up the signals of something different. I scan the area and recognize the presence of Golden Heart energy. It is faint, but obvious, and I can see where it is coming from. Four of the soldiers over there are actually broken Golden Ones. It becomes clearer to me now.

I watch them as they go about their business. They are doing their jobs, just like machines. They have no consciousness of anything but that—no clue about anything else.

One of these four soldiers stands out in particular, and I would say that he is the most lost. They are all lost, of course, but he stands out as the most extreme. If I can Tag him, then Tagging the other three will be automatic. It will happen easily, just by entrainment. He is the one who is the furthest and most lost of all of us, so he is the one I need to focus on, first and foremost. He represents that piece of our Golden Weave that absolutely must not be left behind. He needs desperately to be brought home—without him we will never be whole.

For a moment my own heart aches for him. It aches for all of these four, but in a particularly painful way for him. I find myself feeling intrigued by him and my gaze deepens. Suddenly, it dawns on me that I know this man well. It has taken me a little while to be able to recognize him through the machinery he has become.

My remembrance of him becomes stronger, and my thoughts go back to our original Lemuria. I knew him when he was a Golden Scout Leader. We frequently worked closely together back then, and we became brothers because of it. He was a dear friend of mine. At the time of our original emergence out of Terra, he was the one who went out first. He volunteered, and was chosen to be the First Scout.

His courage was immense, and his clarity and skill were highly developed and greatly respected. We all entrusted him with the job of being the first one out; to scope out what was going on, to report back, to shepherd us, and to be the leader of that initial emergence. We loved him dearly, and he was quite special.

He had done scouting far and wide, even before Lemuria. That was his job and his skill set. He was a true explorer by nature. When the decision to birth Lemuria was put into action, he was the first Scout to travel her terrain for all the rest of us to follow. I can only imagine how extraordinary that must have been for him, to be the first receiver of her in that way, at that time. He must have been filled with Terra's welcoming and beauty, as she showed him who she was and what she could bring to him and to all of us.

He would tell us some great stories about all of that—he knew things that the rest of us didn't, as we all did about our own aspects of discovery—but he would tell us amazing stories about when he first walked through Terra's forests, came upon her waterfalls, and saw her rainbows. He was the first to be touched by her in those ways, and we would listen in awe and wonder. We knew how special those first meetings were, and how those moments would never be forgotten.

We absolutely adored him. He was amazing and entertaining with his stories of adventure, so funny and full of exuberance. He was a giant of a man, with a personality and heart to match. He also had great dreams of what was to come, dreams that seemed beyond the scope of any boundary we might have considered. His was an imagination overflowing with color and creativity, rich in so many unusual ways. He was a great big soul with a great big heart.

All of that was before his own shattering happened. All of that was before he was the first Golden One to emerge out upon the surface of what we thought was Golden Terra as we had known it. But, as we now know, it had become Mondor instead.

I wanted to describe him to you in some detail, because what I see here in front of me now is so completely and radically different. I see that he has indeed become as a machine—locked inside himself, inside the Web of Fear. All traces of what I just told you are completely gone. I know they are in there somewhere, but for all intents and purposes, you could say they have been obliterated. In that way, you could say HE has been obliterated.

How the Heartless Ones could have obliterated the enormity of who he was, I do not know. I am aware that a part of me does not even want to know. However, I put my feelings about that aside now. It's imperative that I do know, so that I can help him as fully as I can.

Clear pictures show themselves to me in my inner eye. What I see is that when he had originally emerged as First Scout back onto the surface of our beautiful planet, he was spotted quickly because of his brightness. He was careful, yes. He was wise, yes. He had not extended his brightness out, because he knew better than to do so at that point, but nevertheless, it generated some heat. The H-O could spot him easily when he came within a certain range of where they were. They could sense the difference in temperature, and they recognized that he was different from them in many ways.

They decided instantly that First Scout was a threat to them, and immediately seized him. They also seized the other scouts that had emerged after him, and at this point, they knew exactly where the rest of us would be emerging as well. There was nothing to be done about what ensued. The desecration, as we have already told you, was immediate.

Now, I am shown that they took him first, and then the others, and tortured them all in ways that were beyond anything imaginable. First Scout was, as I have said, a very strong person—a deeply centered and highly skilled Golden Man. The H-O went to work on him, and there were several different directions that they tortured him from. Some of it was physical, and when that didn't break him, they went to the mental. And when that didn't break him, they went to the psychic and the emotional.

The bottom line is that they hit him from every single angle, and he stood strong for a long, long time. He withstood this torment, because his Golden Heart was so strong. He would never, ever utter a single word.

He never said anything, and would not tell them about our people in any way. And yet, somehow, they made him believe he had betrayed us all. He never did, but he came to believe that he did. This was part of their brainwashing and their tormenting manipulations of his psyche.

They kept First Scout alive so that they could continue studying him. They pulled him apart like he was a laboratory animal, trying to figure out what made him tick; what was his story, what were his secrets, were there any mysteries? They worked on figuring out how to get into his head.

In his battered and weakened state, they brainwashed him mercilessly until they made him believe that he had betrayed the whereabouts of all of us and had told them of our plans. They tormented him into believing that everything that happened to all of us—all the pain, suffering, and desecration of his entire beloved Golden Family—was ALL HIS FAULT. He was the one that they heaped all of this torment on, until finally he could take no more.

His spirit broke, and that was the end of him. They had robbed him of himself.

Can you imagine what this must have been like? Can you imagine what this would be like for someone, for you or for your loved ones? What future would you have after that? That is what happened to First Scout. He died a kind of living death.

There was no shred of him that was left, nothing that could be a person. Instead, he became one of the heartless machines.

Yes, he was still in a body—but it was no longer him. The H-O could now do an automatic takeover. They could make him be whatever they wanted him to be at that point; he was now one of them, as were the other Scouts that had been captured as well.

I am aware of all of this now, as I'm looking at First Scout, as I'm watching the machine he has become. My heart aches for him, because that could have happened to any one of us. It aches for him, because I know who he was, and I see that he knows none of this now. He's just an empty shell, where once there was such a great big, beautiful Golden Being.

My awareness alerts me to the fact that I must not dwell on any of this right now—that will be saved for another time. I have a job to do, and if he sees me, he will capture me. He will take me prisoner. He does not have the wherewithal to recognize me in any way, shape, or form whatsoever, except as the enemy.

How am I going to do this? I focus my sight on where his Golden Heart used to be activated inside his chest. I know that I have to be extremely careful, because if he feels my energy at all, he will sense something is not as it should be. He will sense its warmth. What he's grown familiar with is that it's cold inside of him—always cool and cold, like steel.

He considers himself unworthy of any kind of love, because he believed himself responsible for our demise. He thinks he is forever unforgiveable. That's the conclusion that he is holding inside of himself. That's the belief system that he's now got tucked away, way down in there. I feel this, and I know that this means he will block me, because he believes he is not worthy of love or forgiveness or of being Rescued at all.

I pause to think about this. I'm dealing with a lot of different complexities here. Usually, in a Tagging, there is a willingness to be touched, an eager ache somewhere deep in the heart, however small. However, because he has become like an H-O machine that believes himself unworthy of redemption, all of those doors are shut.

I pause again. What am I going to do? This appears impossible. At that moment, I suddenly flash on an image of the child that he had in Lemuria. I know how much he loved that child. He would put that child up on his shoulder, and he would parade around with a wonderful beaming smile on his face for all to see. He was completely lit up. He loved his child with a passion.

I feel the sensation of this energy with such clarity that I can almost taste it. It infuses itself throughout my whole body and moves over into his, acting like a bridge. Suddenly, I see something in his heart space opening up and I recognize that there is a small ember of light hidden inside of him. Although buried deep within him, it is there, nonetheless. It is the flicker of his Golden Flame, like a speck of electricity buried so far down inside of him that he doesn't even know it's there. And, because of that, he doesn't feel me being aware of it.

I realize that this is my entry point, and that I can Tag him by moving across this bridge of his love for his child.

I'm ready, here I go.

I am also aware of the presence of Avalar and Andar standing right here with me, watching. I feel Master Saint Germain strongly as well. I know I am being witnessed now. I know that this specific moment of Tagging is being witnessed by all the Golden Ones everywhere. We have ached for this moment. We have known it would come, and at last, here it is.

I hear Andar saying to me, *"We honor you. Do your job that you do so well. We are witnessing you now."*

In that moment I feel a huge Golden Cocoon opening, enlarging, and encompassing me, First Scout, and the other three scouts that are with him. It is a supremely quiet space. You cannot hear a sound—not even a pin dropping. It is just pure Golden Light enveloping us all—sparkling, glistening, and glowing. I focus my gaze intently on the First Scout, inside of his heart, inside of the love he has for his child. My heart opens to that wave of sensation, and immediately, the Golden Love moves directly from my heart over into his. It travels deep down inside of his system by its own intelligence and locates the flicker of his inner Golden Flame. As soon as it touches that Flame, his true Golden Heart becomes ignited again. It doesn't burst open or anything like that, but it becomes intense, concentrated, and potentized.

As this is happening, I see the same thing occurring inside the other scouts. Because they are all linked, it is able to move from one to the other by osmosis. I watch in wonder as they all light up inside. They still don't know it's happening inside of them, but I do. It is beautiful to witness.

I take a deep breath, because I know that we have finally hit home base. In some way, this is the end, it is the completion of the Rescues—not that there won't be more to Rescue, but that we have gone to the deepest depths. And now, over time, all the rest of the lost Golden Ones will be much more easily Tagged and physically Rescued, whenever possible.

It is all going to be much easier from now on. It is as if the Golden Circle of Life is restored and has been made whole again. There is still much work ahead, but we have managed to call home all of the most missing pieces.

I know that these four scouts will find their way back home over the course of their own time and their own history, as their Golden Consciousness gradually moves back up into the realm of their physical awareness. Who knows how long it will take? It doesn't matter. Their Golden Flames have been rekindled and reignited. Because they have been Tagged, they now know somewhere inside of them that they are no longer alone, that there is a path home to Golden Wholeness for them—even for our beloved First Scout who has believed himself forever unworthy and unforgivable. He will find his way home to Love; they all will. It is guaranteed.

I linger for only a moment more, offering up a prayer of Thanksgiving. I am thrilled that this has been successful. I know we all are.

I also know that I must leave here now. The job has been done, and it is time to go. Right on cue, I hear Andar's voice, strong and clear. *"It's time to turn yourself around and walk away, and just keep walking. We will take care of the rest. Job well done, our dear Brother!"*

I feel Master Saint Germain's energy literally propelling me out of there. It's as though I am on a fast train to freedom again. As I go, I do my best to leave behind all trace of that depth of the Web that I have just traveled in. I take some deep breaths as I taste the air gradually clearing around me, and I glimpse a ray of daylight.

Finally, I am brought to a standstill beside a clear stream running through the forest. I become aware of beautiful Golden Angels moving me gently into the water, and I hear them singing all around me. Their voices are exquisite, and they soothe me right down to my bones. I feel myself being completely cleansed and cleared of all debris from my trip, with all traces of residue dissolving.

Gradually, I feel my full joy returning as the weight of all that energy finally lifts completely, and I am thoroughly restored and refreshed anew. I am so grateful. That was a load!

I am exhilarated as I splash the cool water onto my neck, shoulders, and arms. I savor the sensation of my wet feet and ankles, of my toes wiggling into the wet ground beneath the water. I feel as if I am glowing with Golden Goodness, and I am truly and deeply happy.

I know that I have been an integral part of a great and most important undertaking. Tears well up in my eyes and roll down my cheeks as I register what just took place. Those lost scouts are not lost anymore. They don't know it consciously now, but they will. I am incredibly happy for them, and for all of us.

I am eternally glad that the mission was successful, and equally relieved that it is now over.

I know it is going to take me a little while to integrate what took place, to let it find its way in my own psyche and heart. It was a big undertaking, and I am exhausted from it in many ways that will continue to reveal themselves.

Now it is time for me to rest. Peace in my soul is mine now and I am enormously grateful. We are truly on the path of regaining our One Golden Heart. Golden Hallelujah for us all!

THE SECOND SCOUT TELLS US ABOUT HIS RESCUE

I am Second Scout, and one of the four soldiers that was Tagged only a few short moments ago.

I want to tell you my story as well, because it is extraordinary. And, as a result of you reading it, I will be witnessed and confirmed. You may not believe some of what I say here—you might think it is all too good to be true, but it is true, every word of it. This is how greatly the Tagging has changed me already—and, because I was Tagged, something even more extraordinary is now possible.

But first, let me paint the picture of how things have been for me up until now.

I am stuck in a cold, hard place. I don't even know that I'm stuck, because I am a machine. I do what I'm told and go where I'm told. I have the ability to destroy; to hurt, disable, and disarm. I don't feel anything personal about any of it. In fact, I don't even know how I'm having this conversation, because these words of emotion don't mean anything to me. I don't have any emotions, I am a machine; I do what I am told to do. I am a Heartless One—a soldier, and I am controlled by other Heartless Ones who can maneuver me in any way they like.

I am one hundred percent obedient to them, because there is no other option. I am their robot, so to speak, and I don't pay attention to anything else, because there is nothing else that I notice. I know that some strange people have been inside our Web for a long time, and that they continue to maintain a presence.

They do their best to hide from us, but eventually I find them; that is my job.

I search out and find these funny little people, these people with feelings. I don't understand or care about them at all. My job is to simply take control of them physically. I get on with doing what I've been told to do, and when I encounter opposition I simply use brute force. I use whatever physicality is necessary and whatever tangible weapons are available, so that I can bring them down and keep them down. End of story. That's all I know, and that's all I do; I am very good at it.

There are other soldiers as well who attend to aspects of control and enforcement that are more mental and psychic in nature. Their job is to lure these odd people deeper into our Web, and to make sure that they stay in a state of mental and emotional distress at all times. The other Heartless Ones excel at constantly confusing the strange people's brains, at scrambling their psyches and manip-ulating their emotions. They are very good at what they do, and the results are nothing short of amazing: these odd little people have been rendered useless, mixed up, and totally at our mercy. They have been turned into cowering pawns for us. The point of it all is that we are able to maintain our control of them at all times, and in every way. Fear is our greatest ally; fear is our ace in the hole.

As I explained earlier, the physical enforcement aspect of this is my particular forte. It is what I do, and do well. I am an excellent fighter, and can hold my ground and outdo anyone at anything in this arena. My stamina and perseverance are unequaled, my focus is razor-sharp and clear, and my determination unwavering. It's simply the way that I am made.

My daily routine is dull, boring, and empty. But of course, I don't know this, because I am a machine—what do I know, except what I am programmed to do?

And then, in an instant, all of this changes.

I would like to talk about the Tagging now. I am conferring with a group of fellow soldiers about our latest plans when I see a flash of intensely bright light. It is golden in color and so bright that it startles me completely and causes me to jump back a step. I watch, and wait to see if it will happen again, but it doesn't. It is so peculiar—I have never seen anything like it.

I want to see more of it. It was such a contrast to the dull gray atmosphere that surrounds us here.

I have absolutely no idea what it was, but something inside of me became radically different. I don't know how, exactly, but whatever happened defies explanation and has changed everything.

It has made me feel quite odd inside. It shocks me to even use the word "feel," because I don't even know what that means. It is all astonishing. Has my machinery been rearranged or something?

I look at one of my fellow soldiers and I see that the same thing seems to be happening to him. I find myself getting even more wobbly, and I don't like it. I don't like it at all. In response, I command myself to harden up. I may not know what it is, but that's how I deal with this sort of thing; I just make it go away, so I can proceed with my orders.

That is that. That is the first part of the change in me.

Following that experience, I decide to leave the other soldiers and get back to my job. I am walking along the pathways of the terrain that I live in. I walk these same pathways every day checking, guarding, and making sure that the way is clear of those funny people. I go about my usual routine, but soon become aware of something in my sight line, a blip on my radar that shouldn't be there.

It is something warm, which is a temperature that is not one of our own—

so I know that it's one of the foreigners. As I come upon this funny person, this foreigner, I notice that it is a female. I know it's my job to do what I can to take her out, or at least take her prisoner. I'm about to call in for specific instruction, but something about her stops me.

I don't understand it at all, but suddenly, it feels as though she is somehow moving her warmth, her actual body temperature, inside of my chest. I have no idea what's happening to me. My whole world is starting to spin. I've never experienced this sensation before, and I don't know what to make of it. Normally, I would be instantly reaching for defensive or offensive tactics, and she would probably do something to resist me. We might have a short struggle, but then it would be over. I always win—always. I dominate—always; it is what I am programmed to do.

But this time, I find that I am suddenly immobilized, and that she is just standing there looking at me. She seems to have no fear. I am surprised by this. I see no fear in her, and she is not shrinking away from me. She is simply standing there, looking at me, not making any sound at all. And then something inside of me is changing again, I find that I'm actually feeling sick inside. I've never felt sick inside. I find my balance is unsteady again, only much more so this time. I've never been shaky like this. I find shortness in my breathing, and I have never even noticed my breathing. I find I literally cannot move.

She continues to stand still, just looking at me, as if she is seeing right through me. What do I do now? My mind is suddenly swimming with images, and I begin to have feelings swirling around inside my chest. I hurt. Why is all of this happening? Why is my chest hurting? I don't understand—I feel so uncomfortable. I feel like my steel skin is going to start cracking any second and that the steel armor I wear, and count on, is going to simply break apart into smithereens.

She starts making a strong whooshing sound now, deliberately focusing all of her breath right into me.

As she does this, it moves straight into my chest, causing more rumblings and generating more and more heat until it fills my whole body. It is beyond anything I can control. The truth of the matter is that it feels good, and that is the very reason that I am so distressed. What now?

It is making my insides feel like they are unraveling and coming apart, and the heat feels like it is literally causing me to melt. I am losing all that remains of who I was, or who I thought I was.

And then she speaks:

"Golden One, beautiful Golden One. I am Aliyah. You don't remember who I am right now, but we were dear friends in days gone by. I know you, and I honor your Golden Heart. I witness you. I know the beauty that lies

inside of you, and I am here to help you remember. I am so sorry for all of your pain. I know how lost you are."

At her words, I collapse completely. I don't know what she's talking about, but I break. I just break. I can almost hear the sound of it—all these pieces of me crackling and spinning themselves away. And even as that is happening, something else starts rising inside of me, something strong and determined—and it won't be denied.

Suddenly, vivid images are flashing in my head of another time and place. I feel like I am actually there, I can see and hear shouts of anger and screams of anguish. There is blood everywhere; it is a massacre of people and Terra alike, and the pain and suffering are destroying her very surface.

I feel stunned. I don't remember ever hearing such cries. There are many, from different forms of life. I feel a heart inside of me that is greatly wounded; it is mine, it is huge, and it hurts.

I see myself standing there in shock, frozen and helpless. I am powerless to do anything. I cannot stop the death and destruction. I am failing my people. I am one of the strongest Scouts, and yet I cannot stop what is happening here—and now my heart is broken.

The images continue on in all of their gory detail. I see myself as I am taken prisoner, as I am brutalized by these machine-like creatures. I am being held against my will and abused viciously, and the cruelty knows no end. I have no control. As strong as I have always been, I am no match for these robotic people who don't seem to care about anything except the darkness of their cruelty and desire for power.

I see clearly now that I became one of these heartless machines because I couldn't stand it anymore. They tortured me until there was nothing left of me to fight back: they broke me, and I literally became a non-person. There was no ME left.

They took my empty shell and made me into one of them. Since then, I have done many horrible things. I don't know if I can ever set that right, but it's most peculiar that I would even want to. I've never thought these things before, and I don't recognize myself right now. I'm a great big jumble of confusion.

I am aware that I feel completely lost in myself. This woman, Aliyah, who stands in front of me now, is certainly right about that. I am utterly lost. I look at her eyes. They are like bottomless pools that show her great depth. A faint memory of knowing her from somewhere begins to take shape in the back of my mind.

She is looking at me with obvious recognition:

"My dear Golden Friend from long ago. Your Golden Goodness runs deep. I

know this about you. You have helped me many times, and I am extremely grateful. You have gifted me greatly, and now I am here to gift you back.

"You are not yet ready to come with me, but you have shown yourself ready to receive me and let me back into your own Golden Heart. In a few moments this meeting will end, and it will be as if it never happened. This is not a day for taking me prisoner. I am here to grace you and tell you that I witness who you are—all the Love of your Golden Heart and all the Beauty of your Golden Being. Everything else is not truly you, and never has been.

"Over the course of your future lifetimes and experiences, you will come to understand this again. In these few precious moments together, your Golden Heart has been ignited, and someday you will follow that and find out what it means.

"You will indeed come home to us all, my dear friend. I love you dearly; we all love you dearly. You are loved, and we are One Golden Family. Someday you will know what all of that means again; someday, some time, some place...until then, know that you have been found. Know that you are no longer all alone.

"Golden Godspeed."

And just as suddenly she is gone. She simply disappears—she's left me. What can I do now? I can't go back and I can't go forward. I realize, for the first time, that I am stuck. I am quite aware of this sensation. I'm not the machine that I was, but I'm also not the Golden One that she spoke of. I am so far from that.

All I know is how to fight, and yet, my fight seems to have abandoned me. It was my strength, the very thing that I have always relied on—being cold, hard, and aggressive was my way, my only way. Now what?

I don't know where I am going from here, and I still don't know why this is happening. I can feel a tidal wave of even more emotions rising inside of me. All these feelings—they're way too much. I don't feel strong anymore, not like the indomitable man I used to be. Instead, I feel exposed and vulnerable.

It's obvious to me that I am wounded, and indelibly so. Even in my present state, I can see that. But the thing is, I can't handle knowing about it; it's too big. Even just thinking about it starts a fire in my belly that would eat me alive, and burn everything in its path—the fire and fury of being so viciously brutalized, the fire and fury about all those that I loved being massacred, the fire and fury of all the pain that's been buried inside of me for so long. I would never be able to contain it. But I also realize that rage would be better than feeling this intense heartbreak that could crack me in two.

I don't know about all this. I feel utterly bereft in this moment; adrift from myself. And I am tired. I am tired of all this "me" that has woken up. I cannot abide feeling the enormity of this pain inside, not for another moment. I consider just walling myself off from it, building barriers around it, burying it deep, deep, and deeper still, and hiding it completely from myself. Numbness would be preferable to all this.

As I'm in the midst of thinking all these things, and doing my best to figure out a way to survive this, I become aware of two Beings standing close by me. They're not really physical, more like strong beams of light and color. I feel that they are there watching me. I am so lonely right now that I lean toward them without giving it a second thought.

They are steady as a rock, their energies strong and clear. One of them begins to speak:

"Beloved Brother, my name is Andar. I am here with my companion, Avalar.

"We know your struggle right now, and we are here to help you, and to witness you in these next few moments. Know that you are not alone, not ever, even though that is how you perceive yourself to be. We understand this. We know and understand you.

"Yes, you are right: everything has changed in you. You have been reawakened, deep down inside of your core. Your Golden Flame of Being, your Golden Heart, has been reignited and fanned. It lies there waiting for you to receive it fully.

"It is for you to decide whether you wish to do so or not. It is for you to decide and choose how you want to proceed with your heart. Although it is painful right now, it can lead you to your new path and show you the way forward, if you so choose.

"A choice, Golden One, is yours now."

I hear his words, and I can feel a reverberation inside of my heart space. I begin to feel a softening and smoothing out of all the questioning and confusion of a moment ago. Believe it or not, there's actually something comfortable and comforting about it; this is new. My identity as a machine is definitely leaving me now. What is replacing it? I'm not sure yet. I just know it's good, and that it's me. Although I understand that I am being given a choice here, the choice seems obvious. I like the warmth—in retrospect, I never did like feeling so cold.

As foreign as this situation is, I am aware that it all feels so familiar. It starts turning my thoughts toward yet another surprising direction. I start to think about a possibility of maybe, someday, being able to set my weapons aside completely, and perhaps discover a new strength and skill in myself that eclipses the lure of power.

It makes me think that perhaps I can put down this tremendous weight that has shackled me to despair. It makes me feel that maybe I can let go of this feeling that I failed—this feeling of tremendous responsibility, of guilt and self-recrimination; this blaming of myself for not saving everyone and for losing myself.

I become aware that just thinking about it this way begins to lighten me up somehow. This is followed by the sudden recognition of how bad I feel and how deeply sorry I am for all the pain that I've caused other people. I was in so much pain which, ultimately, led me to cause others harm. It's hard for me to bear, knowing what I had become as a machine—knowing what I did. I don't know what I'm going to do about all of that. What can I do to make it right? Is it even possible? Is there any chance of forgiveness at all? That's a tall order. I don't know. And yet, something inside is compelling me to think about it.

I do know that there are many others like me; many others that are lost because of all the torment that they suffered, so many others that were broken just like me. I ponder this for a moment, and suddenly a light goes on inside of me, and I become clear. I hear myself saying, "I want to help them. In fact, I vow to help them. I vow to help all of those who are still lost like I was. That is what I dedicate my life to now. I've been there, I understand, and I know it well. This is how I can begin to make it right. This is what I choose to do. This is my choice now."

I suddenly feel strengthened again. There is something that I can do with all of this, something I want to do with all of this. I make the decision that I am going to help, not hinder. This is my choice from now on.

I don't know what, where, when, or how, but I will do my best. I will do my absolute best. This, I know.

"We hear your thinking," Andar says, and there is a smile in his voice. I am aware that there is a smile starting inside of me, too.

"This is a choice you make, my Golden Friend, again and again," he continues. *"There will be many opportunities, many times and places that will give you a chance to fulfill this vow and, through this, to lead and to find your own way Home. You will have blessed yourself in doing this, and so many others will be blessed back into their true selves because of you.*

"We witness your vow today, and we are proud of you, Golden One. Welcome Home to that which is your birthright. Welcome Home to Golden Heart. Follow your path, and you will know exactly which steps to take and when. We love you. Golden Peace."

I feel their love touching me deeply in my own heart. This is brand new, and it rocks my world in a great way. Then, suddenly, they are gone. They disappear, leaving a trail of brightness and warmth in their wake.

And here I am, yet again on my own, but I don't feel alone this time. I don't feel alone at all. My heart is here with me. I know this now.

This is my story, dear Reader. Does it still sound too good to be true that I would be able to start changing from a cold-hearted machine back into someone who actually CARES? I'm surprised, but then, well, I guess that's the power of the Golden Heart at work.

I know I still have a long way to go, but I am determined.

The Oracle Rescue

I am in a dark underground cell. The air is damp and cold, and I can hear the distinct sound of water dripping methodically nearby. Rodents are scurrying across the floor, disappearing into the hidden corners. Besides them, I am the only one here. I can feel the dead weight of a heavy chain gripping my ankle. I can't move.

As weak and immobilized as my body seems to be, there is so much turbulence going on in my head that it's making me dizzy. I feel like I am spinning, as if I could literally fall off my own feet, even though I'm not even standing. I am being bombarded with gruesome images, words, sounds, and sensations. I can't turn it off, and I can't stop it. It's coming at me incessantly.

I wish I could take off my head. I wish I could be dead—anything but this unrelenting torture. I am losing my mind. There seems to be no ME.

I feel like I'm stuck, trapped inside a horrific nightmare that will never end. The details are all too real, clear, and vivid, clutching me in their midst and hurling me around like I am a broken branch in a storm. I am powerless to avoid seeing all these shocking images of people being violently attacked and persecuted, and hearing the agonizing screams of their suffering. It is endless viciousness and heartlessness playing itself out all too clearly inside my head.

As I weave in and out of the excruciating pain, I can see blood everywhere, an endless pool of blood. It runs like a river. All the holy waters that were once pristine, clear, and clean are filled with it. I feel like the air that I breathe, where once it was clean and fresh, now stinks. Of what, I am not sure, but it is noxious, through and through—no longer life-giving.

I can hear the pain from the trees as they sway in the breeze. Theirs is a quiet moaning, as if they are aching deep inside. I can feel that Terra is upset. On the surface of her crust, she is crying. She's longing for something precious to be restored, some kind of natural harmony and caring.

There is certainly no harmony in my head right now. There is only all of this violence, pain, and suffering.

I don't know what to make of it. It continues to torment me. I wish I could die, and then it would be gone; anything but this. But I'm not dead.

No. I am here, and painfully aware that I don't know what to do to help myself. I am a Sensitive, and all of my intuitively receptive conduits of clear-sightedness, clear hearing, and clear feeling are filled up with this gruesome sensory input and cruelty that I just described. I feel so blocked. I feel like my system can't breathe. My energetic incoming and outgoing streams of communion are not flowing properly the way they are designed to. They are obstructed and overloaded by this unrelenting, horrible torture. I feel so vulnerable; too open and too powerless to stop it.

I feel like I'm on the edge of falling into the darkness completely. I'm sure I've lost my mind already, but maybe I haven't, if I can talk about it like this. Maybe I actually haven't.

All of this is hard for me to experience, and I feel deeply alone. There is so much going on in my head and my inner senses, and yet I feel starkly alone in the face of it. I feel cold inside. I ache for all of those being hurt, and for myself. I ache for my own loneliness.

I curl up more tightly around myself, clutching my belly and my heart even harder, trying in vain to warm and protect myself and to hold on to the last remaining shreds of my own sanity. I become aware that there is someone else in the cell with me now. I know who it is; it is the soldier, the guard who comes and checks on me now and then. I don't know if it is day or night, but sometimes he comes in and waits for a minute, only to quietly leave.

I've gotten used to him, and am grateful in a way because it is something else, someone else, that I can feel. Even though he is the "enemy," as long as he isn't hurting me, his presence is comforting in a way. I know it sounds crazy, but that's how deeply alone I feel.

Right now, he is sitting quietly in the corner. He's looking at me, of course, that's why he is here. But he seems to be more than looking at me. His gaze is curious, investigating. Slowly, I realize that I am actually feeling a warmth, a sort of genuine kindness coming from him. I am surprised, what could this mean?

I wish I could say that this kindness was taking away all of the turbulence in my head, but it isn't. It gives me something else, though—a sense that I am cared for enough that this man is kind to me. How odd that I would even consider trusting anything about him. I don't understand this, but that's how it feels. He's not speaking to me or anything, it's simply an energy that I am aware of. He continues to sit there, to be with me.

For a moment, I find something inside of me softly easing up a bit, and my thoughts start turning in a different direction. I still have the "nightmare" spinning in my head, but I'm also aware of a small, clear space opening up. I begin having some of my very own thoughts, instead of being completely consumed by the other madness.

I am aware that I simply never, ever thought I would find myself in this kind of situation and circumstance. I have always been such a clear and fluid person, filled with so much light, joy, beauty, and peace.

I remember now that I am an Oracle, a Golden Oracle, and memories of my past start to tumble forward into my psyche. I am having some lucid moments— it's like a breath of fresh air amidst a toxic sky, and I am grateful for this current of brightness.

I can remember that I am one of only a few Oracles of our Lemurian people. As an Oracle, I have great natural talents for energetically seeing, feeling, hearing, and knowing in ways that go beyond our normal range of sensitivity. All of our people are extremely sensitive and fine-tuned in their own ways and skill sets. My particular abilities in this arena have a different intention and purpose, in that I am also a Sacred Seer and Record Keeper for the Collective Spiritual Consciousness of our people.

I help to hold the treasure of our Sacred Wisdom securely, bringing it forward from the past, holding it clear and strong in the present, and spreading it forth like seeds in a garden. I do this so that it can continue to strengthen, enrich, and inspire us as we grow forward and blossom magnificently. My gift of Sight also enables me to see ahead—far into the future.

As with our other Oracles, I am a highly sensitive instrument, greatly honored and respected by my people.

I love my talents, and I love being an instrument. It makes me feel good; it makes me feel well and healthy on all levels. Under normal circumstances, there is great joy in my incoming and outgoing streams of sensitivity and sacred communion. I experience a level of Golden Wholeness which is far beyond what anyone else in my Golden Family can feel. Even though theirs is also outstanding, mine is bright with song and beauty that haven't been born yet, that haven't been imagined.

It is extraordinary to be me—it is beyond extraordinary. I feel like I am a gem, a gift; straight from God, from the Source, from the heavenly and beauteous realms of life and living. I marvel at myself sometimes, at where all of this comes from. I marvel at the sensations I receive, the love that I experience, the ripples of magnificence that touch me, reaching deep inside and emanating forth. I feel and experience an exquisitely heightened sense of beauty because of all of this.

Before I say any more, let me be clear that this isn't about me as a person, not at all. I don't want it to sound like I have a swelled head, or any such thing. Absolutely not. On the contrary, it makes me feel supremely humble. I know I am a manifestation of God's gifting and God's ability to make the extraordinary become real—and I am a most happy recipient. I have also worked hard to develop and refine my natural skill further, to become this attuned and sensitive. I have the resilience and the fiber in my body to support and balance this and to hold it all steady.

That's always been one of the greatest challenges for someone as sensitive as me. This is also true of all of us Oracles; having balance is necessary to support and sustain these levels of supreme sensitivity. In Lemuria, we would gather at regular intervals to conduct ceremonies designed solely to strengthen and support the ground we needed to keep us steady. This enabled us to continue to hold our sensitivities well. We would reach down deep into Terra and draw up her ground, her steadiness, her stability, and incorporate and integrate that into our systems. It was her ground of Being that helped make our ground so strong and unwavering.

We would also bring forth the energy from her Golden Core Crystal, infusing it deliberately into our design so that we were constantly in tune with the deepest and most sacred part of her, our beautiful planet. This was not only a great source of strength and inspiration for us, but a powerful medicine as well.

These are just a few of the methods that we practiced to maintain and fortify our fundamental balance, so that we could continue holding the fluidity and the flow of our ingoing and outgoing streams of awareness. This enabled us to flourish with our profound and highly developed sensitivities. It was a fine art, and always filled with tremendous joy and celebration.

But that was then. That was who and how I was in Lemuria. And this is now—a totally different experience being me. Sadly, I feel completely cut off from all of my natural flow, inside and out. I feel unable to access anything that would help me here. As I said: I am stuck, blocked, overloaded, and immobilized, on all levels. So far, there is nothing I can do about it.

Somehow, I was captured by the Heartless Ones. I don't recall how it happened, but I know that they knew I was one of the power centers; a key player in our Golden Configuration. They knew that I needed to be blocked and disabled, precisely because of my powers—thus rendering me useless to my people and to the sustenance of our Golden Configuration. I can't fathom how they knew all of this, but I know that they are not to be underestimated.

Once captured, they took me deep inside what feels like a very large energetic hologram; it's like I'm buried inside a matrix of some kind. I am inside the Web of Fear, but I am in the deepest, innermost arena of it. I am not the only one that has been taken in this way. On the one hand, I know they would like to simply kill me off, but I also know they are not going to yet. They are too intrigued by me and what makes me tick. They want to know more about my design and how to block me further.

They torture me in all the ways I described earlier, by deliberately distorting and interfering with all of my ingoing and outgoing streams. Their aim has been to shut down my outgoing streams completely and to just keep pouring interfering overload into my incoming streams. In so doing, they have me right where they want me—disabled, and about to go around the bend.

At the same time, I know myself well, and I know that so much of this bombardment coming my way is actually crystal-clear information—information about what is taking place with my Golden Family who are lost and in the hands of the H-O. My highly sensitized intuitive system tells me the story of all of it.

This is true. It is coming my way because I have the capacity to see, hear, and feel it—to know it all. But at the same time, there is also a deliberate distortion, a scrambling and interference in my circuitry that prevents me from accessing my Golden Power and using my outgoing streams to help those in need. That's why I feel useless; I am normally powerful, and now I feel as if I am nothing.

I am disabled by this interference, while at the same time I am clearly seeing, hearing, knowing, and feeling the travesties of my Golden Family. I think you get the picture; everything is backwards for them. It has all been turned inside out. Where there once was love, there is now fear. Where there was clarity, there is confusion. Where there was faith, there is hopelessness and despair. Where there was strength of self, there is now only self-doubt, despair, and disconnection.

I know they are not able to hold true to that which is most dear and sacred in the face of what they are going through. Interfered with at every turn, their hold is slipping, and in many cases has fallen away entirely. I know that those who are lost are no longer connected to who they truly are—to their abilities. I hear all of the questioning and confusion amidst the cries of their pain and the ache of their loneliness. I feel all of it as if it is my very own.

I hear them being tortured, and I see them being made into pawns. I hear the brainwashing and know they now believe that their children, their families—all those they loved—died because of them. They feel that they are responsible for this suffering and that they are to blame. I feel the depth of this remorse and guilt, which doesn't even belong there, that now controls and pummels them constantly. They believe their light is a threat to those they love and that they represent possible danger for all. They are trapped by this, stuck between a rock and a hard place.

I know they have been imprisoned by fear—rendered quaking, terrified, and weakened by the enormity and relentlessness of it all. I know how deeply and desperately alone they feel and believe themselves to be. I know how vulnerable and unsafe they feel all the time. All of this, ALL of it, is completely counter to who they truly are.

Oh yes, I am crystal-clear about it all—I wish that what I am seeing wasn't true, but it is. I start to feel frustrated by all of the awareness and clarity about my loved ones. What is the point of knowing about it all? What the heck is the point? I'm stuck here, and I can't do a single thing to help them; I can't do a thing about any of it. I can't even pray for them, because my outgoing systems are blocked. I am powerless.

In this way, I am as lost as they are. Again, I wish I could die, just as so many of them also wish. I want to be free; my head hurts, my soul hurts, my heart hurts. I wish the sounds of pain would stop for me, as much as for them. Somebody turn the volume down and off, please!

I look over, and I see the guard still sitting there; I still feel that current of kindness coming from him, and I just don't know what to make of it. I thought he was one of them. What if he isn't? What if he's only masquerading as one of them? Is that why my system seems to trust him somehow when, on the surface, it seems like the craziest, most stupid thing to do?

And just as I think that thought, I hear him talking to me very, very quietly. His voice is almost a whisper as he says:

"Dear friend, yes, we know each other. In fact, we know each other very well, but you are not able to remember clearly right now. There is too much distortion in your system—but have faith, we are going to help you. I can't help you myself directly, but I am going to bring you someone who can, soon. Help is on the way, I promise."

I see him get up and go. What can this mean? I can't make sense of his words, and in any case, I don't dare to believe him.

A short while later he returns, and this time there is a woman with him. Something about her feels quite familiar to me. In fact, now that I see them standing side by side, they both feel familiar to me. I think I understand why I let this man's energy move me earlier. It is not clear who they are or exactly how I know them, but I know that I do. There's still too much noise and commotion in my head for me to answer these questions.

The woman moves quietly toward me, and as she does, I take a closer look at her. I find myself becoming mesmerized by her eyes. I realize they are like mine. She has the Oracle in her eyes, just like I do. It dawns on me that we must be sisters in that way. As clarity begins to seep in, everything changes for me, and I feel an enormous weight of confusion, like the heaviness of a thick, wet wool blanket, slowly lifting off of my head and peeling away from my senses.

Her eyes are looking deeply into mine now. It's like she knows exactly what's happening inside of me; we are both Oracles, and she KNOWS. She knows everything I have been going through. I know that she knows, and I know that I am being witnessed right now. Oh, I am so glad and relieved that someone else understands my plight so thoroughly.

For a few moments there is a stream of pure brightness and light moving from her to me. It is arcing through the air, creating a glowing bridge between us. Suddenly it expands, and we are enveloped by a soft, undulating Golden Energy that cocoons us safely here. Out of the corner of my eye, I am momentarily distracted by something moving slowly around her legs. I look down, and I see the body of a beautiful Golden Mountain Lion: strong, lithe, and powerful. I cannot help feeling its eyes penetrating me as well, those eyes of an ancient animal that need no words. It moves closer to me.

The eyes of the lion and the eyes of the woman are so similar—purposeful, wise, and powerful. My memory is jogged again, and I recall that she is an Oracle of the Sacred Golden Animal Kingdom: She Who Walks with the Golden Four-Leggeds. She and her Sacred Animal Allies are One, and I know that without this lion, this woman would not have been able to make her way in here to find me. I sense that there are several other lions present as well.

The bridge of light between this sister Oracle and me opens up wider now, becoming still stronger and clearer. It's the first time I have felt a clear stream of energy like this in a long time. I take a breath, and oh, how good it feels!

The woman says to me:

"Yes, I am here, my beloved Golden Sister. My sacred lions have guided me here to you and enabled me to penetrate this deeply-buried prison you are in. I am here to Rescue you and to bring you out again into the light of day. I know your Golden Heart well, and I honor you now."

Suddenly, I feel an intense Golden Light coming straight from her heart into mine. It washes through me and begins to awaken the brilliance of my pure joy, deep inside. My own inner Golden Light starts to expand suddenly, and I begin to feel bright again—more alive and more fully awake. I am returning to myself, and I couldn't be more glad. It's extraordinary; I haven't felt this in a long, long time. This is who I truly am.

My whole system starts to become bright with the glistening effervescence of Golden Light. It's creating space in my head, in my energy fields, and in all of my incoming and outgoing conduits. Where they were blocked and distorted, my natural currents are now slowly unwinding and making their way toward flowing more smoothly and clearly again. I am deeply relieved.

I take in a deep breath, and then another and another. I am getting an inkling of a taste of my wellness again. My whole system is filling up with my Golden Light and my heart—well, my heart is positioning itself to start singing again soon. I can feel it coming. It's my ancient memory returning, little by little. I know we are still inside this prison, and it's not over yet, but everything is beginning to change for me. I am filled with gratitude.

I become aware that the energy around us is changing and that we must not linger here. I hear my sister Oracle saying, *"We must go. It is time, and we must go. We will continue this later."*

I see all the Golden Lions moving deliberately closer to us now, actually hugging our legs and pressing up against us in a tight, protective circle. I know they are the only ones who can get us out of here, and I thank them with all my heart and soul for their strength and presence.

The guard comes over to me, unlocks the cuff around my ankle, and helps me to stand up. I feel weak and very wobbly, for sure, and it takes me a few moments to steady myself and find some balance. But I am determined, and somehow I manage to do it. I hear his voice clearly in my ear, as he says:

"Stay focused, put all of your concentration on walking, on moving forward, and you will feel the strength in your legs returning. Go with your sister Oracle now. The Lions will guide you well and keep you safe."

As I turn to go, I see him stepping back. There is another Presence of Golden Light, a female, who has suddenly appeared by his side, and I catch a final look at the two of them standing there, holding hands, watching us, and holding the space for our safe exit. They seem so calm about it all.

Again, he says, *"Just keep walking now. Don't look back, just keep walking."*

My sister Oracle takes my hand and my arm firmly in her grip, and the Lions surround us intently. We are definitely a tightly packed unit now on the go. We keep walking and walking, moving through layer upon layer of dense, jangled, noxious "stuff," completely untouched and unimpeded by any of it. We are in our own Cocoon of Golden Protection, with the Lions moving us as one body on our own clear pathway.

Gradually, the thick, murky haze of the terrain we have traveled through lessens, and the air around us becomes clearer. I know I have emerged from deep inside of a dark pit, both literally and figuratively. Oh my goodness, how grateful I am to be out in the light of day. I know it's not even bright, but it is much better than where I've been.

We eventually slow down and finally come to a complete stop. I look around me, taking it all in. I see we are standing in a small copse of trees. It is beautiful here, and the air actually smells fresh and clean for a change. I know we are still in our blessed cocoon, and that's what makes such a clear space even possible. I take in a slow, deep breath and turn to look at my sister Oracle. She reaches for both of my hands, taking them gently in hers while she gazes deeply into my eyes once more.

I feel her love softly permeating me and seeping right down into my bones. I recognize how fully she is witnessing me, again speaking to me without words. My heart opens wide to her, as I love and witness her in return. We need this. We need to witness that we have just been liberated from a place that was dark, confining, and suffocating to our Spirits.

She continues gazing into me and I feel her love finding, and gently touching, those wounded places inside of me. *"I know,"* she says to me. *"I have been there, right where you were myself. I know."*

Tears suddenly well up in my eyes and roll down my cheeks. They are tears of great sadness for all of the pain, but also tears of relief, as I register how truly seen and understood I am in this moment. I no longer feel myself desperately isolated and alone, lost in that void of disconnect and madness, unable to find myself anywhere.

I squeeze her hands harder. Her healing kindness is a soothing balm, reminding me of the fact that this has been such a long and painful experience, and that my heart still hurts from it. At the same time, I am aware of a sense of freedom, and that there might actually be a positive future ahead for me. The experience inside the pit is over, and I didn't lose my mind after all.

In truth, I didn't lose myself either. I am eternally grateful to her and her sacred animals for loving me so much that they would go into that dark place and do whatever was necessary to Rescue me. I let this realization wash over me, and find myself coming to a state of calm and peace inside. I feel thoroughly warmed by it all.

Gradually, I am aware that my true wellness is waking up and beginning to restore me through its own intelligence. There is a bubbling up of immense joy, as my incoming and outgoing streams of light and communion continue to open up further and flow freely again. This is my wellness. This is my sacred Gift returning to its natural design and rhythm. It moves me greatly and brings more tears to my eyes—this time of great joy and expectation. I begin to absolutely know that I will heal and become whole again.

I turn my focus back to my sister Oracle and see that she is happy too, *"My animal companions and I must take our leave now, my sweet sister,"* she says. *"We still have much work ahead, and time is precious, as you well know. Be well, dearest friend, be well. Until we meet again, joyous Godspeed!"*

And off she goes, gracefully.

As her little tribe moves away, I say a silent prayer of gratitude to her Lions for all their loving action on my behalf. I know that they hear me, and that they send back a silent signal of warmth and caring that caresses my Soul. I know that all of our paths will cross again, and for a moment I look forward to that day when we will all be circling in an unfettered dance of true joyous remembrance and reunion.

Until then I know that I have much ahead that needs attending as well. Now that my circuitry is open and flowing properly again, and I have gained access to the depth of information regarding our Golden Ones lost in the Web of Fear, there is indeed much work to do.

Each one Rescue one; each one Rescued, Rescue more. My purpose awaits me! Off I go, with a smile in my heart and joy in my Being. I will never take my freedom for granted. I breathe it in and savor it now; Glory Be, Golden Hallelujah!

But wait…

Suddenly, I see Avalar and Andar standing in front of me—I knew they were with us back in the cell. At least my senses are clear enough now to know what I couldn't see then. I reach toward Andar first and give him a great big hug, letting him know how profoundly grateful I am for all that he did for me. He looks back at me and his voice is full of love:

"Beloved Golden Friend, we are all so grateful that you have been freed. You would have done the same for me, the same for any one of us, if you could—and you will. Yes, there are many Rescues ahead for you and many gifts that only you can bring to bear in this place of Mondor. We are counting on your skills to help us in the remainder of our purpose here; to re-instill the memory of their Golden Heart, and a vision of their way Home in those who remain lost. I know it sounds like a tall order, and it is, but you are the Golden Oracle. Your outgoing streams of communion, once they are fully freed up again, will be able to accomplish this better than any of the rest of us can. This is your gift, and we know it is what your heart yearns to do.

"Bless you, Beloved Friend. Bless you."

And with that, he turns toward his beloved Avalar, who envelops me now in a giant hug of love and gratitude as well, as she says:

"Dearest Golden Beauty, yes, you have been on a powerful journey inside that complex winding labyrinth of great pain and disconnection. You know it well now. You became it thoroughly, precisely so that you would know. This is the state of so many of our Golden Family, and now that you know it so intimately and have heard the cries of deep loneliness and anguish so acutely, you will be able to respond and help them all greatly.

"You will be a bridge for them to cross from there to here, as you have done so well yourself. No, you didn't lose your mind. You are way too strong for that to ever happen. In truth, you simply became fully informed.

"We are eternally grateful to you, Dear Oracle. Not one ounce of what you went through in there will be wasted. This information that you have now is precious, and we will all be served by it. Know that you were never forgotten in there. It was simply a matter of when and how we could retrieve you, all the while knowing that you were gathering essential information for all of us.

"We could not bring you out until your purpose of discovery was complete. Know this. Let the pain of the isolation you have experienced diminish and dissolve, making way for new heartfelt joy to emerge. Let it now be replaced with your understanding and your remembrance of what your purpose was in being there in the first place. And yes, you did indeed fulfill this purpose extremely well—just as we knew you would.

"We thank you, dear friend. So deeply, we thank you. The rest of our Golden Family will now be able to be brought home—safe, sound, and well. We deeply honor your unwavering Golden Heart, your strength and clarity of purpose, and the profound abilities of your divine instrument. Thank you for all that you are.

"Golden Blessings to you, our Sacred Oracle. May there always be a forever song in your heart."

I am so moved by her, by both of them. The resonance of all of their words pulses through me and quickens my spirit, activating my joy and optimism still more.

Andar turns to me once again, and says:

"Beloved Sister, yours is a great path ahead. All together we will continue to bring each other home. Our successful Rescues are increasing, and our

numbers of restored Golden Ones are rising, enabling us to become much stronger as a united front. We are restoring and reestablishing ourselves back into our original Golden Imprint. We will speak again soon about what specifically lies ahead for you, and what the plans and details are. For right now, however, this is a time of quiet respite for you, to gather yourself and settle into your peace of renewal. When you are ready, we will meet again.

"Until then, dear one, Golden Blessings and Golden Gratitude forevermore. This is a great day!"

And, with a wink and smile, he and Avalar are gone.

As I am left standing here by myself, still bathed in their gratitude, I am aware that I am completely awash in the enormous wave of their love and joy. Their clarity has become my own, as I remember the true strength and profound power of my instrument. My incoming and outgoing streams remember clearly their point and purpose as well—they will not only receive, but also deliver whatever is needed to help all the Golden Ones everywhere. My communion opens again with immense joy and celebration, and I hear the sweet song and glorious sound of Golden Life beating beyond the scope of this place.

I know that I can pray once more. I know I can foster and support, can water and feed this beautiful garden of Golden Life, to help it grow and stand strong at last. My sensitivity opens to the freshness of my renewal and all the gifts that it will bring. I know it won't always be easy, not at all. There is much arduous work ahead, and I sense the enormity of this task in front of me. But my Spirit is strong, my heart is open, and I am centered and steady in my Beloved Source once more. What else do I need?

Lead on, Golden Day, lead on!

THE DREAM RESCUE

I am a baby girl, sitting on my mother's lap. She feels distant to me; not because she doesn't love me, but because her physical presence isn't very strong. She lives more in the world of her spirit, rather than her body.

I am aware that she is hurting enormously, and that it is the reason she doesn't want to be in the physical domain. I can feel her pain. She comes in and out of her body from time to time, but it's not a steady, reliable feeling. It's more like tepid water, neither hot nor cold. It leaves me feeling insecure and uncomfortable; not sure what to make of where I am and who I am with. But I love her, and I know that she loves me as best she can.

She is a dreamer, but that isn't the problem. The problem is that she hurts inside. A big chunk of her is lost. She can spend time outside of her body, but not in her body. She longs to escape all the time. I feel for her, even though I am but an infant still. I don't know how I know this, but I know that I am here to Rescue her. I am here to bring her home in some way. I don't know how I am going to do that; I just know that I will.

Moving forward in time now, I see myself as a young girl about eight years old. I have flowers in my hair that I've picked from our garden outside. I love flowers so much. I relate with them, and find them extraordinary. They are a delight, and that's why I pick them. My mother doesn't always like that I pick so many. I like to make flower chains and wear them in my hair; I love to smell them, and have their blooms around me all of the time—I can't get enough.

My mother suffers, and I can see this. She always wishes that she was dead; it's such a shame, and I don't know what to do about it. Sometimes I wonder what difference it would make, because she is not all here, anyway. My father drifts in and out of the house. I have a brother and a sister. I don't know where they are now; they must be off doing their own thing.

I don't know what I am doing here most of the time. I know that I need to find a way to save my mother, but how am I going to do that? She seems so lost and forlorn that she can't connect with anyone. It's not that they don't like her; they all like her, but she's not present—she's always wishing she was somewhere else.

Moving forward in time again, I find myself at about twelve years old. I go to bed one night, and have a terrible dream. I have a lot of dreams, which fill my nights with all kinds of things. Sometimes the stories are amazing, vivid, and real; when I wake up I am confused, and I don't know where I am. It often takes me quite awhile to quiet myself, to remember that it is only a dream. It is always potent for me.

On this particular night, the bad dream I am having is turning into a nightmare. I know it sounds strange, especially for someone my age, but in this nightmare I am being burned at the stake. It is horrific.

I hear people all around me, yelling and shouting, "You are an evil witch; you are Satan, you are the Devil, you must die." The voices won't stop. I see other women being burned alive as well—at least three or four others. It's horrible. I'm screaming desperately; we are all screaming. And these people, mostly men, are shouting at us relentlessly, "You're evil witches. You're bad. You're the devil, Satan. You'll be damned."

I keep screaming. I keep hearing screaming. I feel the fire on my skin, and the smell engulfs me, devouring me. I am burning.

Suddenly, I wake up. My sheets are drenched and I am dripping with sweat, in the grip of something terrifying. I leap out of bed and run to my mother, asleep in her bedroom. Desperate for her care, I shake her. "Mommy, wake up, wake up. I had a horrible nightmare. I'm so frightened, help me."

She rouses herself quickly from her sleep and takes me into her arms, holding me close to her bosom. For once, I can feel her actually being here with me and reaching into my heart to comfort my fears. I am quaking. She says, "What did you dream? Tell me about it, sweetheart."

I tell her my nightmare in detail. When I have finished she says, "Oh, I've had that same nightmare so many times that I practically have it in the daytime as well. I've had it often, and it feels so real that it makes me wonder whether I'm actually living or dying."

She pulls me still closer to her and starts to quietly cry; I am crying as well. My father is sleeping heavily on the other side of the bed. He doesn't hear a thing, and it is probably just as well. We are here, weeping quietly together, holding each other tight. It is so sad. And then my mother says to me, "I'm sorry. I'm sorry that I'm not more present, but I live in this fear all the time. I'm sorry that you are getting it now, too."

I can't stop crying, and neither can she. What am I going to do? I feel her fear. I feel it seeping into me, into my bones and my heart. Now I understand why she can't be present most of the time. It's so sad. I feel sad for me, but I feel sadder for her because of this grip of fear that she lives in. I never knew any of this before.

I am aware that she feels broken in some way. I don't know how it happened, but I just know that it did.

I finally fall asleep. In the morning I am the only one in the bed. I can hear both my parents downstairs, going through their usual morning routine. Things sound as if they have returned to normal—but for me, the sensations and feelings of the night stay with me in an amorphous but undeniable way.

I have that familiar feeling again and I say to myself, "I am going to save her. I don't know how, but I am." I know that I have it within me to do that. I don't know what it will take, but I know that I will do it—somehow, some way, some day. I am aware that it is a fact, a truth that lives inside of me.

Suddenly, I bounce up and jump out of bed. The nightmare is over. It has given me the clarity and understanding that it wasn't really my dream at all; it was a message from my mother, telling me what has been causing her such pain.

With this understanding, I find that I feel wiser now. I am a different person than I was, and no longer a little girl. I have deepened greatly, and I realize that this particular pain is what I have been looking at in my mother, day in and day out, all of this time. I understand now—I understand perfectly, and I am here for her. I feel grateful to know this and to feel this.

We go about our days and our lives, one moment blending into the next. Then one night I have another dream. In it, I am standing with my mother, watching her. She is fumbling around, lost, and groping for something that she cannot find. She's looking outside of herself in a desperate way to find something that is of utmost importance to her. I realize she is looking for herself.

She says to me, "My sight, there is something wrong with my sight. I cannot see." As I look at her, I see that she truly cannot. It is as if she is as blind as a bat, and whatever she is looking for is hidden, as invisible as what is right in front of her. As I look at my Mother, flailing around in desperation and panic, I suddenly feel a beautiful energy Presence standing right next to me. I see lots of Golden Light, and I hear gentle singing. I know that this is a special Being that has come here to help me. Something tells me that the moment to save my mother has finally arrived.

The exquisite Golden Being says to me:

"I am Avalar. You know me, sweet one, and I know you. You feel like you are in a dream, but this is not a dream. This is more real than anything else. It is your time to give that gift that you have, to do the very thing that you have always wanted to do. I am here to witness you doing this."

As Avalar speaks to me I turn to face my mother, and I feel my own heart opening wide to her. Golden Light begins pouring out of me like a gushing fountain and moves itself right over into her, reaching deep inside her heart. "I see your Golden Heart," I hear myself saying to her. "I know you are a Golden Being, and you shine so beautifully. You always have. I love you so much."

Deep inside her chest, I see a bright Golden Flame flaring up, igniting, and becoming strong and vibrant; it is dancing exuberantly inside of her. She starts beaming from within, and for the first time I feel true joy within her. She is pulsating with it.

She becomes giddy, absolutely giddy. She is smiling and laughing like I have never heard her do. I hear her say, "Oh my goodness, what is happening to me? I feel suddenly alive, what just happened? I don't feel lost anymore. Was this right here all the time? Was this here all along?"

I take her hands in mine and I am beaming with her. I am so happy for her! We dance freely together around the room, laughing at each other with utter joy and abandon. I look over at Avalar, and she smiles broadly at me, and says:

"Yes, you've done it. Indeed, you have done it! You did the very thing that you came here to do. You have successfully Rescued your sweet mother. Bless you, Golden One, Bless you. We are all so grateful. Job well done!"

And with that, Avalar suddenly disappears.

I'm still here with my mother; we are still holding each other's hands and beaming with joy. I'm amazed as I look at her, because she looks like a completely different woman. She looks many years younger and very beautiful, with cheek-bones that I have never seen before. She is glowing and her eyes are twinkling; tall and strong, she is so fully present, here and now with me. I am watching her be amazed, amazed at the beauty and joy of what she has found. I know she has finally found herself.

And you know what? For the first time ever, I feel the intensity of her mother love inside of my heart. I have never felt it before. It pours into my heart like a beautiful mountain stream, overflowing into something big and bold and bright and beautiful. It is palpable and real.

It makes me so happy. Finally, we are here, in this life, together—Golden.

I hear both of us laughing, and as I listen, the sounds wake me up. I realize that I have once again been in a dream—but this one is real. It is truth that has come to get her and me.

I lie in my bed for several minutes, basking in the warmth of love. I know that everything is different now. I know I have fulfilled something that I have been yearning to do for a long time, and there is joy about it everywhere.

At last, I get out of bed and go downstairs. Walking into our small kitchen I see my mother standing by the window, gazing out at the flowers in our garden. She is obviously enjoying what she sees, and I am touched by the Golden Glow that is still radiating from her. It is like a deep inner well of happiness, making her body shine.

I go to her and reach my arms around her body. She responds warmly, hugging me back in a fiercely loving and powerful way that tells me that she is finally here with me—to stay. Oh, what a truly beautiful day this is!

A Man Finds His Freedom

I am trapped in fear.

I am a man in my early twenties, a monk. I live in a monastery that is cold, damp, and often dark, as it is made primarily of stone and built underground. I have sequestered myself away quite deliberately in this silent order, for reasons that I shall explain shortly. I wish I could say it was peaceful and silent inside of me too, but sadly, there is nothing in my existence that is quiet, except for the environment that surrounds me.

Because of our vow of silence, we do not speak unless it is absolutely necessary, and then only in whispered and hushed tones. I like not speaking. I find it comforting that I do not have to make conversation or talk about anything at all. I like having my mouth shut most of the time. It means I don't have to reveal or expose myself; that I don't need to risk anyone's judgment of me. I already feel harshly judged inside of myself as it is, with enough judgmental conversations to keep my internal space quite loud much of the time. I wish this wasn't the case. I wish I could have serenity inside of my head—but I do not. My state of daily existence is a sorry one; I am troubled, deeply troubled.

I began my story by saying that I am trapped in fear, and that is most definitely the case. Fear is one thing that I know a lot about. I feel like I am in its grip all of the time; an iron grip, a trap made of steel. I cannot move. There is fear everywhere inside of me.

I am frightened, and always live in so much panic that I often jump at the sight of my own shadow. I am lost inside, deeply lost. There is certainly a part of me that would love to find myself, but there is a bigger part that is afraid to do so because of what it might reveal. I am a sinner, a true sinner. I believe with every fiber of my being that I am not pure, that I am bad. I wake up in the morning wishing I was not, wishing I could have died in my sleep. I wish that I could die every second of every day.

Perhaps you are wondering why I don't simply take my own life. I know it certainly sounds like I might want to, and the truth is that I think about it often. I even have a plan for that very thing. And yet, I don't actually follow through on it, and I don't know why. I think it's because I'm afraid that God will reject me, too. If I take my life, maybe I will end up somewhere that is worse than here, somewhere even worse than my own insides. I feel trapped between a terrifying rock and a hard place—and I can describe fear to you probably better than anyone.

It's like a monster, devouring me. It is eating me up and spitting me out, all at the same time. I live in it, and it lives in me. It is dark and menacing, and frightens me so much that I am constantly trembling in my own skin. It keeps me perpetually skittish and panicky, hypersensitive to everything all the time, as if I am plugged into a high voltage wire of some sort. It never stops. Yes, I am afraid of life in general, but that is simply a hazy peripheral anxiety. My true fears center on me, inside of me.

I am afraid of myself, of my thoughts and my heart. I am afraid of my impulses, my desires, and my wonderings. Every morning when I wake up, it is not the day itself that I dread, but me in it. It all sounds extremely sad, doesn't it? Well, it is.

On top of all of that, I find I can never fully breathe; my body is always in a state of distress. It's like living in a dark, suffocating hole. I wish I could be numb to it all, but I haven't been able to. So far, I have found no relief or escape from this fear. I feel completely alone.

Let me tell you more about my earlier life, so you can put some of these pieces of my puzzle together.

Let me explain how I was, as a young boy, without the grip of all of this. I would welcome your listening, because it validates me, and maybe, just maybe, I won't feel as alone.

Moving back in time, I see myself around the age of ten. I am growing up in a fairly ordinary family. As a young boy, I am magical; different from the other boys. I am a dreamer, and live in a world of my own, a most special and beautiful world. I am extremely sensitive, and I see and know things that no one else does. I often see Angels, and they are wonderfully beautiful and kind to me. For me, this is all quite normal. I assume everyone sees Angels. I think everyone is like me, until one day, I suddenly realize that no one else is. No one else is like me.

My parents look at me in bafflement, they clearly don't know what to do with me. My mother can be harsh, because she wants me to be like a regular boy, strong and sturdy—typically masculine, I guess you could say. And I clearly am not, so she often criticizes me and says things like, "Why aren't you like your brothers and the other boys? Go toughen up. Go toughen up, you. You're going to be a man. Get on with it."

My father pays attention to my other brothers instead of me, because they are "normal." I can tell that he has already decided there is nothing he can do about the way I am, that it isn't worth trying to mold me into something that I clearly am not. He also has a lot to attend to as the man of the house, and really, I am the least of that kind of priority. I am actually grateful for this, because I know it enables me to escape his harshness and hardness.

What I do is go off by myself. I separate myself from people as much as I possibly can by spending a lot of time outdoors in Nature. I absolutely love this solitude, and it allows me the freedom to slip into the realms of my Angels effortlessly. This soothes me greatly. It is not even something that I make happen. I have never understood how it happens, but I just slip off out of my body, so to speak, into this beautiful space, this sensation of wondrousness.

It is beyond me and I know that. It is beyond everywhere that I exist in my regular daily life. I don't know how to describe this to myself, much less to anyone else. It is my secret. When other people look at me, they describe me as a dreamer, and that basically sums it up for them, so they let me be. In that way, they let me be different.

As I get a little bit older and start growing into a pubescent teenage boy, I realize there is something else that makes me even more out of the ordinary, and this difference upsets me greatly. I find that I like boys. I don't like girls in the same kind of way. I am not attracted to girls, only to boys, and I find that extremely jarring.

I remember the first time I felt the sensation of feeling sexually aroused by looking at a boy. It was such a strong sensation; like an actual pull, something igniting and exciting in my body. I was shocked by it, and then my heart started to go in that direction too. I realized it wasn't only sexual.

The more often I saw that particular boy, the stronger my love grew. It frightened me. I knew this was seriously wrong. No one had to tell me, I just knew; I became confused and ashamed of myself. That's when I first started to feel afraid of myself and my impulses, of this longing that I felt. I continue to be afraid. None of this has changed inside of me since that first episode.

I often wonder if anyone else can see this about me. I do my best to shroud myself, and I wish I could actually pull on some kind of body suit that would keep it all in, that would completely prevent anyone else from ever knowing about it. I worry that they will sense it; that they will find out and do terrible things to me. I am not only frightened of myself, but also terrified that I may be hurt by others.

Every morning when I wake up, I start to pray. I don't know exactly when or how I learned to pray, but I did. I pray every day that this will all go away; that I can somehow tamp it down, stamp it out, and make it go away forever. But no, there it is every day. As I grow and mature, I know I simply have to live with it. It doesn't change at all; if anything, it gets stronger. I haven't actually acted on it yet, because I don't even consider that. I don't allow myself to have thoughts in that direction; I am so rigidly constrained.

My inner world becomes painfully tight and narrow. I am still highly sensitive, and there continues to be times when I seek solitude and find myself, yet again, slipping out of my physical body and into the world of Angels for a time. When I was younger I would always let myself feel their love for me, and mine for them. But as I start to basically hate myself, as I try my best to reject myself, I notice that my ability to receive their goodness, their love and joy, begins to diminish greatly. I feel unworthy and ashamed, bad and dirty.

But even as I believe that I don't deserve them, I also yearn for them, because I desperately need some respite from my own inner torment and self-degradation. I need their lightness and brightness, their love for me, however little I can allow. I try my best to stay open to them, and am grateful that they are with me, that I still have this gift of them that just happens, no matter what I do and no matter what I am.

The inevitable day finally comes when I have a sexual experience with another boy. I don't know if he is like me or if he is only curious about his own sexuality. It actually seems like it's not something that is particularly significant to him, but simply another way of exploring himself. I realize that perhaps our sexual act together means nothing to him—but it means everything to me. It isn't because I love him or want him in my life, but because the physical manifestation of my desire literally rocks my world. It stuns me down to my core. It opens up a zillion sensations and scares me out of my mind, precisely because it feels so good. It feels deeply right to my body and Being.

Acting on my impulses only makes my secret larger and harder to contain, because the physical passion in me that has now been aroused is heightened and seems uncontrollable. I feel that I want to hold my hands crossed over my genitals and hide them forever. And yet they give me such pleasure, and I need something that feels good in the midst of my own torment. I find myself getting more mixed up by the minute, more trapped inside this conflicting nightmare of my experience of myself.

I realize that I need to basically put myself away, and decide to join a monastery to become a monk. Maybe it will wipe all of this out. Is it about God? Am I joining up because I want to be close to God? I don't think so, because I believe that God has already rejected me. I know I may be joining the monastery for some of the wrong reasons, but I don't know what else to do. I believe that if I shut myself up in that place, I won't be able to act on my sexual impulses and longings. This will stop any of that sort of thing from ever happening again. It will serve to protect me from myself.

Of course—and it comes as no surprise to you, I am sure—I am definitely one of those monks that punishes myself religiously through self-flagellation. I do that as much as I can. I am constantly trying to beat the sinner out of me. I joined this particular silent monastery because I knew I would never have to explain myself or have anyone tell me anything that they are observing about me. That remains a huge relief for me.

But the thing is, my impulses aren't going away at all. I had truly thought they would, but they haven't. I had also assumed that, of course, it was impossible that there would be any activity of that nature inside the monastery. However, being in the monastery offers me far more opportunities for sex than I could have imagined.

We find that we need each other. Can you believe that? It's like I went from the frying pan into the fire. Now I know that I am a sinner. I am all of the things that I have heard about people like me; I am evil, of the devil, and I will go to Hell for sure. I am now all of those things, and I believe that Hell is exactly where I will end up. Talk about stamping out my own soul.

When I pray, I know it looks like I'm praying, but I'm not. How can I? I'm not worthy of praying anymore. God have mercy on me? I don't deserve mercy. I go from kneeling in prayer position to hiding in a cubicle with another monk for a few minutes, desperately satisfying our need.

And our need is intense. Here we are, all locked up in this damp, cold place. We try, but we can't run away from the fact that we are mere mortals. We can't subdue that which flows vigorously through our veins. I know there is a belief that somehow our God connection renders us immune to that. I think that this is true for some people, but for many others here, that is clearly not the case. It is a joke and the joke is on us. We are fools for even thinking that it might be possible.

How confusing this all is to me. God always seems to be something outside of everyone and outside of self. The belief that if we say certain prayers a certain number of times, or engage in this or that ritual, obey this rule or that rule—that somehow, we will enter the gates of Heaven. It certainly doesn't make any sense to me. It doesn't make anything any better or any different. It doesn't make me believe that on my deathbed I will be able to say that this or that prayer or ritual, or the amount of times I went to confession, entitles me to go to Heaven when I die, versus someone who hasn't done any of these things.

It doesn't make sense to me; none of it makes any sense. I don't know what does, but I do know that it isn't any of this. I don't feel that things truly work this way. I'm sensitive, and I can feel all of this confusion, not just in myself, but in lots of the other men here too; this is simply my experience of it.

I'm sure there are some monks who have a completely different experience and understanding of all of this. But I am so absorbed with my own inner machinations that I can't think of it in any other way—and we have our vow of silence. There aren't long hours of debate or of revealing our varying perceptions and points of view. I just know that it all looks quite off to me.

On the other hand, as I have already described, I feel off inside, so I imagine it may simply be who I am. I know that I came to the monastery to feel protected from myself and from the outer world stigma—and now I don't want to leave, because I definitely feel safer here. Things are unspoken. I can survive, have sex, and also be quiet and make it through this constant state of fear, shame, and self-rejection that I live in.

Forgive myself? Don't even talk to me about that. Forgive myself for what? I'll forgive myself at one moment, only to go out and sin again. That doesn't make sense to me. I am unworthy of forgiveness. I am unworthy of self-forgiveness, and quite unworthy of God's forgiveness.

Ironically, there are times when I still slip out of myself and see my Angels, although I am afraid to ask them for help. I can't risk being rejected by them as well. I'm grateful that I see them, however infrequently, because those are my times of something beautiful—whether I believe it is deserved or not. Those are moments that ease my pain somewhat, although it doesn't last long.

I feel that I am doomed to be in the pain that I am in for as long as I am alive. Every morning when I wake up, I wish I was dead. And fear—well, I know it exceedingly well. It is a constant for me. You'd think I would have made friends with it by now, but it doesn't want to be friends with me. That is not what fear is about, at least not for me.

I started out by saying that I am afraid of my own shadow, because I do believe in some way that maybe I am dark, that I am not pure. I cannot say that it is one hundred percent so, because if it is, then I wouldn't have the Angel experiences. I know enough to know that. It is more the constant questioning inside, the constant self-doubt; I flat-out don't trust myself. I can't—I am afraid to.

As I have already explained clearly, I don't deny that fear runs my life. I know that it controls me in every way. I often think that if I lived in another time and place, if such a thing existed where people like me could be accepted as part of some kind of norm, then I wouldn't be afraid like this. I might still feel fear around me, and perhaps be afraid in other ways, but nothing like this. And I certainly wouldn't have locked myself away.

The truth is, I am locked up inside of myself. My heart is locked up. I feel like my soul is locked up. There is nowhere to go or be or do inside of me. It is all just one great, big, living pain of fear.

Then one night I have a dream, and everything suddenly changes. I understand that you might not believe this, that you may think it's too good to be true, but this is what happened—and I am living proof of its wondrousness.

In this dream I am a woman with a daughter. I am a similar kind of person as in my current life—sensitive, sorrowful, and lonely—except that I am female. Our plights are different, but our feelings deep down inside are the same. I feel that I suffer deeply; always in conflict and torment. I am in great despair, and I am shut down inside because of it all.

In the dream, my young daughter comes into my room in the middle of the night and wakes me up. She sits on my bed beside me and gazes intently into my eyes. "*I love you, Mama,*" she says to me. "*I love you so very much, and it has troubled me to see you in such pain. I know what is deep down inside of you. I know of the despair and torment that you have been trying to hide from yourself and from me, but I KNOW you, Mama. You cannot hide yourself from me. I know about all of it, and I am sorry for all of your pain.*"

I try to look away from her, but she puts her hands on my shoulders, insisting that I look back into her eyes. She keeps her penetrating gaze locked onto mine. I finally surrender to her, because I don't have the inner strength to do anything else. "*KNOW that I see you, Mama,*" she lovingly continues, "*Know that*

I understand you. I am here for you. I am here to help you. I am here to witness you. You can stop running now."

At the sound of these words my heart breaks. She's right. I have been running from all of this for so long, and I am tired. I feel broken down and weary. I look into her eyes, and even though she is still young, I see a wise soul who is telling me the absolute truth. I know that she sees me totally. I know that she sees all the parts of me that I have buried and been so afraid of. I feel as though she is indeed actually witnessing how deeply lost and lonely I am. She knows I have lost my Soul.

She continues to look steadily into my eyes, into my heart and my Being. Gradually, I feel touched inside by her pure, warm caring and total acceptance. I am vulnerable and raw, but the gentleness of her love soothes me. It is potent, and finds all of the places inside of me that have been locked up for a long time. I'm acutely aware that she has no judgment of me, absolutely none. All I see and feel from her is love—pure love—and it simply opens me up inside; wide open.

I can't control this response and I find that I don't want to. My heart feels like it's breaking, but not with pain; it is a wondrous opening that is happening inside of me. I watch it all take place, and I am amazed by it. I watch and feel as the "inner cell" that I have been locked up in so tightly starts to crack and come apart more and more. As it does, warm love comes pouring out of it and out of me. I never even knew it was there.

It's like I am being witness to the revelation of buried treasure that I didn't know existed. "What is all this, inside of me?" I wonder. "How did I not know of this before? And by the way, how is this happening?" I had felt so unworthy, and now all of that is changing, as if by magic.

I have all of these thoughts tumbling through my brain, but the love inside of me keeps pouring out, as if it simply knows best and has its own plan and intention. It is far more powerful than my ability to control it—and I don't want to. As I continue to watch and witness myself, I notice that my daughter has her eyes closed now. She is humming quietly, trancelike, and the tone of her voice penetrates me in ways that feel right and good, but unfamiliar.

I suddenly feel myself to be someone that I don't even recognize. It is bizarre and wonderful, all at the same time. It is bigger, stronger, and more determined than I am. I want to hang onto my old, despairing, familiar self, but it is slipping right through my hands.

I take a deep breath and decide to simply ride this horse the way it's going. Anything is better than where I have been. I focus my attention on my daughter's eyes. They open, beautiful and clear, full of love and warmth and kindness. For a moment the sensation reminds me of when I feel my Angels nearby. It's soothing and intoxicating, in all the best ways—illuminated is perhaps a more appropriate word. Yes, that's it. I am feeling lit up.

"You are so beautiful," she says to me now. *"I honor you, my beautiful mother."* And with that, all of the light I am feeling begins to turn Golden in color. It has an even stronger vibrancy and strength than what I was feeling before, and it jogs some kind of ancient memory in me that I know is important and indelible. I have the knowing that it has been waiting for a long time, for exactly this moment.

"Your Golden Heart is alive and well," I hear her say. *"This is who you truly are; this is who you have truly been all along. Let this warm you and guide you from now on. Step inside of this, and all will be well. Welcome yourself Home, Mama, welcome yourself Golden Home."*

I begin to cry—large tears rolling down my cheeks. An upheaval of pure joy is taking place inside of me, as though the earth has moved within, changing me forever. I start to sob, and the "let go" feels so good. It is a tremendous relief.

I am aware of a Golden Flame shining bright and strong within my heart, and the pure physicality of it practically throbs inside of me. It pulsates: boom, boom, boom. It is real and pure. It spreads itself deliberately throughout my whole body and mind, washing me thoroughly, as if it knows exactly what it is doing. I allow and welcome it—I even invite it.

After a few moments I feel clean; cleansed and refreshed by all of this Golden Light. I am aware that I am actually starting to glow with it. My skin tingles and my insides feel vibrant, awake, sparkling, and alive. At the same time, the sacredness of it all strikes me powerfully, and I am aware of how holy I feel—and how whole as well. I feel simply me; totally, completely, radiantly ME.

I look at my daughter and I see that she is Golden Radiant as well. We smile at each other in joyful recognition of this most special event and revelation. Everything is being restored to its proper place, and all is becoming right in this moment. There is a sense of pure harmony about it.

And you know what? All the other stuff I had been feeling—drowning in, day in and day out—has completely disappeared. I don't know how, and I don't know where, but it is gone. It has plain evaporated. I didn't have to do anything about it or with it. All I have now is Golden Love—in me, for me, and streaming out from me.

In this moment, I know: if there is such a thing as God, this is it. In truth, I don't need any version of God outside of me. I am God myself. I am "living God in a body," in my own unique way. I am now living as God's gift to me; nothing else matters. I don't care about anything else or whatever anyone else has conjured up about the story of life. I don't care. It isn't relevant to me anymore.

I am Light, THIS light; Golden, Golden Light. I know everything is going to be fine. And then…I wake up.

That was the dream. I wake up from the dream, and for the first time since I was a young boy, I am not afraid. My first thought is not a thought of anxiety or fear or wishing I was dead. Instead, I wake up, open my eyes, and see what I see. I think to myself, "Here I am."

I am aware that everything has changed. That is to say, everything about me and inside of me has changed. Everything on the outside, of course, is still the same, but everything about my inner world has shifted, like tectonic plates underneath the surface of Terra that have rearranged themselves.

My inner workings, with their own intelligence, begin to move quite steadily in a new and most positive direction from this moment on. There are still times when I have flickers of the old beliefs and questionings of sinning and the devil, etc. But whenever that happens, I am clear that it is simply old, outdated history; like reading a story that doesn't apply anymore. It steadily begins to disappear from my inner psyche, from my mind and my emotions—it dissolves away from my awareness, as if it was never there.

I begin to discover what I had never considered possible before, which is that I am peaceful. I experience peace which lasts for longer and longer periods throughout the course of a day. Over time, it does, in fact, start to become my state of Being for extended periods. My experiences with my Angels occur more often once again, and I am pleased about this. Believe it or not, I am able to absorb their love and to receive it one hundred percent. This changes my life still more.

In my heart I understand many things that I had never thought about before. One of the things I know now is how lost I was, and for how long. I look around, and I can clearly see how lost many of these other men are. And, without trying, I seem to have a large reservoir of compassion that bubbles up for them and for myself, for how lost I was and how lost they still are. I know they will find their own way, just as I have miraculously found mine.

My perception of the "me" that I was before this wondrous rebirth is totally different. It is as if all of the old perception was a small thing in a way—all things being relative—when in fact, it had completely consumed my life, inside and out. In any case, the whole thing is different now. I find myself being able to touch it with my heart—even blessing it, in a way. In regard to my sexual preference, I feel perfectly fine about it now. In fact, I simply feel that this is the way that God wants to be through me. I know I am not like other people; I never have been and never will be.

I am gifted in many ways, and my "differentness" and sensitivity enable me to know Angels and sense far more beautiful things, precisely because of who I am. In my heart I can feel and express the tides of emotion, grace, and love that I believe happen because of who I am and how I am designed. I feel nothing but positive about this, and adoring of it. I am grateful. It is incredible.

I know I am Golden; I know I am a special Golden Being. This is clearly my path. I don't know about anybody else's journey, but the bottom line is that I receive my path. I own my path, and I now celebrate my path.

I don't know exactly what I will do going forward. It is not important to know such details, or to bring them forward at this moment. All I know is that I am home inside of myself and comfortable in my Golden Heart. I am glad to be joyously alive and growing stronger every day. And yes, I am immensely grateful.

I know this will all get stronger as time continues. I have that knowing, and it is indelible in me. I hope someday to be able to bless where and what I have been through, to simply feel at ease about all those forces and feelings of fear that terrified me inside and out. I know it sounds amazing, given where I was, but now I don't feel terrified anymore. I'm not even sure I feel afraid at all, frankly.

I no longer question myself. Instead, I question the constructs, those mental constructs of Satan and all of that. All of the rules and regulations and laws that people have created and built up, all "in the name of God." How strange they sound and seem to me now. How pitiful and empty. Many of them seem counter to life. And that is how they run—counter to life. I do not see that they brighten or enhance life at all. They simply erode and corrode the possibility of life before it can even begin to grow. That makes no sense to me.

I am still in the monastery, and I ponder these things because they are everywhere in the air—it's rampant. I reflect on the fact that I need to decide what my particular position on all of this is, but then I lose interest in it after a while. I climb back into my Golden Heart, pleased as punch to even have it and feel it and know it and be it. I am glad and grateful. I have enormous compassion. That's one of the best things that has been born in me.

You're probably wondering if I will leave the monastery. Yes, I think so. It's the right and responsible thing to do, given that I have only been here for protection and not for the right reasons of sacred communion and such. I don't know exactly when, or what this will look like. This is all still quite new, and I am still wrapped up in savoring the goodness of it all and the true goodness of me.

At some point, when I am ready, I do look forward to deliberately building a life, a Golden Life for me that will not only be a gift to my Maker but also a gift to the beauty of Life itself. That would be something that would be totally in alignment with who and how I am.

Again, as I have said already and will continue to say, I am extremely grateful. Saying it feels good, because it is my truth. I am Golden Grateful—every day, in every way.

Thank you for listening, and bless you. Golden Bless you.

Sananda Rescues

I am Sananda, and this is the story of my greatest Rescue.

I came at a time where there was much darkness, when things were going hugely awry. The consciousness at that time was falling farther and farther into despair and confusion, and I knew it was my moment to come. Golden Terra was calling me, and I could feel her beloved spirit from deep within her Core. She needed me. All of the wounded and lost Golden Ones needed me. They needed a tall drink of Golden Water—not just a sip, but a huge tall drink of our pure Golden Water. That was what I provided.

Some say that I came in the name of sacrifice, but that is not true. This was one of the greatest gifts I have ever given, one of my most grand and beautiful expressions. I loved it. I loved it because I could see it all so clearly—and yes, I knew what I was getting into. People get stuck on the outer details of that experience which enables them to stay distracted from the absolute inner core of radiance, from the sublime Golden Treasure that was taking place inside those outer circumstances. That is another way to control: keep everyone focused on and distracted by the outer circumstances—so that as little attention as possible goes into the inner, into the reverent place, into the sacred restoration that was being addressed and attended to during that time of my walk on Terra as Jesus, as Yeshua; as whatever form of that name is wanted and needed by you, the Reader.

It was agreed upon by everyone in Golden Spirit, by the many Masters of the Golden Team of which I am a part, that it was time. All was ready. It was the perfection of all the vibrations and frequencies that would enable me to actually make this reconnect, this deposit, this Golden Restoration that was going to be sustaining for such a long time to come.

The actual incarnation itself was only a small piece of something vastly bigger. It was the "Golden Nugget," certainly, but it wasn't the whole treasure. It wasn't the only time, place, and moment. It was the beginning of something magnificent that stretched far forward and remains strong and clear, as you will see as I talk about it.

My incarnation as Jesus was deliberate. This was by agreement, by choice on my part; by absolute conscious consent and desire. My heart wanted greatly to do this. Again, as I said, I knew what the outcome was going to be, and that didn't matter to me at all. My time was going to be short. There is something to be said for a short incarnation that is filled with potency and power. It is not meant to be sustained for a long period, precisely because it is potent, powerful, and concentrated. That's something to think about. It was short and sweet and to the point—short and Golden and to the point.

I was born as Jesus. Whatever details have unfolded over time, or been inserted throughout history, it is simply that I was born to my mother Mary and my father Joseph. That was our nuclear family: me—Sananda—as Jesus, the Divine Mother Mary as herself, and the inimitable Master Saint Germain as Father Joseph. This was all carefully crafted and divinely orchestrated. It was deliberate; powerfully deliberate. Together, we came to do a gigantic Golden Rescue—a Rescue and a deposit, an integration and a restoration. It was a thoroughly Sacred and Divine Undertaking.

I breathed my Golden Heart, my Golden Soul and Spirit, down through Terra, joining myself inextricably with her spirit. She received me, embraced me, and welcomed me. She had been hungry for me, and was overjoyed, as completely overjoyed as I was to be with her.

I love Terra so much. She is a huge part of me, and I of her. People don't talk about that very much in terms of Jesus, but it was the crucial and central point for my being there. She gave me balance, endurance, power, and stability. She enabled me to walk steadily and to hold myself strong and clear in my physical illumination during that time. It was precisely because of her that the sacred, refined energies of the spiritual domains could be received and integrated into the physical consciousness that prevailed at that time. She was, and still is, the anchor for us all. The power of her gifting to us, and the love she has for us, are immense.

Keep in mind, as well, how much of this sacred deposit was about the people in their mortal state and how much was about reconnecting and reactivating the Golden Etheric Consciousness Lines. The latter was by far the greater piece. Everyone thinks it was simply about the people, and they don't know or realize the greater picture that was being addressed.

We're going to talk a lot about the people, as this book is mostly about them. But there was much more of our family, and many other elements; highly active elements of our Golden Family, throughout the unseen realms—the cosmos, the stars, and beyond. I was a gigantic Golden Powerhouse of Love. Remember that. Remember our Golden Inter-Communion.

And so I am born. I am going to refer to myself as Jesus for the rest of this story.

Many people come to pay their respects to my parents and to gift me for simply being born, for coming here to be with them. They recognize the Sacred

Energies that are being brought in at this time, and they come to share their understanding of this and their honoring and support of this movement.

I love both my mother and my father with my whole heart. I love Terra, life, and all of these people with all of my heart. My heart is unstoppable; it knows no bounds and seeks to love wherever it can. It is the pure joy of giving in its simplest and most pristine form—loving for loving's sake, simply because I do.

As I grow I can see what is happening around me very clearly. I know that I am different, that I am Golden. I know why I am here. I do not have a moment of confusion or uncertainty about any of this. I understand that everyone around me has confusion or uncertainty. How lost are they, these beautiful Golden Ones that I see? How veiled and disconnected? How far from their true Center do they find themselves to be? I know so many of them have lost themselves, have lost their way in the midst of this haze, this darkness, this complete state of heavy unconsciousness.

It is difficult, you know. It is very difficult for the human heart that is activated to survive in this kind of darkness. The activated human heart needs light. It thrives, blooms, and blossoms in the light. The Golden Sun is what it needs, and the Golden Sun needs it. That's one of the central points I wish to state: how much we are loved by the Golden Sun and how much we love it. It is one of the most beautiful communions that has ever been known.

How lucky are we Golden Ones to live these kinds of splendid experiences, these realities, these truths that are so pure and pristine, so innocent, simple, and exquisite? They are all expressions of beauty over and over again.

Moving forward in time, I am now about thirteen years old. I am loved. I am a much-loved son. I'm about to grow into manhood, and I feel my body changing. I am aware of some kind of a quickening in my strength and it feels good. I'm entering a new threshold of being, from which I can see even more clearly. I feel my body and presence supporting me in ways I haven't experienced before. My feet are growing more firmly planted on the ground, and my arms and legs are well-muscled and strong. I like this feeling of physical strength. It is completely right.

I enjoy being in this body. I enjoy it immensely. I am quite aware that I am made of the same materials as Terra upon which I walk, and that pleases me enormously. There is a state of oneness, of union, of intimate understanding because of that. I love this; it allows my communion with her to become even more fluid and deeper than it was before.

As I continue to mature, my view of myself changes, along with how I understand things; the world all around, and myself in relation to it. I am beginning to truly feel my place here. I have such an abundance of love and support from many directions. I am deeply gifted by Terra and the celestial realm, from beyond, and from many people right here as well—my parents, siblings, extended family members, and friends. It's beautiful. It's beautiful to be me and beautiful to be here. I see the love shining in the eyes of those around me when they look at me. That shining warmth makes me feel good inside. I am happy.

Now, I am about eighteen years old. Things have changed quite a bit. I am more aware of turbulence. I am aware of differences and opposites. I am aware of fear, of the suffocating presence and power of fear. I understand how controlling it is, how much it pervades the psyches of people around me, and how harsh they become because of it. The energy of divisiveness that surrounds me is apparent; it is hard and bruising, regardless of whether or not someone is actually physically beating somebody up. It is that air of divisiveness of, "You are not like me, so I don't like you. You don't agree with me, so I don't like you."

These opposing sentiments, emotions, and belief systems create pain and bruising in the body, as if it is actually being beaten up. People don't realize this. They don't realize how much they are being beaten every day. It's in the psyche, the air, the energy fields, and the body—it gets stored. The body doesn't resonate with this kind of attack, abuse, discrimination, and cruelty; the more it escalates, the crueler it becomes, making the impact even greater—and then the survival instinct to oppose it is increased and heightened.

It creates more and more conflict. The Wounded are wounding. Those who are wounded wound back, or want to or try to.

It's all fundamentally a state of self-preservation, in a way. Even domination is a state of self-preservation, isn't it? It says, "I am bigger, stronger, and more powerful than you. I will protect my ground, and I will take yours as well. And in doing that, I become bigger, more powerful, and stronger than you, so I can take even more ground and make that mine, too."

There is no heart in any of that, and that is why I have come. But in order to be, to extend, and to express my Golden Heart, I have to know what I have come into and what the existing conditions are. I need to know the terrain, so I can make the best possible use of my time and energy, because I already know it is going to be short. And so, I get on with it.

I am a fully-grown man now. The things that I know, see, and feel have rapidly matured me. I have come into my own. I have come into my Soul Power, my Soul Grace, and my highly-activated Golden Heart, which has enormous capability. I let it do its thing. I step out of the way and let it do its thing, because I have no knowledge—or inclination to know—exactly what that is going to look like. I do not need to control any of it or arrange it or have any say in any of it. I have already had my say by consenting to be here. That was all that I needed to say. That was my vote of consent, confidence, and faith.

And from that moment on, I have, in that way, taken a back seat to my Soul Power, to my Golden Heart, which is running this show completely. And I am glad, because there is no way I could do this myself. I am not capable of handling what this is about to bring forth, and I know it. Within the human state, I need to let go and let God, in order for my gifts to come through. It is the way of it, because it is something far greater than me.

And that's one of the dilemmas that ensues down the road. People think that I am the one to be revered and acknowledged. It isn't me at all. It's God. It's the Sacred Essence of me, streaming forth from that which is the enormous power of Golden Creation. It is the Sacred Source of us all. That is what should be revered. I am but the instrument. Good at it, I am; I will agree, and I will say yes to that. It is my gift to give, because I am so good at it, but let us be clear: it is God's gift.

One of the reasons that I am so good at it is that I know to let go. I know to let go to this vastness of Golden Power. My Golden Heart sings; it sings as I touch everyone around me. I am asked to hold gatherings, because people are greatly drawn to me. The energy of the gift that pours through me is magnetic, inspiring, and uplifting. Although I will show up anywhere I can, I prefer to gather with people in quiet places—in the pristine purity of Nature that supports me, that supports the words and the energy, that supports this communication, communion, and transmission of Remembrance. It's the Rescuing that I am doing, Golden Heart touching Golden Heart.

I know that the Golden Flames inside the hearts of those who come are being quickly reactivated. These people are hungry. They've been hungry for a long time, these Golden Ones. They come to me for something of which they don't even know how to ask. They come with broken hearts, and here I stand, pouring out water and nourishment on this parched, dry, arid, and empty land. They are drinking it, eating it up, inhaling it, and taking it deeply in with such intent and hunger. Nothing else exists for them, just like nothing else exists for me right now. It is me; it is them. It is them; it is me.

Everywhere I go, as far as I can, I extend my voice. I extend the radiance. The radiance extends itself through me, through my voice, and deposits itself in the Conscious Streams of Awareness. It is a beautiful thing for me to witness, because that is really what I am doing. I am the Golden Witness to the beauty that is here. I am the Golden Witness to the beauty that has always been here. Yes, it is covered by darkness, and it has been for a long time. But how much can this veil of darkness truly cover the strength and power of life? It can put a damper on things, but that is all.

I am here reminding the Golden Ones of how powerful they truly are. This is not the power of domination, not at all. We understand each other. Domination is an outside force of the Heartless Ones. It is a mental construct, and one of fear. Our Golden Hearts govern and have dominion as a construct of loving embrace, loving presence, loving-kindness, and loving and deliberate co-creation. We are devoted and committed to this, so all of it begins to get restored now. Imagine it is like a giant tapestry that is growing and extending itself outward. The Remembrance of our union is being re-pitched. The Golden Note is being re-sounded.

It is strong, and it is embedding itself deeply back into its seat of rightness where it belongs and where it has always belonged. The Golden Imprint has remained since we were here in our original Lemuria together: the Golden Lemuria that we created, built, fostered, nurtured, and claimed as our own breathtaking creation. All of us, all of the Golden Ones everywhere, claim this beautiful dream that we had all poured ourselves into so completely.

We shared it and let it shine everywhere. We gifted it and loved it. We loved the feeling, and we were proud of that. We were blazing in our One Golden Heart, and we honored this. That's what I mean when I use the word claim. We honored it as us, and as greater than us, for all and for all of life.

So, in my short time as Jesus, I am reminding all the Golden Ones that can hear this, feel this, and be touched by this, to remember again that this is our Truth. Remember how it feels; remember what it's like. BE IT, BE IT, BE IT. I cannot do this for them. I can only Rescue them. I cannot, in fact, save them. That is for them to do for themselves.

Once they have been Rescued and their flames have been reignited in a powerful way, then it is theirs to take over and do with it what they will, in their own time and way and fashion and freedom. Their lives and their paths have been rerouted directly back into their true selves. They will never be the same again.

And for those who are not directly in my presence, I am successful in doing a lot of Tagging in this incarnation. And then those Golden Ones that are consciously reverberating the Golden Radiance again—and there are many—join with me, and together, we make more Rescues and we accomplish more Tagging.

There is such a great deal that is accomplished even in this short time. It is the greatest global Rescue ever. It is the most beautiful thing. There is Golden Song everywhere, and for a moment it is louder than anything else. It is louder than the fear and all that the fear brings. It is louder than anything. It reigns, and it is glorious.

All of the universe, and beyond, is singing with it. Deep down in Terra, the core crystal herself is singing Golden Song—bright, light, Golden Heart Radiance. It makes us cry. It makes us cry because it is beautiful, and it feels good and it feels right. There is nothing like truly coming home, being seated in self, and feeling comfortable because everything is lined up the way it's supposed to be. All of us are expressing in our unique ways, with our unique designs and systems. It is a time of exquisite gems shining—Golden Gems shining, Golden Sun shining. It is internal. It is in the conscious etheric lines of Remembrance, and it is deep, solid, and abiding.

I know it will stretch forth; it will reach forward for eons to come. It is renewed hope, a renewal of faith. It is a regathering of many lost ones. It is strong, with strength in numbers. It is potent, triumphant, radiant, glorious, and beautiful. So much beauty is being born from this, so much beauty.

I call it the Christ Heart. Christ Heart is Golden Heart. This is what we're all about: living, breathing, One Golden Heart. I witnessed as many of our loved ones reached out to many beyond them. It spreads like wildfire, and has remained so to this present day.

At some point on my journey, things are not going so well on the outside, and that's a great understatement. But I knew it was coming, and I have prepared for this as well. I have trained and prepared my body. I have prepared my mind. I am ready.

The governing authorities of the day take me prisoner. They torture me, causing me to endure great physical torment and pain. I am hoisted up onto a cross for all to see. Yes, I am a shining example of what NOT to do, so they say. That is the story.

I am hanging from this cross, blood dripping from my body, seemingly power-less and helpless: a clear demonstration and shining example of what NOT to do, with the message being, of course, DO NOT SHINE. Do whatever you have to do to not shine. Cover your light. Bury your light. Repress, suppress, and depress your light. Don't love, because your love will shine brightly. Don't love too much, too far, too open, or too inclusively. It might rub up against the wrong kind of people. Don't show your talents, your God-given Golden Talents—the magic, the mystery, the wondrousness. Don't show the power of your abilities to touch and heal, intrinsic in your design. And for heaven's sake, don't talk about the Light. Don't talk about the Gold. Don't talk about the kindness, the heartfulness, and all that this can generate.

Always be careful, because look what is happening to me. It is what will most likely happen to you, too.

I look out from my vantage point on the cross, and I see everyone looking at me, aching from what they perceive as my suffering. I am, in truth, not suffering at all. My body is bleeding, yes, but I am not suffering. I knew this would happen. I prepared for it. I am able to disassociate from the pain. Don't project the agony upon me that is not mine. Don't make that be my agony. This agony is yours—the agony of the conclusions that you are drawing, the belief systems that you are creating and adopting, the darkness that befalls you because you believe I am your only light.

I am not YOUR light. I am MY light. YOU are YOUR light. We are ALL light. My exit takes nothing away from you. In fact, it says to you that you don't need me to foster this in you anymore. You are as strong and powerful as this love yourself. Live it so. Be all that you have remembered in our time together. Isn't that what it's been? I have been witnessing you. I didn't do it for you. You did it. You showed up with hunger, and you inhaled your own Golden Remembrance. You reempowered yourself. I reminded you; that's all.

I saw you, as you have seen me. I witnessed you, as you have witnessed me. It is the joy of the freedom of owning and knowing the power of God that you are already and have always been. You are that and always will be that.

I look down from the cross and see all of you crying. I know that many of you will stop crying soon, because when you have moved out of the shock of things, you will realize the truth of what I just said. You will know it to be true for yourselves. And I know that you will know, and you will carry it forth, and you will help others to remember. You will do for them exactly what I have done for you.

As I gaze out, I am also aware of the many who are giving in to complete ignorance, loss of self, and loss of Light. They believe that because I am gone, they are gone as well. For them there is no more shining forth of Light for now.

And the other thing is, how do you know that I left at all? Frankly, nobody knows the answer to that but me. Perhaps I didn't actually die, and perhaps I did. Either way, as we know, life lives on, as we have all witnessed many times over. Throughout time you have seen me, felt me, and walked with me again. We have walked with each other, and we still do. The truth is, nothing can get in between us. We are One Golden Heart, one Golden Christed Heart—the greatest gift that we have ever known.

And to those people and authorities who have "condemned me," I can see clearly that they are simply doing what they know to do. Without them having an activated heart, why are we all surprised? But some of them, many of them, are Golden Ones that have become lost. And one of the greatest intentions of my incarnation here is to reach them, because to be lost is the greatest pain of all. Don't you think?

To be broken in spirit like that—so that you can be reshaped and manipulated into a completely different form of consciousness, almost obliterating everything else you have ever known—that is true pain. That is excruciating; the deadening of spirit. It doesn't get any worse than that, because the truth is, spirit never dies, but it can be deadened. And that's like being between a rock and a hard place, as you say, unable to go anywhere, unable to move, and feeling unable to do a thing about it, because you don't even know that you have a choice. You are not even aware.

All the pain has beaten your Golden Memory right out of you, so it's a dead zone of consciousness. And yet, if you listen, there is still a heartbeat in there, isn't there? You can be trapped in that obliterating grayness, and you will still feel it—thump, thump, thump. There's a heartbeat. Isn't it amazing that it would still be there after all of this pain and suffocation of self? Being a complete stranger to self—there is nothing more lost than that.

But I can hear the heart beating. I am clear and I can hear it clearly.

Many people don't want true clarity, even those "in the know" that think they do and say they do. All they want to see and witness is the goodness and the beauty. Will they allow their clarity of sight and insight to take it this far, to where they witness this kind of pain? To where they can feel and allow for this kind of despairing, and through this—and only through this—be able to put their finger on the pulse of the heartbeat that still lives within that deadness, inside the depths of that Golden Being? The Golden Heartbeat is still there. It is buried, deeply buried. It is covered over and layered over and crusted over.

But if you call up your Golden Courage and go into it, you can still hear it. That is the power of the heart, the splendid Golden Heart, alive and well and still beating. It is there as a waiting patient. Does it know that it will be revived and restored to expression? Yes, it knows that at some point it will be. In the meantime, it beats and stays alive, because that is its nature—it is an exquisite pearl that can be trusted, everlasting.

The "dead zone" is the deepest chasm of lostness that our Golden Family knows. We cannot turn our back. We must not turn away, because—let me remind you, Golden Ones—what happens to one happens to all. If there is a deadening of consciousness like that, we feel it in the greater tapestry of our Golden Family Configuration. We know it in some extended place of ourselves, or maybe not so extended. We feel those levels of pain. We know them by osmosis, if not by immediacy. And that shakes everything up, doesn't it? It keeps everything shaken up until it is touched, witnessed, and restored. It shakes up and rattles the framework of Self, creating a sense of unsettledness, a vague but persistent kind of distress within. It also stirs up those feelings that are designed to hide all the uneasiness—like judgment, chastisement, blame, and anger.

This stirring up of everything is the Golden Heart within, creating a crack in the entire composite picture: a crack where it's light can, and will, inevitably get through. That's what happens with those who are lost and broken. Many of you will go forth to Rescue those exact ones. You will see. You will see how far into the web you have to go to look at them, and you will find out what it is like to feel as they do. You will witness what it takes, as you watch your own Golden Hearts reach out to theirs through that crack of openness, to reignite their flame and allow that Golden Heartbeat to increase and strengthen, becoming brighter and broader, making a way for its Golden Fluid to flow properly and freely again.

You do not need to change them, only to remind them. They will change themselves over the course of their history. But never believe that there is nothing you can do about it, because the Golden Stream flows all by itself once opened. It takes hold and begins to navigate a new course; establishing terrain with new parameters, directions, and creations that may seem unbelievable to self, because they are the opposite of the deadened consciousness.

And yet, that is precisely what can and will happen; once Rescued or Tagged it is inevitable that that Golden One will find their way home. I repeat, it is inevitable. It is simply the way of the Golden Design, the way of the true Golden Self. In this you can rest assured. Deep within, you already know this is true.

I encourage you to place your attention not so much on what looks like closed doors around you, or blocked avenues to your freedom, but on the beauty that your Golden Flow is, the beauty that your Golden Heart creates and generates merely by its own nature. Be that to the best of your ability, just like I have been in my incarnation as Jesus. You've seen what it looks like. You've felt what it feels like. I have been showing you all of that, being a good role model amongst other things, with all the joy in my everlasting Golden Heart.

As I gaze down from the cross one last time, I think to myself that there is always much more to life than meets the eye—much more to each one of us than meets the eye. I look at you from here, and I know that there will be many journeys outward from this particular incarnation. There will be times when you will come back to Rescue more and more Golden Ones, newly cognizant of the strength of your Golden Heart than before, more than you could have been aware of before on this planet of Terra.

It is strong in you now when you incarnate. It is strong. Be true to that. Yes, there will be many lifetimes when you will pay dearly in terms of persecution and pain. But you will see, as did I, that the main point was to Rescue and bring everyone home; and the rest of it is the rest of it. You will naturally grow to understand through time, and you will heal. That is inevitable also.

I am with you always, whether you believe in me as Jesus or not. I am forever Sananda, the Golden One, and that is how you know me, in truth. In Golden Heart we are one. We are One Golden Radiant Heart. I love you, my Golden Partner. Good day and Godspeed.

MOTHER MARY RESCUES

They call me Divine Mother Mary. I am a great Golden One, and a great shepherd of the One Golden Radiant Heart. I speak now because there are many things to tell the truth about, many old habits and patterns to shed and walk away from, to release and be relieved of. This can occur now, because there is an absolutely pure and crystal-clear understanding of the state of things—what has happened, what is happening, and what will be happening for all the Golden Ones.

I come with my fellow Golden Ones, Sananda and Master Saint Germain. We each have our piece of the pie to speak about, to convey and express energetically through our words and our avenues of sight and clarity. This is an enormous gift that I give back to you in great joy, harmony, and peace.

I do this because everything is ready. Everything and everyone are ready to receive this now. Every system of life is ready to support this. This is a great, resoundingly joyful gift for all of life in every way, on every level, seen and unseen. Please keep this in mind as I tell my story. Allow yourselves to listen and hear me, and see how it all makes you feel and what comes alive inside of you as I speak.

My time as the divine Mother Mary, mother of Jesus (Yeshua, or however you wish to call him by name), was one of the highest privileges that I was ever granted. It was one of the greatest challenges of my evolution, if not the greatest. It was something that I stepped up to, boldly and brightly. I did it with immense care, tenderness, nurturing, and understanding.

I am the stable base for a beautiful being. I am the mother, the deliverer, the one who holds the parenting battery of Golden Joy for this beautiful being to be ushered forth into the world. It is a time that is filled with darkness, and one that is working under false premises. The people are not connected to their Source and the divine union with that which is of the greatest and highest good.

It is a time of "Lost Man." I use the term man to refer to all human beings, whatever the gender. It is the perfect time for us to come, as receptivity is in resonance for us to regather as Golden Ones and to spread our recognition and witnessing of one another. This enables many Golden Flames to be reignited and brought to full fire; in a sense, engaged and activated.

An extremely highly activated time it is. Our intention is to rescue, remind, and restore, to bring that which is our greatest sacred holiness back up to the surface of conscious awareness. I come back to Golden Terra with supreme joy. I keep talking about the joy, because it is abundant for me, and for all of us at this time in our own way. It is buried deep down inside for most, but I am acutely aware of it.

It is a time of absolute vibrancy, and I am a bright, sacred, holy light in the midst of a dark shroud. I love my light. I love being a Flame of Goldenness in the midst of all the fear in Mondor, the fear that is generated by the Heartless Ones. I am serene and I am glad to be here. I feel completely purpose-driven, mission-driven, and fueled by my great Source of All Being that holds steady. This keeps me strong and completely nourished in my soul center within my body at all times.

I can hardly wait to get pregnant. I was excited even as a young girl thinking about it. I have a lovely family, and they take great care of me. I am grateful to them; there are many women in my family who are strong in their own right. They support me in being fully myself and give me exactly what I need, as do my father and my brothers. It is a perfect balance for me of the male and the female. It is just what I need, with exactly the right atmosphere and energetic environment for me to foster and continue nurturing that which I came in with, which is this powerful deeply-seated strength, clarity, and love.

My Golden Heart is sacred and strong and I know it. I know it well. I am young, in my mid-teens, when I meet my husband Joseph. Soon after being married I become pregnant. He and I make a plan together; we know why we have come and joined together. Our plan is born from our Golden Harmony. We know the best way to proceed with what we are here to do, knowing all the while that we never work alone.

We are grandly guided and directed. We often commune and consult with many great masters, as well as other Golden Life Forms on other domains and dimensions, seen and unseen. I can see well into the future, as can Joseph. Both of us know the depth and breadth of what we are bringing forward and what our responsibility to this truly is. It is the same responsibility that I feel right now at this moment in speaking with you.

I have a natural and easy delivery of our baby. I call it our baby, but he was a Grand Master before he was even conceived. Out he came, and here he is—splendid.

He is special and pure. His light burns brightly inside, and he glows; he Golden, Golden, Golden Glows. Everyone who comes to see him is moved and touched. They are indelibly touched within their hearts, even though he is a newborn baby. His is glory; his is Golden Grace that is to be shared.

It is not about him. It is about what he is sharing and all those who are touched. The sound and the resonance of his light, the pulsation of his Goldenness reaches into the hearts of everyone who comes, making them want to bow down to him. They do it instinctively. They drop to one knee, because they have been seen. They feel recognized and witnessed. All that is holy and sacred and pure inside of them is being witnessed, seen, loved, and adored. How can you not drop down on one knee when you feel this way inside? It is a position of prayer, thanksgiving, and gratitude that finally your essential essence is being seen, understood, and engaged. Nothing else matters, everything else merely falls away.

Those who come are friends and friends of friends who have heard about this most special being. They arrive and bestow riches and material things upon this little babe. We consider the gifts unnecessary, but the gratitude and love that we feel is fully received and appreciated. They are all so touched by Jesus' presence that the outpouring of these gifts is simply their way of conveying their feelings and deep resonance, gratitude, and recognition. We appreciate the beauty of the gifts, as they bring much brightness, lightness, and celebration to our home. Brightness prevails. Our Golden Glow, the Remembrance from Lemuria, is bright and shining. It is wondrous.

Joseph and I know what we need to do to prepare this child to move into his growth and development. We know how much time we have to stabilize him and to have him experience the training that he needs to have in the body in order to survive and succeed in what he came here to do, especially considering the events and circumstances that will take place later on.

We know; the three of us know what is ahead. There are no secrets, and this is not a mystery. We come in knowing full well what is needed from each of us in order to insure the success of this Rescue Mission. Things in this way could not be better. It is a prime open window for us and we seize it.

We seize the day; we go full throttle with full gusto, absolutely shining brightly and with no holding back. It is not even a consideration. There is only forward movement, Golden Steady and one step at a time, with patience and perseverance, and always staying the course. We know full well our Rescue Mission will be a success, and so we proceed unhindered.

We are aware and clear about the future for generations to come. Don't think for a minute we are just isolated in this present moment with Jesus. No, this mission is far, far greater. This is a definite planned event of Golden Restoration for all the future generations to behold, to be a part of, and to be supported by. It sounds big, because it is big. It gives you a sense of how powerful our Golden Hearts really are and how potent the Golden Life Force truly is. It matters—oh yes, indeed, it is significant and it matters.

Jesus has already told his story—some of the ins and outs of it, anyway. My job is to hold the space, to hold the home base space steady as a rock. It is as if I am always seated firmly on the ground with my bottom touching it: solid, secure, and steady like a rock. That is what he needs so he can go out front and forward. Relatively speaking, I am very much in the wings, as is Joseph.

People really don't know what Joseph does in many ways, and he has his own story that he will share. He is very much a part of this and has an essential role which he plays and lives out. I will let him speak for himself when his time comes.

My role is always to hold the juice and the space. I am the powerhouse; I am the mother and the deliverer. I am the balancer. That is my job. I am the gigantic Golden Battery. I am basically tethered to Terra, and she and I together hold all the sustaining power for this huge and sacred Golden Rescue.

Jesus can always count on me. He draws from the power that comes through me, as well as his own source of power. We work as a team, and we rely on each other. That is what the plan is, and that is how it goes. I love this. I am secure; completely sovereign and Golden Secure. I touch many women—I have a profound effect on Golden Women, and on many other Golden Souls throughout the time that Jesus is alive and active in his mission.

I am responsible for spreading the word, touching those lights, making those Rescues, and fostering the entire paradigm of the divine feminine. The purpose is to make this movement larger, more stable, more secure, and stronger, so that it will be able to persevere, to remember itself and be able to carry forward. It is a great purpose that I have, large and far-reaching.

I watch our beautiful Golden Man be torn apart, persecuted by the Heartless Ones. I know that he did not feel this pain physically, because we had ensured in his training that he would not. He needs to keep his Golden Light bright throughout every step of his journey, no matter what is happening. That is a fact, and that is what he does.

He touches many of the lost Golden Ones who had been taken in, broken by the Heartless Ones, and turned into soldiers for them. In his ability to keep his light bright he is able to Tag and even actually complete full-on Rescues for some of them. During the whole period of what looked like his suffering, his light never diminished. His Golden Radiance just grew stronger and stronger. Time is short—we know this; he knows this.

As he is taken and put upon the cross, his communion with God is palpable. His generating of Golden Fluid is tangible. It pours out of him. There he is up on the cross with streams of Golden Power, Golden Love—pouring straight out of him into everyone who is there and everything that is there, all life forms.

He knows that the Heartless Ones are lost. What could one expect from something like that, from that state of lostness? What they do is no surprise. There is such kindness in his soul, a kindness that goes far beyond what is known as kindness to date. That is one of his deepest gifts: the kindness that reaches right into the heart and soul and body and being of everyone.

This is the vibration of Golden Harmony. There is no divisiveness here. There never was, and there never will be. It is the Christed Heart, the Golden Heart within all of us; it is exactly that. How little have you known of yourself? How small and tiny a glimpse have you had into the true breadth and depth of your beauty and Golden-Heartedness?

You think you have loved, and you have loved. I'm not taking that away. I'm not diminishing that in any way, shape, or form. What I am saying is that it is but a minute flicker of the amount of love that you are, that you possess, and of which you are made. What you have consciously coming up to you now, coming back into your memory banks and your conscious awareness, is so much more than your mind can comprehend. Your sight, sound, smell, and hearing; your greater awareness, your Golden Awareness, are all returning to you.

Upon Jesus' departure, there are many of us who still remain to carry on the work and be the ignited Golden Flames of Heartedness that we have become because of him. It is our light now, and I speak for all of us when I say this. It is our light now that is strong, steady, secured, alive, ignited, activated, and well. We do not need him for this. His job is done. He is on to other things that are all relevant to this, but not in the same way and position as he had been earlier.

Now it is for all of us who are left to continue the blossoming, the Rescuing, and the solidifying of the Golden Activation that has taken place during this time with Jesus. We band together, and this is much heightened in the divine feminine. Many, many women are involved in this, as well as those men who recognize the essential importance of the divine feminine. It is the divine feminine in the female and the male that is being fostered, nurtured, and fanned.

We do what we are still here to do. We love a lot and share a lot. We gather a lot, because we need to reunite the Golden Family and Golden Harmony in family form that is fully us as Lemurians. We must do this. It is our pure nature and design, and it is our love.

There are many young children who are born into this Golden Moment of Experience here. These are incredibly special children, all of them. We rely on each other to foster and teach these children to be the Golden Ones again. We teach them to remember and to live their "Goldenness" in the best ways that they can in this time and place—smartly, carefully, and wisely, but with great joy and knowing, with enormous clarity and wholeness. So many beings becoming responsible for all that is carried through in generations forward. People give a lot of attention to all of it being Jesus, and yet there is so much more going on.

He is the catalyst, but it is all of us, as well as him.

Things change even more as time goes on. Things change in terms of the Heartless Ones and their attitudes and aggression toward us. We do not feel safe from it. We are safe in ourselves, but we know the times and circumstances. For me this is no surprise, as it is no surprise to many of us. The question is, what are we going to do and how much will it, in fact, affect us? And when I say affect us, I mean deeply, deeply affect us. How much will it interfere with us?

That's what I want to talk about now, because there are many interfering forces in the midst of this time and place. And there will be in future times and places that we will come back to deal with again, and yet again. These are all tactics of divisiveness. The creation and the fostering of the whole idea of Satan and sinning are like throwing a monkey wrench into a beautiful Golden Pie.

This takeover that asserted itself is designed to counteract the Golden Glow spreading. It is designed to get in the way, and to break apart the Golden Family; to break apart the relationship, the deeply sacred relationship, that we have with one another—and that each one of us has within ourselves, with our Sacred Golden Heart. The more that the Heartless Ones can devise ways to keep us away from our sacred center, the more effective they are, the more successful in keeping us weakened.

It comes in many different forms—different names, different acts of brutality, different brainwashing tactics, different reprogramming. But it is all designed to do one thing, and that is to keep us off our center, to keep us away from our sacred holy centers, because that is where our power lies. If we are in our center, aligned and communed, we know everything Golden. We are Golden Crystal-Clear and our light is blazing. They cannot have that, because they don't understand it, and their hearts can't receive it. But what they can do is to disarrange, distort, tamper with, and divide in a counteractive way. If they can do that, then they can stay in control and in charge.

And the more they do this, the more that any of us are weakened in any way by this, the weaker and more vulnerable we become. So you have all of these mind constructs, these patterns in the Heartless Ones' imprint that deeply affect us Golden Ones—calling us the devil or Satan, calling us witches practicing witch-craft. All of it is designed to bruise us, and to generate fear and fan the flame of that fear, over and over again.

All the way down the line, that fear has been planted through generations and generations. In truth, all of these things—these tactics, these constructs and devices—are all false, completely and totally false. They do not exist in the Golden Design. They never have, they do not now, and they never will.

But this is what I am here to tell you today. Those things do not belong to you. Those patterns, those things, belong to the Heartless Ones' imprint, to their configuration. NONE OF IT BELONGS TO YOU OR YOURS. IT IS COMPLETELY FOREIGN TO YOU—SEPARATE, OTHER THAN, NOT YOU.

It is time to take these off. It is time to see the difference between that imprint and your true imprint and to make choices as to which ones you are going to live by. Even if you think you've never subscribed to any of that stuff, you need to look to see if it's within your arena anywhere, on any level, however on the edges or outside the edges. It is not enough to go into denial if you have been affected by those things and just say, "No, I haven't been. I don't believe that. I don't subscribe to that."

You need to truly look and see if it is in there anywhere. Have I ever been affected by this? Was my family affected, or my parents or their parents, or their parents? Was it passed down to me, and just because I decide that it is not for me, does that make it not anywhere present in my energy fields in some way? Am I affected by this at all?

Of course you are affected by it. There has been no escape from the H-O influence. Be in denial if you want to, but that is what it is—denial. If you are able to admit to having this H-O influence, then offer it up to the Golden Light to be released from you, so that it is gone from your energy field and psyche and consciousness forever. Delete it now, and make a choice about where you belong. Where do you fit in? What is your home base? Who are you without this influence?

Know what needs to be cleaned up, to be strengthened and fostered—and then let the Heartless Ones have their own configuration back. It is theirs. You don't need to change it. You don't need to do a thing about it. Live and let live.

Another area that is important for me to speak about is abuse. Many women and men throughout time have been abused in acts of domination, violation, and excruciating torment in many ways. I acknowledge this, and I witness this. I am sorry for this pain for all that have been brutally harmed.

I want to speak about this as a metaphor. It is a belief system about our One Golden Radiant Heart that has, metaphorically speaking, been abused and violated by the Heartless Ones. This started, of course, in the initial shattering. In this fragmentation and weakening and woundedness we have held our One Golden Heart as being wounded.

Over time, there have been repeated violations of our heart space, as we have been broken-hearted. We have witnessed the persecution of those we love. We have been persecuted ourselves. We have endured much heartbreak and heart-ache. The constant bombardment of emotional, psychic, and energetic battering that's happened to many of us has been crippling. The fact that this bombardment is in the air because it's happening to those we love, both near and far, is further crippling. It's happening to our Golden Family in some time and space basically all the time, even today—very much so today, in fact.

It's a repeated feeling of violation and intrusion—taking away that which is sacrosanct, the robbing of our purity and our essence, the robbing of our soul. It has certainly felt this way. We also see it being done to Terra, to her skies and waters, to all which has been pure and pristine—now abused by aggressive, dominant, controlling forces with cold determination, greed, and cruelty. This need to control and dominate is counter to us as Golden Ones.

This has broken our hearts even more. There is no getting away from it in Mondor, is there? There is no getting away from it at all. It's in the consciousness, in the air and the soil. These acts of violation and brutal intrusion are designed for one thing, and one thing only: it is an attempt to rob that which is sacred. It's designed to get in between you and that which you hold the most near, dear, and holy; that which is of greatest meaning to you. It's designed to keep you separate from that, so that you will not re-engage your power. It will distract you and it will bruise you; it will batter you and it will disturb you.

It will make you weak and cause you to curl upon yourself in agony because you hurt so much. You hurt for yourself, and you hurt for all those whom you love. You hurt for all of that which you love—for the body of Terra herself, and so much more. You ache from this constant battering, and you do everything that you possibly can to survive it. As long as you are here, that is what you do.

Most of your time is spent surviving, and I understand that. I know it well. I am here to tell you something about that. The truth of the matter is that your sacred self is strong, resilient, powerful, and whole. Your sacred self has remained completely untouched, unscathed, unbruised, and unbattered. You are not who, how, and what you think yourself to be. You have been whole this entire time. You've lost sight of this wholeness, yes—all of you have, to varying degrees, some more than others.

Some have become more lost than others, and you have already been told the many reasons why throughout the pages of this book—you will continue to understand it, as more is said about all of this. In truth, underneath it all and inside the center of you—your heart, your being, your core—you are one magnificent Golden Being. You always have been, you always are, and you always will be.

No one, and nothing, has desecrated you. Nothing has desecrated you, ever. All these things that I talked about earlier are on the outer periphery. They are conditions and circumstances of the Mondor imprint. They are that and simply that. You are divine wholeness in your body, within your Golden Body, your Golden Heart, your Golden Mind, your Golden Clarity, and your Golden Understanding.

I urge you to center yourself now in this, back home in you. Turn your full attention to this. *Take your attention off what is outside and place it gently but squarely on yourself, inside of you, right in your sacred center—restoring that which is of the greatest meaning to you. Be and live that, from now on, however you may frame it.* It is the joy and the jubilation of your Golden Truth: free, clear, vibrant, alive, and well. Let me restate that word—well…so well.

I knew in my lifetime with Jesus that all of this was going to be in store for all of us then, and in the future—continual revisits to Mondor. We would have to go through all of this again and again, in a variety of ways; each and every time, in order to survive things. We would have to endure things. There would be a great joy of Golden Restoration, Rescues, and homecoming.

But it is this battering and weakness and falsehood which I am now addressing, so that these can be shed. So that you can simply walk away from all of this, right into that which you truly are, have always been, and always will be. It's okay now. Everything is in support of this now. You are wanted, needed, desired, and valued NOW.

Your Goldenness is hungered for. It wants to be brought in, brought out, and brought forward. All of life wants to witness you, Golden You, and be Golden Witnessed in return. It is the most sacred sharing that there is. It is, it simply is.

Take a deep breath. There's much more to say and tell, but these are things that are directly relevant to Jesus' incarnation, because that is where they were born. Yes, there was great darkness before that, of course. But very particular and specific things were born in that period of time that have been current throughout time ever since.

Today is a new day, just like it was back then when the Golden Light burned so bright. It was a divine homecoming, all of us together with our lights alive and well and bright for that period of time, as if we were being watered and fed and nourished right where we were. It was a glorious feeling, and it remains a glorious feeling, because we are still glorious beings no matter what. No matter what, we are always Glorious Golden Beings. NO MATTER WHAT, OUR ONE GOLDEN HEART HAS BEEN WHOLE, JUST AS WE HAVE BEEN INDIVIDUALLY.

As we speak further through the process of these pages, you will deepen still more into the strength and power and truth of that, and become more fully solidified in this resonance that is the Golden Sacred Heart of you, and of all of us. Thank you for listening. Onward we go. Ever bright, ever joyous, ever Golden. Good day.

MASTER SAINT GERMAIN RESCUES

I came to be a part of Sananda's walk on Terra when he was Jesus/Yeshua. I came because the three of us—he, the divine Mother Mary, and I—had been in charge of this project since its birth. This was part and parcel of our continuing to hold the space of the beautiful Golden Lemuria.

It was an exquisite privilege for me to be the one who was always the main activator and igniter, the one who would propel the Golden Ones forward, who supported them always and helped them to have resilience and steadfastness—to persevere—because persevering is the name of the game of successful creation. It is not just about starting out, or about being in the middle; it is bringing it all the way home to its final and dedicated, devoted conclusion.

This takes energy and stamina. It takes immense self-regard, honesty, and respect for that which is in the process of being born, in the process of being brought forth—for the creation. The creative act is something which most people do not understand. If they did, they would be far more dedicated to standing strong when that is what is called for and needed.

They would not come to the table with anything but self-confidence. They would not come with anything but exquisite envisioning and pure joy over the manifestation of Source, because that's what Golden Creations are. All Golden Creations are manifestations directly of Source. Golden Ones understand that they are but instruments. They are privileged, divine instruments for a tremendous outpouring of God and of Source; of the Divine.

Every time that a Golden One takes a breath, it is done with reverence. Every day in Lemuria was a day that was given thanks for, because it was yet another opportunity to speak, express, and engage with this divine power, this fuel, this intelligence and wisdom. We speak often about the beauty of Lemuria, and it was jaw-dropping—far beyond one's ability to create or manifest, because it goes beyond the parameters of the mind, of mental knowing.

Every day for a Golden One was a day of being birthed anew, of realizing still more the deep and profound capacity of God and of Source; a moving through, magnification, and realization of creations that beautifully continue, because every single creation begets a new creation, and on and on.

This was yet another opportunity to engage in Golden Creation. We have Sananda coming in as Jesus, Mother Mary as the divine mother, and myself as Joseph, the father. There are some people on the planet who know a lot about Joseph, but he is rarely revealed, and there is a reason for this: as Joseph, I am holding the sacred behind the scenes. I am the illuminating space-holder behind the battery that is Mother Mary, who is behind the expresser, the deliverer—the messenger, which is Jesus/Yeshua. From now on I will refer to him as Jesus, because that is what is appropriate and what we are most familiar with.

The divine personhood of Jesus is the fuel of the Source from the battery that Mary is holding that is propelled and sustained by the Source that is coming through me. I am holding that course, that conduit of energy, that Golden Living Stream. I am holding it steady and secure and completely unwavering and sacrosanct, of course. The whole thing is sacrosanct.

Pouring through and holding this steady conduit is also the Golden Light from the incoming stars, galaxies, and universes. It is way beyond that of Terra. This is a co-creation of all Golden Ones everywhere; a most deliberate forthcoming deposit that is being made to reinforce and regather the Golden Intelligence, the Golden Fiber, and the Golden Juice back into that location that we knew as Terra, which the Heartless Ones called Mondor.

In any case, that is my role, and I am basically holding steady behind the scenes. I am in constant communion and communication with Jesus and Mother Mary, and with the many Golden Masters of the celestial realms and other Golden Planets and Places. I am also bringing through the Golden Force Field of the Golden Elementals and the unseen Golden Vibratory Frequencies from Golden Life Forms that are not in the material form. "Etheric" is the appropriate term.

This is a huge undertaking. It is an extremely focused, much directed, and most intentional undertaking. It is more concentrated and more focused than our original Lemurian project, which was far more outpouring and out-blossoming— like a flower opening to the Sun. This is more like honing in with the kind of focus that one uses to look through a microscope. It is honing in with that strong inner eye, inner light, determination, brilliance, and knowing that this is our job and our intention—that this is what we are going to be successful in doing.

Not only are we pulsing through the Golden Energetic Streams into this location that is known as Mondor, but we are also making a tremendous amount of Rescues, as well as deposits for future Golden Rescues. Our thinking is extremely advanced. The lines of energetic communication and Golden Resonance are strong, steady, and sturdy. They are delivered with that intention so that they are able to walk forward on their legs, so to speak. They will remain, and they will sustain.

This is the sustaining part of the creation. How do you make real the sustaining part of a creation? This is it in action. You can see the legs that it has had all the way to the modern day. The sustaining quality and power are palpable; it remains so. It has been adored and worshipped, idolized and revered. Homage has been paid throughout different cultures and times, and it has touched the people, their hearts, and the atmosphere.

It is extraordinary how strong the in-placing, inputting, depositing, and delivery are in the short walk of Jesus' incarnation, at least the part where he is outward and visible to people. This gives you a glimpse of the power of Lemurian Heart. Does it not?

This shows you what is possible, what the Lemurian Heart, the Golden Heart, is truly capable of. It defies explanation, as it goes far, far beyond. It is incredibly powerful, potent, and a remarkable privilege. It is a glorious manifestation of God: a manifestation of Golden Source which is Source itself having gifted us all with this Golden Power to bring forward both in Lemuria as Lemuria and in times since.

Keep in mind that being gifted with this gold from Source was exactly that—a gift. That is why it took Masters to build the creation of Lemuria. It is why Masters, developed and skilled Masters, were invited to become a part of this great endeavor. The gold is not something that can be held by anyone; it needs someone who is deeply sacred, reverent, and conscious of what it needs. It is a powerful, beautiful resonance of Source from Source.

To be an instrument of this Golden Heart is the most sublime and splendid experience that you will ever know—and you do all know this, of course. It is an exquisite gift to be an instrument of, to work with, and to create from.

Back to the incarnation at hand: the great birthing of the savior, the Golden Savior, who comes to remind many Golden Ones who you truly are. He brings you illumination and reminds you of that illumination inside of your beings. It becomes known as the Christ-Heartedness. You are reignited and reactivated as your Golden Being and it is glorious. You love it, you eat and drink it up.

It is a potent, divine, and delicious savoring experience as all the cells in your body suddenly wake up. They have a point and a purpose. They are free and joyous. You haven't known this since Lemuria. You forgot, and now this is like pure exhilaration. If there is ever a Golden Joy Juice, this is it, and you simply take it in. You take it in fully and you become it.

Just like Jesus, you become a Golden Station right here in Mondor. Who would have known that this is possible? Who would think it is possible? Mondor is so dank, dark, and heavy; it obliterates light. It isn't making and turning on light. The odds that you are faced with are now eclipsed by the Gold and the Golden Heart. It is strong, pure, and bright, outshining everything else.

Once the Heartless Ones catch on to what is happening with our gathering of light, which is completely foreign to them, they know what this means for them. This is strong, potent stuff. It is way stronger than they are and they know it; but our numbers are small, and they rally their forces. How are they going to subdue this? How are they going to obliterate it? How are they going to keep this under tight control so they can continue to survive?

Survival is what they know—that is how they think, and their consciousness is in the darkness. That is where they feel comfortable. They take this happening of the rebirthing and restoration of Golden Light and they twist and torque it. They do everything they can to make it into something that holds a counter-perception. This is how the whole thought form of Satan and the devil, of evil is created.

They take a piece of it and invert it in such a way that it begins to collect energy as a negative thought form which is opposing, destructive, and obliterating. This extends to convince anyone who might think of doing the work of light that they are sinners and that it is an evil thing. They want everyone to think that they are basically evil people, and to instill fear throughout.

It cloaks the possibility of light emerging within the population. Many of the Golden Light Shiners at that time are taken and persecuted as Jesus was. This is all done publicly to instill yet more fear in the populace. They want them to be deathly afraid that this will happen to them if they dare speak of this or become like this.

That message then carries its own weight throughout time, up to now. This does not mean forever, but the message is still here in the present day. It carries its own weight of cloaking, depressing, repressing, and suppressing the true Source light within all people. It distorts their thinking and their perceptions of themselves. It makes them small, and in making them small the Heartless Ones have control and dominion over them.

That is how they handled it then, and in a variety of ways since. It isn't always about something religious, although that is often the case. It certainly isn't all about the Christian religion. There are many religions that have their own aspects of this, but it's much broader than that, of course. It is also in many avenues of life's walk—this control, this dominion and cloaking, this ability to keep the people down.

When this is the case, what you have is a people who are largely dead inside. They believe they are unworthy and that they are sinners. They believe they are no good and are broken. They believe they have no power, because what seems to be a greater power is always clobbering them over the head in one way or another.

This is done through the energetic spiral and configuration of fear. Fear is the greatest breeder of smallness. It breeds obliteration of light. It freezes everything and causes one to forget who and what one really is.

You have thought forms that became so strong throughout time that they took hold, just like any creation can do. Creation is creation: it all comes down to the underlying intent. You need to understand that, because it is vitally important. You need to get clear and focused on the creation that you are invested in—whether or not you think you are creating (because part of you is asleep to that), or whether or not you are aware that you are creating (because you have been subdued).

You are creating. Every human being is in the act of creating all of the time, every second. That's what you do, that's what we do, that's what life does. Life continues on, and that means life continues creating. What is important is to identify what parts of you are in control of your creations. If you want to rearrange the game board and put the puzzle together in a different way because you're having more clear perceptions and understandings of yourself, then by all means do that. That will rearrange your creations and set them on a different course. And perhaps you will feel more and more aligned with your Golden Greatness as you do this. If it comes from your Golden Heart, all is well.

Jesus embodied his lifetime splendidly. We understand and know that the H-O put their influence on everything. They thought they were obliterating Jesus and his light, but of course that is the furthest thing from the truth—that was literally impossible. But they did continue to try and obliterate the Golden Lights of other Golden Ones; they did it then and have continued to do it throughout time. They have been quite successful through adversity, pain, and incredibly unconscionable actions, behavior, and persecution that defies life. It is unconscionable beyond bearing.

They would have the people witness the persecution of their loved ones and their children and all that they held dear. Everything created a ripple effect, so that the fundamental message became, "Do not go near your light, because you put yourself in peril and danger." However, to a Golden One that wasn't frankly the most important thing: more to the point would have been, "If you do this, you will put your family and those you love in peril and in danger," and that was, by far, the greater pain for a Golden One.

So, there was a shutdown. "It is not safe—it's not safe for those I love, for my family and my extended family. It's not safe for anyone that I care about. It's certainly not safe for me, so we won't do it. We'll just carry on in Mondor and survive the experience, and it will all be over when we leave the body." That is one viewing window.

Then, you can look at it through the viewing window of the Golden Ones coming back to Mondor for two things: one is to Rescue the Golden Family Members, and the other is to reconnect with Golden Terra. She is, of course, a humungous piece of the Golden Family. The overall goal is to come back and Rescue the Golden Family and be with Terra, because she is holding the gold in her belly. She is holding that most sacred of the sacred treasure for safekeeping inside of her belly.

It was important and necessary for all of these reasons to come back to Mondor, which was a place that we may never have revisited. Although, of course, this is where the Lemurian experience was first created, so that was yet another reason: we had to come back, because this is where it all happened. We wanted and needed to restore that Golden Imprint. We wanted to get everything geared up and activated again, because that was who we were. That was what we chose to do.

We made that choice when we were given a point to re-choose, before we went down into the belly of Terra when the planetary changes happened. We were all given an option to relocate and go somewhere else, but we decided that we wanted to be here, and wanted to be with Terra. We are going to see this through, whatever it brings. Do you remember that?

So here we are. We stayed here, and wow, Terra gave us all the skills that we needed to weather this storm. The time inside of her body was what enabled all of us Golden Ones to grow enormously, to thrive and persevere throughout time and space up until this very day—and this marks a new direction which we are about to open.

We have survived and lived to tell the tale. We are still whole and intact as Golden Ones, and that's the truth. The revisits to Mondor upset the apple cart in that they made you all believe, to one degree or another, that you were something other than what you truly are. Through all of those experiences of being in the dark, dank consciousness of constant interference and obliteration that continually tries to take your light, the repetitive nature of it eventually wore you down, and you "lost it." You lost connection.

Putting on the Mantle of Fear to go to Mondor in the first place made that happen. We are talking in varying degrees, depending on the experiences you all had, of how far that forgetfulness did, in fact, go. How far did you enter into a complete misperception of yourself? How far into the Web of Fear were you taken? Did you choose to go and Rescue? All of those things have had an effect.

That entire impact, and all its levels and aspects are going to be the focus of the next section of this book, which we call the Lemurian sickness. We will be talking about it at length, so rest assured that each step of the way throughout the journey of this book is but one segment of such; it is not the whole journey itself. We have to put one foot in front of the other and follow in this sequence, because this is how it all happens, how it happened, and how it continues to happen.

Bear with us, if you would, and continue on. Let yourselves be present in each step, so that you get it thoroughly. What is the point of just sticking your toe in and holding your nose and trying to get through this as fast as possible? That is not going to make it. You are never going to be able to heal if you do it that way.

Only by engaging in your own totality of this experience will you understand the many different facets of it—within both the wounding, and the Source light that you are that has not been wounded. If you do not experience it wholly, you simply won't get it; you won't get the whole picture, and you won't feel the whole resonance of you. You won't be able to be restored properly to that which you truly are, because you will not have healed the wound.

You need to witness the wound fully, in order for it to heal. You need to experience it and be with it. Once you acknowledge that it is there, you say, "What does this need to heal? Let me provide what I can."

In acknowledging this wound of the spirit and the presence of this wound, you can then go into it, feel it fully, be with it—be present with it, and feel your own compassion, love, and caring for it. Your divine Golden System will then begin to emerge and take over this healing process. That is how this is happening. You don't heal from the outside in. You heal from the inside out: the Golden Inside Out.

Moving forward...

I came in again for Rescues when I was Master Saint Germain in France. It was right before the time of the Illuminati, and I was there to help open a deeper and bigger aspect of the Golden Force Field—to prepare the way and hold steady that current again, so that those who were coming, who had just arrived, would take over and hold the Golden Light strong and steady. The way would be paved, and all things needed for continued support of sustenance would be in place.

I had many incarnations of Golden Preparation in this manner, just as I do in the modern day, and have been a part of the great doorway of "I Am." It is all the same. I do the same thing every time, and I don't mean that as something that is redundant. I simply mean that I am very skilled—I am a great Golden Way Opener and Golden Preparer. I have the ability to lay down the supporting structure that will be needed so that the Golden Energy that rides in that conduit will be strong and have legs; so it will continue to move and flow, to build momentum as it goes into the future, into what we know as the future—far ahead of now.

It will be coursing through time and space joyously and flourishingly. It will do so strongly and become magnified as it goes, growing with joy and jubilation. I will be watching it every step of the way. This is what I do. This is who I am—Golden Way Shower, Preparer, and Activator. There is nothing particularly quiet about me and my energy, although I certainly can have quiet. There is great potency and power in quiet, but nonetheless, it is always potency and power. This is who I am, this is my job: it is what I do.

I have come to remind you of the strength and power of yourselves as Golden Creators. I have also come to remind you that although you may feel as if you have been immobilized, you are not. Although you may feel as if you have been weakened, you are not. Although you may feel as if the divine feminine in you has been violated, you will ultimately discover that you are whole.

If the Heartless Ones can violate in the name of obliterating the divine feminine, they have that power under their control. It is subdued. The divine feminine in life—be it in a female, male, flower, plant, tree, sky, etheric crystal, or energetic space and cocoon—no matter what, the divine feminine is the great birther. It is the most magnificent life giver that there is. It is the mother and all that that means. The mother births, the mother tends, the mother nurtures—the mother is never not the mother.

It is with great pride and joy that the mother brings forth such Golden Grace and Glory. She is a powerhouse beyond anything you have ever imagined. That is the divine feminine within you, and you, and you. And the divine masculine when it finally comes and reveals itself in the modern day will show how steady, supportive, strong, and allowing it truly is.

What you have seen in the male stereotype throughout time has been that patriarchal thought-form patterning that is largely faulty. It isn't that the male doesn't have a space and a place and a job and a purpose—it's just all been torqued around and completely skewed. This is the H-O at work. This is what they wanted. This is a kind of male identity that is not the truth, that is not divine, that does not truly comprehend what the skills and the attributes of the true male are.

It has been this distortion and contortion which has created so much pain, turbulence, and violation of that which is true life—that it has simply gotten out of hand. In the modern day you have an entirely mixed bag of the male energetic. Some of it is looking like it is getting stronger with patriarchal dominance, and then you have a breakdown of another piece of the masculine identity. You have confusion and lostness, while the divine feminine, the women who have been subdued for so long, arise. Everything seems to be bringing itself back to where it is supposed to be, and yet at the same time it doesn't look that way at all.

I will not speak about the greater world at large—I am only interested in the Golden Ones. The Golden Ones, you Golden Ones, don't have these dilemmas. You are clear in yourself about the balance of your divine feminine and your divine masculine. However you want to call it—the yin and the yang. There are many terms to describe this, and even deeper than that, you don't even have the terms to describe these two things as different: it is simply all one thing, it is called the sacred.

It all boils down to that, down to your relationship with the sacred within you. Where do you stand on this? What does this even mean to you? How do you relate with it? What do you do with it? What do you do about it? What role does it play in your life? How does it express within you, and beyond that, through you? What I am most interested in are your internal workings.

One of the things that the Heartless Ones were successful in doing with their interference was to bring you to that almost breaking point where they made you believe—where the interference caused you to believe—that you were not pure. All of this interference made you question: what does this say about me? Who am I? What am I? Am I pure? Am I not pure? Am I good? Am I bad? All this rocking and rolling of the mental psyche is a form of torture. The torture lives in fear, and fear lives in torture. So, all of this questioning, this puzzlement, this agonizing self-doubt runs deep throughout many of you—and you think you've got it handled on a certain level—but if you go a little bit further you'll see it is there still, just at a deeper level and a deeper space.

And deeper still, if the truth be told, if you are being honest, your foundation is actually not very firm in that way. You quake a lot, deep within you. You feel erratic, skittish, and panicky. All of these things are fear states, so that tells you that when you are feeling any kind of a fear state you are still in interference. It's still got you. You're still in that arena of believing something that is not true of you. You have lost sight of yourself.

It goes way inside to that place where you meet the doorway of you, the doorway of your most sacred self—interference can go no further. It cannot touch that. What is inside is completely impervious. It is not able to be violated in any way, shape, or form, not on any level whatsoever. It never has been, and it never will be. This is your natural Lemurian design. This is your Lemurian Golden Being—sacrosanct, Golden Sacrosanct.

But interference will take you all the way to that point. It will interfere with you so that you do not—cannot—go beyond that point; you are so distracted and consumed with all the fear-based mentality and thought forms and energies and dilemmas and quandaries and pains and upsets and commotions and clang, confusion, and chaos. It will keep you so occupied in those spaces where all you can do is scurry to help yourself—to try to get through, to survive this thing, whatever this thing is.

It's one of many moments of trying to survive and feeling like life is so hard. "God, it's just so hard. How do I do this? How am I going to do this? Do I give up? Do I quit? What does that mean to me? Does that mean I would die? Do I have choice in whether I live or die? Is that going to change anything? What would that be like? Do I want to be here anymore? Do I want to shut down so that I'm not here anymore?"

This is a place of despair that is so deep that it makes a Golden One want to give up—and that's what the H-O want. If you give up, then there is the possibility that you become one of them, that you have no more spirit to rise above any of it or see your way clearly through. You are simply too broken—and we understand this. This is heartbreaking.

Or, you give up and go dead inside, which means your spirit has been tamped down. Your life force is no longer going to be an issue for the Heartless Ones—you are basically just another sheep, a part of the herd: you have been nicely controlled.

For those of you who experience yourselves deeply enough to be aware of these depths that I am talking about—those of you who can sense this deep despairing side of yourselves—you are the ones who are lucky. Your sensory instrument is still functioning, albeit in an uncomfortable state. It is painful, and you would do anything to outrun it or run away from it. You already know that is impossible, because you have tried it and it doesn't make any difference. You are still sensitive, you are still feeling things.

Those of you who go to these depths are lucky, because where you can come to is the end of the line for interference—but you can go further. Interference cannot; it is literally impossible for interference to do so. It always has been, and it always will be.

You have arrived at the point where you might believe that there is nowhere else to go. You have reached the end of your rope. It is all too much, and you feel like you can't handle it anymore. It is as if you have reached the end of a very long fall, deep down into a dark, slimy well. It has gotten you, so to speak. You might feel like, "Oh God, I give in. I can't stand this anymore." You feel and believe there is nowhere else to go. You are tired of fighting back. You are tired of doing everything you can to survive this; you are tired of the effort, and your spirit is weary. You feel like your spirit is taking a beating, and it is exhausting—too much overload, overwhelm.

"What is the point," you say. "What is the point of all this?" And here is where you stand on the edge of the splendid: the answer to all of your questions is your Sacred Self. The Heartless Ones have done everything they could to keep you from it, because that is where your true power is re-engaged, and they have needed and wanted to continue to try to prevent that at all costs. They will do anything to prevent that from happening.

But you are still awake enough to be feeling and sensing, to not shut down in the pain of it all—many of the Golden Ones have done just that, and it is completely understandable. If you have not shut down all the way, then thank God, because then you can help others to remember who they are.

The greater your sensitivity, the greater the pain that you will feel—the pain of what's going on in the ethers around you. It's in the air. It's crazy commotion and chaos and clang. We have talked about it at length. So here you are, finally wrestling with that final question: the truth of me, "Am I good? Am I pure? Or am I not? Am I worthy, or am I not?" And that bundle of questioning is exactly that—the final interference. That is interference at work in its grand finale, in unrelenting fashion. If it can keep you in that spot of confusion and questioning and self-doubt, then you are not trusting yet. You have not yet trusted back into your sacred center.

The interference hopes to keep you there forever. But at some point, perhaps even as you listen to me, you hear and resonate with what I say now: this is the end of something, and just prior to the beginning of something else. You take one step toward the unknown, into the unknown. You drop that line of questioning, that attack on yourself—knowing that all of those questions and all of those thought forms have truly nothing to do with you.

In fact, you have no "issues." You have nothing to fix, and none of it is truly who you are. It never was and never will be: none of it belongs to you. All of it is just interference, repetitive interference, going on and on. It goes on one way or another, pushing your buttons, pressing those areas where you feel vulnerable to upset, to angst, to being thrown off. And, while it may look a little different for each person, that is only the content—the form of the thing is the same.

It is called Interference by the Heartless Ones—anything to throw you off your sacred center, anything to keep you from remembering. It is there to keep you from your sacredness, to keep you from completely trusting—with one hundred percent certainty—in your purity, Goldenness, and Godliness. I'm not talking about an occasional trusting here; it's not a random level of self-trust, and it's not self-trust on a good day. I am talking about rock solid, one hundred percent, total self-trust—which takes you home to your Source.

It's so one hundred percent total that you can see clearly that everything else— all this other stuff—is false. It is a fabrication of the Heartless Ones, and remains as a fabrication of the thought forms that have been produced by the Heartless Ones that want to keep this entire unbalancing act alive. They want to keep everyone controlled and down, as slaves to them, as slaves to unconsciousness.

I am talking about a full-on trust that's unwavering, indelible, invincible, and impermeable. It's the truth. It is the truth of you, no matter what. When you take a step out of that confused, chaotic questioning and you let it go and give it up, knowing that it's just interference at work, you fall into your splendidness. You fall right into it and the door to interference closes one hundred percent, and is no more.

You are in the sacred now, the holy now. You are sacrosanct. You are Golden Source, Golden Joy, Golden Love, and Golden Heart. You are the truth of you. You begin to finally realize you have not been wounded at all: you are whole. You are resonant Golden Grace and that is all there is to it. You have found your way back home.

Why am I telling you all of these things? I am sharing this because it will sustain you throughout the journey that this book describes; there is still more to come, and areas that might make you flinch. There are things that you are not going to want to hear, things about which you are going to say, "He doesn't know what he is talking about." I'm not asking you to agree with me, I am asking for you to first feel a resonance inside of you, and then decide. So really, I am asking you to keep an open mind.

We still have some steps to go; this is a journey for the Golden Ones, and it isn't over yet. Consider what I have said, if you would—in the very act of considering, it is like a Rescue has been made—my heart has touched yours and given it space. Now it is up to you what you want to do with it, or have it do with you.

Ours is a wondrous Golden Heart, a profound love and caring, a bright and positive Golden Creation. We are here, and we can do so much and be so much. We don't need to leave this place in order to fully be who we are, but that is a topic for another conversation a little bit further down the road. For now, I honor you and love you. This is a great day. Godspeed.

THE CHILDREN'S RESCUE

This is my Rescue story. Thank you for listening.

I find myself in Mondor. I am a mature woman who has made many Rescues, in many lifetimes, of many children. I absolutely adore them, and am devoted to them one hundred percent. In Lemuria, I was a Sacred Shepherd for the Golden Children. It was my pure joy to teach them; to be with them, listen to them, watch them, and honor them as they grew. I knew that I had a hand in all of that—an important hand—and that my presence with them was inspiring, fortifying, steadying, and illuminating.

I loved my purpose; my Golden Skill Set was strong and masterful in these ways, and I loved the children. We would play for hours and spend much time communing out in Nature, learning much from her. There was always laughter and delight; the pure pleasure of BEING and witnessing the beautiful Golden Sights and Sounds.

The children were taught to focus and adapt to the challenges presented to them, and they thoroughly enjoyed learning. Every day they would find themselves rewarded through their own efforts, as they felt themselves growing and strengthening inside and out. It was an enormous pleasure to watch and witness them BECOME.

Our greatest learning tactic was that we would become like Butterflies. This made us grow even more Golden for one another and with one another. There is a way of Being in that kind of light design, the Butterfly patterning, that made everything easier. It made it easier for me to impart information to them, to teach them and to reach them—and it made it easier for them to receive it, because it was playful and open; it was receptive and light.

Mine was never a heavy experience—it was always light in every way. Aren't the Butterflies beautiful? Don't they always make you happy when you see them? Extraordinary and free, look how gorgeous they are. Being Butterfly was one of our most joyous aspects. Butterflies and children go hand in hand—they are one and the same, in many ways.

My connection to the children of Lemuria is extremely strong, and that is why I have been the leader of many Rescue Missions throughout all of my incarnations. It was my only purpose in coming back to Terra, ever.

My job has been to gather children that have been lost in the maze and haze of the Web of Fear. These children have been lost from their parents, from their connectedness, from themselves, and from one another. The deepest, most penetrating feeling that I have always experienced, of course, is their intense loneliness—their aching cry for Mother, for Father, for safety and protection; their heartbreaking loss of love, warmth, and tenderness. They have felt deeply abandoned, and this has always made my heart weep.

I have clearly heard their sorrow arcing throughout the ethers, "Somebody, please help me. I hurt. I need." My heart has always responded, and I have ached so deeply for them; I have felt their deep yearning and the agony of their need. I have considered it my responsibility to repeatedly return as fast as I could each lifetime to gather more of our Golden Children and bring them home to safety. Sometimes it was just a few, and others even more than that. At times I was doing the Rescues by myself, at others with fellow sister and brother Golden Shepherds.

This time, right now, is my final Rescue journey. As you can tell from previous accounts of Rescues, these last that are being made are the deepest. This current one is the most arduous journey into the maze of forgetfulness and fear, because everything before now has been paving the way for all of us Rescuers to go in further and further. I know what I am going to find, and it will not be pretty. It will not be as I would want it to be—but that won't stop me.

All that matters are the children.

I am weary from all the Rescues I have made. Each one has taken a little bit more out of me, escalating my energetic exhaustion levels further and further—but I have not been able to stop myself from coming. My last two Rescue Missions showed me that I am extremely tired. I am weary, and yet there is this last one to do. Even though I feel exhausted, my devotion keeps compelling me, as my love for these children eclipses everything. If I don't do this, it will keep me awake at night forevermore. I do it for them and I do it for myself—I need to do this for them, as much as they need it from me.

So there is gladness in my heart, although I am weary. I considered that maybe I was too spent to be able to do this Rescue successfully, that it would be unwise to take it on. I now know that this is not true. What I have is a great deal of Rescue experience under my belt, and that is what is going to serve me now. I come alone for this Rescue. I don't want to bring anyone else into this depth of the maze and haze with me. It is my choice to go in deep like this, and I will bear the responsibility for whatever happens. I will do my best. I have asked my Source and those who love me to fill me with strength, clarity, focus, and resilience. I know I have all that I need inside of me to do this. I am ready.

I'm inside the web of fear now—I have been for some time, trying to locate this last group, a handful or more of little ones. I haven't been able to, and I find this alarming—I should have heard them by now. My sensors are acute. They have never failed me, but for whatever reason, so far I hear nothing. I only hear the background buzz of the fear vibration rattling around me—chaotic and full of clang. I know it well.

Because I am experienced and wise, it doesn't bother me at all right now. I couldn't care less about it. I have one focus, one purpose, and all the rest of the jangle is simply what is outside of me. I decide that it is time for me to go even deeper inside the Web of Fear, to levels far beyond those in the past.

I take a deep breath and dive in. The further I go, the more I sense that I am on track. I know it, I can feel it. It's like a faint stream of awareness directing me, propelling me, and compelling me to keep moving. My sight and senses are probing all around, and I find my ability to smell dramatically increasing. I delve deeper still.

I am listening intently, and suddenly hear something; I realize I've been hearing this all along. It's the sound of silence, and I don't mean in a good way. I follow it, and I can feel it bringing me closer to its source. Everything starts to become murky. My eyes cloud over, and I am being substantially veiled by the haze and the maze. My hearing of the silence is still acute, and my sense of smell remains heightened. I can even taste something bitter and noxious in my mouth.

I know that something is very wrong here, and will be even worse where I am going. I know that I am getting closer; all of these sensations are signals telling me so. Everything suddenly becomes dark, thick, and more disorienting. It begins to smell really bad. I mean, truly foul—toxic and nauseating.

Despite all of this, I am able to sense the children and their energy. I am close, and struck again by the ominous texture of the silence and how disquieting it is. Usually where there are children there is noise of one kind or another, but the eerie silence continues.

At last I see them materialize out of the haze in front of me. I am shocked; there are ten children, lying helplessly on the floor of a cold, damp, wretched place. They are all curled up within themselves, not even over and around each other for comfort. They are curled up, each one by themselves, in a teeny, tiny, tight little ball. As I move closer to them, I see that they each have metal chains coiled all around their body, pressing into their flesh. They are imprisoned by these coils of steel.

The children make no sound. They do not even register that I am here. Far gone, they are completely caved in upon themselves—ashen, empty, and numb. Their skin is gray and cold and they look almost dead, but I know they are not. They have retreated deep inside of themselves, and do not see or sense anything. They believe they have been abandoned and are utterly silent. It is the silence of agony and heartbreak, of wandering lost and alone inside in a cold void. "Does anyone even know that I am here, that I exist? Does anybody hear me? Anyone?" If they were calling out, that is what I would hear them say.

I feel like I could stretch out my hand to touch them and I wouldn't even be able to feel their skin pressing back on my fingers—so fully have they disappeared inside. The more I reach out to try to touch them, the further they seem to disappear. It's not actually what's happening, but I'm trying to convey the feeling of how far away they have gone, and how deeply and achingly alone they feel. It's gone beyond their crying out for help, far beyond any ability to connect at all. I kneel down beside them, aching, holding my arms around my own belly, just as they are.

I have a moment of simply being with them, like them, in this way. I do this not only because I can't help it, but because I love them so much. I know it is essential to building the bridge back to physical sensation, if there is any chance of this at all. I take a moment to feel with them, to witness their pain and anguish beyond words. I convey to them energetically that I hear them, that I see them, and that I understand. I tell them how deeply sorry I am for their pain and their loneliness. I let them know, in any way that I can, that I am here, that I am WITH them, exactly where and how they are.

I know this is but the beginning of building that bridge. I know I cannot push this, because time and sensitivity are required for them to find their resolve to return. It takes whatever is needed for these children to come back into their own senses, their own bodies, for them to even begin to register what is around them on energetic and physical levels.

I wait.

I continue to soothe them and to speak in quiet, soft ways. I radiate my energies toward them in loving and reassuring waves, hoping that it will somehow permeate the barriers of their woundedness. I don't know how much time I have. I don't know what the risk of waiting here is, but I carry on, patient no matter what.

I sit here watching, waiting for them to come back into themselves so that they can register that I am here, and that help has finally arrived. But they don't. They can't.

I reach inside my inner wisdom, asking for help myself. I know there is a way, somehow. "How can I bring them back?" I ask my Soul. "How can I bring them back to me so they can be helped?"

All of a sudden, I become aware that Golden Beings, Avalar and Andar, have appeared next to me, one on each side. I feel their strength, their love, and their conviction. They each reach for my hand on their respective side and hold me firmly in their grip. It is solid and steadying. I feel reassured and relieved. I know they are here as an answer to my prayer and I am extremely grateful.

They stand still and steady with me for a moment, focused intently on the bodies of our Golden Children lying here on the floor. Then I hear them start to breathe with a quiet whooshing sound. As they do this, Golden Light is generated and begins to fill the space that we are in.

They continue with their slow, steady whooshing sounds and gradually the temperature changes, warming the air around us. I know they are generating the energy to establish a safe, loving cocoon of Golden Fluid, almost like a birthing sac of sorts. This tender energy now surrounds the children, encasing them gently in a safe, loving pool. It's a safe space, a space of repair and healing for them. I notice how extraordinarily gentle they are being, as if too much energy would, in fact, hurt the children. It would be an overload of some kind and actually cause them pain.

They go over to the children and somehow unlock the steel chains with their breath, freeing them from their imprisonment. I don't know exactly how they have done this, but it doesn't surprise me that they are capable of such a thing. It all happens quietly and quickly.

And then they stand amongst them, continuing to breathe, slowly and gently, patient and unwavering in their stance and outpouring. The depth of their caring for these children, their love and understanding and oneness has become palpable now—and guess what?

I feel the Souls and spirits of the children turning in our direction, beginning to carefully come back toward their bodies. As they do, I am aware they have to reenter the space of conscious pain that they have gone through, and have been doing everything in their power to disconnect from. Now, as they come back to reenter themselves, they meet the pain again. It startles them, but at the same time, they seem to know that they are being carried safely on the waves of Golden Love generated by Avalar and Andar, and by me as well. They continue coming, because they have yearned for this. They have a sense of something familiar and they ache to rejoin. It is obvious to me that they sense that safety has, indeed, arrived.

As they return to themselves, I see their story of pain laid out bare for me to witness. I see what happened to them. I see how they were brutally taken from their families, bruised and damaged. How they were then separated from one another and beaten and brainwashed repeatedly, all in an endeavor to control and reshape them into little Heartless Ones that would grow up into complete robots. I can feel the enormity of their terror and intense vulnerability. Somehow, they knew they were lost to us and that, perhaps, they would never be found. It absolutely terrified them—of course it did.

Our Golden Children were strong, but not strong enough to endure this. No one would be, no matter what their age. And they had no one to protect them in the face of all of this horror. Can you imagine?

In this moment my own senses have joined with their stories, and I can feel their little bodies trembling as if they will never stop. My body quakes and my chest begins to heave with short breaths of pure panic. My mind jumps into heightened vigilance, and I am aware that I cannot move. I am trapped in the jaws of cold steel encasing my body, restricting me completely. "What am I doing here?" I hear the frightened voice of one of the children crying out. "Why am I here? What is happening? I cannot move, and I cannot breathe."

I instinctively reach out to the child, that Golden One who is so frightened and confused right now. I move close to her and wrap her sore little body in my arms. I soothe her with my voice, making sounds that I hope will calm her and let her know that she is not alone. I tell her that she is no longer bound by the chains, that they have been removed and that she is free from them now.

I see Avalar and Andar doing the same with the other children, hugging them, wrapping them all up in an embrace of Mother, Father, Friend, and Family. Together, we are doing our best to provide a safe haven for these little ones to come home to.

And finally, slowly but surely, they register all of this. They begin to become calm and to breathe more deeply back into their little bodies. The children are feeling something besides the pain; there is a spark of hope, and they begin to sink into the warmth of love. They realize, "Somebody is here who loves me and is protecting me now."

Gradually, they each make their way into full body awareness. Their skin changes color and becomes vibrant again. They open their eyes slowly, taking a moment to adjust to the brightness of our cocoon that is in such contrast to where they have been. They recognize me, and they recognize Avalar and Andar—and they start to cry. Huge tears pour unchecked down their beautiful little faces. They hug us back harder, sobbing into our chests and holding on as if they will never let us go. *"We are here, sweet ones,"* I tell them. *"Do not worry. We are here, forever with you."*

Their tears continue to pour out, speaking of how frightened they have been, of how much they have suffered, of how alone and lost they have felt. I am relieved to hear them crying so freely instead of being locked up the way they were before. We hold them without speaking, letting this all wash through until they are spent for the moment.

When they are ready, I look at them and say, *"I'm sorry. We are all sorry for all the pain that you have been through, and for how scared and alone you have been. We are sorry that we could not get to you sooner, but it was very difficult to find you. We knew you were here, but it was hard to get to you, and it took us longer than we would ever have wanted. Please know this, we never forgot you. We never will. And when this is all over, we will explain more to you, so that you will fully understand. Please forgive us for not being able to find you sooner. We love you very much, and have been deeply worried about you."*

They each look up at us with eyes brimming with love. They clearly trust us implicitly, and know that I am speaking the truth. They are loved, and we are here now. They are safe, and don't seem to need to know any more at this moment. They begin to unfurl and uncurl their little bodies, stretching out and feeling the extension of their arms and legs. They can move again, thankfully.

Suddenly, I become aware of the Spirit of Golden Butterfly. She dances close to me, hovering, and I know what she wants to do. She is the one who can reassure our little ones and inspire them to know that all will be well, that everything will get better from now on.

She begins to dance all around the children too, and I know that the moment has come for me to fulfill my purpose of reawakening and reigniting the Golden Flame in the hearts of my dear, sweet children. Avalar and Andar watch and witness me as I get on with the task that I have done so often, and know how to do well.

I gaze deep into the hearts of these little ones, each one separately, and all together as well. I remind them of who they truly are, have always been, and always will be—great Golden Ones with beautiful Golden Hearts, alive and well. They meet my gaze, and they remember clearly the many times that we danced in the open fields of Lemuria with the Butterflies, as Golden Butterflies ourselves. They open their hearts to me, to the beauty of us, to Life in the Golden Way. They are delighted by Butterfly, and their eyes shine and dance with her as she arcs through and around them. Their Golden Hearts soar inside of them—free as Butterflies, free to be aware again of themselves as wondrous Golden Ones.

I keep blowing the Golden Light into their hearts as they join their Gold with mine. Everything is becoming lit up and bright as our union is taking place—our Golden Union being restored and joy-filled. We belong together, and we are together once again.

Our Golden Cocoon is full and bright with love and beauty. I stand here in awe of these beautiful Golden "Little Ones," who are definitely not so little at all. They are the huge Gentle Giants that they always were and will grow into once more. My own eyes fill with tears as I admire them and acknowledge their tremendous courage and strength of spirit, as well as their beauty and love of life—of being alive.

I know that these children are going to be exceptional adults. They are going to be the stewards of a new age; of the true transformation that's based not only on hope and affirmation, but on the wisdom of knowing the pain that went before and on living through such darkness and unconsciousness. Because of all of it, of what they have endured here, they will bring forward great Golden Clarity and Golden Consciousness of the highest order.

This is how they will utilize all the pain that they have experienced, because now they know. Their cellular memory will never forget, and will bring forth great things that will truly make strong and lasting change and positive creation: creations of Golden Goodness.

I know all of this in the moment, clear as day, and yet here we are, still deep within the haze and the maze of fear. We need to get ourselves out of here. It's not over yet.

I look at Avalar and Andar, and Andar nods his head to me that yes, it is indeed time to go. We huddle together for one last group hug, knowing full well that this is the beginning of many more to come.

Andar says:

"It is time to go, dear ones. It is most definitely time to go. In a moment you will turn, you will leave this place, and you will walk. You will continue walking, and you will not look back. Just continue walking forward, following the path that Golden Butterfly will carve out for you. You will remain in the Golden Cocoon, and you will be safe and sound every step of the way, I promise you. Stick close together, and follow her now. Avalar and I will stay here to make sure all goes well for as long as your journey takes. We will meet up with all of you later, and we will celebrate then. Godspeed."

We gather and turn as one body, the children and I, and suddenly we are literally propelled right out of there. We move swiftly, as if on the wings of Butterfly herself, and our way is clear and unfettered. The atmosphere changes, the air gradually becoming less and less hazy as we move steadily through the intricacies of the Web.

It feels like no time at all before we emerge, although I know that, in fact, the journey has been quite a long one, given how deep inside the Web we were. But Butterfly, as always, has made the way easier and lighter, effortless and timeless. I am forever grateful to her.

I take a deep breath and am aware of moisture in the air. I know that water is nearby and my senses lurch toward it. I am so thirsty.

Finally, we stop moving completely, and Butterfly goes to land on a large, round rock that is standing beside a small stream. Water is gushing along, sparkling with life, and it draws us in. Excited, we all rush into it, jumping up and down as we splash ourselves and each other. Washing off all the heaviness of where we have been, it is a great cleansing of our bodies and our spirits. We let the pure joy of this moment and these sensations sweep us up and fill us with renewal.

Minutes later, we are still playfully sloshing water all over each other. The children are giggling and laughing. They are children again. My oh my, how happy this makes me. How exquisite and beautiful they are! My heart opens even more. I am glad and grateful, and I will never forget this moment of freedom for all of us. The children are giddy with it, and so am I.

This is my last Rescue, and I have done it. Relieved and overjoyed, I offer up a prayer of thanksgiving to all those who helped us in this arduous undertaking. In response, I feel great waves of love coming my way and filling my heart to overflowing. I feel very blessed.

Suddenly, all eyes widen hugely as a vast multitude of Butterflies appear as if out nowhere, fluttering all around, landing on our bodies, touching us, and making us sparkle and glow with joy, inside and out. I know my message of thanks has been received and that all is truly well. The magic has been restored.

I look at the children again. I absolutely love them, and this Golden Family of ours. One Golden Radiant Heart we truly are, and always will be. I smile, and know all is blessedly well and Golden. All my children are now safely home in themselves. Hallelujah!

THE GOLDEN ORACLE RESCUES

Dear Reader, The Golden Oracle in the following Rescue is the same Oracle who was Rescued in "The Oracle Rescue" earlier in this chapter.

I am a young woman in my early twenties. I am being burned at the stake for being a witch. It is an experience with which I am quite familiar, as it has happened to me many times before. During each instance I manage to stay more and more clear, to remain less affected by it. It always kills me, of course; that's the point. But the funny thing about it is that the Heartless Ones actually believe that my physical death is the end of me—which of course, it isn't.

I'll be coming back. Many of us will be coming back, over and over again. There will be more Rescues to make, and we will keep coming until all of the Golden Rescues are completed. That's the way it is. So the joke is really on the Heartless Ones, isn't it? They just can't get rid of us. Sometimes, I feel that they are quite frustrated about this.

Here I am, tied to a cross, in the midst of a pile of wood, burning. The flames are blazing hot, searing my flesh. I am sure it's a gruesome sight for anyone who is an outsider looking in, but at the moment, crazy as I know it must sound, the temperature feels quite cool to me. The heat is so hot that I actually feel cool. I can smell my flesh burning, singeing, and very soon I will depart from this particular physical body that I have inhabited this time around. But I am not ready to go quite yet, because there are some things I still need to witness before I do.

Witnessing is part of my responsibility as a Golden Leader. I make it my job to witness both the pain of my loved ones as well as their reawakening into the power of their Golden Heart. It is an honor to Golden Witness, as difficult as it often is to see what I see and know what I know. But on the other hand, as I said, I am also here to witness the truth of their Golden Beauty, and of course, that's the best part.

I am the Leader of this particular group, this band of Golden Light Bringers and Rescuers that have come here to fulfill our missions. We are Golden Sisters, united in purpose and in heart. Right now, it is for me to witness everything that is happening to them, and to acknowledge the enormity of their courage and dedication.

I can see them being burned at the stake, just as I am. You would think I would be hearing them screaming in pain, but I am not. This part of it, inside of it all, is totally quiet. I know they are simply watching themselves, just as I am watching myself. This is because we all know, and are remembering clearly in these moments, exactly why we came.

We know what we hold and stand for—and that we chose to go through whatever it would take to fulfill our purposes in coming here. And we knew that it would simply be a matter of time before this kind of thing would happen to us. This is so often the case for us Golden Rescuers: a majority of the time we end up being persecuted for our Light in a variety of ways, many of which have already been spelled out throughout the preceding pages.

Suffice it to say, that what we have been willing to endure has been a testimony to how deep our love and devotion goes. And the witnessing of it all, as best we can for one another, validates and recognizes our courage and devotion and honors our Souls in the midst of all of this.

Before I say any more about these end moments for us, I am going to move backward in time and tell you our story, my story, up to this point. This will help to clarify how I can be objective right now.

We came to Mondor destined to unite as this band of six women who are now joined in one purpose and one purpose only—to Golden Rescue. We are all close companions of Sananda, who was Jesus in a previous lifetime. We were closely bound in that particular incarnation with him, and our purpose then was to hold steady the sacred Christ Heart Energies that he was birthing and igniting throughout that incarnation. This was before religion got hold of it all.

It was essential then, as it is now, that these Sacred Energies constantly be nurtured, fed, and watered, just like a beautiful garden, so that they could take even stronger hold and have the "legs" to fully walk in generations to come. Those Energies, what we sometimes call the Christ Heart, are the Golden Heart Love.

This was the greater plan at work.

The six of us have come back now to deliberately, once again, foster The Christ Heart Sacred Consciousness—to speak to this, sing to this, and be with this. It is the core of the Golden Imprint that has remained in the etheric consciousness of Terra and, if it is to stay strong and viable, needs loving attention and fostering, just as all life forms do. The six of us will also be guided by this Sacred Energy to Rescue some of our Golden Family that have been taken prisoner by the Heartless Ones, precisely because this is what they were doing here as well. They had come before us to keep the Golden Spirit alive, full and radiant, growing and bright—to hold it strong and steady, just as we have done our best to do.

There are many people, in fact, who will firmly believe that it is dangerous to show their Light—truly dangerous. And, circumstantially, there has certainly been much validity to that. I am not arguing that point; just look at me, burning at the stake.

But what one will need to be really cautious about is internally diminishing and hiding one's Light from self, as well as from others. Just because it is done on the external does not mean that it needs to be done at all on the internal. Why would it have to be? It doesn't.

The union with one's Sacred Self, this sanctified intimacy, can always stay alive and well, can always be cherished and adored—no matter what. It is magnificent. It is the power and beauty of who we all are: God made manifest.

Part of our job in coming here will not only be to Rescue some of our Golden Family, but also to remind our fellow Golden Ones, yet again, that this is so—that they are, in truth, Golden Sacrosanct. As others have come before us to do, we are here now to also help shore up this remembrance inside for as many Golden Ones as we can possibly reach.

With all of this in mind, I came to Mondor and was born into a good family of quiet people. My life appeared to be quite peaceful. I say that because there was a lot of commotion all of the time in the energy fields here—things that were jarring and upsetting. But, by contrast, my inner well-being stayed largely intact so I could basically live, even straddle, these two levels of consciousness at the same time—and stay clear about both, the outer and the inner. I knew about both. The older I grew, of course, the more I knew, the more I saw and felt, and the clearer I became.

From a very young age I was aware that I had to be most careful about the conclusions that I was drawing. I needed to keep myself directly in line with my true perspective, with my truth. I did what I could to stay aligned with my internal wisdom, because I knew I held something sacred and dear. The Golden Heart burned brightly inside of me, brighter even than the flame that would engulf me at the end of this walk. The passion and the heat of my Golden Heart outshone all of that, eclipsing everything else. When I delved deep inside of it, when I let it comfort, soothe, and inspire me, it was absolutely glorious—even a reality beyond magnificent, if you can imagine that.

It was always there inside of me—steady, steady, steady—and I was grateful. It was often a challenge for me to remain ensconced and clear in it, but the challenge made me stronger in many ways. Every time I was pulled by outside influences and felt myself sinking into the Web of Fear, the strength of my Golden Heart would make its presence known. I would return to my inner sanctuary, because I knew that that was my truth—the other, the fear-based experience, was not.

I was grateful for my clarity. It made me dig deeper, get stronger, and keep persevering throughout—all the while knowing that I was here on a mission. I had a specific purpose; multi-layered, in fact—both enabling me, and demanding that I stay focused. It taught me well, throughout.

Focus was probably one of the primary key ingredients in the success of these Rescue walks. Focus, staying focused on the reason for coming, focused on the task at hand, focused on the ultimate joy of why we were truly here. This made all things possible in many ways. It made the extraordinary happen.

I loved the atmosphere that Jesus stood in and exemplified. I carried it forth into this lifetime and was bathed by it. I loved the feel and the taste, the smell and the sense of it. It was a quality of energy, of Being, that was always exquisite and beautiful. It was so right, delicious and divine, as if it was in a cocoon all of its very own. Standing inside this cocoon was a remarkable contrast to what was outside. It was like day and night, light and darkness, Golden Sunshine or oppressive gray clouds.

The air in Mondor, outside the cocoon, always smelled bad. It was stinky and thick. It held a kind of debris made of toxic thought forms, floating unchecked in the air like pieces of ash. Sometimes they would get stuck in my nose and create great pressure on my entire system. I had to watch out for that all the time.

It was extremely toxic for me as a Golden One and for all of us Golden Ones. It was toxic air, toxic water, and toxic consciousness—and when I use the word "toxic," I'm talking about how it was so divisive and counter to life. It didn't brighten life, it dampened it, it literally gummed up the works.

Moving forward in time now...

My sisters and I are gathering late in the evening for a sacred meeting, as we have done many times before. We need to keep our meetings quiet, out of wisdom and complete understanding of counter-forces at work here in Mondor—the H-O.

We often meet deep in the woods. The forest and all the energies in it are our Allies: Nature. The particular place we often gather is filled with protective Nature Spirits that are integral and essential members of our team—Golden Trees, Golden Fairies, and Golden Elementals, to name a few.

Our meetings hold powerful Golden Energy that we thrive in for these moments that we are together. It is exquisite to hear the Golden Elementals sing. I always feel that their song can be heard far out in the galaxy. The energies of our love that pool together are a communion: a holy, sacred communion. We make it a point to savor these moments as much as possible, because we need them greatly to fuel and stabilize us, to balance us and keep us strong and steady—able to be and do what we are here to be and do. We know this well.

Our eyes are brightest during these gatherings and our hearts are filled with joy. It is a deliberate harnessing of all of this Golden Nourishment. It is magnetic and powerful. Our beloved Terra is inspiring and strengthening as she, too, moves her energies up and into our bodies and Beings.

Our gathering tonight holds an air of greater importance than usual. The stars above are bright, and the air is crisp and cool. There is Gold everywhere, permeating our space. As I look around, I notice that the divine Mother Mary has joined us from Spirit. She has materialized into physical form and is greeting some of the women who have just arrived. I had heard rumors that she might come tonight, and I'm eager to hear what she has to say. I'm sure she has some guidance for us before we embark on the Rescue Missions for which we have been preparing. We are set to go tomorrow, at first light.

When everyone is here we form a circle, holding hands and taking a moment to be still. Mother Mary stands in the center of our circle, turning slowly around as she gazes for a moment into the eyes of each one of us here. She is such a splendid Being, and we all adore her. In her eyes I see both encouragement and reassurance. I know that she knows these Rescues will not be easy. I know that she has come to offer us some of her strength and faith to tuck away inside of ourselves for the journey ahead.

Mother Mary says:

"Beloved Ones, Shining Golden Sisters of my Heart, know that all is well as you prepare to embark on your mission. Know that we are with you, many of us in Golden Spirit, riding on the wings of Angels. We will be close. We will be there. We will witness you and all that takes place.

"I have a few last words to share with you that will help you on this particular trek into the labyrinth of the Heartless Ones. Do not be duped by fear, my Beloveds. I know you are already well acquainted with this wisdom, but it needs to be reinforced. I am emphatic about this.

"Do not, for one instant, think or believe that you are afraid. Fear does not exist in you, and it never will. You know this; it never has. It is impossible. It is not your design. But you will see many things that will cause you to feel fear, to recoil, to brace yourselves and to flinch; to lose your breath because of the shock of it all.

"You will be going deep inside of the maze of fear to accomplish these Rescues—deeper than you have ever gone before. And this is no small feat for any one of you. This journey demands courage, strength, endurance, resilience, and fortitude. All the Rescues do, of course, but this one especially so. You are strong; you are strong ones, and you know it. You know that is why you are here; you are the only ones who can make these particular Rescues that are ahead of you.

"As you already know all too well, many of the things that the Heartless Ones do are shocking. They continue to do harm on the physical level—and even more damaging for many, the most devastating is the violation of spirit and of heart, of life and love. The Heartless Ones always do whatever they can to violate, take over, control, and dominate, and then dominate some more.

"I am not telling you anything that you don't already know. You know these are the facts of this time. These are the facts of this Heartless Consciousness. These are the facts of what I have called 'the state of Lost Man.' We know that all that we see in this Web of Fear, and about this Web of Fear, is because of that 'lostness.' We understand this.

"But remember that right here, at this moment, you are on the periphery looking in. Those Golden Ones that you are here to Rescue are no longer

standing on the periphery. They are inside this lost zone. They are in this violation. They are emotionally and psychically devastated, and they are in great, great pain. It is agony of the heart and devastation of the spirit. They feel it throughout their entire systems, and you will feel them feeling it.

"Why am I telling you all this? Why am I speaking about that which you already know?

"Because in this case, when you first locate the imprisoned Golden Ones on a sensory level, it will jar you so greatly that you may lose your focus altogether. You need to be well-prepared for this.

"I guarantee you, you will flinch and you will gasp. You may even find yourselves curling up in a fetal position in an effort to protect and save yourselves. That is precisely what they are doing right now. The emotional and sensory experiencing is important. You need to witness them. You need to let yourselves be receptive to whatever they are feeling. You need to feel it completely yourselves, because that is exactly the call. That is exactly the information that will lead you closer and closer to them—closer into the understanding of their Beings; their hearts, their souls, their minds, their psyches, and their totality. This is what will enable you to help them.

"They are close to being broken completely. They are but a hair away. That is why merging with them in this way is essential. It is the only way you can establish a bridge over which they can cross and return to themselves in one whole piece. That is the only way this Rescue will work and be successful.

"You have all volunteered for this mission. You have chosen to step up to this degree for those you love. I am giving you the full picture as much as I can at the moment, because, again, you will feel it all. You will know more than you've ever wanted to know, and then some. You need to be this fully prepared because the emotional assault will blind you in many ways. I urge you now to concentrate and hold your focus, to be open to input—but also streamlined—to stay steady and on task.

"It is the devotion in your heart that has brought you here, the vow of our sacred Golden Family. It serves you well, and will do so even in the moments to come when you feel that things are at their bleakest. Know one thing: YOU ARE NOT ALONE.

"Not only will I be with you, but several of us in Spirit will be there helping you, protecting you, and doing whatever we can in every way. We know you will do your absolute best. We know that you will persevere until you feel the beating of these Golden Ones' hearts in yours.

"Stand strong. Be your strength and clarity. Let your Golden Heart guide you all the way. Bless you. Golden Godspeed."

As Mother Mary prepares to leave us now, she gives us all one last penetrating look of love. Her eyes tell us exactly what we need to know right now: that she believes in us one hundred percent. We are indeed strong, and we can do this—and she, and many others, have our backs. They always do.

After she has left, we return to the purpose of our gathering and iron out the final details of our journeys tomorrow. Our plan is to each go through the Web traveling in different directions, so that we can cover as much ground as possible. Hopefully, we will all end up joined at the exact same spot—right where our lost Golden Ones are.

With our plan finalized and everything in place, we each try to get some sleep as best we can. Finally, we wake to meet the day, as the time has come to go. Our Rescue Journey begins.

I have entered the maze fully, and feel that I am fogged in and feeling heavy. My steps are laborious, and it seems so slow, slower than I've ever been in here. I am having difficulty breathing, and I cannot see clearly. Everything is dark and murky, making me feel disoriented and spinning. I keep remembering what Mother Mary told us about sustaining our focus and clarity.

It takes everything I have to keep moving forward through this. All I know is that I have to concentrate and keep breathing. I am well aware of the air of violence and cruelty around me, the clang of commotion and conflict, but within my space I seem to remain relatively calm. It amazes me that this is possible.

Again, I gird myself and keep my focus directly on my path. I know how supported I must be by all the Golden Energies Mother Mary spoke about, to be able to do this at all.

The speed of my traveling increases, and I am aware of my senses heightening along with this acceleration. There is a pulse of Golden Life in here somewhere that is drawing me toward it, like a magnet pulling me in. I can see a channel opening up in front of me.

All of my senses, and especially my sense of smell, become much heightened detectors. As I move quickly along I can hear sounds, faintly at first, but growing louder as I travel. I must be going in exactly the right direction. Good.

The sounds become louder and I hear desperate crying and wailing. Agonizing screams of pain are piercing the air. In an instant I am doubled over with agony, shattering inside my own guts. I can't breathe, it is suffocating. I remember, again, what Mother Mary told us, and I do my best to let myself yield to the experience and to these crippling sensations. My heart is in agony. I never knew I could feel this kind of pain inside. It is like the breaking of my Soul.

Suddenly I know, in a flash of images and sensations, everything that has happened and is happening to these precious Golden Ones—the brutal torture of body, mind, and spirit. I feel like my own system can endure no more, and I am losing it. I feel like the most private and precious core of me is being strangled. I am stunned by this.

I labor, as I do my best to breathe and breathe again. I urge my senses to understand that, yes, I need to know all of this, but I also need to immediately take a step back so I can continue on with my job. Things ease up a bit, and I feel the necessary space clearing for my own thoughts and feelings to return to the forefront of this experience I am in.

I wonder for a minute why these Golden Ones are even being kept alive. There seems to be some deliberation about that. I realize that it's because the Heartless Ones want information about their Spiritual Natures. They want to know what makes these particular Golden Ones tick, because they know they are holding considerable power.

The H-O not only want to dominate us and drive us away forever, but they also want the Gold for themselves—they don't even know what the Gold is exactly, but they know they want it. They have somehow realized that this is the power that fuels us and makes us strong—and so they want to rob us of this, to steal it.

It becomes apparent to me that they are holding these Golden Ones alive in order to move things in that direction. That's what they're after. They believe that this is possible and that they can just take it, like they do with whatever else they want. What they don't know is that it doesn't work that way—they have yet to discover that.

The Golden Ones we are here to Rescue shined their light openly and brightly in their walk on Terra, and the H-O saw this. They imprisoned them so they could study them.

I can feel that these Golden Ones held prisoner are in deep trouble. They are being so tampered with that they will soon drown in the H-O configuration completely. If that happens, it could be many lifetimes before they would be found again, much less Rescued at all.

I know that my job here is critical. We cannot let these Golden Ones get swallowed up.

I sense some other incoming energy that feels familiar to me, and before long I see the rest of my Golden Sisters who are on this mission coming toward me. We greet each other quietly. We have, indeed, all managed to find our way to this same spot. Thank goodness.

As we stand together to assess the situation at hand I become acutely aware of the solidarity of us as a team, right here and right now. I start to feel the same sensations that I feel at our gatherings in the woods, as if we are being infused with the power of love and strength. I know the support of the Golden Elementals is here too, because I can faintly hear them singing. Suddenly, I feel more anchored in my clarity. We all do.

I also feel the presence of Mother Mary, and Avalar and Andar as well. It seems like the whole universe has opened channels of Golden Support to us, and it is all coming our way. I have an indelible knowing that we will succeed in our mission precisely because of our strength in numbers and this Golden Support that is here with us now. I feel greatly fueled by this and ready to proceed.

We silently move as one unit toward the direction of the prisoners. Our focus is crystal-clear, and we can see them just ahead in front of us. They are alone. No H-O are here for now. We draw closer still. Their bodies are lying flat on the floor, not moving. Are they suddenly all dead, I wonder?

I stop and breathe, waiting for an answer. As I look more closely with my finely-tuned vision, I can see that they are still alive, but barely. They are drawn so deeply inside of themselves that they don't register anything, much less that we are here. The sensation of their energetic absence is almost eerie.

We start to move still closer to them, only inches away now. How odd they look, these beautiful Golden Ones, so gray and ashen and empty. Part of me is still not convinced that they are even alive, they have vacated their bodies that much—but I know that they are.

I see Avalar coming in now, and she begins to move her arms in gentle wave-like motions, the energy of these gestures slowly weaving a Golden Cocoon around them all. She continues to do this until it encases them in a Golden Sphere of warmth and love. It is so substantial that it's almost physical, like something I could actually touch and feel between my fingers.

One of the Golden Ones stirs slightly. Before long, all of them are moving, little by little. They are slowly coming back into their bodies, and I can tell that what they feel is physically painful—and this is just the start of the discomfort for them. I pray that they continue to return to themselves, no matter what.

Now, Andar and Avalar both take a position on either side of the cocoon. They spread their hands out and hold them with palms facing the Lost Ones. Andar indicates with a motion of his head that we are to join them, and together form an entire circle wrapping itself around the edges of the cocoon. Mother Mary steps into the formation now as well.

We all know instinctively what to do next.

We close our eyes and draw up a breath from our Golden Hearts, from deep inside of our most natural rhythms. We begin to blow this energy outward toward the Lost Ones—gently, evenly, patiently. Our Golden Love ushers itself toward their bodies, and spins carefully throughout the systems of these precious ones here. I watch these Golden Ones come back to life as if by magic, with their bodies being carefully stroked and soothed, their psyches gentled and calmed. The broken pieces of their hearts are now beginning to be put back together again.

It is mesmerizing for me. The intelligence of this Golden Love Energy is deliberate and completely attuned to their every nuance. It needs no instruction from us. It only needs freedom to do exactly what it knows so well.

Slowly but surely, the transformation back into their self-awareness and then, more deeply still, into their Golden Awareness, takes place. These Sacred Souls that have such profoundly deep connections to their spiritual realms and natures begin to breathe properly again and look alive. Finally, they look at us and register who we are and why we are here. Tears come to my eyes and roll down my cheeks as I look at them looking at me. Because of my thorough witnessing of them earlier, I could look back into their eyes and honestly say, "I know. I know of your pain and your suffering and I am sorry for it all, so very sorry."

In the instant that they get this, how seen and understood they truly are, they begin to cry too. Slow tears at first, and then great heaving sobs. Suddenly, they turn away from us and grab for one another in a panic, huddling, clinging as tightly together as they possibly can in a desperate effort to protect and shield themselves from further onslaughts of pain. It is a reflex reaction to all they have been through. I know this, we all know this. They can't help it—but seeing it this way, how desperately they are trying to shield and protect themselves, makes my heart ache even more and my own tears continue to fall unchecked down my cheeks. It pains me to see how much they have been through.

All of us here in our circle stay still and continue to wait with understanding, patience, and unwavering love. At last, the Golden Ones are slowly able to unwind from their reflexive survival positions, and they turn their eyes back to us, reaching, stretching out their hands to us, imploring us to come close and help them now.

We are there in a heartbeat. We move inside their small circle and bring them all into our arms. We rock together, side to side, feeling the glow of our Golden Radiance seeping into their bodies and Beings, soothing, calming, and gradually reorienting them. We stay this way for some time, until things start to feel whole again. This is not something that can be rushed and we all know this.

After a few more minutes we draw back from one another and I find myself looking into the eyes of one of the Lost Ones. I look at her deeply, as I know that my other sisters are also doing the same with the rest of them. I feel my own heart opening up and beginning to flow across to her, directly into her heart. My Golden Love penetrates her and reaches deep inside that beautiful Golden Heart of hers, quickening its flame and encouraging it to rise and spread itself out.

I see in her eyes that she is feeling it now. They close, and she begins to tremble. It's been a long time for her, and the sensation is so beautiful inside of her that it makes her nervous for a second. She winces—a reflex reaction again—as if somehow it will cause her to feel pain. I squeeze her hands in mine, gently reassuring her that she is safe and that this Golden Sacredness inside of her is safe as well.

She takes some deep breaths and I feel her gradually relaxing inside, trusting me and letting go to what is taking place. She moves back into trust of herself and her Golden Heart.

I am aware of the Golden Witness in me rising up to the forefront again, and this time altering its stance with the changing tide. Whereas earlier I was witnessing her pain, now I am witness to her Golden Joy and Beauty. I watch and honor her as I witness her Golden Radiance and glow reasserting its rightful position at the center of her Being again. I sense that this is taking place for all of these previously Lost Ones here, as my Team of Golden Sisters are also doing their job of witnessing this gorgeous Golden Reawakening and Remembrance.

The Golden One who stands before me is no longer lost; she is found. The radiant infusion of her greater Being is soothing her now and bringing her home to herself in peace and understanding. She looks at me with eyes filled with light and life, bright and twinkling the way I knew they could be. She is truly radiant. She gently squeezes my hands in a gesture of confirmation that all is well with her, and instinctively we reach out to hug one another.

I know there is more of a journey for us ahead, and more recovery for her to do, but for now, this is wondrous. I actually feel as though I have witnessed a true miracle, and my heart is deeply touched by it all.

After a few seconds my intuition tells me that it is time to go. I turn my focus to see what's happening with everyone else, and it's obvious that all of the Rescues are done—this part, anyway. Clearly, it's time to go. We still have many steps to take to get ourselves safely out of here.

Andar steps to the center of our group, and says:

"Beloveds, it is time to move on. I urge you to stick closely together and follow the lead of Mother Mary, who will guide you out and make sure you are safe. Avalar and I will stay back to ensure that everything goes well. We will catch up with you on the outside. Job well done, dear friends. We are forever grateful."

And with that, Mother Mary takes the lead and we are propelled out on the power of her wake. We remain protected and safe within our Golden Cocoon and focus ourselves on maintaining our forward motion, no matter what. We keep moving and moving, pulled by her energy, out of this dark place.

The air gradually starts to change as everything around our cocoon begins clearing and lightening. Finally, our motion slows down and stops. I am relieved that we are back in the forest at our own safe haven. We are greeted warmly by many of our Golden Clan who quickly take the women who have been Rescued into their care. I know they are in good hands now, and I breathe a deep sigh of relief that we all made it home safe and sound.

I stand still for a moment, simply listening to where I am. It's dusk, and I can hear the crickets singing through the trees. It's a happy sound for me, a sweet freedom.

I suddenly realize that I am absolutely exhausted, and as I look at the others, I see that they are as well. Of course, it's been a major trek, to say the least—and there is still much healing and restoration to take place for these dear Rescued women, and certainly a good night's sleep for those of us who went in to bring them home.

It feels good to be here again. I stifle a yawn, as Mother Mary approaches me and gives me a great big bear hug of love and gratitude. Her energy is intense, as she says to me:

"Job well done, my fine Sister. I know what this took for you, and I am grateful for who you are and what you did. Give yourself what you need now to recoup, and we will speak again soon. Bless you, my Beloved. Bless your beautiful Golden Heart."

I feel the power of her loving and passion deep inside of me, right down to my bare bones. I couldn't have done it without her. That's the truth. I am enormously grateful to her. I see her congratulating everyone, encouraging us all to rest. There is nothing but this; our time for healing is now.

As I lay down on my bed of earth I feel the Nature Spirits all around me, soothing and nurturing me tenderly. I hear the gentle breeze of the wind comforting me, and I am bathed in the caring and support of the trees as they extend their branches my way. I couldn't feel more supported and loved. I am tired and spent, but I also feel cherished and understood; it moves me. My eyes well up, this time with tears of sweetness and soft joy. I offer up my thanks and soon fall asleep to the Golden lullaby of it all.

Sometime just before dawn I feel the breath of a familiar Being whispering in my ear. I recognize that it's Mother Mary, and she is rousing me gently from my slumber. *"It's time to get up dear one,"* she says, *"We need to have a meeting.*

I'm going to wake the others now, too, so we can gather and speak."

Somewhat groggy from our efforts of the day before, but happy because of our success, the six of us Golden Sisters gather around Mother Mary. We have all been amazingly well restored in the night, and we are here, ready and listening. I know this meeting must be something important, because Avalar and Andar have arrived as well, and they join our circle with great joy and acknowledgement.

Mother Mary addresses our group:

"First of all, let me say Congratulations again, job well done. That was an extremely demanding mission, and you were all exemplary. What fully skilled and strong Golden Ones you are. Everything went smoothly, and what took place within our Golden Cocoon was certainly nothing short of miraculous. We are all eternally grateful to each one of you.

"The Golden Ones that you Rescued are now being well attended to and cared for by others here, so you don't need to have any further concerns for them. All is well with them, thanks to you. Bless you.

"I am here this morning not only to commend you, but also to speak to you about a new kind of opportunity that has presented itself. The moment has come when each of you can make a new choice about the rest of your incarnation here in Mondor.

"Certainly, there are more Rescues to be done here, if that's what you want to continue doing, but there is also another kind of opportunity being offered to the six of you. You can now choose to become something that will offer great gifts to many, but in a very different way.

"This opportunity is about being sublime—literally and actively, Golden Sublime. If you so choose, you can dedicate the rest of this incarnation to shining the full brightness of your Golden Heart, your Golden Light, right here in Mondor—and I mean FULL. There are still many hungry souls here in Mondor, hungry Golden Hearts that are longing for their own brightness to be witnessed, longing to be touched and to be re-inspired. You can do this by extending the full radiance of who you are and letting them see, feel, and taste this again. Through your own unabashed Golden Shining, they will be touched, and they will remember their own.

"But know that this choice comes with great risk. Let me explain.

"If you choose this path, you will have committed yourself to doing your utmost to speak forth boldly and shine brightly, without holding back. You will be the beautiful magnets of Golden Light that you can be in every way, to the best of your ability, knowing that, in so doing, you will most

definitely be seen not only by many Golden Ones all around, but also by the Heartless Ones as well. And because you are being visible in your light, you will be caught. You will be persecuted, probably sooner rather than later.

"But in being so filled with your Golden Brightness and the strength of this, know, too, that you will perceive and experience things, events, circumstances, and insights differently than you would otherwise. You will live from a completely different perspective, and thereby have a completely different internal and external response to it all.

"Also know, that if you choose this path, you will not be doing this walk alone—not a single step of it and not a single minute of it. We, many Golden Masters in Spirit, will join more closely in union with you than we ever have. It will be a bond deeper than you have ever known. I can tell you that no matter what happens, we will be right there in it with you every single breath of the way. No, we won't be physicalized, necessarily, at least not every time, but our energetic resonance and union with you will be abiding and clear. We will be as one powerful Golden Team.

"We understand fully that although this path is a great gift, it is also a tall order. It is up to you, my dear ones, to reach into your hearts and make your own decision about this.

"The bottom line is this: if you choose this path, then SEIZE THE DAY! Seize the day in every single way. Be fully Golden—fully bright, fully bold, and openly passionate about this that has such great meaning for you. Blaze your Golden Path. Shine and share your Golden Heart thoroughly, at every opportunity.

"Can you imagine doing this in Mondor? Can you imagine how much pure Light that is going to be created here in the midst of this darkness? Can you imagine how greatly Lemuria will come to life right here, for as long as you are doing this?

"Ponder on these questions. See how your systems respond."

I take a stand back inside of myself. The mere thought of this reality actually takes my breath away, for a variety of reasons. My first response, quite honestly, is that I...oh, dear.

I find that I actually can't quite imagine anything so BIG happening in this context of life that is small, tight, and constricted—and it actually makes me uneasy.

I register all of this with equal amounts of surprise and understanding. We have not been here before with any intent to shine that brightly and boldly, but only with the intent to Rescue and reassure. There has never yet been any question about coming here, plopping ourselves down, and GOLDEN SHINING for all to see. In fact, the reality has been to NOT shine brightly, so that we could be camouflaged and get the job done.

We have each put on the Mantle of Fear in order to traverse Mondor unseen, in order to even be here at all. How does this change that fact? What happens to the Mantle of Fear, then? Do we discard it suddenly? Is that possible? How do we even do that? What's up with all of this?

"Humph," I think to myself, with so many questions stirring in my mind. "And why now? Why is she suggesting this NOW?"

As if she has read my mind, Mother Mary turns directly toward me, looks me right in the eye, and I know. It's as clear as day: it's simply that "the time has come."

Tears start rolling down my cheeks. I can't help it. There is so much intense emotion in me right now about all of this. I know that, for one thing, it is an opportunity to be outwardly bright in the midst of darkness. I have a sense of what a huge difference this could make for many Golden Ones here. It could carry them for a long time to come. If their hearts are reignited, they will heal and be restored, never having to return here again as a Lost One.

I feel the power of all of this in my heart, as if it has already happened. I know the huge gift that this would be, not only for Golden Ones here, but for me as well. It simply goes outside the confines of any experience I have yet known.

I look inside my heart and Soul for the answer to this choice Mother Mary has presented to each of us, and something deep and abiding within me takes over. It reassures me that, yes, this is absolutely right and timely, and that it will enable me to fulfill my Golden Vow in a way that allows for levels that I have not been able to achieve before. Deep down, the question of "What do I choose?" meets my responding devotion to my Golden Family full on, and of course, the answer is "YES!"

Of course it is.

I don't know how this is going to happen, but I trust this path, and that's that. My heart spreads open like a wondrous beautiful flower inside of me. It's like a long-awaited need for the Sun is finally getting filled. I have hungered and now is my time, my window, to feel fully replenished and to be Golden Bright and Shining here on Terra as Original Lemuria revisited. What immense joy this could be.

I look at my sisters around me, and I know they have each arrived at the same decision that I have. In this, we are yet again united. Yes. Positively and absolutely, YES!

Mother Mary hears us, and there are tears in her eyes as well. She beams at us, looking like a proud mother, full and triumphant. And then she speaks to us about how this is going to be, how this level of shining is going to be possible. *"Bless you, Golden Ones, great heartfelt Blessings! What truly devoted hearts you have!"*

She reaches for our hands and pulls us all into her body in an embrace of such tenderness and love that it makes me cry, yet again. There is something about this path that is so special. I don't know in what way exactly, but simply that it is. It is like a huge gift for all Golden Life EVERYWHERE, shining pure Golden Brightness in the midst of the heavy darkness. Yes, that would be something amazing for all. I can see that, clear as day. I get it.

Mother Mary continues:

"Now that you have made your choice and demonstrated, yet again, the profound power of your devotion and trust, I have a gift for you that will make this possible. It will answer all of your questions about 'how,' and you will be freed from the bondage of the Mantle of Fear, even though you still walk here in the confining configuration of Mondor.

"On the one hand, you might think that this would be easy, that all it would entail would be a change of mind, heart, and intention. But the truth is that it involves considerably more than that. Shortly, you will be entering an intensive training period with several of the Golden Masters in Spirit that will help you understand the complexities of this and show you how to do it. And, after your training, shine on you will, indeed!

"Bless you all, dear ones. You are Golden Heart of the Highest Order."

My sisters and I look at each other as Mother Mary leaves us, and we recognize that this is going to be big—for us and for all. We are eager, though, and certainly most grateful for all the help we can get to make this possibility come true.

Soon, as Mother Mary promised, we go to another space, time, and dimension for a short but intense training program. Unfortunately, dear Reader, the details of this will have to remain a mystery for the moment, as there is still much ahead to be explored before we can reveal those specifics.

For now, suffice it to say that the training is successful, and we once again reenter our same bodies here in Mondor. We gather and collect ourselves; there is not a moment's hesitation. We are free, completely free, of any constraints. Our only task is to shine as brightly and as radiantly as we possibly can, to be all the Golden Love we can be—and that's exactly what we all do in our own unique and beautiful ways.

Each of us shines brightly and boldly, whether we are on our own, or together as a group. In my body, I feel completely different now than I ever have here in Mondor before. I am aware that I am truly LIVING GOLDEN HEART, vibrant and radiant. I am no longer attuned to simply the expression and extension of this shining, but I AM the Golden Brilliance itself in every cell of my body, in every breath I take, in everything I see—and everything I feel. I feel like a bright Golden Light Bulb turned up to the highest setting possible, and my Being pulsates with it constantly.

I am this and only this. Everything else in Mondor and about Mondor is being eclipsed. My Gold is outshining all else, and I mean ALL ELSE. It's a truly glorious sensation. It is indeed sublime, and has changed everything—like Mother Mary said it would.

My sisters and I greet the dawn each day, and the six of us say our morning prayer of thanksgiving to all that are near and dear to us on all levels. We give great thanks for this opportunity for our shining and brilliance and give thanks for all the support that is here with us, enabling us to greatly shine. And I have to say that the support we feel is amazing, astounding, unwavering.

It comes from our entire Team of Golden Ones, from Terra to the Celestial Realm and all points in between. It is almost unfathomable how connected and interwoven we feel in the Golden Brilliance once again, even though we are here in this configuration of Mondor which leans so differently in a different direction and makeup.

We each go about our business. We go about our ordinary day-to-day business, but we do it all in a completely different way, we don't look over our shoulders anymore. We are not hyper-vigilant, we don't feel the need to be careful.

We already know the outcome and we signed up for it, but there's a whole lot of blazing to happen before that time. We do indeed touch many people, and our numbers grow quite quickly. People seem to come out of nowhere and show up and feel the flame of our hearts reigniting their own. There is great love, great sharing, and great community amongst us all. Our Golden Radiance is strong and expanding. It is beautiful—truly breathtaking.

One night, the six of us are on our way to our forest gathering place when we suddenly sense that the Heartless Ones are close by. We know they've found us, and our end is near. We don't stop. We don't go into hiding. We don't run away—we shine. We keep on shining. We are like bright stars in the midst of the night sky. Amazing. Undaunted.

They are coming upon us now. I look into my own heart and I ponder for a moment, knowing they are close. I say to myself, "How do I feel about this?" and all I feel is calm. I have no fear. I don't know what fear is. I know who these people are, these Heartless Ones. I know how lost they are—I understand they are doing exactly what they know to do. It is no surprise, and I don't even put up a fight.

They come out of the trees right for me, expecting me to fight them and resist, but I don't. The same is true for all of us. We couldn't be a quieter and a more peaceful Golden Team. It's time. The time for this, too, has come.

They seize us and incarcerate us. Periodically, during that short time, they parade us out in front of the public, calling us all kinds of incriminating names to slander us, names and false accusations which are designed to deliberately engender fear in the onlookers. The more they do this, the more the people watching are caught up in the frenzy of it all and join excitedly in the theater of attack and accusation. "Evil Witches," they call us, "The Devil, Satan, Sinners, Evil Ones..." and the list goes on.

Every time they use any of those words, I can see the public leering more closely at us. Many of them are throwing rocks, and are so caught up in it all that they seem unable to stop themselves. They are mesmerized, electrified by all of this theater, this drama, these counter-influences being tossed back and forth.

And here are the six of us, the target of it all, being persecuted for our Light.

Whatever it is they are saying, it is all aimed to create more fear and to use us, yet again, as an example of what NOT to do, of what to FEAR, of what NOT to be. The H-O are using us as puppets for their own gain, now and in the future. They are using us as pawns to control the audience through fear.

What is the message that this theater gives its audience? It's quite clear: this is what is going to happen to you if you shine your Light. This is what's going to happen to you—and to those you love.

Beware.

And it goes on and on. I watch it all happening as if in a dream, crystal-clear, and yet hazy, all at the same time. The words, the sensations of it all, simply don't touch me; they bounce off an exterior layer around me. I remain in an untouchable Golden Cocoon throughout.

But as I am observing all that is taking place, the strategic manipulations and the frenzied fever of it all, I wonder to myself, "Will it always be like this? Forever? Will it always be that we will be persecuted for shining our light so boldly? Will it always be thus in the days to come—lifetimes and generations down the road? Always?"

I wonder.

I am well aware that the thought forms created to condemn, suppress, and control the shining of one's light have taken hold as a form of consciousness, and that these thought forms can only grow stronger and multiply the more they are energized and acted out.

Will there ever be a time when people recognize the entrapment of it all? Will they ever realize that their own Light is simply the truth of who they are? And that reclaiming it is their salvation? That they don't need any mediators? That they already are this and that their birthright is to be this, splendidly—unfettered by any fear, much less that of being hurt or killed or putting those they love most at risk?

Will they ever question, truly, whether or not anything else makes any sense at all?

I want to say to the audience around me, who are looking at me with faces of horror, fear, and ignorance, "I am the one who is free. You are not. Someday you will walk right out of this trap that has been set for you and that is controlling you. Someday you, too, will remember who you are and what you are not."

My thoughts are cut off as I am violently hoisted onto a cross standing in the midst of a great pile of wood and flammable debris. I see that the same has happened to each of my sisters, and we all know that soon these piles will be set alight. Each of us will have to endure this.

In this moment, we reach towards one another with our energies and spread out our vast courage to each other. We hold strong. We witness each other here and now, with total clarity, presence, and conscious awareness of what is happening to us and around us. Instead of flinching, cowering, and panicking, we are wide open, calm, and steady.

I know all is well, even though it looks like the exact opposite. Mother Mary appears in our midst, followed by Avalar and Andar. They are smiling at us, reminding us that, yes, we are all here together—solid, steady, and united. They breathe their fortitude into our hearts and Beings, letting us know clearly that they are honoring and witnessing us in these moments. They remind us that soon this will be over—that our journey has come to an end, and that we have done well, all of us—extremely well. We have shined so brightly.

Our shining has reawakened many, and inspired so much Golden Life to sustain itself here now, enabling it to stretch out and move forward with confidence and capability. We have completed all that we came here to do, and much more.

I feel the Golden Elementals. I feel the Sacred Family everywhere cheering us on, blessing us, being grateful for this time of oneness and connection that we've all had here—a beautiful, sparkling gem that will shine on in the consciousness.

And with that the flames are lit: this is where I started my story earlier, dear Reader.

Yes, the fire is hot, but I feel cool inside the searing heat. My body is burning, but I feel no pain. I sense that, for all my sisters here, it is the same. Had we not been shining so brightly, we might have been crushed by this, because we would have been in an internal state of hiding, and in that hiding, there is a certain weakness that happens. We might have been permeable to feeling the unbearable pain of it all, not just of burning, but also the wounding of the words and false accusations heaped upon us. Perhaps all of it would have penetrated us in ways that would have wounded us deeply and that we would, in fact, have to live out and be reminded of again when we come back.

But as it stands now, we are immune. Our shining has, and is, rendering us so. This is unbelievable to you? Perhaps, but it is our truth, nonetheless.

I feel immune to all of it, with my Golden Light as strong and passionate as it is. My Goldenness in me and all around me is literally encasing me in a Golden Universe that renders me invincible to all else. As I said earlier, it outshines and eclipses all else.

I am well aware that the Heartless Ones are doing the only thing that makes sense for them to do. I have no other expectation. I don't waste my time or energy with any of that. These are the facts; this is Mondor. These are the Heartless Ones, and this is what happens. It is no surprise.

Oddly enough, I find my heart simply blesses them. I know that perhaps you don't agree with this, that I should blame them and be outraged. But I find that my heart doesn't want to do that anymore. I don't condone what they have done, what they do, and will continue to do. I just know that blaming them is useless. It is all too obvious to me now that it only adds to the perpetuation of it all. It only energizes all of that agony. It does not bring about any solution, much less balance. It comes from a place of helplessness.

I am not that configuration anymore, so I see it through a different lens now.

Instead, I find myself wanting to bless them, because frankly, it's all crystal-clear to me now that they're ignorant and they don't even know what they are doing. They think they do. They believe they do, and many people believe they do, but the truth is that they don't. The truth is that the power of Golden Spirit is far greater than anything they could ever do in their vain efforts to try to extinguish it, dominate it, or much less truly control it. And it is for me, as it is for those who are awake and aware and bright and shining, to simply carry on being awake and aware and bright and shining. That is the answer for us, plain and simple. I reiterate: Our Golden Heart eclipses and outshines all else.

Speaking for myself, as I proceed with doing this I will continue to see, feel, and know clearly. And I will be strong, not because I am trying to be or praying to be, but because I am Golden Heart, Golden Love, Golden Power, Golden Shining. This is my choice and my path, and I love it.

These are my final thoughts here. Now it is time to go. My body's packaging has served me well, and I am grateful to it. I leave it for the ashes to be returned to the soil, and I am grateful. I say goodbye to my beloved Terra as I rise up.

I hear Avalar whispering to me on the wind, *"Let go, let go, let go."* I feel Andar reaching under my arms and lifting me upward like a feather on the wind. I am light in my body and spirit.

In an instant, I see Sananda, the quintessential Golden Man. My heart reaches toward him, not out of need, but pure love and adoration. He is my rock. He is my inspiration for being strong and courageous now. He shined this way himself, and while here, I have done the same with all that I have.

He reaches back to me with so much caring that it is as if he is holding my Golden Heart right in the palm of his hand.

Sananda says to me gently:

"You are this, Beloved. YOU are the Golden Grace living and breathing all on its own, no matter where you are and no matter what dimension you are in. Your Golden Heart is all the strength and source you will ever need. Know this now. It is the Truth. It is the pure Golden Way."

And in this moment, as I look at him, at Mother Mary, at Avalar and Andar, I know that I have triumphed. I realize I don't feel shattered in any part of me anymore, the way I once did. I am fully and completely whole.

In shining so brightly in my physical body I have taken my power—my true power—back. It is mine forevermore, like it was in Lemuria. I have fully reclaimed my Truest Self, and everything has changed because of it, forever.

I am truly Golden Free again, no matter where I am.

As I continue to rise up with a smile beaming inside and out, I see my kindred sisters rising up alongside me. They are smiling radiantly too, just as I am. We rise up higher and gently move into the Spiritual Realm, where we are greeted by many Golden Ones who are happy to see us. "Come," they say, "Come with us now. We hear tell that there is great news awaiting us!"

As they scoop me up into their luminescent joy I have much to be thankful for. I feel blessed to be me and to do what I do best—SHINE, GOLDEN SHINE.

This is the end of my story. Thank you for witnessing me, dear Reader. I am grateful. Someday, may I do the same for you.

We are One Golden Radiant Heart.

PART THREE

GOLDEN HEALING
AND RESTORATION

CHAPTER ELEVEN

GOLDEN SACRED FIRE CIRCLE

THE GOLDEN WITNESS SPEAKS:
The air is quiet. There is a complete hush everywhere, as if all motion has stopped. I can actually hear the fact that I hear nothing. "What is different here?" I ask myself. "What has changed?"

In answer to my question I begin to notice the sound of The Golden Sea with its magnificent waves crashing exuberantly against the rocks lining the shore. I am even aware of a change in cadence as the waves turn tender, lapping gently onto the sandy beach—one after the other, over and over...

I find it cleansing, as if it is determined to wash me clean all by itself. I love the Sea; I love the wind and the air, the feel and the smell of it all. I inhale deeply.

When I lived in Lemuria of Origin, this is what it was like. I always felt loved and cared for by the Sea, and by all aspects and forms of my beautiful Terra. And here I am again, having this beautiful moment of intimacy with it all. I close my eyes and savor it, letting the Sea purify me, as she always does.

I am shaken out of my reverie by a voice that I know well. It is one of my Golden Sisters, calling to me urgently. "Come on! Come on! Hurry up, there is an important meeting, and it seems there is great news to be shared with us all! Come—hurry!"

She is very excited, and I can see that there is a lot of fuss brewing about this gathering. I pick myself up and join them, wishing I could have had a few moments longer to savor my daydream. It felt so good to be cleansed and cleared. But here I am and all the better for what little time I did have.

Everyone is being ushered into a large meeting place that reminds me of one of the vast Golden Meadows of Lemuria. It is wide open under a huge sky, which is coming to dusk and settling in for the last part of the day. An aura of sweet harmony prevails here.

I see Avalar and Andar up ahead greeting everyone as they arrive and directing people to gather themselves into small groups of twelve. I find I am one of twelve Golden Ones who are guided to sit in a circle around a large campfire. As I look around I can see that each Golden Group has its own separate campfire, and these small groupings are spread out as far as my eyes can see. There are many Golden Sacred Fire Circles in this vast Golden Meadow, and I wonder what is going on.

After everyone is settled Avalar stands at a point on a small rise where we can all see her. Her skin glows Golden and her hair is bright and blowing gently in the breeze. There is something about her countenance that is unusual, a quality to her beauty that I haven't seen shining through for a long time. I think that it is a great sense of PEACE, one that permeates her entire Being and radiates outward. It touches me, as it touches everyone, and it seems to be carrying a new message for us. I melt—something about this is different.

The stars above begin to twinkle and the evening sky deepens into night around us. There is a great hush as we are gently enveloped in her cloak, and Avalar begins to shine even more. Her Golden Aura glows softly at first, then gradually builds until she becomes fully alight, standing on the rise like a Golden Beacon against the starry sky. We are all struck by her Beauty, her illumination, and her love that permeates and caresses each one of us.

And then she begins to sing.

The sound is one of history, ancient and sacred, and her tone is Heartfelt, deep and pure. It's as if she is telling a story. It is the story of our Family, of our love and devotion and our sorrow and pain. The sound gives me goose bumps, and my heart opens to acknowledge everything that she knows and has witnessed in each and every one of us throughout our journey from Lemuria of origin until now.

I start to cry quietly, as others around me are doing the same. It's a let down kind of crying, as if the end of something has come. I feel as though I am coming apart at the seams in some way, as if my body and system know something that my mind hasn't yet understood. I surrender to it, because there is absolutely nothing else I can do.

Her song continues on for some time, and then gradually comes to an end. As the last plaintive notes echo around me and gently fade, I hear the sound of a "whooshing" penetrating the air, gathering energy and strength. After a few seconds, I recognize that it is giant wings—slowly and methodically flapping above us, coming in closer and closer.

I can feel the wind, generated by the beating of these wings, against my neck. It is blowing my hair around, and the sound and feeling is thick, deep, and huge, as if they are encompassing our entire world, right now and beyond. The wings are circling us, over and over again, swooping up and down and in between where our Sacred Circles are positioned.

We are being affected by this sound and motion, feeling as though it is deliberately generating heat and stirring everyone deep inside. For myself, it is actually somewhat uncomfortable, and yet, something inside of me also knows it is necessary. Why? I don't know the answer to that yet.

Again I surrender, because there is absolutely nothing else I can do in the face of it. I feel like I'm breaking apart at the seams even more—until finally, it stops.

I look up at where Avalar was standing and I see that someone else has taken her place. Our beloved White Eagle stands before us: tall, magnificent, and strong.

He is powerful, large and Golden, with his silky wings spread up and out behind him. They seem to go on forever, stretching high into the night sky, and reaching forward toward each of us, enveloping us as well. We become gently but firmly encased in their soft feathers—cocooned, loved, and protected. The sensation is palpable throughout my whole system, and I relax completely into it.

He begins to speak, his voice literally booming forth with Golden Passion and strength, coupled with deep tenderness:

"I am here, Beloved Golden Ones, I am White Eagle.

"I have been watching all of you for a long, long time. I have been part of your journeys and have been with you throughout. I have watched you in all your courage, as you have done things that were far beyond what you ever thought yourselves capable of. I have witnessed you draw forth from within that which has birthed you and enabled you to endure and persevere.

"I have felt your hearts, open and tender, leaning into all of those that you would Rescue, so you could hear them and be with them in their plights and their pain. You have been one with them, and it has pained you greatly as well.

"Your sorrow has been equal to your loving, so much have you given of yourselves in all that you set out to do. I have been there with you throughout it all—and I have watched and waited for exactly this moment to arrive.

"Dear Ones, I am here to tell you that THE RESCUE MISSIONS ARE OVER. There is no more Rescue work to be done. Your purpose of saving the entire Golden Family has been accomplished. It has been successful. It is complete.

"NO GOLDEN ONE, ON ANY LEVEL, ANYWHERE, HAS BEEN FORGOTTEN."

At White Eagle's words, I cock my head so I can hear better. Did I hear that right? Did he say that the Rescues were over?

I am actually stunned by this news. I can't believe it. I can't believe what I am hearing. My system almost doesn't know what to do with this information. I am used to being in constant "GO RESCUE" mode.

I look around at my small circle, and see the same bafflement in the eyes of everyone else around me. Is this true? Are they really over?

White Eagle declares again, *"Beloveds, I repeat: the RESCUE MISSIONS ARE OVER, AND NO ONE AND NO GOLDEN LIFE FORM ANYWHERE HAS BEEN FORGOTTEN.*

"Our ENTIRE Golden Family has been Rescued and/or Tagged and brought back as One. Do you understand what I am telling you?"

Suddenly, I hear the beating wings again, only this time it is a different kind of sound and motion. It is the gathering of the Golden Angelic Realm descending upon us, flying everywhere between us; around us, above us, and even into Terra below. It is strong, light, feathery, brilliant, and true. It seems to underline what White Eagle is telling us, and is confirming that something that has driven us for what feels like forever is over, just plain OVER.

I start to get it. Those around me start to get it; it is true and we are accepting it. Apparently, truly, yes, the Rescue Missions are indeed over. We are done.

And with that knowing firmly in place, we crumple into a heap and cry.

Within our small groups we reach out our arms to each other, hugging and offering support physically as best we can—and then we sob and sob. All you can hear in the night air is the sound of our crying, echoing throughout the entire giant meadow.

It is the heartfelt sound of suffering that has been survived and is finally coming to an end. It's cadence is real, honest, and deeply poignant.

We cry until our tears are spent. Shouldering one another, we let the waves of emotion and release pass through us and disappear into the dancing flames in the center of our circles. We give it all to the Sacred Fire—we give it all, and then some.

The night goes on, and finally we sit quietly together as one—our Sacred Fire Circles joined in compassion, deep understanding, and empathy.

White Eagle speaks again:

"When you feel ready, you need to talk. You each need to 'say your piece,' and give each other an opportunity to be witnessed within the safety of your Sacred Fire Circles. This is a time to empty out whatever is in the deepest parts of your hearts that comes up to be revealed and shared.

"You know each other well. You have gone through so much together. You will hear and see yourselves in one another, and your hearts' tenderness and compassion will soothe those pathways that have been tried and tested, pained and bruised.

"All your wounds, your pain, and your sorrows need to be expressed. They need to be aired and witnessed. And then slowly, because of this expression,

they will be able to heal. Your sorrows will change, your pain will lessen, your wounds will be attended to and cared for. They will slowly transform and be restored by, and back into, love—Golden Love.

"It is time for this. It is time to let go of being in Rescue Mode and instead let go to the Divine caring within you that can heal.

"This you have earned and this you need. Your Beings want this."

With the naked truth of it being finally accepted by each one of us, we proceed exactly as White Eagle is urging us so lovingly to do. We go through the night, each one of us baring our Souls, talking about what has hurt us the most, and what has touched us the deepest in our sadness and pain throughout the journeys we made into Mondor.

We listen to one another with full presence and full understanding, letting ourselves be opened, stripped, and shaken by this depth and power of sharing, by the naked honesty and vulnerability of it. It is so raw.

The wounds are apparent and in great need of being witnessed and healed.

"I hated the pain that my loved ones were in," said one person. "They were in agony, and it broke my heart."

"I was doubled over in the searing pain of such heartlessness," said another. "I didn't know how this cruelty was even possible. I didn't know what to do with it."

"I wanted to go numb, to shut down my senses so I wouldn't hear or see or feel the pain of my family anymore. It was beyond bearing so many, many times."

"I could feel the pain and the fear, and it literally felt like it was breaking me."

"I had never known such pain. I have memories I feel I'll never, ever be able to forget. I was abused many times, in many ways, on many levels. I am still in shock."

"I had never known Fear before, and I never knew that it could have many faces and be so cruel. I felt strangled by it, as if it would completely snuff out my life."

"I never understood what Fear was until it brought me right to my knees and left me trembling. I was powerless, lost, and felt completely alone."

"I never knew that Fear was like a disease, an infectious disease, spreading its sickness everywhere."

"I've never felt so trapped, so completely trapped and alone. I thought I was going to go insane."

"It's the agony that still feels like it's ripping me apart. How will I ever heal this? It makes me sad. My heart aches. I feel broken."

The stories go on and on, the pain pouring out like water releasing from a dam.

And with it all come revelations that, while outside of the realm of what I had personally experienced in terms of their content, contain the same form—Pain, always Pain; Fear, always Fear.

The Sacred Fires in the midst of our circles devour it, suck it all up, turning it into ash and blowing it away. The flames are bright and searing, transforming it and helping us to set ourselves free.

Finally, as the night sky begins to seep into dawn, we find ourselves able to share some of the joys and the incredible feelings and experiences of magic and miracles in the Rescues we had made. Some of us had been Rescued ourselves at one time or another, and we are able to speak fluidly about the cascading events of it, how it had changed us and further fueled our resolve to Rescue others.

The longer we talk, the greater the ease; and the more we share, the greater the comfort. As the Sun rises we find we are spent.

The Sacred Fires begin to die down at last, taking our dross and pain with them. We have burned out what would have crippled us further and saved ourselves from that which we had suffered through. This is OUR Rescue beginning to take place.

Throughout it all, we felt the constant presence and reassurance of Golden White Eagle; his strength was unwavering in both its encouragement and gentleness. I had known of him before, but I had never experienced him like this. To me, he had been a Golden Ascended Master who had strong Native American roots. But now, I see he has expanded to a form that is all encompassing.

It was as though his wingspan cradled us—inside ourselves and with one another. He was our shelter throughout this night, and stood again as our Healer in the light of the morning. We look toward him now as he stands, clearly defined in the light of day. He is breathtaking in his Beauty, and his Golden Eminence shines forth with tremendous joy and compassion:

"Well done, Sacred Golden Ones, well done! You have been through much last night, and you will soon reap even greater rewards from this deep sharing and caring. You have emptied out and cleared a pathway for tremendous healing to be set in motion.

"Know that this marks the beginning of the Journey of Restoration back to Wholeness, back to One Golden Heart, alive and well and, yes, absolutely flourishing.

"At the end of it, it will seem simple. And yet, throughout this healing movement, the levels and demands of even this journey will be complex and multi-layered.

"It is indeed a journey; an active and conscious process. Know this to be so. And as such, it is yet another choice point for you—a choice to heal. It is up to you."

And with that, we see Master Saint Germain, Mother Mary, Sananda, Avalar, and Andar joining White Eagle on the rise of the hill. They are standing strong up there in solidarity as one unit: a shining Golden Team that has our backs and our fronts as well. We know this crystal-clearly.

White Eagle continues:

"We encourage each of you to go inside and ask yourselves if this is what you wish to do—for you and for all. You are so accustomed to putting the needs of others ahead of your own that you have, in a way, lost your ability, and certainly your inclination, to treat yourselves first in the understanding and comprehension that you are now the wounded one in need of help.

"Yes, you have Rescued so many—both in the form of actual physical Rescues, and others in the form of Tagging. As we have said, no stone was left unturned, no Golden One or Golden Energy Life Form was forgotten. You don't need to know any further details about any of them anywhere right now, except that, in great thanks to you and your successful efforts, they are now finding their way home as well.

"Now let them go. Instead, turn toward yourselves.

"ALL Golden Ones everywhere wish to see EACH of you healed and restored to full Golden Health, Wellness, Happiness, and Flourishing. This is imperative if we are to resume our active life as One Golden Heart, One Golden Lemuria again back on Terra.

"Each one of you must consciously choose this for yourselves, if it is what you want. This journey of healing will not happen in the snap of a finger. As I have said, it is a process. It is an unwinding of you and a re-collecting of you; a constant and continuing request of your commitment to YOU.

"This journey is your Rescue, your Rehabilitation, your Restoration back to the fullness of your own Golden Heart Life.

"It is not enough to say, 'Yes, I do,' thinking that it will happen all by itself. It won't.

"There are too many memories, learned behaviors, and fear-based conditioned responses for that to be the case. Each step of your 'unwinding of the Mantle of Fear' must be understood and treated with kindness, caring, and insight. It is an intensely gentle journey. It is an act of pure and engaged self-loving.

"This must be a CONSCIOUS commitment on your part; otherwise, it will not happen. If you decide that this is truly what you want, then all the details will emerge as needed. As always, we are all in this together. You are not alone.

"Take a moment to look inside your hearts and see if your healing is what you feel you want and are ready for. Consider this 'Project of YOU' like every other choice point that you have faced before. Give yourself time and space to reflect upon whether or not this is what you desire and need."

And with those words clearly stated, we all pull back our energies and go deep inside of ourselves to make our decisions. I am grateful for this opportunity because I would have thought it would be an automatic "Yes!", without any choosing at all. Of course I want to heal, but I am also well aware of the POWER of choice—and that this deliberate and conscious choosing is the thing that will enable my whole system to fulfill my next purpose.

It doesn't mean that I won't still care about and tend to others. I will live my life with them in mind as well. However, it means that I am placing emphasis and centeredness on ME, because I am the one in need, and I know it. I respond to this, too. I am "the patient," to also be cared for in my own consideration and awareness.

And judging from what White Eagle said, I know this is going to be a lot more complex than I might think or expect. As in all intricate and demanding journeys, consciously and deliberately CHOOSING it will keep me steady, clear, and stronger on the path of my own wellness. I welcome this.

With this in my understanding, I look inside my heart, only to be met with blazing Golden Light. Okay. Well, obviously it has its own intention, and who am I to stand in the way? I am grateful to be greeted with my own loving in this way. Of course this is what I want—and of course, I am ready for it, because it will be precisely my Golden Love that will guide me and show me the way. It is my own Golden Love that will finally bring me back home to itself.

I ponder on this for a moment, aware of the depth and joy of it, and hear myself saying resolutely, "Yes! Whatever I need to do for my own healing to happen and for my own Golden Shining to be clear, strong, radiant, and free again, THIS is what I want—and I am willing to do this one hundred percent."

With that declared to myself, I open my eyes and look around. And what do I see?

Many Golden Eyes shining back at me. YES! A resounding yes. The choice has been made.

Again, we are in this together and we will support ourselves and each other to the best of our abilities. That is our promise. "Onward!" as Master Saint Germain would say.

Let Golden Freedom BE. I let it begin with me.

I look to where White Eagle is standing and his wings are literally vibrating with joy. They spread out from his body, unfurling themselves to their full breadth and span in their Golden Freedom. Watching this gives me chills and makes me feel electric throughout my whole body. I feel as though I am watching my freedom take place.

"Golden Ones, yes! Yes and yes," he booms. *"We have heard your choice, your voices of freedom, and we are thrilled! Know that we will continue to travel together, as we have up until this point. Know that my heart and my wings are always with you.*

"In sacred Golden Blessings, I love you forever. One Radiant Golden Heart Forever!"

For a moment, my heart absolutely leaps with joy as his exuberant energy touches mine. I watch him and the rest of the Golden Masters who stand there beaming at us. They are clearly proud and respectful and honoring of us. I know that they are indelibly joined with us and that our hearts are woven into one Golden Wave of determination and anticipation of great outcomes.

In my next breath the Sacred Fire Circles dissolve completely, and our small groups disband. We find ourselves whisked off to yet another place in Spirit where there are more details to be revealed, and yet another tale to be told.

Come with me, dear Reader. This should be fun!

CHAPTER TWELVE

RESCUING SELF: HEALING THE LEMURIAN SOUL-SICKNESS

THE GOLDEN RESCUES ARE OVER. Now what?
The Golden Witness continues to speak:

I find myself in a sweet spot. I am deep within a Sanctuary inside the domain of Golden Spirit, and I know that there is much for me to learn here. There are many levels of Interference that need to be understood and shed, and layer upon layer of conditioned, fear-based responses to be known—so that I can let them go.

I experienced many lifetimes of Rescues in Mondor and parts of me have come to identify myself in ways that are not truly me, so that I could be there fully and get the job done. As I explore this sense, I wonder how I am going to actually release all of it. It seems like such an intense layering of "stuff" that has built up inside of me and around me. I realize now that these layers are thick and overcrowded with junk of one kind or another. I hadn't seen that before, and they are sticky too, like glue.

I know I am in Spirit, and therefore these dense layers are not actually being worn by me right now—but I am being given the opportunity to experience them as though they are. This is how I can understand and make new choices about what I identify myself with, and what in truth I will choose to wear from now on.

It's obvious to me, as I stand here seeing things more objectively than ever before, that my healing is indeed a "hefty plate of a task" that lies ahead of me; it is way more complicated and complex than I would have thought.

I understand even more why engaging in this was another Choice Point—it's huge, and I begin to fathom the true choice I have made. It will be worth it in the end, but there are many steps between now and then.

Alright, let's get on with it!

I look around, finally becoming aware that there are many Golden Ones with me. I see that we are feeling equally enthusiastic to get on with things; I can see it in their eyes and feel it in their hearts, and we are all lit up right now.

In my bubbling up of excitement it takes me a minute to realize that someone special has entered our midst. A hush descends throughout our gathering, and we turn our focus toward what has drawn our attention like moths to a flame.

Sananda is standing in our midst—tall, glorious, Golden, and shining. His countenance makes me take a sudden breath. He is beautiful, and my insides completely melt.

The atmosphere is charged with electricity and purposefulness, and as we find our places and settle in, there is a sense in the air that something about this meeting is important and special. We open ourselves to the outpouring of love that is thoroughly permeating us from this exquisite Golden Being.

Sananda speaks:

"Beloveds, you are mighty ones, completely devoted to that which is the Golden Truth. Your hearts are strong and pure, and not a day goes by when you do not touch that which is sacred inside of you and around you. At this moment you have no idea of the depth of your beauty or the power of your touch when you are in this.

"I ask you to listen to me carefully, and to give my words your full attention and consideration. There is a Second Choice Point to be considered now, before you can venture further on your journey of healing.

"Healing yourselves from your travails is something that needs to happen, no matter what future choices you make. This healing and repair are essential for each one of you, regardless of where you choose to go next. You each suffer from what we refer to as the Lemurian Soul-Sickness, and this is something that we will soon address with you in great detail. But first, there is something even more pressing and important to decide upon.

"Yes, for all of you, your healing will take place no matter what. This you have chosen, this you have committed yourselves to. But what is also being presented to you is the choice to heal with another specific purpose in mind.

"Yes, you can heal and restore, and never go back to Terra again—that is one choice. Or, you can choose to heal and restore in precise preparation to go back to Terra shining radiantly as One Golden Heart, One Golden Lemuria, reuniting with her again.

"You can choose to return there to be and live the Golden World, whole and free. This is the opportunity which is being presented to you.

"If you choose this opportunity, the trajectory of your healing—and what it will entail—will be different than if you are just choosing to heal yourself, period.

"If what you want and commit to is full restoration of Lemuria back on Terra once again, then every aspect of what is needed for precisely that to happen successfully is what will dictate the journey of your healing and

restoration—for that purpose, and that purpose only.

"My question to you is this: do you want to heal and restore yourselves for the sake of just your own healing? Or do you want to heal and restore for the purpose of not only healing yourselves, but also for the purpose of going back to Terra and fully restoring Golden Lemuria with her again?

"Do you want to flourish on Terra with all of us together once more as One Golden Radiant Heart? That is the choice that is being presented to you.

"I know this raises immediate questions in all of you; I can hear them, and I understand. I know you are wondering how this can happen, literally. Let me address this.

"You will not go back into Mondor. You will only go back to planet Terra to BE Lemurian, to re-build Lemuria, and to restore our Golden World. We will be Golden Lemuria again. YOU—all of us—will be shining this truth brightly for all to see.

"How can this happen? It is simple.

"Our beloved and most magnificent Terra has the capacity, the heart, and the desire to support many different levels of consciousness. She is capable of doing this very well. She offers this to humans as one of her many exquisite gifts.

"With that said, we can live on the same planet and coexist with Mondor. We will not become Mondor; we will not compete with Mondor; we will not be controlled by Mondor; we will not be thwarted by Mondor. We will basically not have anything to do with Mondor.

"We can have our own Golden World. We can have this again in complete totality.

"How? Same location, different consciousness.

"SAME LOCATION, DIFFERENT CONSCIOUSNESS.

"We would not be there to change Mondor at all. That is literally impossible. Only Mondor can change Mondor. That is not our frequency anyway, so why would we even do that? It is simply not our business.

"We would be there being us, Golden Us. Being Lemurian and letting Mondor be Mondor: live and let live. GOLDEN LIVE and LET LIVE.

"'Unbelievable,' you say? 'Impossible, unfathomable, no way?'

"I can hear it all—and what do I have to say to you in return?

"What I have to say is this:

"IF you make this choice, then
"YOU WATCH!

"The window for this possibility has opened, my Friends. The window that you have been waiting for, preparing for, and talking about for eons—is here.

"It is NOW. It is READY. It is TIME.

"That which heretofore has been impossible is now possible. You know the saying, 'It's an idea whose time has come?' In this case, 'It's a new Golden World whose time has come.'

"In truth, it's not just a possibility; it is a definite. It is our destiny—deep down inside, you know it too."

My insides are in turmoil. Every single word Sananda is speaking is turning on bells and whistles and intense waterfalls of emotion and resonance. My mind is awry, but inside I am deeply quiet.

He has touched pure peace inside of me—pure Golden peace. I hear an Ancient Calling rising up from deep within the sacred caverns of my Golden Heart. It is a longing, an aching, and a yearning for this truth that Sananda is reminding me of that needs to be fulfilled. It's why I AM.

My heart is calling me to come and meet my true Golden Self full circle. My Choice, my answer? Yes, of course. YES—and I know without opening my eyes that everyone else has made exactly the same decision as well. We are aligned; we move forward as One Golden Body.

Sananda continues:

"I know you are wondering HOW. We will address every single aspect of this and what it entails. You will go through further training when you are ready, when the time is right, and all the healing that you need to do to prepare for that has been completed.

"But first, you need to heal yourselves. It will not necessarily be an easy process for you, but I promise you it will be well worth it. It will not be as hard or as painful as what you have already walked through for so long. Unraveling the wounds and attending to them is an act of love for yourself.

"The first thing you are obviously going to need to do is to LET GO. Many of you are so wired for rescuing that you don't even know how to stop. You don't even know how to do anything but RESCUE. You have forgotten all else.

"I know you think I am speaking strong words, but I know exactly what I am talking about. Look at yourselves. Look at each other. You have excelled

at Rescuing—all of you. It has been the driving force of your life experience for so long, and you have done remarkably well.

"You have trained yourselves into it—and now you must train yourselves out of it. If you don't, your internal distress will increase greatly; your systems will only be spinning in place with nowhere to go and no one to Rescue. THE RESCUES ARE OVER. There is no more need for you to be that way, is there?

"Without that, who are you? That is the resounding question you are left with. 'If I am not Rescuing, who am I?'

"Be aware that you are 'wearing' all of this now so that you can dismantle it. I know we are not on Terra right now, that we are indeed in Spirit. Nonetheless, this 'apparatus' is being worn by you so you can see it clearly.

"In the pages ahead White Eagle will be guiding you through the journey of clearly seeing yourselves and earnestly identifying your various symptoms and levels of the Lemurian Soul-Sickness—but before that happens, there are a few more things I would like to say.

"Before you can live the Golden World again on Terra, two things need to happen: YOU need to be healed and reoriented to your natural design and frequency, and the Imprint of the original Shattering needs to be healed. It's as though it's hanging there in the ethers of Terra, suspended and waiting. If this is not attended to, it will take over your lives when you get back there. All of the memories of pain of the Lemurian journey since that original shattering are still alive in that Imprint. It is the whole collection of memories that are infused into our Lemurian Configuration there, energetically and ethereally.

"Once you are healed individually, we can heal that Imprint together. I want you to know about all of this so that you can ponder it from time to time, and be aware of how these things work.

"If conditions are to be a 'clean slate,' they need to be cleaned first on ALL energetic and etheric levels. Do you understand?"

I feel my whole system opening up to what Sananda is saying, as if new lights are being turned on and new frequencies tuned in. It's like I am a radio and my "station" is being pinpointed with extraordinary precision. I feel focused in a new way, with a feeling of fortitude in my body that wasn't there before.

I am aware that there is a Plan, and I love the feeling and reassurance that this is bringing me. I feel like I'm right where I need and want to be, and that

I will have the help I need to get to where I want to go. On top of that, there is a renewed purpose for me; one which I can turn my energies toward—a new direction, focus, and goal. I love this. And yes, I do completely understand what Sananda is saying about the Imprint that will need to also be healed when the time comes.

I am on board and fully committed and devoted to this extraordinary thing: Golden Me, Golden Us, Golden World. I can't imagine anything better anywhere. It seems unbelievable, really, doesn't it? And yet, it feels right—as if everything is already naturally lining itself up inside, as if my own greater Golden Intelligence has already naturally stepped up and taken over.

Who am I to argue with that?

I breathe a sigh of ease and contentment. It's the first time I have breathed like this in what seems like forever. I can tell there are only good things ahead, and that makes me smile.

Sananda Speaks on the Lemurian Soul-Sickness

The Golden Witness speaks:

We are still gathered together in our group, listening intently as Sananda continues to address us.

"Beloveds," he says gently. *"It is time now to clearly know and understand your state of deep internal distress. You are in a state of what we refer to as the Lemurian Soul-Sickness. It is real, and it is true. If you don't believe me, look inside yourselves.*

"It's right there coming to meet you. Its time has come. This is your healing process, and one that has been activated by your consent and choosing.

"I urge you to welcome this; to simply feel, hear, and witness fully all that it has to tell you, show you, and reveal to you now and in the forthcoming days. Acknowledge it and be receptive to it. It is not here to hamper you further, but to enlighten you about your present state and, through this, to be healed. Gentleness, kindness, and self-compassion are what are called for.

"It's time to let down, and let it be."

At his words, I crumple into a heap. I realize I am exhausted. I don't seem to have an ounce of energy left for anything. Even my sense of caring seems to have left me. How am I going to be able to do this?

Sananda steps inside me with his voice, as if he has been listening in on my thoughts and says tenderly:

"Beloved, it isn't about DOING anything. It's only about BEING with it. Your state of sheer exhaustion is the beginning. This is where it wants to start. Let go and be with it. There is more to know."

I am still crumpled in a heap, feeling so spent that my exhaustion is weighing me down like a heavy, wet wool blanket.

"Yes," I realize. "The Rescues are over, and yes, I am completely worn out."

My breathing becomes slow and effortful, as if I hardly even have the energy to do that. I don't know as I'll ever be able to even get up again—much less think about making a life, or anything else.

"My goodness," I say to myself. "I'm so sorry. I didn't even know I felt this way. Oh dear."

My body responds, and I hear it as though it is actually speaking aloud to me.

"Thank you for listening," it says. "This our beginning. There is more…lots more."

I sit gently with myself and realize that these sensations are stronger than my desire to want to avoid the feelings of exhaustion.

Sananda continues gently:

"Beloveds, as you walk through this part of your journey, I urge you not to be daunted by this. It is because of your need to wear the Mantle of Fear, in order to be in Mondor. You have worn it extensively and it has pained you. That is what you will recognize now.

"You may not always want to acknowledge how much you are hurting. In fact, you may not even want to admit that you are at all, but you are, most definitely.

"You need to understand that where you find yourselves now is because of where you have been. This distressed state remains in place today. Yes, this is EXACTLY where and how you are in modern times: stuck.

"You are still 'glued in' to the Mondor Imprint. It is essential that you know and accept how truly stuck you are. You may deny it, and you may avoid it. You may fight with it, and you may try to resist it, but you are still stuck, nonetheless. You may have done your best to liberate yourselves from this Imprint, only to find out that it still 'has you' in one way or another. It may not have you all the time, but it has not disappeared or dissolved completely from your experience.

"No matter how far out to the periphery of this Imprint you have managed to get, no matter if you are hugging even its outermost walls, you are still stuck inside that Imprint. You may feel, relatively speaking, freed up, to

one degree or another, but you are not; you are still wearing, and being manipulated by the Mantle of Fear; you are still stuck inside the Mondor Configuration.

"I know I am speaking bluntly, because I am jogging your memories. I speak for you at this moment, because you do not have the clarity about this to speak of it for yourselves. Presumptuous of me, you think? No, I am speaking the facts that you are too veiled to see.

"Of course, you don't see this for yourselves. You are far, far too disconnected from your Golden Core to be able to remember. You have sunk so deep inside Mondor that your memories of your true Golden Selves have been obliterated from your conscious awareness. But that means nothing; the Sun is still shining behind the clouds, even on a foggy day—so it is with all of you.

"Everything that you experience that is not your Golden Sovereignty is NOT YOURS: it is the Mantle of Fear, and all that it contains. It is relentlessly affecting you in disharmonious ways; it is, in truth, not yours. It all belongs to the Mantle of Fear, it all belongs to the Mondor Configuration.

"Please consider what I am saying: again, it is not truly you; again, it is not truly yours.

"Yes, you still find its interference in your lives unrelenting in one way or another. It will continue to be so until you recognize your present state of disharmony—until you clearly understand and see this dissonant reality that you have been living in and identifying yourselves with.

"Basically, you could say that at this point, you are experiencing a case of mistaken identity. You don't have your Golden Remembrance to see exactly who and how you truly are, but you will. And in the end, it will all end up boiling down to this: misperceptions and realignment with your True Selves.

"As it unravels itself for you to witness, you will see, and you will understand. You will gradually remember and re-own who you truly are. You will remember, because it will remind you of itself.

"We describe it as the Lemurian Soul-Sickness, because that is what it is at the core. You are Golden Soul-Sick because you have had to compromise yourselves in many, many ways in order to fulfill something of greater importance than your natural freedom.

"Yes, you have been thoroughly Golden Soul Embodied upon Terra before, in Lemuria. You know how beautiful, whole, and gloriously loving life upon

her can be. To experience your embodiment as the opposite of that freedom has been tremendously painful in many ways, and on many levels for you.

"I urge you, with all my heart and soul, to realize and embrace that your Lemurian Soul-Sickness is real. Only through this will you be able to be healed by your most true nature and be restored to what you know deep down inside is calling.

"Then, and only then, can you move on. Then, and only then, can you—and your lives—be restored to Golden Freedom."

I continue to sit quietly, listening to Sananda's words, feeling his energy, and my responses in return. Tears are rolling slowly down my cheeks. I don't quite know if they are tears of sadness at the thought of my "Lemurian Sickness," or tears of relief at being recognized and understood at such deep levels inside. They are both, I guess.

I'm being slowly and deliberately stirred; the soil of the deepest ground in me is being turned over and aerated. And so far, there is nothing I want to do to stop it.

Golden Rehabilitation and Restoration Program

The Golden Witness speaks:

I find my eyes closing and feel that I am greatly in need of a rest right now. I doze off for what seems like a few short minutes, but amazingly, when I wake up, I feel completely refreshed. I see that Sananda is no longer with us, but I am still surrounded by all of us who are still here. It's a great sea of beautiful Golden Faces sitting together and waiting in anticipation.

Once again, we hear White Eagle's gigantic wings flapping, and we know that he is near. As he approaches, the sound and motion of his movement gets us centered and clearly focused. We have made our choice to heal ourselves, and we are ready to roll up our sleeves and dig in.

"Great Golden Ones, Good Day!" White Eagle bellows out with joy as he lands, amazingly quietly for one so large, and with wings so huge. Steady on his feet, he carefully folds his wings down by his sides and looks at each one of us with love and patience. His eyes are kind, but penetrating and crystal-clear.

White Eagle continues:

"Steady on, Golden Ones, have faith! This is a joyous journey, and one which will captivate your minds, hearts, and Souls in breathtakingly beautiful ways. You will be glad to be able to tell the truth and be yourselves, to let your Light gradually find its way back to full-on shining.

"First, we must look at exactly this point: are you aware of your dilemma about this, about fully shining? Are you cognizant of your inner conflict?

"I call it the 'Lemurian Lament'; the dilemmas about shining that you have lived with for so long. Now it is time to fully face and understand it. Believe it or not, it will be a challenge for you. It is a good one and well worth your full attention.

"The dilemma is this:

"You have longed to share and shine your FULL Golden Light and yet, you knew and understood there was peril in doing so. You knew you wouldn't, couldn't, and shouldn't. It was risky business, not just for you, but for those you loved as well. You were not in Mondor for that. You were only there to Rescue. But even in your wisdom, it didn't change the inner agitation that this created inside. You are Golden Ones, enormous by design—having to render yourselves so small stifled you. We know it was necessary, but what has it left you with?

"Each of you has been bottled up, quite literally, like the whole universe poured into a tight and constrictive container. It's a good metaphor— imagine that. That is what you have become; that's how squeezed you have been. That is the reality of the identity that you have worn in Mondor and will wear again when you go back into physical form—unless you change it.

"The first step to change is thorough understanding and acknowledgement. Great compassion for yourself is called for here. This inner conflict has been, and still remains, active inside of you—and it needs to be addressed with tender loving care."

As White Eagle is speaking, I feel myself getting short of breath; I am uncomfortable, nervous, and jittery. My Creative Centers begin to heave in rebellion, and I feel as though I could throw up. It feels literally IMPOSSIBLE for me to have crammed myself into such a small, tight, narrow, confining, and restrictive space. How did I do that? I cannot fathom it right now. All it is doing is making me hugely sick and enormously anxious. And I know that this face of Fear is not even my true design. What's up with this?

I know, dear Reader, that I am not in a physical form right now. I am in the domain of Spirit. But, as I said, these revelations are being brought to me so that I can make changes necessary to being able to live freely back on Terra in the future. No, I don't have a clue, either, how this is going to be possible. Bear with me. We will find out together.

While I am here "in rehabilitation and healing," please be aware of how clearly and enormously the physical Imprint is being brought to me, to each one of us, so we can fully know it in this new light; so we can repair and heal ourselves properly for our future reentry back to Terra as fully embodied Golden Ones. That is to say, fully Golden Shining.

I have many automatic knee jerk responses based on my experiences in Mondor, the most challenging of which are a result of the persecution experiences and pain, both my own and of those that I love. The memories are gruesome, hard, painful ones that are stuck inside my cells. Conclusions were drawn and belief systems set in place because of them. It's as though the THOUGHT of going back to Terra re-stimulates those cellular memories, and I am quaking before I've even stuck a toe back in there. My system is already in that mode; expecting, anticipating, preparing for—and bracing to withstand that persecution again.

But what if I am met with something different? What if I am met with silence instead? What if I am met with love, even? How would I be? Would my defenses and defensiveness drop away? Would I trust this? Or would I forever walk around in conflict, braced because I don't feel safe and because I don't want to be the cause of harm to those I love? What if Fear still ruled me, no matter what?

It is obvious to me that I am actually sicker than I thought. I desperately want to shine. I crave to shine, I NEED to shine—but I am also perpetually blocked by my inner conflict about it. Is my "No" louder than my "Yes" when it comes to the reality of my SHINING?

Holding myself back makes me sick. The thought of putting others at risk makes me sick. Not being fully in my Golden Juice renders me sick. Having this constant push/pull, yes/no conflict in action makes me sick. It all makes me sick. Now what?

Its as though White Eagle was listening in on the thoughts whirling around in my head, and I become aware that his energy is here witnessing us spinning in our confusion. I realize it's necessary for this kind of "breakdown" to happen. It's the beginning of a massive "unwinding" of the distortion created by our various experiences in Mondor. We have become tightly wound and bound, and there is nothing better for us than having our insides come apart and unwind themselves in this kind of chaotic, sad, but poignant and understandable confusion.

I am beginning to feel the compassion for myself that White Eagle mentioned earlier. It is emerging from deep inside of me, gently rising up and spreading through me. I can see those around me are having a similar kind of awakening: baby steps—gentle, tender, baby steps.

White Eagle continues to speak:

"First, let's talk more about the Mantle of Fear, and more specifically, about SHEDDING THE MANTLE OF FEAR. Several of us will be addressing this subject at length.

"You can't just rip it off like a band aid. This is a gentle removal, done with care and kindness and patience, above all else.

"Yes, you feel like you've been in a straitjacket, bound and gagged for the longest time. That was the price to pay for your generous and loving endeavors. You'd think that you could stand right up and take that straitjacket off and be clear as day—instantly. But no, that would be way too painful for you. Your system would go into spasms of vulnerability and distress.

"There is much to be learned from that which you have worn. There is much information and training which, once recognized and understood, will serve you in exactly the ways that will benefit you, and everyone, the most when you return to Terra as a Golden One. The thing that you believe has weakened you, has in fact strengthened you as well. It is the growth that you needed to achieve to be of the greatest and most effective service in the future."

My jaw literally drops at what I am hearing. You mean to tell me that the thing I want to "GET RID OF BECAUSE I HATE IT AND IT HURTS ME" is, in truth, the thing that has served to strengthen and educate me? Are you telling me that I need to be GRATEFUL for this? Are you telling me that I actually need to honor this?

Why can't I BE DONE WITH IT?

Dear Reader, I know my frustration and impatience have surfaced—I thought I was feeling such compassion and gentleness. But a few moments ago, what happened? I feel like I'm on an emotional see-saw going up and down, back and forth, with each emotional response having such intensity and drive. When I think about it, though, I'm definitely feeling passionate about it, and I like that. That, I know, is a healthy sign. I've been contained for such a long time.

Yes, this is definitely A PROCESS—and an up and down one at that! Okay. I'm still in.

Now what?

White Eagle continues:

"Who and how you were in Lemuria of Origin is not who and how you will be in the Lemuria of the future. You will be stronger, even more potent and powerful, a better Golden YOU than ever before, precisely because of all you have gone through and what you have learned and now know.

"We are not trying to GO BACK to Lemuria of Origin. That's only our reference point for Remembrance. We are, and have been, MOVING FORWARD through spiritual evolution. It's a new day, a new dawn, a new Golden Consciousness that you will bring to bear to this beautiful planet of Golden Terra.

"The point, as Sananda described precisely earlier, is to be able to vibrate the Golden World on Terra. It is to be fully physically embodied and expanded as Golden Ones—living, breathing, being full Golden Consciousness there again. To establish a complete and whole, fully functioning and fully flourishing Golden World there—coexisting with Mondor.

"Again, as he said: same location, different consciousness—live and let live.

"Right now, I know you feel like you don't know who you are. You are in between configurations, in between patterns, in between Imprints. It's disconcerting in one way and enlivening in another.

"The Mantle of Fear is beginning to loosen up. It is time for a respite, so your system can repair in its own way at this juncture."

WHITE EAGLE SPEAKS
ON THE LEMURIAN SOUL-SICKNESS

The Golden Witness speaks:

We are whisked off yet again, to another place, and I find myself landing gently by myself inside what feels like a Golden Cocoon. I become aware that it is a Healing Pod. I find it soothing to my soul; it is soft, gentle, and undemanding.

I rest and relax as my system lets go, like warm butter melting.

Even though I am resting inside my Pod, I hear the sound of birds singing softly, as if they are happily going about their daily business and somehow including me in their sweet conversation. I don't know what's being communicated exactly, but I love being included in it; being a part of something sweet and beautiful.

My mind is serene and slow for the moment, and my system is humming gently. I feel as if I am enveloped by a soft lullaby, being gently rocked and soothed, comforted and delighted in. I feel like I am in the arms of Love; I am in the arms of Golden Love.

I find I don't need anything else, just this. This is fine; this is Heaven, this is perfect. Everything is a gift to me from now on—a gift of LOVE. I KNOW this.

I hear the Sea again. I hear the waves lapping gently onto the shore, rhythmically caressing the sand. Occasionally, this rhythm is punctuated by a rolling, crashing wave bumping up against the side of a rock, causing my senses to somersault and tumble along with it. It is a comfortable motion, as though I am being washed and cleansed by the Sea. I love her, I love my Golden Sea. She houses such an abundance of life, and her waters are exquisitely pure and clean. She loves me back. She always loves me back.

I am important to her. She includes me in her sound and rhythm, in her motion and steady push and pull across the deep surfaces of my Terra, as if she is stroking my skin. She bathes and rocks me, all the while washing me clean.

I yawn and stretch and return to my dozing. It is quiet. Not a sound. Instead, I just…feel.

I feel myself, as though I am in physical form. I feel the soles of my feet walking barefoot on the warm sand. The Sun, my favorite Golden Sun, is shining high and glorious above me, radiating down and through me, permeating and blessing every cell of my body and Being.

I love my Golden Sun; she is here for me. In her warmth I am soothed, I am created, I am brought back to life. I am regenerated and beautified. I blossom. I can feel myself growing inside as she touches me and reminds me that I am whole and that I have come home.

I breathe a deep sigh of contentment. Why? Because I know she is right. I know it with every fiber of my Being. And for the first time in a long, long time, every level of me, inside, seems to truly and deeply…let go.

In my softening and yielding something else begins to happen, something I have longed to feel for so long: I receive. I receive my Golden Sun.

I receive her nourishment and drink it in. Not in big gulps of desperate need, but long, slow draughts that penetrate and permeate every atom of me. They reach every possible nook and cranny inside my body, my mind, my heart, and my Soul.

I have felt sick for a long time, and right now, in this very moment, I know and understand why. And I am perfectly fine with it. I am not crying because of it. I am not sad, or grieving any loss because of it; it served a purpose, and I know this. My Soul-Sickness is caused by my devotion to my loved ones, and I am nothing but grateful to it.

Whatever happened as a result of retrieving my beloved family was well worth the price. I know this now. Every cell of me recognizes this, and in so doing, each and every one of my atoms and molecules let go. My body lets go. The memories let go. My heart lets go, and every part of me gives thanks. I offer up my gratitude to the Sea, to the Wind and the Sky, to the Soul of my Lemurian Family, and to the Soul of my Source.

I stop walking on the sand and get down on my knees, kiss the ground, and pray. I touch the sand with my bare hands, feeling my palms and the sensors in them beginning to re-commune with Terra again. She becomes my body, as she always was before. She fills me with her prayer of thanksgiving for my safe return back into my Golden Center, knowing that this means great things ahead for us both and for us all, as ONE.

My eyes are closed, but I can see. My Inner Eye is restored to full function again. As before, I can see the gloriousness of the rainbows in front of me, the sun sparkling on the water, the beautiful bridges of Light that have been created out of love and joy for communion by all of Golden Life everywhere.

My mind is dazzled and my Consciousness is awake. My body is tingling. My Soul is soothed. I know I am in exactly the process of being thoroughly healed by all that I intrinsically am.

Sometime later, I wake up. I find myself back in the familiar Great Hall, looking out the windows to the hills beyond. They are streaked with colors of blues and greens, pinks and violets, all in a warm cascading glow. As tangible and substantial as the hills appear to be, they are also light in motion; ethereal, and glowing back at me.

I hear the sounds of yawning and the mutterings of people waking up all around me. We are together again; many, many Golden Ones, back in our "training hall" after our much needed healing treatment. I look around, and I can see that everyone's eyes are softer than before. They are more liquid, and sparkling gently as if they have seen great beauty and been touched by it—re-inspired by that which could reach them deep inside. I feel the same way, and I know my eyes must look that way too.

Returning to what has meaning for us is the greatest of medicines.

I hear White Eagle's voice speaking. He is standing strong and clear in front of us, beautiful and majestic as always:

"Hello again, Beloveds.

"Yes, you have received the first of many such healing treatments, which will punctuate your overall restoration journey. You are in need of these treatments, remembrances, and gifts given to you by the various forms of Golden Life that have been waiting for you to return to them. It is their most profound joy to touch you again and gift you with their love—to feel you receiving them through your entire systems once again. Giving is a joyous gift, but knowing that your gift has been received is one of the greatest joys of all.

"Receiving is all you need to do. It is all that is being asked of you during these specials moments of treatment and regeneration. You need give nothing in return. Your receptivity is your thanks. The entire Golden Family

is glad and strengthened because of it. Know that this is how our inter-com-munion prospered and flourished long ago. We knew how to give, and we knew how to receive. Each aspect of this gifting created our tapestry of Golden Love and Oneness. Our bonds were tight, imprinted, and secure. They still are. You are remembering and reawakening those abilities that would enable you to re-live this in wholeness again.

"Let's practice receiving some more by simply saying 'Thank You.'"

Without instruction, we find ourselves turning to one another; moving throughout the room, and stopping one by one, full facing, full presence, full on, looking into each others' eyes. I stand in front of each Beloved Golden One that I find myself encountering. I take their hands gently in mine, gaze fully into their eyes, and say, "Thank You. Thank you. Thank you. Thank you for the beauty of your Soul and the gifts of your Being."

I look at them for a moment, and I see that they have registered me, that their eyes are not blank and clouded as they had often seemed in Mondor. They are deep and endless and rich with life that becomes even stronger and more textured as I express my gratitude to them. It's as though this exercise, this simple beautiful practice, is bringing them back to life. It's bringing them back to being seen and valued, back to being included in something precious, sacred, and beautiful.

I see and understand that it is soothing the wound of unworthiness that grew as a result of Mondor, as a result of being beaten down and disregarded as nothing, of being punished for no reason and castigated as meaningless. I can see the wounding of spirit that had happened because of this. It is crystal-clear to me—being blamed, accused, and falsely brainwashed into believing we were guilty of causing great pain to those we loved.

All of this is rising to the surface of the eyes of those in front of me, as well as to mine. I recall what it was like to be in that atmosphere of unrelenting accusation and blame, false as it was. The ache in the eyes I am looking at comes up for me to witness. It is the pain of that interruption in one's self-value, that seed of self-doubt planted, growing to overwhelming size.

It plays out in front of me as I continue to simply say the words "Thank You." And to hear, reflected back at me, those same words: "Thank You."

It takes a long while for our practice to soothe that pain, but gradually it starts to take hold and calls up, from deep within, the memories of being valuable and essential to the whole. It is life-giving and life-receiving. We are recognizing all that we are—Golden, Precious, Included, Valued, Needed, and Wanted. We are beautiful again; slowly but surely, beautiful again.

It makes me cry. I didn't know that something this simple could be so deeply penetrating and healing. It is like tilling the deepest levels of the soil with love and shaking loose the dirt so that it can be aerated and breathe life again.

"Yes," White Eagle speaks again. *"We will, during our time together, be calling up within you the wounds that are part of your Lemurian Soul-Sickness. This is a real state of distress, of dis-ease, of imbalance. It can only be effectively healed by love: specifically, Golden Love.*

"You will not know the full extent of this 'sickness' until we touch upon it. There have been many ways, understandably, that you have had to deny yourselves, to subjugate your pain, to ignore your needs for the sake of others and the fulfillment of your greater purpose. We told you before you set out on the Rescues that we would make sure that you were taken care of and restored once this was over. You may or may not recall this right now, but many of us Golden Masters made a vow, a sacred promise, to do this. Now, we are in the process of fulfilling this vow.

"We are here for you. That is the Truth. And we will stand steady and see this through until you are whole again. You have our word on this.

"Again I say, 'Steady on, have faith Beloveds.' The great unwinding is happening, and your Lemurian Soul-Sickness will be a thing of the past. The key, as always, is to simply go as fully into it as it asks of you to go.

"As you have left no stone unturned in terms of the Rescues of your Golden Family, recommit to leaving no stone unturned in the Rescue of you. You ARE love. You are GOLDEN LOVE. You WILL know this fully again. That is a promise.

"It is destined to be."

My mind is a blank.

And my Spirit—well, it is singing.

My sacred heart says, "Thank you."

More from White Eagle on the Lemurian Soul-Sickness

The Golden Witness speaks:

I find I am feeling agitated inside; I find I am feeling unworthy. "Unworthy of what?" I ask myself.

LOVE. I feel unworthy of love.

"Oh dear, I'm not doing this very well, am I?" I think to myself. Much emotion is surfacing, and many seemingly conflicting emotions at that. One minute I'm serene, and the next I'm upset. One minute I'm receiving, only to then reach a wall inside that wants to close the door to exactly that which I ache for the most.

I look out and see a sea of faces sitting with me. Everyone seems to be looking baffled and uncomfortable in some way, like I am. It's an unsettling kind of sensation that we seem to be experiencing.

White Eagle stands up in front of us and looks at each one of us as if we are the most precious of gifts to him. His gaze is loving, his eyes crystal-clear and shining.

"I know what you are feeling," he says.

"This is the process of it, the deepening of your awareness and clarity, level by level, that something is wrong inside. It is like peeling an onion, complex and multi-layered.

"This is the Lemurian Soul-Sickness revealing itself to you ever more deeply, as your journey with it continues on. This Soul-Sickness has affected every single cell in your body, mind, heart, and spirit. It is not something to be treated lightly; to do so would only leave you bereft of yourself. We have spoken of this before.

"It needs to be known on its terms, which are DEEP. You need to continue turning fully in its direction; facing yourselves, being with yourselves, listening, feeling, hearing, welcoming, and loving yourselves.

"Loving yourselves is the thing which you find the most elusive. Odd, isn't it? Since LOVE is who you are. You will find this push/pull happening periodically. It's not a bad thing, not at all. It's a good thing to be aware of yourselves and what's going on inside. Again, as we have said, it is a process—and your emotions are showing you that.

"I heard a story once which I want to tell you. It goes like this:

"There was a young man diving deep down into the Sea. He loved swimming this way and feeling himself encased in the waters of Life. It nourished him inside, as he knew that he was made of these same waters.

"One day, as he is resting briefly on the ocean floor, he sees a fish hanging out in front of him, right in his face. The fish is wearing goggles and a snorkel and has little flippers on its fins.

"'This is a funny sight,' the diver thinks to himself, as he chuckles in amazement.

"He looks at the fish quizzically and says, 'Well, hello there, Mr. Fish, nice to see you. What's up?' The fish looks back at the diver with confusion in his eyes. It's obvious that he's lost.

"'Kind sir,' says the fish to the diver. 'I'm on a quest to find something they call WATER. I've heard it's special, and I want to find it, but I have no idea where it is. Have you seen it? Can you point me in the direction of it, please?'

"The diver can't help himself—he bursts out laughing!"

As does White Eagle! As do all of us! The atmosphere in the room is jiggling with mirth, like a bowl full of jelly!

"Well, that about sums it up, doesn't it?" I chuckle to myself. The thing I am looking for is the thing I already am, the very thing that always surrounds me.

"I know it's a silly story," says White Eagle, still smiling. *"But it makes the point clear. That's how you are with love. You don't remember clearly that it's what YOU ARE, and that YOU ARE BATHED IN IT and BY IT, ALL THE TIME.*

"You have been pummeled out of this knowing. What do we need to do? Get you realigned back into it. The way to do this is to first acknowledge how out of alignment with this you are, and what it feels like. Here we go."

I find my agitation returning again, and growing. It's on a physical level first, but spreading throughout my whole system. I feel like I am indeed bound in a straitjacket, and as if my arms and my legs are pinned and pressed tightly together. I am in a vise of some kind: trapped and stuck, definitely firmly stuck.

"What you are feeling is the Mantle of Fear that has you in its grip. It's like an iron grip, isn't it? You can't breathe properly, and your cells are pressed too tightly together. They feel like they are being suffocated. Your body is going into a panic, and your brain is on overload. Your entire system is in a state of alarm.

"Coupled with that, you also feel drugged: heavy, encased, dulled, unbalanced, and unclear.

"This is the toxicity of it making itself known to you. Register all of it. Feel and witness this state of contraction.

"As Sananda told you earlier, there is nothing for you to DO about it, but BE with it. BE WITH YOURSELF."

I follow White Eagle's voice and let myself feel it all; it's tight, suffocating, and heavy. Yes, it is all of that and much, much more. It seems at first like this will never end, but as I move into it and feel it on its terms, and accept without resistance, something in me begins to shift in relationship to it. Once again, a rising up of my compassion for myself begins to happen. It's an automatic, caring response to my condition. I know it is a response of love to myself for the pain that I am in.

I decide that I will continue to be patient and kind with this process. No, it's not comfortable, for sure, but there is an opening of something deeper and caring in me because of it. I like this, the caring. I need this.

I will allow my unwinding to continue. I will keep moving with it. I will let it keep moving me.

AVALAR SPEAKS ON THE LEMURIAN SOUL-SICKNESS

The Golden Witness speaks:

I am aware of being back, once again, inside the Great Hall in Spirit. Everyone is here, and we are waiting patiently for what is next. My insides urge me to close my eyes. I feel sleepy and wish I could rest for a moment.

My eyes are closed, and I am breathing gently into the sounds inside the room. I begin to hear someone singing softly inside of me, and I recognize the voice of our dear, beautiful Mother Mary. I listen to her song and find myself tumbling gently inside of it.

Her song speaks to me of the perfection of everything as it is right now, reassuring me that I am unfolding, held tenderly and carefully in the arms of love. I feel young again, like a newborn baby, innocent and pure. All I am is love, and all I feel is love, in every way. It is mother's milk; it is the sensation of her warm skin against mine; it is her soothing, cooing sounds. All of this informing me that I am real. That I am alive, and here, and cared for. That I am seen, and that I am valued.

I wiggle around in my skin, feeling myself and discovering the sensation of being me, purely ME. I bask in my reverie for a little while longer, while Mary's song continues to soothe and comfort me tenderly. Gradually it all fades away, and soon thereafter my eyes want to open.

The noises in the room call me back, and I awaken. I open my eyes, feeling calm and settled. I am comfortably warm, and I feel a sense of spaciousness in my energy fields. I recognize I haven't felt this for a long time, like there is simply space for JUST ME. I am certainly not alone in this lovely room, but nonetheless, my sense of space is my very own. I love it, and it feels really good.

I allow myself to gradually adjust to where I am, surrounded by all of these beautiful Golden Ones. A rush of warm gratitude for everyone bursts out of my heart, and I am pleased to be here with them. I love this feeling of Family, this aura of union and dedication to that which is truly essential and meaningful to all of us.

It makes me happy and I take a deep breath. As I do this, I hear the soft swooshing of the Angels this time, as they pass through and around us. It is a soft, sparkling welcoming that fills our hearts and lifts our spirits toward what is next. Up in front of us I see several Golden Masters who are coming to join us.

Avalar moves center stage and focuses her attention toward us. She looks radiant and peaceful, graceful in every way, inside and out. I love her—we all love her deeply.

She speaks with kindness, and obvious joy from her heart:

"Most beautiful and beloved Golden Family of mine, I am glad to see you.

"I know you are going through a great unraveling with the help of White Eagle and others, and I know that it is a process that is stirring in all ways.

"As you are finding out, it is one that is filled with motion, and that which goes from one kind of terrain inside of you to another and then another. Your emotions are intensely stirred up, and your senses are high; all of it leaving you feeling sometimes as if you are being tossed about like a cat tosses a ball of yarn. In that way, it can feel a bit awkward and unwieldy.

"This is a process of your natural fluidity opening back up again. Be like water, and trust the process. The intensity of it will not overpower you. Trust me, it won't. It is the way of this progression, because you have been contained for so long. Once you made your conscious choice to heal, all of this rises to speak and be known. All those places inside of you, wherein you have felt your vastly bigger energies restricted, now emerge and begin their expression of freedom. It is your system's natural response to your commitment to yourself. It is organic. It is life force and life power, setting itself free.

"THIS IS A HEALTHY THING in every way. Yes, you are IN IT, and it is carrying you along to where it wishes you to go. This journey is your Golden Soul speaking. It is the one that is in the driver's seat. It is directing your movement and unwinding you from your previous experiences.

"Your Soul knows what it, and you, need. It knows; it is strong, it is wise. It is you, your steady Center, bringing yourselves back home to YOU.

"IT HAS A PLAN! I encourage you to roll with it! Be like water and trust the process.

"On a different note, as much as you are rolling along with it, you might also occasionally have a sense of feeling out of touch in a way, an amorphous kind of feeling that might cause you to feel uneasy. Do not worry. It is nothing

great, but it is enough to set you on edge and cause you to automatically tense up and contract your awareness to some degree.

"I am urging you to acknowledge this when it happens, and to do your best to soften and relax. It is nothing more than a simple passing through of energy which had heretofore become blocked and thickened. It is not important to know the details of this energy or why, unless it brings that information to you itself.

"Don't go hunting for it; don't go analyzing anything; don't go worrying. That, in itself, is not you. Worrying is not in your intrinsic nature. It is yet another knee-jerk response that lingers in your patterning from Mondor.

"Whenever you feel yourselves becoming overwhelmed by anything in this process, take a deep breath, then another, and another still, until you have softened back into a natural receptivity of grace. It will not take long before THIS becomes an instinctive response for you that will gradually, but surely, bring you back to your original Golden Imprint. On this you can depend.

"It is there inside of you. Know this and keep going. All is progressing beautifully. Carry on, beautiful Ones. All is well."

I find that I instantly know exactly what Avalar is talking about. I am starting to feel sort of out of touch, vaguely disconnected. It makes me want to reach for control and tightness in order to regain a semblance of balance. But what is my true balance, I wonder? I feel like I'm in a kind of "No Man's Land." I notice I'm not feeling comfortable in my skin right this moment.

I do as Avalar advised. Instead of worrying, I soften. Instead of analyzing and trying to figure out what or why, I let it all go. My Soul knows what to do. I yield. I become water; I become fluid again. And lo and behold, here's my grace coming in, just like Avalar said.

I take another deep breath, this time one of savoring this warm and reassuring sensation. I am relieved. I am flowing naturally again, at least for now.

I remind myself that this is a process. "What's next?" I wonder.

Andar, Avalar, and Master Saint Germain Speak on the Lemurian Soul-Sickness

The Golden Witness speaks:

There is some shuffling around at the front of the room as I see more Golden Masters coming to join us. There seems to be an aura of increasing intensity which has settled in, and I have a feeling that it's an indication of what is to come. I start to get fidgety in my seat, and I don't know whether to feel nervous or excited.

Finally, one of the Golden Masters steps up to address us, and I see that it is our beloved Andar. How wonderful! I am happy to see him. I feel his love and caring pouring out to us, reaching deep inside our hearts. I feel his immeasurable gratitude toward us, and my heart opens up instantly in response. I am thankful to him, and to Avalar also, for their constant and loving presence with us. Andar's steadiness is apparent to me, and I welcome its comfort and peacefulness. I drink it in, and am reassured that all is well.

His beautiful voice rings out strong and clear:

"My dearest Golden Friends, I am happy to see you and to be involved in your healing. You have done so much for others, and it is my pure joy to see you coming home to yourselves. You deserve this, and you need this. Both Avalar and I are here to support you in any way that we possibly can, as we always have and always will.

"You may or may not remember that, before the Rescues even started, Avalar and I, and several other of the Golden Masters, made a vow to all of you. We vowed that once the Rescues were completed and everyone was safely brought home or Tagged, we would do whatever would be needed to Rescue all of you who sacrificed yourselves in the name of the greater purpose. We vowed that we would help you heal from your travails and we would remind you of who you truly are—your powerful and beautiful Golden Selves. We made a promise to help you restore yourselves, and this is the pledge that we are fulfilling.

"In reminding you of our promise, I am hopeful that you will keep an open mind and open spirit to the information we give you, and to the experiences you have during this process that we know will ensure your return to yourselves. We are devoted to you and will do everything in our power to fulfill our Sacred Golden Vow that we made to you way back then.

"If there are things we discuss that you are not sure about during this entire process of your healing and restoration, simply let this be. This is a normal response for many of you because of how veiled you have become, and how much your true memory has been buried. Again, I encourage you to let it be. Let the energies percolate and bring to you a sign and signal of what is correct and true for you, when your timing is right.

"Jogging your internal Golden Memory is our main purpose right now. Know this: everything we do and say is geared toward exactly that."

I listen to Andar's words, and it's as though there is an ancient bell going off in the back of my energy fields somewhere. It is sounding a clarion call that comes from ancient times and from an ancient form of me. It sounds distant, but clear. It's calling me, and I am beginning to feel it with every fiber of my Being. It is calling me toward itself.

It opens up a deep yearning inside my heart—something that I ache for. It is a thing that I have wanted for a long time, without even consciously knowing. I am moved, powerfully moved, by my ancient Self.

I instinctively put my hand over my heart and whisper to this call, "Yes, I hear you. I am here. I am coming. Yes." My body is flooded with warmth and tingling. There is such a rightness going on inside of me, and I feel like I am actually waking up—as though a brand new day is dawning, literally. I know it sounds cliché, but that's exactly how it feels. It's as though there is a "crack" in my patterning, and an ancient light is seeping through my framework. It is permeating me, and gently but surely pulling me toward itself.

I yield. Oh, yes, indeed, I yield. This is the best thing I have felt in a long time!

I realize that my eyes are closed, and I momentarily forget where I am. There is no place or space, only me, deep inside of me; soft, warm, coming Home. I relax into it, and let it cradle me for a few minutes.

Soon my attention returns to the sound of Andar's voice. I become aware, yet again, that I am surrounded by many that I love in this Great Hall, and that there is a purpose for our gathering. My focus returns to matters at hand, but I know I am indelibly changed. I feel deeply happy about this.

I look ahead and see our beautiful, beloved Avalar standing next to Andar. They are holding hands and their foreheads are bowed together, touching for a moment. It is a gesture that looks familiar to me, and again, I feel an ancient stirring inside.

As she turns to face us squarely, Avalar says:

"Beloveds, Dearest Family of my Heart. I am here to also remind you of my promise to you in past times. I said I would bring you home, and I will.

"Both Andar and I have walked with you through all of the terrain that you have experienced in Mondor. You have known us as we have helped you, witnessed you, and supported you in every way. I know you have often wondered how we can do this—show up so often. I speak for myself when I say that I have been witness to all of your experiences, and often felt them as my own. I did this on purpose, asking myself to feel everything fully as if, indeed, it was my own. I did this so I would thoroughly KNOW. I did this so I would be able to say 'I have been there too,' and because of this, you would feel my understanding and resonance with you now.

"Through it all, Andar and I have managed to build a bridge back to your

Golden Memories. We are in a position to be able to help you rejoin your present selves with your ancient memories and help you carry yourselves forward, intact, into the future, where you are destined to be flourishing Lemurians once again.

"As a Golden Family, this was the original plan—this was what we all agreed on.

"Now, Andar and I, and the many Golden Ones who pledged along with us, step up to be with you in this, our greatest joy—your homecoming. We celebrate that this time has now come!

"Slow and steady wins the race, as they say. Take advice from our friend Turtle and let this be an unfolding that has no pressure on it, with no push or stress or strain to be completed. As much as it is an unwinding, it is equally, of course, a rebirthing of you. It has its own needs and timing, and all it is asking of you is to respond and be present with it, with all the love and tenderness you can muster.

"You have been sore. You will be sore for yet a while longer. Rest assured that this is the natural course of your healing, and please do your best to be soft inside with this. As I said earlier to you, breathe and soften. Breathe and soften. Breathe and soften; inside and out.

"Yes, it is a process, as you have already been told over and over again. And now, I am to repeat this yet again. It is simply important to accept this, and to therefore be able to walk it one step at a time, with faith and conviction that there is a point to it all—an endpoint where you will rediscover what you have yearned for and been lost without.

"Take it step by step, with thoroughness and presence, as a profound act of love to yourselves."

Suddenly, I feel a great stillness coming over me. I can hear my breath moving in and out slowly and gently. I feel reassured, and my insides are responding with sensations of relaxation and ease. I am at peace. I know I'm right where I need to be, inside and out.

I find myself perfectly accepting that this is a process, and I know from experience how processes typically go. I know that it means movement, stirring up, being flexible and open to change, settling in, and then more movement, and so on, etc. It has many levels and many layers, and that's okay with me.

I know where I'm headed, and this is my journey. It's mine, all mine; I'm going to care for it, and me, as best as I possibly can. I know I can do this, and I haven't felt this strong and self-secure in a long time. I'm here, and that's all that matters.

Oh, and did I mention Patience? Well, believe it or not, Patience is my new best friend.

Oh, and dear Reader, maybe you'd like to breathe in some Patience too, right about now. There's still a way to go! But I can guarantee you this: it's going to be worth it. I know it is.

Gradually, I find myself returning to the Great Hall with full focus again. I see Avalar giving Andar a warm hug and taking her leave. Andar steps forward and addresses us again:

"I know that you are aware of how much we love you and always have. We have been through so much together, right from our beginnings as Lemuria of Origin, great Golden joyous, gloriously life-enhancing days. Gradually, you will remember those days, and all that Golden passion and creativity that you were made of and still are.

"Let us carry on, together, with our walk home, with your healing and restoration, so that you can know all of this yet again. Let me start this next stage of things by bringing up the subject of the Mantle of Fear.

"I know we have talked about this much throughout this entire process, and here it is again. I know I will be repeating some things that you already know well, but you are viewing things now from a different vantage point, and this is information that can be understood in yet a new way, from a new perspective.

"Prior to the Rescues, we talked about the Mantle as something you were going into. Now, we are focused on talking about it as something you are coming out of. There is a big difference, so please bear with me as I discuss this Mantle yet again.

"As you well know, this Mantle of Fear that you have worn so well is amorphous, elusive, and insidious. You have not actually felt the Mantle itself most of the time; you have only felt its encasement, and the subsequent effects of confinement and restrictiveness. Because you have not been able to stand back and see it clearly from an objective position, you are actually not clearly aware of how much, and in how many ways, it is controlling you; your perceptions, behaviors, reality, and identity.

"I emphasize the word CLEARLY. My intention is for each of you to see this Mantle, and everything about it, with crystal-clear clarity—to see everything it is doing. That is the goal. Then, and only then, will you be in a position to do something about it.

"Obviously, seeing something amorphous, that is specifically designed to be completely veiled, is a challenge. In this way, the H-O have indeed created something extremely effective. But, as challenging as it may be to see and identify something this amorphous, it is definitely doable, if you desire. That part is up to you.

"The more you focus your intent in this direction, the more your vision will show you, and the more you will understand. It will become so clear to you that you will wonder why you never saw it before.

"For many of you, exploring this whole issue brings up Fear. You'd rather not know, and you'd rather not see. You'd rather not admit that this is running you. This is because it brings up the charge of being a victim; that discomfort that causes you to panic and be afraid that discussing, much less admitting, to such a thing as being controlled by the Mantle will only make it worse, and make it stronger. You're afraid it will only bring it on more and take over everything. But the thing is: it already has.

"The irony is that, in your natural Lemurian design, you have no Fear. For you to be afraid that even looking at the Mantle will make anything worse is only a demonstration of how the Mantle of Fear is working on you successfully. The H-O do not want you to recognize or admit to any of this. The H-O want you to remain weakened, and better yet, paralyzed, by Fear. The Mantle itself is not going to make this easy. It's designed to keep you in Fear, by whatever means necessary.

"Avoiding it is understandable in one way, but faulty overall: all it will do is keep the Mantle, and its Fear, in place. You'll never come out of the Mantle of Fear by choosing to pretend it's not there—never. It's impossible.

"The Mantle renders you a victim; weakened and powerless. Until you want and choose to change that position, it's got you—period. Only you can choose to see and understand this clearly, so that it can no longer have you in its grip. Only you can choose to be free of this. Only you can choose to be restored to your true Lemurian design, which has no Fear in it; and never has, and never will."

"Wow," I gulp at the strength and directness of Andar's words. They really hit home somehow. I am shaken up, and the "no Fear" part seems monumentally impossible at this moment. It seems unfathomable that such a thing as Fear could cease to exist in me.

"Hum." I hear him, but I don't know. How is that even remotely possible? "Oh, well. Carry on. Keep listening," I think to myself. Let it be.

Dear reader, I know I sound a bit resistant, but that's only because in some ways I feel like he's speaking Greek to me: I don't know where to put it. But at the same time, I agreed to keep an open mind and an open spirit. I'm here...being, listening...and that's that.

Andar continues on:

"Because you have been to Mondor and worn this Mantle many times, it has also become an element of living that is familiar to you. It is like a second skin which you have grown accustomed to in so many ways, that you are not even aware of it on conscious levels: your systems know, but your psyche doesn't. In that way, you have become so used to it that you don't even register that it is there.

"The nature of it as a 'veiling agent' makes it hazy, mysterious, vague, and seemingly undefined. It has no perimeter that you can actually TOUCH and say, 'Oh yes, that's where it is.'

"No, all you have is your feeling body, your sensitivity, and the deeper levels of this in you. Open these sensitivities more, and you will see it. You will see what usually cannot be seen, and you will also see how it is duping you and manipulating you enormously.

"What you know for sure is that ANYTHING Fear-based, no matter what it is, is NOT YOU. It is the Mantle of Fear at work. That is the first thing to acknowledge. The second thing is to be willing to open up those deeper sensitivities of yours and put them to work on your behalf. You might not like what you see, feel, hear, and find, but at least you won't be unaware and powerless anymore.

"Makes sense, doesn't it?

"You know, if you were not healing yourselves, with the goal of returning to Terra and actually restoring the Golden World, we wouldn't even be having this conversation. None of this would matter, because it would simply be that, once you leave Mondor, you drop your encasement and become freed up in Spirit. And that would be that.

"But you have chosen otherwise, haven't you? That's why you are sitting here. As Sananda said previously, if you choose to go back to Terra and restore Lemuria, your healing progression will be different than if you don't choose to do so. This is why I am talking like this. This Mantle of Fear needs to be known thoroughly, period."

Again, I gulp at the strength and directness of Andar's words. I am aware of many conflicting thoughts and feelings whirling around inside me. How do I feel about what he is saying? Can I even see this thing that is so elusive? And do I REALLY WANT TO?

On the one hand, I do not. It seems so uncomfortable. However, on the other, to my surprise, I am intrigued. What if I could actually SEE the Mantle? What if I am being duped, and don't even know it? I certainly want to find out—I don't want anything or anyone else controlling me. No, NO. My determination kicks in.

Additionally, in the midst of my jumble of thoughts and feelings, my absolute trust of Andar remains paramount. SOMETHING about what he is saying is true, and I know it; my inner voice and deeper knowing are telling me so.

Alright, I am determined. I want and choose to do this, and I open my mind and my conscious awareness. I request my deeper sensitivities to get to work and show this to me in a way that I can understand. Once that's done, I return to Andar's words with renewed focus and resolve.

Andar continues:

"I am aware that all of you wish to know more, and have decided that you want to become clear about this. With that in mind, let us recognize again that the Mantle of Fear is like a costume. It has altered your frequencies and your natural configuration many times over. In this way, it has altered your personal Imprint.

"Okay, that you know: but how EXACTLY?

"Again, let us recognize that the Mantle is designed and patterned to keep you down and to keep your true power immobilized. It does this to everyone, and is therefore not personal to you; it's what the Mondor Mantle pattern does—it may feel personal, but it isn't.

"Yes, it strives to keep you weakened, to keep you buying into and believing yourself to be weak. Even if you consider yourself a strong person already, I guarantee you ARE weak, relative to who you TRULY are. That's a fact.

"We must begin by allowing you to identify this state of weakness. We begin by having you look at your state, at where and how you have been weakened. I can tell you that you are going to feel raw in this unraveling. You are going to feel as if your skin is inside out. That is the nature of it, because it IS you emerging from within. It is you coming from your deep insides OUT. Naturally, what first spills out is the toxic matter; the infection, the soreness, the wounds. Clear this out fully, and your Golden Self will emerge.

"Since we cannot truly SEE the Mantle, and how it is working, you will need to rely on your feeling senses, on your emotional bodies. Your sensitivities are acutely aware that something is not right inside, that something is not lined up, not aligned.

"Your sensitivities KNOW that the configuration of YOU has indeed been skewed. It wants to fix this. It wants you to be consciously aware of how uncomfortable you are and how much pain this skewed configuration is causing you.

"Being cloaked and controlled gives YOU, Golden Ones, no room to be and breathe. Acknowledging all of this is the beginning of a great dismantling and healing.

"Take heart, my dearest friends. Find it within yourselves to stay the course of this journey as it continues to wind up and down, through and about. Embrace your determination fully. Have faith, dig deep, and stay the course. This is for YOU and for all the Golden Treasure that awaits your remembrance inside.

"Carry on, and know that we are here with you, all along the way. One Golden Heart!"

And with that, Andar steps back and disappears amongst the gathering of Golden Masters that are huddled up in front of us. I am well aware, yet again; my insides are stirred up. I know I need to trust this, to trust the process and trust myself. I can do this, and I know it.

I look around, and I see determined eyes present and on board for whatever is next. After a few minutes, Master Saint Germain steps up to center stage and begins to address us.

"Alright everyone, let's get started!

"We are going to place you in smaller groups so that you can help each other identify and clarify what your personal symptoms of the Lemurian Soul-Sickness are. These are indicators of where and how you have been weakened by the Mantle of Fear and the experiences of your persecution.

"These weak areas, these symptoms, are not only painful for you, but as you will see later on, they can't help but hinder your forward movement. Because your system is basically caved in on these weakened areas, interference can come in more easily, magnify those weaknesses and the pain therein and use them as further interference to keep you down. In other words, what is already weakened in you can be made even weaker by Fear,

because you are vulnerable in these areas. Do you understand? This is Fear and its manipulation.

"I'm sure you know the saying, 'You are only as strong as your weakest link.' It's true. This is why it is important that you know exactly what your weakened areas are and how deep they go, so you can attend to them and bring them back to their full strength and well-being.

"You need to know exactly where you stand in this regard. Understand this as an information gathering process which will reveal to you what your symptoms are. As you identify these weakened areas together, the process will, at a certain point, turn into a releasing experience all on its own.

"This will happen simply by light being shed, as you focus on yourselves. Imagine it is like looking at a blueprint of an old house that outlines all the details of wherever the building needs repair. The areas of weakness will be obvious. Once identified, they will be expressed and aired. These are your symptoms emptying themselves out.

"We realize that this Soul-Sickness is happening on varying levels and in various ways to all of you. It is not the same for each one. We know this. But what is being presented here, and throughout this process, is the whole array of what this Lemurian Soul-Sickness looks like. Keep that in mind. Some of it is relevant to you, and some is not. Take what resonates for you, and discard what does not. But know that every nook and cranny of this is being explored and presented because somewhere, somehow, some Golden One or some Golden Ones are feeling exactly this way.

"Please understand and welcome that we are covering the whole array. If you are not feeling a particular symptom inside of yourself, simply have compassion for those around you and for that Golden One somewhere out there who is. That will bolster them and give them courage through the ethers; every piece of this 'sickness' is being identified and witnessed for every person. It's the whole picture of our entire Golden Family in terms of the Lemurian Soul-Sickness.

"I encourage you not to try to rush through this exploration.

"You will find that there are several layers to these symptoms and that what you don't see in yourselves may be triggered by what someone else says about themselves, only to be revealed in you later on. As I said: collectively, you will reveal this bigger picture and be able to arrive at clear-sightedness and recognition of it all.

"Whatever it is, welcome it coming up to be known and expressed. Be patient, be gentle; be tender and caring. You may find that you feel sicker at first than you thought you were. You may discover much more discomfort and upset inside of you than you would have ever expected. Please do not get discouraged or daunted by this. This is a natural part of healing once you start 'digging' and giving permission and space for what is there to reveal itself.

"I encourage you to let it be. Make no decisions about it; draw no finite conclusions. It is an unraveling process, and it is here to help you. As you empty out, this will be the beginning of you being able to alter your position with the Mantle of Fear so that you will eventually be able to see it as separate from you.

"You are in a safe place here. You are amongst family. It is time, and your systems are ripe and ready for this liberation. Let us begin."

Master Saint Germain directs us into smaller groups, and as I settle into mine, I see that I am actually surrounded by the same faces that I sat with in the Sacred Fire Circle. I am glad, because that means our deeper bonds of understanding have already been forged, and we will be able to make good headway in this healing process.

Okay, here goes…

I give everyone my undivided focus and presence, opening my heart to each of them, and to myself as well. One by one, we each take a turn to give voice to that which is rising up inside of us. Although I am fully focused on our small group, there are, of course, many other voices that can be heard expressing throughout the hall as well.

Our various voices ring out as many emotions, thoughts, and feelings are unearthed.

"I feel like I've been on mental overload from all of the H-O input over so many Rescue Missions. I realize it has weakened me and made me doubt myself."

"I feel like Fear stripped my nervous system and laid me bare. It has made me feel vulnerable and weak in the face of heartlessness."

"I feel like I'm crawling on my belly. I am tired, exhausted, and spent. I don't feel as though I will ever be able to get up again. This is because I gave everything to the Rescues of my Golden Family Members. I feel like I have no more to give."

"I have no vitality at all, and my personal sense of PASSION is nowhere to be found. How will I ever be able to move forward? I have no juice in my tank, period."

"I feel like I'm in an overcrowded bus terminal; too many people, thought forms, and painful memories flying around inside my head and my heart. My inner sightedness, which used to bring such comfort and joy, now sends me spiraling, with all of these horrible images and upsetting thoughts. I'm ALWAYS feeling pummeled. I'm on sensory overload. I feel weak and unable to control any of it."

"I don't feel safe. Will I ever feel safe again?"

"I feel like I'm completely off my Center. In fact, Center? What Center? Balance, what balance?"

"Everything is chaotic inside of me, like I am living in a hurricane all the time."

"I'm anxious all the time. It's underneath and around everything. It's like a bad bug inside of me. I am quaking and quivering constantly. Will it ever stop? I am overwhelmed."

"I'm in a straitjacket. My hands are tied and my body aches. I can't move. I'm stiff and tight all over, even though I'm not wearing the jacket anymore. It's as though it's permanently welded to me."

"I feel emotionally distraught. My emotions are being torqued every which way, and I can't control them. I feel like I'm being yanked around, like a puppet on a string. Who, or what is controlling me? I feel completely disconnected from myself."

"I feel afraid and disconnected. Fear seems to have gotten in between me and all that is sacred and meaningful. I've never been afraid of myself like this before. I don't trust myself anymore."

"There's been too much chaos, craziness, and cruelty. I want to go home."

"I feel totally numb inside—numb and frozen. Is there any ME at all?"

"My body, my physical body, hurts too much to even move. I feel like it's making me cave in on myself. The pain is sucking up all of my life force, and I can't do anything about any of it. I can't control the pain. I'm terrified it will spread and get worse. I don't know what to do. I feel helpless. I am down on my knees. Please, anyone, help me."

"I can't stand what I see, hear, and feel. I feel the sickness, the pain, and the woundedness of many. I can't stand to know this much anymore. It's too much for me; for my brain, my psyche, and my emotions. My heart aches with all the pain that I see and feel in others. My chest aches. My breasts ache. I'm on information overload. It's making me sick. I can't stop it, and I can't get rid of it."

"My guts ache, and my head hurts. What have I been breathing, eating, and drinking? It feels so toxic. I cannot digest this toxic consciousness and Fear. No wonder I have digestive issues."

"I feel like I could erupt, like I'm a volcano on the edge of blind fury. I know it's in me, this rage. I hate what the H-O have done to my Golden Family. I hate what the H-O have done to my beloved Terra, and all of its creatures. I am so furious about all of it. What will become of me, of us, of our beloved Terra? Will Lemuria ever be a reality again?"

"My legs and feet ache from walking, running, and hiding from the H-O in my Rescues. I feel like I've been moving through sludge, and it seems to have stuck to me. It feels dirty and toxic."

"My mind doesn't feel like my own anymore. It feels like my wiring got mixed up, and I feel damaged because of it."

"I feel heavy, and I don't feel like myself. I feel like I've been wearing too many overcoats of Fear, and I can't breathe anymore. It's suffocating me."

"I'm afraid of the rawness of my emotions and psyche. I'm afraid of the Fear I feel. I'm afraid of what it might do; I'm afraid it will take control over me. Wow, it sounds like it already has, if I am talking this way. I didn't even realize how constantly braced against myself I am. I'm shocked."

"My heart is broken. What do I do with that? Too many little smithereens to even pick up and try to glue back together again. Now who will I be?"

"My body feels like it's on fire for half the time, and stuck and crippled the other. I don't want to be in a body anymore. Everything hurts too much."

"I realize how defended I am. I know it helped me in my Rescues, but somehow, I need to break through this defensiveness and get to the real me. This defensiveness keeps people away from me, which leaves me lonely and sad. It's not who I truly am."

"My throat is constricted from a lack of freely expressing."

"My creative centers are shut down, and in Lemuria I was creative and passionate. That was my life. How do I get this back?"

The voices go on and on and on…

And so does mine.

I didn't know all of this was inside of me, inside all of us, or that it would keep rising up like an endless river that can never stop. Finally, it grows silent.

And here we are, lying in a heap next to each other, unable to move. We can't even talk anymore. With no energy left, we are spent. How sad. How utterly sad this is.

Yes, we are indeed sick in our own ways. We admit it, and now we know. We have been thoroughly honest with ourselves, and with each other.

For the first time, I have no tears. It's gone beyond that. This seems like such a dry desert of lost, aching Souls. I don't really know what to think or what will become of us, of me.

As I lie here feeling like a dried-up wad of paper that has been crumpled into a ball, it slowly dawns on me that perhaps we have fully emptied out, and that is why it feels dry like this—and empty.

"There must be something good about this," I reflect to myself in my exhaustion. "Emptying out is a good thing. Perhaps I need to rest in the vacancy of it and let that be what it is."

And so, I do. I lay my head down again and wait. I wait for what is next. I have no feelings. I'm spent.

It seems like a long while that there is no movement in this hall. Not a sound can be heard when, quite suddenly, the atmosphere changes. I become aware of a smell, a fragrance wafting through the air, sweet and pleasant. There is a soft but distinct humming sound that I hear as well. "I wonder what that is," I think to myself. It grows louder and comes closer.

All of a sudden there is a sensation of people coming toward us, a gathering of a throng of people—it's a vibrational feeling—not physical. It's purely an energetic presence, but so tangible that the room actually starts to feel overcrowded. There are many of us here.

"Who are they?" I wonder, "Why are they here?" I recognize these vibrations, I recognize them all. They are each a part of me, and me a part of each of them. They are other members of our Golden Family coming to join their energies with ours. They are our Golden Family Members that we have all Rescued.

The energy in the hall changes dramatically, and it's as though it is being filled to overflowing with Golden Brightness and dazzling points of light—the way the water looks when sunlight is reflecting on it. My heart changes too; where it was sad and empty a moment ago, it is now warm, soft, and buoyant.

I am opening up unexpectedly; I am being completely touched by and enfolded in love, permeated by its warm radiance. It is deep and beautiful. My whole system feels greatly comforted and soothed, and I automatically melt inside with a knowing that everything is going to be all right.

I feel the energetic touch of the many who love me, and I know that I am not alone. Suddenly, the words "Thank you" are reverberating through my heart, as a powerful wave of complete gratitude is washing through me, over and over again.

"Thank you, Dear Friend, for Rescuing me," I hear a soft voice telling me inside. "Thank you, Dear Ones, for Rescuing us all. Thank you from the bottom of our hearts and our Souls. Thank you all for loving us so much."

The persistent sounds of "thank you" move me, the pulse of it ringing through me over and over again, and the sensation floods my cells with meaning on every level. My eyes, which had been dry and parched a moment ago, well up as huge tears start running in rivulets down my face. I can't stop crying—I just can't. I could cry a river and then some.

I recognize and remember that my pain, and our pain, has been for this, for exactly this. It has been for this pure and holy reunion of our loved ones. The goal has been for family to return once again; to touch, join, and love together again.

I become aware that I am not alone in my tears. We are all crying, sobbing quietly into ourselves, and then reaching to hold a hand next to ours to affirm the physical connection of our Souls' understanding and reunion.

There is nothing but the sounds of sobbing in the room. But you know what, dear Reader? This time, it is the sobbing of grief turning to relief, to union, and then to joy.

The depths of pain that we had shared moments ago finally release from us, are pushed up and out, only to be transformed into light by these even deeper levels of recognition. We not only grasp with our minds and our psyches, but we also feel and absolutely know deep down inside our beautiful hearts. It was all for this.

Healing—deep, deep healing—is truly happening now. It is here, now.

I continue to be powerfully moved by the sweet warmth of this human kindness, by the gentle loving of true and abiding kinship; all of the Rescued are conveying their eternal gratitude to those of us who Rescued them.

This rejoining and pure love of our Golden Family is such a moment of happiness. It all comes together, a pinpoint of clear recognition of the reason for all of the pain we have endured. It is a moment of sharing deep thanks for all the Rescues ever done in the name of our Golden Family everywhere.

The feeling, the powerful sensation of this eternal gratitude, continues to wash through me, over and over again. It cleanses me, offering a haven of giftedness, a sanctuary of Golden Peace. It is the best medicine in the world.

And it keeps on coming—the truth of it all, the reasons why, the joy of the success, and the knowing that we would do it all over again if needed. No stone has been left unturned, and none have been left behind. No part of each of us remain untouched by that which is the Truth of all of us: our One Golden Heart.

Has it been worth it? Yes, yes, and yes again. We are one Golden Family, healing and coming back together again. There is only the sweet sensation of joy pouring through us—One Golden Heart.

MEETING OUR GOLDEN HEALING TEAMS

The Golden Witness speaks:

After a few more minutes we find ourselves being lifted out of the hall and gently transported to yet another realm. The Angels have come and taken us to a large Golden Healing Center, comprised of small outbuildings that are shaped like starbursts. There are flowers everywhere; beautiful, sensual flowers. I breathe as deeply as I can, inhaling the exquisite fragrances that set me free, free to feel beautiful as I am.

We are led first to what seems like a Sanctuary of sorts. Inside it is flooded with Golden Light and arcing rainbows of soft colors. We stop and wait for a moment. I see White Eagle again, along with several other Golden Masters. They seem to be conferring about something important, and we wait while they conclude their discussion.

Finally, White Eagle turns to us, stepping up to address our large group. His Golden Radiance is strong and beautiful, shining like a gigantic halo around his head and body. It extends far beyond him and undulates as though it is beating time with its pulse. It is alive and here to assist us, that is clear.

White Eagle speaks:

"Welcome, again, dearest Golden Ones. Yes, you have emptied out many of the symptoms of your Lemurian Soul-Sickness. Yes, you are understanding the complexities of how much the Mantle of Fear and your journeys into Mondor have pained you, causing you to lose your internal balance with your Golden Core. And yes, your remembrance of what it is has all been for is being regained in its fullness. Savor this remembrance and this gratitude that has come your way. It has honored you for being who you are, and for giving of yourselves so selflessly.

"Feel this love, including your own, as it touches every cell. Let it illuminate you from within. Welcome it and embrace it with your being. It is medicine for you—great, great medicine.

"Your embrace of this sacred Golden Love is paving the way for even deeper levels of you that are reaching out to be healed. As we have stated many times, it is a journey of a series of steps, each one preparing the way for the next to follow. But each level of this becomes easier and more illuminating and illuminated. Please don't be daunted. Continue on, knowing that more emptying out means even more Golden Remembrance emerging forth from you, which brings only greater and greater joy for you—and for all."

I take in a breath at White Eagle's words. Yes, I am grateful to feel love rising up in me again, finally, and to be touched by the love of others as well. But how much longer is this going to take? How far does this go? How much more is there for me to unravel?

Dear Reader, perhaps you are wondering the same. How deep does this sickness go? Will it ever be over? I don't know. I can only yield to it and hope for the best. Please bear with me, dear Reader, a while longer.

Remember that we are all Golden Gentle Giants, and the pain of the contracted state has taken its toll. It simply goes ever deeper; there is still more to know and feel, and I need to stick with it—this is my conscious choice, after all.

And, dear Reader, I hope you'll stick with me, too, and perhaps even find it in your heart to cheer me on in the process. I could use your support, if you're willing. That would be grand.

I finally focus back into White Eagle's voice as he continues speaking:

"In order to facilitate the rest of your healing and restoration, you will each be assigned your own Golden Healing Team. They will work closely with you to help restore your wellness in ways that go far beyond what you can even imagine that you need. In addition, as you have already experienced, you will also receive periodic cleansing and rejuvenating treatments from the Natural Golden World. These will help hugely in your rehabilitation process.

"All in all, you will be in great Golden Hands, receiving the best Golden Treatment possible.

"And what is being asked of you in this? Simply to receive, JUST RECEIVE!"

"I like the sound of that," I think to myself. "Bring it on!"

No sooner do I have this thought, accompanied by tremendous relief about it all, then I find myself transported to a quiet place removed from everyone else. I am inside a beautiful healing treatment room. The atmosphere is peaceful, and the energy is soft and soothing. I begin to feel calmer right away, and more at ease than I have.

I lie back quietly. I seem to be in a lovely "spa" chair, with my neck and head cradled comfortably, and my feet stretched out. My eyes are closed, and there are warming pads resting under my feet, my neck, and my hands. All in all, I would say that I couldn't feel any more relaxed. The fragrance in this place smells soothing and lovely—a mixture of flowers and fresh air.

I become aware of a quiet rustling, and I turn to see three Golden Ones present with me. I instantly know they are my Golden Healing Team. There are two masterful Golden Energy Healers, one male and one female. Next to them is a third Golden One who seems to be more in the role of Assistant to the other two. I sense that there may be others who come in from time to time, but this is my own Golden Core Healing Group, and I am delighted. I feel great confidence in them, and I am relieved that they will be helping me. I love having my own Golden Energy Healers!

They seem to know exactly who I am, although I am not clear as to whether we have actually met before. Perhaps we have, and because I don't recall this right now does not mean that it won't come back to me at some point. All I know is that I feel extremely comfortable with them.

The male Golden Energy Healer steps forward and begins speaking to me kindly. I find his voice reassuring and gentle:

"Greetings, Dearest One. This is a wondrous and welcome reunion for us. You have gone through much, and the three of us are here to help you and to continue to be with you throughout the rest of your restoration journey—and beyond, if you desire.

"Receive us, if you will. Yes, we are your Golden Healing Team. My partner and I, and various Assistants, will come and go, depending on your needs. We will be watching and monitoring you vigilantly throughout your entire rehabilitation process, and we will meet for actual treatment sessions on a regular basis.

"These will be designated Energy Healing Sessions, during which you will simply enter into a relaxed state while we do our work. Sometimes we will talk, and explain what we are doing. At other times, we will work silently. Our work will be focused in your energy fields, and even though you may sometimes feel as though we are actually touching you, we are not. Often, you will find yourself going into your reverie or dozing off. There is no expectation of you at all, except when dialogue is helpful to your treatment.

"All we ask of you is that you receive yourself and us. Your attention needs to continue to be ON YOU. Your regard for yourself needs to be up front and center. You need to fulfill your commitment to yourself to allow further healing and restoration to happen. We are here to help you in any way that we possibly can.

"We encourage you to make yourself your top priority, and to let all other preoccupations slip away. This will be as demanding of you in that regard as everything else you have devoted yourself to, up to this point. You have made this choice for yourself consciously and deliberately. Because of this commitment, you will heal. It is absolutely destined to be, but following through on your devotion to this entire process is imperative in order for this to be so.

"During this rehabilitation period, you will be continuing to receive ongoing information, education, and illumination from the other Golden Masters that are attending to you. This will enable you to understand where you are and where you are going. It is essential for you to hear and consider

every word. You need it all in order to fully understand, and, when ready, to be able to make whatever shifts are absolutely right for you and your greatest well-being.

"From now on, as we have said, we will be available to you during your entire progression of healing. We will help in monitoring and stabilizing you, bringing you moment by moment recalibration as your frequencies change. We will ensure that this entire process takes place as easily, comfortably, and successfully for you as possible.

"You are a Great Golden One, a Great and wondrously splendid Golden Gentle Giant. What you have walked through is the opposite. This perhaps explains to you why your load of distress has accumulated and become so great. It also sheds light on why this process of healing is such an extensive one.

"We are here for you, Dearest One. Let us begin a treatment. Please relax and receive. We will do the necessary work."

Right away, I feel everything changing.

There is a lightening of my load, and my senses feel as though they are being gently coated with a warm, soothing medicinal liquid. Not only are they calmed by this treatment, but they are also cleared and buffered somehow. Whatever it is, I am grateful for all of it.

I become aware of my heart, and how it has gone through a great travail. I feel sad for a moment, deeply sad, and a huge wave of this sadness washes through me and then gently fades away.

I hear the female Golden Energy Healer instructing me in soft tones:

"Let it be, it is all being released."

I appreciate her soothing words of explanation, as I feel my body easing up even more in its natural way. I find I have no resistance to this depth of my emotion, and I am glad.

Things hum along quietly for a few more minutes, and I grow sleepy. My eyelids feel heavy, and there is a slight pressure on the top of my head. It is not uncomfortable, it is simply there.

All of a sudden, I begin to feel an agitation beginning, and I am aware of new insight opening up. A sense of visual clarity is happening for me. It is as if I am watching myself and seeing the picture of how I am and what shape I am in right now—like watching a movie of myself.

I see clearly that I am not only tightly wound and constricted, I am also overloaded with a kind of slime and grime, invaded by a goo that pervades me inside and out. It seems like some kind of toxicity. I see how it is somehow stuck throughout my entire system; it's massive, and no area seems unaffected by it. Wow, this I did not know.

One of my Golden Energy Healers touches my shoulder gently to let me know that everything is all right:

"Yes, this is indeed toxicity. Your next steps in your healing involve understanding the nature and effects of this. We encourage you to welcome the information that is showing itself to you, and to know how positive this is. The fact that you can see it so clearly is an indication of your restoring health—to be somewhat shocked by it as well is a completely understandable response.

"As you already know, wearing the Mantle of Fear thoroughly, and for as long as you did, stressed your natural system in many ways: shrinking yourself down into a size and state that was too cramped and binding for you, and doing so repeatedly, created distressing patterns that are completely foreign to you. This, you already know. You have become tangled up inside—your configuration is skewed, as Andar clarified earlier.

"On top of all of that contraction and entanglement, you witness now, more clearly than ever, the toxicity of the Mantle of Fear and all that it holds. You begin to fully comprehend how it has been systemically poisonous to you. This 'poison' is the toxicity you are actually seeing now. Your inner sight is bringing you clarity about this.

"Please know that there is nothing to be worried about. Worrying is the first clue that you are not in your natural state. If you are feeling worry at all, it confirms to you that you are still not restored to your intrinsic well-being, wherein no Fear and no face of Fear exists.

"Instead, take a deep breath and recognize, yet again, that in truth, you are a Golden Giant. You are in the process of slowly remembering this, and all that it means. Trust your Divine Intelligence and let the course of this have its freedom. The more you trust yourself, relax and soften, the better. Your system will, in time, shed all of this distress, as your Golden Remembrance emerges.

"You will detoxify and you will heal. You will expand your energies once more, and you will emerge restored: that is the Destiny which you have chosen."

I take a deep breath and feel myself being shifted into an altogether different awareness. My inner sight opens up in a new direction, and another piece of my memory is being jogged. I am having flashes of splashing under a Golden

Waterfall, with its cool waters bouncing off my skin. It is refreshing and clear, sweet and joyful. It makes me feel deeply glad inside. Threads of shining Golden Brilliance encircle me, and weave throughout my body and heart, making me feel like I am a rare jewel sparkling in the sun.

I recognize that somehow, this memory is an important part of my first energy healing treatment. I wonder to myself, "How is this?" It dawns on me that this memory is helping me to regain my footing inside of myself. This refreshing and revitalizing memory, now reactivated, is going a long way toward reminding my cells that they are happy, free, and jubilant, just like these moments under the waterfall.

My heart melts with joy at this realization, and a tingling sensation that rises up in my body confirms it. I feel as though I am celebrating a homecoming with my cells. How happy I am to feel them again in this way! It's been so long. I feel complete love and adoration inspiring me inside.

More memories, positive and life-affirming Golden Memories, are sparking all over the place inside of me now. I vividly recall walking in the early morning with the dew moistening my feet, feeling Terra beneath me, loving me with her vitality and passion. I am smelling the leaves and touching the trunks of my special trees, feeling the soft wind in my hair, the clear sound of birds chirping flooding me with delight.

My senses are aroused by these memories, and my body lunges forward with enthusiasm and joy to greet the day. My feeling is one of strength, healthy movement, and renewed passion. My heart is excited and bubbling over with creative ideas. I have not experienced these sensations in what seems like forever, and the motion of them swirling inside of me brings renewal. I know my cells are responding in kind, following suit, gravitating hungrily toward this vitalization and enthusiasm.

Wow. This is amazing! I savor this state and keep on savoring. I have been hungry for this.

After a while, my focus returns to the healing room. I am still reclining in my spa chair, relaxed and happy. I open my eyes. My Golden Healing Team is gathered around me, watching me with eyes of love. I reach for them in pure gratitude.

My feelings are deep, clear, and simple—just the way they used to be. Nothing feels clogged inside of me, and there is no exhaustive effort; no strain, and no stress. I am being bathed in, and by, these wonderful feelings and sensations.

One of the Golden Energy Healers says to me:

"These memory moments are essential to your rebuilding. They are, in themselves, healing treatments. They are infusions of that sensation of

complete non-containment of Golden Remembrances that remind you that you are fundamentally expansive and free, and that your system is, in truth, exuberant and fully engaged in Beauty.

"These memories will come and get you periodically, and they will strengthen, rejuvenate, and re-inspire you. They will give you the awareness again of the actual presence and tangibility of your wellness and Golden Joy. They will nourish you greatly and support you, reminding you of your Lemurian grace. They will bolster you, strengthening your immune system, your nervous system, and indeed, all of your systems throughout. This is YOU, building and crossing the bridge back to your true Self again.

"Know that we are with you: strong, steady, and constant. We have your greatest well-being and re-flourishing in the forefront of our minds. Always, and only, the Golden Best for you, Dearest One.

"That is enough for now. We will meet and speak again soon. In the meantime, we are with you, whether you are consciously aware of us or not. All things are well and will progress beautifully. We guarantee. Blessings, happy, healthy you!"

With their great kindness and positivity still encouraging me, I feel my Golden Healing Team moving out to the edges of my energy fields, positioning themselves there until it is time for us to meet more closely again.

My heart beats with gratitude toward them once more. I am glad to have these great Beings with me. I know I am in superb hands, and am relieved. I feel incredibly supported from deep inside my bones, and I have a new optimism that something grand and wonderful is going to happen in me in the days and times ahead. How fortunate I am.

Everything feels like it has turned in a new direction for me—as if everything is now on the "up and up!" I glow with love inside, as I say another prayer of thanksgiving for my many blessings. I am eternally grateful for all of this bountiful Golden Support.

MORE FROM MASTER SAINT GERMAIN ON THE LEMURIAN SOUL-SICKNESS

The Golden Witness speaks:

We are gathered back in the main Healing Sanctuary. I can tell that everyone is feeling refreshed, revitalized, and stronger—just like I am. Everyone seems more resilient somehow; bright and in positive spirits. Quite a contrast to where we were not too long ago! Our Golden Healing Teams are a vital part of this, I know. I look forward to more time spent with them as I get to know them and myself again.

It's nice to feel my insides becoming clearer, and no longer painfully tangled up. I know my healing continues to be a process, and I am trusting myself, and it, more and more as time goes on.

I take another moment to settle myself, and when I look up I see Master Saint Germain taking center stage. His demeanor is radiating strength and purpose, and I know that his words are going to be strong and powerful.

His voice booms out:

"Greetings again, great Golden Ones. Now that you have the support and skill of your Golden Healing Teams onboard with you, everything will feel much more manageable. Your relationship with them, and your understanding of how you can work together, will become more evident as you progress. We are grateful that you are able to receive them.

"It's important for you to know how supported and cared for you are by them, by us, and by your Golden Family as a whole everywhere—and to embrace this as fully as you can. We are in this together. We have your backs, and we are by your side. We are a Team, and we will continue to demonstrate this.

"You have enormous amounts of support with you in this journey. That is a guarantee. This is not to say that you are not strong and capable individuals in yourselves; not at all. You are all exceedingly so. But recognizing and allowing the full support from the Golden Family to also be an integral part of you is absolutely essential. It speaks to that aspect of your true Lemurian Design. You're not alone, and you are not taking this journey alone: you affect the whole and the whole affects you.

"Every ounce of strength you regain is an ounce of strength for all of us—for our entire Golden Family. We are affected and buoyed by you, as you are by us. That is why it is joyful for me, and those with me, to witness you in this healing and restoration process. Every step is a boon, you see. Every new level of awareness reached is like the Sun shining in the middle of a cloudy day for you, and for us all. It changes everything and everyone and lifts us up.

"It is powerful to witness, and powerful to be touched by all of you regaining yourselves again, thank you. Thank you is what I want to say on behalf of all of us right now. I honor you and respect you all enormously."

I am poignantly touched by the power of Saint Germain's words, and by his passion. I can feel the depth of love that reaches solidly toward us; the love that he feels for us, and our Golden Family, is palpable. His care is like a giant, bolstering Golden hug that reaches straight down into my bones, making me feel like I can do anything, climb any mountain, overcome any obstacle.

I am well aware of this profound support that he delivers to each one of us, like a package, every time we meet with him. I know it is up to me to receive and open that package to utilize what is inside—it is my choice to let myself be gifted.

He is a great, steadying, and motivating influence for me. He makes me want to keep going, reaching, and touching all that is sacred, holy, and meaningful inside of me. Plainly put, he deeply inspires me. I make a point to receive his support inside of me even more now than ever, because of what he just said.

I love it, and him, so much. I also know that he is a great Golden Activator. When he is around, more often than not, it means "action now!" Speaking of which, he continues.

"Alright everyone," he says with passion. *"Let's talk about:*

TOXIC CONSCIOUSNESS

"You have recently identified many of your personal symptoms of the Lemurian Soul-Sickness. You have opened to them deeply, felt them, and heard others. You have felt yourselves raw and turned inside out to release the voices of your pain inside.

"You need to know that these are only that: symptoms. They are not who you truly are. They are only the wounds and weakened areas that are pouring out to make way for your authentic selves. That is not to minimize them, but simply to clarify the picture as a whole.

"As we have stated, these symptoms, these pockets of energy, need to be felt and witnessed. This will continue to be so as they come up, level by level, to be cleared. Through this, their Imprints will actually be transmuted by the light of your understanding and love, and you will gradually find yourselves freed up by your Golden Selves emerging again.

"This process of your personal healing is well underway and has taken on a life of its own. Your Divine Intelligence is in the lead and will continue to direct you and illuminate your way. With this movement humming along so well, we are free to look at the more collective focus too, and at those external influences that have also been affecting you adversely. It is a sign of your increasing inner strength that I am able to address these influences now.

"Toxic Consciousness is absolutely a loaded subject; it is the toxicity of Fear in the atmosphere, and all the interference that this generates every

moment, of every day, for all of you.

"For you Golden Ones, living in Mondor is like living in a toxic jungle all the time, and swimming in a toxic soup. It is so foreign to you, foreign to your design, and counter to what is truly in your heart. You know this already. We have spoken of it at length before, but we are at a deeper level now. We haven't approached, in this way, how sickening this is for you; we have yet to explore it as thoroughly, and from this particular vantage point.

"Let me explain further. As we know, Mondor is controlled by the Heartless Ones. Therefore, the Imprints in the Consciousness are Imprints of Heartlessness; all that this means and looks like, and all that this generates—heartless thought forms from heartless people. They are everywhere, permeating everything, and deeply affecting everyone.

"These heartless thought forms are counter and corrosive to life, to one degree or another. They are not uplifting, and they are not Life Enhancing. Let us be clear about this: it is why we refer to them as toxic.

"These toxic thought forms create actual Imprints and patterns in the air waves and in the atmosphere. They build up over time, laying down texture, so to speak, layer upon layer. They repeat themselves, and they are constantly generating new concepts of the same kind and intent.

"Imprints, in general, also contain the energies of actual etheric memories— the history in the Consciousness that has built up and often repeated itself. If these Imprints are of a positive nature, you have the continuation of positivity. If they are negative, they spawn the continuation of negative creation.

"In this case, these heartless Imprints are of a negative charge and toxicity, as we have said. They continue to replay Imprints, and spawn new ones of the same nature, over and over again. This is their Consciousness, alive and well and at work. Of course, this is Mondor. This is the land of the Heartless Ones. This is what they want, and their Imprint is governing the outcome.

"Nothing can change until the Imprint is changed. And, since this is the Imprint of choice in Mondor, then only Mondor can alter it—if it ever even wants to. It's the Consciousness of Mondor. It is not about the body of Terra herself.

"It's the Consciousness of HUMANITY in Mondor. It's not what all humans are like, by any means. But it is what governs the atmosphere, the air waves, and the energy fields which thereby affects all of life, to one degree or another.

"As I said, and as we know, this Consciousness is toxic for all of you. It is fine for the H-O—but not for you. What is essential for you Golden Ones to see clearly, is the level of sickness that you feel because of this atmosphere, and because of the debris and toxicity that comes at you, every day.

"This Toxic Consciousness controls you in many ways—and you feel out of control in many ways because of it. It makes everything slimy, gooey, and slippery. It's like you are always slip-sliding around in the swamp of it. This toxic mess is thick and sticky. It's like layer upon layer of thick plaque that has built up, and it pulls at you and sucks you in. Sometimes, it's like quicksand; other times it's like sticky black tar that you can't get off of you—and that you can't get out of.

"And yes, as I said earlier, this is what you are swimming in all of the time. It affects every single aspect of you ALL the time—your thoughts, feelings, emotions, beliefs, and consciousness. It affects your body and your health on all levels.

"It affects every single decision and choice that you make. You are always being adversely affected by this toxicity and everything in it. It is fear pollution which causes pain pollution for you Golden Ones.

"Who's cleaning that up? No one. Why not? Because it's Mondor, and so you simply can't. It will breed more and generate more. That's what it does; that's its program and consciousness.

"In a while we will look at what you can do about this for yourselves. But first, we have to acknowledge the state of where you are right now and become crystal clear about what is going on for all of you.

"Your sickness is because you are swimming around in this toxicity— breathing it in, eating it, drinking it, thinking it, believing it; you are being affected by it all the time. You are constantly trying to digest this, and your systems will not do so!

"Your systems don't know where to put all of this. In your efforts to survive and do something with it so you can carry on, you are doing your best to digest it, process it, and make sense of it—but you can't. Your systems are not designed for this.

"Therefore, you always have an inner conflict at play. Your true health and well-being is continually wrestling with this toxicity, trying to keep it at bay, to discharge it—prevent it from contaminating you further.

"It's a heavy toxic load for you, and no wonder many of you feel like you are losing the battle against it. It's totally understandable to feel that you are losing a grip, like you're slipping down a toxic slope. Many of you are caving in, or have already caved in, under the weight and stress of it. You do your best to keep your head above water, while at the same time you are always cognizant of the sensation that you are close to sinking fast.

"This toxic poisoning shows up on all levels of you: physically, mentally, emotionally, psychically, and spiritually. As I said, many of you are trying hard to adapt to, and even digest, this toxicity when it is not yours to do so. Your systems will NOT digest this—they know better.

"But you don't know what to do with it, do you? You don't know where to put it. No, of course not.

"That creates this overload which, in and of itself, becomes a toxic buildup. Subsequently, most of you are in a state of constant agitation, anxiety, and distress which makes you feel constantly on edge—and on the edge. Sometimes it's in the background, and sometimes in the foreground, but it is always there.

"It keeps you all stirred up in Fear of one kind or another, and to one degree or another. It pokes at you and prods you—and then it dupes you. How are you being duped by Fear?

"Do you sometimes get caught up in the herd mentality, and sucked into the intense Fear pockets of the masses? Do you get plugged into Fear by something you read or something you hear? How malleable are you? Are your emotional strings being pulled around, and yanked and manipulated by the Fear?

"Are you caught in it? Are you being sucked in? Are you buying it too? Are you losing your sight and connection to self? Are you inadvertently giving yourself away to it? Are you beside yourselves with Fear?

"Stand back and assess yourselves. Check it out. Be honest about this. The H-O know how contagious Fear is. It is a like a disease; in an instant, it can be built up into a massive crescendo just by plucking a few emotional strings and sounding some well-chosen Fear notes. Oh, yes, they know well how powerful a tool this is, and they are using it masterfully.

"It manipulates your emotional bodies and tampers with your psyches, so that you are like that puppet on a string that we spoke of in earlier chapters.

It creates thought forms and foods that are corrosive and upsetting to the physical body.

"And, as I said earlier, it's a toxic jungle that you're walking in all the time. Not only are you swimming in it, but you are surrounded by it. There is no escape from this, because this is Mondor. Fear is in the air, and coming at you and pummeling you all too often.

"Debris and toxicity are flying everywhere, clogging up the natural pores of life, on all levels. Fear—divisiveness, disruptiveness, disharmony, and its many other faces—are all designed to disconnect you, and to keep you disconnected from yourselves and your natural intelligence.

"Fear is flying at you to keep you unbalanced and contracted; it is chipping away at you to keep you afraid. All of this just from Fear-based toxic thought forms floating around the air, joining with each other—and all are well aimed for a desired outcome: the FEAR GAME. And you, Golden Ones, are many of the pawns on the board.

"At this point, I am asking you to stand back, regard yourself, and assess HOW you are being affected by this, and how you are being duped. How do you see that the Golden Ones are being duped? Sometimes it is easier to see in others than yourself. But that will give you insight and enable you to look at yourselves to see if that applies to you also.

"Let me spell it out on its various levels, and give you some examples that will help you begin to specifically identify this for yourselves:

"PHYSICAL: It weakens your physical body and makes your attention and energy go there—rendering you unable to function and rise up above it. When you are 'down like this,' it is easy for interference in the airwaves to blast you further. You can find yourself in a downward spiral that is difficult to reverse, much less rise out of. When this occurs, it means that worry and Fear have taken hold.

"Do you ever FULLY relax inside? Fear keeps you unhealthy and gagging by toxifying the food, the water, the air, and the soil. It tries to poison your cells with its toxicity.

"EMOTIONAL: Fear keeps you in a constant state of feeling vulnerable to one degree or another. It invades your self-esteem and self-worth. It causes you to doubt yourself in ways that are fundamentally unhealthy.

"Fear keeps you distracted and spinning, so that you are never able to stop

and pay attention to what is TRULY going on inside of you—so that you never need to actually sink into how good you DON'T feel.

"It makes you believe that you are not good enough and that you are always in need of fixing. This makes you completely unable to appreciate who and how you are simply by virtue of being.

"Fear keeps negative perception and judgment of self and others constantly alive and well and floating around everywhere. It keeps you overwhelmed by itself.

"MENTAL: It causes you to lose sight of your clarity, inside and out. It distorts your perceptions.

"Fear creates mental thought forms that are designed to trigger direct emotional response and contraction of the emotional and physical bodies. It creates faulty thoughts, misperceptions, and misunderstandings about yourselves, others, and life in general.

"It distorts your thinking and conjures up faulty beliefs, which become magnified by the herd mentality.

"Fear keeps you out of your heart and in your head as much as possible; preoccupied with 'issues' and things which are unimportant and meaningless.

"It tries to take you out of the 'feeling range' altogether.

"SPIRITUAL: Fear seeks to upset your relationship between you and your Source.

"It erodes your spiritual self trust. It gets in between you and that which has sacred meaning to you, so that you won't seek out or trust your inner voice—or yourself with it.

"Fear keeps you disconnected from yourselves, from Terra, from your Source, and from Life. That is its main purpose: to keep you disconnected from you and your Divine Power in whatever ways it can.

"In standing back and choosing to see Toxic Consciousness clearly, you'll find it shocking. It is invasive and it is strong. It is everywhere, and it can bring you to your knees.

"Toxic Consciousness is not a delusion. It is real and alive, and it is affecting you daily; in every single moment. The reality is that for many of you, it has already brought you to your knees and left you feeling weak, trembling, and powerless in its grip.

"The facts of it—the truth of it—are overwhelming, aren't they? But this is how it has been for you Lemurians.

"ONLY by seeing this Toxic Consciousness and realizing its effects on you, can you begin to clear the air for yourself. Only by realizing the Imprint you have been swimming in, can you make a new choice if you want to. It begins—and ends—with Awareness.

"TOXIC CONSCIOUSNESS—it's REAL. Think about it."

Oh, my goodness. Wow. I'm in complete overwhelm listening to what Master Saint Germain is talking about. It is taking my breath away—uncomfortably so. It seems like too much to even hear, but, of course, I believe him.

I become aware that my vision is shifting, and I am seeing a great sea of humanity undulating inside what could only be described as a cesspool. I see that everyone is coated with this tar-like sticky slime, and it is gross and noxious. It smells and it is making them smell. They can't get it off—it's too sticky and slimy.

I see everyone having a level of panic about this, whether it is low, moderate, or high. Everyone has it, because everyone knows that something about this is not right; it's just not right. I see the Golden Ones trying to peel this sticky grime off, while saying to themselves, "What is this? This is not me. This is not my skin. How do I get this off me? Why am I stuck and why is this painful in my head, my mind, my heart, and my body? Why am I feeling so badly?

"What is this debris flying around me? Looks like a crap storm for sure. Yikes!

"Where's my helmet? Where's my mask? Where's my filtering system? I don't want to breathe anymore. I don't want to hear any foreign thoughts anymore. I don't want to feel anymore, because I know I am being controlled, duped, and wagged by it.

"None of it is truly me. If I am not this, then who am I? WHERE AM I?"

Master Saint Germain's voice enters into my thoughts as they whirl around frantically in my head.

"Yes, I know your thoughts and I know your feelings. I understand. I know it can be truly shocking when you see it clearly. Most of you haven't wanted to see it, and that has been a big part of the problem.

"I urge you to stop trying to hide from it. Stop avoiding and ignoring it. Stop making excuses in an attempt to pretend it's not there. Stop resisting and fighting it. Let all of that go and stare it right in the face.

"Look at it full on. Admit it. Admit what you see, feel, and hear. Admit what you have already truly known inside—that something is not right; it is not clean and it is not healthy for you. That's a good start. Then you can

see exactly what it is, and you can see your position in relationship to it.

"Then, and only then, will you begin to gradually, but automatically, separate from it. There will be some distance between you and it, some objectivity about it. You will see that it is clearly NOT YOU; that it has never been you and never will be you.

"You will see and know that you are completely and totally different from it. You are a different Consciousness vibrating—same location...different Consciousness.

"Now, you've got it. That's the Truth—same location, different Consciousness.

"My dear Friends, where do you want to go with this? You have a choice. You can spin in place and do your best to survive—or...what else do you suppose you can do?

"You can stand still, see it clearly, and BE DIFFERENT. Here is right where you can trust yourselves and your sensitivities. Here is when you can dig for that vast wealth of wisdom and insight that resides inside of you. Here is where you can draw from within, to alter your relationship to that which is affecting you, and to that which is around you. Here is when you can make a choice to stand strong and steady and peace-filled in the midst of this toxicity, this manipulation and yanking around—all of this interference and disconnection.

"You can choose to be, and do, the opposite. You can dig deep and reconnect. You can hold onto your connectedness with yourself, with your Source, and with that which is meaningful to you—and hold onto it with all your might.

"You can be still and calmed by your love. You can let go of the frenzy. Let it be what it wants to be and let you be what you want to be. There is nothing you can do about THAT, but there is something you can do about YOU.

"You know things can be different. YOU have been different here before. New decisions need to be made on your clarity about this; new insights, understandings, and choices.

"Are you ready for that now? Bold, brave, brand new choices await."

LAST WORDS FROM SANANDA ON THE LEMURIAN SOUL-SICKNESS

We are still in the Sanctuary. Yes, we feel pretty shell shocked, and are hoping for a respite right about now. It seems that we have a window of quiet time on our hands, so I am going to call in my Golden Healing Team and see if they can help me. It's been a lot to hear about and see; a lot to no longer try my best to make sense of and digest. How do you make sense of craziness anyway?

My Golden Healing Team is here right away, and time flies as they work with me. I fall asleep somewhere during the session, and when I wake up, I feel rested and refreshed, as if my wiring has been reassembled somehow. I am feeling more at ease and am grateful—that was an uncomfortable load.

"Don't try so hard with this, dear Friend," they say to me before they go. *"It's simply part of the process, and the gentler you are with it, and yourself, the better. You don't need to have the answers; let it reveal itself. We remind you again: it's a process, and a natural one at that. You are bringing back your true health. Have faith."*

They take their leave, letting me know again that they are with me always, and are a breath away when I need them for treatment. I feel them in my heart, and their reassurance and love for me are gentle but palpable—and I love them in return. Again, as I know I say often throughout this book, I am grateful. That is the plain truth of it.

I stretch out and prepare to wake up fully and get focused in the room again. I can see the many beautiful ones around me doing the same. It seems we seized the opportunity for some energy healing treatment and restoration.

As I'm gathering my wits about me, I see Sananda entering the room to take his place at the stage in front of us. He is completely and utterly Golden, shining strong and bright. The pure radiance of him reaches out to touch us, and I feel it shimmering and dancing on my skin. I become enveloped in his Golden glow, and a pure peacefulness blankets me softly.

I focus my attention on his words as he begins to address us:

"I am here to summarize this entire subject of the Lemurian Soul-Sickness.

"I know many of you feel like you have already heard so much about it that you are done with it. But, in the interest of bringing crystal clear clarity to it, we have repeated ourselves often with the intent of systematically pulling apart and loosening the veils. We wish to separate the strands at deeper levels, so that release of all of this can ultimately happen. If you could have seen how tightly woven and bound the veils were when we started, you would now appreciate fully how loosened they are.

"With that in mind, let me put the last remaining pieces of this puzzle in place. And yes, I will be repeating some of it again—but this is the last time.

"*This is what I see from my vantage point. In a nutshell, your condition looks like this:*

"*What you are all feeling is varying levels of despondency. This is the true Lemurian Soul-Sickness at work. Underneath everything, there is this hopelessness that is setting in; a Fear and desperation at the escalating crescendo of interference in one form or another.*

"*Being in Mondor has become ruinous to you Golden Ones. There is great distortion throughout, and it is only escalating. The H-O are literally playing THE FEAR GAME and you are stuck on the game board as one of many pawns.*

"*Your Emotional Bodies in particular are being yanked around mercilessly, and there seems to be little room for escape from this; you are being wagged and duped at every turn. Make no bones about it. This is the way it is in Mondor. FEAR is up and it is controlling and running everything and almost everyone.*

"*Many of you are doing your best to free yourselves, to return to inner peace, and to find that which is sacred and central to sustain you. But it is in the context of Mondor. You are still stuck inside the Imprint of Mondor, no matter what.*

"*Many of you have done much to disentangle yourselves in this regard, but it does not bring you out of the confines of this loop, this Imprint, this taut and restricted configuration. Your lives are still operating only in relationship to Mondor.*

"*Many of you are frustrated as you find the whole thing so maddening. In fact, many of you are beside yourselves with frustration because, of course, you want to do something about it, but you feel like you can't.*

"*Many of you wonder, what is the point in living? Many of you are awake enough to feel the confinement, the restriction, and the parameters binding you. And, because you are awake enough, you wonder what exactly is the point? How can I truly be here? You realize, 'I can't.' You are increasingly aware that you cannot be truly free and expanded in this Imprint. You may or may not have consciously admitted this to yourself. You may still be hoping that there is a way, but there isn't.*

"'*What do I have to do?' you ask. 'Do I have to just survive and get through it until I die? Will I ever be able to be free, fully free, in my body?'*

"No, there is no full life for any Golden One in Mondor. There never was, there never is, and there never will be. It is virtually impossible; the Imprint and the configuration is too small for the hugeness of the Golden Gentle Giant. Don't expect it to be so.

"But don't give up yet, either. There is a way and it is coming.

"But first, you need to continue admitting how sick this is making you feel; the toxicity and the Interference in all its forms and faces. Admit that you are affected deeply by it.

"Why is this essential? Because your systems will know that you hear them and that you care. Then, and only then, will you have a chance to heal the many levels of your woundedness. In truth, it only happens through your hearts.

"If you can feel and allow and accept this, you are beginning to fathom the contrast that is creating these sick feelings and this despair and frustration. You KNOW there is something else about you that is bigger and freer than all of this. You may not know what exactly, but you know there is SOMETHING. If there wasn't, you wouldn't even feel sick, would you? You wouldn't feel sick because there would be no inner conflict. There would be no 'Bigger Self' inside wanting freedom.

"You wouldn't feel the torment of the repression and confinement and restriction. You wouldn't feel up against something else. You wouldn't feel sad and despondent, and as if something is becoming hopeless. You wouldn't feel your inner life force ebbing away in the face of it. You wouldn't feel hopeless, helpless, or powerless at all. You wouldn't feel weighed down by it, repressed and suffocating.

"Yes, there is indeed something bigger inside of you trying to get out, to reach, express, soar, and stretch out—to then expand even more. You know this in your understanding, but you have yet to fully FEEL and BE this all the time.

"You Golden Ones are in Mondor. Without the purpose of Rescuing as your reason to be there, you are lost. Being in Mondor made you lost anyway, but at least it gave you a reason and a purpose. As this is no longer the case, now what?

"You do not know what to do, where to go, how to change all of this. You are getting even more disturbed and disrupted and frustrated. Fear of the Fear has set in. Fear of increasing and escalating Fear has set in.

"Interference, Toxic Consciousness, and other disruptors are increasingly threatening human life. An unsettling panic has set in. Overwhelm and hopelessness has set in. Powerlessness is setting in. It seems too big and overwhelming and out of control.

"Now what? What to do to help yourself and others? Where to go? Where to turn?

"In truth, the greatest pain you have is your disconnection from your true Selves and your disconnection from your Source. That is where your greatest area of weakness lies. That is where interference has a field day. And that is what Toxic Consciousness thrives on.

"Because of this disconnection, you do not remember who you are or the true power you have. All of that power, that vast resource inside, is useless to you. Yes, indeed, you sense there is something more inside of you. You HOPE there is, but it is elusive. It is like something present somewhere that you cannot touch or even know for real. It is too far away. It is veiled, unavailable, and inaccessible.

"There is a despondency about this. You are sinking fast, and you are under the pressing weight of the torment of that which is NOT you—Fear, Fear, and more Fear.

"This is what we have been talking about. THIS is the Sickness, the disconnect, the not remembering; and therefore having no access. It is depressing, literally. It is depressing you and your unremembered hopes and dreams.

"Because that's the thing, you see. You Golden Ones have known complete freedom in the physical body upon our beautiful Terra. You KNOW the wondrousness, the beauty, and the Golden Light pouring forth through and out of you which stretches beyond to the Stars and other Golden Life Forms everywhere. You know that this is what your sensitivities are for, and about; to enable you to commune, engage, communicate, foster, adore, witness, and cheer on because you are in touch with yourselves and the entire Golden Family everywhere!

"So, yes, you already know what it is to have this on Terra. To not be able to feel that in the context of Mondor now that the Rescues are over, makes you feel overwhelmingly sick, disconnected, and depressed. You feel as if you are dying inside. It is slowly but surely crushing and crippling you.

"What is the point of being here beyond just surviving this?

"This is where you finally hear your Golden Soul speaking up, loud and *clear, urging you to listen to it and follow. There is no other place to go. There is no other support for you Golden Ones as long as you are in the body—except for one place: Terra, Golden Terra.*

"She is the ONLY true support you have. SHE IS YOUR ANSWER."

I hear Sananda's voice, but I am not sure what he is saying. What does he mean exactly?

I feel his energy intensifying hugely, becoming like a laser beam; pinpointed and direct. I feel like he is right in front of me, his face before mine, his eyes staring at me with total concentration. I know he is doing this with every one of us here.

I look at him looking at me full on. His gaze is piercing and penetrating into my core. The magnitude of his love opens up and pours inside of me, radically shifting everything. I feel like it is, in fact, piercing layers and levels of stuff inside of me, breaking things apart, bushwhacking, unearthing, vigorously making space and deliberately and determinedly opening up a pathway. It is not a soft and gentle movement. Rather it is one of sheer groundbreaking and finality.

"The time has come," he says in a voice that shakes the room. *"I ask you, are you willing to not be sick anymore? Are you willing to let go of Mondor now? Are you willing to let go of its identity, its configuration, and all that it holds?*

"Are you willing to actually walk out of it all? Are you finally willing to walk out of it, leave it all behind, and walk back into Terra?"

For a moment, I wonder why he is even asking us that. Of course we are. Of course, I AM.

And something startling begins to happen. My whole body starts to quiver and shake uncontrollably—so much so that my teeth feel like they're going to start rattling in my head. I feel an intense vibration reverberating inside of me making everything shake, rattle, and roll. There is no time to think about it, about what this is. The gyrations are intense and I'm automatically grabbing to hold on tight to any semblance of balance.

But I can't, I can't. I suddenly register this fully—and as soon as I do, in an instant I decide to let go. I LET GO. Yes. Yes. Yes, I do…

In an instant, I am drifting. I feel like I am a whole complete planet unto myself, and my ground and everything about it is shifting deliberately and intelligently. The feeling of it is strong and purposeful. I am amazed, and somehow hypnotized by the motion of how it is moving around and rearranging itself. The intent is strong. The message is clear. Freedom. Space. Now!

And then as quickly as it came, it all stops and everything is silent and still. I am drifting again, and I can hear the Sea—her waves breaking up on the shore-line. I can feel her and her waters calling me in.

The sound of my beating heart whispers in a voice of pure joy, "I am free. I am me. I have walked away. YES. My ground is free, free for me now—free for me again."

CHAPTER THIRTEEN

GOLDEN RESTORATION AT LAST

PEACEFULNESS

THE GOLDEN WITNESS SPEAKS:
I find myself moving out into the wide universe, I am not sure exactly where.

I am floating upright in an open space, a space that feels neutral, that has no life form—except me. I am alone with myself in a pure and uncontaminated way. There is no toxicity here. There is no pollution on any level, of any kind.

I am serene and still. It is completely quiet, and all I can hear is the sound of my heart beating inside my body. I become aware that I am inside a safe space.

Soon, the sound of the heartbeat of the universe reaches me, blending with mine so that we become one: United, Constant, Present, Pulsating.

I register that this, somehow, is how life begins. I don't know exactly what that means, except that it's true; it's the birthing of sound which gathers and grows, becoming all of life.

I am the Soul of this Universe right now because my heartbeat has merged with its heartbeat, and I am happy.

It's not an emotional happy, but a Soul Happy; it's intrinsic to me and has no basis in anything outside of my self. I AM Soul. I am one with this Universe. This Universe and I have combined: we are one peaceful, happy heartbeat.

I feel as though I could float forever. I find it soothing and I welcome the absence of stimulation. It's nice to feel nothing for a change; nothing except this true pulse of me, this true pulse of Life.

I wonder about God for a moment—why, I don't know. As soon as I have this thought, I wish I hadn't, as it distracts me. It's odd what I see about this: God, it's all mixed up. It's completely mixed up. I'd never thought of God in this way before—so loaded and scrambled with all kinds of incongruent stuff.

And then I hear the sound of Master Saint Germain's voice gently whispering in my ear—as if he is standing right next to me.

"Beloved," he says. *"This is the last piece of toxicity that you need to look at and understand; this Sacred Source that has become convoluted and twisted up, contaminated and polluted. It has been manipulated and reconfigured and is full of so much pain and Interference—all 'in the Name of God.'*

"Fractured.

"Dissonant.

"Distorted.

"Discordant.

"This concept has been greatly interfered with, as you can now see.

"When you speak the name of God, recognize what has happened to it. If you choose for this to be the sound of your Source, you must be clear on your deep internal resonance of it. You must be absolutely crystal clear about this, and only this, and hold it close and sacred. Otherwise, you risk having your perceptions distorted, and you continue to be at the effect of interfering contamination.

"Or, you can decide to re-choose. It is for you to clarify anew your intimate connection with YOUR Source—its face, its feeling, and its name—what it means to you and what it means as you. What is it that has given you life?

"Oh, Divine Love. Isn't that where you started? Isn't that what you are? Isn't that where you begin, and never end?

"Oh, Divine Love.

"Magnificence.

"Beauty.

"YOU."

I am so surprised that I am rendered speechless by what Master Saint Germain is saying. He is right.

I don't know quite what to decide at the moment, but it's as though a giant "elephant" has been pulled out from under the rug.

God has been my Center, and yet it is so obvious to me now: the entire package of God has clearly become tainted and twisted, torqued and toxified, and so filled with fear! How had I not seen this before? It is as clear as day.

I simply had no idea how mixed up it had become. Being inside of Mondor kept me stuck inside the confusion; there had been no opportunity to stand back far enough to be able to see things as clearly as this.

Now I can and I am stunned.

Master Saint Germain continues:

"Keep your focus on what is showing itself to you, Beloved. Let yourself have reactions, and allow your clarity to reveal itself. An emergence is in progress, unraveling everything right back to the core. Notice, be aware, and allow.

"Imagine you are being 'washed' through and through, literally."

I know that I need to do exactly what Master Saint Germain is suggesting, that I need to witness how this has become toxified and interfered with. Even though it seems like a big plate full of confused energy, I also know I will eventually emerge clearly embracing the pure truth of me: Oh, Divine Love.

That is my core. That is ME.

Whatever other name I might wish to attach to it will be something I will decide upon later, if I choose to.

I take a deep breath and let myself unravel and evolve. I know this is part of my healing in process.

GOLDEN TERRA CALLS US HOME AGAIN

Golden Witness speaks:

Out of nowhere I hear yet another voice. Its sweet resonance takes me so completely by surprise that I am jolted out of my thoughts, and I instinctively and eagerly lean right toward it.

"Oh, Beautiful One, where are you?" It calls to me.

I hear the sweet sound of this voice so long loved, and I know instantly who it is.

My Terra.

My TERRA!

My Golden Terra.

Her Spirit has come to get me…

My eyes fill with tears of loss that turn to joy as her heart touches mine, which reaches hungrily back to hers. We join and we are ONE. What bliss this is!

In an instant my memories of being inside her body long ago open, filling my senses to overflowing. Within them I am Golden, and cradled inside her Golden Womb. It is warm, reassuring, and secure. The atmosphere is filled with magnificent joy, passion, and reverence; it is profound beauty.

She rocks me tenderly as she sings sweet lullabies to my soul. I am her delight, her Treasure. I know she knows me better than I know myself.

My memory of it all is opening back up again. Is she really here to bring me back? Is this true?

"Yes," her sweet voice reassures me.

"Come back inside me, my Love," she says gently. *"Come back inside of me again. I have longed for you.*

"I have waited, and finally the time has come. Are you wanting?"

"What a silly question that is!" I think to myself. YES, of course! Oh, yes, I do.

Instantly, my entire Being gravitates toward her and I can feel her pulling me gently, steadily, toward her body. I realize how I have ached for this reunion.

I find myself finally falling back inside of her, inside her belly, her Core Crystal. I move inside her heart, into her Soul. I become ONE with her powerful sound, the pulsating heartbeat of her, this most beautiful, most magnificent Planet.

I am HOME, back inside of her once more. I am HOME inside of Terra, my great Mother and inspiration.

I am HER and she is ME. All that I have wished for is being fulfilled. She is passion embodied, and because of her, so am I.

As I land on Terra's inner solid ground I feel as though my feet have become physicalized again. I am aware of the re-forming of my physical sensations even though I am also well aware that I am only in here energetically. Somehow, Terra is holding the Imprint of my physicalized form, and because of this, I am fully grounded in my body Imprint, my physical mind, and my heart.

Dear Reader, I know this may sound impossible, but you know well how this can be when you accept that we are all energy, fluid and flowing, in and out of our various formations and different levels of awareness. It continues to be so.

I am physicalized again, and yet I am operating on purely energetic principles of this inside Terra's body, as I did long ago.

I am here, once again. I am returned to that haven of wellness and love that is huge and constant. Terra: magnificent, wondrous, magical, inspiring Terra.

I adore her, I simply do—and she adores me back. This I KNOW: she adores us all.

I take stock of where I am and what I am aware of. I can't wait to be reminded—I am totally present.

The first thing that strikes me when I am back inside of her body is the scent; the air is moist, rich, and rejuvenating. I can hear the sound of water as it runs in merry rivulets, dripping and falling throughout her deep inner caverns. Far off, hidden tunnels return the echoes, bouncing them softly from wall to wall.

Crystals and crystalline formations are being birthed everywhere; the walls, floors, and ceilings are all glistening and glowing with intense beauty and magic. The air is charged with reverence, and all is holy, deep, ancient, wise, and strong.

My senses are overflowing. All of this is familiar and reassuring. Oh my, it is so good to be HOME.

As my system continues to adjust to this environment I begin to hear other noises, and as I look around, I realize I am not alone—certainly not. I am thrilled as I recognize that many of my Golden Friends are here with me. And I know there are many more beyond what I can see right now. I have the sensation that we are ALL here right now. We are all reunited together, inside of Terra, just the way we were way back when.

What a glorious homecoming this is!

And then, without further thought, I feel myself, and all of us, being gently lifted up. Transported like one huge river flowing, we are being taken back into the Great Golden Hall where we had first established our original Golden Configuration. We are going back to where we had declared the original Golden Vows of our One Golden Heart, long ago. Such a powerful place, and with the richest of memories.

There is a hush of reverence as we enter and feel its spacious glory once again.

It is exactly the same as I remembered it: one giant hall with arched doorways, opening up to small sanctuaries around its perimeter. The walls are still glowing and shimmering with dancing light, the enormously high ceiling arching gracefully toward its majestic sovereign peak. The floor is still solid Gold, glistening under my feet.

As I enter, I vividly recall how profoundly inspired I felt by the Golden Soul of Terra and our Golden Family; our declarations of devotion and all that we stood for. Right now, I feel exactly the same, as if time has not changed a thing.

Once again, here it is. Once again, here we are...

There is a great aura of excitement in the room and our celebration is escalating as the moments go by. How happy we are to be back in this glorious place once more.

I see the presence of the Golden Masters among us, and of Avalar and Andar moving through the crowd to greet us, their faces alight with love. Eventually we are ushered into a semblance of order as we find our seats, holding hands and greeting one another with total joy and jubilation.

Everyone gradually settles down and all becomes quiet. I remember this as well, the profound stillness inside this exquisite and massive Great Golden Hall.

I notice we have managed to form ourselves into one large circle, with many Golden Ones standing behind us. There are Golden Ones from the Stars, and the Life Forms of many of the Golden Energetic Ones present. Golden Angels are with us as well, standing tall and regal at every corner of the hall, and interspersed among us.

Our gathering creates a Golden Radiance that emanates from this special place in a huge and magnificent way. We glow intensely but quietly, and the air is hushed and expectant. Soon, that which we have been waiting for arrives: the exquisite Golden Soul of Terra.

She manifests herself in a spiraling energetic form and "stands," undulating within the center of our vast circle. Her Golden Energies dance and swirl gracefully around her Center as if she is weaving rainbows out of pure Golden nectar. They feel warm and substantial and as soft as silk. Reaching toward us, they caress us tenderly as we sit mesmerized by her pure grace and Beauty.

And then we begin to hear her unique sound.

At first it is a tone, a vibration that moves through us, through our energy fields and our cellular memory. It touches everything and everyone, making an indelible mark of love and welcome and homecoming. Gradually, it formulates itself into a beautiful, lyrical note.

"Welcome, welcome, welcome!" her voice rings out joyous and bright. *"I am glad and grateful that you are here and that you have returned to me so that I can help you make your final returns to yourselves. This is a significant moment. It signals the end of an era, the end of a way, the end of a long and arduous journey.*

"When you've been in here with me before, it has been for entirely different reasons. The first time, we were focused on building our initial Configuration of Lemuria, and subsequently, when you chose to remain with me when the cataclysms were coming, we were preparing and strengthening you for what lay ahead. No, you did not know what that would be exactly, but I did. I knew of the possibility of what might take place, because I knew what might happen when you resurfaced. I did all that I could to prepare you for what that may be, and for what could follow as a result. We worked hard and were diligent together. You grew and stretched tremendously, gaining so much.

"Remember, again, that you were given a choice about that: whether to leave me in the face of the oncoming planetary changes and re-create somewhere else, or stay with me and continue to evolve no matter what. You made the choice to stay with me, in the name of our continuing Lemurian freedom. You wanted more for yourselves with me, as I did with you.

"We had become inseparable.

"But your choice meant that you were also signed up for whatever that choice would bring with it, the entire package of what that might become and whatever twists and turns would come with it. At that time, you believed you were choosing ongoing Lemurian freedom.

"And yes, I can hear you saying, 'Well, what kind of freedom was that that I ended up having? No freedom at all. Quite the opposite.'

"But I say to you, please don't judge—there is still more to know and understand about it. You are moving on. You are about to open up a new way. You are about to create a brand-new era.

"The time for the Golden Age has come again, my Beloved Ones. The time for you as great Golden Gentle Giants has arrived, to walk upon my surface tall and free again. Somewhere inside of you, you knew it would and here it is.

"I hear you wondering, 'How will this be possible?' All in due time, my loves; all in due time. You will see, I promise.

"Yes, your 'process' of restoration continues, at these levels and in this way, with me. Remember, if you will, that I have housed your Golden grace and glory, your true deep Golden Treasure in order to keep it safe and sacrosanct. This was our arrangement way back then. THIS was our need, our agreement, and our choice together. I made a vow to do this for you—and I have done this.

"Yes, you have been missing these deepest and most sacred parts of you while you have been traveling throughout Mondor. But these treasures were not ever lost. They were here with me, inside of me, for safekeeping.

"You have come back inside of me to retrieve them, to reclaim that which is by rights your very own. But first, there is still more that we need to do to prepare the way for this reintegration and receiving of that which is the Golden Treasure of YOU. I urge you to roll up your sleeves and get ready for some more work together."

TERRA OUTLINES THE HEALING SEQUENCE

"Let me outline for you exactly what we will be doing so that you know what is needed and what to expect.

"We will be covering a lot of ground together and moving through the specific sequence of layers that are in need of restoration. This is done, once again, by exploring certain aspects of each layer so that the energies within them will be able to move and realign freely when the time is right. Each layer hinges on the one before it. In order to be successful in reopening the proper flow of them, we must be thorough in making sure each one is clear and cleansed. Subsequently, the entire sequence of reactivation can happen properly when the time comes.

"Let me clarify the layers and the sequence to which I am referring.

"First, we will reexamine the Imprint of the Original Shattering which happened when you reemerged onto my surface long ago. We will go inside your personal shattering from that experience, and that of our entire Golden Family as well. Understanding this Shattering Experience to its fullest, in all of its intricacies, is the only way for you to heal and be restored fully. This is where and when the original wounding took place. All the pain that has followed was because of this original wound; this original wound is what all of the ensuing pain has hooked into, on all levels.

"Second, once you have understood the intricacies of your original Shattering Experience and brought this wound to a true state of healing, you will then be able to reconnect fully with your Divine Source. This will enable your Divine Wholeness to become intact again. You will literally 'anchor back in' to your authentic, true selves again.

"Third, once the foundation of you in your Source, as your Divine Wholeness, is complete and activated again, you will be able to successfully shed the Mantle of Fear that you have been encased in. Once this happens, the contracted state you have been in will open up and your natural expansiveness will be reawakened. Your natural flow will return, and your pathway to Golden Remembrance will be fully cleared.

"Fourth, at this point, you will be ready to consciously remember, receive, and re-embody the full Gifts of the Gold originally given to you by your Source. All of your Sacred Golden Conduits will be reconnected, reawakened, and reactivated as well. All of this will be like 'reinserting the key' back into your full Golden Heart, thus allowing your deepest loving to become radiant and outpouring, your Power Centers to change shape from being concave to convex, and your Golden Creatorship to be reawakened and reactivated again.

"Fifth, once all of this is complete you will find that you have firmly reestablished a solid, steady, and secure platform to support you in continuing to expand and express your Golden Love freely. You will purposefully create forth in it, with it, and as it again. You will be able to finally flourish as your Lemurian Golden Selves upon my surface once more. Together, we will stand strong and radiant as One Golden Family, One Golden Heart; alive, joy-filled, and well.

"Sixth, our task will be to roll up our sleeves even more, hold our beautiful Golden World steady, and continue to strengthen and expand it through *our powerful love and devotion. We will spread forth our exquisite Golden Creations to the best of our abilities: this will be our deepest passion restored and celebrating.*

"Yes, we will have the grand opportunity to thrive again, to shine brightly, and to thoroughly flourish in our Golden freedom. Yes, it is time. The 'window' for this is open and ready.

"And we will do all of this, while at the same time allowing Mondor to be exactly what and how it wishes to be. We will be here together; one planet, two completely different realities expressing. Same place, different consciousnesses. Same place, different frequencies sounding.

"We will both thrive in our own ways, and with our own purposes fully and freely expressed. Golden Live and Let Live. Why not?

"This is the 'upgrade' everyone has been talking about and working toward for so long. This is our Golden Destiny fulfilling itself.

"How do you feel about all of this?"

Terra pauses and gives us a chance to ponder what she has said so far.

⌘

"Wow," I think to myself. "Well, okay." This certainly is a solid plan, and it sounds like it has a great ending! I'm excited, and I feel like I've been like a little mole buried in the ground and am coming out to feel the sun shining on my back. I look forward to breathing fresh air, to having a lightness in my heart that makes me want to sing my Golden Song and blossom on Terra's surface again. I haven't a clue how this is going to happen, but if Terra says this is so, I believe her. As she said, "Why not?"

Terra's voice returns to my awareness:

"This is the picture of the work that you and I are going to do together. I am spelling this out for you, step by step, so you will know what is coming, and not waste precious time in wondering about the point of it all or about what comes next. Once again, it is a process. Oh, I do know how much you love that word!

"Nonetheless, love it or not, the journey through this sequence of layers is a specific undertaking, an instinctive, deliberate progression outlined by your Soul and the Soul of our Collective Golden Family. Its request of you is the same as mine: that you commit to remaining present with each moment of it, and that you stay steady, patient, and aware throughout. This is the greatest evolutionary step that you have taken to date: it outdoes

even your original entrance into Lemuria.

"Why? Because it brings with it so much, and is a shining testimony to who you are and where you have been. It is your entire history catching up with itself and enfolding into a new blueprint, an enhanced Golden Configuration appropriate to modern times. Through this, you will come to see that no effort has been wasted, no mistake made, and nothing out of alignment with the true intent of your purpose and Golden Evolution, individually and collectively. Everything has happened for a reason—everything.

"Again, I ask that you simply remain present and don't attempt to think ahead. Let the movement unfold without pressure, without pushing, and without the strain of wanting it so much that you press yourself out of it and make this freedom impossible. That kind of push only creates restriction and binding, which is the last thing you need any more of.

"I ask that you return to your instinctive Lemurian way of allowing, of being present, honoring, and allowing still more. This is your true Lemurian Design expressing. If you call this ability up, it will arise effortlessly inside of you.

"Do this for yourselves, please. Do this for all of us.

"Take charge of your patience and sink into it. Bless you."

In response to Terra's words I immediately feel something inside of me changing, altering. I feel a sense of confinement that is foreign to me preparing to leave. I am aware that Terra is telling us there is more work of unraveling to be done, maybe a lot more. And I am good with this.

Knowing that there is a future for me, for us again—which is different than Mondor—enables my heart to relax deep inside. I don't need the details; I will not try and hurry this up. Knowing that there is an end point that includes my full Golden restoration is enough to reassure, encourage, and enable me to stay allowing and present. It helps me to be the picture of patience in each stage of what reveals itself throughout this continuing process.

I am totally focused on Terra and whatever this brings. And, finally, happily so, my focus has optimism all around its edges. It's beautiful and uplifted. I have a renewed vitality for living!

Terra's voice is heard again, *"Let our work begin!"*

Never have I been so happy to roll up my sleeves and dig in.

Exploring the Emergence Shattering Experience

The Golden Witness speaks:

Great shuffling can be heard throughout the Hall as we prepare ourselves for whatever is next. The air is thick with anticipation and absolute focus in the present. Everyone is ready.

I am aware of many Golden Masters with us, along with Terra.

Terra continues:

"Dearest Ones of my heart and Soul, let me take you back. Let me jog your memories and reiterate some things to make the entire picture crystal clear. Let us go back to our beginning.

"Originally, before you even came to me that first time, before Lemuria was built and established, you were offered this wondrous opportunity. You, and many others along with you, were asked if you wanted to come to me to create this beautiful Golden Empire of Lemuria. You eagerly said 'yes,' and as a result, you were given the power of the Gold from our Creator as a gift to utilize and express forth in this project. This Gold would endow you with great powers of Creation, even bolder and brighter than any you had known before. The Golden Energy has profound alchemical properties which, when utilized with positive intent, can create pure magnificence beyond that which you could even imagine. Such was, and is, the power of this great gift.

"Perhaps you remember when you chose to volunteer for this project, our beloved Lemuria.

"Perhaps you recall that we came together to create this civilization of immense love and beauty. We did so to foster and generate more of the same for the benefit of the many universes and Golden Life Forms everywhere— and for the great times and futures ahead, when such gifts of beauty and love would be sorely needed.

"This you did out of love. This you did with love. This you did IN love. This was your loving in action, Golden Loving action.

"Powerful.

"Potent.

"Deep.

"Magnificent.

"Right at the beginning, we carefully and deliberately built our Golden Configuration together in this very place. Upon this energetic platform we made our sacred pledge to our One Golden Heart—that it would become strong and soar; it was our love and devotion made manifest.

"As our One Golden Heart we proceeded to flourish for a long time, creating prolifically and powerfully here, and throughout the cosmos, in ways that exceeded any and all expectations. It went far beyond possibilities previously known.

"All of our experiences of Lemuria wove an indelible and beautiful Imprint, a tapestry of sheer beauty on all levels of life. This is the Imprint of our Lemuria of Origin. It became a living thing which can never be snuffed out, no matter what.

"The Imprint of our entire experience of flourishing is still vibrating and alive.

"Do you understand? Simply because you cannot yet fully connect with it again, does not mean that it is not so.

"Where is it? It is here, right inside of me, where it is still very much alive and well and activated. It is also still on my surface, beneath everything else. There, it lies sleeping. It is not activated, but it is still very much there.

"It was built and established there, and there it will remain, forever: a living memory, an indelible record of our original Lemurian Life together, before the great planetary changes came. It holds that complete story in all its detail and richness. As I have said, it is still there underneath everything else that has played out since then.

"All that has transpired is a like a new layer of patterning, an additional weave, an additional Imprint. But that does not mean the Original Imprint of when we flourished as Lemuria is not still there.

"Do you understand? Can you open your minds to accept this?

"Again, because you cannot connect with it, does not mean this is not so. You are going to reconnect with this flourishing Lemurian Imprint again. You are going to remember this fully when all is ready for you to do so. You have so chosen.

"Take a moment to connect with how this is making you feel inside."

I pull my focus back into myself and look inward. It feels like Terra is deliberately restoring the building of our structure of who we are and where we came from. She is systematically putting the pieces of us, and of our original journey, back together like building blocks, one on top of the other. She is restoring our memory of our foundation and our flourishing back into our conscious psyches. She is restoring our history in this way and bringing it back to life again. I can actually feel it inside my body, as if I am regaining substance and vitality as she speaks.

Terra continues:

"Let us talk about your connection to Source, your remembrance of your true state of Divine Wholeness. This is the base and platform of YOU, of your Life Expression. You will never be able to stand tall again without this firmly in place, no matter what you want and no matter what you do. It is time to reestablish your solid connection with your Source, and to become as Whole as this, again.

"Let me jog your memory and clarify something else for you. Prior to embarking on the Lemurian Project, your Oneness with your Source was solid. Your Sacred Wholeness was already firmly established. If it hadn't been, you wouldn't have been approached to participate in this undertaking.

"You had already developed and matured this Wholeness, and you knew what this meant. You lived, breathed, and created forth from this. You were fully conscious of yourself as Divine Love made manifest, period. It was precisely because of this that you could be gifted with the Gold from our Source. To your base of Wholeness was added the potency of this rare and precious Golden Gift.

"The Golden Energy required this platform of Sacred Wholeness to stand on, and to be supported and stabilized. Your Sacred Wholeness held it steadfast and secure, enabling it to flourish forward and have strong legs of its own.

"Do you understand? Do you remember?

"Throughout your time in Lemuria on my surface, and your subsequent time inside of my body, all of this was brought to even greater levels of strength and ability—until the Emergence back to my surface took place.

"That is when your shattering happened, and your identification of Wholeness was disrupted. That was when you and your fundamental Divine Connection broke.

"Yes, it took place in the instant after you resurfaced, when you were met with the Heartless Ones trying their best to annihilate you. In those moments during that precise experience, within that intense pain and

violent destruction, your Imprint of Wholeness felt like it was shattered—for you and for the entire Golden Family everywhere.

"This has already been discussed at great length. But it comes here, again, because it is imperative that you more clearly understand that this is where and how your original wounding happened. The shattering not only felt like it broke apart our tapestry of Lemuria, but it also felt like it broke apart each one of you. And, in the process it created a tear, which rendered an increasingly vast chasm between you and your Divine.

"Some of you, many of you perhaps, will say that you disagree with me, that you have no breakage between you and your Divine. You may say that your relationship to that which is your Source, however you name it or perceive it, is intact and whole.

"I would like to question that, and to offer you the opportunity to gaze at and assess this again, all things being relative. I would like you to ask yourselves: what are you capable of as a Golden One?

"This tear is the wound. This wound broke the Sacred Connecting Point in your design. This wounding caused a complete collapse in the structure of your Sacred Connection, thereby creating that chasm of separation between you and your True Being, between you and your Divine Source. Once thoroughly solid and strong in this regard, you became wobbly, insecure, and disconnected—and vulnerable to becoming even more so.

"Do you understand?

"I would urge you to give consideration to what I am saying, and to see if the shoe fits.

"Know also, without question, that your travails in Mondor, right from the beginning, have caused you to be interfered with precisely in this disrupted and torn area. Interference has capitalized on your weakness, on your collapse, and has gone right into that torn place, pummeling it and making it stay weakened. For many, there has been even more wounding, thus rendering any weakness even weaker still.

"Let us be clear, again, that Interference has deliberately done everything it could to not only KEEP you weakened and disconnected, but to increase this disconnect and separation from your Divine Wholeness. It has been unrelenting in this, and still is. This has been, and continues to be, its main purpose.

"I know you know all of this already, and I am sure you do not want to *talk about it yet again. But what you don't know is the complete picture of your shattering; the tear and your collapse. We will look at this now. Stay with me, please.*

"Let us go back to when you were originally ascending up to my surface after our sojourn together inside my body. You had been well prepared during our time together. You were strong, you were clear, you were eager, and so hungry to be back out on top. You were keen to call forth your creative resources to build again anew on my surface. You were ready and open, wide open.

"Even though you didn't know what it would look like or what you would find on the surface, you nonetheless couldn't help but expect that it would be exactly the same energetically as it had always been before—LOOKING differently, of course, but BEING the same.

"You had no expectation of anything else. Why would you? No amount of telling you otherwise, or telling you not to have this expectation, would have changed this. Why not? Because the Imprint of how Lemuria had been was indelibly inside of you. It was a given.

"At the instant that you emerged onto my surface you were met with violence, destruction, and brutality. This was the precise instant that you, and the entire exquisitely woven Imprint of our Golden Family, felt like it exploded and shattered—it was in that very millisecond.

"Why? Because you were taken completely and utterly by surprise, and with such intense violence and pain. It came absolutely out of nowhere, with a force that was literally abrupt, sudden, intense, and shocking.

"And, as I said, you were wide open. Why wouldn't you be? That was your Lemurian Design.

"No, you were certainly not expecting what took place, nor were you capable of such a thing. You had never experienced, nor did you even possess the ability to imagine, such a thing. This was completely contrary to you."

At Terra's words, my breath becomes shallow and my hand rises instantly to my heart. It is almost impossible for me to stay focused on her, as my insides begin to tremble. I realize that, yes, there is still more to know, but hearing about it and feeling it again is painful.

After another moment, her voice reaches inside me, somehow bringing me back so that every word becomes crystal clear again. I know she knows what we are going through.

"*What you need to remember fully,*" she continues, "*is that, instantly, at the precise second that you were shocked, your systems recognized that something had gone horribly wrong. Alarm bells went off inside all of you—emergency, CODE RED, 'take action to protect and safeguard,' is what your inner signals were commanding.*

"*And you knew exactly what you needed to do. Your systems went into high gear and, of course, you instantly went into instinctive preservation mode over all that was sacred and dear to you.*

"*But you knew that it was not only about protecting those you loved around you, it was also about protecting your Sacred Golden Gifts and the doorway to them—the Sacred Golden Conduits and the access way to all of that inside of you. Your Sacred Golden Centers within KNEW that the preservation and safeguarding of all of this was imperative: it was an absolute number one priority.*

"*And so, you shut off and closed down inside, like shutting off the breakers on a circuit box panel.*

"*You literally slammed closed the doors to your deeper Sacred Goldenness inside, and all aspects connected to that, so that all of it would be protected and safe from the Heartless Ones, no matter what. That was the sheer devotion of your wise Golden Self in action.*

"*And in that instant, I MET YOU.*

"*In that fraction of a second of need, we were in clear and conscious agreement that I would safeguard all of this for you. It was automatic. You gave your Sacred Golden Centers, your Sacred Golden Conduits and all of that Sacred Golden Treasure, to me for safekeeping. I received it and deposited all of it inside of my Golden Heart, and I have been the Guardian of it all ever since. It has remained safe and sound inside of me, inside of my Heart.*

"*I have been devoted to protecting this. I have been devoted to you. We have talked about many parts of this already, but it wasn't time yet to fully examine and grasp the finer details, the power of those moments and their repercussions, and the many instantaneous decisions and choices that were set in motion because of them—until now.*

"*This intensely shattering experience caused its own reverberation, and subsequently its own Imprint. It created a new layer and weave of patterning and sound, and it is alive and vibrating inside of every one of you; it remains vibrating inside every Golden Life Form everywhere.*

"Yes, this Emergence Shattering was the original wound, and this wound is still inside of you; reverberating, alive, and active. It is precisely this wounding, and the pattern of its Imprint, that needs repairing. THIS is what needs attention and complete healing.

"This will alter everything that has happened as a result of it. This is Consciousness shifting, going from sickness to health, Golden Health. Your entire picture of yourself will change accordingly.

"Let us take a few moments of time out.

"Breathe slowly and ask yourselves to soften more inside. I know it is painful to go through all of this again, but it is what is needed in order for healing to be successful. We are in this together. Remember that."

I do as Terra suggests and focus within, breathing deeply. I breathe a deep sigh of relief, feeling grateful that I am not here alone, and that Terra is here to guide us. I trust her with my heart and soul, and that leaves me reassured, no matter what. All is indeed well.

Dear Reader, maybe you even want to take a breather right now too.

Maybe you want to put this book down and go take a walk or get a cup of tea or something. This is pretty intense, I know. It's one thing to go through it once, but to keep rehashing it is definitely challenging, and for good reason—this is not easy stuff. I remind myself that the experience itself is not happening now, that at least it is already over. That helps me to stay open with this exploration. I know it's necessary, and I do my best to welcome it. That seems like a kind and loving thing to do, don't you think? After all, it is a piece of me, a deep part of my story; it is a living, breathing energy that is in great need of my caring. I find I trust it, and I trust myself. I let it be.

After a while, Terra resumes again. Her tone is purposeful and loving and it feels as though she is holding us tenderly in the palm of her hand.

"Yes, I know the shattering experience left you dazed and in shock—still.

"Prior to that moment, you were solid. The next instant you and our entire Golden Family union felt ruptured and broken, like splintered pieces hurled forcefully out into the vast universe, seemingly forever. In many ways, it's as though the shattering of it only just happened, the reverberations of it are still acute and intense inside of you.

"PTSD? You got it. Deep inside of you those feelings of being broken, wounded, and collapsed still remain. They generate a constant sense of agitation.

They give rise to the FEAR THAT YOU ARE NEVER SAFE.

"And, because of this, you continue to be vulnerable to unrelenting Interference which finds its way into these areas that have been weakened, that feel torn, stripped, sore, and fragile—that seem unsafe. You believe you are simply not safe. This shows how disconnected you are from your Wholeness. When you are fully in your Wholeness, safety becomes a non-issue. It's not whether you are or are not safe. It simply doesn't even enter into the equation of your Consciousness. Life is what Life is. That is that. You meet it and do your best.

"The tear, your wounding, is still in place. The disconnect is still there, and yet there is good reason to fully appreciate this. Why? Well, the fact is that you needed to be small in order to traverse Mondor and not be recognized by the H-O.

"Hasn't this woundedness, and everything about it, kept you small and in a state of contraction? In that way, hasn't this also served your greater purpose? Yes, of course it has.

"I urge you to find it within yourselves to honor this. Let it be that which it is with all of its complexities, all of its faces, and all of its feelings. Yield to this. Honor and Witness this."

I know Terra's right. None of this feels good, but I do like that there is some kind of a silver lining about my admittedly weakened, suffering state. Nonetheless, I don't like feeling like I'm still stuck in it. I don't like this at all. How will I ever climb out of this pit, this collapse inside of myself?

"I hear your questions," Terra says in my ear. *"And my answer to you is this: by witnessing your woundedness and weakness even more deeply, by going inside of it, listening to it, and giving it what it needs to repair and restore its balance and support again. You go into it fully and meet it graciously on its terms. It will then have a chance to heal and repair itself, regain its strength, and bring you back your Wholeness. This is how you will regain your Wholeness.*

"Your insides will bring it back to you. You've been whole before and you can be whole again. It's there, it's within you. You already know it. In truth, you already ARE it."

"Okay," I say to myself. "I hear you, Terra, and I certainly hope that, somewhere inside of me, all of this is true. But why don't I FEEL it? Why does it still feel impossible to me, like this weakness and woundedness are simply never going to change?"

"I hear your questions, Dearest One. And, again, I say: trust this, trust this process. It's time to dig deeper still. It's time for you to find out these answers for yourselves.

"Shortly, you will re-experience for a few moments that which shattered you. Why? Not to make you uncomfortable, but so you can crawl INSIDE of it and see the decisions and choices that were made in that instant; so that you can be inside the wounding as it happens and understand what the wound truly is. You can open it up and read it like a book, in its totality. That's the ONLY way you will know what truly happened in that instant. And that is therefore and thereby, the only way you can make repair now.

"Please don't be daunted by this or shrink from it in any way, on any level of you. Remember, the actual event itself is already over. This exploration is but for a few moments of conscious, clear insight and understanding.

"In the interest of your proper repair and healing, please be present with this and be thorough. All aspects of this shattering need your attention. All of its nooks and crannies need the light of your caring and your crystal-clear understanding. They all need Witnessing. This is your clear loving in action. This is your healing.

"Are we one on this? Are you with me? Are you willing?"

I feel Terra's invitation and I know it is a reflection of my own to myself. Am I willing to do this for me?

Okay, I'm in. Game on.

I take a deep breath and relax. Bracing myself won't get this job done. I know that I must be open and receptive. I must be fully open and aware in order to witness myself successfully.

Suddenly, out of the blue...it comes. The Shattering happens.

Instantly, I am doubled over in agony. I hear screams piercing the air. There is violence everywhere. I feel like my heart is being crushed, as if something deeply precious inside of me is being smashed and broken into smithereens. I hear an agonizing scream. It is mine. I don't know which pain is the worst, the outer or the inner. It's so much pain, on many different levels of me, and for all of us.

It's the splitting pain of our totality, the breakage in our family Whole. One moment we were Golden Whole, and in the next instant we are broken.

I am broken. We are broken.

Things slow down dramatically and the whole theatre being played out opens up like a tight ball of twine being pulled apart, separated strand by strand, so that it can be felt from the inside. It's happening in slow motion.

I hear Terra saying to us:

"Look at it and feel it. Grasp it, Dear Ones. Let it inform you. You know it is in the past, and yet it still remains alive and active, as if it is happening in this very moment. This tells you how much it has been affecting you, and everyone, ever since that very first instant: it still breathes and has a life of its own.

"Understand this. Understand it with your presence right here, right now. Give it the room and space it needs to show itself to you."

I hear another crack, and watch as I witness the actual tear itself happening. It's happening inside of me, and it's happening to all of us as a whole.

It's intense. It's agony. Again, I am screaming. I am inside that sound, inside that moment...everything abruptly stops. It stands still—as if the theatre of it has been put on pause.

A window inside my psyche opens up and something else, besides my pain, rises up urgently: it's my Golden Wisdom. I recognize my wisdom making a decision.

I recognize my KNOWING that, right this instant, I need to find a safe place for my inner Golden Treasure; that this sacredness which is dear to me must not be discovered, must not be put at risk, in any way or on any level, period. It must be protected at all costs.

I am not frantic about it. On the contrary, I am perfectly steady and aware. I know that this is what needs to be done. It's an absolute.

I turn purposefully to seek refuge for it, and suddenly, Terra is right in front of me. She is right in my face. Her arms are wide open. Her heart is wide open.

"Give it all to me, Dear One," she says. *"I am here for you, and for this. It will be safe with me. Give it all to me now. I will take it and protect and safeguard it for you with my life. I promise. This is my sacred vow."*

And in that instant, I know. I know that this is where it will be safe. Yes. I yield myself to her; I allow that which is so deeply and powerfully sacred inside of me to break away from me because I love it SO MUCH. I not only allow it, I insist upon it. It is my clear, conscious, deliberate choice.

It is a choice I make from my deepest wisdom out of love and understanding that this place of heartlessness, this consciousness wherein I find myself, cannot and will not support or uphold something so precious. It would destroy it, one way or another. I cannot allow this to happen, and I won't. None of us can and none of us will. It is far too precious; we know this.

And, we know what to do. In one instant, as one united decision and motion, we do it. We give all our Sacred Golden Treasure, and everything related to it, to TERRA.

Once done, it is done. That is that.

In the next instant, the movie theatre of the shattering experience opens again and returns to normal speed. The experience plays out and the agony continues, but that which we have been devoted to is taken care of and kept safe. Like a mother with her children, they are safely tucked away and protected while she has to carry on and face and endure. But at least she knows THEY ARE SAFE NO MATTER WHAT. They are safe.

So it is with us. Our Gold is now safe. Our Golden Selves are now safe. Our One Golden Heart is now safe, and it has remained safe all this time inside the Golden Heart of Terra.

As my recognition of this sinks in, as this "penny" drops into place fully, my whole system goes into noodle mode. I become limp with relief and a humongous weight begins lifting from my heart. The intense pain that has been enshrouding it begins to dissipate, and the light of day starts to dawn for me.

Yes, I see through both my new understanding and my eyes that this has been the greatest wound of all for me: being disconnected from myself.

Yes, the shattering experience broke me apart, no question. But my deliberate choice to put away my Golden Sacredness for safekeeping kept me unable to repair myself, and unable to find my way back to my platform of my Source inherent in that. Seeing this clearly has brought an entirely new element into the picture of my understanding. I know it was the right and only thing to do, and I would do it again if I had to.

But it left me abandoned by my true strength; absent from my deepest and most powerful resources, and disconnected from my true power. It left me without this vast resource from which to draw, and with my Sacred Golden Conduits unavailable. It left me without my deepest Golden Self or Wholeness intact. Yes, indeed, it left me broken and weakened greatly.

Yes, I still had enough Golden ME to function and draw from, but not the wealth that I truly am, not by any means.

But it was a choice point; I knew I needed to protect the Gold, this powerful gift that we had been gifted with by our Source. We needed to protect our deeper Golden Selves until such time as we could reunite with them safely again.

We needed to protect our Sacred Golden Conduits from ever being discovered by the H-O. We needed to keep all of our Sacred Golden Treasure, and everything connected with it, hidden from their sight and sensors.

But what I realize, is that in making that choice to save that which I love deeply, I inadvertently hurt myself in these ways. I gave my power away, and caused myself to only limp along thereafter. That was the trade off and I chose to make it. We all did.

I not only disconnected from my sacred Golden depths and Treasure, but also from my Divine Source upon which it stood. It happened in the same moment, because it had all become contained in, and part of, the same package.

Would I make that same choice again under similar circumstances? Yes, of course I would. Yes, of course, we all would. I see the choice was for the greater good, and that rules, first and foremost. Yes, I acknowledge this.

But I am also recognizing the other side of it: the price and the repercussions of that choice and sacrifice—and then there's the wound: it is wide open and waiting for what's next. Now what?

"This is where we will stop for now, Beloveds," Terra says ever so gently.

I am surprised; this doesn't seem like a great place to stop. What? My insides are wide open and strewn all over the place!

But as I look closer, I see that the cells of my insides are actually beginning to shine softly, to glow. It does look like some kind of newness is being born, "Humph," I say to myself. "Interesting, okay."

I turn my attention back to Terra. She knows best. I know that.

"This is the first layer of the sequence of healing and repair of which I spoke earlier. Yes, your state of woundedness is wide open and, because of this, has been successfully prepared for what will transpire next.

"We need to let this be, and go into the next layer of the sequence and undertake a similar investigation.

"As I mentioned earlier, when each of these layers have been fully attended to, we will be going into the final repair of all of them. That is when you will find yourself anchored solidly back into your Source again. Then, your Divine Wholeness will indeed be restored, I guarantee.

"But not yet, first things first.

"Let's move on to address the next layer: The Mantle of Fear."

Exploring the Mantle of Fear

Terra's voice can be heard loud and clear.

"Ah, the Mantle of Fear, your old and dear friend, your costume for Mondor—that which enabled all of you to accomplish the Rescues success-fully, that which enabled you to reconnect with all the lost Golden Ones so that now they can find their way home.

"As enshrouding and veiling as it was, as painful as it was to be in, it was the ideal, and ONLY, camouflage. It was THE instrument through which you could locate and Rescue our Golden Family."

I recall White Eagle saying something about honoring this, and I recognize that this is exactly the attitude that Terra is having about it as well.

It becomes obvious to me that it is much easier to honor than it is to judge. I realize I've been holding this Mantle tightly in my psyche as something which only caused me pain and distress. Why haven't I also been as acutely aware of the gift it gave me? I couldn't have done any Rescues without it. Does my true Lemurian self judge it, or does it know its value?

Yes, it knows its necessity and its value, and is potently grateful for it. I feel that gratitude flooding through me.

I can also feel that my world is changing, as if everything is shifting on its axis toward a new balance of comprehension and blessing. Simply put, my Consciousness is changing, and I know it, just like Terra said it would.

Terra's beautiful voice enters my thoughts and gently brings me back to what she is saying:

"Do you remember the first time you ever put the Mantle of Fear on?

"Do you remember feeling that sensation that you would never be the same again? There was nothing 'good or bad' about that. It was simply an observation at the time. Do you remember that?"

I ponder for a moment. It seems so long ago, but yes, I remember. It was definitely a sensation.

At that moment, I had no idea what I was doing, what I was in for, and what would happen as I wore the Mantle. I remember KNOWING that, once I donned it, there was no turning back. I could only go forward into the complete unknown. It was like jumping off a cliff.

My vow to Rescue was first and foremost, and I would do whatever it took, including jumping off this cliff into the vast canyon.

In looking back at that very first time, it's obvious to me that yes, indeed, I have not been the same since. I am radically different than I was before that first time I donned the Mantle of Fear.

Silence, there is silence in my head. All is still in me. I take a deep breath and blow it out slowly. I simply had not realized how different that choice and that moment made me. It made me hugely different—and I mean, HUGELY.

It's so enormous that it's actually taking my breath away. I feel a little stunned as I realize that the thing that has been so elusive all along has finally been found and unveiled. The Mantle of Fear itself is that elusive thing. Now I am unveiling the actual veiling itself—that's interesting.

My Consciousness is shifting again as it's in the process of this unveiling. I can feel it, it is moving. Something is disengaging from me. Layers upon layers of veiling, enshrouding Interference perhaps?

It becomes obvious to me that Interference is encased in, and ONLY in, the Mantle of Fear. Once the Mantle is shed, there is NO Interference—NONE! I see that so clearly. It's as if I have been at a masquerade ball wearing a pair of virtual reality head sets.

Inside the Mantle of Fear there are many, many layers of enshrouding, of veiling. It is texturized and thickly woven, like a super-duper heavy, chunky winter sweater that is knit so tightly that it's almost watertight. There are tiny little gaps in the thing; tiny little holes where the light still gets in and through, but they are TEENY TINY!

Yes, this Mantle is tightly woven, and it holds ALL the controlling influences of the H-O inside of it—layers upon layers of all of it. But without this Mantle, NONE OF THIS EXISTS! It is all being held inside the Mantle, as if the Mantle of Fear is holding the entire world of Mondor inside of itself.

I get it. That's the Consciousness. Once the Mantle of Fear is shed, that Consciousness and everything contained in it, is no more.

No, we Golden Lemurians do not need the Mantle anymore. Why not?

Because the RESCUE MISSIONS ARE DONE, and we have no need to go back into Mondor ever again. We have no need to wear that Consciousness ever again.

We get to shed all of that and be ourselves again. And without the Mantle of Fear, who are we exactly? Who am I exactly? What is that like, exactly?

Terra says:

"I hear your thoughts, Beloved. I hear your questions and I know you are wondering how this 'shedding' is going to happen.

"The truth is that you have gotten so used to wearing this 'shroud' that you don't know or comprehend who you would be without it. You have each adapted and aligned yourselves with it so thoroughly that it has simply woven itself right into your identity. It IS you now, in a sense. It is how you view and identify yourselves. It is how you control your lives and everything in them. You project from this Mantle, you expect from this Mantle, you believe you are MADE of this Mantle.

"But you are not. You are not made of this Mantle. You are made only of love, and Golden Love at that.

"Who would you be without this Mantle of Fear? That is up to you to find out. This is the hinge upon which everything else will follow. The key back to your Golden Self is your free will.

"By choosing to let go of the Mantle and retrieve your Gold you will anchor down deeply inside your Golden Being. Without making that choice and that FULL commitment, you will not. It is that simple.

"The choice is yours, entirely. It is yours, alone: FREE WILL—what do you choose?

"The Mantle of Fear? Or freedom from the Mantle of Fear and everything contained in it, everything that goes with it and all the ways it has adversely affected you?

"This is not to say that you have not learned valuable lessons and grown immensely because of the Mantle. This will be discussed shortly. But first and foremost, is addressing your decision about whether or not you even want to shed the Mantle? Perhaps having it on gives you a sense of control, a sense of identity and aliveness, albeit it through the window of pain. It is familiar, after all.

"Perhaps you want to keep fitting in with everyone else. Perhaps you have built a life around and upon it, and you are not willing to let that go to find out who and what your life would be without it. I understand these dilemmas you are possibly engaged in. I understand them well.

"Yes, it takes guts to let go of this Mantle. It takes tremendous courage and faith precisely because it is a leap of faith—one hundred percent so. Donning the Mantle was a leap of faith long ago, and taking it off is a leap of faith now.

"It takes supreme self-worth and self-honoring to do this. In a word, it takes deep self-love. Why? Because it is a leap back into love, pure Golden love—plain, profound, and simple.

"It is the very thing that you have been clamoring for, for so long, and which you have believed would 'just happen,' and would ask nothing of you. So many of you have been convinced that you would be the recipient of this profound and dramatic alteration in your awareness and consciousness.

"This will not happen this way. Why not? Because, as in all of life, it is the journey THROUGH that will get you there and keep you there. What good is a shift like this if you can't sustain it and build a whole new world precisely because of it?

"What good is having your consciousness 'upgraded' for a split second, a minute, an hour, a day? What good is it if you don't know how you got from A to Z, and therefore can't help yourself stay there, much less help anyone else to get there and stay there too?

"Yes, it gives you a glimpse of what is possible in you and for you. Yes, there is actually value in that. But without 'legs' to walk and without a foundation to build from, what good will it actually be in terms of the greater possibility and the greater substance and manifestation of it here in the physical domain?

"As I said, taking this particular leap of faith is actually you taking the 'leap of love,' isn't it? And isn't LOVE what this is all about? Isn't your HEART what this is all about? Isn't the heart of all life what this is all about? Golden Love and Golden Heart.

"You can stay contained in, and by, the Mantle of Fear if you want. But I can tell you that without wearing it for a specific reason and purpose such as the Rescues, it will end up being ruinous to you.

"Why? Because you have no reason and no greater purpose for wearing it anymore. Because your power of your true Being is already being activated. If this power has no place to go and no avenue for complete and full expression in a free way, it will cause you enormous and unrelenting pain of a different kind than what you have known. This would be the pain of unexpressed power and unexpressed love. It would be the pain of repression of an entire system of glory and shining.

"Can you imagine how that would make you feel? Can you imagine that kind of internal pressure on your system? Something so huge trying to burst forth that can't because it is being blocked by your free will trying to override it at every turn? It will spiral around on itself. It will be whirling intensely in place inside of you with no way out and nowhere to go, doors slammed and locked shut.

"This would create intense internal conflict to varying degrees depending upon how awake you are. This inner conflict between you and your Greater Self would give rise to great internal commotion and upset. Plus, it takes enormous amounts of energy to hold something like this back, to suppress it. It's flat out exhausting.

"Yes, you have already made the choice for freedom, but your free will stands guard at the gate. You can thwart your choice if you want. You can

deny your choice if you want. You can convince yourselves that you are in charge and that your Soul will obey you, if you want.

"But the Truth, my friends, is this: whose dream are you really here to live? The dream of your Will or the Dream of your Soul?

"Are you here to remain your Small Self or are you here to truly be, and live, your BIGGER Self, your Golden Self? That 'something else,' that 'something special' that you have always known was inside of you, that you have always felt was there?

"You can refuse to shed the Mantle. Your Free Will can decide you're not having any of this. Maybe you'll get to it another time, in another lifetime. Maybe Lemuria will be restored at some point in the future. That is, IF I am still here...

"Yes, my friends, healing and freedom are what you have already chosen. You chose that back during the Sacred Fire Circle when your healing path began. Remember? It's not a question of IF, it's only a question of WHEN.

"But you don't have to have it now. You can refuse to shed the Mantle of Fear. That is entirely up to you.

"What will it ask of you, exactly? Well, that's the leap, isn't it? That's the leap right back into LOVE, Golden Love.

"That's a power to behold. I wouldn't want to be trying to hold back that force of beauty if it was me. But, like I said, it's your call."

EXPLORING RECEIVING BACK OUR GOLD

Terra's energy is still strong and clear, and she hasn't yet given us a break to even ponder her many questions and input. Personally, I would like some time out, but I'm sure she has a reason for charging forward the way she is. I am aware of intense motion inside of me, especially great stirring inside my head. Maybe things are moving on their own and don't need my reflection right now.

Terra's questions continue, without skipping a beat:

"And how, exactly, do you feel about fully receiving back the gift of your Gold anyway? Let's talk about it some more.

"Are you willing to do whatever it takes to have that restored in you, AS YOU? Truly, are you? Let's explore that now."

Terra is not being easy on us, and I know why: it's because the doorway is here, now. It's not off in the vague future somewhere. It's not a fantasy or an illusion.

It's REAL, right here, right now—and she is pressing us up against the wall of our Beings, making us look at what is getting in the way of us making that leap of love which will bring back our Greater Golden Selves.

We have been told that this is our Destiny, that this is destined to happen in the physical world again upon Terra. We have been told that each one of us, and our Lemurian Family as a whole, will only truly heal and be restored again by doing the repair and remembrance here in this physical domain where Lemuria was born and built.

So, here we are, in this physical domain, and the window is wide open, the doorway is wide open, the way is free and clear. Are we going to take it? Am I going to do it? Are we going to set ourselves free now? If not now, when?

We need each other to be free, that's the other thing, isn't it? Restoring our Golden World is up to each one of us. It's up to enough of us saying "yes" and actually doing it, that will enable us to have a strong platform for MANY to have, to be, and to restore our full Golden World.

Yes, I can be a Golden world of my own, but wouldn't it be much better to be a world of many Golden Ones restored?

Don't we want and need each other for support? For building as a Team? For manifesting this sacred Golden Treasure in its full breadth and depth once again? Haven't we all felt so desperately alone all this time, wanting and needing the comfort and remembrance of all of us as one celebrated unit?

Golden Lemuria was, and is, a family affair. It is a whole tapestry woven tightly and lovingly together, strand by beautiful strand. It's not a solo journey, is it? It never was. It was never intended nor designed to be. Nor was it birthed and brought forth as such. Rather, it was a glorious multidimensional and inter-dimensional family experience.

Isn't that our destiny? To be this again, and not isolated Golden Ones here and there, but to be a whole One Golden Heart with many standing sovereign together and breathing as One? That's right—One Golden Heart.

My thoughts continue to stream forward until I hear Terra's voice clearly in my ear:

"Yes, Beloveds, this is OUR destiny together and I am here for you. You are here for yourselves, for each other, and for me. We are ALL in this together. We are One Golden Family, One Golden Heart.

"In the past you have felt Fear about being free, about shining outwardly and sharing your love openly without restraint. You have felt all of this to be unsafe. You have known it was not wise to do so and because of this your "NO" was firmly in place—immoveable and absolute, and wisely so.

"But that whole construct belongs with the Mantle of Fear, and when that is

shed the issue of safety and everything that goes along with it will no longer exist, no matter what. That perception, the framework of it all, will no longer be controlling you and running the show. That will no longer be the patterning you will be living in and perceiving everything through, not anymore.

"Many of you have spent much time trying your best to resist, outrun, and fight Interference and the obstructing, divisive influences of the Heartless Ones—the heartbreaking and seemingly unconscionable injustice of it all. You have felt fury and outrage over the unrelenting heartlessness you witness all around you, and you have felt your own rage over your feelings of powerlessness to do anything about it. You have felt small, like your Being was not enough to make a difference or to change anything in any real, lasting way. You have felt controlled and dominated by forces and powers seemingly greater than yourselves.

"You have been alternating between sinking and treading the waters of Interference which has been constantly thwarting you and making your lives difficult, inside and out. You have thought and believed that any reasons for your lives not working successfully, or for you feeling a lack of harmony inside of yourselves was only your own 'issues' that have been getting in the way. This has actually NOT been the case at all. Not that many of you don't have things in yourselves you wouldn't like to improve upon, places inside of you that you want to strengthen, develop, and even transform, but the Interference sensation of all of it has been only and exactly that—Interference at work.

"We have talked about this at length already, I know. And right here, right now, it needs to be spoken of again. Interference will continue to thwart you in whatever way it possibly can. It will stop at nothing and it will never stop. Why not? Because that is its JOB!

"If there is one single point that I hope you truly grasp, it is this: you live and swim in the land of Interference. You are being interfered with all the time. You think it's you, or yours, and, yet, NONE of it is. As we have said, it does its job exceedingly well.

"My point is this: do not expect that to change. Don't expect there to be any difference in such a patterning of life in Mondor. No, absolutely not.

"It's time for you to decide if you want to keep staying in that game, or if you want to get off the court. Once you've gotten fully off that court, out of that Fear based patterning, you will experience a rising up inside of YOUR truest nature. Your true patterning will reassert itself and you will be left *standing alone, outside of and separate from Mondor.*

"You will be a different person, with different perceptions and perspectives both about yourselves, about others, and about Life in general. You will realize that you are no longer part of the maddening crowd, part of the sufferers, part of the victims, or part of the 'vulnerables.' That won't be your position, it won't be your vantage point anymore. Instead, you will stand strong as the true Golden Creator that you are, with all the understanding of what it means; of what it can bring forth.

"You will feel, see, hear, and sense differently. You will behave differently, and you will respond differently—all of it from the vantage point and patterning of your enormous and profoundly loving, wise, joyful Golden Self.

"You will realize that you are, indeed, standing out and that, initially, you are standing alone as an island unto yourself. But soon, you will see there are other beloved Ones who are joining you there…until such moment as you are many, many Golden Ones shining, all standing steady together—sovereign, strong, supported, loving, Beloved.

"It will be a different world for you. You will be a different 'you.' Once Golden restored, your world, inside and out, will look, feel, and BE Golden throughout. You can expect this. To say this is a dramatic and radical change for you is an understatement: it is a massive change. This is how enormous and positively power-filled YOU ARE.

"I know it is impossible to fathom exactly how this will feel. It is literally impossible. You have not yet taken the steps necessary to have this regained in your fiber and body of Being. You cannot even imagine really what this will actually be like.

"I'm asking you to listen and to keep an open mind. It's important for me to say my piece, and for you to let it resonate where and how it will touch inside of you. You see, I already KNOW these things; I am here to tell you these things because, again, I am jogging your individual Golden memory patterns and the collective Golden memory pattern at large. Again, this is our Destiny and I am here to open that pathway up again.

"You may not be able to truly fathom the reality of being this right now, as it is such a change from a 'smaller identity' to a 'Bigger Identity.' I know that, nonetheless, you feel the yearning and the intense NEED and DESIRE for this fullness and well-being to be restored.

"Deep down, you KNOW who you are. Deep down is where this is going to rise up from, if you consent.

"Here again, my dear friends, FREE WILL determines the way. As we spoke of earlier, shedding the Mantle of Fear is done by consent of your Free Will. And once the shedding is complete, the next step of receiving back your Gold is also done by consent of your Free Will.

"Think about it—you decide. Are you willing?"

WELCOMING OUR PERSONAL GOLDEN TEAMS

The Golden Witness speaks:

I feel jostled and overwhelmed. Terra has been pressing me up against myself in ways that I hadn't anticipated and have not had any time or space to catch up with. Perhaps that is a good thing—it feels like it is blowing my mind, and I know that's precisely what it's supposed to do. What is there, really, to catch up with?

Nothing, it's about LETTING GO. Alright...I surrender.

Terra speaks with a new lightness in her voice:

"Beloveds, I know you have found this to be somewhat uncomfortable, as I have been presenting you with the facts of how you have been holding yourselves in ways that you were not fully aware of. That's what happens when something is so familiar—it can sound foreign to hear that this wasn't really you at all. The mind has to translate what it's being told and try and make sense of something, which, on the one hand seems like nonsense, but on the other feels utterly true.

"What does the mind do in that situation? It waffles back and forth, because it is struggling to make sense and survive, trying to hold onto that which feels the most familiar. But in this case, which one is it that is the most familiar? That is its quandary. And that's precisely why I didn't give you space and time to ponder it. All you would have found yourself doing, if I had, would be pacing back and forth, confused about what's what, and vacillating on the fence.

"By keeping your 'train moving,' you were able to flow through it. And here you are at the end of it, still not firmly clear, but nonetheless considerably more connected with that which is true to you, instead of that which you had adopted as you.

"The Mantle of Fear still remains in place because we have not yet begun the actual shedding procedure, and you still need even more clarity about

your Free Will in this regard. Of course, the process of exploring it still continues.

"In order to help you along in your freedom journey, and support that which you wish to truly support in yourselves, we are going to bring in personal Golden Teams for each one of you. These Teams are different than your Golden Healing Teams. Although some of the members may be the same, the intention is different, and they will explain themselves to you so that you can understand the distinction.

"Of course, this is a personal decision on your part as to whether or not you wish to receive them. Keep in mind, they are here on your behalf. If this is your choice, I urge you to open your hearts and welcome them in."

I feel my heart expanding like a flower in the morning sun. I have felt Golden Presences around my being, off and on, for some time now, and have secretly hoped that this was a sign of loving support and help just for me. I know I already have my Golden Healing Team that is with me always, and I have begun to understand and establish their place in my life. This, as far as I'm concerned, is an extra boon—like icing on top of the cake! I am extremely grateful and yield to them even more.

I am enveloped in a warm, rich Golden Glow. It starts to spread throughout my entire system, but I feel its warmth, especially in my heart and down my backbone. It is soothing, comforting, and inspiring, all at the same time. It makes me feel relaxed, peaceful, and quiet.

I know my Golden Team has arrived and that this is how they are making their presence clearly known. It is not only an emotional feeling, but an actual physical sensation too. I appreciate that. It makes it feel all the more tangible and real.

Gradually, their energies start to swirl around me, and I am aware that there are three distinct "presences" here with me. They feel strong and beautiful, and I register them as old and dear friends of mine, Golden Ones that I have known and that have known me, truly forever.

They are Teachers, Masters, Angels, Guides, and Guardians—but, above all, they are my friends. They are my truest, deepest, oldest, and dearest Golden Friends of my Golden Heart. And my response to them is to absolutely BLOOM in their presence. I cannot even help it. Everything about me is sparkling and energized and creative. I am small no more.

"What is this transformation that is happening in me?" I wonder. "It matters not," I answer to myself. All that matters is that it makes me feel great; it is so right, and I am truly happy to feel them here with me.

"Dear, dear Friend," one of them finally speaks with much love in her

voice. *"We have longed for this moment, for this window in time that would be perfectly aligned for our reunion and restoration together from this moment forward. There has been much ground covered and much experience gained throughout the long journey from inside Terra way back when. Here we are to tell the tale and come back into each other's hearts consciously once more.*

"Yes, we are members of your Sacred Golden Team. There are three of us here, but there will be others who come in from time to time in the days ahead, depending on your needs and the circumstances involved.

"Your Golden Healing Team that you are already familiar with is with you to address your health needs on all levels, whereas we are here to encompass the broader spectrum of you and your life. We each have our place and position, and you will see how this works together as time goes on. For now, it is only important that we take the time and space to reunite and begin fostering what will be a wonderful and fruitful relationship.

"We love you deeply and dearly, and we know you are feeling this love. It will always be thus. We are of One Golden Heart, here to support you and help you in rediscovering your Golden Self and living a full Golden Life in whatever way your Soul has planned for you.

"We will never do it FOR you. We will only always help you to do it yourself. That is our intention and our way, but we are thoroughly here for you, just you. And we will stand steady and strong with you for as long as you desire. We are your personal Sacred Golden Team and are overjoyed to be so!

"Yours is a path of Golden Freedom, a path that is filled and virtually overflowing with creativity and wealth of all kinds. On this path, you will experience yourself sometimes as a newborn baby: young, innocent, and wide-eyed. At other times you will feel firmly ensconced in yourself as a Golden Master: strong, mature, and well wizened. Both are equally important aspects of you; one growing back into the other until it reaches full maturity, and the two blending into one gorgeous, grace-filled Golden Presence.

"You are a Golden Soul in a Golden Body, and your physical expression is your Soul pouring itself forth with passion and joy-filled purpose. We are here to help you remember this and make this fully come alive again. We will help you in whatever ways are needed, in this regard, throughout your daily life. We will be there with you in your daily comings and goings, and throughout all that transpires from now on, both inside and out.

"No aspect of your life is too mundane for us to be a part of. Our purpose with you is one of totality, and that means we are available to help on all levels and in all aspects: big or small, significant or seemingly inconsequential. Much of our relationship is also about your remembrance of how multidimensional you truly are. Our bond together is going to foster your opening back up to this reality of you, and help you in remembering that you are an essential and beloved part of a greater whole—a huge, beautiful Golden Family that is awake, inspired, and ready to restore and thrive.

"Golden Life is on every level of awareness, not just one. Our Golden tapestry spreads far and wide so that when you finally come to fully remember its magnitude your jaw will drop! Our Golden embrace is huge! But all in good time...

"You know that we are always available to you, and sometimes you will even sense our presence standing right next to you, showering you gently with our love and support. We will talk together. We will walk together when you want. We will listen to you and you will know that we hear you. Ours is a deep, sacred connection, and as your Golden Eyes and senses return, our communion will become more and more clear and sustaining for you.

"We urge you to be patient in this recognition and knowing, and we encourage you to please call upon us often whether you clearly feel us or not. Know we are there and that we hear you no matter what. This is not a fanciful dream. Our connection and communion are real and solid, and over time you will remember.

"What are you feeling right now, dear Friend? What are you aware of? Tell us, please."

I have been listening to the sensation of them so intently that it takes me a moment to actually stop and think. I am well aware of how comfortable I continue to feel with them, as if I am simply sinking into a soft and gentle place of complete safety. I don't know why that word "safety" keeps arising for me, but it does. It makes me realize how unsafe I have felt for a long time. It's as though my entire system is enormously relieved to let down in this deep kind of a way. I have ached and longed for it. There's no denying that. It's been a long, long time, and I am aware, yet again, of how tired and spent I have been feeling for what seems like forever.

I realize also how sore I have been in my efforts to be so vigilant and constantly "on guard," a state of gripping heightened awareness that I know was necessary for survival in Mondor. The penny drops that I don't need to be that way anymore.

Do you mean that I can really honestly and truly RELAX?

"Yes, dear Friend, yes indeed," I hear one of my Team say back to me. I hadn't even thought I had asked the question, but I am aware that this was proof that they heard me in my conversation. That is how close they are, and I like that. I am glad.

"Yes, your system needs to remember how to relax, how to let down, how to let go, and how to let BE. This will happen more and more as you reawaken to your self-trust, your Golden Trust of your Golden Self. All of this will evolve naturally. You will see.

"This is a conversation that will be continued along with many others of its kind. There is a lovely road ahead for us and our bond will only deepen and become more tangible as everything moves forward. Know this, trust this, trust yourself. All is well, and will only continue to be so. That is a guarantee.

"Our Beloved Friend, know that not only are we your Golden Team, but you are also our treasured Golden Teammate. You are the one in the physical. Through your physicality, we will also gain greatly. Together we make a great Team, a great family of Golden Love.

"We treasure you. We love you. We are here for you and always will be, for as long as you desire."

I feel their loving and kindness washing through me and making me feel clearer than I have in a long, long time. Much of the grogginess and fog that I have been plagued with for so long seems to be evaporating and my thoughts are focused and peaceful. I become acutely aware that something else is about to happen. It's as though my body and brain know it before I do, and my system is preparing itself for what is next.

"Yes, dear Friend," my Team says. *"You are soon to make the actual transition back into our One Golden Heart. But, before that happens, there is one last preparatory meeting to have with our beloved friend, Master Saint Germain."*

Off we go!

TIME OUT WITH MASTER SAINT GERMAIN
LESSONS LEARNED AND PERCEPTIONS EXPANDED

I feel myself shifting out of Terra and being whisked away to some other energetic place in the stratosphere that I have never been to before. It is a soft cocoon of lavender light that permeates everything, including myself. The scent is tangible and thick, like a blanket of perfume that soothes my senses. I know the energy and I know the fragrance: this is Master Saint Germain's domain. I feel privileged to be invited here, and as I adjust my sight to where I am, I see many of my friends feeling the same way. We nod our heads to one another in appreciation of this beauty that surrounds us, as we recognize that this is a rare moment of honor.

This is a sacred place, one which needs to be revered.

We are gathered together, sitting on a floor of soft velvet cushions, their color so deliciously purple that it just about makes my mouth water. The walls and ceiling are covered in varying materials of different textures that are luxurious and rich to the eye. If time allowed, I would love to go around this room touching everything, absorbing the feel and beauty of it all. There is an atmosphere of elegance that holds within it a quiet respect and honor for all who enter. Again, I feel privileged and grateful to be here.

I see both Avalar and Andar standing on a small platform at the front of the room with their foreheads touching, bowed in the loving communion that is so often their way. I'm thrilled they are with us as well. I have missed seeing them for a while, and it makes me feel whole to have them with us, standing together like this.

After a few moments, as we wait in silence, Master Saint Germain graces the room. I realize I have missed him too, even though I know he has been watching us from a distance as we have been communing inside of Terra.

He speaks, his voice full and tender:

"Welcome, my Beloved Golden Ones, welcome to my hearth and home. I am happy to see you, and happy that this time has come. So much of our time together so far has been intended to see you through difficult and trying times, to prepare you for what's ahead, and to bolster your strength and resilience. You have all done outstandingly well in your travels and challenges throughout many lifetimes since our original Lemuria together. I am proud of who you are, what you have accomplished, how you have accomplished it, and who you have become because of it.

"Soon, you will be taking your last steps toward your recoveries of your Golden Treasure. This body of work that we will be doing will enable you to sail through the final 'eye of the needle,' and land safely back inside your deepest Golden selves once again.

"Standing in front of you and witnessing the steady strength of your radiant

loving hearts is breathtaking. You may not see it for yourselves, but it's obvious to the three of us.

"You have grown enormously. You were beautiful and strong before any of this even started, but now you are even more so. You are deeper, richer, bigger, and broader than you have ever been before. Ironically, this is thanks to your 'tutelage' from your journeys in Mondor, and the devotion that took you there many times.

"All of this is what we are going to explore together.

"Before we begin, however, there are two questions I wish to ask you. It's time to sum up your understanding of your journey since Lemuria of Origin, and to bring it into clear focus and position for release. With this in mind, if you were to summarize your assessment of the Heartless Ones and all that you have learned about them, what would you say?"

I draw inside and look at what I would say in answer to this question. It comes to me simplistically and without any judgmental overtone at this moment. "They are like machines," I hear myself offering. "They have no emotion. They are robotic. They generate only Fear and perpetuate the same."

I know he is addressing all of us, but I find myself only able to hear my own response.

"My second question is this," Master Saint Germain's voice returns. *"If you had to summarize what you know about Interference in this moment, what would you say?"*

Again, I draw inside and listen for my own response. "It is a specific kind and quality of energy that has kept me down and controlled me. It is called Fear. This is what the Heartless Ones have used to dominate us: it is the Mantle I have worn." As I offer forth my response I am aware of feeling relieved. Maybe it's the act of bringing it to a bottom line, but something about it is definitely crystallizing and moving into a new position inside of me. Something about it is lightening up.

"Good," Master Saint Germain continues. *"Now that you have expressed this succinctly, we can move forward and view some of this from yet another perspective.*

"I pose the question to you, what have you learned about yourselves?

"In order to answer this question, we will be closely examining the many lessons learned from Mondor, the strengths you have gained, the muscles you have built, and believe it or not, the many 'gifts' it has given you. There is no doubt, from where I stand, that you have been enormously enriched,

both individually and collectively, by your experiences there in ways that you have not been able to witness before because you were so thoroughly 'in it' in order to get your jobs done. You are in the process of separating from it, inch by inch. You can now appreciate the many complex layers of you which have been developed and matured by it.

"Even though this may be the last thing you expected, we will also be focusing on Interference, yet again. I guarantee this will be the last time. What will make this time entirely different from the previous discussions of it is that, this time, we will be hearing about it from ITS point of view.

"Yes, this may come as a surprise to you. But there is much to be learned from understanding the inside view of what has been your constant companion throughout Mondor, and this understanding will enable you to better navigate the future and all that it will hold.

"You cannot deny that Interference has indeed been a constant traveling companion throughout all of your moments in Mondor. Today will bring you an important body of information that will help you understand some new things both in yourselves, and about that which has walked and talked with you for a long, long time.

"This is a great opportunity to extend gratitude toward yourselves and the consciousness that has gifted you greatly in ways that you may never have imagined. I know you are surprised by what I am saying, but you also know that this has been the case. Experiences are never wasted. They are never insignificant or meaningless. When our time here together is done, you will be standing in appreciation with me. I guarantee it.

"Let's move onward!"

As I listen to Master Saint Germain's words, I have to admit I am intrigued. I never would have thought that Interference even had its own point of view, so lost was I in my survival of it. Listening to it in a truly receptive way has definitely never been my desire. In fact, in regard to that, I have absolutely resisted it. I have never truly, much less graciously, "let it be." Why would I do that? I always needed to be on the alert for it.

In reflecting on this, something in my perception about it is changing even more, and I am aware of my whole system moving in a new way.

Yes, I know that during the Rescues, Interference was always there. I had been taught to manage myself in the face of it. I had been trained to survive it and to make the journeys through it. But I had never dropped my guard in the face of it and turned toward its voice in actual receptivity. I had never relaxed myself and let it be. There was always something in me that wouldn't, couldn't, and was plain determined not to. I believed that in doing so, I would be giving my power away to it and that would have been a disaster.

Surviving Interference was part and parcel of the experience of being in Mondor. I was there to Rescue, so I had to be deep inside of it, and always on guard and prepared so that it would not derail me. Interference didn't want me there, I knew that. Of course it didn't, any more than I would welcome it into my land and country.

But now?

I feel a distance slowly beginning to grow between myself and Interference—and with every inch of separation that is taking place, I find I can breathe more easily and let both of us somehow have our separate spaces. This is brand new for me, and frankly, it seems like a miracle. I am amazed, truly amazed. Any distance between me and Interference is like the best thing in the world.

"I wonder what will happen?" I think to myself. "I would dearly love to be at peace about it."

My thoughts take a turn toward Master Saint Germain as I hear his voice in my ear.

"Beloved," he says to me gently. *"There will be plenty of time for this to reveal itself. First, it is essential to look at what you have learned from your experience with Interference and exactly how your journeys in Mondor have made you stronger, bigger, and better."*

I realize that I've never thought about any of this before. I've never had a chance to because I was always so "in it" and on Rescue mode. It's as clear as day to me now that, yes, I do feel remarkably different than I did before all of those Mondorian travails. How so? I'm about to explore this when I hear Master Saint Germain's voice addressing us as a group:

"I would like you to gather yourselves into small groups and discuss this together. Help each other to identify the strengths you have gained and the lessons you have learned. Ask yourselves these questions, and see what your responses are that come from the various levels of your awareness.

"How have I grown exactly?

"What 'muscles' have I developed?

"What strengths have I gained?

"What lessons have I learned?

"What have been some of the personal 'gifts' of these experiences besides

the rescuing of those I love?

"What do I understand about myself now?

"What do I clearly know about myself now?

"Who and how have I become because of these journeys I made?

"Start with any of these questions and explore them as best you can, knowing with certainty that this is but the beginning of many answers to come. For now, listen to yourselves and each other, and be inspired. You will learn a lot, I guarantee it."

And with that, Master Saint Germain steps back and the energy starts gathering intensely in our direction. Okay, here we go: our focus is on.

I am in a small circle with five of my dearest Golden friends. We are huddled together, looking into each others' eyes and searching deeply. Yes, I see what Master Saint Germain is talking about. There is a depth, an enormous upwelling of fierceness and character that is gazing back at me from new rivers and valleys within those eyes. That depth is bright and bold, it is incredibly strong and strengthening to witness. I didn't understand how truly empowering our task of rescuing has been, over and over again—but I can see it in the eyes of those around me, and feel it as well. It is rising to awareness inside of me and about me. I have grown enormously, and I do feel much stronger.

What lessons have I learned?

Well, let me see. I have learned how incredibly resilient I am, for one thing. I have developed an ability to "roll and rise" that I didn't possess before. I am even more adept at shape shifting: I can adapt myself to just about any environment or frequency, and blend into its background at will.

I have sharpened my vision and acuity, and honed my senses in many ways to new and heightened levels. My inner sight, hearing, feeling, and gut instinct have all improved dramatically. I have become truly adept in these areas, and realize that it has opened me up to the abundant richness of the entire universe of Golden Life.

I also recognize that my instinctive sensitivity has grown in ways that enable me to receive a much broader range of input, including the rise and fall of intensely withheld emotional reactivity—and all its repercussions. Sometimes it can be quite uncomfortable for me, but I have improved dramatically at managing that side of things. Witnessing has enabled that to happen.

I notice that my ears have developed new abilities to detect sounds at levels that were not possible before; I can hear the "something" that is present in what sounds like nothing. I am also aware that my sense of taste and direction has somehow combined, birthing an entirely new sensory ability. I know there is still much more to say about all of this. My sensitivity now knows no bounds.

As I ponder and express these things, I hear what the others from my small group are discovering about themselves in response to the questions posed. I shift my attention to them, welcoming what they have to say. I have a feeling that their voices will reflect my own as well.

"My trust of myself and of my inner and outer senses has deepened immeasurably. In Mondor, I learned to listen to this more carefully than ever before, and to rely completely on my senses. They helped me to know exactly when to make a move, and when not to. I proved to myself over and over again that I was worthy of my own trust and that I knew exactly what was needed—when, what, and how. I am even more confident in this than I ever have been. This has given me a great gift of myself."

"I have learned much about the depths of pain and how fragile and brittle it can make us. I understand that pain can be like a huge and gripping force unto itself that can change many things about who we are, how we are, and how we behave; how we react and respond. Within that fragility, there is also great strength that is brought forth. It doesn't always show up right away, but it is always there."

"I've learned much about witnessing pain and finally bringing myself to being able to honor it simply because it is there. If I cannot change it, at least I feel I can do something in the face of it that is respectful and kind, something that recognizes and listens with love to the experience instead of flailing around feeling useless. If it's going to happen and be there anyway, I want to witness it as valuable instead of flinching and turning away from it. Pain is a deeply altering experience, which from other vantage points can be seen for the exquisite mosaic that it creates. I want to honor its masterpiece, whether inside of me, or someone else. I don't want its power, depth, or beauty to go unrecognized."

"I have learned that kindness has many faces, and enormous power within its gentleness that can move mountains. I love how much kinder I have become because I have been through so much pain myself. I want to reach out with gentleness more than ever before. I want to let others know that I see them and understand. I truly want to touch the heart of the Soul of those I come across."

"I have grown to become a really good Witness. In the past, I did not understand the true power in it, did not realize how much the presence of this awareness and ability changes me and the person I am being present for. Its effects run so deep on both sides, consciously fostering every breath and moment of this incredible creation that is ours, that is us. Witnessing someone is an honor that teaches, enlightens, graces, and humbles. Actually being witnessed by someone empowers and strengthens me, it makes me know I am seen, heard, felt, included, respected, and valued. It is always a win-win for everyone, and flat out makes us stronger and more beautiful in every way. I have grown to feel that it is truly like touching and appreciating Source made exquisitely manifest through all of us—it is yet another way of adoring the sacred."

"The fine art of Teamwork: that's something I have learned much about and become strong in. I love doing something as a Team, thoroughly trusting and relying on each other and knowing that we are solid, that we have each other's backs. I love the sensation of our group purposefulness, of efforts being pooled and our skill sets being interwoven and utilized. I love it. There is simply nothing like it for me. It's my family in action and in skill, all on behalf of greater love."

"I realize how much stronger and better my connections regarding Teamwork have become, especially with the unseen Golden Energies, and the Elementals and other levels of Golden Life that I work closely with. All those connecting pathways and communication lines have become much clearer and stronger. All of these Golden Allies are near and dear to me, and I am eternally grateful at how touched I am by them and what they have done for me, for all of us throughout our journeys in Mondor. I simply would have never known their depth of skill, love, and dedication otherwise. Those were hard days in Mondor, and all levels of Golden Life had shown up to save us and bring us home."

"It's the same for me in regard to my Golden Animal Family. I never knew what they would be capable of in these kinds of challenging circumstances, and I am touched at how supportive they have been and what they have done for us. I trust them now, more than ever, and am moved by how much closer we are and by how much stronger and clearer our connections have become. I feel honored and privileged to be with them in this way. Everything we have experienced together has deepened and cemented our bonds in ways that nothing else would have. I realize this is true for all my relationships; something wonderfully indelible has taken place here."

"And Nature, where would I have been without her? Where would any of us be without her? She is our solace, our comfort, our respite, our haven, our nurturer, our strengthener. The list goes on and on. Without any doubt, our trust in her and our abilities to know and receive her have increased quantumly. We have turned to her fully and relied on her for so much, and she has done nothing but show up and give to us endlessly. My passion for her, and with her, has grown so big that it practically leaves me breathless. Without her, I would not have made it through."

"I have deepened hugely in my understanding of how much I love our Golden Family. I knew it before, of course, but it has been taken to new heights and breadths in every way and on every level of me. I have been amazed at the lengths I have been willing to go through in the name of the Rescues—all without a moment of hesitation. I didn't always know I would be successful in what was being asked of me, but I always knew I would do it to the best of my ability and then some. I never, ever flinched, never even thought of walking away, not one single time. My heart is full to overflowing with unending love for all of you."

"I have become much more skilled at building energetic bridges and being able to hold one end steady while building the bridge as I go—then stabilizing it on the other end and being able to hold it in place so that others can cross it with ease. Talking about it makes me even more aware that this is no small feat! The Rescues gave me a lot of practice and I feel strong in this ability. I know it will serve me well in many ways."

"I appreciate that I am much more skilled at wearing many hats. More to the point, my attention can be focused on more than one level at a time, and I can draw from varying skill sets to meet the different kinds of challenges that I face. When it comes to variety in the demands, I have become flexible even though it is consistently a stretch in one way or another. Juggling many balls in the air at once is a challenge, and can be really tricky and often exhausting. That said, I am fluid, and these muscles are strong now."

"Throughout my experiences in Mondor I have learned that I can always rise to meet any challenge presented. My abilities, in whatever ways are needed, always show up. Furthermore, I know without a doubt that whenever I have a need and reach within, more is always there. ALL that I need is always there. My experiences in the Rescues showed me this, and I am grateful for it."

"My resourcefulness has reached new heights. I am amazed at times how creative I have become—at how I stop at nothing until I find the vantage point that provides me with insight into a solution for whatever the "problem" may be. My sightedness, and my ability to shift my perspective until I find that correct window that shows me the remedy, never ceases to amaze me. It feels electrifying when everything simply clicks and lines up, telling me that the energy of solution and resolve is activated and present. I believe there is a solution to every problem and an answer to every question; otherwise, none of these things would even present themselves. I learned this from the various array of situations in which I found myself in Mondor."

"I am now even better at shape shifting, camouflage, and stealth. I know there are lots of us who have become highly skilled in these areas, and I'm hoping that these fine tuned muscles of mine will serve a purpose that is quite different in nature than what I developed them for in the first place. I don't know how this skill set can be applied in other ways, but I hope to find out. In the meantime, these muscles are well developed and strong."

"I have learned much about staying the course, and here I am, still doing so. I wouldn't have missed one minute of it. I keep putting one foot in front of the other. I keep eyes, ears, and nose open, breathing one breath after another. I keep it moment by moment. Be present and keep walking, as Master Saint Germain always says, 'Onward!'"

"I have grown markedly in my ability to stay Centered, to stand steady and strong in me, as me. Isn't that one of the best gifts of it? Having gone through such dire circumstances, I have been left with something incredibly valuable— trusting me and all that I am, no matter where I am, and no matter what state of energy I am traveling through; knowing who and what I am, and who and what I am not. I have gotten much better at this. The contrast of dramatically different energy streams—my peace, and the chaos and clang of Mondor, all in the same place—has become so clear to me now. Repeated 'practice' in Mondor has enabled this to happen. I also learned that it was essential that I acknowledge and accept that this contrast was there in order to stand steady in it. I am grateful for this gift of my growing steadiness. I know it's something that I can, and will, perfect even more."

"Yes, I have also learned that I can finally walk in two worlds, and not get lost in the shuffle. It's been a tricky thing to learn and I have wobbled a lot, but the repeated Rescue Missions have made me stronger and more capable of straddling worlds, dimensions, and domains of awareness. I never thought I would learn to do this! There's still more skill to learn, but I am well on my way. I own this ability—no one can ever take this away from me, and I know that now. There is simply more to me than meets the eye and I am honoring and loving this more and more every day."

"I have learned that I feel at my best when I am actively focused and engaged in a purpose that demands my creativity, no matter what level. This is what calls up my strength and my sense of confidence and wellness. It simply resides inside of me, and when I'm engaged in a conscious, creative purpose it automatically rises up. I am fully in it and fueled by it. When I'm not engaged in this way, I have learned that my energies tend to swirl around looking for their direction and not having any point. It's like my creative energies feel lost, have no place to go, and don't know what to do about it. I can get confused, lazy, sleepy, and unhappy. I love being creative, and exercising and stretching those specific muscles, whatever the purpose may be, even if it's an uncomfortable one. I am skilled and want to utilize and keep expanding these abilities. Doing the Rescues showed me that. They stretched my creative self in ways I would never have imagined; I am a better person because of it."

"I discovered I am fearless. It turns out that in the face of Fear, I am fearless. When the stakes are high, that's when my fearlessness shows up. When they're not, I tend to forget this and can sometimes lose sight of it in the swamp of things. The bottom line is that I am fearless, that's one of the truths of me."

"Heartless, Heart-full—what a difference; one feels cold, barren and empty, the other warm, touching, and life-giving. Being in the same place with these two is an extraordinary experience and sensation. There is nothing more to say about that because it speaks volumes for itself."

"Honoring everyone's Soul Path, however that looks and whatever twists and turns it takes, that's something that my travels in Mondor, and the Rescues themselves, taught me. It's not for me to judge—good or bad, yes or no. Everyone's growth is their very own and mine is only mine."

"I've witnessed thoroughly that Golden Life can never be taken away. It's there, inside every single Golden One, no matter how dire the life journey has been or will be. It is an eternal Golden flame, and that's the way of it, period."

All of these voices in our group have much to say. It's as though a giant treasure trove has been discovered at the bottom of the sea, and we become aware of things about ourselves that we simply couldn't take note of before. It shifts everything for us.

All that we have gone through is seen through a new light. It is filled with awareness, appreciation, and gratitude for the empowerment we have received because of it. It is radically different from our prior perspective.

I listen, and am moved because I realize, more clearly than ever, that we share so much and have gained enormously. Additionally, in whatever areas we have not developed strongly, we can gain further strength and learning from one another. All of my beautiful friends can share the strength of their muscles with me, and we all benefit because of the bigger and better "us" we have become. All thanks to Mondor.

Finally, on top of these lessons learned, I turn back to my insides, becoming aware of one last thing I long to share: my Heart, my Golden Heart. It has deepened powerfully, and I mean…powerfully. I know I speak for everyone on this.

I realize that it wasn't just my sensors that guided me to where I was going in Mondor, but more accurately, my Golden Heart. My Golden Heart told me everything I needed to know: when, where, and how. It was the voice of my Heart, the response of my Heart, the knowing of my Heart, the clarity of my Heart that led me right to those I was there to Rescue. It enabled me to find them in all of the depths and hidden corners of that crazy maze of Fear. It enabled me to build a bridge to them and communicate and commune with them. My Heart was the one that made these discoveries and reconnections even possible. Listening and loving, that is the art of my heart.

My Golden Heart always kept me in its sacred grasp. It never lost sight of me; it never lost sight of those I love.

My Golden Heart was my guide and sustainer throughout. It is my LOVE.

Yes, the power of my loving and all of its abilities has grown tremendously. I have seen, heard, felt, and experienced both the excruciating pain and pure joy of hard-won reunion like never before.

My Heart has deepened hugely. It has been crafted into new shapes and formations by the depths of pain I have known and witnessed—both my own and others. It has been honed into awareness far beyond my previous experience.

And my compassion?

It is difficult to accurately describe what I have learned when it comes to compassion; it has become a giant of me. I can honestly say that as much as I might wish, on the one hand, that I hadn't known the pain I did—on the other hand I wouldn't trade it for the world because of what it has given me in terms of my compassion. All the pain was the very thing that made it grow into such a beautiful and exquisitely powerful force inside of me.

Oh, yes, I have grown. Oh, yes, I have deepened enormously—I am a much stronger and better person because of it.

I start to cry at this realization. I FEEL it. I FEEL ME and what I have become: such a kinder, steadier, more compassionate and infinitely more grateful person than I ever was before. My tears are mostly because of the enormity of me, but also because I am glad; I am glad that there is this huge gift of it to take home with me. It's not only that I was able to rejoin with my beloved family, but that I have also been able to grow into and become something that is greater than I ever was before. I had no idea I would have ever become capable of this immense depth of love, loving, compassion, caring, and kindness.

Had I not suffered as I had, I would never have BECOME who I am now.

It has carved, honed, and polished me into something deeply beautiful. I have grown tremendously and am grateful that I am alive to know this.

I look around at my dear friends and they are looking at me tenderly with tears in their eyes. They are feeling the same thing in themselves. In the end, it can be distilled down into one thing: Our Devotion. It pours forth from our Golden loving. It's the depth, the presence, and the hugeness of our Devotion that made all of this happen.

My devotion and our devotion is full, rich, and abiding. And throughout everything we've been through, I know that we would do it all over again, if needed. I know I speak for everyone, for all of Golden Life everywhere, when I say that my devotion to our family simply knows no bounds. It makes me cry, again, at how devoted I feel; it makes my bones weep with meaning.

Love is indeed an incredibly powerful thing.

The "Voice" of Interference

The Golden Witness speaks:

We have been sitting quietly together for some time before Master Saint Germain speaks again. I can see Andar and Avalar conferring with him up front for a moment before they each go to stand at opposite sides of the room, flanking and facing us with their hearts shining powerfully upon all who are present. Their love is palpable and their support as enduring as it has been since the beginning of our lives together.

I become aware of my recently welcomed Golden Team as I feel their enveloping protection placing itself around me like a soft blanket. It feels warm, cozy, and safe.

No longer huddled in our small groups for discussion, we are now all tucked in with our Golden Teams. It's perfectly lovely, and all feels so well.

Master Saint Germain is standing up in front of us. I notice he is looking expectantly in a specific direction as if he is listening and waiting for something himself.

"Dear Ones," he says, as he finally turns his focus back to us. *"This is an important moment and one which I am asking you to be fully open to and receptive of. The energy of Interference itself has agreed to 'speak' to you and share its perceptions on the subject of its nature and purpose. Soon you will hear its 'voice.' Know, however, that it is not actually here in this place with us, but only a transmission of information that we have been granted to know.*

"Please let it inform you. That is its only intent right now; it is here to offer you an opportunity to listen and learn."

Suddenly, the aura in the room changes as a "voice" is heard throughout. It is not loud, but it is clear. I notice that it has no feeling to it; it just is.

"I am Interference," it says. *"I am the voice of Fear expressing itself to you. I have no other power other than what you give me, but you have never known that. Because you have never known that, I have had GREAT power over you.*

"It's simple, really, at least from my perspective. I can completely overwhelm

you. I can bring you down, roll you over, and make you plead for mercy in a millisecond.

"I can make you tremble, quake, and shake until your teeth rattle inside your head. I can spin you in circles until you are a blur, even to yourselves.

"I can manipulate you and upset you with sensory overload and emotional chaos of all kinds. I can divert you from your path, distract you, and preoccupy you with meaningless 'junk.'

"I can create divisiveness between you and others. I can upset your faith in yourself, in others, and in life.

"I can disrupt your connection to all that is meaningful and sacred to you. I can disrupt your trust of yourself, making you feel doubt at every turn. I can disconnect you from you, I can derail and disempower you and keep you enslaved to me.

"I can make you AFRAID; making you afraid handles everything of which I just spoke. I can do all that and more.

"Who has been in charge? I have. If you thought otherwise, well, then you're the fool.

"I know it seems unlikely that I would be here telling you these things, but it's obvious to me that you are clueless about any of it. You have believed otherwise, and this has always given me the winning hand.

"Oh yes, that's right, you think YOU are in charge, don't you? And yes, that's exactly what I want you to think.

"If you never spot me, then I can carry on and do whatever I want. If you never see the control I have, and had over you, you won't do anything to alter it. Your ignorance of me, your lack of acknowledgement of my true power and the many ways I wield it will continue to render you powerless.

"You're quite malleable, you see. It's incredibly easy for me to manipulate you: your emotions, your psyche, your perceptions, and your projections. It's easy for me to stir you up into a panic and watch as you get sucked right into the panic of others, like a giant herd of sheep running frantically in whatever direction I want you to.

"It's easy for me to do all of this. Frankly, it's so easy that it's almost pathetic."

My jaw drops. I am speechless as the words of Interference sink in.

Of course, none of this is new to me. And yet, the way it is being summed up and delivered so bluntly shocks me into a new level of stunning clarity. I know that it is true, that this is exactly what is contained inside the Mantle of Fear that I have been wearing and being duped by. Hearing it in this way makes my resolve to shed this Mantle of Fear absolute.

I want to just drop it—ALL of it, for once and for all. I don't choose to have any of this in my life anymore, period.

"Keep listening, Beloved," I hear Master Saint Germain say in my ear. *"There is more. Stay open to receive this valuable information please."*

I return to the sound of the "voice" of Interference as it continues:

"Why am I telling you these things? Why am I exposing myself like this to you now? That's a good question, and one that I am not going to answer just yet.

"What I can tell you, is that I want you to leave me alone. I don't want to be changed, altered, or fixed. It will never happen, so stop trying. The only way for us to co-exist is for you to be you and me to be me.

"I repeat: don't bother trying to change me. It will never work. Leave my space and I will leave yours.

"I repeat: leave my space and I will leave you alone. Goodbye."

And with that, the "voice" is gone.

Everyone is hushed, frozen. I don't know exactly what just happened, but it was something major, a resolution perhaps. All of us getting to the bottom of what we've been dealing with, at last, and comprehending the option of being freed of it on Terra.

"Leave its space?" That's the shift in Consciousness that we've been told about. Now, I understand better than ever. I know there is only one place to turn—ME.

Yes, I choose to return to who I truly am, to MY true Golden Sound and vibration of MY true Golden Consciousness. I choose to trust this absolutely. I choose to live this absolutely—Absolutely Golden Me.

There is no more room for compromise in any way or on any level. This is the ONLY way I am free from the Heartless Ones and their interfering forces. This is the only way I am fully free to be Golden Me on Golden Terra again.

I get it fully now; it's crystal clear.

I am grateful for this information, and to the energy of Interference for bringing it so clearly to me. My resolve is absolute and I feel solid in it.

I greatly appreciate that I understand this and know the option that I have, and I'm choosing it one hundred percent. Bring it on.

Golden Restoration at Last

The Golden Witness speaks:

In a heartbeat we are back inside Terra, back inside her beautiful Great Golden Hall. Master Saint Germain is with us, as are all of our Sacred Golden Teams. There are many blessed Golden Ones here, and the atmosphere is vibrating with enormous love, support, and encouragement.

Even though we are deep inside Terra, instead of on her surface, I feel much more physicalized in my body. I know that this sensation is only an energetic imprint of my actual physicalized form. I am feeling this in such a substantial way, and because of this my Golden restoration will be triggered and reactivated in my physical cellular memory as well. In this way, all levels of me, including my physical body, will be restored to my memory and imprint of my Golden Grace.

I know this is a great big event for us, and to my surprise I find myself totally calm, as if I have been waiting for this for a long, long time—which, of course, I have.

I am quiet within myself, feeling as though I am standing at the entrance to great Golden Gates. I know with complete confidence that I am finally, and fully, ready to walk through them.

"Yes, dear Friend," I hear one of my Sacred Golden Team members saying to me. *"It is time. You are about to make the actual transition back into your Golden Self. Terra herself is going to lead you through the sequence of layers and levels that will enable this complete transformation back into your Golden Radiance.*

"We know this is your choice, loud and clear. We have known it since the beginning when you made your first Golden Vow to our One Golden Heart so long ago. You have remained ever devoted, no matter what, and we admire your strength, your courage, and your love that you have shown throughout the long journey from then until now.

"We bless and honor you in this great and wondrous moment.

"Take a deep breath and gather yourself. The time has come. You have prepared yourself for exactly this. And yes, indeed, you are...ready."

I am aware that I am standing right on the edge of my Sacred Golden Opening, and everything else falls away. I know my Free Will was given up a long time ago to that which I hold the dearest in my heart and ever in my sight line, our One Golden Heart. It is my reason for Being. It is the gift my Source gave me for my entire existence, longer than I can remember.

Pure Divine Golden Love, I am here. I am ready to shine. Come to me, rise up in me again. Fill me up, re-enfold me back into you and birth me anew. Yes, please, now.

Terra's energy comes front and center as she swoops in and takes over the atmosphere in every way. She is holding us carefully inside her embrace. I know she will not let go until we are each finally "Home," and ready to stand on our own. I trust her with my life, as I am in her wise and loving hands. She is my most brilliant Leader and Ally. She will deliver back to me what I transferred into her safekeeping long ago.

"All right everyone, settle in, it's time," her voice rings out steady and clear.

"Let me remind you that we will proceed through the entire sequence of layers that I outlined for you earlier. Each one will be fully and finally repaired. When this is completed, your Golden Remembrance, your Golden Selves, will be restored and reactivated.

"Soften into yourselves, yield inside to the deepest desire of your Golden Heart. You have done every inch of prep work possible to ensure the success of this restoration. Trust and have faith.

"OPEN. NOW IS YOUR TIME. LET THE GOLDEN RESTORATION BEGIN!"

I feel Terra trembling beneath my feet and my body along with it. I am so excited and eager that I can hardly contain myself. It has been such a long journey.

"Breathe, my Beloveds, breathe and breathe, and breathe some more; slowly, steadily, in and out. The course of events will take care of themselves. You are simply the beautiful, ready recipient. Receive yourselves now."

First, I sense the Imprint of what was the Original Shattering coming into view again. I can see it clearly in my sightline. This time, however, I see that it is no longer broken. I am amazed at the difference, actually. There is no tear, no torn threads, no little shards of anything broken or broken apart.

What was the shattered picture has now been completely healed and restored to the Imprint of our lustrous and healthy Golden Tapestry of Being. We are one whole unit, tightly woven in beautiful splendor as if it had never been anything else. It is more brilliant in texture and color than it ever was before. And, yes, it is most definitely WHOLE!

I am thrilled! I breathe into it fully with my joy, abandoning myself to it completely. I sink into it, hungrily inhaling its scent and feeling its texture on my skin—soft, yet strong and sturdy. It is radiant, whole, and sacrosanct. It is absolutely the most beautiful thing I have ever seen!

My eyes fill with tears of joy and profound relief. I take in another deep breath, this one filled with immense gratitude. I am so happy about this that I could burst!

In the next moment, all of this gives way to me falling...falling...falling.

I feel as though I am doing somersaults, tumbling through space or rolling like a giant beach ball down a hill. I am not being jarred by this sensation at all; rather, it feels like the natural pull of gravity. I am aware of my Source coming to take me back into itself, to re-enfold me into its Center.

I become acutely aware of the ABSENCE of what was, the lack of what had been here for so long: a great, gaping chasm between me and my Source. Now, there is no chasm. It is simply—gone.

There is no vast, empty hollowness. I am not flailing around groping desperately for something I can't reach, the way I had been in the past. Instead, I am steady. I am sinking in; gravity is pulling me down inside itself in a great way. I am aware that I am ANCHORING; I am being anchored back inside my Source. The sensation of completion and groundedness that comes with it is intensely solid and secure.

I feel tremendous sensations of pleasure throughout my whole body, throughout my entire system. My heart is ringing with pure joy and exuberance that defies anything I have felt before. I have a sudden flashing memory, an insight of the pain of disconnect. It makes me much more grateful for this conscious re-embrace of my Soul and my Source. I am inside of this great Center of Creation and Beginning—that has no End.

I am INFINITE; I am REMEMBERING this now. It is remembering me. I am infinite and I am whole.

I am solid and steady in this. I am anchored and cemented right where I belong and exactly where I was originally birthed. I am HOME—plain, simple, and perfectly splendid HOME.

I feel totally comfortable, satisfied, and at peace. I need for nothing, and feel as if I never need to go anywhere else again. I luxuriate in this for what seems like a long and lovely time. It's simply sublime.

At some point, I hear Terra's voice gently calling to me, as she says warmly:

"Welcome home, dearest One. Life is good again, isn't it? Your internal foundation is restored and strong. Now it is time to release the Mantle of Fear, that camouflaging garment that served you so well. Be grateful to it and wish it Godspeed as it makes its way back to its home of Origin. You can set it free to fly—to fly away from you forevermore."

I take a deep breath and feel my gladness and gratitude to this garment that once cloaked me and enabled me to retrieve that which I love the most, my Golden Family. I am grateful to it for all it has done for me. I welcome its freedom to return from where it came, and to be restored to its true home.

I feel as though I have been in a masquerade ball and it is finally over.

I take off my mask. I take off my coat. I take off my costume, my socks, and my slippers. I stretch out my bare feet and feel the sensation of my toes wiggling happily without containment of any kind. I stand strong and squarely in my feet and I tingle from head to toe.

I don't stop for what feels like many minutes. I am tingling all over, every single part of me, inside and out.

I look down at my body and I see the vibrating that I am feeling inside. "Is it Terra that is actually vibrating or just me?" I wonder to myself.

"It is definitely just you, Dear One," I hear Terra's voice chuckling in my ear. *"It is most definitely YOU tingling with Life, with Source, and with Freedom! Inhale this fully and feel your joy. All is progressing beautifully.*

"You are waking up, indeed. You are BEING BIRTHED ANEW!"

I find myself stretching out and extending my arms, legs, and neck; luxuriating, yet again, in this novel sensation of pure freedom from confinement, restriction, and containment. As wonderful as it feels, I notice it also feels sore inside some of the places and spaces in me that have been cramped for so long. I take a while to extend myself, working through those tight and sore sensations as Terra urges me on in my rediscovery of self:

"Keep stretching out, Dear One," she says with glee. *"It won't take long for you to feel your fluids restoring their steady streams of health and well-being inside of you. You are like a river with many outgoing streams, all of which have been dammed up for quite a while. Letting loose is the name of this game—simply letting loose to flow, reach, touch, enjoy, and revel in the sensation of release and renewal.*

"Keep on breathing and letting this have its time and space. You are being fully restored to YOU. It is a natural and thoroughly enjoyable experience. Be fluid, be free. Enjoy the sensations. Remember what it's like to be truly YOU, and only YOU.

"Delight in this. Revel in it—your freedom is now!"

"Wow," I think to myself, "this is my freedom! I have forgotten it so thoroughly that I hardly even remember it!" I know that sounds absurd, dear Reader, but you get the picture, I'm sure. This is THE thing which I have ached for—and now, here it is. It's actually happening; I am actually FREE! It's not something that I'm simply talking about or thinking about: it is truly in process at this exact moment.

I start to feel overwhelmed for some reason, as if it's all kind of blowing my mind. I don't know why—you would think it wouldn't be, because it's entirely natural and I have desperately wanted this. I realize, in the process of it, it is doing exactly that—blowing my mind. Every other part of me is jumping up and down with joy, letting out great whoops and hollers of enthusiasm and exuberance.

But my mind, my poor, sweet mind, it's always the last to know. It's always the last to understand, always the last to agree, to yield. And now, I finally feel it letting go too. Why? Because this is way too big for it to prevent, much less have a say. My heart is much stronger, and all of this birthing is way too filled with love for my mind to do anything but dissolve into it completely.

Finally, I feel the sensation of the ENTIRETY of my self deliberately folding into this beautiful and exquisitely pleasurable flow. I let go and let myself truly be.

My energies feel like beautiful currents of air and bubbling streams of fresh water all at the same time; humming along, vibrating to my natural sound and frequency of pure joy. It is the most natural thing in the world for me. It is easier, by far, than anything else ever was.

I continue to delight in my expansiveness and well-being until I hear Terra's voice gently in my ear once again.

"Sweet One," she says. *"Now that you are yourself again, it is time for the Golden Treasure to be given back to you. It is time for it to be reawakened, restored, and reactivated.*

"Is this your choice, Beloved?

"Once chosen, there is no turning back. You will no longer be asleep to this. Your Golden Radiance and Golden Power will be strong. You will be your Golden Love, embodied and bright again.

"Do you choose for this now? What does your free will consent to, my Dearest One?"

At Terra's words, I start to feel the sensation of Golden warmth glowing in me even before the process has started. I can't help but want more of this; I simply can't help it. It's all that I am and want.

I know that deliberately stating my choice is essential to what follows and that, once declared, there is no turning back. Forward motion will be activated, and this train will indeed leave the station.

I declare my conscious choice emphatically: "YES! ABSOLUTELY YES!"

And suddenly, everything in me, and around me, changes.

It's as if I have entered what feels like some kind of a Golden container and am lying stretched out inside of it at the bottom of the Sea! It feels like I am inside a seashell, maybe an oyster shell, and I am the pearl inside. I register that my outer shell is my protection and buffer.

It becomes still clearer to me that the shape of the container I am in is more like a Pod. Yes, that's it, it's a Pod—a beautiful, huge Golden Pod, and I am "The Golden One" resting peacefully inside of it.

I feel my Golden Pod, with its outer encasement tightly sealed, resting gently on the bottom of the ocean floor. I know instinctively that it is a Golden Ocean. I sense strongly that all of this is from an ancient time, long ago, and that I have now returned to my awareness and consciousness of this. It is my Golden Destiny fulfilling itself. I have returned to my Golden Memory.

The rhythm of the waters and its steady, slow push and pull is shifting my Pod ever so slightly from side to side, and I feel lulled and soothed by its gentle swaying motion. My overall sensation is that ALL IS WELL; I have been here, whole and happy, for what feels like an eternity. I am totally peaceful about this.

I am Beauty, clean and shining and radiant—Golden so. I am GOLD. I am pure gold.

Every inch of my awareness within this beautiful Pod is of Golden shimmering Light, inside and all around. My knowing tells me it has been thus throughout my entire history. I feel it. All of time is converging in this present moment inside this beautiful Golden Pod.

I am so deep inside the Golden Sea that I don't hear the waters themselves moving—I feel them. All is quiet, completely quiet.

And yet, in the center of that quiet, I do hear something. It is perfectly beautiful and sacred: the Golden Heartbeat. It is the Great Golden Heartbeat of my own, of the waters, the Sea, the ocean floor, and of the family of ocean life around me—and the ENTIRE FAMILY OF ONE GOLDEN HEART and beyond.

At different levels and to varying degrees I realize it is all right here, inside of me, inside of my sweet, sacred Golden Heart, right inside of my beautiful Golden Pod. It makes me happy.

After a while of listening to the steady rhythm of this wondrous heartbeat, my attention is drawn to reach deep down inside myself. In doing so, I discover a labyrinth of pathways, a weave of intricate conduits and inner streams that have yet to be fully discovered again. There are what appear to be doorways to them that are not open. I find my curiosity rising, as I gently touch these doorways, acknowledging and honoring them—and they yield, opening effortlessly.

They are Life Giving; my Golden Sacred Conduits and Golden Inner Streams that had been hidden for so long are opening up again, becoming a complex patterning. They are beautiful, expanding, and fluid. I feel like I am lighting up like an exquisitely adorned Christmas tree that has been waiting for the electricity to be turned on. My deeper Beauty is right here for me to witness, feel, adore, and BE once again.

My heart begins to throb once more, but with an ancient kind of reverberation this time. It's a pulse of such intense glory that it literally fills me to bursting with radiant passion and brightness. I feel myself blazing with Golden Power! The network of my Golden intricacies is coming alive as my Golden "juice" is coursing through me. All of my Golden Sacred Conduits are activating, and my Golden Inner Streams are flowing with absolute abandon again.

What a sensation of pure, intense joy.

This is followed by a sudden undeniable yearning to open up the outer shell of my Pod. I am SO FULL with Golden Light that I need more room and more space—I need to literally burst out.

I hear a sudden Crack, and see a place in my outer shell that has, indeed, unceremoniously split itself open. My Golden Light instantly lurches forward to pour through. I am ready!

There is the sound of an even bigger Crack, and another still. After a moment of pure silence, I hear the creaking sound of something opening, and finally the entire lid of my outer shell opens wide and my Golden Light bursts forth with exhilaration.

My freedom! Oh, how wonderful this feels. What a celebration this is.

My Golden Energies instantly begin stretching out, and as they do I become aware that the entire body of the Ocean is celebrating with me. It is hearing, feeling, and seeing me—gathering me to itself to be embraced warmly. Here again, I am being witnessed and welcomed with an enormity of love.

As I find myself fully receiving this generous warmth and welcome, it's as though I begin to purr like a Cheshire cat. And...suddenly...my Golden Sound is born again.

At first, it is a quiet, low tone, and gradually, the more I spread forth, the louder, stronger and more vibrant it becomes. Oh, it feels good to sing in this way again, from deep inside my heart. All of my inner pathways that I hadn't felt for such a long time are alive, fluid, and flowing again. My true health and well-being are returning. This makes me incredibly happy.

As I spread out my energies still further, they reach intently across the vast expansive beauty of this deep Golden ocean floor. I notice, to my delight, that there are many other Golden Beings that are being born here alongside me. We have been MANY Golden Pods resting here peacefully together on the ocean floor waiting for exactly this moment. I am delighted to see them!

The tendrils of their Golden Energies welcome me as we welcome each other, and together we weave our Golden streams of love for one another into a beautiful pattern of Golden Harmony and synchronization. Together as one, our deep

Golden Love covers the vast expanse of this wondrous and sacred ground at the bottom of the Sea. It feels fantastic.

We continue on, steadily mingling and weaving together the strands of our Gold. This glorious sensation of our intertwining brings us much pleasure and joy. I savor it for many moments as I notice how natural and organic it feels—something from long ago that is but new again.

I hear the sweet, ancient sound of that which truly and simply defines us: our One Golden Heart. It's as if we have given conscious voice to this sacred frequency at exactly the same moment. And, as we do, our threads link up still more intricately, finally interweaving themselves indelibly into this particular patterning of our Golden Tapestry once again. The patterning spreads out and reaches toward other dimensions as well, as if it is searching out other Golden Life Forms who are sounding this same note, this same frequency, this same song again—One Golden Heart, steady, strong, and sacrosanct.

It is profoundly moving. And, to my surprise, a sudden and deep sensation of pride wells up in me like a fierce wave rising up from the sea herself. I ask myself, what am I proud of?

I'm proud of us, of all of Golden Life everywhere that has struggled enormously to arrive back at this moment. I know this is but the beginning of our restoration to our Golden World, but it is, unto itself, a magnificent event, just like we were told it would be.

It is a Blessed Golden Reunion, literally. Again, I savor it; I love and inhale it. I could drink forever.

And, then, just like that, I feel so FULL! It's like I have eaten this huge glorious feast and I simply cannot have another bite. I am completely and deliciously satisfied and stuffed: Golden sated.

I reflect on the state I find myself in, deliciously happy, fat, and full. In the process, I find myself quietly wondering, "Now what?"

I look around and sense that my other Golden Friends are wondering the same thing. There must be further to go. There must be air somewhere to experience breathing in. There must be more to explore in this new and fabulous way.

"I hear you, dear One," Terra says to me gently. Is that another chuckle in her voice?

"You are Golden Restored, but you are still inside of me. You are still amidst my Golden Birthing Waters.

"There is one more thing that needs to be done before your full reemergence back onto my surface can take place. I know that's what you are starting to

yearn for, and that this is what your system is naturally gravitating toward. It wants still more freedom. It needs and wants to reconnect with its memories of our beautiful Lemuria of Origin, once again, in a completely physicalized and materialized way, up on my surface. I know this, this will come.

"But first, we need to give a gift. Understand that without having already restored your Golden Light to this point, you could not give this final gift.

"Conversely, without actually giving this final gift, you cannot be restored to your FULL Golden Capacity either. You cannot return back into your physicalized Golden Body on my surface until you have given this gift successfully. This is a situation of balance, the pure balance on both sides of the scale that, once addressed, will restore the Golden Whole.

"That gift that you are ready to give, 'What is it?' you ask.

"It is the Gift of Forgiveness. It is the Gift of Forgiveness to all the Heartless Ones everywhere."

I gulp. I hadn't seen this one coming.

"I know," Terra continues, *"that what I am suggesting is taking you by surprise. But know, that without this, your heart is still bound in a certain way and you cannot be FULLY GOLDEN FREE. You are the one who will continue to suffer because of this.*

"Do you understand?

"Ponder this for a moment. See if you are, in fact, willing to give this gift without restraint, without condition, and without hesitation.

"Again, is this what you consciously choose to do, dear One? Are you willing and ready to give this gift—truly, freely, and fully?"

"Oh," I think to myself. "Wow, that seems like a tall order doesn't it?" And, yet, I absolutely know I cannot move forward any further without doing this. I know that I will be the one who suffers if I don't.

I know that as much as I love being healed and restored here in Terra's Birthing Waters, I also want and need ground upon which to stand and rebuild Lemuria on Terra's surface—the way we did before, only even better this time.

I know that I need to stand out. I want and need to express my Golden Shining on dry land. I want to have it and to be it all. I cannot remain hidden and tucked away, albeit as beautiful as this freedom is under this beautiful Golden Sea.

I yearn and ache for more. I know that I need to do this for myself, my Golden Family, and the Heartless Ones. I know this is the Final Repair.

I think for only another moment; I find that I trust this. It's simple, I Golden Trust.

As soon as this dawns on me, my heart rings out with a resounding "Yes!" I am shocked by its enthusiasm and eagerness, but given that its full freedom is dependent upon this, I can understand why.

My intense eagerness rises up inside of me and takes over. Yes, I am indeed ready. I am indeed willing and grateful for this opportunity to extend my love so generously. In the past, I wouldn't have even begun to consider doing such a thing. In the past, prior to now, I was wounded and unable to release myself from that wound, let alone forgive anyone for having any part in it. I simply couldn't go beyond that or even tolerate the thought. I was far too wounded, sore, battered, and bruised. I felt too raw and vulnerable.

But, now? I am none of those things. Now, I am healed. I am Whole, and free of the Mantle of Fear. I am Golden Restored and reactivated. My Golden Memory has returned intact, huge and bright—and there is the possibility of still more to come.

I am capable of this forgiveness, I know it. I am most definitely GOLDEN LOVE; that's who I am. Forgiveness is my middle name. Bring it on, I'm in!

In a flash, my energetic sensors are back on top of Terra, out on her surface, standing alongside throngs of Golden Ones who are here with me. Even though we are actually only here energetically, it's as though we are fully physicalized and standing tall together on her surface once again. This is where we need to be in order for this Forgiveness to take place; this is where the Heartless Ones are.

Yes, again, I reiterate, forgiveness is my choice.

This gift of Forgiveness is my KEY. It is me inserting the key back into the full flow of my Golden Love and back into the full range and freedom of my Golden Heart. I know this. I know this is true of ALL Golden Ones everywhere—seen and unseen, here, far, and beyond.

With this made crystal clear, we stand in solidarity together and sing out our vibrant One Golden Song, the Song of brilliant and powerfully loving One Golden Radiant Heart!

Forgiveness of the Heartless Ones, Golden Forgiveness, it is fully our choice.

Who knew, dear Reader, that this was where we would end up? Makes sense though, doesn't it?

We've been preparing and waiting for this moment, this inevitable moment that would finally SET US ALL FREE. Forgiveness is indeed a most powerful thing.

CHAPTER FOURTEEN

THE POWER OF FORGIVENESS

THE GOLDEN WITNESS SPEAKS:
Here we are, together on Terra's surface where the Heartless Ones live. Let me state again, dear Reader, that we are only here energetically; our physical states, which have yet to be fully realized, are still back in the birthing Waters of Terra. We are certainly in full force, energetically speaking, and that is all that is needed in order to get this job done. As Terra made clear earlier, we need to give the gift of this forgiveness thoroughly and successfully before we can actually resurface in a physical way and BE our full Golden Embodiment again.

I look around and take in the sights and sounds of my Golden Family members who are with me. I feel tremendous courage welling up within me, and I know that this is due in part to the fact that I am surrounded by the purposefulness and strength of these others. There are so many of us who are ready and wanting to give this gift of Forgiveness. We stand strong in ourselves, and even stronger in our togetherness.

I hear a voice that comes out of the blue, speaking loud and clear. *"You cannot go forth in your full Golden grace if you don't forgive the Heartless Ones, because without that forgiveness your hearts are still in a certain state of contraction and binding—in that sense, you cannot evolve."*

My ears perk up and my heart skips a beat. I know and love that voice: Sananda. Of course it would be, he knows about forgiveness, doesn't he?

I can only hear him, but he is crystal clear and strong as he continues:

"I know you are wondering; how does this forgiveness happen? How can it happen when the Heartless Ones are still at work everywhere, all of the time, dominating everything and everyone?

"And I ask you, who rules?

"And I hear you say, 'It seems they do.'

"Well, look again. Yes, they rule THEIR domain, but who rules YOURS? You do!

"And I can hear you respond, 'But we have to operate under certain rules of Mondor.'

439

"Well, yes, for now this still applies in a certain way to the physical, materialistic side of things, but that is all. Your Consciousness governs everything else about your lives, and these physical, materialistic aspects will fall into place over time; it is a given—you don't need to know how right now.

"The only thing you need to pay attention to is CONSCIOUSNESS. Consciousness rules. Be YOURS and only yours. Everything else will follow suit.

"You are not here to change Mondor; you are not here to change the Heartless Ones. They have told you loud and clear that they don't want that, that it would be futile to even try.

"No, you are not here to change them; you are here to change yourselves. You are here to be YOU, GOLDEN YOU, reestablishing the Golden World.

"It has to happen sometime. Someone has to do it: why not you and why not now?

"This is where it originated, and you can simply pick up where you left off. Only now, you're even stronger, wiser, and more fully equipped.

"Now, you can pick up some of those Golden Creations that were built in Lemuria of Origin long ago for precisely these moments. It was 'for the future.' That 'future' has come and is now the PRESENT.

"Stand tall. Stand proud. Stand Sovereign. Stand Golden."

Sananda's voice fades away, but his words linger and vibrate in the atmosphere.

We are still standing in a large group. The patterns of Mother Nature are with us and we are ALL listening. I can see it and feel it. The trees, the birds, the air—ALL of life is listening to this right now. ALL of life is present and participating. I can feel the pondering happening in the atmosphere. It is hushed, but active and acutely listening.

I understand what Sananda is saying and I know that I stand tall in my Goldenness—that I am filled with love and generosity of spirit. I want to create forth and not be hung up on this "obstruction" of the pain of the past. I don't want to give myself, nor my life, over to this anymore. I have no intention of doing so.

I only intend to stand Golden Strong from now on—and yet, there is so much history with the H-O, isn't there? There is, and has been, so much Interference in the harmony of Life.

Forgiving the H-O? How, again, is that going to happen? Exactly, how?

Yes, I want it. I've certainly made it clear that I choose this. We all have, but frankly, now that we're here I cannot fathom it actually happening. I don't know how this is going to be truly, deeply, and abidingly successful. Even though, as I said clearly, I do want to forgive, but wanting and doing are two different things. And in this case, they are two VERY different things indeed! Forgiveness is not something that can be faked or done half way.

So…now what?

I look at those I love and see that as bright as these eyes are around me, as caring as they truly are, they are wondering the same thing too. It seems like such a tall order. But, more essentially, the question being asked, is how? That is what I see as the most outstanding quandary.

Sananda's voice comes in, crystal clear again, as he says:

"As you already know, your Golden Freedom depends upon this. Let me clarify it for you even more.

"You're actually not doing this for the Heartless Ones. In truth, they don't care whether you forgive them or not. They don't care at all. That is not within their domain of consciousness. It's foreign to them. They frankly have no relationship to forgiveness—that side of it is a completely moot point; their viewpoint is basically, 'So what? Who cares?'

"So, as magnanimous as this 'Gift of Forgiveness' sounds, the real point is: yes, you are actually doing this predominantly for yourselves. You cannot carry this heavy burden around in your hearts anymore.

"Blame, anger, frustration, hurt—any part of it weighs a ton after a while. It compromises your health on every level and distorts your vision and ability to create beauty and freedom.

"Bottom line: you cannot move forward without forgiving the Heartless Ones. You know this. You know you will never be fully free if you don't do this. However, the DOING of it, and its successful delivery and completion, is entirely up to you, isn't it?

"Take a look at one another and notice what you see about this. It's actually more complex than you would have thought."

I turn to the Golden One standing on my right. Such beautiful eyes he has; filled with purity, joy, and longing to progress forward. I can see that his heart remains troubled, which looks at odds with where we have, in fact, arrived in ourselves. We have already restored ourselves so much, and it looks completely out of sync for this "troubledness" to even be there. In a way, it doesn't even make sense. "What is wrong with this picture?" I think to myself.

I can see that his heart looks compromised. He is still hurt, and holding on to both it and blame.

"It's a shame," I think to myself, because I can see that it squashes his heart, constricts it, and makes it small and hunkered over on itself. It is not wide open and free when it comes to the subject of the Heartless Ones.

I understand it. I have absolutely no doubt that this is also what is in my heart as well. There has been such a tremendous amount of pain and hurt. How can we ever actually let this final woundedness go?

I turn to the other Golden One standing on my left. She is such a sweet Soul, and I can see that her heart aches. It aches because it wants to love fully but cannot. It cannot set itself free to love fully until it has resolved this issue regarding the Heartless Ones. Her longing to love is palpable, and it bothers me to see the additional pain she feels from being held back. I can feel it in myself too. It is in my heart. I get it; I get what Sananda said. He's right. There is no freedom until this has been completely released and set free; until true forgiveness has been successfully given.

We have restored ourselves enormously with Terra's help and guidance, but there are these last important threads that remain to be healed.

However, it takes willingness on our part, doesn't it? We already know this; it takes a choice, right? WE have already declared this. What still remains is the HOW.

Here is the reality of it. There is still more to know before we can get on with things honestly, successfully, and truly.

After a few more moments of trying to figure this out, Sananda directs us to form our smaller groups again. There is obviously more to know and understand, more nooks and crannies that have remained hidden until now.

Master Saint Germain suddenly appears inside the center of our small circle. He gazes steadily at each one of us, and I feel as though my spirit is inhaling his clarity and benevolence. He, too, knows how to forgive. Perhaps I can have some of what he has, in order to bring myself to the other side of this.

"Beloveds, dear Golden Ones," he says to us. *"Your hearts, in truth, are incapable of holding a grudge, blame, or punishment. Whatever you are feeling along these lines is not truly your own, but actually only the last vestiges of 'smallness' from your Fear based travails.*

"In truth, you Golden Ones have never understood why someone would want to hold a grudge; it hurts the holder more than the person doing the hurting. It is self-perpetuating pain. Your hearts have always known better. They have always known that only those who are wounded, wound. Only those who are hurt, hurt.

"Your Golden Hearts are longing to rise up and see this clearly again, to embody this and to live such knowing fully again.

"I know your questions, I hear your quandaries. Let's spill them out and see what they sound like—to you, and to one another.

"Speak now. Empty out what is in your heart and soul."

I see both Master Saint Germain and Sananda standing quietly as we unload ourselves yet again. It always seems like there's more, doesn't it? And in this case, there certainly is. I hadn't arrived yet at this juncture of opening inside, so knowing exactly what is in the way hasn't had a chance to be seen or heard yet. Now that the way is cleared for this, there is no stopping us from letting it spill out into this safe and secure atmosphere of supportive love and kindness.

Our voices reveal our anguished concerns openly.

"I'm afraid if I let this go it will mean that I am condoning the behaviors of the H-O."

"I'm afraid that letting go, and forgiving, sends the wrong message to the H-O. They will think the message is that I am okay with what they have done and continue to do. They will interpret this as me being on their side."

"I'm afraid if I let this go then I am saying to those I love who have greatly suffered that I don't care about their pain anymore. Holding onto this blame and refusal to forgive lets them know that I am with them, that I am on their Team, no matter what."

"I'm afraid that letting go of this hatred will give me too much freedom. I am used to the contraction this hatred provides. I don't know if I can manage without the small space in which it confines me. What if I am not good enough on the other side of this?"

"I'm afraid of letting go of this hurt and blame. I'm afraid to do so."

"Do I dare? Do I dare set myself fully free? Do I even know how?"

"What will I do with that 'bigness' if I release this contraction and smallness? What will I do without this 'conflict' to engage me and keep me occupied?"

"What will I do with that harmony, all that loving and goodness that is on the other side of this?"

"What will I do without 'the wounded identity' to explain who and how I am? Will I have to be BIG? Will I have no excuse to hide behind if I fall short somehow?"

"What will I do with all of that Golden Power? Can I trust myself with it?"

"What will I do with all of that freedom?"

There are many questions, and while some of them sound absurd, all are genuine. Many of the queries reflect the smallness of our Selves, and how afraid we still are to own our true joy and wellness. These are the areas that need the most healing, because they are stuck and continue to block our freedom. It is tripping us up like little nail heads sticking up out of a wooden floor, just enough to cause our feet sharp pain and make us walk gingerly, still braced and limited, contracted and afraid. It is enough to cause us to still vibrate in the Mondor configuration without hardly even realizing it, behaving as if we are still in that configuration, when in truth that is no longer the case.

For myself, my biggest concern is the message it sends the H-O, or at least how it could be interpreted. That said, I realize they won't even register that forgiveness has taken place. As Sananda said, "They won't even relate." So why give that one any more energy?

In terms of staying within the confines of pain because I believe it sends a message of support to those I love who are suffering—oh dear, it may be well-meaning, but isn't it just plain backwards? Wouldn't the greatest show of support be to provide a shining example of letting go, and cheering everyone else on to do the same?

Originally, when this whole conversation first began, I was sure that forgiving the H-O would be the biggest release. Now it is clear to me that letting go of all the hurt and pain and its burden and control is equally important, if not more so. Isn't this my ultimate freedom? Giving up all attachment to, and notion of, my own woundedness? Admitting that I am, in truth, healthy, well, wise, and free—and that we all are.

Letting the Heartless Ones go so I can let myself go. Letting the Heartless Ones be so I can let myself be. Yes, I choose this. I choose Golden Freedom and I choose GOLDEN ME.

I honor every Golden One who has suffered; I have suffered myself. I honor them and I honor me. I honor their right to be free and I honor my right to be free.

Suddenly, in the midst of my thoughts finally coming together in a clear fashion, there is a great spinning and spiraling energy that practically bowls me over. It is a powerful wave of emotion and turbulence. Yet again, I hear the cries of pain that we have all suffered. I hear the clang and the chaos, the divisiveness and despair. It is painful—it is heart wrenching and gut wrenching. I realize I simply cannot live with this anymore. I don't want to be attached to this anymore. Frankly, I don't want to even give this any energy anymore.

It underscores my decision again. Yes, I choose to let go. I choose to forgive the Heartless Ones and, in the process, to forgive myself for holding on. I AM DONE.

It's part of our history and I honor it as such. It's what we have walked through to arrive here, but I'm done being it anymore. I want to step out and move on.

I want to be free. I want to happy, healthy, and harmonious in my body and in my life. I want this for my whole Golden Family as well. I want to focus on TODAY. I want to decide how I want it to be from now on. I want to be in charge of my life, and I want my Golden Life. I want to be in Golden Charge.

In order for this to be so, I will do whatever is needed—and right this moment, I know that all those around me feel exactly the same way. Finally, we are ready. The "how" is a moot point. We're just going to do it, period.

Sananda, Master Saint Germain, Mother Mary, Avalar, Andar, and many other Golden Masters enter where we are. Suddenly, there is a thunderbolt of energy, and pure strength electrifies my body and makes my insides quiver. I stand up straight, my backbone strong and steady, my heart open and all senses on alert.

Within our inner sight we see a huge gathering of the Heartless Ones standing right in front of us.

As we gaze at them from our newfound understanding and viewpoint, we see things we haven't seen before. Yes, we see their hardness, their non-caring, their coldness, and their "robotic-ness." But we also see, for an instant, that something brought them to this point. What was that?

As we continue to look, their robotic metal falls away, only to reveal to us what look like a group of pale, emaciated, wounded looking waifs. They have hollow eyes. Pale and wan, their mouths are gaping open, hungry and crying to be fed. How pitiful and weak they are!

I am shocked by what I am seeing. I think to myself, "These are the 'monsters' I have been afraid of?" I am aghast in a way—shocked and utterly confused.

How could THEY create all THAT? How could they create all of the upset, pain, and divisiveness we have walked through? Right now, they seem incapable of any of it. I am still confused.

"Let me remind you, Beloveds," says Sananda. *"The wounded, wound. The hurt, hurt. Keep looking. There is more to see."*

I look more closely still. I become aware that some of those faces actually look familiar to me.

"Oh, no," I think to myself. "Oh, please God, no."

My heart automatically lurches uncontrollably, as I admit to myself that some are the very lost Ones from long ago. Now deeply wounded and traumatized, they have been literally taken over; these former Golden Ones are now H-O themselves.

My heart begins to break. Oh, I truly ache for them. My fingers instinctively reach toward them through the vapor and mist. Can I not help them? Can I not save them?

I realize something. I absolutely HAVE to forgive the H-O, because some of them are part of our Golden Family; any one of these lost ones could have been me, or any of those standing beside me.

I start to cry quietly. I hear others crying around me as they are witnessing the same thing and acknowledging the same truth.

"I thought all the Golden Ones were Rescued," I think to myself. But I realize that no, many were only Tagged and haven't even begun to follow the threads of Golden Light to find their way home.

I begin to weep uncontrollably. My heart aches and breaks for this demise of Heart and Soul and Being, and I sob and sob. This is the saddest thing I have ever seen; it is the saddest thing I have ever known.

I knew there were those of us that were quite lost. I knew that before, as we have spoken previously, but I had never seen them in this way. I'd never seen them revealed and exposed at this level—this pitiful and this "gone" from us.

"Oh, you poor, poor Golden Ones," I think to myself. "I am so sorry for your pain. I am so very sorry for your pain."

I realize, without further need for convincing, that forgiving the Heartless Ones is ALL I want to do. I don't care how many of them are Golden Lost Ones or not. In order to save some, I have to forgive all. Given their state of obvious woundedness and lostness, why ever would I not? Is my heart not so much bigger than that?

Of course it is. I am Love. I am Divine Love. I am Golden Love.

Instinctively, my heart goes over to each and every one of them. I touch them with my witnessing, my recognition, my understanding, and my compassion.

I include those that are not of our kind, knowing full well that they are like desperately wounded children who have not known better. Whatever it was they found to compensate for their pain was how they survived their neglect and rejection. It felt like they had come to this planet because they had been banished from some other place; rejected, unwanted, tossed out—exiled.

It seemed like they had gotten their hands on a game, a game they called Fear, which they discovered gave them power and a control they had never known.

Dangerous? Yes. Destructive? Yes. Unconscionable? Yes.

The wounded, wound. The hurt, hurt.

Are they forgivable? Yes. Does that make me a "bad" person for wanting to forgive? No.

It makes me one who understands, who sees the picture properly and responds with compassion. It makes me one who deeply cares for all of Life, everywhere, no matter what.

And for the Lost Golden Ones who have been taken over and turned into Heartless Ones themselves? It is the only thing I can offer that will help them save themselves. They consider themselves unforgiveable for having become so lost, and for doing whatever it is they have done because of it. They cannot turn to their hearts because their hearts are shut down. It's as though their own hearts have cast them out, cast them away, and want to punish them forever—which, of course, is not true.

I know it is only through OUR forgiveness of them as a Golden Family who loves them, with this forgiveness REACHING them, that they stand a chance of coming home at all. I hope and pray with all my might that they hear my forgiveness of them.

I WANT them home. I NEED them Home. WE need them Home.

I open my heart wider. I deliberately create a bridge for my forgiveness to cross over to them and stand, fully facing the doorways of their hearts. I am patient. I wait.

I continue to stand there, at their doorways to their hearts, and I will do so until they hear me, feel me, and let me in—however long it takes. I am their family. I have to believe it is only a matter of time.

My heart aches for them, and I honor them. They have been through a tremendous amount, more than I can even fathom. I touch them. And…suddenly…one of them feels me, one of them responds—tentatively.

I feel as if my hand of love is being touched back. Yes, tentatively at first, and then more strongly. I wait as our link together grows firmer as our connection becomes clear. Finally, the moment is ready; my mouth opens, and words of love spill out unchecked.

"I am here to tell you that I forgive you, my beautiful Golden Friend. We all forgive you and it is time for you to forgive yourself. You could have been any one of us. Everyone has their breaking point if pushed to that final edge. We understand.

"We forgive. We love you. You are Golden Heart—you can forgive yourself. And, if you feel you need and want to, you can even make things right somehow. Somehow your loving will do this, I know it."

Slowly but surely, I feel a response; a warmth growing, a small, but distinct light going on: hope.

He begins to cry; stunted, stilted sounds at first.

It's as if his tears have been as dry as a desert, as if the waters won't come out of the faucet. He has been dry for so long, and at last it has begun to flow. In the midst of his tears, he cries out and bends over clutching his stomach. He is so lonely I can hardly bear it. I cannot force him to respond to me, all I can do is stand here, patient and available. Without thought, he finally reaches for me, his hand shooting out to grab mine in a sheer grip of desperation.

"Don't let me go down again," he whispers to me in a frantic plea for help. "Please, don't let me go down again. I can't go back in there. Help me. Please, please help me."

I hold firmly onto his hand clutching mine. I don't let him go. All the while I am talking to him like a lost Soul about to go under. My sounds are soft, my voice is soothing. I don't know what words I use, only that I have to keep talking softly in order for him to stay connected to me through his grief and sorrow.

Finally, I hear his voice speaking up in such obvious pain. "I'm so sorry," he says through his muffled sobs. "I am so, so, so sorry for all that I have done to hurt you, or anyone, anywhere. I am so sorry. I am so, so sorry. I will be forever sorry."

As he empties out his burdens, I see him finally being able to look at me. It is hard for him at first, but as my gaze continues to hold him in tenderness and love, he finds himself able to look back at me. What I see in his eyes takes my breath away.

It is as though I am looking into the deepest canyon of despair; a kind of bleakness that I have never imagined possible. "Empty and lost" is a complete and utter understatement. I have never experienced such intense void and disconnection. I have known a lot of this, in myself and others, but never anything as bleak, barren, and empty—like a Soul that has lost its Soul.

I stand in that cold emptiness with him. I know well that he needs a witness in order to climb out and stay out. He needs to know that SOMEONE, SOMEWHERE sees and knows.

I breathe. He breathes.

Soon, I realize that there are other Lost Golden Ones here who are going through their "pit of despair" as they are being lovingly attended to, cared for, and witnessed by those of us here to help and forgive. Gradually, a soft but palpable wave of energy permeates everything, and a warm caress of complete caring takes over. It gently sweeps throughout all the Heartless Ones as well, not just our lost Golden Ones here.

It matters not whether they respond. We are really only interested in making sure that those of our Golden Family are brought back to life. We know it is not for us to change the others, and yet, our compassion cannot help but extend to them as well. Lost is lost, after all.

Our forgiveness becomes obvious. It has begun, and the "let go" happens in an instant all by itself.

Suddenly, all of the judgment, blame, anger, and frustration, the desire to punish and make "them" suffer for "what they have done to us," has vanished. It has vanished into thin air.

How? Simple—with understanding and clarity. The wounded, wound. The hurt, hurt.

They are so lost and desperate that they literally don't know any better. It doesn't make anything "right." That is for them to decide. But it does set us, and them, free.

It disentangles us from one another, and each person can then decide for themselves how and what they want to do and be.

In our case, we want to bring these Lost Golden Ones home. Once we have done this, our Golden Family will truly be restored and complete again. We will then be able to be whole as our Golden Family, and our One Golden Heart.

And from here on out, WE can be US; and we can live and let live.

Our forgiveness continues to ring out, strong and clear. Our Golden Hearts are open, and we flood this gathering of Heartless Ones with such love that they don't know what to do. It's as though the ONE thing for which they have ached is actually touching them. They didn't know that they needed this, but here it is—LOVE.

Our Golden Love continues to stream out, like a fire hose that has no intention of stopping. We are not trying to change or alter, we are simply unable to stop what, for us, is our most natural and instinctive drive and flow. It is our wellness expressing, sharing, caring, and being.

The more the moments pass, the better we feel. Any lingering traces of our personal burdens, and the charge of their memories that we have carried in our hearts, lift and dissolve away in the face of this outpouring and out-streaming of pure love. We cannot help it. Loving is what we thrive on, loving is our instinct and our passion. Loving is our health and well being. Loving is our grace.

We are restoring ourselves.

Sananda was right. We are setting ourselves free, free to be that which we truly are once again. Free to flow. Free to care. Free to love—no matter the outcome.

I find I never want to stop. I have simply never ever felt this good. I have never felt this relieved of pressure. I have never felt this easeful inside. Who knew that all of this angst, contraction, pain, and frustration that I had experienced for SO long was only because my loving river was stopped up, blocked, restricted, and contained?

Who knew?

Who knew that SIMPLY LOVING would be the final answer for me, and for all of us?

It turns out, as I witness, that even those "Heartless Ones" who are not of our Golden Family are so bathed in this love that they cannot help but want more. It's there if they want it and it's not for us to have a say in the matter.

I see that it is by osmosis that they, too, are remembering something about themselves, from whatever their point of origin, and from wherever they herald. It's as though their light is slowly turning on inside. They are registering that they are indeed of value; that they are indeed valuable, worthy of being cared for, cared about, and yes, maybe even loved.

To my amazement, where they had only organs for hearts, mechanical organs, they now have an actual organic muscle that is throbbing and pulsating with something warm, gentle, and tender. Is it possible that their "hearts of love" are being born, or perhaps reborn, and activated somehow?

Yes, I do believe so.

What will become of them? I don't know. What will they do now? I don't know. And I don't need to know, really, it is not my business.

But...I find I truly care.

My final decision about all of this is exactly that: I care. I care about loving. I care about myself. I care about all of my Golden Family. And I care about those previously called "Heartless Ones."

I realize my Golden Loving knows no divisiveness. It doesn't exclude, it only INCLUDES. In truth, it loves purely for the sake of loving, not for the intent of changing. It simply loves because it loves.

And that is fine by me. You know why? Because I FEEL GREAT when I am loving!

Suddenly, my life is open, and my heart is open. My Soul is singing, and I AM FREE!

I AM GOLDEN FREE! I AM FULLY GOLDEN FREE! And so is everyone else around me.

This is a great moment! This is a great day! HALLELUJAH!

❧

Aftermath:

Dear Reader, did we accomplish what we had chosen to do? Did we succeed in the task of giving our gift of Forgiveness truly, fully, and successfully? Did we actually accomplish this?

Yes! Oh yes, we absolutely and most certainly did—splendidly so!

PART FOUR

GOLDEN
REACTIVATION

CHAPTER FIFTEEN

BIRTHING ANEW

D EAR READER, this next chapter of our book is focused on re-engaging our Golden Heart Powers on all levels. At first glance, you might think that we are revisiting what we did in the beginning of the book. You might say, "Been there, done that. Why are we here again?"

Please know that we are only stepping back into these important fundamental arenas so that we can tap into them again and re-engage the Golden Life Force fully. We are not building them in the same manner as we did at the start of Lemuria. This is the only way we can re-engage, and thereby reactivate our Golden World.

Yes, once again, it is a step by step process, with each stage building upon the last. We invite you to stay with us a while longer and hold your attention steady throughout these different levels of Golden re-engagement. Soon we will succeed in completing the process!

OPENING THE SACRED BIRTHING CONDUITS
AND RESURFACING ON TERRA

The Golden Witness speaks:

Once again, we find ourselves within Terra, inside her Great Golden Hall. We can hear the distant waters of the Golden Sea pulsating faintly in the background, and we know that in some small way we are there as well.

Our hearts are light and Golden. There is a great hush throughout the air as a deep feeling of relief and completion floods us, permeating everything.

"Blessings, my beautiful Ones," Terra's voice sings out proud and clear. "JOB WELL DONE!

"You have done a great thing and given an enormous gift indeed. Yes, your forgiveness of the Heartless Ones has been absolutely thorough and successful. You are complete with this in every way. This is evidenced by the 'hush' throughout, something you can feel in the air and which you will see and know upon my surface when you emerge there soon. You will find that you have thoroughly cleared the space for your true vibration to re-embody itself and create new life.

"Please understand that this clearing that you have accomplished has created distance between you and the Heartless Ones; there is now absolute separation between you. You are no longer overlapping energies in any way. You are as two separate worlds and two distinct separate realities.

"Let me reiterate that YOU have created this space and this clearing for yourselves. YOU did this intentionally, deliberately, thoroughly, and thoughtfully. And now that you have created this clear, empty space, what exactly do YOU want to do with it? Something will need to be done, because Nature does, after all, abhor a vacuum; if you don't fill it intentionally at this time with possibility, it will fill up with something else: It could perhaps even return to what it was before.

"You must decide what you wish to put there. You must define and delineate this exactly, and then you will make it so. YOU are the Creators.

"Think of it as a garden; a garden of possibility, with you as its Golden Gardener. YOU are also the tools and the instruments that are needed to design, cultivate, build, and sustain this beautiful garden. It's all yours and it is up to you.

"It is time to put your Golden Creation Abilities back to work. It is time to open back up those Sacred Birthing Conduits that have lain dormant in you for all of this time. That is the only way that you will even be able to surface at all. It is through reactivating and re-utilizing your Golden Creation Skills that you literally become physically Golden embodied again. You will see what I mean.

"Let's talk about this. Let's talk about the HOW TO.

"First, you begin with your sacred Golden Heart. You climb inside of it and listen to its sweet song of desire. What does IT want to create? What does it want to grow?

"Once you have identified the feeling of this, you welcome it expanding inside of you, filling you as if you are being blown up like a birthday balloon. This is the energy of the dream of your pure Golden Love which is longing to be materialized. It is right inside of you, waiting for this moment to offer itself to you and show you what it can do and be.

"Your Golden Creative Juices run deep and powerful; they are ancient and adept at what they know and do. You are highly developed in this arena already. Putting yourself into a position of creating again is what will stir this memory, reminding you of that which you already are. You

will be 'waking yourselves up,' and deliberately calling up all those Golden creative muscles back into play. You already have them, and you already know them—give them a chance and ride the wave of their natural ability.

"All that I am describing is the deliberate birthing forth of Consciousness. Consciousness is the root of all Creation. In this case, of course, Golden Consciousness is the root of your Golden Creation.

"Go inside of yourselves and spend time in communion with your hearts. Define the sensation of what your heart wishes to create and what it desires to pour forth. Let it move you with all its might. It is not in the details right now, but only the sensation and its 'body of desire.' You will know exactly what I mean when you feel it.

"As you continue to feel it rising inside, it will grow and soon become an actual sound, a pulsating kind of frequency which you will be able to hear and feel. It will ring true through you, as you, and when it is ready, it will usher itself forth and create vibrantly—literally manifesting from the frequency of its vibration. This is your Golden Consciousness in the act of its creation. You are its instrument and its vehicle; and at the same time, you ARE this yourself as well. You are made of this. You are fueled by this and as this; it all becomes one and the same.

"The more you understand this and consciously yield to it, the greater your natural sense of empowerment and responsibility will be. I urge you to open happily to this. This is your Mastery at work: witness yourselves making that which is so important and meaningful to you.

"This is you birthing yourself forward. This is literally the 'setting in position' of your Golden Creation Energy—strong, clear, and absolutely steady. Once born, your deepest sacred Golden Heart's desire and intent will continue to fuel your creation, causing it to expand even more and grow ever stronger and brilliant.

"You will continue to sustain this creation with your intense love for it and your full commitment to it from here on out—giving it whatever it needs, whenever it needs it. Through your commitment and dedicated support and fostering, it will eventually grow so strong that it will develop 'legs' of its own, and expand forth further from there. Again, as I said, this is your Mastery at work.

"This is what I call Responsible Creatorship.

"There is nothing 'sloppy' or 'wishy washy' about it. It is not happenstance

and it is not by default. It is strong, clear, and deliberate. You create FROM great inner wisdom WITH great inner wisdom. In this way, you instinctively know exactly what you are doing, and you give it what it needs to follow through and to be established correctly and sustained well.

"This is an act of pure Golden love which becomes an actual Golden Creation that can live and breathe, thrive and multiply. That's how it works.

"As I said, in this creative act and ability you are already highly skilled. This is exactly what Lemuria of Origin was about for us—Conscious Golden Creatorship. You know the ins and outs of it well. It's time for each one of you to remember how adept at this you already are. This is your Golden Memory returning in these most exciting ways!

"Are you ready?

"Go inside of yourselves and harness this. You will know exactly what I mean."

As I listen to Terra's instruction, I feel deeply excited and my insides are powerfully stirred. Something is definitely "percolating" inside of me, deep within my cells. Yes, I can see how she would describe this as "waking back up" because that's exactly what it feels like to me. It's deep, strong, and present: its time has come and I love it.

After a moment, I manage to sink quietly into myself and prepare to listen, hear, and feel. This is mine to do and mine to know.

My heart opens wide. I enter it and bow down in humility, respect, and receptivity. In response, there is a powerful wave of energy that begins to rise inside of me, one which I recognize as being most familiar. I remember it now. It is strong and deliberate, deep and broad. I recognize it as my true source of Power, something confident and life giving that I haven't felt in a long, long time. It deliberately comes to me, enveloping and permeating as I kneel quietly inside the center of my Golden Heart.

My Remembering continues as I feel into the sensation and find the ability to create; to birth and deliver forth in this powerful Golden way. I am being consciously re-empowered by this knowing and capability once more. I recognize how deeply WELL this makes me feel, on every level.

I know these are my sacred Birthing Conduits opening up and flowing properly again; activated intently by my Source through the center of my Golden Heart, fueled by my deepest Golden passion and power. It is Golden Love in action, full on. There is no question that what this creates is of higher purpose and greater benefit because that is all it ever seeks to do. That is all it knows.

I know that this is ME doing what I love to do the most, being in the way that draws new dimensions of strength, vision, power, and further ability—and through it all, pure joy. If I had to describe the ultimate joy that breathes, exhilarates, laughs, and lives me—this would be it: this feeling and this sensation, THIS experience of BEING the power of pure Golden Creation, with all my senses awake and aware; working, dancing, and delivering.

I remember vividly that there is nothing else like it. It's what would catapult me out of bed in the morning in Lemuria! It was incredibly empowering, inspiring, strong, and rejoicing. Every day was a discovery and revelation of this Creative Power and I reveled in it and let it revel in me because, after all, doesn't this pure power of loving LOVE to feel itself happening and creating? It isn't just about me, the instrument through which it comes forth. It is equally about the energy itself which thrives on its freedom and expression of making pure beauty out of itself. It's the magic of it—up close and personal, intimate and splendid. I adore this in me. I adore that my Creator moves me and moves through me, as me, like this. It's exhilarating and rejuvenating, splendid and free.

You get the picture, Dear Reader. I could talk about this for days, I love it so! And, isn't it just heavenly to be able to focus on and feel something so purely glorious and life affirming for a change? I certainly appreciate it much more because I haven't had it for a long time.

My, oh my, I'm drinking this in. Are you, dear Reader, remembering your own perhaps? Are you remembering what it's like to create like this yourself? Are you being stirred in these ways too? I hope so, because it's right there inside of you as well. You'll see.

Okay, back to focus now.

As I was saying, the great wave of my creative memory is rising up inside of me and scooping me into its arms. I ask my heart, "What do you yearn to create?" And it answers me with still another wave of energy and flooding of sensation. I can tell that it is trying its best to start slowly, but its eagerness is almost getting the better of it.

My inner senses experience what it would be like to be as a beautiful fireworks display exploding in the sky. It is a pure, bright, pulsating display of color and electricity. This is combined with the steady strength of my creative power coming up from underneath, and the result is something that absolutely KNOWS it can BE. It will only go forward; there is no stagnation and no back peddling. It's powerful drive and intent is to deliver forward and deposit itself into the space upon Terra's surface; which has been made ready for it to "ground in" and anchor; rooting down, deep and secure.

I continue to sit, letting all the colors and patterns of light burst open with life inside of me. It's absolutely exhilarating, and I understand the intensity of my heart's desire and the gentle yet strong force of its power. It clearly knows what it wants, and it has what it takes to get there and deliver itself.

After a few moments the atmosphere inside of me quiets down, leaving a wonderful sensation of soft shimmering lightness with my inner energies weaving and blending themselves gracefully together into yet more new patterns and shapes. I would describe this as creation in process—blending and merging its energies and bringing new life out of itself. It swirls sensually around inside of me, and I feel as if I am being stirred by Golden snowflake-like crystals, only they have substance, intelligence, and purpose.

That's what I am acutely aware of, that this power of Creation has such Intelligence. It IS Intelligence. It is teaching me about itself—not from an outside point of view, an "end product," but from its deepest inner process and movement and the intricacies of its evolvement. It gradually becomes like one body of feeling, as Terra said it would. It has substance, texture, taste, feel, and almost smell. It's tactile, a beautiful living energy dancing to its exquisite song.

As I feel and clearly understand these things, I become conscious that, yes, my Golden Memory in these ways, and at these levels, is indeed returning—and this makes me feel so happy.

As for my response to Terra's earlier question about what, precisely, I want to create in the open space up top?

This, I have decided, is exactly what I choose to plant when I get there: all of this Golden energetic substance will be going into the soil in my garden. It will provide food and water as well, and the elements my Golden Self needs in order to rebuild my Golden Body and my Golden World.

"Yes, Beloved," I hear Terra's kind, motherly voice in my ear. *"All of you will be deliberately generating forth a brand new field of Golden Consciousness into the physical world; a brand new platform that will sustain complete Harmony, and all the elements therein: balance, co-creation, responsibility, and leadership. Golden Love will be your Leader. Golden Love will be the gift you give from this time forward.*

"You are clear now. You know what you want to do and how to do it."

In the midst of listening to Terra's voice, I hear a distinct pulsating note being born from deep inside me. It is the Golden Frequency finally sounding inside of me the way Terra said it would. It literally vibrates in my body, and my cells respond eagerly. My insides light up like a panel board of circuitry being switched on. My inner Birthing Conduits and creative pathways become even more highly charged and activated. It's as though I, as a "divinely inspired creative machine," am being moved into full gear. It is so strong in its momentum that I am literally aching to express this fullness and readiness to deliver. I know it is time.

"Take a deep breath," I hear Terra say. *"Focus on your breathing. Soon you will be overtaken by it, and you must simply let go and trust this process in its infinite wisdom.*

"The time has come, and you are ready to be born anew. There is no turning back. There is only forward motion ahead.

"Yield to this, beautiful One. This is the greatest act of Golden Creation that has ever moved you. YOU are both the recipient and deliverer of this. Give birth and be born anew."

The frequency sounds more intensely, so much so that it seems to scoop everything up inside of itself, including all of my awareness. I am no longer sitting in the Great Hall. Instead, I notice my energies relocating, moving in two distinctly different directions and patterns—each one with the same intent, but from completely different angles.

I become aware of my energies moving upward to Terra's surface again. I sense that I am there to "check it out," to see the state of things and make my discovery about it. As my sensors emerge out on top, I become aware of that "hush" all around that Terra spoke of earlier. It is totally and completely quiet, with no sound except for that of empty space.

I am absolutely thrilled. I can see for myself that we did indeed successfully give the gift of Forgiveness in an absolutely complete and thorough way. There is certainly no question about it. All that is here now is peace, stillness, quiet, and emptiness…open space.

As I stand here listening to and witnessing this wondrous sensation of open space, I notice a flavor of questioning beginning to form in the air. It's as if this place and space is asking me why I am here, what do I want: are we joining or not? As I feel this, I realize that it is actually offering itself to me and saying, *"I am here for you. The choice is yours."*

I am touched by its gifting and this rekindles deep memories of my original arrival on Terra so long ago, in that time before Lemuria was even born. My intense longing to be on her surface rises again, and I meet this open space with all my heart. "Yes, oh yes, I long to be here with you, my dear Terra, and to plant myself in full Golden physical awareness again, if you would be so kind as to have me."

In response, the energy immediately joins with mine in a clear statement of agreement and affirmation. I am aware that this is the initial stage of preparation for my physical emergence yet to come, and I know exactly what I need to do next.

Instinctively, I gently return into Terra's body without breaking the connection I have made, knowing full well that I have created a "bridge" for what is to come. Once back inside, I focus my attention on my breath of Golden Creation, inhaling deeply and exhaling fully. I blow it directly up through the body of Terra, up through the many layers of her fabric and "flesh" until it reaches the deep roots that stretch down from her surface from its place of "open space."

I continue to blow my Golden Breath into those roots, watching as it moves up through the actual cells of Terra's soil and merges into that Intelligence that makes up the crust of her body. I delight in this tangibility and awareness. I greet it again and it receives me warmly. We are joined. It is no longer just "empty space." I have begun to fill it with active Golden Life Force with new point and purpose. Now we're cooking!

I continue with my breath of honoring and appreciation. I know this energetic preparation is essential for this intelligent "body" of ground, this atmosphere, and for me. As I breathe into it, I know I am gradually Golden "texturizing" the cells, atoms, and molecules of it. I am creating a platform upon which I will land and into which I will deepen and integrate. I am consciously harmonizing with it, and it with me.

We are aligning perfectly. In this way we will be able to receive each other easily and comfortably when I emerge in full Golden body—and with full cognition of what is taking place. It is also the most respectful and honoring thing to do. I am loving this. I love being this conscious about creation. And I know, of course, that I am not the only one doing this. Although I am not focused on my other Golden Family members right now, I know they are doing exactly the same thing as I am. We are in this process of deliberate Golden Creation together. I delight in this knowing, and again it stirs my Golden Memory banks, reminding me of happy and fulfilling times back in Lemuria of Origin.

After a few more moments, this energetic blending and "texturizing process" feels done for now and my energies shift completely toward another direction entirely. I start to feel myself swimming again, deep inside Terra's Golden Birthing Waters, the Great Golden Ocean of Love. My whole focus turns toward this blessed Golden Sea.

And I see so many of my Golden friends around me!

There are many of us Golden Ones here, swimming together, reaching with long slow strokes, as we move gracefully through the waters. There is only the sounding of the great Golden Frequency that carries us, moving us along steadily. It is our music and we are its shining Golden dancers in this beautiful water ballet. The Birthing Waters are warm and sensual, and we are delighting in them.

The Golden Frequency alters, and our direction shifts along with it. We start to move upward, swimming toward what we know will soon be air and light, free of the sheltering waters. Our limbs become stronger and we stretch further and reach up hungrily as we feel our Souls aching to break through that final layer of wet, even though it is still well out of reach.

We continue to strive, deliberately and fiercely, as we rise up and up. Our power of passion and purpose propels us as we continue to lift ourselves higher. The Golden Frequency sounds ever louder, and our energetic crystalline structures begin to form actual physical shape and substance.

We are truly beginning to re-embody! I begin to hear and feel my breath in a way that I haven't for a long time; it is deep, clear and resonant in my lungs, potently enriching my cells throughout. There is no sound but that which is the Frequency Sounding, lifting us determinedly and returning us to our bodies and our Golden Homeland.

We are giant Golden Beings, beginning to glow with sheer Golden physicality. I stretch my arms out as far as they will reach with each upward stroke, and I can feel the joyous buoyancy of the waters as if they are intently lifting me as well.

My tactile senses are alive, alert, and receptive to every nuance of where I am and what I feel—the sensation of gliding, the thrust of upward heaving, the inner heat being generated inside my physical torso. With each second passing, I am becoming more and more solid in my body. What an extraordinary feeling! I don't have time to stop and take it all in, but I am acutely aware that it feels both familiar and new. The higher I go, the more physically strong and substantial my body feels, and I know my Golden friends around me are experiencing the same.

We continue to hoist ourselves upward—getting to the top is the only thing that matters.

At last we see the soft diffused light filtering down from above the waters! My heart literally lurches toward it as it beckons to me. I reach with one last lunging stroke and break through the top of the waterline.

Yes!

My solid Golden Body rises up silently and slowly out of the waters, tall and hovering on the glassy surface of the sea. I am vibrating and glowing with both exertion and Golden Radiance fully shining. My glistening wet body is poised, vigorous, and fully Golden vital! What a picture this must be! This is outstanding!

I become conscious of many things, the most central of which is the feeling of many Golden Ones rising out of the sea to join me. We are as one body of Golden Gentle Giants that have emerged from the depths of ancient time. What a sensation of remembrance this is; what a sensation of knowing that this, exactly this, was destined to be...NOW.

I am completely overtaken by this TRUTH for a moment as it arcs keenly through me, and I quiver inside and out. It cements in this reality, stamping it in place, telling me unequivocally that only great and blessed things will come from this.

And then, there is nothing to do but...INHALE.

I have waited to breathe in this great, glorious fresh air for a long time, and it feels fantastic!

I breathe in deep gulps of it, deep down into the bottom of my lungs. It feels so fresh, fine, and invigorating! Oh, what a sheer delight this is: the power of my physical body coming to life! I look down at myself in wonder as I feel the strength of my muscles, alive and well. I love this physicality! I LOVE being physical again—and so Golden glowing too!

The Sounding of the Frequency continues even out here, its purposefulness still obvious by its tone and intensity. I look around, and my sight sees only our beautiful body of Golden Ones, beginning to glide silently and effortlessly across our brilliant Golden Sea. She is shining beneath our feet, and we can feel her happiness over our successful emergence.

We can see the beach ahead, and move in that direction. Soon, I know that my feet will stand on the solid surface of Terra once again. It is a dream coming true. I close my eyes for a brief moment, and feel the sensation as my feet touch her ground at last. She feels solid, spongy, and substantial.

I have finally landed, literally.

We Golden Ones continue to move as one great Golden Body, walking through the gently caressing waves to meet the sands of the beach. Our beautiful Golden Beach—I remember her so well. What an exquisite sensation this is, with my toes curling into the Golden grains of sand as they yield under my feet, greeting me home again. The smell of the moist salt air combines with the freshness of this beautiful morning. It is dawn and it is, once again, that sacred time when we would gather in Lemuria to greet the glorious day, to herald the joy of being awake and one with that which is wondrous.

We are doing it again as if we hadn't skipped a single beat.

The Golden Frequency pulsates more quietly but is still steady and clear. Our voices merge with it, rising up in absolute joy as we sound our collective Golden Frequency. The sound echoes around in complete celebration, signaling our victory. We have arrived! Our emergence is complete, and our physical Golden Homecoming is real. We are here now. We are Golden Gentle Giants ready to set forth and reestablish our glorious Golden World!

HALLELUJAH!

My attention wants to focus on looking around and feasting on the immense beauty that is everywhere—but my energies stop me, directing me to focus only on this family of Golden Ones who stand here with me. I become aware that there are throngs of us—many more than I had thought. I follow my inner directive and stay focused on them, on our frequency sounding, and on the sensation of finally being out in the fresh air; breathing deeply and deliciously.

Slowly the Sun rises. Oh, my glorious Golden Sun, I have missed you so much!

I begin to feel its warmth caressing me, gently making my skin tingle all over with its glow and greeting. I am thrilled to receive, to experience this divine and blessed energy again. I close my eyes and drink it in for a moment. I am touched, and I say, "Thank you, thank you dear, sweet Sun. Thank you for all the Golden Blessings of love that you are. Thank you."

I feel a strong, compelling sense of purpose, and I know there is something important that I need to do now. I hear Avalar's voice nearby; it is the soft, sweet lilt of her song that seems to be riding the glow of the sun in its shining. I look in the direction of her voice, and see both her and Andar walking toward us.

As they join us, we hug and take some time to simply enjoy this reunion, this celebration of huge success and completion—in many ways and on many levels. We have tears of joy running down our cheeks as we embrace one another, and let our triumph slowly begin to sink in.

Finally, it is time to get on with our purpose that is intensely calling to us. We move to form one large circle which is joined by another circle of Golden Ones around it. Soon, we are a splendidly giant weave of several Golden circles, each one surrounding the other, completely connected through the holding of happy Golden hands.

We are still singing our frequency softly as we savor one another through our physical touch—warm Golden bodies and pulses beating; we are all here in flesh and blood. Our vibrant Golden physicality makes our hearts sing and our eyes shine with gratitude, relief, and wondrousness.

We are indeed enormously happy to be here, on the surface of Terra's beautiful Golden Body—to be back in our Golden Physical bodies again!

I take a moment to drink it in, savoring as much as I can.

I still know there is yet another greater purpose calling for attention. I don't know what it is, but I am well aware of its urgency. I respectfully wait for it to inform me; I know there will be plenty of time.

But, oh, dear Reader, isn't it grand that we finally made it here? YES!

ReConnecting and ReActivating
Our Sacred Golden Configuration

The Golden Witness speaks:

Once we are in position, Andar and Avalar move into the center of our inner-most circle. They are holding hands, and their energies are weaving and blending together through their bodies, just the way they used to do back in Lemuria of Origin. Back then we would see this often, this beautiful heightened picture of their loving and understanding. In witnessing them standing unified in exactly this way in the midst of our circle, I know, yet again, that all is going to be well. Everything about this moment is describing the harmony and perfection of it—the way it used to be back in Lemuria. So it is now, and so it will be. I can feel it; I can feel the "rightness of it."

Slowly, Andar turns and circles his gaze around to meet all of our eyes. He is taking us in as he looks at us, and I feel his love touching me in a deep and comforting way. After a moment, he begins to speak with such tenderness in his voice:

"Great Golden Ones, I welcome and honor you, my dearest Golden Friends. You are so powerful and beautiful. You are now re-embodied and whole with your Golden Light and Love powering through you for us to see and rejoice in. You have made it! You have made it through to this 'end place'—the accomplishment and triumph of Golden Spirit. You are strong, sovereign, and free; and I am extremely proud of you. I am proud to be able to call us One Golden Shining Family back on Terra's sweet surface again.

"Congratulations! This is a great triumph for you, and for all of us. I know you will gradually reintegrate yourselves physically as our adventure starts anew. It is a great Birthing and we are here now to nurture and support it to the best of our Golden Abilities.

"Before we can get on with the process of daily living in our Golden way, there is something important which needs to be completed in order for us to physically flourish here again. Avalar will be guiding you through these last parts of our Golden reintegration. My role in this is to hold the space steady for this powerful reconnecting of your energies with our Sacred Golden Configuration. Avalar will explain the situation thoroughly, and I urge you to simply listen and follow her lead."

Gently, with the sounding of the Golden Frequency still humming along quietly in the background, Avalar steps forward and begins to speak. Her clear, melodic voice is poignant.

"My most beautiful Beloveds," she says, with so much warmth and love that it brings tears to my eyes. *"Congratulations! Yes, you are finally here! You have all arrived back on Terra's most beautiful surface with all the space that you have now created for yourselves to build Golden Life anew. This is a rich moment, and one which will be a central part of our Golden History Storytelling in the future.*

"This marks a great triumph for you; a victory on many, many levels—more than you even know. I honor you, and bow down in praise of your enormous strength and determination to rise again. It is with tremendous pride that I witness the love and devotion that has carried you through so much, and which brings you at last to this sacred moment right here, right now.

"Bless you, Golden Ones, bless you. I celebrate you and your triumph.

"Now that you have successfully arrived, I know that you are eager to taste and savor everything that Terra has for you. But first, there are some final pieces of our Golden re-embodiment that need to be attended to. I know you have been sensing the urgency of this, and I am grateful for your willingness to stay focused on birthing for a while longer.

"Our next task is to reconnect with our original Golden Configuration and invite its energies to wake back up and reactivate fully. This will allow us to draw on its wealth of stability and support. You remember, dear Ones, that this Golden Configuration is what we so painstakingly built through our love and intention, way back at the beginning of our Lemuria of Origin. Without that base, if you recall, we would have had no solid foundation to support and anchor our growth; the grounding energies would not have been there to hold us steady. Without it, there would have been no Lemuria to even remember, because our creations would have toppled over like twigs being blown around in the wind. Before we can firmly reestablish our Golden World here, this supporting base of our Golden Configuration needs to be activated and in full operation again.

"Once this Configuration has begun, it will re-stimulate and re-illuminate the massive network of Golden Lay Lines and Conduits that run beneath Terra's surface. It will move all of those Golden energies back into the elements that make up her crust. This will stretch out and become the great Golden Grid which will sustain us ever forward on Terra's beautiful surface. This ground will have become illuminated as our Golden Land upon which we will build our Golden World.

"Through the process of this happening, the memory of this configuration and Golden grid patterning and life force will also be reawakened and reactivated inside your bodies and physical cellular structures. You hold all of this thriving, illuminated memory inside of your cells, and now it will be brought back into your active conscious awareness again. In this way, your internal base, and that of Terra's ground and surface, will be realigned properly in this Golden Way. You will recognize and know the life force and supportive power of it inside of you once more. It will, of course, be enormously strengthening and empowering for you.

"In doing this conscious reconnecting and reactivating, we set the course for our new future. We bring back into play, and into memory, all of our flourishing history and the many gifts that we created FOR PRECISELY THIS TIME NOW. We re-source ourselves as our One Golden World physically embodied and manifesting on Terra's surface.

"We, as Golden Embodied Ones, are here to flourish and thrive—not just survive. We are here to undertake a great project the way we did back in Lemuria of Origin together. Yes, we are here to bring forth the Gold, to be the Gold, and to gift the Gold forward through our deliberate and conscious Creations again.

"This is what you feel calling to you, and now is the time to meet it. In doing so, you will see that this marks one last Choice Point that needs to be declared.

"I know you are perhaps surprised that there are so many Choice Points along the way of our Conscious Creation, but each one leaves an indelible stamp of commitment which lights your way forward. As I have made clear, reactivating our Golden Configuration, and thereby resetting our Golden Grid, needs to happen in order for us to move forward in our Golden purpose. This is a deliberate and conscious undertaking on our part, and is to be done together. It is not something to be taken lightly, nor accomplished in any way that is less than fully thorough.

"That is why it is a Choice Point for you: it is the choice to reactivate the configuration and reset this Golden platform, thereby becoming the recipient of its tremendous power and multilayered Golden Gifts once more.

"In your choice making, also be clear and cognizant of your pledge, of your conscious commitment to follow through and stay this new course. KNOW THAT SAYING 'YES' TO THIS CHOICE IS FULLY SETTING YOU APART FROM ALL THAT HAS BEEN REGARDING MONDOR. IT IS SETTING

YOUR COURSE SOLIDLY AS GOLDEN LEMURIA, EXCLUSIVELY, FROM THIS MOMENT FORWARD.

"*Once chosen, this will be activated, and you will be on a 'moving train.' Nothing will ever be the same again—nothing.*

"*You will reach far beyond anywhere you have ever been, both inside and outside of yourselves. You will bring to bear all of your fruitfulness from Lemuria of Origin PLUS all that you have gained and learned from your experiences since then. You are incredibly strong and powerful Golden Ones—wiser and happier than you even know, and far, far more capable than you can imagine. All of this will reveal itself soon.*

"*In consciously and deliberately choosing to live this Golden Life, and in choosing to reactivate this Golden Power and Intelligence on all levels, you also choose to hold yourself fully responsible for all that you are and TO all that you are. You choose to actively RESPOND to, and support, the greatness of you and the greatness of our one Golden World. You are fully Golden capable:*

"*SHINING,*

"*SPLENDID,*

"*EUPHORIC,*

"*LOVING,*

"*COMPASSIONATE,*

"*CAPABLE,*

"*CONFIDENT,*

"*CLEAR,*

"*AND*

"*RESOURCEFUL.*

"*These are but a few descriptive words that do not even touch the long list of attributes of which you are made. My point in expressing them is to jog your memory, yet again, and to fill you in on what will be expected of you. This is not because I am expecting any of this, but because YOU are. Isn't that why you came—to respond to that which is your inherent greatness?*

"*You know there has always been more to you than you have expressed. You know there has always been something 'special' waiting inside of you. The very thing that has always made you feel different is the very thing that has been waiting to be given space and permission to express and manifest itself. It is the very thing that has been waiting to be known and brought forth by you.*

"Well…it's time has come: now is that time.

"I urge you to make this final choosing another clear and conscious move forward. Step up with all of us because YOU WANT TO, because YOU CHOOSE TO, and because YOU COMMIT to this and commit to YOU: Golden You, Golden Life, Golden World—One Golden Heart.

"It is, again, your choice."

I feel the power of Avalar's message as I listen to her words, and it makes me almost tremble with the unexpressed life force that is hungry to break forth from inside. There is so much being said between the lines, and I know this crystal clearly. I am being greatly stirred and rekindled, and every choice point I meet in this process empowers me and brings me more and more back to life.

I continue to be amazed at how many choice points there are in this creative process. I am well aware that each one needs to be met, and to be made with absolute clarity and consciousness. I know there is no waffling room—it is either all in or all out. I know that this indicates the power of who we are and what we are capable of bringing forth. I know that this is why these choice points are not small, nor are they presented idly. Conscious Golden Creation is exactly that: CONSCIOUS Golden Creation!

Each step is deliberate and thought provoking. Each one asks me to show up and be present one hundred percent. In so doing, I can receive and be the complete fullness of what is possible. Nothing less will do if we are to truly reestablish a Golden World. That, I know. There is nothing small about this, absolutely nothing; and there is nothing small about me. Anything "small" is over for me, simply over.

Avalar's voice joins my thoughts as I hear her say:

"Yes, everyone, once again, this is Conscious Golden Creation at work.

"Remember in Lemuria, how you loved to step up in your natural excellence? Remember how you loved the fullness of committing to your splendid creations with absolutely no holding back? Remember what it felt like to trust yourselves, your Source, your Heart, and your Gold one hundred percent and more?

"This is where you find yourselves once more—deciding if you want to be and live that way again. It is in you; it is all in you. But, as always, free will remains the deciding factor.

"So…take a moment and make your choice.

"Remember, in saying yes, you also say yes to following through and staying the course, no matter what.

"You know the drill: Decide. Declare. Do.

"This is your moment, and a great moment it is. The one for which you've been waiting—Golden Physical World, One Golden Heart thriving. Here again? Yes, it is. It is a great moment, indeed.

"You choose.

"I ask each of you to consciously declare your choice now."

Looking around, I become acutely aware of the passion and commitment in all that surround me; the strength and dedication is palpable. We have come through so much, and to make this final choice for the next undertaking is an honor and a privilege, a true blessing for each one of us. Our heart's desire is surging forward toward this new challenge of self-expression. WE are the ones who will benefit after all, aren't we? Wouldn't you want to do this as well, dear Reader?

The thought of being an active and integral part of something as delicious, wondrous, and magnificent as Lemuria flourishing again delights ALL of my senses! I vividly recall the feeling, and of course I want this again! I can't wait for the surging of such immense creative power inside of me and through me: a brilliant Body, Being, and instrument of Divine Golden Love!

It makes me hunger and long for it. I love it and it is all that I want. Yes, I will commit and stay the course—no matter what. I know that only great things can come from this, I simply know it. I will stretch and be stretched, and I will love the challenge. Isn't this perfect?

Onward! I choose YES—absolutely one hundred percent YES! I'm ALL in! Let's go!

And, of course, I know that everyone else is on board too. We all declare this choice exuberantly as we rally ourselves for our future here together: the Golden course has now been set.

"Take a deep breath in," says Avalar joyously.

"Finally, we are ready! Let's get started!"

I breathe as fully as I can. It feels great to feel my lungs, my actual physical lungs, filling up with this splendidly fresh and invigorating air. I love it!

I exhale slowly, and I can tell that something has already inexplicably shifted: in less than a heartbeat this "train is in motion!" I can hear the wheels turning, the motor revving up, and everything moving deliberately into higher and higher gear.

Avalar's presence becomes full on and powerful, focused and directing, and her voice guides us clearly:

"Let us stand strong and clear as we meet our Golden Configuration again and take a bold step forward in inviting its power back to this surface and back into our cellular memories. It is yearning to meet us again. Let us consciously realign with it and receive it so that we can be supported and empowered by it—and create forth successfully because of its strength and steadfastness, once again.

"You are such strong Golden Ones of such powerful and dedicated heart. Let this be."

I feel Avalar's energy so strongly, it is as though she has come to me and is squeezing both my hands in hers. I know that she is doing this with all of us, giving us her ample strength to become crystal clear about this truth. She is enabling us to be physically Golden sovereign, right here and right now, so we can see this through properly. She is certain that, together, we can do this.

She knows that we have this ancient memory inside of ourselves, and that the destiny moment has come for us to call this back up, and to hold it steady in our position of present time. We are restoring our Golden Configuration to full power again, harnessing this base of our Golden World, and remembering what we are truly capable of. When the process has been completed, we can express it openly and fully once more.

"Breathe deeply and slowly," Avalar instructs us. *"Breathe this Golden Sustaining Power up into your bodies, minds, hearts, and emotions. Own it once again. Do this now, as you did so thoroughly long ago."*

I breathe; we are all breathing intently.

A harmonizing with something ancient begins to flow up from the ground beneath Terra and ourselves. It hears our calling and responds in turn, and I feel the ground shifting beneath our feet. With my inner eye I can see the Golden Configuration in all its beauty beginning to undulate and swirl, in and around itself, as it reawakens and begins to stir. It is coming back into its Remembrance in this yet deepest of ways.

As the ground quivers beneath my feet, I sense our Golden Configuration recognizing that this pivotal moment in our history has arrived. I feel it responding to our devotion and commitment. In response it is saying, *"Yes, I am here. I am coming back home to you. And, yes, we will rejoin in pure Golden strength, purpose, and abiding love."*

I begin to feel enormous gratitude for this beautiful Intelligence and its kind way.

"Let your hearts go to this," Avalar says gently. *"Let your hearts travel back deep inside our original Golden Configuration that was, and is, so precious*

to us. Let it receive you, and receive it, once again. Share yourselves and be shared with."

My awareness moves deep inside the labyrinth of this Configuration below Terra's ground. I continue to feel great motion and activity, and I can hear sounds like the popping and gurgling of energies breaking out and flowing again—streams undammed, opening up to find their dry river beds once more and moisten them anew.

Of course, these are the same pathways from Lemuria of Origin, but they are reinvigorated with new purpose and drive, refreshed conscious sentient expressions of themselves. They have a plan now that they have been stirred and invited to exercise and express fully again. They make their choice to participate, to move and to flow in the name of our one purpose together: OUR ONE GOLDEN HEART.

I am reminded, once again, that we are one Golden Family, including ALL of Golden Life in its rich array of multitudinous forms everywhere. Ours is a family that is vast, deep, broad, high, full, and rich.

I reach further inside and feel my love meeting these flowing energies. In so doing, I deeply touch the heart of this configuration itself and its labyrinth of pathways and conduits that are part of its beautiful design. I feel it as its very own, and yet I also feel it as a part of me. I breathe my love into it. I am reminded of how deeply I care for it and how much I appreciate this beautiful living creation and its loving intelligence. It is the supportive and sustaining base of all that I have physically been before in my pure Golden embodiment.

Its energies are literally touching me back, caring for me, merging and aligning in me, into my cells which are hungrily reabsorbing it. My Golden Cellular memory of it is waking up and systematically realigning itself into perfect position with this powerful Golden foundation.

I begin to feel its strength, purpose, and support beneath me and inside of me. It is holding and supporting me as if I stand right in the palm of its strong and steady hand. I am absolutely secure. From this base, I feel I can do anything and will remain steady and secure. What a deep, empowering, and sustaining feeling this is! Dear Reader, I feel like I could do anything! I had forgotten the pure strength of this beautiful blessing we had created long, long ago.

For a brief moment, I flash back upon when we originally made and set this Golden Configuration. I remember how painstaking it was to build, and how careful and deliberate we were in that process of birthing and setting it up perfectly for its greater purpose. It was the first of our Golden creations and, of course, the one that would support and sustain us throughout.

I am reminded of my original relationship to it, and how deeply supported

I always felt by it in Lemuria from that first moment on. I am aware that my feeling about it is exactly the same. I can literally feel how solid and steady, how completely adept and capable it is. I am also aware of how much it wants to support me, and the many others that make up our Golden World.

I am quite moved by how devoted, loving, and strong this configuration truly is—and now it is alive and well and activating itself fully again. I am also aware of its pure joy of being, and how grateful it is to be free, inspired, enlivened, and UTILIZED again. I feel it deliberately breathing itself back into full life through its intelligence and the rekindling of the memory of its devotion and purpose to all of us and our One Golden Heart.

As I feel this happening, I also feel it deep down inside my body, a knowing that I am this steady and secure in myself once more. I am remembering it all inside of me, as me. My cellular memory of this is back and I am grateful with every atom of my being.

I hear Avalar's voice coming back into range as she gently guides me toward shifting my focus, now that this base is "up and running" again.

"Please continue to breathe deeply, Golden Ones," she says. *"Only this time, breathe your Golden Love into the soil itself, into the microbe families, into all the filaments and life bringing elements that make up this outer layer of Terra's beautiful body. Remind all of these precious life forms, cells, atoms, and molecules of what once was and how they flourished as the foundational Golden elements of our glorious Golden World. Remind them of your love for them. Touch them and let them feel you. Breathe into them. Breathe deeply, quietly, and slowly."*

I yield to this completely. I fully and freely let go, and as I do so, I begin to cry. My tears come from a huge river of profoundly deep yearning and caring that is opening back up inside of me. My deep ache to love this soil, this ground, and everything that is a part of it is intense and moving; my love is pouring out of me with abandon. I embrace and sweep and infuse this sweet soil, this sacred and precious ground, with my breath, my tears, and all of my heart.

After a few moments of doing this, I stop and wipe my eyes, and I feel it receiving me. It is receiving me and I know it and feel it!

In the next heartbeat, it responds to me with its ever sustaining love, moving me to tears once more. I feel as though it is breathing me in exactly the same way I am breathing it. Golden breath is moving gently back and forth, until we have merged and blended completely into one exquisite Golden pattern. It continues to flow smoothly, and to spread out further still in an exquisite sensation of the pure "rightness" of it all. This is a memory of mine which has become fully clear once more: it is Communion, Glorious Golden Communion. I know this is the beginning of that vast memory being rekindled, and am humbled to be standing on a ground of such pure beauty and love.

I continue to stand quietly, completely immersed and rejoicing as this beautiful ground celebrates in, and with, me.

Gradually, I can feel it beginning to glow and vibrate strongly with renewed Golden energy, life, and purpose.

I know with absolute clarity that this marks the start of the resetting of our beautiful Golden Grid. It permeates, spreading far across this beautiful land, and I am borne along, as it holds and illuminates me. All of Golden Life is reawakening itself throughout these lay lines, conduits, and pathways. It is sharing its intelligence and joy for life all across this sacred surface of Terra—ours once more.

At the same time, this is happening inside of my cellular structure, my body, and my internal "Golden Land" as well. I breathe, this time a deep sigh of relief and pleasure as I savor it; I love all of this completely, and it feels absolutely right.

Finally, the sensations begin to slow and become quiet. They gently fade as our intimate communion winds down for now. I have a clear knowing that our purpose here is complete and successful. I know that all things are now strong and steady, and right where they belong.

Before long, out of the quiet emerges a low, steady, happy "hum." I have a knowing that it is the purring of Golden Life sounding itself. I smile at the success of our venture, appreciating that all is secure, happy, and well—ready for whatever is next in a Golden way.

I hear Avalar's voice in my ear, as I feel her words touching my heart:

"Yes, indeed, the Golden Configuration is now fully reactivated. It is complete in its restoration and reintegration into our beautiful ground and all its elements, into our physical systems, and our One Golden Heart Consciousness here on the surface. In addition, this stage of the Golden Grid has been re-illuminated and successfully reset across this land. Now we can move forward into the last and final piece.

"Another great job well done, Golden Ones! You certainly are utilizing your Golden Creation abilities well. Yes, indeed!

"Congratulations!

"Hallelujah!"

AVALAR'S GOLDEN CLARION CALL TO ALL OF GOLDEN LIFE: FINAL GOLDEN UNION

The Golden Witness speaks:

Our triumph continues! We seem to be having one success after another.

We are all feeling really good right now—good about ourselves, about what we have done, and excited to see what is next. With each completed stage of our creative birthing, our systems are becoming brighter and stronger, and there is a true vibrancy and vitality that is beginning to emanate from each of us. It is our Golden Glow. It's so nice to feel it again and to be restored.

Avalar says with such joy in her voice:

"Beloveds, Beautiful Ones, yes, I know how well you are feeling, and I am happy to see this. It has been a long time since you have tasted your true and inherent wellness, and it becomes you. Your joy is beginning to find its natural way out, and your Golden Energy Fields are radiating and shining powerfully. As we continue completing this final process of moving forward, you will become even stronger still.

"Each step brings you back into your proper place as a Golden Gentle Giant, and your whole system responds—awakening and reactivating more and more. It is a thoroughly rejuvenating and revitalizing remembrance for you, and brings nothing but goodness inside and out. Bless you all; bless you for your steadfastness and commitment to reach this final turn."

Avalar's beautiful voice fades gently into the background as I get caught up in my experience of how physically comfortable I am feeling. As I stand here quietly appreciating this, I also become aware of how incredibly grounded I feel.

Yes, I remember this feeling distinctly. It's the way I always felt in Lemuria of Origin. It is safe, secure, and solid, and makes me totally comfortable and at ease in my body: all is peaceful with my world. I am perfectly stable on Terra, and she is perfectly stable within me. I am completely physically Golden re-secured, physically Golden Grounded again. I inhale deeply and truly let myself take a moment to thoroughly acknowledge and appreciate this.

I become aware of my cellular memories and pathways flowing properly as well, with all my conduits of Golden Illumination shining brightly and clearly through me, within me, and as me. The more I appreciate this and the longer I stand here, the more I realize fully that I am Soul in Body again. I haven't felt this way in a long time.

I am my Golden Soul standing strong and steady on my two Golden feet, right here in and as my Golden Physical Body on Golden Terra. There is no feeling of separation between my Soul and me. As I said, I am Golden Soul, Golden fully embodied again.

I remember this reality from Lemuria of Origin. Back then, I never had any thought that it could or would be otherwise—it never even occurred to me. Now that I am this again, I am so thankful and relieved. I am Home; I am thoroughly and fully "home," in me and as me.

Dear Reader, do you have any idea what a special and extraordinary feeling this is? Perhaps you can imagine. I know the "small state" well, but I realize it is indeed gone. It has disappeared—poof.

Here I am in my glory and Golden Love, completely physicalized as a huge and substantial radiant Golden glowing physical Being. I feel my power in this and I own it. It illuminates me fully, and I feel enormously strong and resilient because of it. Joyous? Inspired? Grateful? I would most definitely say so.

Suddenly, it dawns on me—I feel…FREE again! I am free in my physical body in my physical world.

I'm almost shocked by this sensation for a moment, and humbled as well. It vibrates through me powerfully; I am tremendously alive! I savor this feeling, letting the reality of it sink into my senses. I breathe deeply into it and embrace it, letting the words roll around on my tongue as I repeat to myself, "I am free, I am free, I am totally Golden Free."

I become aware of how much I have missed and ached for this. It makes me realize how potent and precious this is; that it is something I will never take for granted again. I am deeply grateful for its return to me now.

I hear Avalar's voice entering my thoughts, as she calls to us excitedly:

"Come, everyone, the sacred Golden Ground has been fully prepared, and we are now ready to call in the rest of the Golden Family. It is time.

"We are bringing everyone home to Terra again to thoroughly reactivate the tapestry of our Golden Imprint in the present time, in all its fullness and glory. This will complete the setting of our Golden Grid and our universe will be a closed unit unto itself in this physical world once more.

"As you know, our Golden Imprint holds the memory of our history as Lemuria flourishing—as our Golden World thriving—on Terra's surface long ago. Its fully reactivated frequency, vibration, and illuminated patterning are essential to the continuation of our thriving consciousness from here on out. It feeds us continuously with its memory and beauty, inspiring us constantly to keep on creating ever more beautiful things and experiences to add into its weave. All of this will be up to speed again once the whole family has returned home here.

"So...let's get on with it, shall we?

"They have been waiting for this moment, and I can already feel their energies gathering eagerly far and wide. Let us bring them all home now and give them the great welcome they deserve.

"Are you ready everyone?"

My heart bursts open with joy as I realize what we are about to do. I know there are many more of us Golden Ones spread throughout Terra and the Cosmos; there are so many of us in our huge array of physical and non-physical forms. I am aware of how long everyone has been waiting for this moment.

YES!

We gather around, holding each other's hands and joining our hearts as we prepare to call them all home, back here to Terra. Even though there are many Golden Star Ones who will continue to remain active in those far off regions, their central focus will be here with us as a part of our Golden Age right here again. It will be, again, as it was in Lemuria of Origin when ALL of us joined through our hearts right here on Terra.

I see Avalar standing in our midst, her face radiant and shining with a glow that is more brilliant and serene than I have seen before. I know that she has been diligently preparing for this moment for a long time. Her face reflects that joy as she prepares to express her divine purpose in all its power and presence. I know this is her job to do, and I know that she is the only one who can do it. I respect her enormously as I watch her prepare to deliver her greatest gift of all.

A great hush descends upon this space and place, and an aura of reverence spreads throughout. I look at Avalar. Her eyes are closed, her hands folded in prayer position over her heart. She raises her face as if in communion with the Sun, and opens her mouth. In the midst of our deep quiet we hear this most beautiful sound permeating the air: Avalar's Golden Clarion Call.

It is the sound and song of pure Golden Love calling to all the Golden Life Forms everywhere, inviting them to stir, to awaken, and to return home to us here. She calls to the sacred memory of our one Golden Family union, asking it to return here as our One Golden Heart beating. She calls to the memories of sacred Golden Physicality asking that this state of awareness and reality reemerge in totality and be whole and flourishing and brilliant. She calls to the memory of this sacred Golden World whose time has come again.

Her notes sound through the air and travel vast distances to touch the many forms of Golden Sacred Souls that are waiting to hear and feel her in this moment, calling to them. I know we are standing here on this beach, but we are also standing everywhere throughout the universes—gently but surely arousing all the Golden Life Forms everywhere that have ever existed. It is time and the time is now. That is the Sounding of Avalar's Clarion Call. We are moved to raise our voices, and together we are sounding this call of love with her. Together, we sing to that which we love and have loved forever: our One Golden Heart.

It is our collective Golden Clarion Call. It is telling the Golden Life Forms everywhere that it is time to wake up, to get up, to live and flourish again.

Avalar's sound increases, intently leading our call through the atoms of time and space, reaching and touching the many Golden Ones throughout the globe and beyond, into the Stars. Our collective sound goes far and wide into hidden places and secret crevices where Golden Life Forms have been living and holding their energies in, close and safe. As our call reaches them, they hear us and respond with their senses unfurling, their veils dispersing, their shields of protection lifting, and their internal Golden Glow beginning to rise and radiate forth in total joy and eagerness.

Yes! We instantly feel the energy of their response. We are heard! Yes, we are heard!

Those Golden Life Forms are calling us back, joining in our song and doing their part to spread the word. Yes, to Golden Life everywhere—yes!

Our song grows exponentially with every new Golden voice joining in. It is the Sound of Golden Song rising and being generated everywhere.

I feel it—I feel it inside my body, and my heart is bursting with what feels like a sudden jolt of electricity and "joy juice" spreading its current through me on every level.

I am aware of the huge variety of forms of Golden Life, waking once more to move again on all levels and in many different ways. It is a vast network of Golden Life, too intricate for me to even fully grasp.

I am nonetheless aware of the fact that we humans are only ONE portion of this Radiant Golden Family, as I feel the incoming energies and responding calls from the animals, birds, insects, and flora and fauna. They are joined by the Devas and Nature Kingdoms, the Trees, Waters, Airs and Ethers, the Star Systems, Angels, Archangels, Sacred Guides and Guardians. ALL of Golden Life of every kind, here on Terra and beyond—far, far beyond.

It is incredibly vast, enormous and much more than I even remembered. Our Golden World is absolutely HUGE! This is MY FAMILY.

What a glorious sensation this is! I feel it with every cell of my body and Being, penetrating my mind and memory. It courses through me as if to say that I need to quickly rouse myself and make room for everyone in this beautiful, multilayered exuberant family. As I do so, I am reminded of how much they love me as I love all of them.

Yes, I had forgotten how deep, and how far and wide our love for one another goes. I had forgotten the reality of ALL of this love and support that we give to one another—and how immensely strong we are because of it. I had forgotten the depth and breadth of this huge and beautiful Golden brigade of wondrous Golden Shining Ones. How BIG and BRIGHT we are!

I had forgotten how deeply connected and interwoven it all is, how intimately we know one another, how profoundly sacred we are to one another. I am remembering it all now.

Communion: such a small word for something so huge, deep, and meaningful—and yet it describes the sacred, intimate beauty of it all perfectly.

Harmony, GOLDEN HARMONY—Golden Harmony is activating again. It is alive and well and flourishing, and there is nothing like it. It is how we are; it fills our Golden World because it IS our Golden World.

As I continue to absorb the profound strength of our union and feel the sweet resonance and perfection of our Golden Harmony, I become aware of something else stirring. I recognize it as our beautiful, sacred Golden Imprint, the Tapestry that is the energetic patterning of our One Golden Heart. In response to all Golden Ones reawakening, it is automatically reactivating itself again as well.

I feel its beauty touching me, reaching all and infusing us with its gentle weave and inspiration. It is the Golden Tapestry of us at our best. It is the interwoven design of our Golden Love Story brought into this glorious present time. It will vibrate anew, stretching out once more to gather new beauty and new experiences of great Golden Love to weave into itself as we move forward.

I take a deep breath as I allow its energetic sensations to merge with me. I feel as if I am becoming one with the actual tapestry itself. I am its richness and beauty, its sweet rhyme and rhythm, interwoven with divine Golden threads. It makes me feel silky and shining just as it is. I am aware that I am being inspired by its Golden history and power, and embrace it fervently as my appetite for it is strong.

Golden Love is the center of this tapestry and the center of my heart. It is the center of the heart of all.

I feel myself being blessed by it for a few moments longer, until gradually the sensations fade. I find I am returned to stillness once more. My eyes are closed and I feel utterly peaceful. Everything is quiet and motionless.

Suddenly, I hear another sound, and this time it is the low reverberation of a heartbeat that is constant, steady, and strong. I feel it starting to beat methodically deep inside of me and hear it sounding all around.

I recognize it, of course: the Great Golden Heartbeat of our One Golden Heart has finally arrived. It echoes throughout my entire body, mind, and heart. I know, unequivocally, that all Golden Ones from everywhere have made their way home to Terra again. They have heard the call and are awake and present. They have returned, eager and ready to thrive as our One Golden World once more.

With this recognition, I also know that our Golden Grid is fully set and complete. It is set, airtight and sacrosanct, and will remain ever thus so—just as it always has. Our Golden World is now a closed system unto itself, as Avalar said it would be.

"Yes, Beloveds, absolutely Yes, Yes, Yes!" says Avalar, with deep joy resonating through her words.

"Our entire Golden Family everywhere is awake. Our Golden Imprint is vibrating and our Golden Grid is set and airtight. We are a Golden World once again; we are whole unto ourselves, exclusive and sovereign in every way.

"What a triumph and a celebration this is! Let yourselves truly feel this as much as you possibly can. Yield and sink into it. BE it thoroughly. THIS is what you committed yourselves to: this is yours to have."

In response to Avalar's words I breathe slowly and let go even more. Deep inside of myself I can feel the rightness of it and the precious beauty of us here, settled in together again in this way. My whole Being "drops anchor" inside as I truly yield to this truth. The enormity of my Golden Family and its love for me touches and moves me even more.

It is me; it is inside of me. It breathes me and I breathe it. We are ONE, inextricably ONE again—and this makes me profoundly happy.

I embrace this rare, sweet, and precious gift, savoring it in my heart and in my soul. I will always treasure this and keep it safe. I will always appreciate and adore it; I am grateful for its return into my life, my consciousness, my every living, breathing moment. I love and treasure my Golden family as my Golden Family loves and treasures me.

We are One Golden Family, One Golden Heart, One Golden Life, and One Golden World.

Here it is again. It is mine—all mine again. It is ours—all ours again.

Tears of joy slowly roll down my cheeks as I fold my hands in prayer over my heart. I do not need any words to express what is in there. But there is one: gratitude. There is pure Golden Gratitude overflowing everywhere.

Terra's Golden Beauty Abounding

The Golden Witness speaks:

Avalar's joy is infectious as we hear her declaring our triumph again, *"Yes, we did it, my dearest Ones! We did it!*

"We are One Golden Family and One Golden Heart completely restored. Our Golden Grid is set and airtight and our One Golden World is here to stay! Thank you so much for your part in making this such a resounding success. Again, JOB WELL DONE. Congratulations!

"And, finally, with all of this completed, it is time for each one of you to simply enjoy being here!

"Yes, it is time for you to savor and receive anew the many gifts of Terra's beauty here on her surface. Let her move you with her wondrous creations which will reengage your Golden cellular memories of our Lemuria in these ways. As you already know, it is about reawakening and revealing the many layers of your memory, step by beautiful step. Give yourself the time and space you need to take in all of Terra's majesty. Receive it. Rejoice and revel in it!

"It is yours, All yours! It is ours, All ours."

With this, my focus shifts to only myself and my physical resonance. Everyone else disappears, and I am standing alone with Terra's magnificence shimmering and shining all around me.

My eyes open wide as I am eager to take it all in. I look out around me, absorbing every nuance; every form, shape, and color that I see. My whole body feels like the lens of a camera—receiving it in a magnified and finely focused way. Some parts look similar to long ago and others entirely different, new and intriguing. I am intensely curious about it all.

As I see the horizon that greets me, I am aware of how I have longed and ached for this. Nothing but pure beauty meets me in return, softening my pupils, causing me to well up with tears of adoration and gratitude. It is sheer, utter beauty everywhere.

I am engulfed in smells, sounds, sights, and sensations that are beyond my wildest dreams and imaginings. "Oh, Terra!" I sigh. "You are so much more beautiful on your surface than I even remember! How glorious and generous you are. How captivating!"

A great big smile bursts open inside my body and lights up my whole face. I am positively beaming. Why do I feel like Terra's beauty is smiling right back at me in exactly the same exultant way? There is such recognition going on, back and forth, between me and all of this. It's like bridges of caring from long ago. I can feel Golden Receptors being reactivated inside of me, enabling the reabsorption of this on a deeply cellular level.

I start to turn in a slow, tender circle...inch by little inch. I don't want to miss a thing. In doing so, I am gifted with a whole kaleidoscope of images, joined together and punctuated by the distinctly familiar energy of Lemuria, our Golden Land. I know I am still standing here on the beach, but it seems like Terra is giving me the whole panorama of her different creations, directly where I stand; she is bringing it right back to me.

As I move, my eyes feast on the green rolling hills, wide open blue sky, and mountain peaks rising up to touch the Sun; the rainbows and billowy cloud formations floating lazily above. Everything is shining against the backdrop of Golden Glow, sparkling and glistening. It practically makes my mouth water.

I inhale the fresh, clean air with all of my might, letting it fill my lungs, welcoming it into my whole body. I keep taking slow, deep breaths, allowing it to deepen each time. It is absolutely delicious! How sweet it smells and how wonderful it feels. This divine air is fresh and clear, and its energies are fully vitalizing and replenishing. I close my eyes, savoring it completely.

I can hear water in its glorious variety of expressions: flowing like a happy stream, babbling brook, clear mountain spring, wild river, ocean wave, and clear streaming waterfall. Somehow, for a moment, I can even hear pouring rain, then sleet and hail. I can "hear" the peacefulness of the snow falling and coating everything with its beauty and purity.

There are so many different bodies of water happily reminding me of their potent and vitalizing life force. My ears are tingling with the sensations of it all.

I open my eyes again and my gaze lands gently on trees and bushes, greenery and flowers—endless flowers of all kinds. Oh my! The sweet and sensual fragrance of all of it, the aromas and exquisite beauty that reaches right into me and virtually caresses my soul. I am in pure awe that such immense and exquisite beauty could ever be fashioned like this. And out of what?

Of course—the soil!

Terra's soil; it is thick and rich, and right under my feet. I immediately drop to my knees and grab a handful, pressing it eagerly to my face. The pungent aroma of this incredible life-giving material makes my nose crinkle with glee. I rub it over my hands and face, pressing it into my pores and praising it fervently for all that it brings to me, to all of us. I am grateful.

Finally, happily smeared with dirt, I stand up and gaze again in awe at the many beautiful expressions that make up this, our resplendent Golden Land. Indeed, how lucky and blessed we are.

As I am having this thought I become clearly aware that, as I give my love and adoration to these natural wonders, they are sending their love back to me with equal enthusiasm! These beautiful creations of Terra's are as happy to see me as I am to see them. In this moment I am joyously reminded of our special and sacred communion, of how supremely life giving it is.

I am also reminded of their innate intelligence. They are made up of crystalline elements of Golden Light. They have their version of cells, atoms, and molecules, just as we two leggeds do. They are alive, and as they vibrate and speak to us—we vibrate and speak to them. We are all Energy after all, simply manifesting in our different ways.

I am an important part of Nature's life; I adore her, she adores me. As I feel the energy of both her beauty and caring, I become poignantly aware in a deeper way than ever before; we are indeed one heart space—ONE GOLDEN HEART SPACE.

I stand here, continuing to witness and admire her as she does me, and I realize that at this moment we are deliberately reawakening our ancient memories. We are reminding one another of our true sacrosanct Goldenness in these ways. Our communing deepens, becoming like a beautiful dance with our loving energies swirling, blending, and merging—layer upon layer, inside and out, back and forth.

Before long, I notice that my body is feeling far more texturized and Golden substantial. It is radiating a much more powerful Golden brightness than it was before, and the same is true of all of Terra's creations that I am seeing. It is apparent that we are becoming stronger, literally, in our Golden embodiment because of our intimate and powerful communion, this conscious co-creative harmonizing.

I also become aware of how incredibly healthy and vibrant it makes me feel. My cells are expanded, happy, and alert; free, fluid, and flowing. I am aware that my energy centers are focused in an outward way, and that they are convex in their design instead of concave and contracted the way they had been previously. This enables the proper flow of my energies to move freely, openly, and outwardly. I can almost hear my cells popping open inside as my memories of health and vitality are deliberately being triggered back into motion, into life. I feel replenished, re-nourished, and revitalized. I feel strong, vibrant, clear, and healthy!

And…I am totally lit up with all of this Golden Power.

I am completely and outrageously lit up, Golden Fire burning! I feel my Sacred Birthing Conduits even more intensely activated, revving up again for action. I feel intentioned, intelligent, strong, and compelled. My Golden passion is overflowing.

"Now, what am I going to do?" I think to myself. "What am I going to do with this power and life force generating and vitalizing me?"

What is that I hear? Oh, it's Terra and she is laughing at me.

"Beloved," Terra says chuckling. *"I am so happy for you! I am happy for how vitalized you feel and how much you now remember and are reactivated in your true Golden Creative Power. It is a strong and mighty gift, isn't it? It is always a blessing to be directed and utilized wisely.*

"And I am thrilled that you are thoroughly reabsorbing my beauty and splendor again. It is all for you, Beloved. May your days ahead be filled with visions and sensations of me pouring my beauty forth for you to enjoy. I want you to feel inspired by my beauty, so much so that it fuels you to create your own. I want to move you. I want to shelter and feed you, to provide all that you need. I am here for you. It's really that simple isn't it? You are my gift and I am yours. It will always be thus.

"Rest assured that there will soon be many clear avenues for your Creative Abilities; they will beckon to you in obvious ways when the time is ripe. Know this: Golden Creation is your path for the rest of your days here. You are a great Golden Creator, and nothing will stop you nor get in your way.

"Understand the path of flourishing. Receive it, stay fluid with it. Always honor its sacred intelligence. Golden Life recognizes you now, and knows that YOU possess unique skill sets which are essential to the health and growth of our Golden World in a Golden Way. There is no need that exists in Lemuria that doesn't have a savvy and developed Creator to answer that need. It is the way of it for us.

"Soon, you will identify your special Skill Sets and you will express them powerfully with absolute freedom and joyous abandon. You will flourish, and because of you, our Golden Family will flower as well. Everyone is an important piece of our Golden Pie. This is true of all Golden Life Forms. We know this to be true. It's the best, isn't it? How much we honor and appreciate and value each other. How much we know the value of ourselves and our unique gifts."

My heart warms at Terra's loving words and I know that what she says is true. I am truly happy and glowing. Everything in me and around me feels in complete harmony and balance. I belong and I know it: I know that I am about to flourish.

"Remember, Beloved," Terra's voice continues. *"In the days ahead, when you need a friend, I am here. I will always be a refuge and haven for you in every way. Your Golden Soul beats in tune with mine, and in this way we are one and the same. I understand you—you know this. I love you so deeply both inside and outside of my body and Being. WE have a long*

and beautifully intimate history together, and I will always be here for you—always.

"As long as you are in physical embodiment, I urge you to remember that I will always be your balance. I will remain your secure ground. Know that it is in this that you will register your secure physical grounding in yourself, and feel confidant and steady on my surface.

"Being grounded in me is the only way that you will be able to hold steady and stable, and clear the vastness of your actively interdimensional nature. It is the only way you will be able to be anchored enough to create forth in physical ways from this Golden splendidness of yours. In knowing this, I urge you to inhale me and my beauty as much and as often as you can. I urge you to drink deep from me, and let me fill your well when you need it. I urge you to savor me, to revel in the strength that I infuse you with and the sheer beauty that I shower upon you. This richness will always make you a bigger, better, and bolder person. Why? Because you will feel steady and fed on this ground. You will know that you are secure in your base—you in the base of me, and me in the base of you.

"And...you will know how beautiful you truly are because you will see the reflection of your beauty in mine. We will witness one another, care for one another, love, enrich, and enjoy one another thoroughly. This will be the case for the rest of your life with me—as it always was in Lemuria.

"Always make time with me, and in me, a priority. In this way you will be continually reminded of who you truly are and you will feel refreshed, stabilized, and balanced anew. I will not only be your companion, support, and ally, but your 'medicine' as well. Remember this, please. You will be greatly relieved if you do.

"Now that you are strong and texturized even more, you are ready for what is next. Yes, you are good and ready to start flourishing again!

"Bless you, my dearest Golden One. Bless you for all that you are and all that you give to me. Bless you. I love you and I thank you. You are my love forever. Thank you for being."

As I hear Terra's words and feel her tenderness and love for me in every cell of my body and Being, I am moved again. Tears are pouring down my cheeks unchecked and it feels incredible. They are tears of love, loving, and being loved. It is such a great feeling. It doesn't get any better than this. "Thank you, my Beloved Terra," I whisper back to her. "Always and forever, I love you and thank you." I know she knows. She is forever my sacred heart gift.

CHAPTER SIXTEEN

DELIBERATE SACRED GOLDEN CREATIONS

THE GOLDEN WITNESS SPEAKS:
Terra's love still warms our hearts as we leave the beach and move ourselves over to a lovely, quiet clearing nearby. There are small trees and rocky outcroppings around the edges of our gathering place, and pieces of driftwood scattered around. I breathe the moist, salty air as I hear the waves breaking on the shore in the background. I smile at the constant song of seagulls overhead, busy at work. It's a beautiful day and this is a sweet, joyful place.

There are many of us Golden Ones here, filled with much excitement and enthusiasm. At first, it's challenging for everyone to settle down. Avalar and Andar come to join us, and take a seat on a log over by the trees. They gaze out at us, and we settle in and take a moment to appreciate the warm, loving glow that we share.

Soon, Andar stands, and with obvious purposefulness in his voice, declares joyously:

"Okay everyone, let's talk about where we are and how we wish to proceed.

"Now that we are One Golden World, let's talk about Golden Living in our modern times. You have stepped out of Mondor and left it behind, along with "all things Mondor." You no longer vibrate with that frequency, but instead sound out your Golden Frequency loud, clear, and joyously. Mondor is still thriving, alive, and well unto itself. It is somewhere 'out there,' but it has no relationship to us and what is happening where we are.

"We Golden live and let live.

"From now on, we will be referencing Mondor from time to time, in order to show you the contrasts of where you were then and how you are now. Mondor and the Golden World are two different frequencies with two entirely different constructs existing together on Terra.

"As we point these out, you will see that these constructs are both strikingly obvious and strikingly different; the contrasts between the two are blatantly apparent. I know you know this to some degree already, but believe it or not, it will become even more crystal clear to you. This will

put you in an even better position to make new choices for what you want, and how you want to live in our present time.

"Observing some of these contrasts will also reveal to you certain patterns and thought forms that you are still holding from Mondor that need to be consciously and deliberately shifted; they are not you.

"Yes, of course, the veils of Mondor have been lifted; otherwise you wouldn't be where you are right now. But in your Golden freedom you will still notice some areas inside of you that were especially weakened in your travails, that still need monitoring and strengthening back to full Golden Resonance. In some cases, it will mean a complete change of mind and perception altogether. You will see what I mean as we move along.

"These are opportunities to grow and stretch, both personally and collectively, so that we express the fullest range of our freedom and the multitudinous gifts that we can bring. We want to be ALL that we can be, don't we?

"We want to be living in a Golden Way, as our Golden World is RADICALLY different from what you were engaged with during your many lifetimes in Mondor. And, even though you have restored your Golden Remembrance and your Golden Bodies, there is still vastly more freedom to attain. Imagine that! (Well, actually, it's still beyond your ability to even imagine, believe it or not.)

"Our Golden World is far more beautiful, powerful, and loving than you can comprehend. Your personal Golden Beauty is far more brilliant and shining than you even know. We have had to do this Golden Remembrance in stages, not only because that was the only way it would be successful, but also because our Golden World is so remarkably and radically different from where you have been. It is quantumly more radiant and magnificent than you would have been able to absorb—it is still a work in progress, step by step.

"What I am asking of you is to please continue to maintain an open mind. And, I mean TRULY an open mind. Let any and all parameters go—and then some. Opt to have the full picture of our Lemuria restored far exceed anything you have imagined possible. Can you do this? Please do this for yourselves and for all of us. Keep that open of a mind. Please do. It will be the greatest gift you bring to yourselves and to all of us.

"You have brought yourselves home, and you continue to find out more about the richness of Gold that you are and the vast magnificence that our Golden World is truly about.

"Let me remind you as well, that even though we are on the same beautiful planet as Mondor, EVERYTHING vibrates differently in response to our different sound frequency. This is an essential point to understand. The vibration of our Golden Frequency changes EVERYTHING about our experience here—in every way and on every single level.

"Yes, this is one of those striking contrasts between us and Mondor: how the life force in everything vibrates differently to differing sound frequencies and intentions. The same is true for us in return; even though the planet herself may appear to look the same, we experience everything differently because now we are viewing everything through our Golden Heart, Golden Eyes, and Golden understanding. Thus, our perceptions are different, and again, everything responds differently back to us. Do you understand? Let this in please. It will open up your mind more to the truth of this reality. It will help you to adjust to this true new version of you and your life.

"Over time, you will experience this personally as you witness the Golden Resonance that you are putting out coming back to you in the myriad of its beautiful ways—and then you will know exactly what I am talking about. That will motivate you still more to stand strong and steady, embracing all the emerging treasures of GOLDEN YOU.

"Step by step, the process of active Golden Remembrance continues. Remember, let your mind stay open and flexible."

Andar stops talking for a moment and takes a couple of deep breaths. I feel my energy following his lead, and also breathe deeply. I hadn't realized how gripping this was, realizing that I've been "on the edge of my seat" listening to him. His words are thought provoking and make perfect sense to me. I feel motivated, and my excitement level in response has shifted back into high gear. Yes, I am definitely on whatever train he is. I wouldn't have it any other way.

Andar resumes speaking again, still with great purposefulness in his tone and posture. I can't wait to hear what's next.

"Okay, everyone, we are going to shift gears because we have some exciting Golden Creation work to do.

"Let's first begin by talking about you and your Golden Life. What, exactly, do you want and choose to do? HOW do you wish to live your life from this point forward? What do YOU wish to express and deliver that will be the gifts of your truest nature to yourself and the whole? What passion excites you? What makes you feel alive? What feeds you and makes you strong and radiant in your Golden joy? What, exactly, makes you thrive?

"These are essential questions to ask yourselves so that you can get started on Golden living.

"Go into your Golden Hearts, and there you will find the answers. Reflect also about yourselves in terms of 'excellence' again. In Lemuria, you always reached your best, for the best. Anything less than the fullest of you was literally unthinkable. You craved this, calling it up from deep within, and powering it forward with joy and enthusiasm.

"Well, so it is again, my dearest Golden Friends. Excellence is the natural state of your Creative Self. Own this in all of your glory; you will find it both liberating and energizing. The truth is that it has been so tiring for all of you to hold this back. You set yourselves free and your energy frees up because of it. It is natural, fluid, and restorative for you. You are each Golden Excellence. What do you want to do with this now?

"While you are letting these thoughts and questions percolate, let's talk more about our Golden Consciousness. I can tell you that I will be repeating myself to some degree, and I do this deliberately. Some things bear repeating and this is one of those times. I need to jog your Lemurian Memory thoroughly about the importance of this again, so that you can be consciously deliberate in your creations, and clearly focused in the direction that your lives are now going. Please bear with me and let this sink in and recharge your purposefulness at these levels.

"Now that we are fully activated as One Golden World again, we need to pay close attention to reinforcing the substance of our Golden Consciousness Etheric Field. Since all Creation is Consciousness first, this is essential, as it is the seed and substance of it all.

"Picture this energetic field of our Golden Consciousness as an atmosphere that we swim in. See that it surrounds us as Golden etheric streams and crystalline patterns that are moving together to establish our 'consciousness atmosphere.' It may seem and feel like 'thin air' but it is not. In actuality, it has energetic substance, texture, and vitality. It is filled with the energies of our thought forms, our belief systems, our hopes and dreams, our desires and expectations, our experiences and our creations. It is the collective energetic result of who and how we are. It is Golden Intelligence. What, who, and how we are creates it, and in turn, it fuels and inspires what and who and how we are.

"It is like making a scrumptious meal and eating it—ingesting its ingredients. It is entirely up to us what ingredients we put into this meal, what we flavor *it with and the quality of ingredients we use—and more importantly what energy do we instill in our cooking. All great cooks speak of the ingredient of love being the most important one. So, of course, everything we put into this meal is going to directly affect our eating experience and how we are, or are not, nourished by it.*

"Our Golden Consciousness is beautiful. It feeds and fuels us. We draw from it and nourish it in return. We are beautiful people that are striving to live beautiful lives. We radiate Golden Beauty, and all of this, all that is inherent within this, comes from what our Golden Consciousness is made of. It is the direct reflection of us and all that we are in our Golden way of being, thinking, creating, and loving. Yes, it is the Golden Consciousness of our Golden World; our Golden World is our Golden Consciousness made manifest. The two are one and the same.

"We want our atmospheric field of Golden Consciousness to always remain strong, positive, and healthy; and grow ever stronger and more brilliant and substantial as time moves on. We want it to continue to buffer us and be the atmosphere that supports and sustains us in growing strong ourselves. That is up to us as a collective family of Golden Being. This is our etheric atmosphere that we vibrate in constantly. We draw from it and nourish it in return with the outcome of being our brilliant Golden Selves. It behooves us to be alert and conscious of this; as we thrive, it thrives—and in turn, as it thrives, we thrive. Each one reflects and nourishes the other.

"In our daily awareness, it is essential to be conscious of our Golden Consciousness vibrating—always respecting, honoring, appreciating, and witnessing its wisdom and beauty as both a reflection of our own, and an inspiration from which we can draw. It is helpful to express our gratitude toward this beautiful Golden Intelligence, blessing and loving it through our actions and thoughts. Our loving of it will only create more loving that comes back our way to feed, strengthen, and support us and all that has meaning for us. It is the gift that keeps on giving. Consciousness is a living, breathing thing; always be aware of this and our responsibility to this.

"Yes, this is our Co-Creative Responsibility.

"If we want to be a Golden World of Golden Ones thriving, we need to take full responsibility for the consciousness we generate. We need to do everything we can to positively support, nourish,, sustain, and reinforce it. Yes, we do this by who and how we naturally are in our daily lives, but we also need to periodically add positive power and loving kindness in order

to reinforce it even more. All of this is highly important.

"It is imperative to be clear that WE ARE RESPONSIBLE FOR THE CONSCIOUSNESS WE GENERATE AND, THEREBY, THE NATURE OF CONSCIOUSNESS THAT AFFECTS US IN TURN—CAUSE AND AFFECT. WE MUST TAKE FULL OWNERSHIP OF OUR RESPONSIBILITY IN THIS: IT IS THE KEY TO THE THRIVING OF OUR GOLDEN WORLD.

"Let me remind you that this cannot be a sloppy, wishy-washy affair. Ours is not 'consciousness by happenstance.' Our Golden Consciousness is deliberate, intentioned, and responsible. That is who and how we Lemurians are. Remember this in yourselves. Be crystal clear about this and the impact that you have every single second of your existence. It reflects in the Consciousness, the collective energetic formation of it. Our consciousness field is the vibrating energetic imprint of all that we are, do, and be. We are One Golden Family. We are One Golden Team, and it is entirely up to us, individually and collectively, to ensure that our consciousness field is everything that we need and want it to be. It is entirely up to us, period.

"Understood?"

I know Andar is being emphatic, and I appreciate this. He is definitely jogging my memory banks powerfully. It's almost as if he is "knocking the sense back into me." He's waking me up and shaking me up, and I'm getting it, thank goodness. I'm excited about all of this. It is making me remember that I'm powerfully capable of having a direct affect on my life. It is making me crystal clear that I am responsible for, and to, this. Yes, I am certainly grateful for his message and the power of his energy that is delivering it.

Andar continues:

"Let me jog your memories again about a different subject: Deliberate Golden Creations. This is where you get to step up and start delivering what has meaning for you in regard to our Golden Consciousness.

"It's time to talk about how we can intentionally strengthen this field by increasing its substance and power—not just by loving it, but also by deliberately and consciously infusing it with strong, positive, life-enhancing, and reinforcing energies. We want a REALLY STRONG force field of Golden Consciousness around us and this is one of the things we can intentionally do to make this so.

"In a few moments, I will ask you to decide upon a gift of your loving energy that you wish to add to our Golden Consciousness Field that will support and strengthen it. We will call these your Deliberate Golden Creations.

They are like 'packages' of strong life-enhancing energy that you will be deliberately planting into the atmospheric field. Let me remind you that these are not flighty, airy-fairy things. These gifts are deliberate, strong, and fully intentioned. You have the power to generate these with as much quality as you choose, and the wherewithal to deliver them successfully.

"When the time comes I will be inviting you to gather and draw up these positive energies from within yourselves, and pour them forth through your heart and breath, intentionally delivering them into the etheric consciousness patterning and energetic crystalline forms that make up our Golden Consciousness.

"This is our intention at work.

"In order to 'remind' you of how to do this successfully, I am going to take you through it step by step, beginning with the foundation of it all. It starts with inviting forth the skills of both your Golden Masculine and Golden Feminine Divine Natures. This is not gender specified, by the way. Everyone has both of these in them. Both of these aspects of the Creative Impulse work in tandem, hand in hand, each with their own forte to bring to the creative table.

"As Lemurians, we understand that the Divine Masculine Principle is based in the gentle art of 'holding the space' and supporting the base steadily, so that the Divine Feminine Creative Principle can relax into delivering the Birthing gifts. The Masculine is not threatened by the Feminine power in any way. The Feminine is not threatened by the Masculine in any way. Neither one dominates the other.

"Our construct in this regard is one of balance and understanding, of mutual respect between the two, each one admiring the skill set of the other and doing what is needed to support it properly so that the Creation can happen successfully. There is great tenderness and honoring between these two aspects of ourselves. They trust each other implicitly and they are in full harmony always.

"There is much more to say about these principles of Divine Golden Creation, but this is plenty for now. I invite you to take a moment and sit with yourselves. Explore how you feel about your Golden Divine Masculine and Feminine Aspects. Do you know them inside of you, the roles they play and how they feel when they are 'working'? Are you conscious and respectful of them? Are they where and how you want them to be? Do you feel balanced in this way?"

I focus my energy inside of me as Andar is asking us to do. To my surprise, my Inner Being immediately shifts my attention outward instead, over to where Andar and Avalar are sitting, and I feel compelled to observe them being together. They are holding hands and their heads are bowed closely in deep conversation. It is such a sweet and poignant picture; I am acutely aware of the true depth of love for one another that is flowing effortlessly between them.

There is great tenderness there, a joining and blending that is born from absolute trust in themselves and in one another. It is completely natural, and feels like a beautiful blessing that touches everything and everyone around them with sweet peace. In this moment it comforts and inspires me, stirring something deep inside—an ancient sense of belonging and longing; it sparks a craving to want to know more.

As I continue to observe them, I realize that I am looking at two people who are both perfectly balanced within themselves, and as a sacred couple as well. In this case, Andar represents the Sacred Divine Masculine, and Avalar the Sacred Divine Feminine.

I know that us Lemurians used to have both of these aspects perfectly balanced inside of ourselves, and of course, did not even think about it. But since our travails, I have felt myself somewhat askew in this arena. Now that Andar has brought this up, I can see clearly that there is something out of balance about these two principles inside of me. There is confusion and an actual disharmony there. This is not by intent or desire, but because something has gotten out of alignment between the two.

As I take stock of myself, I can see that I am relatively comfortable in my Divine Feminine Nature with my Birthing Conduits flowing. But nonetheless, I do know that I am only just coming back from a long time of these creative energies having been suppressed, repressed, blocked, and held back. That was Mondor's way with the Feminine. It will take time and patience for these to be restored fully and freely. I know this.

What is glaringly obvious to me, however, and which I had not realized before, is how upset and skewed my Divine Masculine became in the process of our travels and travails. I realize that is the part that is still throwing the whole thing off. I seem to have actually lost sight of my Golden-hearted Divine Masculine Aspect. Where is it?

In Mondor, the Masculine Energy was of an entirely different construct, one which was definitely not right for me. It was as if the true Divine Masculine had been frozen away somewhere and replaced with something else altogether. It was something of the willful, ego-centric mind that was about domination and control. It was a fabrication of its own making, something void of heart. That was Mondor, and I know it is long gone.

It is time to retrieve myself in this regard. I know that my authentic Golden Divine Masculine Aspect is somewhere inside of me. I do know this, but where exactly? I feel disconnected from it, and would like to have it restored properly again.

In focusing on Andar, I feel my memory stirring about the perfection of this Principle: that of peacefully organizing and establishing the strong base and holding the space steady so the Feminine can give birth, free of concern. Once a creation has been birthed, both aspects step up to fulfill their roles of directing, nurturing, providing for, and fostering those creations into maturity—each in their unique way, depending upon circumstance and inclination.

There is complete love, peace, equality, and respect between these two aspects. Both of them are fully cognizant of their roles and responsibilities, their unique skill sets and natural talents in the whole picture. They love and they listen to one another, they support and honor each other. It is always a team effort, and there is always tenderness and honoring throughout. There is harmony—beautiful, peaceful harmony. Both aspects are born from love, joined in love, and compelled by love toward the same goal of love.

Deliberate loving Golden Creation: yes, this is the way it is done. This is the way it was done by us Lemurians before. Gradually, I feel my system remembering and becoming clear. I feel those aspects of me beginning to settle back into a position of harmony, balance, and peace. It's perfect; everything is right back where it should be, as I breathe a deep sigh of relief.

I quietly extend thanks inside of myself to Andar and Avalar for modeling this so well for me. I know that what they show me continually in their loving and respectful relating is the beauty of sacred coupling at work. It is beautiful to witness and a privilege to be a part of. I look forward to having a similar kind of coupling relationship myself at some time when it is right. In the meantime, I feel well balanced and at peace about the internal "sacred coupling" of my Golden Divine Masculine and Golden Divine Feminine Energies.

As I sit waiting for further instruction from Andar, I breathe another sigh of relief and relax into how comfortable I am feeling.

Avalar stands to speak:

"Dear Ones, I can see that you are feeling much more peaceful and harmonious inside. It feels really good, doesn't it? It is a restoration long overdue.

"You recognize that your many Rescue journeys took you into a different construct and caused your system to come out of alignment in terms of these Principles. Mistrust was introduced—mistrust between your Divine Masculine and Divine Feminine, mistrust based on constructs and ways of

thinking about this that were not true for you. This mistrust subsequently caused you disharmony and confusion.

"In Mondor, the Masculine Principle was, and is, one of patriarchal dominance. This does not ring true in our systems. To us, it is false. It has an incoherence that is not ours, that is not harmonious. Instead, it creates divisiveness and imbalance.

"Now that those travails are long gone and you have given that configuration back to Mondor, you need to re-identify your Golden Divine Masculine Aspect and allow it to resettle back into its proper position. I see that many of you have recognized this and have managed to do it already. I say, well done! But I am also here to tell you that you will need to stay vigilant about this for a while longer.

"In your Golden Remembrance and Restoration, it is helpful to stay alert to monitoring and continually reinforcing balance and harmony in the specific areas that need it. This arena of your Divine Masculine and Divine Feminine is one such area. The relationship of these two principles working harmoniously together to create will need continued nurturing from you as you move forward. I know you will do this for yourselves.

"With that having been said, there are a few things that I want to emphasize to reinforce this beautiful balance that is restoring itself inside of you.

"Remember that the Divine Masculine within you is always the Steward of the birthing process. This is the aspect of you that skillfully prepares and secures the space and proceeds to hold the feminine steady 'in the palm of his hand' with gentleness, respect, and tender loving care. When ready to birth forth, the Feminine gives way to this completely and yields to the secure and steady base of the Masculine Principle. She deepens, softens, and yields herself one hundred percent to the Creative Divine Intelligence that is moving through and forward from her. Once the birthing is complete, both aspects step up to direct the energy and sustain it properly, each in their own ways and always as a team—ALWAYS.

"TRUST, TRUST, TRUST. All of these principles that are an integral part of your Creative Nature trust one another. Because of this, they join seamlessly and trust still more as one harmonious unit in the creative journey.

"I am inviting you to yield to this knowing and recognition inside of you in a much fuller and deeper way.

"This is your inherent creative nature at work. This brings Golden creation

to its peak ability and success. The deeper your trust and the deeper your joining, the deeper you yield. The deeper you yield, the better Creator you are. This is it in a nutshell."

Yes, of course, I think to myself. Thank you, Avalar for your clarity and wisdom. I see it perfectly clearly now.

As the moments pass, I find that I am feeling more patient and peaceful inside of myself than ever. I'm aware that there are still deeper levels of health and wellness rising up inside of me, and my knowing tells me that I am reaping the rewards of my inner harmony. I am restoring and I am loving it!

Andar comes back in, and says:

"Well, it's time everyone. You are ready to begin the actual process of your Deliberate Golden Creations. First, we need to identify exactly what you wish to contribute.

"I ask you to reflect on specific Deliberate Golden Creations that have meaning to you. What do you want to energize and foster in your lives and in your world? What 'packages of heart energy' would you like to deposit in our Golden Consciousness that will enhance and strengthen it, making it more beautiful and vibrant?

"You are in the process of consciously practicing this. In Lemuria, you didn't need to do so. You were already supremely adept, and this all came automatically. But because we are RE-building and RE-texturizing, this needs to be looked at and thought about as if through a magnifying glass. It's the only way your memory of automatic instincts will be jogged. Please be patient. Practice with care and consideration: give it some serious thought and see what you come up with.

"What would YOU like to contribute in the way of Deliberate Golden Creations?

"Consider yourselves and consider your Golden Family as a whole."

I close my eyes and take a deep breath. OK, I can do this. I go inside and ask myself, "What qualities of energy do I wish to support and energize for myself and our Golden family?"

My answer from my heart is RESPECT. This encompasses self-respect, respect for others, respect for our lives, respect for Terra, and respect for all of life. This is the positive energy that I would like to add to fortify our Golden Consciousness. I would like to energize this with my love, planting it like a seed in our garden which I will feed and water with my continued love and attention. Respect is a quality that is already inherent within our Golden Consciousness. I understand that, but I would like to reinforce its presence and foster it so it will increase. This is a gift of my love that I want to contribute.

Andar continues:

"I ask you to center yourselves in your strong, but gentle, steadying, and supporting capacities. The Masculine is now lined up in ready position with your strong, creatively empowered birthing conduits; the Feminine, lined up as well, will birth forth and deliver shortly. Notice the perfect balance and steady rhythm of both, joined and engaged in this conscious and harmonious way. Notice how good this feels.

"I ask you to also bring the energy of playfulness and lightness to add to what may feel intense at this point. Creation responds well to these qualities of energy, making the whole process more effortless and streamlined, thereby holding it on this platter of buoyancy—light and playful, deep and powerful. It all works together to ensure successful delivery."

As Andar is speaking, I am aware that, yes, I am fully centered in a gentle, strong, and sustaining way. There is a secure peacefulness that stands strong inside of me. At the same time, I am aware of my inner Birthing Conduits shifting around, aligning perfectly into their intelligent positioning for delivery.

Both aspects are wise and intelligent. Each aspect loves, understands, and respects the other. They are both active and they each have their role. They are both ready. I am ready in them, and as them. As a final touch, I add a generous scoop of playfulness and lightness. I feel the energies brightening and lightening as a result. I am aware of a joy bubbling up from within and feel more confident, as if this is going to take care of itself: it knows.

"Now, you are going to deliver. Is everyone ready?"

I take a deep breath and feel myself instinctively preparing to gather momentum. Yes, I feel good and ready.

"Center your focus in your hearts and take a moment to appreciate and love them. In whatever way has meaning for you, thank your hearts for all of their beauty, presence, and kindness, and for their generosity in sharing their gifts so willingly. When you feel ready, invite the gift of the positive life force energy you have chosen to contribute, doing so with gentle care and absolute awareness.

"Feel your heart responding, eagerly offering this energy to you, expanding and magnifying it so that it overflows—filling you completely and enveloping you fully. Absorb it with all of your senses. Taste it. Savor it. Inhale it deeply. It has become your totality for these moments. SIMPLY BE IT.

This special energy is your gift to us.

"It is time to deliver your gift.

"Feel yourselves instinctively and automatically hunkering down into the secure, steady, solid base of support inside of you, as you yield. Yield and open, and let Creation be born through you!

"Yield to the deliberate and exhilarated force of your creative energies, pouring themselves through your Golden Birthing Conduits. Be aware of this strong, steady energy moving through you like a swollen river—with you as its riverbed. Soften and open yourselves still more to give it as wide a berth as it needs. Let it pour through; it knows its way, so let it run free and be available.

"Open your mouth and start breathing with intentioned breaths, giving this potent energy a clear, open pathway for delivery. Your breath becomes like a hose through which this energy pours and is directed by your conscious intention and desire.

"As you breathe steadily, feel it pouring itself through this gateway and following the path and intention of that breath right out into the etheric fields of our Golden Consciousness. Deliver this with total generosity, focusing on your desire to fully and completely give this gift. It is all love, coming from your love and being shared with love.

"Feel yourselves lightening and becoming more buoyant, with everything happening effortlessly. Lighten up even more as your breathing becomes light and easy as well. You are still intentioned, deliberate, directing, and focused, but in a lighter and more playful way.

"Now you become more like joyous fountains bursting forth, naturally and effortlessly outpouring these beautiful gifts, these packages of Golden Loving Life Force Energy. These packages of Golden Energy are freed up, cascading through the air, aiming for and depositing themselves straight into our Golden Atmosphere. They go exactly where you directed them to go, and yes, they have landed!

"Wait for a short moment, and you will see that they are being received by the Golden Etheric Fields and are being thoroughly absorbed. You will notice that the crystalline structures inherent in our Golden Atmosphere have altered their shapes to accommodate these beautifying Deliberate Golden Creations. They are vibrating these energies within themselves with more clarity and greater intent than they were before.

"See it and feel it. Thanks to you, these particular energies are stronger and more vibrant and have multiplied. You have succeeded! Hallelujah!"

I focus and pay attention to what Andar is describing. Yes, I see that our Golden Atmosphere has become brighter, more buoyant and resilient. It feels even more vital and nourishing than before. I hadn't known the effect that energy could have in this way—or perhaps I had forgotten. I love it! It feels positive and completely life enhancing. I am already literally feeling showered with the well wishes and positive Deliberate Golden Creations that have been generated by all of us. It feels amazing, and I feel great being a creator in this way and contributing to our Golden Family.

I hadn't realized it would be this way. I hadn't thought about the fact that this would bring such an immediate gift back to me. Not only is this a great boon to our consciousness, but it is also an immediate boon to each one of us individually as well. As Andar said, "it is the gift that keeps on giving." How positive, uplifting, and strengthening. How brilliant—and it is easy! What a wondrous way to contribute to ourselves and our Golden Consciousness.

"Now," says Andar. *"You get to enjoy the benefits of this conscious Golden Planting and pour forth more Deliberate Golden Creations whenever you choose. Remember to always do this with careful consideration. It must always include your commitment and willingness to foster and nurture these Deliberate Golden Creations along until you feel they are complete and thriving. You will know this, not only by instinct, but also by how YOU FEEL, by how much you are receiving the gift of what you gave.*

"In terms of fostering these Deliberate Golden Creations along in our Golden Consciousness, you do this by touching in with them, by witnessing and admiring them. You continue to easefully and playfully infuse them with even more Golden Love and Energy. This will enliven them even more, increasing their quality and power. That's part of the sustaining responsibility of creating. Creating, supporting and sustaining—that is the full package of successful creative outcome.

"Job well done everyone. You can watch as these loving Deliberate Golden Creations grow and thrive. Our Golden Consciousness thanks you, and we thank you.

"And that, my dear friends, is how it's done."

Andar steps back with obvious pride and delight and returns to his seat next to Avalar. They are both positively beaming with joy.

CHAPTER SEVENTEEN

YOUR SACRED GOLDEN SENSITIVITY

T HE GOLDEN WITNESS SPEAKS:
I look up and see Avalar standing in front of us, preparing to speak:

"Beloveds, I am happy for you. You have brought yourselves to this present time and are beginning to see the effects of your Golden Frequency in your lives. The gifts of your Deliberate Golden Creations are powerful and the more you 'remember this,' the greater their effects and benefits will be. You are outstanding Golden Creators, as we have said, and this is the beginning of you truly integrating and applying this consciously into your present daily lives.

"Andar spoke about the end of an era—that you have walked out of Mondor and left that behind. Let's talk about what this means in reference to your current daily life.

"Living your Golden Frequency, being in our Golden World, does NOT mean that you are separating from, nor leaving anything or anyone in your current lives. It is not about separating from and walking out of your current lives. It is about bringing your Golden Awareness TO your current lives, every second of every day that you remain in your body. It is about changing your lives to reflect who and how you are now. It is about holding your Golden Consciousness—all that you have become and all that you are with joy and gratitude—and letting this prevail and govern. As we have said, changing your frequency changes everything. It alters your perception, and thereby your understanding and clarity about what truly is.

"Give yourselves full freedom to stand out and to no longer be 'one of the herd.' Radiate your Being freely and respect yourselves for your difference. Value and stand by who you are, how you think, how you believe, how you perceive, how you feel, and how you understand. Soon you will find that you are not alone in this.

"One of the first things you will realize is that you are surrounded by Golden Ones that are in your lives right now. All those members of your family and friends that you love are ALL Golden Ones too, and although

you have not seen them as such before, you will now. It will become clear and obvious to you.

"This will enable you to understand many things about them that you might not have even thought about before. The same will be true for much that you see from now on. You will be surprised by how your perceptions continue to change, how your position on things will as well, and how you respond differently to people, situations, and life circumstances—yours and others. You will literally be seeing and understanding things through a different 'lens of life' than you have before.

"Let this be; let this revelation and metamorphosis happen naturally.

"We urge you to examine your lives and gracefully release whatever aspects of them are not working for you, are not of positive service, are not in harmony with you. We urge you to make changes accordingly, to shift things around in a creative way so that the picture of your life is singing in harmony with all that you are now. Let this natural alignment take place. It wants to—so let it.

"If there are painful circumstances in your lives that you absolutely cannot alter in any way then alter your relationship to them. Greet them and resolve to grow stronger through them, knowing that they are teaching you something valuable. Bring your Golden understanding to bear and watch how you naturally shift according to it—and how your circumstances shift according to you.

"We urge you to be gentle with yourselves and your lives, truly embracing yourselves and this discovery of Golden wondrousness that is revealing itself to you on a daily basis. Let this direct and govern you throughout your life.

"It is happening. You are already well in motion. Golden Life is in process. Your emerging Golden Heart is shining, and it is making a difference everywhere. Watch and witness. You'll see it. You'll feel it every single day—more and more."

I listen to Avalar and know she is right. As you can tell by what I shared with you earlier, I love the changes that I'm starting to see and experience in direct ways. I eagerly look forward to more. Frankly, I'm hungry for it, as I've waited a long time for this. I've been hoping for something that would be uplifting and make a huge difference in every area of my life.

Now it is here and it is beginning to happen. I am glad, relieved, and extremely grateful. I know there is nothing airy-fairy or idealistic about any of this. These are solid changes that will reflect in my life energetically as well as practically. I know and feel this. I resolve to be flexible and fluid about it. I am feeling stronger and more empowered by the minute—and yes, I love it!

I return my attention to Avalar's voice as I hear her announcing:

"Alright everyone, it's time for another Conscious Choice Point.

"This one is about whether or not you choose to fully open once more to your sacred Golden Sensitivities. Yes, you have already been using these skills wisely and well, both in your Rescue Journeys in Mondor, and recently in your reemergence and re-embodiment. But there are considerably more to these skills than what you have experienced to date. There is still more remembrance about this awaiting you. Be clear that these are a skill set; you have developed them through eons of time to enhance your life and to help you—not to undermine or weaken you in any way. Be crystal clear about this.

"The question is: how willing are you REALLY to open back up to your full sensitivities in your current lives in current times? Let's talk about this—the ins and outs of it. These waters are somewhat muddy right now. It's essential to see the whole game board of what this looks like before you embark on your conscious choice.

"I know you know that in order to participate in our Golden World, you have to be your Golden Sensitive Selves. It is your true design and that's that. If you hold this back, you will not be able to commune and communicate in a Golden way and you will not be able to receive the true magnificence and gifts inherent in our Golden World.

"The more you open to and retrieve these skills inherent in you, the more you will be able to benefit by what they bring to you, what they enable you to do and be. If you want to be a fully participating member of our Golden World, this is a requirement—it's obvious. To even discuss this as a 'choice' may seem ridiculous, I know. But once more, we have the issue of your free will and what YOU are willing to allow, or not.

"Let's talk about it, and when we're done you can make your choice in a way that you will be able to fully support, from an informed place and position.

"We know that this whole issue of sensitivity is a loaded one. It is actually the 'crux' of the matter for Lemurians in our modern times because it is about feeling, sensing, and knowing. Some of it feels really good and some of it does not. If you're open, yes, you feel many more things and you feel

many things more. It's a trade off. You enjoy feeling the 'good stuff' but because of the pain around you, you're feeling things that you wish you weren't. I understand this. It can be overwhelming and greatly upsetting.

"'Who in their right mind wants that?' you say.

"Thus your QUANDARY is whether to allow your sensitivities to be fully engaged or not. I know that when many of you think about being open and sensitive in your current lives, your immediate reaction is, 'Yikes! Get me out of here! It's WAY TOO MUCH! NO!'

"I can hear you saying this. It's a knee jerk reaction to levels of pain that you experienced in Mondor as well as what is in the world today. But my question to you is, 'Would it really be that way, now that you are living at a Golden Frequency as a Golden One?'

"It is true that with your sensitivities once fully open again, you are going to feel the pain of what is going on around you, but you will also feel the great stuff as well. You will feel all of the beauty and positivity and love and much more. If you are shut down, you'll be numbed to the pain, yes, but it is also guaranteed that you will be numbed to all the goodness and positive aspects as well. Yes, you'll be able to get some of it, but relatively speaking, given who you are now it will be very little.

"The 'teaching and value' in being aware of the pain is that, if it is not yours to change, you can at least witness it and touch it with your compassion and understanding. Doing this is an act of healing, as you well know. And, if it is yours to change in some way, you'll know about it and that will lead you to the solution for it. However, if you are numb to it, you will end up doing nothing and the pain keeps persisting.

"That's simply the way it is.

"When you were in Mondor, you relied on your skills of sensitivity to do the Rescues. Without your skills being activated and utilized you would have not been able to fulfill your Rescue missions. You know this.

"Nothing has changed about who you are, but there is much more on the table that needs to be looked at, not only in regard to your own skills and what they would bring to you, but also to the whole issue of 'being sensitive' in current times.

"In the construct of Mondor, sensitivity is often maligned. It is stigmatized in many ways by many people. Being 'tough' is what counts. This is another one of those 'contrasts' between Mondor and our Golden World which I

want to highlight because it collectively reinforces the negative spin on sensitivity as a valued skill.

"The construct in Mondor has always been to shut down one's sensitivity, to become more mental, and as a result, often more hardened. Many people steel themselves to the world, and in so doing they do the very same to themselves. This is done in the name of survival. We understand this.

"In addition, many people choose to become disengaged from their sensitive natures, considering them a form of 'weakness.' This is a cover for their fear of feeling too vulnerable—not only to possible pain but also to love and its natural consequence of caring. The outcome, for whatever reason they have chosen, is to shut down and become inured to things that otherwise would have them outraged, making them rise up in protest against the hurting nature of these things.

"And, for many, this hardening becomes as a thick encrusted shell which disables the ability to be connected to caring. Getting inured to pain, or getting apathetic because it is overwhelming, both end in the same place—nowhere. Nothing changes and no one is listening. It causes a complete disconnect.

"All of this was, and is, Mondor. This is Mondor's choice, not ours. But notice the contrast. Notice how that repression of sensitivity disables the ability to care and commune. It closes the door.

"Ironically, for a mindset that denies the value of sensitivity, people in Mondor often speak of 'gut instinct'—following the sensation of how things feel, whether they feel right or wrong in making decisions. They often take pride in this in themselves. However they wish to frame it, those are all signals offered up by their sensitivity.

"But, as I said, they don't want to own these as such, because to own themselves as sensitive would imply weakness in their minds. It would also tend to keep them more open which would lead them to feel more vulnerable. It would cause them to feel more. In Mondor, hardening up is invariably the prescription to the callousness and heartlessness.

"Yes, those who in are Mondor do what they do to survive. We understand, that's Mondor. It's about survival and those who go there to learn about survival are learning a lot. But again, that's not us.

"Why am I talking to you about these things? So, you can see all the conflicts regarding the issue of sensitivity and how these waters got muddied the way they are.

"Your experience of being sensitive in Mondor was that it caused you pain. It made you feel raw and out of control, vulnerable, and too open. If you open it back up to its full resonance, what will happen? You are, of course, leery of that. The pain in the world today adds greatly to that hesitation and understandable concern.

"For all these reasons, most of you are still facing this dilemma about what to do with your true sensitive nature. Do you truly accept and embrace it? Or do you try to keep repressing it to whatever degree, and hide from it, keeping it from yourselves and others?

"The rub, if you will, is that your sensitivity is still there, clear as a bell, whether you want it to be or not. Repressing it doesn't make it go away. It gives you a major pain somewhere in your body and Being. The truth is IT hasn't gone anywhere. YOU may have but IT hasn't. There is nowhere to run and nowhere to hide. Your sensitive nature is what gifts and governs you as a Lemurian—I mean this in the best of ways. It is way smarter than any plan you have to ever escape it. You can try and override it with your free will, but it will cost you greatly. It will, in all likelihood, make your life miserable in the process."

As I listen to Avalar talking, I know she is right. I know the quandary I have faced in myself about my sensitivity. On the one hand it has brought me much joy, but on the other I feel enormous pain. I have wrestled with it often, wishing it would go away. I have tried, at times, to override it, squash it down out of sight, and even to numb it. I have given myself "tough love" talks, commanding that I brace myself and toughen up, "get a grip girl, get it together." And I have wept because these were to no avail.

I still felt sensitive and still was sensitive—much more than I wanted to be. I wished I was different. I wished I was more "normal," more like how I thought other people were. Until one day I saw that many other people felt the same way I do. They simply hid it, but because I was sensitive, I could see it. There it was: they were sensitive like me. And yes, they had their own quandaries about it, their own dilemmas and their own angst. We seemed to have the same question. Where did it fit in the scheme of things? What were we going to do with it? How were we going to survive being this sensitive?

Now that I am Lemurian Remembered, I know my understanding and viewpoint of this needs to catch up with the truth of where and who I am now. I still have some soreness inside of me about it and I know that. Being sensitive in Mondor, as essential as it was, was difficult and painful in many ways. I have healed to a large degree, but there is still more to go. This is yet another one of those "weakened areas" that I need to keep an eye on.

Avalar continues on:

"Sensitivity is a great thing because it always alerts you to exactly what is going on. Some of the information you receive is useful to you, and some of it is seemingly not. And yet, informed you are and will be. If there is pain involved in what it informs you of, you need to know about it so you can do something about it. Pain is not there to be shut out. It is there to alert you that there is a need for attention and change.

"The truth about your sensitivity is that it is your greatest gift. It is the gateway and doorway to receiving all of our Golden magnificence and love—and infinitely more. In regard to this, without your sensitivity you would feel empty.

"You need to reclaim your sentient and sensitive natures. You need to release the faulty perception of sensitivity as a weakness and reclaim it as the true gift of enormous strength that it is. Your sensitivity is the one thing that will propel you forward as Golden Ones and open you back up to the majesty and power of our love and caring in our world. It will literally blow your minds! And that is a good thing.

"Now that we have examined the whole game board and talked about every other aspect of this, let's address the CENTRAL TRUTH about your sensitivities: how great they are! They make you available to life.

"Look at some of the benefits that you know about being sensitive, about being 'a sensitive' in your own way. Let's focus on the 'up' side.

"Let's talk about sensitivities as a set of SKILLS that YOU have developed deliberately. Why? In Lemuria you relied on them to commune, to be enriched by, to explore, sense, know, feel, and expand. They brought you the information that was needed and wanted, as well as all the gifts that were available to you. Without them you would have been unable to receive any of it.

"Where does this leave you? Re-identify, redefine, and re-decide.

"These are powerful skills that you have deliberately developed. They are THE most powerful skills you have. Why did you develop them in the first place? Why were they prized in Lemuria? If you hadn't had them fully prepared, you would not have been invited to participate in our Lemurian Project. What do you want to do with them?

"In the end, doesn't it seem odd to you to have such a quandary about something that is so powerful, useful, and empowering for you and for all? Why would you ever opt otherwise? Why would you choose not to have these up and running fully?

"List the reasons and what they do FOR you, the difference they make in your lives: why you need them and what you can rely on them for."

The Golden Witness speaks:

I look forward to when I can truly appreciate the fullness of my sensitive nature as the true strength and gift that it is, and not have anything contrary thrown into the mix of my perception. I need this back fully, I know this. My Golden Life depends upon it.

"Dearest Ones," Avalar continues. *"Your sensitivity wants to gift you. That is its plan. That has always been its intention. It is who you are. Do you choose to have this back fully?*

"My question to you is this: do you want to keep these shut down? In which case you are the one consciously blocking your Golden gifts, both in giving and receiving them. Or do you wish to open these skills back up fully in order to thrive as a Golden One in our Golden World?

"It's up to you. It is your choice."

I take a deep breath. Of course, I know what my choice is. I've already been activated in these ways. But I know Avalar is talking about increasing my awareness and refining my skills still more so that they can fully support me in my daily life. I vow to keep an open mind and an open heart to regaining my sensitivity skills and LETTING GO of whatever I need to in order for this to happen. It makes me wonder if, in the end, it will be about letting go of my misunderstandings about myself.

My hunch is that I'm going to realize that, as Avalar said, my sensitive nature is absolutely my greatest strength. I care deeply and that's a fact. That is a great thing. And if I reclaim this truth, all the skills of my sensitivity will be powered upon my behalf, and on the behalf of Golden Goodness. This clarity is all that I need to know about the choice I'm going to make in this regard.

"Take a moment to acknowledge your sensitive natures. Understand and appreciate how truly refined you are. Make a pact with yourselves that you are going to support the continued opening of your sensitivities so that you can relearn what they mean in the context of your new Golden Life. Open up your mind to the reality that they will bring you immense, truly immense, joy.

"Stand up and reclaim this inside of yourselves now. A world of pure joy awaits you!"

AVALAR SPEAKS ON SACRED GOLDEN COMMUNION

The Golden Witness speaks:

I am smiling contentedly as I watch Avalar standing tall and beautiful ahead of us. She takes a moment to fold her hands in prayer, closing her eyes and placing them, one on top of the other, over her heart. She is in complete stillness for a moment and it seems to make us, and everything around us, also become still. Her energy of love moves softly toward us as I feel it touching me, and all of us, ever gently and tenderly. It moves carefully inside of me, checking with each passing nanosecond to make sure that it is invited. Of course, it is. I take in a deep breath in response and close my eyes as well. I soften.

Her love continues to reach and spread inside of me. Its growing warmth and comfort soothes my heart and soul. I can feel how deeply she cares about me; how much she wants to support me. Her kindness is present and patient.

I am moved. My eyes well up with tears and I naturally open in return. Everything becomes timeless and seems suspended for a moment. All is quiet and still.

Finally, she begins to sing—quietly and gently. Although I know she is singing to all of us, I feel like she is singing only to me. It is a love song, from her to me. I am aware that while she is singing, she is also listening attentively for any response from me, any indication that this is what I want as well. She is respecting my right and choice to engage. Even though she knows full well that I am already open to her, she is doing this anyway. She is teaching me something through this. I know this.

Her song fades gently, and I am left with a pulsating sensation of quiet joy. Whatever it was that she wanted to teach me, I have learned.

"Beloveds of my Heart," she begins to speak. *"I am teaching you about Sacred Golden Communion. I have built an energetic 'Bridge of Caring' between my heart and yours. As you were aware in the process, I carefully checked every step of the way to see if I had your permission to do so. I did not blatantly impose myself upon you. I did it with care and respect for you, and with you. This is how I created the energy of this 'bridge.' Once you willingly received me, you softened. That was my signal that our bridge of love was in place and I could continue.*

"Please keep your eyes closed as I continue talking to you, and let yourselves feel the energy of this communion and of my message in an even deeper way.

Sink in and yield please. I am still teaching—and you are still learning.

"Again, feel how the energy of my love for you has intentionally become like a bridge of caring between you and me. Again, feel my love crossing that bridge to you. It is a bridge of trust and understanding, of listening and responding. It is a bridge of love engaged.

"Recognize that if you were in any way distressed, my loving caring would have a way to soothe you because of this bridge that connects us deeply, intimately, and caringly.

"Recognize that if you wanted to dance with me and sing my song, you would know exactly what that song would be.

"Recognize that if we both wanted to deepen our union and create something together, we would be able to do so because we are engaged and listening, learning and sharing in this deep way with one another.

"Recognize that if we wanted to inspire and bolster one another we would be able to instantly do so by virtue of our love flowing back and forth intimately on this beautiful bridge.

"This is our Sacred Golden Communion. This is Sacred Golden Communion in action.

"Our Golden Communion is one of the greatest gifts that we Lemurians can engage in. It is our heart speaking and singing, and it has more meaning to us than anything, as it is this most intimate expression and exchange of our profound caring. It is Golden Heart to Golden Heart. It is not restricted by time and space, form or dimension. It literally knows no bounds.

"It is the deliberate and active engagement of loving for the purposes of sharing, listening, learning, teaching, expanding, and deepening in our family of love. It is sacred: it is Sacred Golden Communion. It is our sacred connection in conscious sacred engagement.

"We use the word 'sacred' often in reference to all things Lemurian because that is what we are and what everything in our Golden World is. The truth is that all of life is sacred as it is our Divine made manifest. I want you to remember all of this about sacredness and to fully appreciate what this means—that YOU are a Sacred Divine Treasure and the entirety of life is a Sacred Divine Treasure.

"And it is also so with our Golden Communion: it is sacred to us and unto itself. It is a sacred act of pure Golden loving."

As Avalar is speaking, I can feel this sacredness reverberating in my heart, and I feel that I have come home in an even deeper way. I feel profoundly seen, understood, and respected; valued, considered, and acknowledged—all of this in a profoundly meaningful and sustaining way. I am truly grateful.

"Understand that in order to commune in this way and at these depths, one has to understand themselves as sensitive and attuned to life and what they care about. It is time for you to fully remember and embrace this again, and to BE this in your daily lives in our modern times.

"As Lemurians, you were always deeply and actively in communion with all of life, and most especially, of course, those aspects that resonated personally with you. This was integral to everything for you and for all of us. Our sensitivity was fully engaged and fully activated. We relied upon it for most everything.

"Through our highly developed skills of sensitivity, we were able to communicate and commune in ways that were extraordinary and rich. We were able to relate and form deeper relationships that were most meaningful because we were able to be intimate, highly attuned to one another, and responsive in our caring and sharing.

"We communed and communicated through the language of energy which went far beyond words and was not confined to any dimension, time, or space. Our language of Golden Energy was communicated via our intention and had the ability to reach and engage with any level of Golden Life anywhere. Our language of Golden Energy brought our family together and enabled us to resonate and share with one another whenever we wanted and in whatever ways we wanted.

"We could read the energy, receive the energy, send the energy, and connect through the energy. We could say the loving intention of our energy through words, we could sing it through sound, and we could whisper it through our breath. We could vibrate it through our feet, we could transfer it through thought, and we could convey it through emotion. Whatever way was appropriate for our communication was what our language of Golden Energy could express accurately and effectively.

"Our Sensitive Natures enabled us to be the powerful instruments for our language of Golden Energy. Our Golden Sensitivities of sight, sound, and sensing were amazing in their breadth, depth, and abilities. Indeed, if it wasn't for our skill sets of sensitivity, we would have had no Golden

Lemuria, no Golden World, no One Golden Heart at all. And we would not be sitting here today talking about this.

"In everything I have said, do you more fully grasp the loving presence, power, and purpose of your Golden Sensitivity Skills? Do you more fully appreciate them in you, as you? Do you understand their importance and the essential part they play in your lives as Golden Ones?

"You cannot turn these off. You cannot be true to yourself without them.

"Dear Ones, as discussed earlier, I know what it is like to be sensitive in our current times. I know the many conflicts about your sensitivity that you have wrestled with for a long, long time. I know what it is like to be sensitive and open even though there are many times when you wish you weren't. Being sensitive is the one thing that makes our lives as Lemurians extraordinarily rich, blessed, and beautiful. And yet it presents the most pain because we feel the pain of those we love, and we feel the pain of the modern world that we live in.

"I know that I'm being somewhat repetitious as we discussed this at length earlier, but it bears repeating in the context of Sacred Golden Communion.

"I know your deep pain about this, and I know the pain of the world. I know what it's like to feel as though you are going to drown in the sorrows or be broken by it all. And yet your sensitivity continues on. Our hearts are open, and we care—and there is simply no denying this. It is because of our deep caring that we feel everything that we feel.

"I know the dilemma that faces you; the dilemma of staying open vs. shutting down. I know how it feels to collapse inside because you feel too much and too often. 'How do I protect myself from this? How do I buffer myself from it?' These are questions that I know you ask often as you are attempting in vain to shield yourselves from the hurtful realities of our present time.

"The fact is that it's not an option for us Lemurians to harden and become inured to pain and suffering. It's not an option for us to stand there and witness injustice without feeling the pain, without flinching, without aching, and without being outraged. But it becomes too much after a while, I know this and I understand.

"What to do? How to live in the current times as a Lemurian whose heart cares and has senses open, wanting to shut down and go numb—but, in truth, never being able to. You care. We care. And caring this much and being this skilled as a sensitive, always attuned to the language of energy *that is informing us and affecting us, seems like a big trade off. There is all the goodness, the magnificence, the beauty—and then there is also the pain. We are not inured to it and we never will be. We are not numb, and we are not hardened. We may try to be any one of those things, but we are not. Our sensitivity is still there no matter what. It is clear as a bell and informing us in all ways, like it or not.*

"*The reality is that we are living our Golden World in these modern times and we have to deal with things that we never ever encountered in Lemuria of Origin. We know about the contrasts between the different frequencies of Mondor and our Golden World, and they point to what seem like challenges every step of the way.*

"*I know all of this and I know how hard it has been for you in many ways to find resolution about it and still be true to yourselves. You often think and believe that your sensitivity 'weakens you and makes you vulnerable.' But is this really true? Isn't the greater truth that it is precisely this that makes you strong?*

"*I am here to remind you of something—something which you have long forgotten.*

"*There is a piece of you that is still missing. Even though you are now Golden re-embodied and you are bright and shining, there is still a piece of you that you ache for, that you don't even know by name: it is that forgotten.*

"*It is your Golden Mastery.*

"*It is the underpinning of fundamental strength, underneath all of your sensitivity, that holds it steady and perfectly balanced. It keeps it intact with you and you intact with it. It is the foundation underneath these skills that is the base from which you have since grown and expanded. Your base of Being in this regard is well developed, solid, and confidant. On this you rely and have always relied. Do you understand me? There is nothing weak or weakening about your sensitivity skills or about you as a Golden Sensitive One. It is quite the opposite.*

"*Yes, you are all Golden Masters. Your Golden Mastery is the strength and fortitude that holds your sensitivity intact and steady. It is ALWAYS keeping you masterfully aware and attuned to the delicate vibrations of energy that are around you, that you vibrate and commune with, that you share.*

"*Your Golden Mastery is what always keeps you strong and propped up in ALL of your sensitivity, empowering you to stay strong, steady, and standing.*

It enables you to ALWAYS respond, instead of collapsing. It gives you the ability to ALWAYS hear with accuracy and see with clarity. It supports you in BEING the powerful Golden Creator you are that was so strong and well developed that you could meet the demands of our creative project called Lemuria.

"This is still YOU. THIS is still WHO YOU ARE!

"Yes, I know of everything that you have gone through that has made you feel small, weak, and overwhelmed. I have been there with you when you felt yourself collapsing, or on the verge of collapsing, under the weight and intensity of what you felt. Beloveds, none of this is who you are. Those were stages that you went through so that you could be here now.

"It is time to reclaim the truth that, no matter what, you are still the Golden Masters that you were in Lemuria of Origin. That has never left you, nor has it gone anywhere.

"What does this mean for you in the context of modern times?

"It means that you are sovereign. It means that you stand strong as Golden Witness and Golden Creator, and that you can hold yourself upright with eyes, ears, and hearts open. It means that you stay strong and steady and standing no matter what. You are Masterful; you are Golden Masters—no matter where you find yourselves, no matter when, no matter what the circumstances are, inner or outer. That is the Golden Truth of YOU.

"You know that what I say is true. You remember now. You need to give yourselves time and space to catch up with this Remembrance.

"Welcome Home, Shining Golden Masters. Welcome Home."

CHAPTER EIGHTEEN

Your Sacred Golden Skill Sets

The Golden Witness speaks:
As I sit and listen to Avalar speak, her words touch me deeply and I am aware that something inside of me is shifting. What I am hearing seems almost too good to be true—is it too much of a tall order? There has been much throughout this Golden Remembrance journey that has often seemed beyond belief; that being said, everything has proven itself to be real and accurate, judging by how I have experienced myself coming back to life in these ways. But this most recent piece really takes the cake: me, truly, as a Golden Master?

Even as I ask this question, I am clearly aware of things slowly but steadily shifting around inside my ground of Being. Some new kind of alignment seems to be happening—or is it actually ancient? It feels like another long ago memory returning, something that I could only receive again once everything before had been chosen. No matter what my mind might be doing with it right now, there is no question that this is starting to feel completely right to me.

I surrender; I accept this. I will allow myself to catch up to it.

I look around and see all of my beautiful loved ones. It's obvious that I'm not the only one having this kind of response; we all are. This is a deep, deep reintegration.

I see Andar coming to join Avalar and I feel his encouragement as he speaks to us:

"Beloveds, indeed you are Golden Masters, and always have been. In fact, you couldn't have gone into Mondor as many times as you did, nor could you have succeeded in doing the Rescues, if it had not been thus. Now you can let this Remembrance return fully to your conscious awareness. Give it time and space, and it will.

"Reintegrating this truth brings the question of 'what now' to a whole new level.

"It's as though you have arrived at a new mountain peak after climbing ever higher than before, with a longer and more panoramic view. What I suggest is that you look around—enjoy this view! You have earned the right to see it again, and to be the recipient of its vast beauty.

"Take it in as much as you can; this is a time to receive and let be. It is not a time to plan and put your energies forward. Take this moment to pause and to recollect, to celebrate this ancient sacred gift of Golden Mastery returning.

"We now stand strong as Golden Masters in full Golden Heart. We receive once more into our conscious awareness the true power of what this means: the true strength and passion of our One Golden Heart.

"Yes, we are a truly strong and powerful Golden People. This is our One Golden Heart Truth. Let us give thanks for knowing this again.

"We have brought this back to ourselves, at this time, for a good reason."

I watch Andar standing tall and proud, regal in his posture. I realize that I am sitting up straighter, as though my backbone has stretched and grown taller. I am aware of a growing self-confidence, a sense that I am becoming stronger than I could have foreseen. My self-respect is deepening by the minute. I love this feeling of being Golden Masterful; it belongs to me, and I have earned it. I honor this and I honor myself. I know it is of the utmost importance to let myself reabsorb this entirely once more; my future hinges on it.

"Your Mastery is Golden Heart powered," Andar says. *"It is essential that you let yourselves have it fully, without your mind being concerned that it is going to make you arrogant or self-absorbed. That is not our nature as Lemurians. Thinking along those lines will only distract you from your Mastery and keep you disconnected from the true purity of your Golden Heart.*

"As Lemurians, our Mastery makes us appreciate and honor our Divine Source even more. We know that this is from where it truly births; it is a position that we have earned through our devotion. We carry it proudly, knowing full well that we are responsible to this level of maturity and wisdom.

"We do not take it lightly, but we do let it bring us Light, Golden Light—and then we spread it throughout our lives!

"As I said, we have earned it, and we know what this means: it means that we are powerful, capable, strong, and self-confident. It means that we know full well that we must always move forward and through, with great consciousness and awareness for everything that we do. It means that we are constantly aware of the impact that our actions have, both now and in the future.

"Re-centering yourselves as Golden Masters will empower you greatly, making your Golden Creations even more potent and life giving. This is an integral piece of you, and it is imperative that you let yourselves have this again. Please do this."

I feel the power of Andar's words, and I know he is right. I ask my mind to simply be quiet for a while as I allow the wisdom of my body and Being to lead the way. I am welcoming my Golden Mastery, and I vow to do great things with it. This is a truly great day!

After a while, I see Andar stepping back and letting Avalar take center stage again. She looks purposeful and excited about what is coming up next.

"Well, shining Golden Masters, I can see that you are arriving back into your masterful positions more and more as the moments pass. Well done, carry on!

"We are going to let this percolate while we move on to something else that you will find empowering: we are going to explore and restore your memory of your individual Golden Creative Skill Sets. This is the beginning of a wondrous path of revelation for you. It is a daily opportunity to receive the blessings of these skills from long ago and spread them forth with great joy in your heart.

"We can do this now because the 'baseline of foundational skills'—those of your sensitivity, ability to converse in the language of energy, and to Golden Commune, have been restored and are powered up properly again.

"Although they are officially known as your Sacred Golden Creative Skill Sets, I will be referring to them as 'Golden Skill Sets' for short, or even just 'Skill Sets' from now on. It is much less of a mouthful to keep repeating, but know that these Skill Sets are GOLDEN CREATIVITY driven.

"You are Masterful Golden Creators, first and foremost. This, as you well know, is what our project of Lemuria of Origin was about. Keep this in mind—holding the perception of your skills from a context of creativity enables them to 'roll on out' in a way that they wouldn't otherwise. It brings a completely different and unique flavor to the process; one of great buoyancy, effortlessness, and juicy life force. You can feel your Creator moving exuberantly through you. The creative process loves this!

"As always, the actual process of remembering and retrieving your Skill Sets will happen step by step, beginning with the fundamental base of loving intention that drives it. No matter what form your skills take, they are always driven by your love and by YOU as love. That is how we Lemurians are.

"Remain open and receptive and let the process take it's course; your Golden Skill Sets will be reemerging from deep within you, as if after a long sleep.

"Each one of you has a particular Golden Creative Skill Set that you bring to the table. Your chosen desire and responsibility is to express this skill set to the best of your ability. That is why you are here. It is not for you to spread yourself out too thin and try to accomplish what is not in your particular 'wheelhouse.'

"The beauty of our Lemuria is that we each have our piece and we each do our piece. This is not to say that you won't grow and learn in other areas as well—but for the foreseeable future, you will focus in on and hone that which is inherently, organically alive and fully developed inside of you. It is a memory that will be restored; it is your MOST natural ability surfacing.

"This is a skill set that comes from the inside out, not one that is decided upon by the mind and expressed as such. Also, it is not one that is imposed upon you through expectations, either your own or others. This belongs to you; it is uniquely yours. It is what you chose for yourself before you were born, what you came here with, and what you had every intention of expressing fully.

"In your daily lives, I urge you to pay close attention to what makes you thrive and puts a smile on your face when you think about doing it or being it. Notice what makes you feel good and what feeds you inside and out. Your true Skill Set will always nourish you—not drain you off. That is one of the signals that you are aligned properly with what you are meant to be doing. Focus on you and your willingness to 'retrieve' these Skill Sets, and you will indeed reconnect with them inside of you joyously again. Give it time, space, and invitation to reemerge effortlessly.

"It is important to also acknowledge again how powerful you are; that you are, indeed, Golden Masters and amazingly gifted and adept Golden Creators. This means that a state of powerlessness is not an option for you. You will never be able to sit back and do nothing about something that you care about. There is always SOMETHING that can be done to bring about greater harmony and beauty in everything—no matter what it is, no matter what it looks like, and no matter what it feels like.

"Some of you may already be cognizant of your natural skill sets to varying degrees, and some of you may not. Those of you who are already expressing your 'God given natural talents' successfully will find that bringing deliberate Golden awareness to them is going to make them quite a different *experience for you. There is an even greater plan that your Soul is wishing to express. Trust this.*

"Your Golden Skill Sets are born of and expressed from deep within you, united with the desires and direction of your Golden Heart. It is one and the same, becoming one complete creative system in motion. You experienced this recently with Andar in bringing forth your Deliberate Golden Creations.

"As I said earlier, your Skill Sets do not come from your mind, your head, or your mental will. They come from your Divine Source THROUGH you. Let us be clear about this.

"Are you willing to move into this position in your lives? Are you willing to be conscious instruments and vehicles for that which is constantly greater than yourselves—always Golden Love directed, purposed, and intentioned?

"Of course you are! You are Lemurian and that is how you work.

"Remember this, and allow yourselves to make this shift in your everyday living and breathing reality. It is not that YOU don't get to do what you do or be what you are, it's that your consciousness about it is different. You understand yourself as Source inspired and compelled. You are your Golden Soul involved and evolved in the realization of a greater plan.

"Your life takes on this meaning and this purpose. From the moment you wake up in the morning until you close your eyes at night, and during your sleep as well, you know you are blessed with direction and guidance and purpose that comes directly from your Source and our One Golden Heart. That is your purpose in everything you do and be from now on.

"One Golden Heart is our Master Plan. You are a fully participating and contributing member in this beautiful Master Plan. Yes, given that you are Lemurians, I know you know this already—but most of you have forgotten that you know this. I would like you to remember and KNOW this consciously and clearly now. Everything in your lives will shift by degrees to accommodate this Golden clarity, this heightened understanding of why you are here—everything in every way.

"Yours is the glorious privilege of being One Golden Heart right here, right now, and for the rest of your Golden Lives here with Terra.

"Take a moment to reflect on this, letting it settle into place. It is a change from how most of you have been living your lives to date. It is a shift in your consciousness, perception, purpose, and drive. Let us take a moment and let this realignment happen."

I take a deep breath and follow Avalar's instruction to let this settle in where it may. It's funny, because I feel that I already know this to the level that she is talking about—but I am also aware of the sensation of having forgotten it as well. Those two perceptions are meeting each other inside of me—meeting and greeting; and one slowly but surely gives way to the other.

Golden Remembrance takes the lead, and I feel something glorious beginning to happen inside my body. It is not of my mind, nor am I mentally able or willing to define it. It is bigger than that, and I know the most important thing is not to think, to simply let this be.

Avalar continues:

"We are going to invite in your Sacred Golden Teams to help you with this and to begin the formation of a greater bridge between you and them that will continue to greatly assist you in your lives as much and as often as you want. As you already know, your Golden Teams are your Spiritual Guides, your Helpers, your Companions, and your Confidantes.

"Some of them herald from the realm of Spirit, while others come from the unseen Nature Realms and other aspects of Golden Life that are directly helpful to you and your specific Skill Sets. This will vary for each of you, depending upon what arena of the Golden World you are engaged with. No matter what realm they are from, they are with you to offer assistance and support in any way that you need. You have but to ask. Remember this—you have but to ask.

"As you also already know, their purpose is never to do your life for you. Their purpose is to support you in doing it for yourselves. Continue to be clear on this as well. They are indeed your Team and you are indeed a part of their Team. You are the one in the physical body; they need you as much as you need them.

"They are equally as invested in our One Golden World, as this is also their dream being made manifest. You have a Golden Team that is inter-dimensional and multidimensional because that is how our Golden World is. This is our interweaving of Golden Consciousness far beyond what the eye can see.

"Shortly, your Golden Teams will help you in re-accessing your Golden Creative Skill Sets, and they will support you in expressing them successfully in your lives. Your Golden Team is always on your side—available, willing, and wanting to support and assist. Their greatest joy in this is supporting and fostering your abilities to make our Golden World manifest on Terra.

This is what it is about. This is why we are here—for this purpose and this purpose only.

"The first part of our motto is: when you need or want their help, YOU HAVE BUT TO ASK. The second is, YOU HAVE BUT TO RECEIVE; ASK AND RECEIVE. There will also be countless times when they show up when circumstances call for major miracles.

"None of this is to imply that you don't have what it takes to do great things by yourself. That is not what we are saying. Remember that the nature of our way as Lemurians is Family, Golden Family. We have always worked together as a Team. We each have our role, we each have our piece of the pie to be and to express, but we always work as part of the Team—and we always march to the beat of one drum: One Golden Heart.

"Remember this, and stay open and available. Drop the expectation that everything is on your shoulders, because it isn't. Let go of any traces of memory from Mondor that you are alone, because you are not.

"You are reconnected deeply inside to your Source, and this has already repaired that chasm that would ever cause you to feel alone again. However, beyond that, be aware in your daily life activities that you are also not alone. You have help for the asking when, where, and how you want it. Reflect on this as well. Are you willing to have your daily life be filled with resources at your fingertips? Are you willing to expand yourselves and your identity to include this reality as a way of life?

"Some of you are already interdimensionally active, expressive participants within an interdimensional team. You may already be hooked up and fluid in this regard, fully aware of your spiritual team and whatever allies and supporters are part of your spiritual family. Again, your Golden Frequency upgrade changes and alters even that.

"Golden Life everywhere has been waiting for this shift in consciousness to become a reality. They are eager to step up in this new way of engaging from now on. You will see what I mean; give it a chance and give it some space, and you will see. I know you will be happy about it—what was already great will be even greater.

"And for those of you who are 'new' to this way of daily living, you will be pleasantly surprised. You will see how easily this comes to you. Why? Because it is the memory of how you are designed and how you truly operate. It is the restoration of your most natural way, period. It's not a 'learning curve' so much as it is a 'remembering curve.' It's that easy.

"With this having been said, let us invite in your Sacred Golden Teams!

"Make this your internal request by simply offering up your invitation from inside your heart. For example, you might say, 'I invite my Sacred Golden Team to connect with me now in a way that I can feel, know, and understand.' However you wish to phrase this will work. They'll get it. They'll hear you because that is your request and intention and they are standing ready and available—waiting for your invitation. Remember, good teams always know where their teammates are, and these are GREAT teams! Trust this and be available.

"Take a moment, Beloveds, to invite them in please."

I sit back and take a deep breath, quietly moving into my heart until I feel warm and settled in there. I say my prayer of invitation to my Sacred Golden Team and, in what seems like less than a heartbeat, I feel them right here with me. It is great to feel them again. We feel like such "forever comfy family" to me. Somewhere inside of me I feel like I know them so well already—and I know for certain that they know me too.

"Greetings, dear Friend of our Heart," one of them says to me quietly. *"We are happy to be here with you today to help you in retrieving still more to your Lemurian Heritage.*

"Remembering your Creative Golden Skill Sets is such a splendid thing. It makes us happy that it is finally time for Golden Love to be made manifest in the physical domain again—and for us to step up and make this happen. It is our greatest joy. We are right here alongside you, always. We are available to you as much, or as little, as you choose. We respect you and your choices, always. Know this.

"We are not here to hover. Just as you are a well developed Golden Master unto yourself, a Team of Masters is simply that much more support. Wouldn't you agree? Besides, the ins and outs of physical daily living and the expression of deliberate Golden Creative Skill Sets is always full of challenges and opportunities which are often well served by the efforts of a Team. This is especially true when it comes to an interdimensional one such as ours. That is our Golden way.

"Let us settle in together with the intent of bringing back into your conscious awareness your beautiful, fully empowered Golden Creative Skill Sets. These skills of yours are unique to you, and are a gift from your Divine wellspring. Simply get comfortable and breathe easy. All is well and ready."

I feel my heart beating faster than before; I love my Golden Team, and I love that they are here with me. I am excited about what is coming. I can feel energy moving inside of me, and I am conscious of trying to stay relaxed so I don't miss anything.

"Yes," my Golden Team member continues. *"Stay soft and easeful inside. Be aware, consciously aware, of how it feels to be open like this. Notice the sensation of it in your abdomen and your pelvis. Keep paying attention to dropping down further, softening more into your lower back and your sacrum so that you are sitting comfortably in your wellspring of Being.*

"Allow your attention to gather there. Take a few deep breaths and enjoy this sensation. Be present, noticing it thoroughly, so that you can call it up at any time you desire. It's easy; press your hand to any area of your body for an instant as a way of focusing and feeling. This will enable you to automatically call it up whenever you want.

"In a moment we will begin the multilayered process of inviting forth your unique Golden Creative Skill Set. It may end up being a set of several skills, but it begins right now, right here, where it wants to. It will inform you of itself and you will simply be its receiver.

"Before we proceed further, please drop whatever you 'think' you know about yourself up to this point. Drop any identification of yourself as a 'certain kind of person with a certain skill and way of expressing that.' Drop it as if you had never known anything about it, ever. Let it go for the moment. It is that simple.

"It's like taking off a hat that you have constantly worn; take it off and put it aside. Give yourself full permission to be in a state of 'not knowing,' of being receptive and allowing. This is you being open to what is waiting to show itself and come through you. This is you being open and available as the instrument of the Divine Revelation that you are. This is you getting out of its way, inviting it up, and saying YES to that which is being reborn inside of you—your Golden Creative Skill Sets.

"Drumroll, please!"

To my surprise, whatever I had identified myself as has evaporated into thin air! I wanted it to, I asked, and I let it. It was simple.

I am totally comfortable in myself, and open in a way that feels deeply and indelibly familiar. I feel as if an old friend is about to come and be with me again. Without meaning to, I hear my question piping up, "Why have I not been this way all along? It is so ME." My Inner Wisdom responds crystal clearly to me, "Because it wasn't time. There wasn't space and a place to support this. Now there is. Receive it now."

Okay, I am. I do.

My Golden Team continues, *"Feel yourself becoming that which you authentically are. You may have thought you already were, but there is still more, much more.*

"Breathe in and out slowly, letting this conscious memory return and restore itself. Ask yourself, 'Who was I in Lemuria of Origin? How was I in Lemuria of Origin? What was I like? How did I feel? What did I know of ME?'"

I ask these questions, as instructed, and allow the energy of them as a package, altogether, to drop deep down inside of me. I wait. The energy is swirling around gently, as if seeking its own answers. It's as if the answers have been safely tucked away inside of me, inside my cells and my organs and my blood. My body knows, my body remembers. I respect this; I wait patiently. There is nothing else. I can wait for as long as is needed.

Finally, I begin to feel something; a response, an energetic response. It's as though someone pushed up the lever on a movie set and the lights and engine suddenly turned on, revving the motor. Something inside of me is rising up to touch my heart, to reach my psyche and convey a message that any minute will become substantial and real. I know it and I can feel it coming; a body of energy is being reborn within me.

A message has been delivered and my whole body is waking up to a memory of long ago. It is something timeless and ancient, something that was my birthright and my gift to bring forth. I was born with it, born to be it and to make something out of it.

I have a sudden flash of a "reminder." When I came to Lemuria of Origin, my gift was further blessed with Golden Light, as I was christened anew and put on a new path with even greater meaning for its purpose ahead. This new path challenged me. It took what I already had and asked me to stretch it further in deliberate and life giving ways. It said it would guide and direct me so that I could bring forth these sacred and miraculous gifts to our world and greater universe.

It would be a major challenge, an opportunity to explore and expand myself in ways that I had never even imagined. It would ask that I constantly surrender to its greater wisdom and divine intention, all the while knowing full well that every single breath, creation, and moment of my existence was a blessing. It was a great profound Golden Blessing for me to BE; for me to know, to witness and to share.

I was often astounded by the sensation and feeling that I was consciously and devotedly part of a greater plan, one with its own wisdom, direction, and ability. I would pinch myself that I had landed in such a place, with enormous opportunity and gifts to bring forth and to be. I had not fathomed that such a blessed way of living could ever exist, it went far beyond what I had ever conceived.

And here I was; an essential, valued, and important piece of it all. I mattered and made a difference. I contributed something special that was needed and wanted, that was received gratefully on many levels of Life. My unique Golden Gifts were destined to be, designed to gift me and many others with love, Golden Love.

It was the greatest power of love I had ever known or experienced. It took the tremendous power of my love of my Divine that created me, and made it glow and shine more fully and brilliantly; my life, all life, was enhanced and enlivened to a more brilliant degree.

And then there is the Golden Energy. We were honored to be given this gift by our Source in full knowledge that it was powerful and could ONLY be given to those who would know how to use it consciously, wisely, and well—and only for purposes of pure goodness.

As you know, we responded and moved forward, creating with the purest and highest of intentions. When conditions were such that our world became jeopardized, we buried the Golden Energy deep within Terra and kept it safe.

I receive this again and it heralds a confirmation that, yes, the right time has come: all conditions and requirements, both inner and outer, have been restored fully so that this incredible and precious power of Golden manifestation can express forth and deliver itself again. I know this with absolute certainty, otherwise these events would not be occurring.

Yes, I know I am ALREADY my Golden Self and Golden Shining; we all are. However, this remembrance and re-utilization of our true Skill Sets is the VERY THING that will manifest our Golden World back into full Being once again. It won't just be about shining, it will be about deliberate creation and Golden "physicalizing" in every arena. That is our Golden World being restored and filled back up to overflowing as Golden everything—Golden Consciousness, Golden realized and materialized. This equals our brilliant and shining Golden World, absolutely thriving and with much to show for it!

This is my response to those questions as a package; this is what sets the ground for me to ask next, "What is my place in it all? What are my gifts exactly?"

In response to that question I am lit up again. The sensation of the energy inside me becomes more substantial, more physical and touching, more knowing.

I can hear it; I can feel it; I can almost taste it.

My heart warms and begins to beat in a way I had not known before—more richly and happily. I feel grateful and purposeful. That's it; yes, and proud of it too. This sense that I can do anything, climb any mountain; reach any peak because my sense of compelling drive and purpose to create is clear, strong, and made of Golden love overflowing and powering through.

My gifts are those of creation, first and foremost—my Skill Set is that of creation. At this moment, I am having a direct experience like none other: I feel like I am a powerhouse, a Golden Powerhouse of creative ability.

This is vastly different than anything I have felt before. I am experiencing this so totally that there is no room for anything that could get in the way. This powerhouse of me is so strong and Golden filled that there is simply nothing else. I am free, freedom personified. My life is my opportunity to revel in this and do whatever I choose to do with it.

What will this look like exactly? What are the details of my unique Skill Set that is mine, and only mine, to bring and share? I know those details are coming, but what I realize is that THIS direct experience of me as a creative medium for Golden Love is what I need to absolutely KNOW in every way, on every level once more—BECAUSE EVERYTHING IS GENERATED FROM THIS.

I am aware of feeling internal qualities of myself in a way I haven't in the past. I become aware of the sensation of my kindness, of how far it reaches. I feel my deep caring, and the sacred place from which it comes. As I connect with the root of my compassion, it seems endless; I feel it for everyone and everything, including myself. I feel my reverence and adoration for all of life, how precious it is and has always been. My heart warms and expands even more.

This is my answer to this one simple question—BEING LOVE, BEING GOLDEN LOVE—supreme and splendid. This is my intention, and through this, everything else comes forth, as this.

"It begins with BEING," I hear My Golden Team saying. *"Every single skill you have starts with this, and is born through this, because of this. THIS unto itself is a Divine Skill. THIS is where we will begin.*

"Be conscious.

"Be aware.

"Be present.

"Be grateful.

"Witness.

"The vibratory frequency that emanates from you is extraordinary, not only as a person who is Golden Shining, but also as an instrument of Divine grace coupled with the gift of Gold. Everything that you express is the voice of this, every accomplishment that you make is this 'physicalized.'

"If you were to do nothing else but consciously BE your love, vibrate your love, enjoy your love, and extend the love and kindness, the compassion and caring that comes from this, you would realize that this truly is a skill unto itself. You would realize that you would already be delivering and manifesting plenty. It begins here. It truly begins here.

"It is imperative that you truly grasp the power in, and the enormity of, the gift of SIMPLY BEING. When you fully understand this, your power of manifestation will be able to deliver forth easily and successfully.

"It is imperative that you recognize and know that ALL that you are and ALL that comes forth through you is our Creator at work. It is not you as a person, but indelibly YOU as ONE with the Source of all of life.

"Your true power is set free, and your true ability as an Adept Creator is put into motion again.

"Re-center yourself firmly in this knowing. Take a deep breath and sink into it with totality. Feel it filling you up and enveloping you completely. Once you do that, you can move to your unique Golden Creative Skill Set which ushers forth from this."

I do as my Golden Team requests. I sink in and allow myself to be re-centered in my instinctive knowing from long ago. Yes, this is my creative baseline, and I remember it fully now. I feel a sense of pressure lifting, an expectation to perform that I hadn't recognized previously, attached to my personal Skill Set emerging.

When I stay true to my center of BEING, I trust and know that my skill set, which is an extension of this, will inform me when it is ready. Its expression will be crystal clear, easeful, and fun. Yes, it may be a challenge, as it often was in Lemuria before, but it will also be fun and enlivening for me. I look forward to it, and to stretching myself out in that way.

I feel relaxed, and I have a big smile on my face. I feel like I ate the whole pie! THIS was it. Everything else that comes forth from here are the creative threads embodying themselves in the world. Okay, I get it. I know that it will bring unlimited fuel to foster all that I do for the rest of my life.

Now that's power unlimited: Golden Power.

Imagine a well that never runs dry, that flows abundantly forever. It makes my mouth water to think about it.

I hear my Golden Team chuckling as one of them says:

"Job well done, dear One. You are thoroughly ready for what is next. We can now explore the Golden Skill Set that is absolutely unique to you.

"Let us start by asking you some more questions.

"What enlivens you?

"As Avalar asked earlier, what are you aligned with? What do you enjoy? What are you instinctively attuned to? What do you love doing?

"It could be simple or complex. It could be large; it could be small. It is all equal in value as a contribution to the whole.

"Looking at your inclinations and feeling into what makes your mouth water when you think of it, examining what juices you up, inside and out; registering this will bring you your answer about what your natural Skill Set is. THAT is what your Skill Set consists of.

"Once you have those answers, it is simply a matter of the actual design and details of manifestation.

"We will leave you to Avalar's expertise once more, but before we step back, know that we are here and listening. Again, job well done Beloved. This is fun!"

And with that, I see my Golden Team stepping back to the periphery and holding themselves there. I am grateful to them, and glad they are in my life and my world. Bless you, my Golden Team. Bless you, and thank you.

As they fade into the background, Avalar steps forward again and begins to speak:

"Dear Ones, you have established your firm base of creative power and now you can receive your Golden Creative Skill Sets. Everything is in position and ready for you to define what naturally wants to come through you and manifest itself outward into our Golden World. I encourage you to be easy and fluid with it, letting that memory rise up in you at whatever pace and in whatever way it deems right.

"Let me start by giving you some examples of Skill Sets. Certainly, anything within the realm of the Creative Arts is a given, but, in truth, everything is a creative art. We expand upon this construct of what is typically considered creative and open it up to include all Golden creations no matter what field of expertise they are. As Terra said earlier, 'for every need in Lemuria there was a skilled and adept Creator to fill that need.' And so, it is again.

"I urge you to open up your inner windows to this; open them wide. The more open to possibility you are, the more you will clearly receive the information that you need to express and fulfill your purposes.

"Some of your Lemurian Skill Sets were talked about in the earlier chapter on Rescues, but they weren't referenced as such at that time. Let me delve further into this arena and highlight a few for you. This will jog your memories, enabling you to reconnect with them.

"Some of you, for instance, are Golden Water Masters. You work directly with the crystalline formations that make up our water. Water is in everything that has life; therefore, the impact of this particular Golden Skill Set is far reaching. It affects the waters everywhere—the waters in the Cosmos, in your bodies, and on Terra.

"They all communicate with each other across the globe and throughout our atmosphere and universe. As you know, Terra and your physical bodies are made up of a large percentage of water—Golden water.

"Communing with these Golden crystalline water intelligences can shift many things in many significant ways, depending upon which particular aspect of water your unique Skill Set is responsible for addressing.

"Other Skill Sets would include Prayer Masters. These individuals offer a profound influence which affects everything that is generated forth in our Golden World. These Golden Ones are adept at creating the energetic blueprint, and nurture the vision that will steadily carry what will ultimately be made manifest. This is a crucial piece in our Lemurian outcome. Golden Prayerfulness is the base of our creations; it seeds in the love that will be made manifest. It is the base, the ground, and the beginning.

"Obviously, you are adept at the art of prayer and envisioning, and we encourage you to use these skills often. However, these Prayer Masters take the art to deeper levels beyond that which anyone else has even known or imagined. They are devoted to this arena one hundred percent.

"For those of you of the Golden Stars, you are able to carry and hold the gifts of our 'Golden Beyond.' Yes, we need these here, as you already know. They are part and parcel of our Golden World and are instrumental in the beautification and strengthening of it. Ours is not a limited, three dimensional world, it is vast and all encompassing. Those of you who are Golden Star Ones already know that you have a base here on Terra, and that this is where your gifts can flourish as part of our unique and bigger plan.

"These are but a few examples of Golden Skill Sets that I have described, but it is enough to get you started on your exploration and retrieval.

"In addition to utilizing your Golden Skill Sets in manifesting your creations, you will be aware at times that direct Golden Healing is also being asked for. In these cases, you will use your Golden Communion skills to gently and respectfully bring your compassion and healing to those energies that are requesting it. You will connect and engage with these energies and let them know that you witness their state of disarray and disturbance.

"By BEING with them and acknowledging their distress and their pain, you will touch them and they will receive you. In letting them know that you hear and value them, you will lift their spirits and rekindle their joy for life. This is the kind of healing that I am talking about—being FULLY GOLDEN PRESENT in this way with them.

"Through your love, compassion, and witnessing, their inherent Golden love and beauty will reemerge, thereby naturally dissolving their pain—guaranteed. When ready, all of life responds this way to loving kindness—ALL of life. It begins with Golden Loving Consciousness, which seeds the possibility of all things miraculous happening on physical levels too. Through this Golden Awareness and Healing, physical action to repair and heal is bound to happen.

"As with people, this same exact healing Golden Communion process can be done with all life forms everywhere, whether it be in the realms of the trees, air, plants, animals, Elementals, Stars, etc. The list goes on and on. Golden Life responds to your Golden Witnessing, caring, loving, and understanding. Simply make yourself available for this, and see if this is what is being asked of you. If it is, then engage in this way. If it is not, simply respect that and let it go. Perhaps it is for someone else to do, and perhaps the timing is not right.

"As I did with you when I was building the Golden Bridge between us earlier, always listen—each and every step of the way. Remain aware of asking for permission, and of doing so with the greatest of respect and attentiveness. This is our Lemurian way.

"Having clarified this aspect of what might also be asked of you as you express your unique gifts, I am going to give you an opportunity to reconnect with your unique and wondrous Golden Skill Sets.

"I ask you to take a few moments and listen inside of yourselves, inviting up the resonance of what feels like your particular area of expertise. Ponder where your unique affinity lies. What part of our Golden World do you most resonate with, feel most attuned to, and drawn to engage with further? Let your inner wisdom and Golden Heart show this to you.

"As you become clearer, I encourage you to speak up and share what you are discovering. Listen to each other and let your voices declare that which has meaning to you in these ways. Everyone will be able to witness you and at least have a taste of the array of creative talents that are here amongst us."

Many voices speak out in great joy as they deliver their vision and awareness:

"Yes, the Waters, the Golden Waters. They are the essence of my heart and my life. I have such a deep affinity for waters everywhere. I love them, I always have. They love me, they always have. I have glimpses of pure Golden Waters flowing everywhere, touching and blessing with holy wellness. Waters have the power to do this, you know.

"Water has a profound power to heal. It is alive and intelligent, strong and beautiful and free. I have learned much about freedom from my Waters. I would love to bring my Golden Awareness to these life forms now, these crystalline beautiful life forms. Where they are in need, I know I can witness whatever 'troubledness' they are holding and admire their Golden Beauty, facilitating their Golden restoration and wellness once again.

"I have much to say about my love for this, and I am grateful to be able to work openly again with these beautiful crystals of Golden Love. Thank you. Thank you for reminding me of this which I greatly love and can gift back much more fully."

"Yes, the Stars. I have longed to bring my gifts of knowledge of the Golden Stars back to Terra again and to assist other Star Ones to fully remember their sacred Golden Connection with Terra. They have long missed her in this way, as she has them. We need to have our entire Golden Star System restored in its glory as ONE. I can help with this, because it is my forte.

"I have much to bring from afar and Terra is my Golden Base of Creativity, as it was in Lemuria of long ago. Back then, I was invited to join our Golden Family to call forth many Golden Star Ones who wanted to be here as well. I knew how to build these necessary Golden Star Bridges that fostered this kind of interconnected birthing and harmonization. It brought many glorious and supremely beneficial gifts to our world back then. I would be honored to do this again, and would love to.

"My heart yearns to do my part in helping to bring home the Golden Star Ones. I want to do whatever I can to bring the wisdom, beauty, love, and wonderous gifts of the Golden Stars, to be received and utilized by us here again for the greatest benefit of the whole. It would be my Golden 'star dream' come true. Yes, absolutely YES. I have been waiting, aching, to fulfill this purpose for a long time. In this, I too will finally feel free, settled in myself, and at peace."

"I work with the Fairy Kingdoms. They have long felt that their wisdom and brightness had to be withheld because there was only a 'shallow ground of consciousness' here after the fall of Lemuria. They cannot deliver into that kind of frequency. But now that we are here again, they are exhilarated at the chance to shine forth, to inspire, contribute, and make magic.

"I am intimately engaged in the world of the Fairies, and love them deeply. I even feel myself to be more Fairy than person; they have made all the difference for me throughout my experiences in Lemuria of Origin, and since. They saved me often when I was suffering during the Rescues, and kept me going in ways that I never could have managed without them. I am eternally grateful.

"I also know that there is a need for healing and Golden Restoration for some of them as well, and I want to do whatever I can in this regard. I am a living testimony to the power and love that Fairies have for us, and I want to help them bring their beauty and Golden power forward to touch our world the way it did in Lemuria before. They bring the magic of wonder, lightness, and brightness to our world, as well as their profound wisdom, power, and skillful knowledge. I am an indelible part of this, and to continue to do so in our shining Golden way is my heart's greatest desire."

"What I want to do is simple: I want to bring everyone together. I want to be my heart, my Golden Heart, and to share it. Inside of my Golden Heart is the heart of my family, and family is something that I know and care about tremendously. That is my Golden Skill Set. That is what I am most attuned to—Family, our Golden Family.

"I know the art and heart of Family; family throughout our Golden World's arenas. The heartbeat of every family is sacred and dear, and a Blessing. I have the ability to call family together and to hold the space and vibrational sound for collective family harmony to happen. It comes from my heart, from me *BEING* my heart, my Golden Heart.

"I am also naturally attuned to the Golden Heartbeat in all Golden Beings, and I long to bring them together and encourage them to remember more about who they truly are, just as I have. This would make me and my heart extremely happy.

"It would mean a lot to me to stand clear as a Beacon of Golden love shining to shepherd and steward this fully again. I know this will help to strengthen our Golden Family and bring still greater harmony and joy to everyone everywhere. This would be my greatest gift, both to others and to myself. I have much love inside of me to share, and this would make my heart burst open with joy!"

"I have a profound affinity with Trees. I love them, they love me. I talk to them, they talk to me. We are one and the same somehow. I have enormous admiration for them, and they have brought such wisdom and love into my life and my world. They are great Golden Wise Ones, to be sure. It would mean much to me to be a Steward of their Golden Grace, as well as helping to lift any veils of pain from them that they have experienced or taken on. I long to be there for them in this way, and I know I can also make a difference in facilitating the restoration of their infinite wellness through touching their Golden Hearts. They are great Golden Ones themselves, and I worship them."

"Animals are my family. I feel more like one of them than I do an actual, two legged person. The Golden Animal Kingdom is where I resonate and feel most at home. I have turned to them often in the past when I ached for shelter and union. They showed up and loved and cared for me.

"They have been there for me in my bleakest moments; they have helped to protect me, and to bring healing to other loved ones when it was sorely needed. They are my support, my Golden Sacred Allies, and I love them deeply and know them well. I want to always be there for them. I can bear witness, and re-enliven their Golden Hearts. I would be grateful to do this for them, and to offer more love than ever before. It would be an honor to run openly and freely with my Golden Animals again. Yes, I would dearly love that."

"My Golden Skill Set is anchoring, and my calling is standing still and strong. I am embodying the Golden Energy that is being birthed and reawakened through a variety of different projects for our Golden World.

"I hold it steady while it travels, journeying from inception to completion. I do this exceptionally well. I remember this; it makes me feel 'immovable' sometimes, like I am a solid rock that will not yield. That is because I am not supposed to yield when I am fulfilling my purpose and doing my job. I stand strong, steady, and staunch in my purpose. I am immovable as that solid anchoring into Terra, the Golden Ethers, or wherever I need to be holding steady.

"I see this clearly and am grateful. I have long judged myself for not wanting 'to move.' I understand what this is truly about, and that it is a natural skill set for me that goes into gear whenever I am being called to Golden Anchor. This is the role and part I play in the stabilization of our Golden Life. I am honored and deeply grateful to be able to do this, because I know how much it is needed for the balance of what we are here to do and to be. I would love to continue in what is already an impassioned role for me."

"The Children; what can I say? Mentioning them brings tears to my eyes. They are profound blessings, and I love them deeply and dearly. They are our future, and I consider them to be the most important part of our family; the children of all Golden Life Forms are everything to me.

"I feel intensely passionate about this as you can tell. Whatever I can do to help, heal, inspire, uplift, honor, and love our children is all that I ever want to do. It is why I am alive. I want to be an integral part of helping them build and establish a strong platform of Golden Self in their little bodies and in their awareness. I know how to do this and do it well. I can help them have a strong beginning, so that whatever is added as they grow and develop will remain steady throughout. This fundamental base of Golden Love, well integrated and balanced, is most important. I know I can make a difference in this way and it is what I yearn to do."

"Our developing young people are where I feel drawn to put my Golden energies. As they gradually mature and develop, I am able to clearly see their Golden Soul Configurations, the paths that they are here to travel, and the gifts they wish to bring and express. They are our Golden future. I take this responsibility seriously, because I know how important it is to everything they do and become as adults. They will spread their special gifts out into our beautiful world, and it is up to us mature ones to give them what they need to learn, grow, flourish, and be wise about it. It would be my absolute joy to help steer and cheer them along. I have strong abilities in this arena, and I know exactly what to do. How soon can I get started?"

"Gardening and the Soil: creating new life out of dirt and raw elements that are here to gift us, make us strong, and inspire us with beauty. I love gardening of all kinds, but I have a particular affinity for foods—Golden Life of the soils creating Golden Life of foods, creating Golden Life for us.

"I am in awe of the soil. Whenever I touch it, smell it, or work with it—it works with me. We have a communing bridge that goes back and forth which teaches and encourages me. I am a profoundly grateful recipient of the wisdom and intelligence of our Golden Soil. It's all that I am."

"The Air: I have an affinity for that which others think is transparent, the air that keeps us alive and well. Not many people think about it, but I do. It has life and intelligence. I talk to it, caress it, and sing to it. It responds to me.

"Clean, clear air? Yes, I can contribute to this—or rather, I can invite it to be that for itself. It wants to gift us. We can gift it first by cleaning it up, talking to it, loving it, honoring it, and witnessing it. We can lift its particles of pain with this kind witnessing and caring. Who says we can't do this? I can do it and I have and will continue to do so."

"Music: I am a Musician in my heart and Soul. It is what I am and what I live for. Music in Life—have you ever heard, felt, or been touched by it? Of course, everyone has. That's my point, that's how potent and powerful it is.

"It would be my honor to bring forward gifts of Golden Music again, and to hear the sweet, splendid notes of Golden Love sounding out everywhere across this beautiful Planet. How blessed I would feel if I could do that. My heart bursts with joy at the thought of it.

"The blessing of doing this fully and freely again would be my blessing too. Sacred Golden Life through the sounds of song and music touching, moving, and uplifting everyone everywhere. I consider it the greatest healer. Thank you for bringing me home to my Golden Music again. This is my gift to give."

"Flowers: I have such an affinity with and for flowers. I dream of flowers, and smell them most everywhere. I wear flowers in my hair and I wear garments made of flowers. Even my shoes and slippers have flowers embroidered on them. I cannot get enough of flowers. I am a Flower, a Golden Flower. I remember this, and I feel privileged to be counted as one who is among these beautiful, sacred, divine, exquisite Golden Creations.

"We, the Golden Flowers, have our language and our stories. We have our hopes and dreams, and wish to inspire and touch many—as we certainly have. However, to do this with Golden Awareness fully restored will make it all the more special.

"We are each unique and splendid in our own ways, and it is for us to admire the beauty of that which birthed us forth in the first place. We are a reflection and manifestation of our Creator, and one of our gifts is to celebrate ourselves in this way, as well as celebrating the beauty of all of life in its beauty.

"We bring many gifts to our world; not only of beauty but also of healing and balance. I would be delighted and moved to grace our Golden World with our many talents and gifts in ways that far exceed even what we have been doing to date. This is splendid. Yes! What a sweet smelling, exquisite celebration this will be."

"Art: I am a Golden Artist. I always have been, even when things were hard for me and I had forgotten—now I remember.

"All energies Golden are what I paint. All things Golden are what I draw. All shapes and figures Golden are what I sculpt. The energy of Gold moves me and always has, indescribably so. But that is its property, to transmute in such a way that defies description. It just does!

"My Golden Heart absolutely LEAPS with joy at this prospect of birthing forth Golden Art with absolute clarity, conviction, purpose, and power. The power of Golden Beauty is immense. I want to be an outstanding part of this in any way that I can. As art always does, I know it will move and inspire many. I know it will be a Golden Doorway into their Golden Remembrance and inspiration. Art is my gift. I will bring forth Golden Art with great joy indeed!"

"The Devic Realms: this is my universe that I love and am already well developed in. I would love to bring my conscious Golden Awareness to this arena. In fact, I'll probably find the Devas laughing at me, wondering what took me so long for goodness sake!

"I can only imagine the power of Golden Heart this will bring forth in many ways and on many levels. This is no small thing; no, this is huge. For those of you who are aware of the Devic Kingdoms, you know what I mean. For others, let's say, 'Hold onto your hats! Golden Power Up! I'm all in!'"

"Technology: I know there is a way to organize this that is Golden and that will make a huge difference. I am going to 'start somewhere' in this glorious universe, letting my Golden Love guide me. I am eager to see what happens. I am eager to see what it feels like and what will be created with full Golden Heart intention. Yes, the thought of it thrills me to no end. This would be an honor."

"Numbers: the secret life of Numbers, I know it well. They often dance in my dreams. It is my language, and it is not only what I relate to, it is how I relate. It makes perfect sense to me. Numbers talk to numbers talk to numbers, like all of life. What would it be like to touch the Golden Heart inside their world, I wonder?

"We would have Golden Numbers, and thus life begins anew. This is my adventure, and I look forward to diving in as deep as I can. This is my terrain and I am grateful for this 'window' opening again."

"Listening: that's what I am really good at. I know that we all listen, but I'm exceptionally good at LISTENING. I seem to have an extra set of ears or something. It is a talent that I know can enable me to do many things. What excites me about it the most, is how it enables me to build bridges between people to help them. It also assists me in building bridges between systems, clusters of creative projects, and dimensions, etc.

"But right now, it is the people part that draws me in the most. I want to be around people in a meaningful way, and to listen. Golden Listening would be incredible, I know. Yes, I remember this. I was called The Golden Listener, and I could feel the planet move because of it. I could hear Terra shifting, heartbeats thumping, rainbows glowing, children laughing inside their dreams. I could hear so much. I am hungry to experience that again and see where it leads me!"

"Storyteller: yes, that's me, the Golden Witness. This is what inspires me and brings me joy. I have discovered that I have a natural talent for painting pictures with words. Endeavoring to describe that which is usually only left as 'indescribable' is a challenge that I love. I believe it to be my responsibility as a storyteller to never leave the listener or reader out—which means ALWAYS finding the right words to convey my meaning, never saying it is beyond description and walking away from sharing the treasure.

"How else do they get to have the experience? Golden Storytelling, yes, I look forward to my expansion of this. And the more our Golden World expands and thrives, the more stories I will have to tell and write about. This is a dream coming true for me, and it moves my heart deeply. Thank you, dear Reader, for listening to me share my stories in this book. You have been a generous Witness indeed. I am truly grateful."

"Dearest Ones," I hear Avalar's voice collecting us again. *"This is enough for now. Yes, you see what I mean about how far and wide your Golden Skill Sets go—how vast and varied they are. You see how expressing your unique Golden Creative Skill Sets is a way of letting go and allowing something bigger to happen.*

"Rest assured that your remembrance of your unique talents and Skill Sets will continue to emerge in the days ahead. I urge you to continue being receptive to this and celebrate each occasion of clarity. Don't put pressure on it. Simply let it evolve naturally and show you the wisdom of its Golden way.

"Trust yourselves as Golden Creators and as the Masters that you are. As you rediscover your Golden Skills, let your Golden talents soar and fly freely—and always remember what Andar said about the spirit of playfulness and lightness. Always include those ingredients to ensure greater ease and better outcome. You'd be surprised at what a difference this makes!

"And finally, also know that this active expression of BEING and DOING lifts any final traces of the veiling left from the Mondor experience. This is the actual building of our Golden World; it is the recollection and restoration of our capacity to generate Golden materialization. It lifts any final veils and traces thereof. They get deleted by virtue of our Golden materialization into manifested form, which literally 'pushes them away and out.'

"Step aside everyone. The Golden Builders are here and busy at work!

"In your daily activities and situations, ask yourselves, how can I apply my Golden love to this? How does this want to be Golden made and expressed? Simply by intending Golden Heart as the inspiration and drive behind everything you be and do will shed light for your path. It will also 'Goldenize' all the current skills you have been using to date. These will become brighter and bolder, and if needed, redirected in whatever ways are most appropriate and aligned with who you intentionally are now. This will become obvious to you and will expand your success and the joy of it in a truly Golden way.

"Yes, you are Golden Heart through and through. You are its desire, expression, and instrument. You are the physical pathway that will open this up for creation to flow and for everyone else to be Golden inspired. You can only begin to imagine the tremendous and enlivening power of this, as well as the outcome—and YOU make the difference in all of it.

"Know clearly that all that you be and do has impact on all of life—it reverberates far and wide. Think about the ripple in the water and how the energy of its original motion continues on. It is the same with all of you, you all affect the whole. You are Golden Heart generating more of the same. We feel you and we welcome you; we need you. It begins with Golden Consciousness, and from there everything can happen on energetic as well as physical levels.

"Also know that every cell of life communes with one another, no matter what arena you are engaged in and no matter what you may think. Life continually talks to life—always. That's the way of it. Remind yourselves of *this as well when you are generating forth Golden beauty and skill. Take a moment to reflect and smile about the fact that you are at that moment inspiring, enhancing, and uplifting everything everywhere!*

"Everyone, set your talents free to soar and fly! Plant them, spread them out, support and sustain them with your love and devotion. Let them lead you where they may, always guided and impulsed by your loving Golden Heart. This is how we will re-manifest our One Golden World filled to the brim with ALL things and ALL energies Golden—a Golden World that is even better and brighter and stronger than it has ever been before.

"Set yourselves free!

"There is plenty of room for each of you and your unique expressions. We value your differences and will always do our best to support you in finding ways to fulfill your dreams of expressing who you most naturally are. Each one of you makes THE DIFFERENCE in our beautiful Golden World that only YOU can make. We salute you and are enormously grateful for you!

"GOLDEN BE.

"GOLDEN CREATE.

"GOLDEN MANIFEST.

"That is our Lemurian Way.

"Bless you Golden Creators! Bless you! We thank you!"

CHAPTER NINETEEN

Your Sacred Golden
Illuminated Body

THE GOLDEN WITNESS SPEAKS:
I find myself opening once more to the awareness of my Golden Family that is with me. Everyone is beaming and radiant, as am I. We are feeling empowered in ourselves, emboldened and bright. It's exciting to feel the "motion" of our Golden Creative Skill Sets already beginning to take shape, and to realize that we will be establishing actual Golden Heart made manifest.

I sense there is a lot of change ahead for me, and for all of us. I am excited about this. There is a solid knowing of freedom inside of me, true freedom that knows no bounds anymore. The days of having to fit myself inside the confining pathways of Mondor are over, and the feeling of contraction brought on by that frequency are gone.

I take a deep breath, a Golden Breath, and give thanks that I am free again, free to BE ME. I look forward to even more clarity about my Golden Creative Skill Sets that will solidify my stand and presence as an active Golden One contributing prolifically to our beautiful One Golden Heart World.

This is a time of "tall order" change and challenge in the best of ways—I can feel it in the air. Yes, on the one hand, it will be the easiest thing ever because it's who I am naturally, and who and how we all are. On the other, it's about stretching out again isn't it? It's about extending ourselves far beyond the parameters that we have been encased in for so long. It will most likely feel challenging in a great way, and for good reasons.

I know that this is a "season of change" in a Golden way and I am extremely grateful.

I see Andar and Avalar talking quietly between themselves. Finally, Andar steps forward to speak:

"Beloveds, now that you have witnessed for yourselves the emerging Skill Sets that are inherent within you, and heard about those that your Golden Family have as well, I can see that you are feeling authentically empowered. This pleases Avalar and myself to no end. We have waited a long time for

539

you to feel this way again, and it is something for us to truly celebrate.

"This leads me to talk about the state of the current world that you find yourselves in. Yes, you are Golden in our One Golden Heart World. It is for you, and for us, to substantiate this and to make our world strong and vibrant. This we know.

"The reality is that we are here on Terra alongside Mondor as well. As you already know, Mondor lives its own frequency as we live ours. There will be many times, however, when you know you are vibrating your frequency, and are also aware of the movement and state of reality around what is happening in the Mondor frequency as well. This is precisely where some of the 'challenge' begins. The 'challenge' will be to hold your sovereign Golden ground and see Mondor through your Golden Eyes of clarity and under-standing.

"You won't necessarily be able to get away from it every time. You won't be vibrating it and you won't be victimized by it, but you will be aware and cognizant of it. Being able to hold your position as a Golden One in the face of Mondor's motion will, in itself, be an opportunity to exercise your muscles, to 'dig deep,' in order to remain strong and sovereign in your Golden clarity.

"Do not be daunted by this. This will not be a time to close your eyes, but to open them as wide as possible and witness what is going on there. Turn back and focus on what is yours to be responsible for, letting that be unto itself—live and let live. We will be saying this many more times.

"Mondor is a world of pain, struggle, and suffering. You already know this from your first hand experiences there. As I have stated before, people go there for various reasons—all of which we honor without needing to know any details. It is not ours to know.

"The question that I pose to you is this: as you stand apart from it, and see through your Golden Eyes, what do you notice? Is there anything that you want to say?"

The Golden Witness speaks:

I look at Mondor and feel shock and great sadness at the lost world that I see. Swimming around on itself in pain and suffering, it is in a constant struggle for life. A consciousness engaged in the struggle for power, it is at war in many ways and on many levels. That is its patterning and that is its game—its reality.

It has always been thus and will remain so until the consciousness of Mondor changes, as we have spoken about at length previously. What I also see is the struggle to gain a foothold on freedom—the valiant struggle for goodness to "rise above" and prevail. While it does so to some degree, it is always a supreme struggle to get there.

I look within and am aware of my ABSENCE of struggle and any identification with it; it has completely disappeared from all frameworks of my self and my consciousness. I feel only my natural inclination to glide forward, to yield to a greater power that dwells within me, and to LET IT HAPPEN. There is no struggle—there is only allowing.

And yet, I remember well those days of struggle, and how painful and arduous it was; the supreme effort that was required to make headway, and how much of an ENORMOUS challenge everything seemed. The obstacles made for extreme levels of difficulty.

One could certainly say that it was creative in its own way for sure—navigating an obstacle course always is. And there was triumph at the end of the accomplishment, providing I succeeded. But would I want that now? No. Did it make me stronger? Yes, indeed it did in its own unique way. Struggle often has a way of making us stronger if we don't give up. But I choose a different way for myself now: I choose my most natural way again.

This awareness brings me to a place of honoring the consciousness of Mondor and why many souls choose to go there. Yes, there is much to be learned in that kind of arena. It allows me a greater perspective to stand back and allow the experience of those who are there.

That's how I see it. I witness it, and simply let it be.

There is great suffering there which still pains me to see. I am aware of this, and I am wondering about it. I wish it was not the case; I would rather not even see it.

"Beloveds," Andar says. *"I see where you are, and I understand how you feel. Does it make you want to reach out and touch it in compassion? Does it make you want to do something about it? Does it make you want to lift the pain and soothe the soreness of it? Is that yours to do, or not?"*

I look and assess. No, it is not mine to do. No, as odd as it sounds, it is only mine to witness and honor. I do not feel my Soul being called to change anything there. If I did, I would.

I am about to turn my attention away from that "world" and back to my responsibilities when Andar steps in again:

"Golden Ones, as much as it is not yours to change, there is indeed something

you can do besides witnessing and honoring, which in and of themselves are gifts enough. What you can do is consciously attend to the part reflected in you that you see is causing the greatest pain in the world of Mondor: the disconnection of the Spiritual Body from its true authentic Divine design. This is the crux of the matter.

"Let us first be clear on what your Spiritual Body is. It is that aspect of you that is the direct expression of your soul, your spirituality, and your spiritual nature in your physical domain. This also includes your spiritual identity, your spiritual belief systems, and your spiritual values. In Mondor there is a great deal of confusion and disconnectedness regarding this. Many people might not agree, but there is; it's everywhere.

"Do you remember how I spoke about the true Divine Masculine Aspect having been put away on ice for a while? How it was shut down and basically buried underneath this fabrication of 'masculine identity' that was, and still remains, the stronghold of the patriarchal system in Mondor?

"Also, do you remember how you felt when you had let that go and re-owned the true Lemurian Golden Divine Masculine in you? Do you remember that you felt like 'everything was right with your world again?'

"Well, this case of the Spiritual Body and the subject of Spirituality are similar to that. The Heartless Ones do not hold connection to their Divine Source, their Divine Spirituality, or to their Divine Spiritual Bodies. They have disconnected from this whole framework of themselves, thus rendering their systems greatly distorted and confused in their woundedness. The sad truth is that this has left all of Mondor living in that same paradigm.

"The Nature of Spirituality in Mondor is askew. There are many religions and practices that have nothing to do with the reality of one's true Spiritual nature—at least not for us Lemurians, that is.

"This piece of your intrinsic design has to be put back into its proper place, redefined according to YOUR truth, and re-owned in this way. Your Spirituality is the extension and expression of your Divine Source. You need no Mediator, no religious context, no practice, and no dogma. YOU ARE THIS ALREADY. It is not something that you make a date for, whether that is once a week, once a day or once a minute. You ARE this, period, ALL THE TIME.

"You already know this. You have already connected back in, securely, to this base of who you truly are. That was the first step that Terra walked

you through in your Golden Re-embodiment process. I know this.

"But there is this last portion of it to be consciously recalibrated. I speak of this because it comes up mostly in contrast to the frequencies between you and Mondor; that is where you would see this aspect of you possibly becoming confused and perplexed, disoriented and overwhelmed.

"Become clear about the difference and contrast between your understanding and identity of this and that of Mondor, so that when you are in the midst of people who are still vibrating the Mondor frequency you don't get lost or even mildly confused.

"Being disconnected from one's true Spiritual Body is a set up for pain. It guarantees it; that's simply the way it is. For us Lemurians, our Spiritual Bodies govern our entire systems. If there is trouble in this arena, there will be torque and trouble throughout.

"In the Emotional Body there will angst, worry, fear, dislocation, panic, and anger. In the Mental Body there will be confusion, crossed wires, faulty thinking, fabricated belief systems, and mental overloading. In the Physical Body there will pain of all kinds. Some of this you are aware of, and some you aren't, but it is corrosive—you can count on that. It causes things to break down instead of being continuously re-nourished and rejuvenated.

"And there's the Spiritual Body. Well, because of your travails in Mondor and taking on that construct of spirituality as part of the veils of fear, it has felt confused and lost; it has not been able to be sovereign and outshining the way it is truly designed to be. This is a result of the Mondor construct of Spirituality being inherently confused and lost: it is false because it is primarily constructed and imposed by one's Will, and not by Divine Source. Much of it is built on confused and confusing falsehoods.

"Remember, Golden Ones, this may be a perfect fit for Mondor. Obviously, it has its place there because it keeps on perpetuating itself throughout eons of time, but it is no fit for you.

"You as Lemurians are not designed this way. You must choose to leave this confusion behind forever and re-adopt that spirituality which is true for you, and only for you. It is your natural way.

"Speak about your Spirituality, your Spiritual Identity, your Spiritual Body. What does this truly mean to you? Define it according to that which is authentically true for you."

The Golden Witness muses, "Oh my, more to look at."

The first thing that comes to me are the words 'Golden Communion.' I am always in this sacred state of Being; my Spirituality is my Divine Love inside of me, as me. It is that simple. It is pure; it is sovereign, it is sacrosanct. It is holy. I meet it through my sacred awareness, and my sacred awareness is the entirety of me and everything that I know and love.

In my authentic Golden Spiritual Body and nature I feel nothing but clear waters. I do not need anyone else to tell me how to think, what to believe, what to do, and how to behave. I don't need anyone to explain right and wrong to me, to tell me how or where to "find God," or that I need to detach from myself in order to feel my Truth.

As far as I can tell, the biggest sickness that Mondor has is the sickness of being disconnected from Source. That sickness presents itself in many different forms, all of which have one thing in common: THEY CREATE AND PERPETUATE FURTHER SEPARATION BETWEEN SELF AND DIVINE CREATOR.

What happened to true, heart-centered, intimate devotion which only happens between Self and one's Creator? It is private, it is sacrosanct, it is sacred. It can be expressed and honored in many ways. It has deep centered MEANING for me and nourishes me through every cell of my Being. It's ONLY about me and my Source—and it's ALWAYS cause for celebration!

That is my Golden Spiritual Body thriving and in its proper position of leadership and inspiration for the rest of me. It is my Soul. It is MY Divine Creator as Soul as Me, period. It is that simple and that profound.

"Yes, Beloved," Andar says. *"You've got it. Feel the impact of this on the rest of your body, emotion, and mind. Feel that kicking in and realigning you still more perfectly into your Divine Golden Patterning.*

"We will be deliberately deepening you in this process.

"What you have remembered and re-owned in regards thus far is only a small taste of what is the true breadth and depth of it. I will hand this over to Avalar, and she will lead you deeper into this great treasure of you as Golden Illuminated Body.

"Welcome Home, Beloveds, yet again!"

And with that, Andar steps back as Avalar is about to come to the forefront. I am eager to see what more there is to know and remember.

I am aware as the minutes pass that re-identifying and reclaiming my true Divine Golden Spiritual Body and Spiritual Nature has made a HUGE difference in me. Everything has shifted dramatically inside of me, yet again, according to this recalibration. I am simply centered from a whole different place and position.

I feel solidly connected into my Divine Source in ways that I hadn't even known I was missing. It has made all the difference for me. Any trace and memory of wobbliness is gone. I am solid and steady like never before. Yes, I feel sovereign in a much stronger way, and I feel like my Mastery can start to truly shine forth as well.

I see Avalar getting ready to speak and I move my attention in her direction. I am listening.

"Dear Ones," she says gently. "This is such a momentous occasion for you, and for us together as a Family. As Andar has said, your Divine Golden Spiritual Body is the linchpin around which everything else revolves, and if this is not fully intact and vibrating the way it is naturally designed to then there is indeed 'trouble in Paradise.' That is what you have witnessed and experienced in Mondor.

"But this is the case no longer.

"You are reclaiming your Spiritual Body and Spiritual Nature which is your true birthright, and which is the exquisite design born within us from our Divine Source. The blueprint of this holy body has been dormant within the memory cells of your physical body. It is in the process of being both fully restored to its rightful place and fully reactivated.

"As you can see and feel, this alters everything. For Lemurians, your Spiritual Path is the most important thing in your life. Continue to make it so and all will remain well, I guarantee. This is your Golden Mastery expressing.

"Now that your Divine Golden Spiritual Body is recalibrating for your whole system, let us take a look at how your Golden Creative Centers, your Golden Chakras, are doing and feeling as a result. You will witness them vibrating and resonating differently than before. You will be most pleased, I believe!

"Simply stand and feel your feet on the ground. Notice how the grounding centers in the soles of your feet feel—how they are supporting your body as well as how they are connecting with Terra's body absorbing her grounding energies."

I notice that my feet are feeling warm, tingly, and alive—especially on the bottom—as they connect with Terra's body. I feel strong, supported, and secure; everything feels peaceful.

"When you are ready, I invite you to witness yourselves. Do you see how shining and Golden Radiant you are? Look down at your bodies and take note of what you find. Take note of what you are aware of. Look at yourselves from an outer perspective first, witnessing what you see about

your physical bodies and the glowing radiance of one another. This is the first time that you have had a chance to do it in this way."

I look down at my body as Avalar has suggested, and I see that I am wearing a beautiful shimmering Golden Cloak. I lift up my arms and the sleeves feel like silk, caressing my skin. It is light and airy, while at the same time it is definitely a material that has substance to it. I can see its Golden threads sparkling in the sunlight.

It is a beautiful garment, and I feel right and comfortable wearing it. I feel as though I have earned the right to proudly wear something this exquisite and beautiful. I have walked through a lot and I am here to tell the tale with grace and maturity. Yes, I have grown; I have indeed grown immensely through my time and travels on this planet.

I look up at the sun that is making my cloak sparkle brightly and I welcome its warmth, light, and love. I have a moment of pure peace. I have arrived—I am home in me.

These many layers and levels of homecoming, each one more full and complete than the last, have brought me to this beautiful moment of peace. I welcome this. I feel grounded and solid in my body and in my Golden grace.

"Look more closely still, Beloveds. Look at what lies underneath your garment. What do you find inside?"

I look down again as I open the outer garment to reveal what is underneath.

I am amazed at what I see! I knew I was radiant before, but I hadn't seen it quite like I am now. My whole body is glowing with warm Golden Light, and I register that I have a body that is Golden Illuminated. It is strong, vital, and shining—inside and out. I am aware that my physical cells are turned on and Golden Restored. They have their story to tell of their journey, which has ultimately brought them back home to themselves.

I am a collective harmony of Golden Life force with each one of my Golden Creative Chakra Centers lit up and blazing with great feeling, balance, and vitality. I am in complete physical harmony with myself, inside and out. I know I have not experienced this state of pure wellness and vibrancy since Lemuria of Origin long ago. I am no longer contracted in any way like I was in Mondor. Instead, I am fully expanded and free.

"Yes, dear Ones," Avalar's voice says softly. *"Let yourselves FEEL what it's like to be free, Golden ALIVE, and STRONG!"*

I can feel the pure Golden power of me; it is thick and solid, light and illuminated—all at the same time. I sink into it and breathe it in.

I hear Avalar's melodious voice again. *"Let us call in your Sacred Golden Healing Teams so that they can work with you while you engage physically at these levels of awareness. Their assistance in this next process will be helpful."*

I settle into myself and send out my request to my Golden Healing Team to come and connect with me in a way that I can feel, know, and understand. Right away, they are here. I can feel them shifting quietly around me, the same three that I had met earlier in our storyline. They greet me fondly and I feel instantly at ease with them once again.

"Good Day, Dear One," the female Energy Healer says to me. *"We are glad to be here and to help this along in any way that we can. We will lead the way and let you take over after we've gotten things in motion.*

"We will begin with your Creation Center in the base of the body; the sacrum, the pelvis, and the base of the spine. Breathe in deeply as you become aware of Golden Energies moving up through Terra right into your body. You are familiar with this sensation. Greet it warmly and hold it close in that part of your body and awareness. See the spirals of passion illuminating this chakra center, sending waves of strength and resilience up into your entire system. This is such a Divine Center of Health, as it is the life-giving, grounded, life-sustaining center of you.

"Breathe in and up. Connect it with your Golden Heart and your heart with it—Golden Love shining and Golden Life Force pulsating. Be Golden Power aware."

My focus engages into my Creative Center of my pelvic bowl. I am aware of Terra's energies moving up into this region and I am also aware of my Golden Energies. Everything merges together as one. As I feel the vibrancy of it, I become aware of everything changing in yet another way. All is being brought to this Golden "pitch" of vitality and health in every way. I am aware that this is affecting my emotions, my emotional body, and my mental body. Everything is rearranging itself as renewal.

I watch my pelvic bowl being lit up with the forces of my creative energy heightening and brightening. There is power in there. It is the power of ground, balance, passion, and vitality. It is the ground of my sexual and sensual nature that brings pleasure and the gifts of pro-creative drive. I feel great strength and self-confidence—bold and balanced and invigorated. I feel impassioned.

"Is there a message this Golden Creative Center has for you at this time?" asks my Golden Healing Team. *"Listen and you will hear and feel it."*

I open my inner ears to this, and the message comes easily to me. *"I am your Golden Sacred Ground of Being. I support you unconditionally. I am the ground, the base of that which you bring forth. I am strong and steady. I am Golden passion that rises up inside of you and brings you vitality and power, pleasure and fire. Consider me like 'rocket fuel' that powers everything in a physical way. Trust in me; it is trust well deserved. I love you, and I serve you to the best of my ability, always. You can count on me."*

I am touched by this feeling and its message and my loving heart goes right to it to join still more. I send it my gratitude and deep appreciation as I find that in doing so, the feeling of it increases greatly. I love this feeling. It is solid, secure, and impassioned. I am grateful for this in me and as me.

My Golden Healing Team speaks again:

"Keep following your energy as it rises to meet each Golden Creative Center. In each one there will be a message for you. Keep breathing and stay soft. Listen and feel."

I take in a deep breath as I watch as my Golden radiance moving upward into my second Golden Creative Center. It is quiet right now, quiet and serene. There is a sense of complete and utter safety, serenity, trust, and quiet joy. I know this is my Golden Center of Birthing and that it also holds the delight of me at the earliest times and experiences of my life. It is a peaceful, happy place. The Birthing Energies are quiet, but I know that won't be for long. Soon, it will be stirred again, activated with creative motion and power for delivery. I welcome it.

I love this center in me. I send my love into it and give thanks for what it does for me and brings to me. I admire its strong instinct and I trust it completely.

"I am your Golden Birthing Center and I know only freedom. I have always had a strong instinct for what is right for me and I have delivered this forth. I bring beauty and sacredness for you to enjoy and partake. Ours is a union of joy—pure, succinct, and sacrosanct. I am thriving as Golden Love being born every minute of Golden Life. I thrive on this! I take great care of you always and I am well, very well."

I am touched by this message. Everything seems positive and filled with upliftment. I receive it totally.

I pause for a moment longer, watching my Golden Energies collect and settle in before my attention is drawn upward toward my Golden Solar Plexus Creative Center. I see and feel robust Golden Energies. There is something phenomenal about this Creative Center of me; it is intricate and sophisticated. It is my Golden Sun Center. Powerful, bright, warm, and caring—like the Golden Sun in the sky—this Center brings me life in a "sunny" kind of a way.

Many things come together for me in this location of my body. It is my Intuitive Golden Brain, my Golden Think Tank that looks like a high level communication center. There are incoming and outgoing energetic and etheric communication lines, busily working to give and receive information about what is happening; what's up, what's around, and what's coming. Add to this the intelligence of the complex physical digestive system and you have quite a remarkable combination of expertise.

I watch as my Golden Healing Team steps in and begins to do some things with the energetic patterns and frequencies of this Golden Center. As they do, I feel tremendous relief and easefulness inside me. I had not known that something inside of me actually felt "stuck," and was apparently not flowing properly.

After their "adjustment," I feel like everything is flowing along smoothly again, and I am grateful. I also see my Golden Healing Team addressing some aspects of my physical digestive system and bringing that into its proper place and comfortable positioning as well. That makes a big difference for me, too, and I can see clearly that everything is lining up in harmony with my recently repositioned Divine Spiritual Body. I like it, I like it a lot.

"Take some deep breaths, if you would," my Golden Healing Team asks of me. *"Feel these pathways coming back into harmony and balance the way they are supposed to be."*

Any sensations of tightness have vanished, and I am infinitely more relaxed than I was before. I had not realized that I had been holding myself in that state of tension. It had become the "norm" for me in Mondor, and now there was no more need for it. I am grateful to my Golden Healing Team for that which they are doing and supporting in me.

I continue to watch this Creative Center as it takes care of its various jobs and activities, energetic and physical. I see that this activity is normal for this Golden Creative Center and that, basically, it doesn't "bat an eye" at the intricacies and demands of its station. It simply does it—happily. I touch it with my gratitude and shower it with love and appreciation for everything that it is and does. I can hear it almost purring in response, like a cat!

I feel its joy as the wellness it brings circulates in, around, and through its amazing array of pathways and streams of Golden intelligence. It is strong, power-ful, dedicated, and impassioned. The Golden Life Force here is self-confident, self-governing, and self-contained. I love this. I realize I have worried about this Center inside of me in the past travails through Mondor; it always felt overloaded with information and sensory data, but not now, not anymore.

It is stretched out fully, and exhilarated at the tasks that it rises to meet. It knows its skills well and is happy in their implementation.

"Talk with me, walk with me," it says. *"Know me as a friend and intimate companion; I am here for you. I can take good care of myself and that of which I need to attend. This is what I was designed for. I can take care of you, too, if you let me. I am your steady confidence and ability to digest life—in the myriad of ways it presents itself. I do this well and I do this with great joy. Trust me, all is well."*

I am amazed at the good feeling that its message brings to me, and I relax even more than before.

Next, my Golden Energy gracefully rises up and settles happily inside my Golden Heart Center. That's Golden Home for me, the Creative Center of all the loving that spreads out throughout my system—my touchstone for it. My Golden Heart is solid, steady, steadfast, pure, sacrosanct, sovereign, resilient, loving, grateful, forgiving, wise, compassionate, all-knowing, wondrous, and beautiful. It is Golden Beautiful through and through.

This Golden Creative Center is the stanchion, the glue, the reverberation of Source pulsating with every beat. My Golden Heart speaks to all Centers and Cells of me. I remind myself of the remarkable wealth of this magnificent Golden Creative Center; the total generosity that it pours forth as if it does, indeed, have a never ending supply of glorious Golden Love, which, of course, it does!

It is full of abundance, wealth, and richness with an eternal supply. These are words that describe the Truth of this. I am born to love, to love what this Golden Heart does! This Heart of my Soul is alive and well and expressing itself openly and freely, with total joy throughout.

"Greet me," it says. "Greet me with a hug every morning and a hug goodnight at the end of every day. Bless me as I bless you. It is that simple. Gratitude, it means everything to me—and it is who we are."

I am touched in such a simple way, and yet so profoundly. It is like still waters that run deep. My heart, my beautiful sacred Golden Heart, I love you. I am grateful for you.

My heart expands still more and my whole body along with it. It is like the sun bursting over the horizon in the morning. My heart slowly but surely bursts open with Golden Love glowing everywhere. I have never known my heart to feel this happy; happy to be and to be doing what it does best—love, loving, sharing love. I welcome this flooding of warm energy as it courses through my veins and brings my whole body to a state of pure joy and radiance. I continue to be grateful.

I watch as my Golden Energy moves from my Heart center and rises upward deliberately to land comfortably in my Throat center, the Creative Center of my heart's voice and song. My voice is the physical sounding of my Soul as it catches the airwaves and reverberates its joy and wisdom throughout the land and sky.

It is a song of jubilation, coupled with painting pictures in words that have meaning. It is fun and full of laughter and noise and cheering. It is sharing, caring, giving, and receiving. My words are like bridges to my outer experience that reveal what is going on inside of me. My song is my sound of love releasing to that which I love.

My voice—it is much more than even the words themselves. It is a special instrument through which I can share myself and include those that I love inside my stories; a sacred vehicle to inspire and uplift, teach and commune.

This Golden Voice of mine is everything Golden. *"Love me,"* it says. *"I am free. Trust me. I will please thee, and I will share your pleasure with others."*

I am moved by this voice of mine and its integrity and purpose. It has a reason to be and it loves its purpose in countless forms—spoken and energetic. My Golden Voice LOVES TO BE ALL THAT IT POWERFULLY IS.

"Speak up, speak out, and stand steady for me," it says. *"I am all you have ever wanted to be—Free. I am a voice that is Golden Free."*

I see and feel my heart energy pouring through this instrument of this voice, in the right and most perfect of ways, taking over the space that has been prepared and waiting for it to sound and speak and sing forth. Never will anything get in its path again. Never will anything bind or restrict it again.

It will stand for all that it believes in and support all that is goodness and grace. It will not waver in the face of anything else and never, ever back down again. It is a Golden Voice, full and free; Golden and beautiful, happy to BE.

Golden Power—it is the Sound that is and will be heard. That is the Truth of that.

I am shocked a little bit by the power of my voice, its intensity and determination to be its full freedom. I salute this. I love my voice, I am grateful for it and know what it can bring. It expresses my Soul, my Golden Heart, and I will spread it around everywhere.

I will delight in it and be empowered by it. It has its own path set—strong and clear. Freedom is what it expresses in full voice, and I am proud of it.

I feel it responding to me with waves of pleasure washing through me. I gently touch my throat with my hand as a gesture of thanksgiving and I know that all is well with it and me. I find myself starting to hum and I smile.

At this point, I see my Golden Healing Team stepping back in again, smoothing the whole area and bringing it to even greater comfort than before. Automatically, my whole chest area, neck, and head start to shine more brightly, and I feel enlivened throughout. I keep humming and smiling!

Moving upward from my throat Center, my Golden Energy travels into the Golden Creative Center of my Brow Chakra. This is my Golden Third Eye. It looks like a rare and special gem that is shining brightly. It is shaped like a large egg and it sparkles with Golden light. This is the Sacred Golden Seer of me. It sees and knows much; it understands and witnesses. It is always in tune with the Golden Universe at large, as well as with whatever other information it needs for its purposes to be expressed.

My Golden Third Eye supports my physical eyes in seeing everything and everyone through the Golden lens of compassion and understanding—witnessing, being present, seeing clearly. That is the gift of this Golden Creative Center for me. I see and understand everything through Golden Eyes.

My Golden Healing Team steps back in, and this time they are wiping something away from both my Third Eye and my two physical eyes as well. *"Just cleaning the windows, Ma'am,"* I hear them say as they turn toward me chuckling. *"Making them squeaky clean for you to see through properly again!"*

I chuckle and take a look through my Third Eye to see what's up. Yes, it's definitely clearer, there is no question about that.

"Have faith in me," it says. *"Trust in me. I bring clarity, insight, and the gift of harmony to everything I touch with my eyes. Trust me. I will show you the way. I am able to see far and wide as well as up close and personal. I LOVE to see, I love what I see, I am Golden Eyes, I am Sacred Golden Seer.*

"I will show you everything you need so that you know your path ahead clearly. I will make it crystal clear and obvious to you that FREEDOM is here, and what you have to do is seize it and stand strong as it. I will show you how beautiful you are and how beautiful life is. I will gift you beyond your imagining as I reveal to you ALL that is Golden and has always been.

"I am grateful to you and for you. I love you. I am clear, ABSOLUTELY GOLDEN CRYSTAL CLEAR. I always am and have always been. Golden Clarity and Perception, inside and out, is my gift to you. Take this and see your life and everyone and everything in it, including yourself, through this viewpoint of Golden clarity and understanding. You will be most happy, as will I. Thank you for giving me freedom to see freely this way again. Life is beautiful for me. I rejoice in this."

I am moved by this message, and especially grateful because I would love nothing more than to see my entire life through Golden Eyes. I can only imagine how this will change everything for me, alter my viewpoint, and my understanding along with it—giving me broader and clearer insight and greater compassion as well. I have a hunch this is going to be revealing to me in many ways, and again, I am grateful. I feel like I am becoming a renewed and better person as each second passes.

My Golden Energy moves up again from my Brow to my Golden Crown Creative Center Chakra at the top of my head. The sensation is of soft, shimmering Golden Light dancing and swirling gently in patterns of perfection. It delights my whole body and Being thoroughly and washes through me as though I have drunk a glass of Joy Juice! It feels supremely healthy—the best way to describe it is to call it sparkling "Golden Beauty Wellness."

I also feel like my Golden Brain inside my head is being stimulated with this joyous vibrancy. It becomes more alive and clearer than ever, as if it has been fully turned on and is being tuned up by this Golden Light. I see that it's as though my brain has been lying dormant for a long time and is waking up, stretching out, and reaching for more oxygen to clear the cobwebs of time. It feels alive, alert, and eager for new experiences. It is exhilarated with purpose and passion, as my whole body is in turn.

I can feel the pure joy of the Golden Creative Center showering itself down through my body, making it feel juicy, shimmery, and bright with lightened life throughout. I know it is a great Golden gift.

"I am your pure heavenly awareness," it says to me. *"I am that Golden Light which vitalizes you in this sacred and special way every single second. I am holy. I am also pure delight; I am grace and I am glory. I constantly remind you of and infuse you with the vibration of your higher purpose and possibility beyond imagining. Only I can bring that level and quality of beauty to be made real. I love you forever. Know this and drink me in as deeply as you possibly can."*

I become aware of my whole body as this gathering of Golden Creative Centers, as well as the multitude of cells, atoms, and molecules of me. They have different purposes and qualities, but they are joined up and working as a Team, a Golden Team. They are my fuel and my power, lifting and inspiring me with the intention of balance, harmony, and pure wellness of the highest order.

I become aware of these aspects of me communing and communicating in a way that I hadn't been before—since Lemuria that is. I register Golden Communion. Here it is again, right inside my body. I am in active Golden Communion and am benefitting enormously.

I realize that my whole system is united in this one harmonious Golden dance of pure joy. It is Golden Wellness of the Highest Order. That is what this Golden Body knows. That is how it is—pure and simple. It is perfectly exquisite and exquisitely perfect.

I'm aware of how much pure love my body is and how much love I am. My senses are awash with this physical love as I realize how separate I felt from my body in Mondor. I actually felt dislocated in this way because I was always out of sync with it. Something was not right with that picture.

I remember feeling afraid of my body and what it might do next. I remember feeling uncomfortable and awkward in it; not comfortable in my skin. Now I know why. It was simply because of this disconnection, this strange and unfamiliar separation from me. Once again, the word "disconnection" applies. It keeps boiling down to that, doesn't it? I truly understand this and the pain that it causes on any level where it is showing up. I get it, fully and completely.

Happily, I don't feel any of those ways anymore. I am fully connected again. I am Golden Whole.

I am well aware that this process of communing with My Golden Creative Chakra Centers has been vitally important. It has shown me my different aspects and centers that are vibrating in their unique ways. It has brought me to new heights of appreciation and understanding of myself as One Golden Illuminated Body. This is my Golden expression and manifestation of my self in my physical domain. I get it totally, and am suddenly flooded with the pure joy of celebration!

"Dearest One," my Golden Healing Team whispers to me, *"take a moment to savor the sensations and feelings that you are having. Enjoy the richness of you in this divinely physical way—your Golden Physical Body, the radiance made manifest of your Golden Soul in this physical domain once more.*

"Your instinctive drive is always Golden Wellness of the Highest Order. How could you be anything else? This will always be the case no matter what, no matter what you may think. Take a moment to register this and be inspired. You are Golden Illuminated Body through and through."

I do take a moment, and I pause—I stop, look, and listen; I feel.

I repeat the words, "I AM FULLY PHYSICALLY GOLDEN ILLUMINATED BODY" to myself a number of times, and everything in me starts to sing with this vibration of pure Golden Harmony. It is a sensation of absolute pure pleasure throughout.

I flash on how much I always loved the feeling of my physical body back in Lemuria of Origin. I would inhale its joy deeply, and it always made me feel fantastic. I am remembering this, the sweet, divine pleasure of feeling this well. There is nothing like it. It is Golden Wellness of the Highest Order. It is my Golden Gift to myself.

I hear My Golden Healing Team chuckling again. They are happy too and I can feel their happiness right inside my heart. They are delighted and smiling, and I love their sense of humor and their lightness. I am reminded again of Andar's advice about playfulness and lightness. I sense that these qualities play a big part in my physical well-being and health as well.

Life in my Golden World, I feel like there is abundant laughter and lightness. I look forward to experiencing that more and more in myself. I know it is part of my natural design, and that makes me happy.

In the midst of this joy, I become aware of a great stream of Golden Energy that is cascading down from above my head, entering through my Golden Crown Center and moving slowly down my body, into every single cell of me, right down into my toes. Along the way it is lighting me up with its beauty and shimmering crystalline energy. I feel veritably flushed with it.

Once in my feet, it moves through them and down into Terra, down into her Core Crystal, where it settles and collects for a moment. It joins and blends with her crystalline energies. Those energies wind their way back up through my body and back out the top of my head into the Celestial Realms. This sequence repeats itself several more times. The Golden Celestial Energies pour down through me again, into Terra, and Terra's Divine grounding energies travel back up into the Celestial Realms. This two-way motion is constant and continuous.

With each sequence I am feeling more and more energized, balanced, and present with absolute comfort and ease throughout my whole body and Being. By the third time, I feel as though I am like a giant Golden pillar that is filled up with this beautiful, undulating combination of both the heavens and the depth of Terra; perfectly balanced, nourished, and revitalized. It is pure exquisite Golden pleasure throughout.

Talk about wellness! Does it get any better than this?

I hear Avalar's voice coming back in:

"Beloved One, you are all of this—splendid in every way, top to bottom, inside and out. You are perfectly balanced and illuminated with this Divine Golden beauty, and that is why you are so illuminated. You cannot help but be. That is you—that is who you are.

"There is much that has taken place in this last short while. Know that everything is continuing to move in this direction, and that its pathway is open and momentum steady.

"You understand the effect of having your Golden Divine Spiritual Body back in its proper position. You can see how it has shifted everything else accordingly. You have experienced how this repositioning has opened up the freedom of your complete Golden Illuminated Body blueprint again. You are the happy recipient of these shifts. Simply let them continue on as they may.

"Before we conclude this, I would like to take a moment for you to check in with your Golden Emotional Body and your Golden Mental Body, so that you can appreciate the new alignment that has been brought into those areas. These shifts are a direct result of your Divine Golden Spiritual Body being restored to its proper positioning. You will see how powerful and potent this recalibration has been.

"Let us begin with your Golden Emotional Body. Be easy with this and ponder for a moment. Notice what you see and feel and know."

I feel my emotions. They are like clear streams of water washing gently over and under each other. They move in a rhythm together, always in harmony. I focus more closely for a moment because this is radically different from how my emotions were in Mondor.

There, they were all kinds of things, intensity of all kinds, and ranges that were upsetting and jangling to my nerves. My Emotional body felt at the effect of Interference—always. It suffered and was yanked around the most; it was brought to crescendos of highs and lows and everything in between, and all was absolutely exhausting.

Now that I think about it, I don't know how I did it. I really don't know how I kept any balance. I managed somehow, but the contrast between then and now is striking, to say the least. My Emotional Body is no longer feeling frail, flinching, or flailing. It is no longer vulnerable or victimized, or getting pulled and yanked here, there, and everywhere—upside down and sideways.

Instead, what is it like? It is calm, peaceful, and poised.

Oh yes, I still have much emotion, but it is harmonious within itself and that makes it harmonious with everything outside of it—the Golden Emotional Harmony simply IS.

The wealth, depth, breadth, and richness of my Emotional Body were always something that I prized in Lemuria. I could breathe pictures with it into the sky. I could shower it upon something that I loved and make a brilliant gift of it. It was beautiful, sweet, serene, passionate, impassioned, gay, bright, loving, kind, mellow, powerful, excited, and enthusiastic. These are words that convey to you that which is inherent in my TRUE Emotional Body.

I was full of emotion in Lemuria, yes, but it was of a completely different nature than the experience that I had in Mondor.

I hear my Golden Healing Team speaking gently:

"There is space for more repair, and we are here to provide this for you. Your love of your true Golden Emotional Body is what will restore it to its fine balance and harmony—and your appreciation of this will enhance the situation even more. Your Golden Emotional Body is sacred; it is a sacred instrument which enables you to experience and express Golden Life in a way that has color, texture, vibrancy, and richness. It is your Golden Emotional Body that MOVES you with the beauty and richness of your life. Love and appreciate this right now. Love this with all your heart and soul, and it will respond in kind and gift you profoundly."

Whatever it is that my Golden Healing Team does next for me changes everything. What were clear, calm waters before have become like a dance of pure heavenly delight. There is fluid movement everywhere inside of me. I can feel my emotions bubbling and sparkling with joy, resilience, and total enthusiasm to an even greater degree than before.

Avalar whispers in my ear:

"Yes, Beloved, your Golden Emotional Body is a treasure. It brings texture and richness to everything that you are. It is the special vehicle through

which you move and have a vast array of richness and beauty. Without this splendid instrument you would feel flat, empty, and barren. It is your Emotional Body that allows the power of Beauty to be known and felt, Golden so. Savor this, you beautiful Being; savor this wealth of you. Give thanks to it, for it is what makes the experience of your life rich with color, texture, and depth."

I sink into this fluid motion within, and allow myself to become awash with the profusion of it. I love it. I feel as though I have come to myself in yet another way somehow, and again, I have a realization of how healthy this feels. I'm truly glad.

After a few moments more, the heightened sensation of it calms again, and this time it is like a steady hum of glorious well-being. Emotional Health, I love it. I feel only stable and steady poise throughout my Golden Emotional Body. It is graceful and fluid and allowing; it moves harmoniously.

I hear my Golden Healing Team moving back in with their voice once more, *"Dear One, that completes the process here. Let's move on to your Golden Mental Body. What do you see about this?"*

My Golden Mental Body: it is clear, it is concise. It weighs and considers, making decisions which contribute to the whole. It has its own vote that is respectfully acknowledged and included in the final outcome of the wisdom of the whole. It doesn't override, control, or take over. It is part of the Golden Team and it is a great Team Player. It loves and thrives on being so; it brings in the practical perspective and is able to show me the bigger picture in a way that I wouldn't otherwise have seen.

I reflect for a moment on my Mental Body in Mondor. It was in a different state there—agitated and torqued out most of the time. It was another arena in us Lemurians that was affected by the constant broadcasting of Interference. I often felt mentally weak and weakened; that sensation of the "slippery slope," and losing my grip on my clarity and mental balance that I spoke of in the book earlier. It was distressing, as I have already explained.

I feel like this aspect of me still might have some lingering traces of memory which need release as well. I am wondering if my Golden Healing Team can help in this regard, when I hear them say:

"Yes, dear One, we were waiting for you to see this for yourself. We ask you to bring your compassion to your mental state and memory, and we will do our work to repair whatever traces of distress still linger. Know that, as you already said: it is the memory of distress that is there. That's all it is—a memory with lingering traces of non-specific debris which will now release.

"Be kind to yourself, send your loving to this part of you and witness this

*being transmuted into Golden Love. That is how this will be healed from
now on—through the reverberation of your Golden Love.*

"Your Golden Love is the Healer."

I do as my Team suggests, and gently send my love and compassion into this
arena. It vibrates in there, holding itself in place, and gradually I can feel everything changing as a result. My Golden loving quietly takes over and transforms
all else. It feels entirely and completely clear and free.

My Golden Mental Body is glowing. It is happy, peaceful, steady, and clear.

I feel my tremendous gratitude for it, and send it a message of my appreciation for all that it does so generously for me. I let it know with my heart that
I love what an adept, skilled, and sustaining part of me it is. It always has my
greatest well-being at the center of everything, and its steady nature is infused
with kindness and love.

"Dear One," my Golden Healing Team directs me. *"You are ready to take a
look at your Golden Mind. This has also been recalibrated back to its true Golden
Nature. What do you know about this?"*

I focus in on this, and am surprised yet again. My mind, as an aspect of my
Mental Body, is thoroughly clear as well. It is peaceful and quiet. It is happy to
be here—unfettered, completely and totally free. I see and feel the pathways of it
as it weaves and winds its way throughout my whole body. It travels lightly now.

It is inspired in a way it hasn't been since Lemuria of Origin, and I appreciate
this. I can hear it thinking its thoughts, waxing and waning from loud, to quiet,
to utterly silent—with an underlying base of peace no matter what.

I can feel the gentleness of it throughout my system. Its nature is cheerful
and kind and loving. I see that it is happily traveling the patterns of its Golden
Labyrinth inside the Golden World of me, feeling blissful because it is home
and restored to its rightful position. It is happy and harmonious, just the way it
always was in Lemuria.

Harmony, there is Golden Harmony—inside and out.

Dear Reader, can you truly imagine this for yourself in this way?

Go ahead and try; it's real, I guarantee.

My Golden Healing Team speaks joyfully:

*"One more thing before we go, dear One. Don't ever forget that Golden
Wellness of the Highest Order is yours, always. Reflect on this more and
more when you can, so that you truly REGISTER this truth of you. Every
time you do this, your capacity for it in your daily world will increase and
deepen. You will benefit outstandingly from this, we promise; it is your
Golden Body blueprint that is alive and well and completely reawakened
and re-inspired as you.*

"Have it thoroughly and have it with gusto! Say Yes!

"And finally, with this Golden Illuminated Body that you now are, we are going to help you practice stretching out and expanding your Golden Energy Fields. Before we do this though, feel them and tell us what you know about them."

I reach my focus further out from my body as I witness my Golden Rays of Light and Well-being radiating gracefully outward from me. I know that all is well in my Golden Energy Fields. I hear myself breathing in an enormous sigh of relief. Why is that? I wonder to myself. What is this feeling of relief that I have? I recall how tense and in turmoil my Energy Fields always were in Mondor. The contrast now is that I feel and sense only freedom, grace, and joy spreading forth from myself in every direction.

I am aware of my Golden Healing Team moving through my Golden Energy Fields, waving their arms slowly in a gentle clearing motion. As they do so, my Energy Fields begin to vibrate and hum. I am aware that they, too, are being swept clean of any lingering traces of memories that are not of my Golden Frequency.

Finally, my total Golden Resonance becomes complete. The sound of the humming increases, growing still sweeter and ever more peaceful. All my energy fields are freed up again, and I can feel them beginning to reach and radiate out further. It feels amazing.

My Golden Healing Team continues:

"Dearest One, you are ready to put into practice again that which is your most natural design and capability. Reach out your Golden Energy Fields as far and as wide as you possibly can. Recognize that you have all the space in the universe, and you can take up all that you want. Your vibration is Golden Beautiful, and the entirety of Golden Life feels you and loves you. Revel in this knowing and reach out to feel the breadth of your physically generated freedom in this way. You are Golden Illuminated Body radiating out Golden Light as strongly and as freely as you choose.

"Try this, again and again. Expand it with each breath, letting your Golden Heart lead the way. Your radiance is your Golden Love shining. This, as you know, is what illuminates you. Light up your world; light it up as far and wide as you want—this Golden World is all yours to spread out and inhabit freely and fully. Enjoy this thoroughly!"

As they finish speaking, I feel my Golden Heart opening wide and pulsating through me, spreading itself outward on the rays of my Golden Light. I am literally outshining, and it feels splendid! My Golden Love is my Golden Light.

It is radiating out in every direction. With each exhalation it expands still more and more—and more.

I am aware that not only am I generating and extending my energy fields of Golden love and beauty, but I am also creating a kind of buffering for me which holds me stable, steady, and sovereign throughout. I am strong in my center. I am strong in my physical body. I am strong in my emotional and mental bodies. I am strong in my energetic fields. Yes, indeed, I am thoroughly Golden Illuminated inside and out!

I register how incredibly well and strong I feel. I register how beautiful and radiant I am. I am like a Golden Lighthouse, doing what I do best. I hear my Golden Healing Team surrounding me, cheering me on with absolute joy:

"Great job, well done! Look at you. You are Golden radiant indeed. How utterly splendid you are! You have accomplished this total reunion of you. All parts of you are singing in harmony together and ready for what's ahead with enthusiasm and passion. Yes!

"Know that we will continue to be supporting you, cheering you on, and helping you to integrate this still more powerfully in the days ahead. It will take still more time and conscious attention for this Golden Illumination to be absolutely solid and complete, but we are with you on this and the process is well underway.

"Continue to be attentive to your Golden Creative Centers, your physical sensations, emotions, and mentally focused aspects as well. Commune and communicate often with this glorious richness that you are. Thoroughly celebrate your Golden Illumination. Enjoy being you!

"We love you and bless you!"

And with that, they are off—and here I am, left blazing, beautiful, and bright. Well, I'll take it!

As I am savoring this Golden abundance of me, I hear Avalar's sweet voice talking to us.

She speaks with obvious pride and joy:

"Yes, you are Golden Beings as Golden Illuminated Bodies. It is you. You know this. Be this and fully live this.

"We are aware of your pure Golden radiance and your loving beauty that touches us and lights up our world. Yes, you are indeed Sacred Golden Lighthouses and we are grateful for you!

"Bless you!

"Congratulations!"

CHAPTER TWENTY

You are Sacred Golden Lighthouses

THE GOLDEN WITNESS SPEAKS:
I am a Golden Lighthouse. I love this, and I love what it means about me, about us, and about our Golden World.

I look around and see many of us shining bright and Golden. What a splendid sight to behold. I am reminded for a moment that this was how it always was in Lemuria. Everyone and everything was inspired and lit up in this Golden way, everywhere and always. We were surrounded in a vibrant Golden glow.

As I remember this, it warms my heart. That's how it was back then—heart-warming. It was special. It was Golden love shining warm and bright, soft and strong, permeating everything. What a wonderful "climate" to live in, such wonderful air to breathe and a glorious way to be.

That was then, and it feels like it's starting to happen again.

I feel my shining Golden Rays touching and interweaving with those other Splendid Ones who are with me. It creates a wonderful mosaic of Gold and I can hear its harmony singing. The sound is soft and lilting.

Avalar stands tall and proud in front of us, and she is splendid. Her Golden Light is extended around her, reaching up high toward the heavens. She is glowing more than I have ever seen her since Lemuria, and she reminds me of myself and how good it feels to stretch out and feel energetically free and natural again.

"Blessed Ones," she says, *"You are each radiant Golden Lighthouses. This is what you were in Lemuria of Origin, and it is what you have finally remembered and restored yourselves to again. You have gone through much in your journeys throughout time between then and now. You are standing bright and tall and brilliant—and all the stronger for it.*

"You have done a great, great thing during that time, doing what was necessary to bring our Golden Family home. We have told you frequently how grateful we are to you, and for all that you have done. I wish to tell you this, yet again, right here and right now.

"I am deeply grateful to you. I will forever be. Because of you, we all stand beside one another and shine together again.

"Look around you and see the many faces of our loved ones and feel the presence of many unseen Golden Ones who are with us as well. It is thanks to you—you and you and you."

With the motion of her hand she encompasses all of us. I feel her love permeating my heart and I melt. She is telling us something. She is asking us to fully recognize in this moment how extraordinarily special this gift is that we have given. I know that she truly wants us to completely understand what this has meant. My eyes begin to fill with tears.

"You each gave your whole heart and soul to our Family," she continues. *"And you were willing to walk through pain and peril for us so that we could, indeed, stand together again, the way we are right now—Golden, shining bright, whole, healed, happy, and together.*

"Know that your gift will never be forgotten—never—not by any one of us, not ever."

She pauses, giving us a chance to really let this sink in.

I slowly reach for the hand of the Golden Ones on either side of me. Tears are rolling down my cheeks unchecked as I surrender to this wave of warm gratitude flooding me. I completely surrender. This love is as deep as it goes. It has withstood the test and trials of time and has remained unwavering, no matter what. Our devotion to one another is what kept us moving forward, regardless of any obstacle.

I know what Avalar is saying, I know it exactly. Just as my gift will never be forgotten, so will the gift that I have been given. My heart will forever remember and treasure this powerful gift of loving that my family has given me; they brought me back to life.

I look into the shining Golden eyes of those I love, eyes that are moist with tears as well. We gaze at one another deeply and share this precious moment of thanksgiving, counting our many blessings of one another. Blessed are we to know and feel the love that we do.

Avalar continues:

"Yes, Dearest Ones, this is a precious moment in time. It is the beginning of something rare and special, something that will gift yet more and more as time moves forward. You are the Golden seeds of great things to come, and I want to speak about this.

"Yes, you are beautiful, strong, powerful Sacred Golden Lighthouses. As such, you are as great Golden Beacons that shine the way for others to

come home. *You are the unwavering presence of illumination that others will see and be drawn to.*

"That is who you are. That is what you do, automatically, by virtue of BEING.

"From this moment on, and for many years to come, we will devote ourselves to being the Lighthouses that we are, so that we find each other again in the present day. We will endeavor to regather and recollect, consciously bringing all Golden Ones together again as one Golden Family of love in our present physical domain.

"It will be a period of Conscious Golden homecoming for all the Golden Ones everywhere, on all levels, two legged and otherwise, all across this beautiful planet. We are going to make this a conscious regathering. We are going to wake up whoever is left that is still asleep. We are going to offer healing wherever that is needed. We are going to gather everyone together and celebrate our Golden Union.

"How do we do this? We do it by continuing to be everything that we have become—by being Golden conscious, by shining our Golden Light consciously and joyously, by knowing that we are Beacons of Golden Love and that we are being seen and experienced; AND ALSO BY KNOWING THAT WE ARE VIBRATING OUR GOLDEN LOVE SO PALPABLY THAT THE WORLD SIMPLY CAN'T MISS IT. It is naturally being positively affected by this, just as we are by one another. This is what happens. It is who we are and that is that.

"This is our purpose. This is our Golden Path. This is what our Golden Shining will automatically do. This is what we are about—regathering our Golden family in our current times and celebrating this. Dearest Golden Ones, can you imagine anything better than this?

"The Golden Rays of your light will encompass and scan the globe as a splendid example of Golden Being. Those of like mind and heart will see this and they will be drawn to you. You will recognize them, and they will recognize you—although they may not know exactly why at that moment. But you will know.

"Your Golden Love will spark something inside of them and they will wonder if they, too, are Golden. You will encounter many people with whom you will naturally talk with about our Golden Heart. They will look at you and ask, 'Am I Golden too?'

"And what will you say to them?

"Perhaps you will suggest that they look inside their hearts and see. They will. They will tell you that they see, sense, or feel a spark of Gold. And you will say, 'Well, there you are. That spark will grow, count on it. Trust this.' And they will go on their way feeling their Golden spark awaken inside. Gradually—or perhaps even more quickly for some—they, too, will be restored to full conscious Golden Remembrance. This question and its answer will move around the globe, I guarantee.

"Together, we will reach ALL levels and forms of Golden Life everywhere—across the globe and beyond.

"Besides shining your light as the Golden Lighthouses that you are, when appropriate, you may also be drawn, and invited, to be an avenue for Golden Healing. In these circumstances, you will be a Golden Witness and express your compassion intentionally through the process of Golden Communion. This, as you have already seen, will allow for Golden Remembrance and Restoration to happen in the arena that is calling for it.

"Sometimes it will be a case of standing still, of witnessing, and saying, 'I hear you; I understand. I'm sorry for your pain. I witness you,' and making that be the first step. It will always show you how far it wants to go.

"You will do this in whatever arena you are called to, whether that be with people, animals, birds, insects, all aspects of Nature, the Elementals, or the Stars. No matter where, no matter what, no matter when, if it is your personal calling you will do this. Why? Because it your Golden devotion expressing. You care and you can, and you have the Skill Sets to do so.

"As a Golden Family we are coming together again in a conscious Golden way—reconnecting our conscious Golden Awareness, loving and being loved, recognizing and being recognized, sharing the joy of our reunion, and celebrating our Golden family. We are continuing to shine our Golden Light and Love.

"That is our calling.

"Not only will you inspire and uplift, but you will be the Clarion Call of Golden Remembrance yourselves, without doing anything more than what you are doing right now—breathing, caring, loving, sharing, radiating, and extending.

"That is your gift that keeps on giving.

"Your joy of being you is contagious. Know this.

"Your loving of being you is contagious. Know this.

"YOU are each Golden Inspiration, literally. Know this.

"I urge you to realize exactly what this means, now and for your future. Together we are going to light up our world. Together we are going to bring everyone home and celebrate our conscious Golden Reunion.

"Over time, our Golden World will indeed come together; our Golden Light will shine forth from all forms of Golden Life, and our Golden Communion will be in full, flourishing motion again. We will be indelibly interwoven and vibrating our One Golden Heart strongly and clearly again. It is destined to be as we have said.

"Dearest ones, go forth and shine.

"You are the gifts that keep on giving, by virtue of being alive and by virtue of Remembering how Golden you are.

"Extend your Golden Energy fields out as far and as wide as you want. Show your joy with abandon. Let your love be felt and received by many across this beautiful planet. Touch, Golden Touch, and be Golden Touched as others are lit up because of what you remind them they are.

"Sacred Golden Lighthouses, you are. You continue to be gifts for us all. We continue to be grateful to you, forever still.

"We are in this together—One Golden Heart. Thank you.

"Thank you, beautiful Golden Ones!"

I've got goose bumps from the power of Avalar's words. I know she is absolutely right, and my light is blazing brighter in confirmation of this truth. My illumination itself is eager to spread and share, seek and find, reunite and celebrate.

I can't imagine any greater, more fulfilling, joy-filled purpose than this. Dear Reader, can you? The thought of it warms me from head to toe. I am one happy Golden Lighthouse!

CHAPTER TWENTY-ONE

OUR SACRED GOLDEN TEMPLE

THE GOLDEN WITNESS SPEAKS:
We are still gathered at the clearing near the Sea, shining bright and bold as the Golden Beacons that we are. We are ready to begin actively creating and applying our Golden Skill Sets. In addition to this, we are standing strong and steady as completely Golden Illuminated Lighthouses. I feel deeply anchored and strong as my steady Golden Being—I know we all do. We are eager to get started with building, creating, and shining forth in our new lives and our new Golden World.

When I think about it, it seems like such an absolute miracle. I never thought I would be here, much less in this way. The thought of it is huge, don't you think? What I know is that it feels completely right.

It feels wonderful to be expansive, with my Golden Centers convex instead of concave, filling up my entire system in a balanced way—shining and expressing outward, pouring out of me. I feel I am being the best of me in the way that was originally intended.

I become quiet, feeling my inner peace and listening to the wonderful sounds of nature all around me. I still hear the birds calling and let the comforting sounds of the Sea lull me deeper into a serene and restful space. There has been a lot of excitement lately with us becoming increasingly Golden Illuminated, and I feel like I need to close my eyes and rest for a while in the warmth of the sun. My Beloved Golden Sun—I have come to feel and look like a Golden Sun myself!

I let my beloved Sun caress my skin softly as I feel a gentle breeze picking up. I am glad to be here, glad to be with my family. All is right with my world, and so I take a short nap.

As I awaken and open my eyes, I see that everyone around me looks like they have been napping too. We definitely all needed a break.

Before long, I sense in the air that something is about to change. Without warning, our entire group is lifted up and transported away from the Golden Sea into a completely different landscape. I don't know how it happened, but it did! We have landed gently in a field of green grass, wet with dew under our feet. The air is misty, and I can't quite make out where I am, but I am aware that something feels familiar.

After a minute, the air clears and I see the most beautiful piece of land stretching out in front of me. It is a huge Golden Meadow which opens up to surrounding forests, with tall mountains rising up in the background, reaching for the sky. It feels perfectly heavenly. There are gorgeous wildflowers everywhere and the bees are buzzing, the insects chirping, and the birds singing. It is altogether a beautiful feast for my senses.

I gaze at the wonder all around me, simply drinking it in, *"Why does this feel so familiar and special to me?"* I ask myself quietly.

I see Andar and Avalar are still with us as well. They are standing together and holding hands, their Golden Lights blazing. They look up at us and I see big smiles on their faces. Something is up, I can tell. They are both positively beaming with joy, pride, triumph, and celebration.

Andar begins to speak in a rich and celebratory voice:

"Great Golden Ones, we honor you.

"Congratulations on finally receiving back into your Conscious Remembrance all the Golden Illumination that you are, inside and out. What a triumph this is for you. How perfectly amazing you all look!"

I have to agree.

We take a moment to look at each other and it is an awesome sight—so much Golden Luminescence, health, vitality, and radiant Golden outpouring!

Andar continues:

"It has been a long journey, I know, but look at where you have arrived in yourselves and in our Golden World. A great celebration is called for, and we will enjoy it in abundance soon enough. Our lives will be filled with this rejoicing and you will know it on a daily basis.

"Job well done, yet again, my friends.

"I know you have been savoring Terra's beauty, and many of you have been wondering why this place feels so familiar.

"Well, I want to officially welcome you back to this site where we had our Sacred Golden Temple in Lemuria long ago. That is why it feels familiar to you. You know the energy of this place and space thoroughly well.

"If you recall, we used to gather in our Temple for many purposes, one of which was to re-infuse ourselves with the energies of our Sacred Golden Configuration and the united energies of the Sacred Golden Ones everywhere. The imprint of this still vibrates here, just as it did long ago. If you recall, you would visit our Temple often when you needed to feel refreshed, realigned, and reinvigorated with the harmony and life-giving energy of our union.

"It served many purposes, this Sacred Golden Temple. However, its fundamental intent was to serve as our Touchstone for our Golden Oneness and Peace. This is a most appropriate place to start our new life, don't you think? Whether or not we actually build a temple again isn't what is important. All that is important is that this place—this site, and what it held—was special to us. It was sacred, and still holds all of that energy coalesced here."

I feel myself automatically going back to my remembrance of this, of how beautiful our Sacred Golden Temple was and how much I loved it. I loved being in it and I loved looking at it. I loved everything it stood for and everything it meant to me. It was exquisite both inside and out, but what I remember most about it was its heavenly feeling and how it literally pulsated with the energy of Golden Harmony. I could almost touch it with my fingertips, it was that substantial.

I drink in that palpable sensation again. There is nothing amorphous about it. Golden Harmony is alive and well on this site, and inside of me. I am grateful, and I say a small prayer of thanksgiving to this wondrous Temple that stood here proudly long ago. It lives on.

I hear Andar's voice:

"We begin again, right where we left off long ago, but with all the wisdom, strength, and maturity we have gained. It is a new beginning with ancient memories still intact, alive and thriving. Being back at the place that was the capitol of our Golden Lemuria marks a great new beginning for the reality of the full physical realization of our Golden World and all of its great beauty to come—on all levels.

"This reconnection will serve to strengthen us still more as we focus on building our land anew and reaping the rewards of our wondrous creations—both physical, and non-physical. This is our Golden land, gifted to us by Terra, to design and build upon as we see fit. It is our masterpiece to create in every way, on every level of existence, tangible and intangible, form and non-form. It is truly OUR world to consciously create and foster as we so choose and desire.

"Our journey of our Golden World anew begins, right back at our sacred capital. Yes, our Golden Day is here, and our Golden Time is now.

"Our Golden World is a rare and precious gift to have, to hold, and to share from this day forward.

"You adept Golden Creators, as Sacred Golden Lighthouses, are the pinnacle of it all. Avalar has already spoken at length about bringing our Golden Family back together in a conscious way so that everyone remembers and

recognizes one another on this physical plane in this current time. And this we will do in our own ways as we so choose. As our numbers grow together, our strength as a people and as a nation will grow as well; we will grow and expand exponentially.

"Let us give thanks for who we are, what we have, and what we will be. Blessed are we because we KNOW our One Golden Heart. We KNOW of our goodness and ability to create and spread love and beauty everywhere. We KNOW of our abilities as adept and conscious Creators. We KNOW that we can vibrate this world as this beauty and Golden Creation every day.

"It is not always the big things that are important; it is the small things that add up and sustain our growth in a daily way. These are the things that make the biggest difference as we embark on our conscious physical re-flourishing.

"Ours is a Golden Consciousness. Our frequency is our very own Golden One. Hold strong to this NO MATTER WHAT.

"In the days ahead there are many things to remember and keep in mind. One is to GOLDEN LIVE and LET LIVE. There are other levels of Consciousness on this planet as you well know; we are not here to change anyone nor judge THEM for whatever consciousness they have chosen to live and abide by.

"Our Golden World is our own. It is ours to have, to be, and to love—to be true to.

"GOLDEN LIVE and LET LIVE. Keep this in the forefront of your minds always.

"Secondly, BE ALL the Golden Power that YOU ARE. BE it with gusto!

"YOUR unique splendor is an ESSSENTIAL piece of our Golden Whole. WE NEED YOU. We need YOU to be and express yourself to the fullest of your capacity and capability. In this way, you will each thrive, and our Golden World will thrive. It will thrive because we are each standing tall and pouring forth that which we do best: GOLDEN LOVING, GOLDEN LIVING, GOLDEN BEING, GOLDEN CREATING, AND GOLDEN THRIVING. It is our most natural instinct and we are here to do this again."

Avalar steps up and says:

"Yes, Golden Ones, this is true. As we said many times before, you have grown enormously and are stronger than you have ever been. Life will be richer and more beautiful than it has ever been for you. That which you intentionally create and offer forth will be stronger and more deliberate *than ever before. Your power of the gift of your Gold and the gifting of your Gold will hold and yield greater meaning for you, and therefore generate even better and greater substance and results when you spread this forward and out.*

"BE IT! BREATHE IT! LOVE IT! LIVE IT! ENJOY IT! Give yourselves full permission to revel in it with all your might—and then some!

"That is what our Golden World wants and needs: JOY-FILLED PEOPLE LIGHTING UP THE WORLD! Yes, indeed!

"The bigger the better, the more the merrier!"

I smile broadly as I listen to Avalar and feel the impact of her words. Yes, I know it is up to me and up to all of us to choose what we live by and what we energize. Joy has great energy to it, doesn't it? Dear Reader, you know, I have a feeling that my life is about to become much more fun than it has been for a long, long time! We have had a dearth of it for far too long and I, for one, am ready to get on with it!

Andar steps back in with merriment in his voice:

"Beloveds, yes, you are remembering what fun we had in Lemuria! Stretching our creative selves was always many things, one of which was outstanding amounts of celebration and fun in the mix. Again, it is important to feel lightness, playfulness, and ease in our hearts because it is what generates more and more of our Golden Juice.

"We are fueled by it in this way and we magnify that when we spread it outward. It is an essential part of our health, our wealth, and the total well-being of our Golden Creative Natures. Yes, fun is indeed an important ingredient, but it's also simply one of the great benefits of us being truly us. The bounty of our natural Golden joy creates that."

Andar's voice fades away for a moment, and I feel my Golden Third Eye vibrating intensely. My Golden Eyes are wide open, and I look around and see only brilliant Golden Shining Ones standing strong and tall around me. I look down at my feet and see Terra's ground brilliantly glowing with such warm Golden Illumination that it makes my heart melt. Everywhere I look and everything I feel is as pure, pure Gold. Even the natural sounds I hear of birds singing and insects chirping are pure Golden Song.

I listen.

Amidst the natural sounds around me, I become aware of an ancient call sounding in the air, faint at first but growing increasingly louder. It is a Destiny Call.

I know it and I remember it.

I remember when we gathered here together long ago and vowed that, when the time in the future was ready and right, we would shine again in exactly this way. And now, here we are.

Our Golden Destiny is fulfilling itself. What a truly wondrous thing this is. I breathe and let it register and sink in.

Finally, my attention returns again to our sacred site and I see the many Golden Ones that are with me, their faces smiling broadly with sounds of joy, passion, and excitement resounding everywhere.

My eyes take in the beautiful vistas. There are birds and bees everywhere and a song of joy throughout this land. This is the best day ever!

My heart reaches toward it; it is beautiful and enchanting.

Suddenly, I see throngs of other Golden Life Forms coming our way to join with us. I see herds of many different kinds of animals and flocks of all kinds of birds. There are collections of different forms of Elementals, groups from the Golden Devic Kingdoms, the Golden Fairies, and many others. There are swarms of more Golden Bees buzzing nearby and the sensation of many, many Golden Energetic Life Forms gathering with us as well. The Flowers are swaying gently, and the Trees look like they are waving their branches on the breeze to be included as well. There are so many of us. What a sight and what a sensation! Golden Life is TEEMING with giant outpourings of pure love and joy!

As if that wasn't already enough, I see incoming wings—giant ones, smaller ones, white ones, multicolored ones—Angels everywhere, Divine Golden Angels with their wings beating louder in celebration of this grand event. I also see many incoming Golden Star Ones along with many, many Golden Masters and Companions from other Star Systems.

All of our Companions of Golden Heart are with us, and those who are not are represented in some fashion or other. Everyone from everywhere is indeed included in this celebration.

I realize I had forgotten how truly immense our Golden Support Network and Family was. They are here to celebrate our fully realized strength and power, our One Golden Heart fully radiant and blazing once more in this gloriously physical way. They are happy and they are proud. They are preciously PRESENT.

As I gaze around in pleasure, I am reminded yet again that this, our One Golden World, is what everyone has been waiting for—to be a part of this grand undertaking. Only now it is even better, stronger, and more brilliant because of all that we have learned since our original time before; it goes far beyond anything that has ever been conceived.

Andar and Avalar come to stand in our midst again, and this time they are joined by several Golden Masters, those who have traveled through the pages of this book with us and been such amazing companions and guides.

I also see several blessed Golden Archangels that are stationed around our throngs of Golden Ones, standing strong with their enormous wings unfurled and stretching out to touch the Sun.

It is a sight to behold and makes my heart burst with passion and joy.

I feel the enormity of the support—the vast resources available to me and to us, the great wealth and richness of Gold vibrating on every level, in every way. Wealthy are we! Rich are we! Blessed are we!

We are utterly splendid!

There is only pure Golden Brightness everywhere. Everything is intensely vibrant and illuminated as if there has been a veritable explosion of Golden Light itself. The Golden Brightness is showering jewels of Golden Love everywhere like a huge geyser that was switched on. Golden Love Brightness—Intense, Beautiful, Exquisite, Magnetic, Mesmerizing. I take a deep, deep breath and feel it all. It's Home. It's GOLDEN HOME.

Dear Reader, I must go now.

I must leave these pages and walk right into that pure blazing Golden Brightness myself. I belong there. I want to live there; I want to breathe the air there—and only there.

I thank you for traveling this journey with me and for listening to the many stories I have told of my experiences and others of those I love.

I have been grateful for you. I have felt you, as my traveling companion, and this has made a difference for me. I have felt supported by you and have enjoyed sharing all of this with you.

Thank you for Being. I hope you have been deeply touched, Golden Touched. Bless you.

I wish you all great Golden things to come.

ONE GOLDEN HEART.

The Golden Witness waves goodbye, turns and walks right into the sacred, blazing Golden Light, disappearing into it. . .

CHAPTER TWENTY-TWO

FINAL WORDS

Avalar Speaks:
"*Dear Reader,*

"*The story has been told and the journey of healing is complete. All is well. We are all here together—Golden once again.*

"*What is important is to simply get on with our Golden Reality. This is not a dream; this is not something fantastical that you park away somewhere. THIS is our Golden Reality NOW—HERE. It is up to us.*

"*In closing, we would like to talk about GOLDEN TEAMWORK.*

"*This whole book has been about our Golden Family and how much we rely upon and need one another. This is the way it is meant to be. We are Family designed and Family governed. We do need each other AND we do rely upon one another to make the whole thing work—to think otherwise is faulty.*

"*Our Golden Family THRIVES because it is a consciously intentioned, deliberately designed, Co-Creative Golden Effort. That is exactly what makes it work.*

"*If you are feeling, dear Reader, like you are in this alone and that you are the only one waking up and being challenged to go Golden Forward without help, then think again—and hold onto your hat!*

"*There is SO MUCH support, encouragement, reassurance, and help in store for you that comes from all levels of Golden Life everywhere. We have demonstrated this throughout these pages.*

"*To know which levels of support you are particularly attuned to and resonant with is of utmost importance. Then, when you are ready, you can grab that support with gusto and flourish in that Golden Communion and assistance in all the ways that you feel you need.*

"*Remember: WE ARE ALL IN THIS TOGETHER, DOING THIS TOGETHER. THIS IS OUR CO-CREATIVE GOLDEN WORLD!*

"*In light of this, we leave you with some wonderfully supporting messages from some of our Golden Team members that are intrinsically involved in this entire Golden Project.*

"*They are available to help you whenever you ask for them. Know this. They are here for you—you have but to ask. That part is up to you. That is always your choice.*

"*But no matter what, know in full faith that you are a beloved part of our beautiful Golden Family. We love you and care about you and your well-being and life.*

"Let's join Golden hands and hearts and get this Golden Co-Creation moving!"

Sananda's Final Golden Gift

"Great Golden Ones, I am immensely proud of you all. Through this journey you have truly walked right through a gauntlet and come out the other side shining brilliant and bright. I salute you and honor you.

"I know it is not easy to do what you have done. I know it is not easy for any of you to live in the current world, but you bring the balance. You bring a state of grace and harmony that is greatly needed.

"You make a beautiful, kind, and loving difference. You help balance the scales so that goodness and beauty can shine and thereby enable our Golden World to prevail again.

"Never think that you are alone in this. There are many all over the globe who are hungry to deeply touch the greatness and brilliance that is already inside of them; who yearn to feel and know the power of their true goodness; who want to be free of identities that would bind or restrict them in any way. They long to stretch out and be their bigness. They want to BELIEVE. They want to KNOW. They hope somehow, someday, they will.

"They are waiting for someone to believe in them enough, so that it Golden activates them. They wait for something or someone to confirm to them that there is something still more beautiful and sustaining to their lives and that this is who they truly are. They want to fully and freely be their beauty and love. They ache to be this, and why not? It is exactly who they are.

"You are those great Golden Lights that are shining so brightly that they finally get the confirmation they have been waiting for. Your resonance and shining example inspire them to get on with it.

"You will find many people crossing your paths in the future that will feel and believe as you do. It will surprise you, in fact. There are many Golden Ones on the planet right now. They are here because of this Clarion Call for Golden Awakening. They are here because they are part of the Golden Family Remembrance and Reunion. This is where it's happening.

"This heralds a most special time in history. You may often feel like you are living way ahead of your time. I understand. But remember, you are also right on time as well; otherwise this wouldn't even be occurring.

"I love you. I bless you. I walk the path of Golden Love with you with every breath I take and every single step I make. Call upon me if you wish. I am glad to be here and honored to be your Golden Companion always, if you desire.

"That choice is yours. I am here and available.

"May your Golden Love shine forth its glorious joy always.

"Golden Blessings of great Golden Love.

"ONE GOLDEN HEART.

"I AM Sananda."

White Eagle's Final Golden Gift

"Beloved Golden Ones, I am as the Golden wings beneath your feet; I am as the Golden wings that help you take flight and soar. I am as the Golden wings that keep you steady in your flight and secure in the wind that propels, lifts, and carries you. I am always here for you. Please know this.

"My arena is the Great Golden Heart. This is my forte and this is what I will address. I find that most everything is tied into this in one way or another. I have made it my purpose to speak of this and only this as it applies to all things and to all arenas of Golden Life.

"It is simple really. We are love, we love, we are loved.

"Many of you know only parts of this, but all of this is the Truth.

"You know that you are Golden and this adds even greater wealth to your bread basket of Being.

"You are Golden Love, you Golden Love, you are Golden Loved.

"Strive to know all of these things equally well. Pay attention and be present. When you do, you will prosper greatly, inside and out. I guarantee.

"Your love is your wealth. How you be it, live it, know it, give it, and receive it dictates your well-being and flourishing.

"Be strong in your Golden hearts. Know that you are a great Golden Gift, and that you are indeed greatly gifted.

"I love you. I am here when you need me.

"Call upon me and I will spread my Golden wings and help you to fly. I will help your Golden Heart to soar and continue to be free.

"Wondrous Golden Ones, I love you—forever.

"I am here.

"ONE GOLDEN HEART.

"I AM White Eagle."

MASTER SAINT GERMAIN'S FINAL GOLDEN GIFT

"Beloved Golden Ones, you are Great Masters and you are supremely kind and loving Souls. It is with much gratitude that I come to you and say thank you for your endeavors on behalf of our sacred Golden Family everywhere.

"I know what you have gone through and what it has cost you. I know what it takes to regain your Golden footing again. You have made huge strides in this, obviously, throughout the steps of this journey we have shared—and it continues to be a work in progress.

"What lies ahead will be times of joy beyond measure, plus times when you feel the challenge of differing frequencies as you work to hold your Golden Sovereign Ground. You will, however, remain undaunted throughout; that's simply the truth of you. It is because you already are Golden Sovereign and these are passing periods of 'strength training.' You will move through them and always come out shining again—I guarantee. I know you.

"I see your grace and shining Golden Beauty that is ready and able to take steps toward a better world—a far more beautiful, kinder, and more love-manifesting world.

"At times you will wonder exactly how to do this, even though there are many suggestions about that throughout the pages of this book. But still, sometimes you will ask yourself, 'What can I REALLY do that will make a difference in what I see and experience in these current times.'

"Change is everywhere. It always is, but right now it is heightened and is the kind of change that can feel uncomfortable. This is right where I challenge you, because you are already Golden Masters—you can do this.

"I am challenging you to stand apart from the current world reality and look at your true world reality—your One Golden Heart Reality. I challenge you to see what, in fact, you truly and deeply know about yourselves.

"YOU are conscious Golden Ones. The days of feeling powerless are over for you. The days of not knowing what to do and how to make a difference in the face of this change are over. You begin the Golden Wave of Change now. You become the creation of whatever it is that you want to see, know, and feel.

"If it is instability that upsets you, then STAND STABLE. Govern your space with your Golden Power, Golden Love, and Golden Knowing. Stake your claim to your Golden Reality and draw your sovereign boundaries.

"If it's clarity that you crave, then draw up your clarity and BE IT. Be a clear resonance of loving clarity in this seemingly confused world.

"If it is kindness and gentleness that you ache for, then BE that kindness and gentleness. Extend yourselves as often as you can—both to yourselves and to others.

BE the heart of compassion that you seek. It is who you are.

"If it is joy you have lost track of, then look into your heart—and underneath that sadness that you feel on the surface, you will find your joy. You think that the sadness runs so deep that it is all that you feel, but it isn't. I know the enormous wealth of joy in you that you feel simply in the privilege of being alive and pulsating with your Divine Golden Love. BE this.

"Make it your personal responsibility to find joy in the many moments that life is bringing you—in the faces of those you love; in their hearts, in the beauty of Terra, in the kindness that is actually around you in an enormous way. Focus on those things. Make it your personal challenge to energize that which is already there that makes you feel good, inspired, hopeful, and resilient—and that can and will make a difference for those around you as well. This is vitally important.

"If it is love that you want to see in the world, then open your eyes. It's everywhere. Grab hold of it and say a prayer of thanks to it. Add to and multiply it. Savor it, bless it, and witness it. It hasn't gone anywhere—it's still here, inside of you and all around you. Open your eyes and your heart. Let it touch you again, even more deeply this time, so that your life is indelibly changed and charged by it. Let it uplift you and carry you forward. Ride its wave and don't look back.

"If it is Beauty that you want to see, well then, look in the mirror because YOU ARE IT—in spades.

"As much as anything, it is a challenge of perception: the truth of the matter is that the sun is still shining, even when you are experiencing cloudy skies. Go behind the clouds and be with the sun and you will feel warmed and inspired by it. That's the truth.

"Yes, it is a time of great change, and your Goldenness is an enormous part of that change.

"Awakening—it usually means being stirred in some way, doesn't it? Take heart. BE heart. YOU be the difference you want and ache to feel.

"You are strong. Gather yourselves up from within and join together. You'll be amazed at what you discover about what is truly going on. You can do it, you've got this—you are Golden Trail Blazers!

"You, Golden Ones, are so powerful and strong, so beautiful, and such bright, shining Golden Lights. BE YOURSELVES and your blessing will bless us all. Thank you.

"ONE GOLDEN HEART.

"I AM Master Saint Germain."

MOTHER MARY'S FINAL GOLDEN GIFT

"Blessings, all of you beautiful Golden Ones. I am extremely proud of you and everything that you have accomplished. You bring great strength to our Golden Family and great resilience that inspires us all.

"I have been honored to walk this path with you. I know it has seemed daunting at times, but truth be told, your steadfastness has never wavered and you have shown only commitment and compassion all along the way.

"Your Golden Hearts are big and strong. You are capable of vast wells of forgiveness and compassion that might surprise even you. Your Heart always speaks loudly to you, and as Golden Ones you will always listen. That is the way you are made.

"I admire you greatly, and I love you enormously.

"If there is one gift I could leave you with, it would be that of greater kindness and love toward yourselves. It would be to break through that previous barrier of discontent, and truly and deeply be kind and benevolent to yourselves. Why is it so much easier to give that to others, and not so easy to give it to ourselves?

"It is only by giving this kindness, truly and sincerely—to yourselves—that you will ever fully know you are Divine, because that is what your Divine is. That is already you.

"Find the space in your hearts for YOU and shower yourselves with the same kindness and caring that you give so freely to others.

"You are worthy.

"You deserve.

"You are valuable.

"As Golden ones, you already know this. Please don't forget to tend to yourselves, that's all I'm saying. Don't let that somehow get lost in the flurry of life that surrounds you sometimes.

"Be the governing force of your well-being and happiness. Apply the truths to yourself and love yourself with all of your heart and soul. In this way you will melt, again and forever, inside your sweet Source—everything else will be dissolved.

"You are One. You are Whole. Live this.

"Say a kind prayer for yourselves each and every day. Make this important. Make this special. It is a reflection of you and it is part of your wellness plan.

"Stay true to this and I guarantee you will reap great rewards. It's often the small things that have the biggest power.

"Bless you, Golden Ones. Bless you for all that you are, be, and do.

"I love you with all of my heart. You know this. I am right here, always.

"Happy travels. The adventure continues!

"ONE GOLDEN HEART.

"I AM Mother Mary."

TERRA'S FINAL GOLDEN GIFT

"Dearest, dearest Golden Ones, what more is there to say to you that I haven't already said? So much we have shared throughout this entire journey from long, long ago—and it continues!

"Now is the grand time. Now is the treasure that we have been waiting for, and it is the time to revel in and receive this beauty and bounty again. Isn't that a great thing?

"I have only one thing to remind you of and I know you already know it well. But I will say it again.

"Spend time with me. Spend time in Nature. Let the entire natural world lift any dross you feel. Let this be your soothing balm, your clearing, cleansing, and restoration.

"Please don't forget about this. Don't put it at the bottom of your list and don't fool yourself that you don't need this in order to stay balanced, healthy, happy, and well.

"Nature is your Key. It is your Golden Key to stability, restoration, grounding, and peace. It will always soothe you, inspire you, uplift you, listen to you, care for you, support you, and love you.

"It will clear you and keep you aligned in your heart, mind, emotions, body, and Soul. This is your true design.

"Visit me consciously whenever you think to. Let us link our hearts energetically, and I will shower you with love, joy, and splendidness. All that you truly are I will bring back to you whenever you lose sight of any of it.

"Look out at me and you will see yourself:

"Splendid,

"Miraculous,

"Wondrous,

"Beautiful.

"All that you are I am. All that I am you are. WE are One.

"Go in Golden Love now with every beat of your heart and mine. We are indelibly joined forever.

"Blessings, my sweet Ones, Golden Blessings for all things and for all times.

"Thank you for inspiring me. I love you forever.

"ONE GOLDEN HEART.

"I AM Golden Terra."

THE GOLDEN ANGELS FINAL GOLDEN GIFT

"Dearest Golden Ones of our Hearts, Bless you. CONGRATULATIONS and JOBS WELL DONE!

"We have been watching over you throughout this whole time together, and will continue to do so.

"As you deepen in your own Golden Remembrance, you will recognize more and more clearly that we are here, standing right next to you on this beautiful planet of Terra.

"We are strong, steady and, yes, grounded. You might not think of us Golden Angels as being solidly grounded, but as Golden Consciousness rises, we are able to be here more substantially. Although we remain in energetic form, the more you remember your Golden Selves, the more you will experience us as tangible. You will see us, hear us, and feel us. You will recognize that our hands and hearts are outstretched toward you, always ready and waiting to help.

"Reach for us.

"That is our message to you.

"REACH FOR US.

"We are right beside you, standing strong, clear, and unwavering.

"We are here to help you.

"We are here to uplift, support, encourage, and inspire you. We are here to fortify, comfort, and soothe you. We are here to remind you how strong, resilient, and capable you are. We are here to illuminate your way and to help you in whatever ways you need and ask, including helping you to help yourselves.

"We are passionate about this. It is our pure joy to be here with you and assist you as much as we possibly can.

"Smile. You are beautiful and your smile lights up the world.

"Reach for us and you will feel our joy responding.

"We are right here.

"We love you.

"ONE GOLDEN HEART.

"We ARE the Golden Angels."

CLOSING MESSAGE FROM ONE GOLDEN HEART

"I am the sound of your joy laughing.

"I am the song of your voice calling.

"I am the heartbeat of your body.

"I am the love that moves you, touches you, and cares for you.

"I am the love that moves you to care for others and for sacred life itself.

"I have been here all along—alive, well, and free.

"But you did not remember this for a while.

"Now you do.

"Now I am truly free again to be all that I am, all that we are, and all that we reach for.

"I am free to touch and be touched.

"I am free to connect, teach, learn, understand, soothe, comfort, inspire, and celebrate.

"I am free to sing our song of Golden Family as One.

"This is my joy alive.

"Hear me singing my song of Golden Love.

"I am everywhere,

"Always.

"I am you and you and you and you.

"I AM ONE GOLDEN HEART."

ANDAR'S FINAL GOLDEN GIFT

"Golden Ones, dearest friends of mine, I am extremely honored to be at this closing place with you.

"I am extremely proud of you all. The journey you have been through has been no small feat and now you stand here with me, tall and strong. You have traveled through a great deal and you now have a sense of what beautiful, full-fledged Golden Masters you are. My prayer is that your awareness and understanding of this continues to deepen and expand into full knowing as you move forward in your lives.

"Before we embark fully into this next adventure of our beautiful Golden Co-Creation, there is one last thing that I wish to speak to you about. Please bear me with as I explain.

"This last discussion takes us back to the beginning of our trek through the Gauntlet of Fear and enables us to see the events and shattering that took place then through a new light of clarity and understanding now. Please give consideration to what I say here, letting it move within you, bringing you yet greater insight into all that has happened to you and all that you have become as a result of the experiences you have gone through.

"Let us go back for a moment to that time when we surfaced above ground on Terra with such excitement and intention to rebuild our beautiful Lemuria. Certainly, things did not go the way we had planned, thought, or envisioned. This is a major understatement, I know.

"I have been well aware of moments along the way when all of you have wondered and asked yourselves, 'Why did we not see this coming? With all of our heightened perceptions and intuitive abilities, why did we not see, sense, and know what was coming, what would befall us once we reemerged on Terra's surface?'

"That is the question that still remains niggling in your consciousness; wondering, waiting, and needing to be addressed.

"And I respond to you in this way: THE GREATEST GIFT YOU HAVE IS THE GIFT OF PERSONAL FREEDOM WHICH AFFORDS YOU THE GIFT OF CHOICE.

"Remember, first and foremost that, collectively, we made the choice to stay with our Beloved Terra when we knew the earth cataclysms were coming. We chose to stay with Terra and see the journey through no matter what it would bring. We spoke about this at length back then, as you well know.

"We did not know what would unfold as a result of our choice, but we were all on board that trajectory one hundred percent.

"Understand clearly, again, that your Gift of Choice springs from the Gift of your Freedom. And the Freedom that I speak about now is the Freedom of your Soul; the Freedom of you as an evolving, SACRED BEING.

"This is not about your mind, it is not about your will, it is not about your own personal physically inhabited power. This is about your Higher Power, your overriding and over-guiding Life Force. This is about your SOUL EVOLUTION.

"Your physical incarnation is an expression of this, and for this.

"To come into physical embodiment is your Soul's choice. You know this and it bears repeating. You need to remember this now at a deeper level. You are a SOUL INCARNATE.

"With this as your Central Knowing, consider the possibility that your Soul chose, and agreed to, this entire experience with the H-O as a strengthening and eventually expanding, self-empowering experience.

"You were already enormously strong. Ask yourselves, 'what circumstances would it take to challenge me, my already strong and steady fiber of Being?' You know that the answer would be that it would have to be something very powerful to match and 'press through' your own growth of Self.

"From this point of view, it makes sense that, whatever came down the pike from the H-O might well weaken you, disable you, bind you, blind you, veil you, confuse you, shatter you, and maybe even break you. It would do whatever it could to disempower you, even destroy you, so that it could remain in control. And, through all of that, you would rise up, again and again and again—as unrelenting in your persistence of Being as the very forces that were trying to keep you down.

"Indeed, to the H-O your unrelenting presence was a constant source of frustration!

"The truth is that whatever 'came at you,' it never ultimately worked, did it? The one thing the H-O so wanted to do, and tried so hard to do, was to annihilate you. And that was impossible. They could destroy your body, but it was impossible to annihilate your Soul. You would live on and on and on, regardless. They could not extinguish the true and fierce power of your Spirit, your devotion, your LOVE. They could not vanquish your Heart, nor the Golden powerhouse within it.

"In considering and understanding all of this as a challenging and supremely strengthening experience, you can see that the original H-O experience was the catalyst of enormous change for you, within you, and around you. It catapulted you into a specific set of circumstances which you would then travel through for many, many lifetimes to come.

"Throughout that journey it cornered you into pain that would cause you to choose, yet again— repeatedly—who and what you would stand for, devote yourself to, and honor. With each repetition, it would deepen and strengthen you mightily.

"Yes, you would be cornered, again and again and again. You would be painfully squeezed and with each deepening of your insides, your Soul would have greater and fuller access to your consciousness in the physical realm. With each break through the pain, you became stronger and stronger and stronger, far stronger than you ever were back in Lemuria. And you were strong then, but nothing like you are now.

"Through each and every experience you would choose your Golden Heart. In each one, you would respond powerfully through the strength, perseverance, devotion, and LOVE of your Golden Heart and the One Golden Heart; thus making you stronger in all of this, each and every time. Do you understand me? Do you see how much you have grown through it all?

"Consider the possibility that your Souls knew you would need this strength in the future. And that future is now upon us.

"Let us now bring ourselves right into the present day.

"We see that the current world reality of our modern time is not unlike Mondor, in that a substantial part of the global mass consciousness is power hungry, confused, cold-hearted, callous, greedy, unconscious, and lost—Heartlessness. In that particular regard, not much has changed, has it?

"Is it Mondor? Can we continue to refer to it as such? That is for you to answer. No matter how you term it, today's mass consciousness reveals itself as largely fear-based. Because of this disconnection and brokenness, great destruction and suffering is created. Where is the Heart, the caring, the kindness, the balance to all this other? There is certainly a measure of this here already, but more is greatly needed.

"Reenter YOU, Golden Ones.

"It takes a much stronger Golden YOU to be here now and THRIVE.

"Certainly, you can be here and survive just about anything; you've already shown that over and over again. But, to be here and thrive? As in SHINE? As in shine BRIGHTLY? As in shine BRIGHTLY, BOLDLY, CLEARLY, FREELY?

"That takes major strength, the level of strength that you would not have now had you not had that experience with the H-O back then—and everything in between. You have been honed to greater internal strength with access to vastly greater reservoirs of Golden Love than ever before. You have brought this to yourselves by the walk you have made and the challenges you have faced. You have grown into, and grounded yourselves, as solid, radiant, and magnificently powerful Golden Gentle Giants. Here. Now.

"Each one of you is truly a GOLDEN POWERHOUSE, a bold and bright illumination that can outshine all else in its path.

"And that, my dearest friends, is my response to your question of, 'Why did we not let ourselves know ahead of time what was to befall us.' The key words here are, 'NOT LET OURSELVES.'

"You had the ability to, but that was overridden in this circumstance. Your Souls had other plans.

"The strength you have now is the level of strength that stands you in good stead to be FULLY YOU in our modern time. And because of circumstances being the way they are, you are sorely needed for the balance of things; to shine and shine brightly, boldly, brilliantly—as clear, steady Golden Stations right here, right now.

"The brilliance and brightness of your Golden Illumination is also much more powerful now than it has ever been—more so than in our original Lemuria. In all ways, you have evolved and grown; you have gained. You are each one mighty, brilliant jewel of a Soul. You are present, clear, and becoming increasingly awake to your depths, to your capabilities, to your vast Golden Power.

"You can, and are, making a difference, a huge difference—simply by virtue of knowing yourselves, embracing who you TRULY are, and by being your beautiful Presence and natural outpouring of illumination. And you will continue to do so.

"Why? Because YOU have so chosen.

"It is also essential that you accept the truth that YOU ARE BEING RECEIVED. This is not something to deflect, deny, or diminish.

"I urge you to continually embrace the strength and beauty of YOU, to recognize that you are being seen, heard, understood, and felt in all of your Golden Grace. Know clearly that there is much gratitude for you from all of us, and from ALL of Golden Life everywhere as well.

"YOU ARE HAVING IMPACT. ACCEPT THIS TRUTH.

"Yes, indeed.

"Let yourselves own this Truth. Know that, at the end of each day, our entire world, our entire Cosmos is far better off with you in it. These are not idle words I speak.

"Each and every day of your being YOU, Golden Ones, you are making a Golden difference. You are BEING your Golden Light, your Golden Love, your Golden Radiance and Blessedness. You are spreading your kindness, your caring, your beauty all over this world. You are touching ALL forms of life, seen and unseen, elevating them to a greater awareness of the true kindness within themselves, the goodness within their own hearts, the steadfastness of purity and Truth that creates such wondrousness, beauty, and seemingly miraculous transformations.

"YOU are that miracle that is constantly and steadily birthing forth yet new miracles; tending to them and giving them the support they need to grow and have 'legs' of their own.

"Go deep, go conscious, go connected, go kindness. Go Golden. YOU are the difference that you have always yearned to be. YOU are the expression of all of the gifts that your Source gave you. YOU are a birther of Golden Love through your breath, heart, mind, body, and Being.

"STRONG are you.

"Sovereign are you.

"Sacred are you.

"Blessed are you.

"Shine on, shine on. Shine on, Golden Ones.

"You herald a great day, every day that you are here. And we all thank you for this, Great Golden Illuminated Beings that you are.

"We all thank you for BEING.

"Shine on. ONE GOLDEN HEART FOREVER.

"I love you all.

"I AM Andar."

Avalar's Final Golden Gift

"My sweet friends, all of you Golden Ones are so precious to me. I have expressed myself fully and freely throughout these pages and you know full well how I feel about you.

"You have done a valiant job every step of the way, and you have your shining Golden grace and glory to show for it.

"I am honored to be sharing my life with you. It is a privilege to be in your presence and call you Golden Family, Friends, and Teammates. You make such a

difference in my life and, as I have already said many times, I am forever grateful for you all.

"Andar and I have done what we set out to do. We have fulfilled the promise that we made to you long ago, and done everything in our power to bring you back home to yourselves and to enable you to REMEMBER THAT YOU ARE GOLDEN.

"We have done our best, and succeeded. And you have done yours, and succeeded as well.

"All together, I would say that we make a Mighty Golden Team, don't you think?

"Onward we go now, with Golden Consciousness remembered and activated once again.

"We know that what's in front of you now is a transitional period. As you make this transition to the greater fullness of your Golden Being and body in the present day, you will witness in yourselves the entire array of contrasts between you as you have thought yourselves to be, and you as you now find you truly are: Golden Awakened once again. Feel free to be constantly reminding yourselves that this is a transitional process and one which asks of you that you remain kind and gentle with yourselves, and ever appreciative of your powerful strength which Andar just talked about. We encourage you to persevere no matter what.

"As you have seen in the Lemurian journey detailed in this book, the once painful parts of our history have all been transmuted and dissolved by virtue of love, compassionate witnessing, understanding, and forgiveness. Let it go. Through your Golden Hearts, you have transformed yourselves and our circumstances of adversity into new and glorious heights of Golden Love and Light. Embrace this thoroughly.

"As you move forward now, you will soon feel yourselves not only truly aware of your liberation and updated freedom, but you will also begin to witness in yourselves an aching need to love more, and more deeply, than ever before. You will yearn to find ways to express your deep kindness and caring in the smallest and largest of ways. Coupled with this will be a powerful urgency to appreciate and create beauty as much as you possibly can. All of these will be the natural responses to waking up in a Golden way and recognizing that there is space and freedom for you here now. You will find the natural ability within you to express and communicate your loving effectively and with great ease. And you will feel deeply grateful for this, as you feel yourselves being met by those you love and by life itself. You will have moments of profound gratitude for being so alive, clear, loving, and loved.

"I can assure you, your experience of Life will look and feel different. You will sort it all out and you will find yourselves consciously creative in meeting the challenges presented to you in your modern-day world. You will be acutely aware

that there is always a solution: another option, another way. Perhaps it is simply a question of shifting your vantage point in order to know what is possible. Seeing through Golden Heart with Golden eyes changes everything.

"In this book, we spoke about the principle of 'live and let live' as being neces-sary for different frequencies of consciousness to successfully co-exist on the same planet. In present day times, you now have the opportunity to freely be your own loved-based consciousness to its fullest while living alongside the current mass-con-sciousness frequency that is fear-based. During this upcoming transition process you will often feel as though you are straddling both worlds, walking with one foot in the fear-based reality and the other in our Golden reality.

"How does one navigate this exactly?

"You live and let live, but in doing so, this does not mean that you deny the pain of those still stuck in the fear-based consciousness domain. You care deeply, you are kind, you are sensitive. You Golden Ones feel the pain of many and it is hard to watch and feel. You are often affected by this. It all seems like too much, too often, and the pain and suffering can be overwhelming to the point of losing one's self in it.

"But getting lost in the pain and going down with it helps no one.

"This is when you remind yourselves, and each other, of our Golden World, the Golden Love frequency that you are. You remind yourselves of what you are gifted with: Love, Heart, Inspiration, Compassion. You remind yourselves that Golden Love is your design.

"And you remind yourselves here to simply stay present. Witness. Stand compas-sionate and steady. Remain intact and authentic.

"By adhering to the tenet 'live and let live' you recognize both worlds, but you have the choice of which one you live in, which one you energize, which one you are. You may feel affected by the pain of the fear-based world, and you may react to this in a way that, in fact, causes you even more pain, but, gradually, you will find a way to not be deluged by it. You will find yourselves becoming less reactive and more resilient and clearer.

"Instead of being overwhelmed by it all, you will slowly but surely begin to notice a feeling of distance from it, an ability to see it clearly and acknowledge it while also knowing that you are separate from it. You will begin to honor the choices and paths that people take without needing to understand details nor reasons why. You will also remind yourselves that you cannot change people, only they can change themselves. But if it is part of your purpose to help change circumstances where you can, you will be shown. But first, you will give yourselves permission to stand back, let it all be, and let it go so that you can give yourselves

SPACE *in order to feel and know who you truly are.*

"And then you will pivot. You will shift your focus.

"You will consciously turn toward and choose to fully sink in to the depth of who you are—Golden Mastery, standing solidly in your Golden Frequency with grace and freedom. And only then, from this Golden position, will you be freed up and able to make clear choices and see clear solutions. Only then will you know how you wish to express your Golden Way and affect change where and how you are called from within to do so. If it is your Golden Expression to do something about specific circumstances, you will know exactly how, when, and what action to take. If it is for you to establish new paths, create new patterns of creativity, birth forth completely new frontiers, then it will be crystal clear to you in a Golden way. You will feel and see the path laid out in front of you, and you will know this is right because of all the Golden joy, passion, and gusto that rises in you to accomplish these goals.

"In short, you will be Golden alive, well, and fully inspired with a momentum that will enable you to stay the course and be continuously guided and fueled by your activated Golden Hearts. Each of you will indeed be flourishing in your Golden Zone and there will be no stopping you. Although I make it sound effortless and easy here, count on the fact that it won't always be. It may well ask a lot of you—just the way our creating in Lemuria was often stretching and demanding. Oh, but how rewarding it is at the end of the day to feel that your gifts have been fully expressed and that you feel 'fully utilized' in that remarkably nourishing and life-giving way. It's called a great life worth living greatly!

"Isn't it exquisite, after all we have been through, to now have the opportunity and freedom to live our true Golden Way in this present time and place?

"It's an honor. Let's give it all we've got.

"In closing, I encourage you to continue to be kind and gentle with yourselves, and feel the smile in your hearts as you revel in the Golden delight of you.

"Beloved Golden Ones, I love you and celebrate you all.

"Thank you for GOLDEN BEING.

"I leave you with this poem which can be enjoyed as an affirmation for Golden Well-being.

"ONE GOLDEN HEART FOREVER.

"I AM Avalar."

FINAL GOLDEN GRATITUDE PRAYER

"Always, always every day,

"I create forth in a Golden way.

"I am Golden true and gifted free,

"It's a blessing and honor to be Golden Me.

"I treasure this time,

"This moment right here,

"When I can be all that's so dear.

"I am a gift born forth,

"From all that's Divine.

"I am Golden Being in Heart, Soul, Body, and Mind.

"Blessings, blessings Golden Be,

"What a privilege it is to be Golden Me.

"I give thanks for this life, for this time, for this grace;

"To be Golden Family again in this Golden Place.

"One Golden Heart, radiant and true,

"Happy and shining in me and in you.

"Blessings to us all, my Golden Family this day,

"Golden Blessings of love in every way.

"ONE GOLDEN HEART."

AFTERWORD

Dear Readers,

It is with great celebration that we arrive at this point! It has been a long journey of delivering this material and we are grateful if this book has found its way into your hands and heart. You are one more Golden One who is regaining conscious awareness of your true Golden Self and this only brings beautiful gifts of love to you and all of us as well. We are all in this together, One Golden Family, and each one who remembers, uplifts us all.

Living One Golden Heart, as our magnificent Golden World, is not a dream.

You may have moments when you wonder if it is, but give it time and that "dream" will suddenly dawn on you as a full-fledged reality. You will realize that your body and Being is Golden Love materialized and you will feel your Golden Illumination fully outshining and splendid. This will give rise to great passion about living and expressing your own Golden way.

Your unique Golden goodness will plant new creations of love, beauty, and harmony in our world. The more the many of us do this, the more love, caring, beauty, and harmony there will be. Through our daily loving and living here on this beautiful planet, we will know that, yes, we are generating powerfully positive, Golden life-enhancing energy, and we will witness the blessings and transformations that occur as a result. This will motivate us to bring our Golden gifts forward even more, thus setting a solid stage of Golden Love for future generations to come. A new ripple effect will then have taken hold.

It is important to understand that your Golden Remembrance is not a linear process; it is multilayered and fluid. For this reason, it will be very helpful for you to return to this book and read it through several more times. We urge you to do this. Each time that you do, you will remember more of your Golden Self and your Golden pathway will become increasingly harmonious and clear. We encourage you to utilize this book as a guide, a support, a coach, and inspiration. Use it as a reference, a reminder, and a source of Golden love and upliftment.

Lest you think that this book is all we plan to contribute, rest assured that there will be more to follow! Our personal goal is to re-inspire as many of our Golden Family as we possibly can in the years that we remain here on Terra. This is not just in regards to you Golden Ones who are in body, but also to all the expressions of Golden Life everywhere. We are committed to doing our best to support the reactivation of this Golden World and plan to provide continued materials of support along with our endless love and devotion to this awakening Golden reality, whose time has come.

This is the Call to Golden Remembrance, and through that, the Call to Golden Action.

We welcome all of you who wish to shine your Golden Light, standing tall and joyous in this as well.

Blessings, our dearest Golden Family.

We love you. We honor you. We thank you.

WE ARE ONE GOLDEN HEART.

WE ARE GOLDEN FREE.

In Golden grace and gratitude always,
Deborah, Jack, and the Golden Team

WITH GRATITUDE

We want to thank all of you who participated in our work throughout the past 35 years. We feel honored that you came forward to be a part of what we had to offer. Each of you contributed to our own awakening, education, and well-being as we hope we contributed to yours. Thank you!

In regards to our work in the past 8 years, it is with profound gratitude that we give special thanks to our dearest Golden Seven: Stacy Bowman, Barbara Brooks, Leslie Lintner, Francis Kirkpatrick, Joyce Tattelman, Bob Rudorf, and Amelia Belle. You each showed tremendous love, courage, and devotion in participating in The Golden Remembrance series, and the entire Golden Family everywhere thanks you as well. You are so special to us all and we are deeply touched and inspired by you. Forever, thank you!

We also wish to thank our three "test readers" of this book, Frances Kirkpatrick, Teryl Chapel and Tina Brown, who were able to give us invaluable feedback early on. Thank you for that and for reading through the manuscript so quickly.

Next, we want to thank our editors and book designer. Aaron Rose was extremely helpful and a pleasure to work with early on with the manuscript. And then along came Lorien Sekora. What a gift you have been to us throughout the editing process and soon with the marketing. Your perseverance and sensitivity to the manuscript, your editing professionalism and expertise, and your kindness, caring and sweet spirit are so appreciated. We love you Lorien, and are so grateful that you are in our life.

And Chris Mole, book designer, your contributions are so appreciated. We have valued your input and your expertise. Thank you, Chris, for seeing this project through.

And then there's our Golden Team. Birthing and producing this book have been an interdimensional experience of profound love and joy. Our immeasurable gratitude goes to our Golden Team of Masters, Angels, Terra, and so many others in the physical and non-physical realms of Golden Life. We have been inspired, educated, illuminated, and supported by all of you at every turn, and between the turns as well! You have buoyed us, shown us the way, and uplifted our hearts, Souls and Beings in ways that we had never even known existed. Thank you are two simple words that contain a universe of gratitude. This has indeed been one great big Golden Family creation of love.

And, finally, to our beautiful family, and all of our friends of like mind and heart in the physical world who have listened so kindly to us talking about this book and its process for the past number of years, who have been patient throughout our constant refrain of, "it's almost done!" We say thank you with a beaming smile on top! Finally, it's true! It is done!

Big blessings, gratitude, and great love to all.

ABOUT THE AUTHORS

DEBORAH AND JACK BARTELLO have been forward thinkers in the field of personal and spiritual development since 1986. In addition to many years of providing one-on-one therapeutic work and conducting intensive workshops with clients, they have continually focused on bringing through and developing new material that would help restore the conscious blueprint of love, personal freedom, and wholeness.

They began their work together in the mid-80's, teaching people about energy and healing. In 1990 they discovered Northern California's Mt. Shasta, where they joined with Golden Masters in developing and subsequently conducting their Ascended Master Intensives.

In 2001, Deborah and Jack began their conscious journey of the Lemurian Golden Remembrance, which resulted in *The Golden Remembrance.*

Working as a couple, Jack and Deborah offer both the male and female perspective as well as their understanding of conscious, harmonious relationship on many levels. Their union is unique in its conscious and complete devotion to spirit and the common goal of love and beauty with which they are so perfectly aligned.

Throughout their journey together, in addition to being partnered with the Golden Masters, Deborah and Jack have also been deeply partnered with the pulse and heartbeat of the Earth. Every step they have taken has been in concert with this communion—they have always been guided and directed by her, bringing this depth of relationship to all that they put forth.

Deborah and Jack are both Sensitives, and through their "life training" have come to better understand the challenges and opportunities of this remarkable way of Being. They strive to express the depth of their loving and understanding in everything they do, and wish to contribute as much as they can to foster the gift of Golden Love thriving for as long as they remain here.

Deborah has also developed programs on Interdimensional Creativity. You can view her pictures of the Golden Masters as well as other Golden art at onegoldenheartvisionaryart.com. Her artwork has served as windows of Light, love, and healing for many people over the past 36 years.

The Golden Remembrance is Deborah and Jack Bartello's second book.

Visit onegoldenheart.com to learn more.